Marketing Management and Strategy

A Reader

3rd edition

Marketing Management and Strategy

A Reader

Edited by

PHILIP KOTLER
Northwestern University

KEITH K. COX
University of Houston

PRENTICE-HALL, INC., *Englewood Cliffs, NJ* 07632

Library of Congress Cataloging in Publication Data
Main entry under title:

Marketing management and strategy.

Includes bibliographical references and index.
1. Marketing—Management—Addresses, essays, lectures.
I. Kotler, Philip. II. Cox, Keith Kohn.
HF5415.13.M3524 1984   658.8   83-26944
ISBN 0-13-558248-2

Editorial/production supervision and
  interior design: Maureen Wilson
Cover design: Wanda Lubelska
Manufacturing buyer: Ed O'Dougherty

Printed in the United States of America

10 9 8 7 6 5 4 3 2 1

ISBN 0-13-558248-2

PRENTICE-HALL INTERNATIONAL, INC., *London*
PRENTICE-HALL OF AUSTRALIA PTY. LIMITED, *Sydney*
EDITORA PRENTICE-HALL DO BRASIL, LTDA., *Rio de Janeiro*
PRENTICE-HALL CANADA INC., *Toronto*
PRENTICE-HALL OF INDIA PRIVATE LIMITED, *New Delhi*
PRENTICE-HALL OF JAPAN, INC., *Tokyo*
PRENTICE-HALL OF SOUTHEAST ASIA PTE. LTD., *Singapore*
WHITEHALL BOOKS LIMITED, *Wellington, New Zealand*

Contents

v

II
Analyzing
Market
Opportunities

III
Researching
Target
Markets

VI   **Controlling the Marketing Effort**

Preface

Marketing continues to be a fantastically varied discipline, a fact that was brought home to us as we tried to assemble a useful collection of readings that would appeal to students and practitioners of marketing strategy and management.

In positioning this reader, our primary target market was defined as the MBA marketing core course. Other markets include senior-level marketing strategy courses and executive development programs.

In selecting the articles in this reader, our first principle was to choose those readings that are of obvious interest to marketing management rather than to the specialist or technician in marketing research, advertising, or sales management. Our second principle was to select articles that range over many types of marketing situations—consumer, industrial, services, and international. This was done to avoid a common tendency to overemphasize consumer marketing situations. Our third principle was to select many articles that deal with real marketing situations treated analytically. We wanted to avoid textbook-like explanations devoid of illustration and application, and to give instead analyses of situations facing such companies as Anheuser-Busch, Crown Cork and Seal, McDonald, Emery Air Freight, and Docutel. Industries analysed in depth include the banking, steel, and electronics industries. Articles that provide anecdotal material for their intrinsic reading interest, backed up with the derivation of important concepts in marketing were deliberately chosen. Our fourth principle was to choose articles that illustrate the best in modern marketing analysis and management, particularly as derived from the use of behavioral and quantitative concepts. Hopefully these articles will increase the appreciation of readers in regard to the potency of these scientific perspectives in aiding effective marketing performance. Our fifth principle was to blend classic articles representing the finest statement of certain marketing problems and strategies with more recent articles that open new analytical pathways. The collection shows the continued growth of fine analysis in the emerging science of marketing management. Our sixth principle was to increase the number of articles that deal with marketing strategy and strategic planning.

These six principles led to the choice of the final thirty-nine articles. The readings book is divided into six major parts, starting with understanding marketing management and proceeding through analyzing market opportunities, researching target markets, developing marketing strategies, planning marketing tactics, and controlling the marketing effort.

PHILIP KOTLER
Northwestern University

KEITH K. COX
University of Houston

Marketing Management and Strategy

A Reader

Understanding Marketing Management

The scope of marketing management has been broadened over the last twenty-five years. One recent trend has been the addition of strategic planning and strategic thinking concepts to the area of marketing strategy.

The readings in this first part set the tone for a strategic overview of the marketing discipline.

After reading this part, you should have a better understanding of:

1. What the marketing concept implies as a way of thinking for management.
2. A clearer distinction between selling and marketing.
3. Some major strengths and weaknesses in using marketing.
4. The ways strategic planning helps in developing marketing strategy.
5. Product/market options available to marketing managers.

1

Marketing Myopia

Theodore Levitt

Every major industry was once a growth industry. But some that are now riding a wave of growth enthusiasm are very much in the shadow of decline. Others which are thought of as seasoned growth industries have actually stopped growing. In every case the reason growth is threatened, slowed, or stopped is *not* because the market is saturated. It is because there has been a failure of management.

FATEFUL PURPOSES

The failure is at the top. The executives responsible for it, in the last analysis, are those who deal with broad aims and policies. Thus:

The railroads did not stop growing because the need for passenger and freight transportation declined. That grew. The railroads are in trouble today not because the need was filled by others (cars, trucks, airplanes, even telephones), but because it was *not* filled by the railroads themselves. They let others take customers away from them because they assumed themselves to be in the railroad business rather than in the transportation business. The reason they defined their industry wrong was because they were railroad-oriented instead of transportation-oriented; they were product-oriented instead of customer-oriented.

Hollywood barely escaped being totally ravished by television. Actually, all the established film companies went through drastic reorganizations. Some simply disappeared. All of them got into trouble not because of TV's inroads but because of their own myopia. As with the railroads, Hollywood defined its business incorrectly. It thought it was in the movie business when it was actually in the entertainment business. "Movies" implied a specific, limited prod-

Reprinted by permission of the publishers from Edward C. Bursk and John F. Chapman, eds., *Modern Marketing Strategy* (Cambridge, Mass.: Harvard University Press, © 1964), by the President and Fellows of Harvard College; originally published in the *Harvard Business Review*, 38 (July–August 1960), pp. 24–47. The retrospective commentary was published in the *Harvard Business Review*, 53 (September–October 1975), copyright © by the President and Fellows of Harvard College; all rights reserved.

3

uct. This produced a fatuous contentment which from the beginning led producers to view TV as a threat. Hollywood scorned and rejected TV when it should have welcomed it as an opportunity—an opportunity to expand the entertainment business.

Today TV is a bigger business than the old narrowly defined movie business ever was. Had Hollywood been customer-oriented (providing entertainment), rather than product-oriented (making movies), would it have gone through the fiscal purgatory that it did? I doubt it. What ultimately saved Hollywood and accounted for its recent resurgence was the wave of new young writers, producers, and directors whose previous successes in television had decimated the old movie companies and toppled the big movie moguls.

There are other less obvious examples of industries that have been and are now endangering their futures by improperly defining their purposes. I shall discuss some in detail later and analyze the kind of policies that lead to trouble. Right now it may help to show what a thoroughly customer-oriented management *can* do to keep a growth industry growing, even after the obvious opportunities have been exhausted; and here there are two examples that have been around for a long time. They are nylon and glass—specifically, E. I. duPont de Nemours & Company and Corning Glass Works:

Both companies have great technical competence. Their product orientation is unquestioned. But this alone does not explain their success. After all, who was more pridefully product-oriented and product-conscious than the erstwhile New England textile companies that have been so thoroughly massacred? The duPonts and the Cornings have succeeded not primarily because of their product or research orientation but because they have been thoroughly customer-oriented also. It is constant watchfulness for opportunities to apply their technical know-how to the creation of customer-satisfying uses which accounts for their prodigious output of successful new products. Without a very sophisticated eye on the customer, most of their new products might have been wrong, their sales methods useless.

Aluminum has also continued to be a growth industry, thanks to the efforts of two wartime-created companies which deliberately set about creating new customer-satisfying uses. Without Kaiser Aluminum & Chemical Corporation and Reynolds Metals Company, the total demand for aluminum today would be vastly less than it is.

Error of Analysis

Some may argue that it is foolish to set the railroads off against aluminum or the movies off against glass. Are not aluminum and glass naturally so versatile that the industries are bound to have more growth opportunities than the railroads and movies? This view commits precisely the error I have been talking about. It defines an industry, or a product, or a cluster of know-how so narrowly as to guarantee its premature senescence. When we mention "railroads," we should make sure we mean "transportation." As transporters, the railroads still have a good chance for very considerable growth. They are not limited to the railroad business as such (though in my opinion rail transportation is potentially a much stronger transportation medium than is generally believed).

What the railroads lack is not opportunity, but some of the same managerial imaginativeness and audacity that made them great. Even an amateur like Jacques Barzun can see what is lacking when he says:

I grieve to see the most advanced physical and social organization of the last century go down in shabby disgrace for lack of the same comprehensive imagination that built it up. [What is lacking is] the will of the companies to survive and to satisfy the public by inventiveness and skill.[1]

[1] Jacques Barzun, "Trains and the Mind of Man," *Holiday* (February 1960), p. 21.

SHADOW OF OBSOLESCENCE

It is impossible to mention a single major industry that did not at one time qualify for the magic appellation of "growth industry." In each case its assumed strength lay in the apparently unchallenged superiority of its product. There appeared to be no effective substitute for it. It was itself a runaway substitute for the product it so triumphantly replaced. Yet one after another of these celebrated industries has come under a shadow. Let us look briefly at a few more of them, this time taking examples that have so far received a little less attention:

Dry Cleaning. This was once a growth industry with lavish prospects. In an age of wool garments, imagine being finally able to get them safely and easily clean. The boom was on.

Yet here we are 30 years after the boom started and the industry is in trouble. Where has the competition come from? From a better way of cleaning? No. It has come from synthetic fibers and chemical additives that have cut the need for dry cleaning. But this is only the beginning. Lurking in the wings and ready to make chemical dry cleaning totally obsolescent is that powerful magician, ultrasonics.

Electric Utilities. This is another one of those supposedly "no-substitute" products that has been enthroned on a pedestal of invincible growth. When the incandescent lamp came along, kerosene lights were finished. Later the water wheel and the steam engine were cut to ribbons by the flexibility, reliability, simplicity, and just plain easy availability of electric motors. The prosperity of electric utilities continues to wax extravagant as the home is converted into a museum of electric gadgetry. How can anybody miss by investing in utilities, with no competition, nothing but growth ahead?

But a second look is not quite so comforting. A score of nonutility companies are well advanced toward developing a powerful chemical fuel cell which could sit in some hidden closet of every home silently ticking off electric power. The electric lines that vulgarize so many neighborhoods will be eliminated. So will the endless demolition of streets and service interruptions during storms. Also on the horizon is solar energy, again pioneered by nonutility companies.

Who says that the utilities have no competition? They may be natural monopolies now, but tomorrow they may be natural deaths. To avoid this prospect, they too will have to develop fuel cells, solar energy, and other power sources. To survive, they themselves will have to plot the obsolescence of what now produces their livelihood.

Grocery Stores. Many people find it hard to realize that there ever was a thriving establishment known as the "corner grocery store." The supermarket has taken over with a powerful effectiveness. Yet the big food chains of the 1930s narrowly escaped being completely wiped out by the aggressive expansion of independent supermarkets. The first genuine supermarket was opened in 1930, in Jamaica, Long Island. By 1933 supermarkets were thriving in California, Ohio, Pennsylvania, and elsewhere. Yet the established chains pompously ignored them. When they chose to notice them, it was with such derisive descriptions as "cheapy," "horse-and-buggy," "cracker-barrel store-keeping," and "unethical opportunities."

The executive of one big chain announced at the time that he found it "hard to believe that people will drive for miles to shop for foods and sacrifice the personal service chains have perfected and to which Mrs. Consumer is accustomed."[2] As late as

---

[2]For more details see M. M. Zimmerman, *The Super Market: A Revolution in Distribution* (New York: McGraw-Hill Book Company, Inc., 1955), p. 48.

1936, the National Wholesale Grocers convention and the New Jersey Retail Grocers Association said there was nothing to fear. They said that the supers' narrow appeal to the price buyer limited the size of their market. They had to draw from miles around. When imitators came, there would be wholesale liquidations as volume fell. The current high sales of the supers was said to be partly due to their novelty. Basically people wanted convenient neighborhood grocers. If the neighborhood stores "cooperate with their suppliers, pay attention to their costs, and improve their services," they would be able to weather the competition until it blew over.[3]

It never blew over. The chains discovered that survival required going into the supermarket business. This meant the wholesale destruction of their huge investments in corner store sites and in established distribution and merchandising methods. The companies with "the courage of their convictions" resolutely stuck to the corner store philosophy. They kept their pride but lost their shirts.

Self-Deceiving Cycle

But memories are short. For example, it is hard for people who today confidently hail the twin messiahs of electronics and chemicals to see how things could possible go wrong with these galloping industries. They probably also cannot see how a reasonably sensible businessman could have been as myopic as the famous Boston millionaire who 50 years ago unintentionally sentenced his heirs to poverty by stipulating that his entire estate be forever invested exclusively in electric street-car securities. His posthumous declaration, "There will always be a big demand for efficient urban transportation," is no consolation to his heirs who sustain life by pumping gasoline at automobile filling stations.

[3]*Ibid.*, pp. 45–47.

Yet, in a casual survey I recently took among a group of intelligent business executives, nearly half agreed that it would be hard to hurt their heirs by tying their estates forever to the electronics industry. When I then confronted them with the Boston street-car example, they chorused unanimously, "That's different!" But is it? Is not the basic situation identical?

In truth, *there is no such thing* as a growth industry, I believe. There are only companies organized and operated to create and capitalize on growth opportunities. Industries that assume themselves to be riding some automatic growth escalator invariably descend into stagnation. The history of every dead and dying "growth" industry shows a self-deceiving cycle of bountiful expansion and undetected decay. There are four conditions which usually guarantee this cycle:

1. The belief that growth is assured by an expanding and more affluent population.

2. The belief that there is no competitive substitute for the industry's major product.

3. Too much faith in mass production and in the advantages of rapidly declining unit costs as output rises.

4. Preoccupation with a product that lends itself to carefully controlled scientific experimentation, improvement, and manufacturing cost reduction.

I should like now to begin examining each of these conditions in some detail. To build my case as boldly as possible, I shall illustrate the points with reference to three industries—petroleum, automobiles, and electronics—particularly petroleum, because it spans more years and more vicissitudes. Not only do these three have excellent reputations with the general public and also enjoy the confidence of sophisticated investors, but their managements have become known for progressive thinking in areas like financial control, product research, and management training. If obsolescence can cripple even these industries, it can happen anywhere.

POPULATION MYTH

The belief that profits are assured by an expanding and more affluent population is dear to the heart of every industry. It takes the edge off the apprehensions everybody understandably feels about the future. If consumers are multiplying and also buying more of your product or service, you can face the future with considerably more comfort than if the market is shrinking. An expanding market keeps the manufacturer from having to think very hard or imaginatively. If thinking is an intellectual response to a problem, then the absence of a problem leads to the absence of thinking. If your product has an automatically expanding market, then you will not give much thought to how to expand it.

One of the most interesting examples of this is provided by the petroleum industry. Probably our oldest growth industry, it has an enviable record. While there are some current apprehensions about its growth rate, the industry itself tends to be optimistic. But I believe it can be demonstrated that it is undergoing a fundamental yet typical change. It is not only ceasing to be a growth industry, but may actually be a declining one, relative to other business. Although there is widespread unawareness of it, I believe that within 25 years the oil industry may find itself in much the same position of retrospective glory that the railroads are now in. Despite its pioneering work in developing and applying the present-value method of investment evaluation, in employee relations, and in working with backward countries, the petroleum business is a distressing example of how complacency and wrongheadedness can stubbornly convert opportunity into near disaster.

One of the characteristics of this and other industries that have believed very strongly in the beneficial consequences of an expanding population, while at the same time being industries with a generic product for which there has appeared to be no competitive substitute, is that the individual companies have sought to outdo their competitors by improving on what they are already doing. This makes sense, of course, if one assumes that sales are tied to the country's population strings, because the customer can compare products only on a feature-by-feature basis. I believe it is significant, for example, that not since John D. Rockefeller sent free kerosene lamps to China has the oil industry done anything really outstanding to create a demand for its product. Not even in product improvement has it showered itself with eminence. The greatest single improvement, namely the development of tetraethyl lead, came from outside the industry, specifically from General Motors and duPont. The big contributions made by the industry itself are confined to the technology of oil exploration, production, and refining.

Asking for Trouble

In other words, the industry's efforts have focused on improving the *efficiency* of getting and making its product, not really on improving the generic product or its marketing. Moreover, its chief product has continuously been defined in the narrowest possible terms, namely gasoline, not energy, fuel, or transportation. This attitude has helped assure that:

Major improvements in gasoline quality tend not to originate in the oil industry. Also, the development of superior alternative fuels comes from outside the oil industry, as will be shown later.

Major innovations in automobile fuel marketing are originated by small new oil companies that are not primarily preoccupied with production or refining. These are the companies that have been responsible for the rapidly expanding multipump gasoline stations, with their successful emphasis on large and clean layouts, rapid and efficient driveway service, and quality gasoline at low prices.

Thus, the oil industry is asking for trouble from outsiders. Sooner or later, in this land of hungry inventors and entrepreneurs, a threat is sure to come. The possibilities of this will become more apparent when we turn to the next dangerous belief of many managements. For the sake of continuity, because this second belief is tied closely to the first, I shall continue with the same example.

Idea of Indispensability

The petroleum industry is pretty much persuaded that there is no competitive substitute for its major product, gasoline—or if there is, that it will continue to be a derivative of crude oil, such as diesel fuel or kerosene jet fuel.

There is a lot of automatic wishful thinking in this assumption. The trouble is that most refining companies own huge amounts of crude oil reserves. These have value only if there is a market for products into which oil can be converted—hence the tenacious belief in the continuing competitive superiority of automobile fuels made from crude oil.

This idea persists despite all historic evidence against it. The evidence not only shows that oil has never been a superior product for any purpose for very long, but it also shows that the oil industry has never really been a growth industry. It has been a succession of different businesses that have gone through the usual historic cycles of growth, maturity, and decay. Its overall survival is owed to a series of miraculous escapes from total obsolescence, of last minute and unexpected reprieves from total disaster reminiscent of the Perils of Pauline.

Perils of Petroleum

I shall sketch in only the main episodes:

First, crude oil was largely a patent medicine. But even before that fad ran out, demand was greatly expanded by the use of oil in kerosene

lamps. The prospect of lighting the world's lamps gave rise to an extravagant promise of growth. The prospects were similar to those the industry now holds for gasoline in other parts of the world. It can hardly wait for the underdeveloped nations to get a car in every garage.

In the days of the kerosene lamp, the oil companies competed with each other and against gaslight by trying to improve the illuminating characteristics of kerosene. Then suddenly the impossible happened. Edison invented a light which was totally nondependent on crude oil. Had it not been for the growing use of kerosene in space heaters, the incandescent lamp would have completely finished oil as a growth industry at that time. Oil would have been good for little else than axle grease.

Then disaster and reprieve struck again. Two great innovations occurred, neither originating in the oil industry. The successful development of coal-burning domestic central-heating systems made the space heater obsolescent. While the industry reeled, along came its most magnificent boost yet—the internal combustion engine, also invented by outsiders. Then when the prodigious expansion for gasoline finally began to level off in the 1920s, along came the miraculous escape of a central oil heater. Once again, the escape was provided by an outsider's invention and development. And when that market weakened, wartime demand for aviation fuel came to the rescue. After the war the expansion of civilian aviation, the dieselization of railroads, and the explosive demand for cars and trucks kept the industry's growth in high gear.

Meanwhile centralized oil heating—whose boom potential had only recently been proclaimed—ran into severe competition from natural gas. While the oil companies themselves owned the gas that now competed with their oil, the industry did not originate the natural gas revolution, nor has it to this day greatly profited from its gas ownership. The gas revolution was made by newly formed transmission companies that marketed the product with an aggressive ardor. They started a magnificent new industry, first against the advice and then against the resistance of the oil companies.

By all the logic of the situation, the oil companies themselves should have made the gas revolution. They not only owned the gas; they also were the only people experienced in handling, scrubbing, and using it, the only people experienced in pipeline technology and transmission, and they understood heating problems. But, partly because they knew that natural gas would compete with their own sale of heating oil, the oil companies pooh-poohed the potentials of gas.

The revolution was finally started by oil pipeline executives who, unable to persuade their own companies to go into gas, quit and organized the spectacularly successful gas transmission companies. Even after their success became painfully evident to the oil companies, the latter did not go into gas transmission. The multibillion-dollar business which should have been theirs went to others. As in the past, the industry was blinded by its narrow preoccupation with a specific product and the value of its reserves. It paid little or no attention to its customers' basic needs and preferences.

The postwar years have not witnessed any change. Immediately after World War II the oil industry was greatly encouraged about its future by the rapid expansion of demand for its traditional line of products. In 1950 most companies projected annual rates of domestic expansion of around 6% through at least 1975. Though the ratio of crude oil reserves to demand in the Free World was about 20 to 1, with 10 to 1 being usually considered a reasonable working ratio in the United States, booming demand sent oil men searching for more without sufficient regard to what the future really promised. In 1952 they "hit" in the Middle East; the ratio skyrocketed to 42 to 1. If gross additions to reserves continue at the average rate of the past five years (37 billion barrels annually), then by 1970 the reserve ratio will be up to 45 to 1. This abundance of oil has weakened crude and product prices all over the world.

Uncertain Future

Management cannot find much consolation today in the rapidly expanding petrochemical industry, another oil-using idea that did not originate in the leading firms. The total United States production of petrochemicals is equivalent to about 2% (by volume) of the demand for all petroleum products. Although the petrochemical industry is now expected to grow by about 10% per year, this will not offset other drains on the growth of crude oil consumption. Furthermore, while petrochemical products are many and growing, it is well to remember that there are nonpetroleum sources of the basic raw material, such as coal. Besides, a lot of plastics can be produced with relatively little oil. A 50,000-barrel-per-day oil refinery is now considered the absolute minimum size for efficiency. But a 50,000-barrel-per-day chemical plant is a giant operation.

Oil has never been a continuously strong growth industry. It has grown by fits and starts, always miraculously saved by innovations and developments not of its own making. The reason it has not grown in a smooth progression is that each time it thought it had a superior product safe from the possibility of competitive substitutes, the product turned out to be inferior and notoriously subject to obsolescence. Until now, gasoline (for motor fuel, anyhow) has escaped this fate. But, as we shall see later, it too may be on its last legs.

The point of all this is that there is no guarantee against product obsolescence. If a company's own research does not make it obsolete, another's will. Unless an industry is especially lucky, as oil has been until now, it can easily go down in a sea of red figures—just as the railroads have, as the buggy whip manufacturers have, as the corner grocery chains have, as most of the big movie companies have, and indeed as many other industries have.

The best way for a firm to be lucky is to make its own luck. That requires knowing what makes a business successful. One of the greatest enemies of this knowledge is mass production.

PRODUCTION PRESSURES

Mass-production industries are impelled by a great drive to produce all they can. The prospect of steeply declining unit costs as output rises is more than most companies can usually resist. The profit possibilities look spectacular. All effort focuses on production. The result is that marketing gets neglected.

John Kenneth Galbraith contends that just the opposite occurs.[4] Output is so prodigious that all effort concentrates on trying to get rid of it. He says this accounts for singing commercials, desecration of the countryside with advertising signs, and other wasteful and vulgar practices. Galbraith has a finger on somthing real, but he misses the strategic point. Mass production does indeed generate great pressure to "move" the product. But what usually gets emphasized is selling, not marketing. Marketing, being a more sophisticated and complex process, gets ignored.

The difference between marketing and selling is more than semantic. Selling focuses on the needs of the seller, marketing on the needs of the buyer. Selling is preoccupied with the seller's need to convert his product into cash; marketing with the idea of satisfying the needs of the customer by means of the product and the whole cluster of things associated with creating, delivering, and finally consuming it.

In some industries the enticements of full mass production have been so powerful that for many years top management in effect has told the sales departments, "You get rid of it; we'll worry about profits." By contrast, a truly marketing-minded firm tries to create value-satisfying goods and services that consumers will want to buy. What it offers for sale includes not only the generic product or service, but also how it is made available to the customer, in what form, when, under what conditions, and at what terms of trade. Most important, what it offers for sale is determined not by the seller but by the buyer. The seller takes his cues from the buyer in such a way that the product becomes a consequence of the marketing effort, not vice versa.

[4] *The Affluent Society* (Boston: Houghton-Mifflin Company, 1958), pp. 152–60.

Lag in Detroit

This may sound like an elementary rule of business, but that does not keep it from being violated wholesale. It is certainly more violated than honored. Take the automobile industry:

Here mass production is most famous, most honored, and has the greatest impact on the entire society. The industry has hitched its fortune to the relentless requirements of the annual model change, a policy that makes customer orientation an especially urgent necessity. Consequently the auto companies annually spend millions of dollars on consumer research. But the fact that the new compact cars are selling so well in their first year indicates that Detroit's vast researchers have for a long time failed to reveal what the customer really wanted. Detroit was not persuaded that he wanted anything different from what he had been getting until it lost millions of customers to other small car manufacturers.

How could this unbelievable lag behind consumer wants have been perpetuated so long? Why did not research reveal consumer preferences before consumers' buying decisions themselves revealed the facts? Is that not what consumer research is for—to find out before the fact what is going to happen? The answer is that Detroit never really researched the customer's wants. It only researched his preferences between the kinds of things which it had already decided to offer him. For Detroit is mainly product-oriented, not customer-oriented. To the extent that the customer is recognized as having needs that the manufacturer should try to satisfy, Detroit usually acts as if the job can be done entirely by product changes. Occasionally attention gets paid to financing, too, but that is done more in order to sell than to enable the customer to buy.

As for taking care of other customer needs, there is not enough being done to write about. The areas of the greatest unsatisfied needs are ignored, or at best get stepchild attention. These are at the point of sale and on the matter of automotive repair and maintenance. Detroit views these problem areas as being of secondary importance. That is underscored by the fact that the retailing and servicing ends of this industry are neither owned and operated nor controlled by the manufacturers. Once the car is produced, things are pretty much in the dealer's inadequate hands. Illustrative of Detroit's arm's-length attitude is the fact that, while servicing holds enormous sales-stimulating, profit-building opportunities, only 57 of Chevrolet's 7,000 dealers provide night maintenance service.

Motorists repeatedly express their dissatisfaction with servicing and their apprehensions about buying cars under the present selling setup. The anxieties and problems they encounter during the auto buying and maintenance processes are probably more intense and widespread today than 30 years ago. Yet the automobile companies do not *seem* to listen to or take their cues from the anguished consumer. If they do listen, it must be through the filter of their own preoccupation with production. The marketing effort is still viewed as a necessary consequence of the product, not vice versa, as it should be. That is the legacy of mass production, with its parochial view that profit resides essentially in low-cost full production.

What Ford Put First

The profit lure of mass production obviously has a place in the plans and strategy of business management, but it must always follow hard thinking about the customer. This is one of the most important lessons that we can learn from the contradictory behavior of Henry Ford. In a sense Ford was both the most brilliant and the most senseless marketer in American history. He was senseless because he refused to give the customer anything but a black car. He was brilliant because he fashioned a production system designed to fit market needs. We habitually celebrate him for the wrong reason, his production genius. His real genius was marketing. We think he was able to cut his selling price and therefore sell millions of $500 cars because his invention of the assembly line had reduced the costs. Actually he invented the assembly line because he had concluded that at $500 he could sell millions of cars. Mass production was the *result*, not the cause, of his low prices.

Ford repeatedly emphasized this point,

but a nation of production-oriented business managers refuses to hear the great lesson he taught. Here is his operating philosophy as he expressed it succinctly:

Our policy is to reduce the price, extend the operations, and improve the article. You will notice that the reduction of price comes first. We have never considered any costs as fixed. Therefore we first reduce the price to the point where we believe more sales will result. Then we go ahead and try to make the prices. We do not bother about the costs. The new price forces the costs down. The more usual way is to take the costs and then determine the price; and although that method may be scientific in the narrow sense, it is not scientific in the broad sense, because what earthly use is it to know the cost if it tells you that you cannot manufacture at a price at which the article can be sold? But more to the point is the fact that, although one may calculate what a cost is, and of course all of our costs are carefully calculated, no one knows what a cost ought to be. One of the ways of discovering . . . is to name a price so low as to force everybody in the place to the highest point of efficiency. The low price makes everybody dig for profits. We make more discoveries concerning manufacturing and selling under this forced method than by any method of leisurely investigation.[5]

Product Provincialism

The tantalizing profit possibilities of low unit production costs may be the most seriously self-deceiving attitude that can afflict a company, particularly a "growth" company where an apparently assured expansion of demand already tends to undermine a proper concern for the importance of marketing and the customer.

The usual result of this narrow preoccupation with so-called concrete matters is that instead of growing, the industry declines. It usually means that the product fails to adapt to the constantly changing patterns of consumer needs and tastes, to new and modified marketing institutions

[5]Henry Ford, *My Life and Work* (New York: Doubleday, Page & Company, 1923), pp. 146–47.

and practices, or to product developments in competing or complementary industries. The industry has its eyes so firmly on its own specific product that it does not see how it is being made obsolete.

The classical example of this is the buggy whip industry. No amount of product improvement could stave off its death sentence. But had the industry defined itself as being in the transportation business rather than the buggy whip business, it might have survived. It would have done what survival always entails, that is, changing. Even if it had only defined its business as providing a stimulant or catalyst to an energy source, it might have survived by becoming a manufacturer of, say, fanbelts or air cleaners.

What may some day be a still more classical example is, again, the oil industry. Having let others steal marvelous opportunities from it (e.g., natural gas, as already mentioned, missile fuels, and jet engine lubricants), one would expect it to have taken steps never to let that happen again. But this is not the case. We are now getting extraordinary new developments in fuel systems specifically designed to power automobiles. Not only are these developments concentrated in firms outside the petroleum industry, but petroleum is almost systematically ignoring them, securely content in its wedded bliss to oil. It is the story of the kerosene lamp versus the incandescent lamp all over again. Oil is trying to improve hydrocarbon fuels rather than to develop *any* fuels best suited to the needs of their users, whether or not made in different ways and with different raw materials from oil.

Here are some of the things which non-petroleum companies are working on:

☐ Over a dozen such firms now have advanced working models of energy systems which, when perfected, will replace the internal combustion engine and eliminate the demand for gasoline. The superior merit of each of these systems is their elimination of frequent, time-consuming, and irritating refueling stops. Most of these systems are fuel cells designed to create electrical energy directly from chemicals without combustion. Most of them use chemicals that are not derived from oil, generally hydrogen and oxygen.

☐ Several other companies have advanced models of electric storage batteries designed to power automobiles. One of these is an aircraft producer that is working jointly with several electric utility companies. The latter hope to use offpeak generating capacity to supply overnight plug-in battery regeneration. Another company, also using the battery approach, is a medium-size electronics firm with extensive small-battery experience that it developed in connection with its work on hearing aids. It is collaborating with an automobile manufacturer. Recent improvements arising from the need for high-powered miniature power storage plants in rockets have put us within reach of a relatively small battery capable of withstanding great overloads or surges of power. Germanium diode applications and batteries using sintered-plate and nickel-cadmium techniques promise to make a revolution in our energy sources.

☐ Solar energy conversion systems are also getting increasing attention. One usually cautious Detroit auto executive recently ventured that solar-powered cars might be common by 1980.

As for the oil companies, they are more or less "watching developments," as one research director put it to me. A few are doing a bit of research on fuel cells, but almost always confined to developing cells powered by hydrocarbon chemicals. None of them are enthusiastically researching fuel cells, batteries, or solar power plants. None of them are spending a fraction as much on research in these profoundly important areas as they are on the usual run-of-the-mill things like reducing combustion chamber deposit in gasoline engines. One major integrated petroleum company recently took a tentative look at the fuel cell and concluded that although "the companies actively working on it indicate a belief in ultimate success . . . the timing and magnitude of its impact are too remote to warrant recognition in our forecasts."

One might, of course, ask: Why should the oil companies do anything different? Would not chemical fuel cells, batteries, or solar energy kill the present product lines? The answer is that they would indeed, and that is precisely the reason for the oil firms having to develop these power units before their competitors, so they will not be companies without an industry.

Management might be more likely to do what is needed for its own preservation if it thought of itself as being in the energy business. But even that would not be enough if it persists in imprisoning itself in the narrow grip of its tight product orientation. It has to think of itself as taking care of customer needs, not finding, refining, or even selling oil. Once it genuinely thinks of its business as taking care of people's transportation needs, nothing can stop it from creating its own extravagantly profitable growth.

Creative Destruction

Since words are cheap and deeds are dear, it may be appropriate to indicate what this kind of thinking involves and leads to. Let us start at the beginning—the customer. It can be shown that motorists strongly dislike the bother, delay, and experience of buying gasoline. People actually do not buy gasoline. They cannot see it, taste it, feel it, appreciate it, or really test it. What they buy is the right to continue driving their cars. The gas station is like a tax collector to whom people are compelled to pay a periodic toll as the price of using their cars. This makes the gas station a basically unpopular institution. It can never be made popular or pleasant, only less unpopular, less unpleasant.

To reduce its unpopularity completely means eliminating it. Nobody likes a tax collector, not even a pleasantly cheerful one. Nobody likes to interrupt a trip to buy a phantom product, not even from a handsome Adonis or a seductive Venus. Hence, companies that are working on exotic fuel substitutes which will eliminate the need for frequent refueling are heading directly into the outstretched arms of the irritated motorists. They are riding a wave of inevitability, not because they are creating something which is technologically superior or more sophisticated, but because they are satisfying a powerful customer need. They are also eliminating noxious odors and air pollution.

Once the petroleum companies recognize the customer-satisfying logic of what another power can do, they will see that they have no more choice about working on an efficient, long-lasting fuel (or some way of delivering present fuels without bothering the motorist) than the big food chains had a choice about going into the supermarket business, or the vacuum tube companies had a choice about making semiconductors. For their own good the oil firms will have to destroy their own highly profitable assets. No amount of wishful thinking can save them from the necessity of engaging in this form of "creative-destruction."

I phrase the need as strongly as this because I think management must make quite an effort to break itself loose from conventional ways. It is all too easy in this day and age for a company or industry to let its sense of purpose become dominated by the economies of full production and to develop a dangerously lopsided product orientation. In short, if management lets itself drift, it invariably drifts in the direction of thinking of itself as producing goods and services, not customer satisfactions. While it probably will not descend to the depths of telling its salesmen, "You get rid of it; we'll worry about profits," it can, without knowing it, be practicing precisely that formula for withering decay. The historic fate of one growth industry after another has been its suicidal product provincialism.

DANGERS OF R & D

Another big danger to a firm's continued growth arises when top management is wholly transfixed by the profit possibilities of technical research and development. To illustrate I shall turn first to a new industry —electronics—and then return once more to the oil companies. By comparing a fresh example with a familiar one, I hope to emphasize the prevalence and insidiousness of a hazardous way of thinking.

Marketing Shortchanged

In the case of electronics, the greatest danger which faces the glamorous new companies in this field is not that they do not pay enough attention to research and development, but that they pay *too much* attention to it. And the fact that the fastest growing electronics firms owe their eminence to their heavy emphasis on technical research is completely beside the point. They have vaulted to affluence on a sudden crest of unusually strong general receptiveness to new technical ideas. Also, their success has been shaped in the virtually guaranteed market of military subsidies and by military orders that in many cases actually preceded the existence of facilities to make the products. Their expansion has, in other words, been almost totally devoid of marketing effort.

Thus, they are growing up under conditions that come dangerously close to creating the illusion that a superior product will sell itself. Having created a successful company by making a superior product, it is not surprising that management continues to be oriented toward the product rather than the people who consume it. It develops the philosophy that continued growth is a matter of continued product innovation and improvement.

A number of other factors tend to strengthen and sustain this belief:

1. Because electronic products are highly complex and sophisticated, managements become top-heavy with engineers and scientists. This creates a selective bias in favor of research and production at the expense of marketing. The organization tends to view itself as making things rather than satisfying customer needs. Marketing gets treated as a residual activity, "something else" that must be done once the vital job of product creation and production is completed.

2. To this bias in favor of product research, development, and production is added the bias in favor of dealing with controllable variables. Engineers and scientists are at home in the world of concrete things like machines, test tubes, production lines, and even balance sheets. The abstractions to which they feel kindly are those which are testable or manipulatable in the laboratory, or, if not testable, then functional, such as Euclid's axioms. In short, the managements of the new glamour-growth companies tend to favor those business activities which lend themselves to careful study, experimentation, and control—the hard, practical realities of the lab, the shop, the books.

What gets shortchanged are the realities of the *market*. Consumers are unpredictable, varied, fickle, stupid, shortsighted, stubborn, and generally bothersome. This is not what the engineer-managers say, but deep down in their consciousness it is what they believe. And this accounts for their concentrating on what they know and what they can control, namely product research, engineering, and production. The emphasis on production becomes particularly attractive when the product can be made at declining unit costs. There is no more inviting way of making money than by running the plant full blast.

Today the top-heavy science-engineering-production orientation of so many electronics companies works reasonably well because they are pushing into new frontiers in which the armed services have pioneered virtually assured markets. The companies are in the felicitous position of having to fill, not find, markets; of not having to discover what the customer needs and wants, but of having the customer voluntarily come forward with specific new product demands. If a team of consultants had been assigned specifically to design a business situation calculated to prevent the emergence and development of a customer-oriented marketing viewpoint, it could not have produced anything better than the conditions just described.

Stepchild Treatment

The oil industry is a stunning example of how science, technology, and mass production can divert an entire group of companies from their main task. To the extent the consumer is studied at all (which is not much), the focus is forever on getting information which is designed to help the oil companies improve what they are now doing. They try to discover more convincing advertising themes, more effective sales promotional drives, what the market shares of the various companies are, what people like or dislike about service station dealers and oil companies, and so forth. Nobody seems as interested in probing deeply into the basic human needs that the industry might be trying to satisfy as in probing into the basic properties of the raw material that the companies work with in trying to deliver customer satisfactions.

Basic questions about customers and markets seldom get asked. The latter occupy a stepchild status. They are recognized as existing, as having to be taken care of, but not worth very much real thought or dedicated attention. Nobody gets as excited about the customers in his own backyard as about the oil in the Sahara Desert. Nothing illustrates better the neglect of marketing than its treatment in the industry press:

The centennial issue of the *American Petroleum Institute Quarterly*, published in 1959 to celebrate the discovery of oil in Titusville, Pennsylvania, contained 21 feature articles proclaiming the industry's greatness. Only one of these talked about its achievements in marketing, and that was only a pictorial record of how service station architecture has changed. The issue also contained a special section on "New Horizons," which was devoted to showing the magnificent role oil would play in America's future. Every

reference was ebulliently optimistic, never implying once that oil might have some hard competition. Even the reference to atomic energy was a cheerful catalogue of how oil would help make atomic energy a success. There was not a single apprehension that the oil industry's affluence might be threatened or a suggestion that one "new horizon" might include new and better ways of serving oil's present customers.

But the most revealing example of the stepchild treatment that marketing gets was still another special series of short articles on "The Revolutionary Potential of Electronics." Under that heading this list of articles appeared in the table of contents:

"In the Search for Oil"
"In Production Operations"
"In Refinery Processes"
"In Pipeline Operations"

Significantly, every one of the industry's major functional areas is listed, *except* marketing. Why? Either it is believed that electronics holds no revolutionary potential for petroleum marketing (which is palpably wrong), or the editors forgot to discuss marketing (which is more likely, and illustrates its stepchild status).

The order in which the four functional areas are listed also betrays the alienation of the oil industry from the consumer. The industry is implicitly defined as beginning with the search for oil and ending with its distribution from the refinery. But the truth is, it seems to me, that the industry begins with the needs of the customer for its products. From that primal position its definition moves steadily backstream to areas of progressively lesser importance, until it finally comes to rest at the "search for oil."

Beginning & End

The view that an industry is a customer-satisfying process, not a goods-producing process, is vital for all businessmen to understand. An industry begins with the customer and his needs, not with a patent, a raw material, or a selling skill. Given the customer's needs, the industry develops backwards, first concerning itself with the physical *delivery* of customer satisfactions. Then it moves back further to *creating* the things by which these satisfactions are in part achieved. How these materials are created is a matter of indifference to the customer, hence the particular form of manufacturing, processing, or what-have-you cannot be considered as a vital aspect of the industry. Finally, the industry moves back still further to *finding* the raw materials necessary for making its products.

The irony of some industries oriented toward technical research and development is that the scientists who occupy the high executive positions are totally unscientific when it comes to defining their companies' overall needs and purposes. They violate the first two rules of the scientific method—being aware of and defining their companies' problems, and then developing testable hypotheses about solving them. They are scientific only about the convenient things, such as laboratory and product experiments. The reason that the customer (and the satisfaction of his deepest needs) is not considered as being "the problem" is not because there is any certain belief that no such problem exists, but because an organizational lifetime has conditioned management to look in the opposite direction. Marketing is a stepchild.

I do not mean that selling is ignored. Far from it. But selling, again, is not marketing. As already pointed out, selling concerns itself with the tricks and techniques of getting people to exchange their cash for your product. It is not concerned with the values that the exchange is all about. And it does not, as marketing invariably does, view the entire business process as consisting of a tightly integrated effort to discover, create, arouse, and satisfy customer needs. The customer is somebody "out there" who, with proper cunning, can be separated from his loose change.

Actually, not even selling gets much attention in some technologically minded firms. Because there is a virtually guaranteed market for the abundant flow of their new products, they do not actually know what a real market is. It is as if they lived in a planned economy, moving their products routinely from factory to retail outlet. Their successful concentration on products tends to convince them of the soundness of what they have been doing, and they fail to see the gathering clouds over the market.

CONCLUSION

Less than 75 years ago American railroads enjoyed a fierce loyalty among astute Wall Streeters. European monarchs invested in them heavily. Eternal wealth was thought to be the benediction for anybody who could scrape a few thousand dollars together to put into rail stocks. No other form of transportation could compete with the railroads in speed, flexibility, durability, economy, and growth potentials. As Jacques Barzun put it, "By the turn of the century it was an institution, an image of man, a tradition, a code of honor, a source of poetry, a nursery of boyhood desires, a sublimest of toys, and the most solemn machine —next to the funeral hearse—that marks the epochs in man's life."[6]

Even after the advent of automobiles, trucks, and airplanes, the railroad tycoons remained imperturbably self-confident. If you had told them 60 years ago that in 30 years they would be flat on their backs, broke, and pleading for government subsidies, they would have thought you totally demented. Such a future was simply not considered possible. It was not even a discussable subject, or an askable question, or a matter which any sane person would consider worth speculating about. The very thought was insane. Yet a lot of insane notions now have matter-of-fact acceptance —for example, the idea of 100-ton tubes of metal moving smoothly through the air 20,000 feet above the earth, loaded with 100 sane and solid citizens casually drink-

[6]Barzun, *op. cit.*, p. 20.

ing martinis—and they have dealt cruel blows to the railroads.

What specifically must other companies do to avoid this fate? What does customer orientation involve? These questions have in part been answered by the preceding examples and analysis. It would take another article to show in detail what is required for specific industries. In any case, it should be obvious that building an effective customer-oriented company involves far more than good intentions or promotional tricks; it involves profound matters of human organization and leadership. For the present, let me merely suggest what appear to be some general requirements.

Visceral Feel of Greatness

Obviously the company has to do what survival demands. It has to adapt to the requirements of the market, and it has to do it sooner rather than later. But mere survival is a so-so aspiration. Anybody can survive in some way or other, even the skid-row bum. The trick is to survive gallantly, to feel the surging impulse of commercial mastery; not just to experience the sweet smell of success, but to have the visceral feel of entrepreneurial greatness.

No organization can achieve greatness without a vigorous leader who is driven onward by his own pulsating *will to succeed*. He has to have a vision of grandeur, a vision that can produce eager followers in vast numbers. In business, the followers are the customers. To produce these customers, the entire corporation must be viewed as a customer-creating and customer-satisfying organism. Management must think of itself not as producing products but as providing customer-creating value satisfactions. It must push this idea (and everything it means and requires) into every nook and cranny of the organization. It has to do this continuously and with the kind of flair that excites and stimulates the people in it. Otherwise, the company will be merely a series of pigeonholed parts, with no consolidating sense of purpose or direction.

In short, the organization must learn to think of itself not as producing goods or services but as *buying customers*, as doing the things that will make people *want* to do business with it. And the chief executive himself has the inescapable responsibility for creating this environment, this viewpoint, this attitude, this aspiration. He himself must set the company's style, its direction, and its goals. This means he has to know precisely where he himself wants to go, and to make sure the whole organization is enthusiastically aware of where that is. This is a first requisite of leadership, for *unless he knows where he is going, any road will take him there.*

If any road is okay, the chief executive might as well pack his attaché case and go fishing. If an organization does not know or care where it is going, it does not need to advertise that fact with a ceremonial figurehead. Everybody will notice it soon enough.

1975: RETROSPECTIVE COMMENTARY

Amazed, finally, by his literary success, Isaac Bashevis Singer reconciled an attendant problem: "I think the moment you have published a book, it's not any more your private property. . . . If it has value, everybody can find in it what he finds, and I cannot tell the man I did not intend it to be so." Over the past 15 years, "Marketing Myopia" has become a case in point. Remarkably, the article spawned a legion of loyal partisans—not to mention a host of unlikely bedfellows.

Its most common and, I believe, most influential consequence is the way certain companies for the first time gave serious thought to the question of what businesses they are really in.

The strategic consequences of this have in many cases been dramatic. The best-known case, of course, is the shift in thinking of oneself as being in the "oil business" to being in the "energy business." In some instances the payoff has been spectacular (getting into coal, for example) and in others dreadful (in terms of the time and money spent so far on fuel cell research). Another successful example is a company with a large chain of retail shoe stores that redefined itself as a retailer of moderately priced, frequently purchased, widely assorted consumer specialty products. The result was a dramatic growth in volume, earnings, and return on assets.

Some companies, again for the first time, asked themselves whether they wished to be masters of certain technologies for which they would seek markets, or be masters of markets for which they would seek customer-satisfying products and services.

Choosing the former, one company has declared, in effect, "We are experts in glass technology. We intend to improve and expand that expertise with the object of creating products that will attract customers." This decision has forced the company into a much more systematic and customer-sensitive look at possible markets and users, even though its stated strategic object has been to capitalize on glass technology.

Deciding to concentrate on markets, another company has determined that "we want to help people (primarily women) enhance their beauty and sense of youthfulness." This company has expanded its line of cosmetic products, but has also entered the fields of proprietary drugs and vitamin supplements.

All these examples illustrate the "policy" results of "Marketing Myopia." On the operating level, there has been, I think, an extraordinary heightening of sensitivity to customers and consumers. R&D departments have cultivated a greater "external" orientation toward uses, users, and mar-kets—balancing thereby the previously one-sided "internal" focus on materials and methods; upper management has realized that marketing and sales departments should be somewhat more willingly accommodated than before; finance departments have become more receptive to the legitimacy of budgets for market research and experimentation in marketing; and salesmen have been better trained to listen to and understand customer needs and problems, rather than merely to "push" the product.

A Mirror, Not a Window

My impression is that the article has had more impact in industrial-products companies than in consumer-products companies—perhaps because the former had lagged most in customer orientation. There are at least two reasons for this lag: (1) industrial-products companies tend to be more capital intensive, and (2) in the past, at least, they have had to rely heavily on communicating face-to-face the technical character of what they made and sold. These points are worth explaining.

Capital-intensive businesses are understandably preoccupied with magnitudes, especially where the capital, once invested, cannot be easily moved, manipulated, or modified for the production of a variety of products—e.g., chemical plants, steel mills, airlines, and railroads. Understandably, they seek big volumes and operating efficiencies to pay off the equipment and meet the carrying costs.

At least one problem results: corporate power becomes disproportionately lodged with operating or financial executives. If you read the charter of one of the nation's largest companies, you will see that the chairman of the finance committee, not the chief executive officer, is the "chief." Executives with such backgrounds have an almost trained incapacity to see that getting "volume" may require understanding and serving many discrete and sometimes small market segments, rather than going after a perhaps mythical batch of big or homogeneous customers.

These executives also often fail to appreciate the competitive changes going on around them. They observe the changes, all right, but devalue their significance or underestimate their ability to nibble away at the company's markets.

Once dramatically alerted to the concept of segments, sectors, and customers, though, managers of capital-intensive businesses have become more responsive to the necessity of balancing their inescapable preoccupation with "paying the bills" or breaking even with the fact that the best way to accomplish this may be to pay more attention to segments, sectors, and customers.

The second reason industrial-products companies have probably been more influenced by the article is that, in the case of the more technical industrial products or services, the necessity of clearly communicating product and service characteristics to prospects results in a lot of face-to-face "selling" effort. But precisely because the product is so complex, the situation produces salesmen who know the product more than they know the customer, who are more adept at explaining what they have and what it can do than learning what the customer's needs and problems are. The result has been a narrow product orientation rather than a liberating customer orientation, and "service" often suffered. To be sure, sellers said, "We have to provide service," but they tended to define service by looking into the mirror rather than out the window. They *thought* they were looking out the window at the customer, but it was actually a mirror—a reflection of their own product-oriented biases rather than a reflection of their customer's situations.

A Manifesto, Not a Prescription

Not everything has been rosy. A lot of bizarre things have happened as a result of the article:

☐ Some companies have developed what I call "marketing mania"—they've become obsessively responsive to every fleeting whim of the customer. Mass production operations have been converted to approximations of job shops, with cost and price consequences far exceeding the willingness of customers to buy the product.

☐ Management has expanded product lines and added new lines of business without first establishing adequate control systems to run more complex operations.

☐ Marketing staffs have suddenly and rapidly expanded themselves and their research budgets without either getting sufficient prior organizational support or, thereafter, producing sufficient results.

☐ Companies that are functionally organized have converted to product, brand, or market-based organizations with the expectation of instant and miraculous results. The outcome has been ambiguity, frustration, confusion, corporate infighting, losses, and finally a reversion to functional arrangements that only worsened the situation.

☐ Companies have attempted to "serve" customers by creating complex and beautifully efficient products or services that buyers are either too risk-averse to adopt or incapable of learning how to employ—in effect, there are now steam shovels for people who haven't yet learned to use spades. This problem has happened repeatedly in the so-called service industries (financial services, insurance, computer-based services) and with American companies selling in less-developed economies.

"Marketing Myopia" was not intended as analysis or even prescription; it was intended as manifesto. It did not pretend to take a balanced position. Nor was it a new idea—Peter F. Drucker, J. B. McKitterick,

Wroe Alderson, John Howard, and Neil Borden had each done more original and balanced work on "the marketing concept." My scheme, however, tied marketing more closely to the inner orbit of business policy. Drucker—especially in *The Concept of the Corporation* and *The Practice of Management*—originally provided me with a great deal of insight.

My contribution, therefore, appears merely to have been a simple, brief, and useful way of communicating an existing way of thinking. I tried to do it in a very direct, but responsible, fashion, knowing that few readers (customers), especially managers and leaders, could stand much equivocation or hesitation. I also knew that the colorful and lightly documented affirmation works better than the tortuously reasoned explanation.

But why the enormous popularity of what was actually such a simple pre-existing idea? Why its appeal throughout the world to resolutely restrained scholars, implac-

ably temperate managers, and high government officials, all accustomed to balanced and thoughtful calculation? Is it that concrete examples, joined to illustrate a simple idea and presented with some attention to literacy, communicate better than massive analytical reasoning that reads as though it were translated from the German? Is it that provocative assertions are more memorable and persuasive than restrained and balanced explanations, no matter who the audience? Is it that the character of the message is as much the message as its content? Or was mine not simply a different tune, but a new symphony? I don't know.

Of course, I'd do it again and in the same way, given my purposes, even with what more I now know—the good and the bad, the power of facts and the limits of rhetoric. If your mission is the moon, you don't use a car. Don Marquis's cockroach, Archy, provides some final consolation: "an idea is not responsible for who believes in it."

2 Marketing Muscle

Edward G. Michaels

The evidence suggests that marketing will be tomorrow's competitive cutting edge in many nonmarketing-oriented industries, including apparel, textiles, consumer durables, transportation, utilities, financial services, and retailing.

What do Miller Beer, AT&T, Levi Strauss, Canon, and Taylor Wine have in common? They are in different industries. They range in size from under $100 million to over $10 billion. Yet all are committed to essentially the same innovative strategy. Each operates in an industry virtually devoid, until recently, of marketing skills as understood and practiced by excellent consumer packaged-goods producers. And each has decided to change the game and bid for leadership through the simple but unorthodox tactic of out-marketing its competitors.

A notable early demonstration of the power of superior marketing muscle was the spectacular success of Miller Beer following its takeover by Philip Morris. Philip Morris used its packaged-goods techniques to re-

Edward G. Michaels, a Principal in the Atlanta office of McKinsey & Company, has advised a variety of industries on issues of marketing strategy.

position Miller, tripled its marketing budget, and achieved a sixfold increase—from 4 percent to 24 percent—in market share. So far, because of the high cost of the added capacity, commensurate financial rewards have eluded Miller's grasp, yet the company remains a classic example of successful game changing and a testimony to the power of marketing muscle. The moral of the story has not been lost on Miller's competitors.

Strohs and Coors, among others, are now moving to build marketing muscle. Strohs, for example, has hired marketing pros from Heublein, PepsiCo, and Procter & Gamble; expanded its line and markets; and repositioned its product as a premium-priced, "in" beer. Coors, which knew how to allocate—not market—beer, has begun to use market research, expanded its product line, and increased its advertising spending by a factor of 10.

Reprinted from *Business Horizons* (May–June 1982), pp. 63–74. © 1982 by the Foundation for the School of Business at Indiana University. Reprinted by permission.

Clearly, the beer business will never again be quite the same. In an industry that ten years ago relied on distribution and advertising, substantive marketing skills have become indispensable for competitive survival, let alone success. Just ask Schlitz, which, at the same time Miller turned to marketing, was trying to drive its cost down the learning curve by reformulating its product—and slid almost into bankruptcy.

In a number of other industries no more advanced in marketing sophistication today than the beer industry was when Philip Morris appeared on the horizon, there are straws in the wind to suggest that a similar development may be impending or already taking place.

One example is apparel. A major marketing success story of the 1970s was Hanes' use of classic packaged-goods marketing principles to revolutionize the hosiery market with its creative product "L'eggs." Hanes improved its product with memory yarn, developed an innovative plastic egg package, entered grocery stores and drugstores, and advertised and promoted heavily. Imitators have followed but never caught up. More recently, Blue Bell (an outstanding performer) and Munsingwear (a laggard) have hired senior-level line marketing executives from packaged-goods companies. And Peter Haas, Levi Strauss' chairman, describes Levi as a consumer products company that just happens to be in the apparel business. In the 1960s, Levi was lucky to be in the right spot at the right time—but it was marketing skill, not luck, that carried them from a 10 percent to a 20 percent brand share in the 1970s. Prospects are no longer bright for competitors who refuse to pick up the marketing gauntlet these and other apparel companies have thrown down.

The wine industry is witnessing a similar evolution. With its acquisition of Taylor Wine and several California vineyards, Coca-Cola is changing the focus of the industry from production and selling to marketing. Coke has segmented the wine market, broadened Taylor's product lines to target products toward various price segments, repositioned Taylor as a California wine, used controversial product comparison tests in their advertising, and is investing heavily. In an uncharacteristic public forecast, the head of Coke's Wine Spectrum Division has projected that the division will grow from under $100 million in sales in 1978 to $1 billion by 1990. Coke's aggressive entry and apparent success is changing the basis for competition in this low-key, almost "clubby," industry from production and channel selling to marketing. Observers say the wine industry will never be the same again.

Developments in these industries, I suggest, are early signs of a pattern that is likely to emerge more clearly in the 1980s—a pattern that may significantly change the dynamics of competition in a spectrum of traditionally nonmarketing-oriented industries: apparel, consumer durables, textiles, financial institutions, transportation companies, even retailing and utilities. Already, isolated competitors in these industries are beginning to turn to packaged-goods marketing techniques. Some are rapidly gaining share as a result. Sooner or later, their success will compel their competitors to start building marketing muscle of their own.

Is your company's marketing muscle equal to the competitive challenges you are likely to face in the 1980s? The accompanying simple checklist (Exhibit 1) may provide some preliminary clues.

FORCES AT WORK

If the examples already mentioned really do mark the beginning of a move to marketing across a range of industries, at least three precipitating factors can be identified:

EXHIBIT 1

Measuring marketing muscle

The following checklist provides a quick self-test for a company that wants a rough measure of its marketing capability.

1. Has your company carefully segmented the consumers that it serves?

2. Do you routinely measure the profitability of your key products or services in each of these consumer market segments?

3. Do you use market research to keep abreast of the needs, preferences, and buying habits of consumers in each segment?

4. Have you identified the key buying factors in each segment, and do you know how your company compares with its competitors on these factors?

5. Is the impact of environmental trends (demographic, competitive, lifestyle, governmental) on your business carefully gauged?

6. Does your company prepare and use an annual marketing plan?

7. Is the concept of "marketing investment" understood—and practiced—in your company?

8. Is profit responsibility for a product line pushed below the senior management level?

9. Does your organization "talk" marketing?

10. Did one of the top five executives in your company come up through marketing?

If you answered yes to:

9 or 10—you have a strong marketing capability.
6 to 8—you are on the way.
fewer than 6—you are vulnerable to marketing-minded competitors.

1. The battle for market share is intensifying in many industries as a result of declining growth rates (as illustrated in Exhibit 2). A recent study by Chase Econometric predicts that the aging of the postwar baby-boom generation will not provide the marketing bonanza many companies have confidently hoped for. "People are

EXHIBIT 2

INDUSTRY SECTOR	GROWTH RATE IN THE 1960s	GROWTH RATE IN THE 1970s
Airlines	12.90%	6.8%
Beverages	5.50	4.9
Food	3.50	3.0
Household appliances	7.00	1.5
Leather	0.02	(2.5)
Textiles	4.90	2.0
Utilities	7.00	3.2

SOURCE: Federal Reserve Board, Industrial Production Indexes.

counting heads, not dollars," they say. In the 1980s, the number of the affluent (including many two-income families) will increase slightly and the number of the poor sharply, Chase predicts—both at the expense of today's large, reasonably affluent middle class. If true, most current forecasts for the 1980s for consumer durables are overoptimistic.

Faced with virtually "no growth," companies will be grasping for new weapons to help them win share—and sophisticated marketing methods can provide important extra firepower in these competitive shootouts. Philip Kotler and Ravi Singh[1] predict that marketing competition will heat up considerably in the years ahead. The battlefield concepts of frontal attack, flanking, encirclement, guerilla warfare, and counteroffensive, they suggest, will become current boardroom language in the 1980s.

2. In several industry sectors, deregulation is mandating a move to marketing. As a result of substantial regulatory changes now under way, the airline, trucking, banking, and telecommunications industries are becoming dramatically more competitive. In the past, competition in these industries has been along prescribed lines. Jurisdictions

[1] In "Marketing Warfare in the 1980s," *Journal of Business Strategy*, Winter 1981.

have been protected. Prices have been regulated. As a consequence, the marketing function has been rudimentary. Now, with the winds of competition blowing, the need for marketing muscle has become urgent and some companies are already moving to meet it.

Consider the case of AT&T. Five years ago, by bringing in Archie McGill, then senior marketing vice president at IBM, the nation's largest company signaled its intention to become more marketing-oriented. Since then, McGill has built a large marketing staff, perhaps half of them newcomers to AT&T. He has established new customer-based ways of measuring service to replace the old measures based on internal efficiencies. McGill has been instrumental in attempting to reorient the company's product development process from research and engineering to market and consumer needs. At the same time, the company has reorganized around three main business sectors—residential, commercial, and network (long distance, WATS, overseas, and so on). Within the commercial sector, they have organized by customer industry instead of location as in the past. (In one state, more than half of AT&T's 400-plus sales representatives were obliged to relocate as a result.) To service its big customers better, the company has moved to centralized account management. Finally, it has built a professional sales force, reportedly recruiting no fewer than 2,000 MBAs in its Long Lines Division alone. Not surprisingly, in an organization of about a million people, many of these changes—notably central account management, cutting across operating-company lines—have met with resistance. No doubt, there will be further problems and further false starts. Especially for a giant company, becoming marketing-oriented is an enormous job—one AT&T

has estimated will take them ten years to accomplish. But, progress has clearly been made. Slowly but surely, the whole value system of a vast organization is being reshaped.

3. Numerous packaged-goods producers are acquiring companies in hitherto non-marketing-oriented industries and moving to gain share through massive injections of marketing capability. The discouraging growth prospects in most packaged-goods industries have spurred many large companies to look for greener pastures. Many see the opportunity to use their marketing strengths to gain share, or change the nature of competition, in traditionally nonmarketing industry sectors. Exhibit 3 shows a few of the more aggressive of these moves.

A good many of these marriages have worked so well that other companies in the sectors affected find themselves under real pressure to build marketing muscle fast, simply in order to survive and compete effectively.

EXHIBIT 3

ACQUIRER	ACQUISITION(S)	INDUSTRY SECTOR
General Mills	Izod, Ship 'n' Shore	Apparel
	Kenner Toys	Toys
	Parker Brothers	Toys
Esmark (Swift)	Playtex	Apparel
	STP	Additives
Coke	Taylor	Wine
Philip Morris	Miller	Beer
	7-Up	Soft Drinks
Consolidated Foods	Hanes	Apparel
Interco	Broyhill	Furniture
PepsiCo	Wilson	Sporting Goods
Chesebrough-Pond's	Health-Tex	Apparel
	Bass Shoes	Shoes

These three trends threaten all competitors, but they pose an especially acute hazard to companies that are blinded to the gravity of the challenge by misconceptions about the true nature of marketing. Thanks to the Madison Avenue mystique it has somehow acquired, many managers lacking first-hand exposure to marketing people and marketing concerns think of marketing as an arcane, theoretical, "ivory tower" activity practiced by bearded eccentrics in red underwear. At best, it is irrelevant to their real world; at worst, a kind of black magic that no sensible businessman would ever want to dabble in.

Equally misleading is the widespread notion that marketing equals advertising, and advertising means megabucks. Pick 100 executives at random from nonpackaged-goods consumer products companies and ask them for a definition of marketing. If your experience is like mine, more than half will say, in effect, "advertising." Few will mention consumer satisfaction; fewer still will speak of integrated planning. This misconception is understandable; thanks to advertising people, advertising is indeed the most talked about element of the marketing mix.

Early last year *The Wall Street Journal* introduced a new weekly marketing section; of its first fifty articles, more than half were on advertising. What's more, there is an understandably widespread impression that any national advertising program worth its salt costs at least $5 million or $10 million annually—and the economics of many product lines simply won't support that kind of advertising budget. Marketing doesn't always mean big money. Some share leaders are consistently outspent by their competitors yet achieve superiority by emphasizing other elements of the marketing mix: for example, sales coverage and skills, dealer service, or product performance. Where a major communications task does require large advertising expenditures, marketers arrange or rearrange their business system to accommodate this expenditure. Expenditures for advertising and promotion to create awareness, trial, and repurchase are an integral part of the P&L—not what is left over.

While a good many companies continue to shy away from marketing as something too exotic or too expensive, others have written it off as a quick fix that doesn't work. They know: they promoted their best sales manager to corporate VP, marketing, and nothing happened! Or they sent a hand-picked group of managers to a two-week marketing course, with the same result. Or they started a small market research department. Or they worked out a corporate "marketing plan"—and then proceeded to file and forget it.

Unfortunately, most of these actions taken piecemeal leave companies undernourished and dissatisfied with "having tried marketing." Marketing is a line activity; to be effective, it must permeate the company. Middle management must practice marketing daily to build an organization's marketing muscle.

WHO NEEDS IT?

It seems clear that in any industry composed, figuratively speaking, of 97-pound marketing weaklings, the first company to build real marketing muscle should have a solid competitive advantage. But the extent of that potential advantage will vary from industry to industry, depending on such factors as true product differentiation, importance of personal selling, and agility of competition. Let us look a little more closely at some of the consumer goods and services where the gap between current marketing capability and the potential competitive advantage attainable through marketing muscle appears especially significant.

Apparel

Marketing in the apparel business is unmistakably an idea whose time has come. "L'eggs" is history. Levi and Blue Bell have signaled their efforts to strengthen their marketing. The designer jeans media hype worked. Formfit Rogers is currently introducing a new line of panties in a way even P&G would approve: they have conducted extensive consumer research, test-marketed in three cities, and plan to spend $9 million to introduce a product whose first-year sales are estimated at only $20 to $25 million.

When marketing-oriented consumer products companies purchased apparel companies, things started to happen. Chesebrough-Pond's has made Health-Tex into the leading marketer of children's apparel. They tripled Bass Shoes' sales in three years by a calculated application of marketing muscle—broadening the product line, raising prices, investing in efficient manufacturing and distribution, and promoting Bass's already well-regarded brand names. Over the past ten years, General Mills has done much the same with Izod (the alligator shirt).

As a result of all this, the realization is spreading among apparel manufacturers that they can benefit from segmentation, market research, and investment spending—indeed, they may have little choice. As this fragmented industry continues to consolidate and strong brands continue to gain share, the trend will accelerate. If marketing muscle can make the difference between winning and losing in such mundane businesses as toilet paper and toothpaste, it should certainly help to differentiate ego-intensive products like jeans, dresses, and swimwear!

Textiles

Most textile manufacturers have long had a manufacturing mentality. Often they have relied on their apparel, industrial, and retail customers for marketing insights. The textile companies with large positions in the household-furnishings market (towels, sheets, and so on) are selling a consumer product through a retailer just as Procter & Gamble does. Most have already developed brand names and advertise to some extent; some even employ name designers. As yet, however, the sort of thorough consumer research, careful segmentation, and aggressive advertising and promotion that are taken for granted among packaged-goods producers are uncommon in the textile industry. Not that the opportunity is lacking. American-made household furnishings —towels, for example—are a luxury item on world markets. The textile company that first develops real marketing muscle will reap handsome rewards, both at home and overseas. Yet most textile makers are still alarmingly casual in their approach to exporting.

Other parts of the textile industry are still further behind. How should a fabric manufacturer select its markets and decide whether to invest $20 million to $50 million in a corduroy (or denim or carpet yarn) plant? Shouldn't management find out what consumers think of corduroy—whether it is becoming an all-season fabric, what international trends affect demand? Beyond studying industry association estimates of existing supply and demand, such investment decisions, in my experience, are commonly made with surprisingly little knowledge of consumer preferences, other than what little information the company may have gleaned from its customers in the trade, who are often credited with a knowledge of consumers' needs that they don't in fact possess.

True, many textile companies boast "product managers," but these usually turn out to be glorified sales or technical service positions. Markets are not rigorously segmented or analyzed; integrated marketing plans are rarely prepared; investment spending is unheard of. But now that many textile companies have already invested heavily to modernize their plants and equipment, marketing muscle offers the next logical means of achieving competitive differentiation.

Consumer Durables

In other segments of the consumer durables sector (in addition to apparel)—notably consumer electronics, sporting goods, and toys—aggressive companies are flexing marketing muscles. Rather than relying on their distribution channels to "push" their products, they are utilizing packaged-goods "pull" marketing principles—often with outstanding results. Smart consumer durables companies are borrowing pages from the packaged-goods book on marketing (see Exhibit 4).

Consider Canon's strategy with its cameras and tabletop copiers. In each case the company started by identifying unfilled consumer needs: no one made a simple-to-operate 35mm single-lens reflex camera, and no one made a very small, fast copier. So Canon developed these products and poured on the marketing resources. For their new AE-1, they used TV advertising—a first for 35mm cameras. Then they extended the line with new models—simpler versions for the casual snapshot-taker segment as well as more sophisticated models for the photography buff. They used microprocessor technology to develop a small, typewriter-size copier; then, to launch the product in the

EXHIBIT 4

The marketing spectrum

	Industrial Products		Consumer Durables			Consumer Packaged Goods
Typical product categories	Industrial machinery and parts	Motor vehicles	Major appliances —Furniture —Musical instruments —Home furnishings	Small appliances —Consumer electronics —Watches —Batteries —Educational materials	Apparel —Sporting goods —Toys	Food Cosmetics Tobacco
Market size ($ billions)	$260	$75	$50	$30	$120	$460

Typical Success Factors

Sales force management Cost control R&D Product quality	Channel relationships After-sales service Product features	Advertising and promotion Brand name Market research Product positioning

Appropriate Marketing Approach

Push	Push/Pull	Pull

United States, they spent 10 percent of its list price on advertising and promotion. Now, in a "total war" against Xerox, faster models and color copiers are being introduced. Canon has reported 1980 sales of more than $2 billion and profits of $119 million. Not bad for a company that had to suspend its dividends in 1975!

General Mills, one of the premier packaged-goods marketing companies, bought its way into the consumer durables sector and has given these businesses new vitality by direct injections of brand management know-how. In marketing their Star Wars toys and electronic games such as Merlin, General Mills' Kenner Products and Parker Brothers subsidiaries applied General Mills' product management system. Each of these two toy brands has increased its share significantly, growing to almost $100 million annually. It is a fair guess that General Mills has also sprinkled its Izod, Ship 'n' Shore blouses, and Monet jewelry subsidiaries with product managers from its food division. Competitive pressures are already beginning to push other consumer durables segments—furniture, appliances, home furnishings, even consumer electronics—in the same direction.

As even outstanding companies like Hewlett-Packard and Texas Instruments have learned, technically superior new products alone won't save a giant from being outmuscled by a smaller but more marketing-oriented competitor. HP's first big step into consumer electronics, the massive HP-01 gold watch targeted at the affluent senior-executive market, failed because most of the intended customers didn't want a heavy watch and those who wanted fine jewelry didn't think first of Hewlett-Packard. TI, in contrast, stuck resolutely to a technology-based, low-cost strategy, making no attempt to add features. Meanwhile, Seiko and Casio, which were busy researching and segmen-

ting the market, had discovered a large segment unserved by either the HP or TI strategies: namely, the middle-income customer who wanted the accuracy and reliability of the new technology, but not at the expense of elegance. To appeal to the preferences of potential customers in this group, simultaneously gaining share from the makers of "utility" models and attracting new customers from the more conservative high-income segment, Seiko and Casio blanketed the market with a dazzling array of models in every price range. They offered not only almost every imaginable combination of functions but also a wide variety of styles, including a number of high-fashion quartz analog models designed to woo customers away from the likes of Omega and Rolex. By 1980 the two Japanese manufacturers had garnered a large share of the U.S. market for men's watches.

Is much the same scenario being played out in personal computers? Can small personal-computer makers really compete with giants like HP or TI? Yes, if the giant is weak in marketing muscle. Apple Computer spends 5 percent of its sales revenues on advertising its successful personal computer, versus a reported 1 percent for HP. More importantly, Apple concentrates on building in features the consumer seems to want—a bigger screen, a larger memory, more applications, and easy-to-use software. Apple is prospering, while TI's personal computer, the 99/4, originally designed to sell for over $1,000, has had to be repositioned (for "home enrichment" instead of home entertainment) and repriced at $525. Even Radio Shack is beating HP and TI. Consumer research and test marketing could have prevented this embarrassment. With IBM's recent entry, the personal computer battle is certain to reach even higher levels of intensity. Yet, for all its commercial marketing expertise, the unfamiliar world of consumer marketing could prove a daunting challenge for IBM. And any competitor without a thorough understanding of consumer marketing could lose disastrously in the coming struggle for share.

Clearly, the handwriting is on the wall for makers of high-technology consumer products who still let engineers alone control their product development, do little market research and no market testing, and view marketing more or less as a matter of keeping customers in an orderly line. They need marketing muscle, as well as technology strengths.

Transportation

With deregulation, competitive pressures are beginning to force airlines, railroads, and trucking companies to develop some marketing capabilities in a hurry. The case is clearest in airlines. Until recently, fixed prices and traditional routes effectively limited competition to offering free champagne, getting pilots to greet you at the door, advertising such imponderables as "friendly skies," and wooing travel agencies. Now a flock of other elements have become critical: pricing, promotions, adjusting service levels (number of flights), all based on careful segmentation supported by research. Airlines that don't take the trouble to understand and manage all elements of the marketing mix—not just advertising and service—are going to be at a competitive disadvantage.

Much the same is true in railroads and trucking. In the trucking industry, for example, various segmentation schemes are possible—for example, less-than-truckload versus full shipment, specialty versus general carriers, price versus service, geographical areas served, type and size of company served, and so on. In selecting target segments, each carrier now needs to match its strengths (distribution, service capability, etc.) carefully

with customer needs, and to consider its competition, actual and potential—including not only other carriers but internal fleets and leasing arrangements as well. Most truckers have been functionalized and centralized. The winning trucking companies in the 1980s will be those that find the most effective ways of decentralizing profit responsibility and untangling the web of network cost-allocation problems to provide the sort of cost data on which timely pricing decisions can confidently be based.

Financial Institutions

Too many banks still lack the means to determine the profitability of their various products or customer groups and accordingly lack a clear sense of priority among their market segments. Few have researched the habits, practices, and attitudes of their retail customers, and fewer still have developed integrated marketing plans outlining a coherent set of tactics—pricing, products, services, systems, sales efforts, advertising, and so on—for attracting more customers from target segments. With NOW accounts burgeoning, Reg. Q being phased out, Merrill Lynch's Cash Management Account competing for their core deposits, and the possibility of interstate banking looming on the horizon, both regional and money-center banks would do well to embark on a program to build marketing muscle.

They could start by segmenting and setting priorities for customer groups. Next, line bankers in the commercial sector should prepare marketing plans for priority segments, while branch managers in the retail sector should work out market development plans. Creative advertising and promotion approaches can be put to work. Product managers can be established to direct "product development." Entrepreneurship can be stimulated by management information systems that yield timely insights into product and relationship profitability.

Likewise, as deregulation progressively blurs the traditional distinctions among them, other financial institutions ought to be rethinking their need for marketing muscle. Insurance companies, for example, might do well to consider organizing along market or product management lines. Most would also benefit by introducing rigorous marketing planning systems.

Utilities

The financial performance of most utilities in the 1970s can only be described as dismal. Most earned less than their cost of capital. Some paid out more in dividends than they earned. Today, with construction costs and cost of capital at record levels, many are trying desperately to avoid building new power plants. They are confronted not only with complex technology choices but with an urgent need for fundamental improvement in their financial performance.

Here, marketing muscle can play a vital role, for it can be applied just as effectively to get consumers to use less electricity rather than more. Market segments can and should be ranked according to priority, and integrated marketing plans developed. Many tactics can be employed, including price (e.g., time-of-day rates), products (e.g., meters), services (e.g., energy audits), and advertising (e.g., consumer education). Potomac Electric Power Company and Carolina Power and Light are two utilities aggressively pursuing "de-marketing."

In a broader sense, utilities need marketing approaches to help them determine who their more attractive customers are and how to win them. Increasingly, utilities are considering out-of-system sales and entering new businesses—both high-risk areas for the company lacking marketing sophistication. As one thoughtful utility executive said to me recently, "Marketing ought to be a coequal function along with operations, finance, and external affairs."

Retailing

Among retail chains and department stores, some—including K-Mart and Wal-Mart, Kroger and Jewel, Neiman-Marcus and Macy's—have developed winning formulas. But most have not done the thoughtful quantitative research necessary to develop a strategy that will position them most effectively vis-à-vis segments and differentiate them most clearly from their competitors. Notably, A&P, Food Fair, S.H. Kress, and Abercrombie & Fitch had no marketing vision of target customers, merchandising proposition, or competitive advantage. Even Sears still seems to be groping for a strategy.

Too many retailers are still merchandising rather than marketing oriented. For example, only four of the Associated Merchandising Corporation's thirty-one U.S. member companies have a senior vice president or vice president in charge of marketing. Too many are still retail generalists, seemingly unaware of the need to project a clearcut image to the consumers. Since we are so "overstored" in the U.S., more retailers, I believe, will fail in the 1980s if they do not adopt a marketing orientation, develop a clear picture of their target consumers, and position themselves carefully against these segments. They can do this only by understanding what they are now and what is unique about them; deciding what they want to be and what they want want to deemphasize or abandon (in terms of target consumers and product categories); and communicating this image consistently to their target segments.

WHAT IS A MARKETING ORIENTATION?

Insight can be gained by examining the characteristic features of leading consumer packaged-goods marketers as a benchmark. Five of these characteristics are particularly worthy of note.

1. The most effective marketing organizations are consumer-oriented. They do extensive research on the final customer. Consumers' habits, practices, and attitudes are well understood and constantly monitored. Unfilled consumer needs drive product development efforts.

2. They take an integrated approach to planning. All elements of the marketing mix—not just advertising and selling—are fitted together into a sound business plan to build a sustainable competitive advantage. Moreover, the most effective marketers have a preoccupation with top-quality products. Proctor & Gamble, Johnson & Johnson, and General Mills are alike in their determination to produce a better product. All elements of the marketing mix, emphatically including product quality, are used to create a package that will maximize consumer satisfaction. By the same token, marketers in these companies influence the configuration of the entire business system, from product design through to customer service. Their domain is not confined to marketing per se.

3. They look further ahead—typically at least 3 to 5 years—in order to build a sustainable position with the consumer. They are willing to invest to build market share, and they often count advertising, temporary price reductions, and promotions as investments just as they would the cost of a new plant.

4. They have highly developed marketing systems. Typically, profit responsibility rests with product managers below the profit-center level. Their information systems have been honed over the years to provide product managers with real insight into what's currently happening at the consumer and market level. All new product introductions and major modifications to the marketing mix of existing products are based on careful market testing.

5. Marketing dominates the corporate culture. The executives at the top are typically marketers, and they set the tone. Everybody talks marketing: issues of market segmentation, the habits and practices of consumers, marketing plans, new products, and test-market results dominate their attention. Along with this goes an entrepreneurial spirit: middle management is apt to be notably young, bright, and aggressive.

As Exhibit 5 suggests, successful marketing organizations contrast sharply with sales-, manufacturing-, or technology-oriented competitors. Good marketers think like general managers. Their approach is unconstrained by functional boundaries. Without neglecting either near- or medium-term profitability, they concentrate on building a position for tomorrow.

BUILDING MARKETING MUSCLE

Unfortunately, there is no such thing as an effective crash course for building marketing muscle. No one person, system, or technique will make a company marketing-oriented. The elements of a solid marketing capability—that is, a consumer orientation, integrated planning, a long-term outlook, effective marketing systems, and a marketing culture—cannot be implanted overnight: developing a marketing capability is at least

EXHIBIT 5

Four kinds of companies compared

	MANUFACTURING-ORIENTED	SALES-ORIENTED	TECHNOLOGY-ORIENTED	MARKETING-ORIENTED
Typical strategy	Lower cost	Increase volume	Push research	Build share profitability
Normal structure	Functional	Functional or profit centers	Profit centers	Market or product or brand; decentralized profit responsibility
Key systems	Plant P&Ls Budgets	Sales forecasts Results versus plan	Performance tests R&D plans	Marketing plans
Traditional skills	Engineering	Sales	Science and engineering	Analysis
Normal focus	Internal efficiencies	Distribution channels; short-term sales results	Product performance	Consumers Market share
Typical response to competitive pressure	Cut costs	Cut price Sell harder	Improve product	Consumer research, planning, testing, refining
Overall mental set	"What we need to do in this company is get our costs down and our quality up."	"Where can I sell what we make?"	"The best product wins the day."	"What will the consumer buy that we can profitably make?"

a three-year endeavor, requiring change in at least six areas:

1. Investment by top management. To achieve a marketing orientation, management must be willing to invest the financial resources required to build marketing position, and it must be prepared to tolerate a degree of organizational turmoil as old dogs are taught new tricks. The CEO in particular will have to make certain that new role models, new incentives, and new information are made available to managers. By consistently investing his time, he has got to signal and lead a change in the culture of the company, creating an environment that fosters innovation, encourages risk taking, and tolerates failure.

2. Injection of outside talent. In almost every one of the successful cases I have cited, experienced line marketing people were brought in from the outside to spearhead the effort. I know of no instance where major success came through retraining or repositioning. New blood does not ensure success, but it is almost certainly an indispensable ingredient. From my observation, the best results usually come from hiring a single seasoned high-level line marketing executive and letting him add to his team over time.

On no account, however, should the company try to accomplish the transformation at a stroke by hiring a large staff of P&G-type brand managers. A major transplant of this kind is almost certain to provoke such severe rejection symptoms as to jeopardize the entire project. In part this is what happened when Esmark brought forty or so outside marketing people into its ailing Swift division. The marketing "fix" did not work.

3. Develop a clear sense of direction.

As the saying has it, "If you don't know where you are going, any road will take you there." If well-thought-out strategies for key brands or the company overall do not exist, this is the logical place to start.

Target consumer groups must be agreed upon, after careful segmentation and research. Product categories should be assigned priorities based on their market attractiveness and a company's ability to compete in each category. Distribution channels have to be selected. The objectives and roles of advertising and promotion must be agreed upon. Pricing strategies should be explicit. "What is unique about us"—the raison d'être—should be clear.

Such decisions need to be reached at the company, brand, and product-line level. All too often, these key decisions are not explicit and not updated as competitive and environmental factors change. Inertia seems to carry many companies along.

4. Refocus on the consumer.

Nothing is so destructive of marketing muscle as the tendency, common among manufacturing- or sales-oriented companies, to rely on the trade to keep in touch with the consumer. The possible consequences are illustrated by the sad case of Easco, a manufacturer of hand tools that were sold by Sears Roebuck under its well-regarded "Craftsman" label. For years Easco had no marketing department; it depended on Sears' marketing insight. Then Sears stumbled—and Easco fell. Now Easco is learning marketing by building a marketing staff, promoting the Easco name and adding 500 new hardware and home-center stores, including K-Mart and True Value Hardware Stores. Easco is also, ironically, now helping Sears to market its Craftsman line more effectively. Easco's president concedes wryly, "Remaining just a manufacturer as long as we did was probably a mistake."

5. Use of market research.

You cannot have a marketing organization unless product development and customer selection are driven by intimate knowledge of target consumers—their identity, location, and buying power; their needs and wants; the ways they use the product; and their attitudes toward your company and what it makes. Such knowledge can only come through painstaking market research. For the company without a research capability, the most realistic course is, again, to hire a market research professional and let him or her build up a research staff. The alternative—"growing your own"—takes too long, and the results are uncertain.

6. Introduction of genuine product management and product-line planning.

It is at the middle-management level that marketing muscle can begin to develop most quickly. If the business is broken into the proper pieces, product managers assigned, and a supportive environment created, fresh and more aggressive thinking can flourish. Pushing profit responsibility down below the division or profit-center level to product managers can help build entrepreneurship in formerly dull, unaggressive companies. Product managers should exert a strong influence on product economics, research and development activities, even product costs.

They should also be responsible for preparing an annual marketing plan that drives their division's action in their respective product categories over the coming year. Where marketing has been a weak link, annual product-line marketing plans can fuse functions together and sharpen a company's focus on consumers and competition. An effective annual marketing plan reviews market conditions, assesses competitors' actions, recommends tactics for the coming year, and outlines expected financial results. Annual marketing plans—within the parameters set by company, brand, or division strategy statements (step 3 above)—are a "big idea" for the marketing-deficient company. They can act as the catalyst needed to get middle management thinking like marketers.

Many companies have—but underutilize—product managers by relegating them to product design or technical/sales roles. Often the charter of these positions can be enlarged to confer responsibility (though not authority) for the manufacture, marketing, and sales of a discrete line of products. To make this transition work, incumbents will have to be retrained, coached in their broadened roles and, on occasion, replaced. Marketing pros are needed to do this "hands-on" coaching and training; one cannot learn it at a two-week seminar or in a textbook (although both are useful supplements).

TOO MUCH MARKETING?

It has been forcefully argued by some observers that U.S. industry in general is suffering from an excess rather than a deficiency of marketing muscle. They point to a decline in innovative new products, depressed productivity, and a tendency to avoid entrepreneurial risk in favor of safe, short-term returns generated by bland product-line extensions and product faceliftings supported by heavy advertising. Too many companies, they would argue, are

losing out to foreign competitors at home and abroad largely because they are marketing muscle-bound.

It would be hard to dispute that innovative drive and manufacturing knowhow are at least as vital to the long-term competitive vigor of U.S. industry as what I have referred to as marketing muscle. Nor would any sensible observer refuse to concede that overemphasis on marketing can be just as damaging to a company's health as one-sided preoccupation with any other major function.

The damaging aspects of marketing referred to frequently today are associated with companies where marketing is overdeveloped and out of balance with other functions, especially technology. These companies are so marketing muscle-bound they have trouble exercising other muscles—and their other muscles atrophy.

But it would be harder still, I submit, to deny that the most glaring competitive weakness that afflicts most consumer goods and service companies outside the packaged-goods industry is not an excess but a deficiency of marketing sophistication and marketing capability. Their marketing muscles are underdeveloped. Few non-packaged-goods companies are muscle-bound; the great majority would do a lot for the competitive vigor of U.S. industry if the weaklings developed marketing muscles.

It is, of course, easy to overstate the case for marketing. The apparel business is fashion driven, success in the electronics industry is built on superior technology, and banking is fundamentally a service business. Without a superior product or service and low, or at least competitive, costs, the most outstanding marketing will not accomplish much for long. And because consumers often cannot articulate the needs that new technology can meet, a science push is just as vital in many industries as a marketing pull. Yet even though it would be fatal to ignore the importance of competitive costs, good service, and superior technology, the evidence suggests that marketing will be tomorrow's competitive cutting edge in many nonmarketing-oriented industries, including apparel, textiles, consumer durables, transportation, utilities, financial services, and retailing. Sooner or later competitive forces in their own industries will compel many of these companies to build marketing muscle if they are to prosper. Those who act earliest to do so on their own initiative have the best chance of being among the winners of the 1980s.

3

The Misuse of Marketing:
An American Tragedy

Roger C. Bennett
Robert G. Cooper

While American firms cannot neglect market forces, it is time for a new philosophy to emerge, based on the concept of product value and providing superior products at competitive costs.

The automobile industry, a microcosm of the American economy, entered 1981 in a state of shock. At one time, the industry, like America, was efficient, industrious, innovative, and very profitable. But by 1981 this was no longer true. Imports took 30 percent of the market; $80 billion was needed for design and retooling; Chrysler obtained a federal loan guarantee; and Ford and General Motors reported record losses. What is happening in the North American auto industry may offer a glimpse in miniature of what ails the entire U.S. economy.

Has America lost its competitive edge? In the *Harvard Business Review*, two writers argued that America's economic malaise can be traced to a failure of the entrepreneurial spirit, a lack of technological innovation, and a short-sighted view of the future.[1] Pundits

[1] Robert H. Hayes and William J. Abernathy, "Managing Our Way to Economic Decline," *Harvard Business Review* (July-August 1980), pp. 67-77.

claim that the auto industry is in trouble because of cheaper imports that get better fuel economy.[2] This is too simple an answer. A more incisive diagnosis reveals the hard truths. The European and Japanese car makers have simply been better competitors: they anticipated market needs; they built a better product—one that is more reliable, has better workmanship, and is better engineered; and they did it effectively. In short, these manufacturers delivered better value to the American consumer. While "domestic auto makers regarded small cars as low-technology, cheaply designed products aimed mainly at buyers unable or not willing to purchase a large vehicle,"[3] the foreign manufacturers produced high-quality small

[2] See "When it Comes to the Bottom Line on New Cars, Buyers' Yen for Imports is Hardly Surprising," *The Wall Street Journal* (August 25, 1980), p. 32.
[3] See "Detroit's New Sales Pitch," *Business Week* (September 22, 1980), p. 79.

Reprinted from *Business Horizons* (November-December 1981), pp. 51–60. © 1981 by the Foundation for the School of Business at Indiana University. Reprinted by permission.

cars that were recognized as better by the American consumer.

The auto makers are not the only vulnerable companies in North America. In countless other manufacturing industries, North American firms are facing tough competition from foreign producers supplying products which offer better value. The television receiver industry, once dominated by domestic suppliers (RCA, GE, Sylvania, and others) has faced an onslaught of foreign brands for over a decade. Now Sony, Hitachi, and Toshiba appear to be the product leaders, with American consumers actually paying a *price premium* for certain of these "superior" imported goods. The same thing has happened in many other markets. Electronic goods and other moderate- to high-technology items such as cameras, small kitchen appliances, stereo equipment, motorcylces, and bicycles are a few that come to mind. Industrial products face similar competition: Japanese and French tire makers have made major inroads into the U.S. industrial tire market based not on price, but on product and technological superiority. Even America's computer industry is nervously watching Japanese computer makers take aim at the U.S.

The failure to deliver product value to the customer is the prime reason for this lack of competitiveness. Twenty years of adherence to the marketing concept may have taken its toll on American enterprise.[4] The marketing concept has diverted our attention from the product and its manufacture; instead we have focused our strategy on responses to market wants and have become preoccupied with advertising, selling, and promotion. And in the process, product value has suffered.

In this article we examine how this has

[4]Roger C. Bennett and Robert G. Cooper, "Beyond the Marketing Concept," *Business Horizons* (June 1979), pp. 76–83.

happened and we look at some of the major changes that are needed to correct the problem. In apportioning the blame, we are particularly scornful of the efforts of our own profession, namely marketing academics. We suggest that many professors, in relative isolation from the business community, have rigorously and expertly pushed back the frontiers of knowledge, but in the wrong direction. We personally have sometimes been involved in this ourselves. *Nostra culpa*. We have since seen the light, and in this article, one of our many messages is an appeal for others to do the same.

THE MARKETING CONCEPT: CULPRIT?

Three decades ago, the marketing concept was advanced as a guide to corporate strategy. What is this "marketing concept" that has had so much impact on American business direction? Simply stated, it is a business philosophy that places the customer at the top of the corporate organizational chart. It states that the firm should be "market-oriented" and the "satisfaction of customer needs is the key to corporate profits." The philosophy begins with the argument that corporate fortunes are decided largely by the customer because customers, through their purchase "votes," decide the fate of the firm. Further, the most effective way to create a customer is to market products aimed directly at his needs and wants. An integrated program of product, price, promotion, and distribution is considered to be essential to this approach.

The intuitive logic of the marketing concept is difficult to refute. It is impossible to name any commercially successful product or invention that failed to cater to some type of human need. Of course, many of the "needs" were after-the-fact explanations for the product's success, and often the need was not readily apparent at the time of the invention or product development.

This strict adherence to the marketing concept has damaged American business. It has led to a dearth of true innovation and it has shifted the strategic focus of the firm away from the product to other elements of the marketing mix, elements that can be manipulated very successfully in the short run but which leave the business vulnerable in the longer term.

PRODUCT INNOVATION: THE VICTIM

The impact of a market-responsive strategy has been most strongly felt in the field of product innovation. According to a recent U.S. Senate report, product strategies in the U.S. now emphasize short-term returns at the expense of significant innovations.[5] A market-driven new-product strategy provides little encouragement for technological discoveries, inventions, or significant breakthroughs; the "technology push" model has given way to the "market pull" model. Two researchers, Donald A. Marquis and Sumner Myers,[6] report that of 567 new products they studied, about three-quarters were derived by using the market pull model; this study was made in 1969, and we suspect the figure is even higher today.

The market pull model is the antithesis of the technology push approach. With the latter, scientific discovery or the availability of new technology leads to the development of a product. Ideas come from scientists and

[5] Ellis R. Mottur, *National Strategy for Technological Innovation*, report prepared for the U.S. Senate Committee on Commerce, Washington, D.C., October 1979.

[6] Sumner Myers and Donald A. Marquis, "Successful Industrial Innovations: A Study of Factors Underlying Innovation in Selected Firms," *National Science Foundation*, NSF, 1969, pp. 69-71.

The market pull model

The market pull model has been perfected by the packaged-goods industry. They search the market for clues and examine people's needs exhaustively. The result is usually a carefully focused product that is moderately successful. As an example, consider the market pull model for the development of a new breakfast food by a hypothetical company:

Step 1: Do extensive market research to identify an unsatisfied need, segment, or niche in the marketplace. Using sophisticated market research tools if necessary (multidimensional scaling, trade-off analysis, and so on), determine the ideal product's attributes. Let the market "design" the product.

Example: for breakfast foods, a semi-sweet, easily prepared, baked breakfast product, with attributes somewhere between toast and a sweet roll.

Step 2: Ask the R&D group to develop a product that meets these market specifications exactly. No technological breakthroughs or inventions are necessary—just give the market what it says it wants.

Solution: a waffle-like product, frozen, suitable for a toaster, with a sweet filler, say strawberry jam.

Step 3: The next few steps involve the refinement of the product design (including consumer preference taste tests) and verifying the financial attractiveness of the project (test marketing, for example).

Final Step: Launch the product. Position it in people's minds as a great tasting, "fun" breakfast food, which is easy to prepare (hot from your toaster). Give it a name to reflect its position: "Pop-Toasties." Package it attractively, and saturation advertise on television.

engineers, not from consumers. This does not mean that these companies push ahead developing products for which there is no demand. But the initial impetus for a good new product does not always come from the consumer. Indeed, we argue that innovative ideas will rarely arise there. Technology push proves a far more fertile ground for new ideas. Well-known examples of technology push are the laser and transistor, two scientific breakthroughs which are used in a number of successful products.

The market pull model generally yields good results, especially for industries such as packaged goods. And it seems to work in the short run. But whether such a model is desirable for a company or an entire industry in the long run, and whether it suits high technology and more complex product classes, is certainly debatable. Yet, encouraged by the successes of these market-oriented new products, higher technology and industrial goods firms are now emulating the model. As one senior R&D manager in a huge multinational firm put it: "Our consumer division has a market pull new product model that really works. Now we in the industrial division want to do the same."

Much industrial R&D, as a result, has become a technological response to requests from the marketing department. One effect has been the diminished investment in R&D by American industry, dropping from 2.07 percent of GNP in 1960 to only 1.76 percent today. Another result, with serious implications, is that much of the R&D community, after two decades of being shackled, may have lost its creative and inventive capability. As one senior manager said: "Our advertising says we're the 'discovery company.' Hell, we haven't discovered anything for fifteen years!"

A market-oriented R&D strategy necessarily leads to low-risk product modifications, extensions, and style changes. Product proliferation, a disease of the seventies, has been one result. Market-derived new-product ideas will usually result in the ordinary. Market researchers have become expert at encouraging consumers to verbalize their wants and needs, but people tend to talk in terms of the familiar, about what is around them at a particular moment. For example, ask a commuter what new-product ideas he would like to see in the area of rapid transit and, chances are, he will list a number of improvements to his bus or subway system—tinted glass windows, air conditioning, better schedules, and the like. Rarely will he be able to think in terms of totally new and imaginative urban transporation systems. The latter are the domain of the engineer, scientist, and designer.

Managers therefore learn only about the familiar needs of consumers, expressed in the consumer's own terms, for a particular point in time. As a source of innovative and significant new-product ideas, the consumer is limited in three ways:

1. Consumers' perceptions of their needs are restricted to the familiar, to items consumers can relate to. By definition, a true innovation is very often out of the scope of the normal experience of the consumer.

2. Consumers' ability to express these needs, to verbalize what they want, particularly when they do not know what is technologically feasible, is limited.

3. Because of the dynamic nature of these expressed needs, they may well have changed by the time the new product is designed, tested, and manufactured, the Edsel being a classic example.

The eventual result of a market-based R&D strategy is the slow death of product innovation. Original and creative new products, once the lifeblood of American enterprise and one key to America's competitive success in the world, are sadly missing. Consider some more evidence:

In 1960, industry's expenditures for R&D were 87.5 percent of those spent on advertising. By 1977, the proportion had fallen to 75 percent. America is spending a relatively constant percentage of its GNP on advertising, while the proportion devoted to R&D is falling.

We have decided that it is easier to *talk about* our new products than actually to develop them. And so we spend billions more convincing the customer that the product is "new and improved" rather than spending the money in the lab to develop a significantly superior product. In the world of new products, we have become a society of tinkerers and cosmeticians rather than true product innovators.

SHIFTED FOCUS

The strategic focus has shifted away from the product, away from its design, development, and manufacture. Lacking significant product advantages, many firms have been forced to rely on the other selling tools: advertising, promotion, and distribution. And through the supporting elements of the marketing mix, the firm maintains its competitive edge. We call this approach a "non-product strategy," even though the approach is more tactical than strategic.

An example of a company that went from product leadership to relying on other elements of the marketing mix with unfortunate results is the Singer Sewing Machine Company. At one time, Singer *owned* the sewing machine market. It invented the sewing machine, and the name Singer almost became a generic term for sewing machine. The firm was the undisputed product and market leader.

During the fifties and sixties, Singer turned away from product as its core or central strategy. Distribution and a worldwide chain of Singer stores became a leading component of its strategy. And so did heavy advertising and promotion, mostly featuring Singer sales and dollar rebate specials; remarkably little advertising focused on product attributes and quality. As a result, product leadership—technology, design, and quality—began to falter.

The Europeans attacked the high end of the market with technologically superior and better quality machines. Names such as Bernina, Pfaff, and Necchi became synonymous with product reliability. The Japanese, meanwhile, took aim at the middle and lower ends of the market, offering machines comparable to Singer's, but often of higher quality, and usually at lower prices. Today, the major market contender for Singer's dominance is a private brand machine sold by a national retailer, but made in Japan.

The dilemma in which Singer finds itself occurred because the company created a product leadership void in the industry: it turned its attention to promotion, advertising, and merchandising, and left the door open to others to develop and manufacture superior products. Singer moved to a non-product strategy with serious consequences.

In fact, this non-product strategy may succeed, although normally in the short run and in domestic markets. After all, how can one go wrong simply doing what the customers say they want? For a decade or two, cosmetic changes and style updates, backed by intense advertising and promotion, will keep the product competitive. Success in the home market is guaranteed . . . for a while.

The American automotive industry went through this phase between 1955 and the late 1970s. The "new" models were unveiled each fall with great fanfare and little that was substantially and technologically new. In contrast, and with much less hoopla, foreign car manufacturers were busily perfecting new technologies: fuel injection, the diesel engine, front-wheel drive, pollution-free engines (rather than catalytic converters that attempt to deal with the pollution once it has been created), fuel-efficient engines, better quality control methods. The American auto industry's credo appeared to be: where our product is lacking, we will make up the difference by aggressive selling and heavy promotions. In recent years, the hard sell and dollar rebates signified trouble in the automobile industry.

Such a non-product strategy does not work well in international markets either. Here, a product must stand on its own much more than in the home market. Several studies have reported that the product offering (and this includes price) is the key to international success. One reason is different customer expectations. Europeans, for example, are often characterized as being more interested in the functional and technological aspects of products than are North American consumers.

More important, the other elements of the marketing mix are not likely to be as effective abroad. Advertising is bound to be less concentrated and hence less influential as many and diverse markets are attacked; the firm also loses some control over its promotional, selling, and distribution efforts as it moves to foreign lands and relies on intermediaries. In third-world and state-controlled economies, the normal supporting elements of the marketing mix are likely to be either ineffectual or controlled by others. Product must compete against product; and so product strategy becomes preeminent.

Unfortunately for many North American firms, our global economy and the multinational corporations are rapidly making the notion of a "home market" obsolete. As one British manager put it: "Our home market has become someone else's international market. Either we must build products for international markets or not build products at all." The same is happening on this side of the Atlantic. *World products* are the logical outcome. The implications are clear: if America's home market is really an international market, then the rules of international competition apply. More than ever, a non-product strategy begins to fail.

The non-product strategy is weak also because it is a short-term solution. The strategy fails because no market remains stable forever; needs change and technology moves ahead. Somewhere, a company—at home or abroad—introduces a new product that represents a significant improvement over existing ones: a front-wheel-drive car; a radial tire; a word processing machine. The product may be better because it is a technological breakthrough. It might be simply a significant departure from existing designs. It almost certainly better anticipates users' needs. And the firms that have not heeded the central role of product strategy are suddenly vulnerable. The product cosmeticians and tinkerers are suddenly left in the wake of the firms seeking the technological advances.

A familiar example illustrates this point well. The American kitchen used to be dominated by American products, heavily promoted and, incidentally, sold at a relatively low price. But, in the last five years, of the three major technological innovations, two—the food processor and the convection oven—came from overseas, and the third—the microwave oven—illustrates the problem that U.S. manufacturers have in competing. The Japanese producers dominate the market.

THE ROOTS OF DISASTER

In the short space of twenty-five years, American business has shifted from a product strategy to one which emphasizes non-product variables. Why the sudden reorientation? The marketing concept as a doctrine of business has been cited as one reason. But this is merely an explanation of a phenomenon, and not its cause.

We submit that two major forces have

created this non-product movement. One is the fault of business educators. The other is the method used to evaluate academics.

Let us look first at management education. For the last twenty years, business schools have been the fastest growing educational units on university campuses. In the 1950s, schools of engineering led the way; but today management is king. The dramatic growth in graduates is further evidence: in 1950, only 4,000 MBAs graduated in America; by 1979, this number had grown to almost 50,000. Add to this the many undergraduate programs and executive training courses and we begin to appreciate the extraordinary growth of management education. The influx of graduates of these schools and courses into American business is bound to have had an impact.

Have you ever wondered what management teachers—those people charged with educating today's and tomorrow's managers—concern themselves with? Consider a recent convention of marketing educators, the 1980 American Marketing Association convention in Chicago. A quick perusal of the program reveals some startling facts. Over 50 percent of the sessions were devoted to techniques: understanding and reaching the consumer, measuring the consumer's behavior and desires, and developing new models and methodologies in this area; 18 percent to educational methods; 5 percent to techniques of planning and strategy; only 4 percent to general marketing strategy; and *nothing at all* to new products.

This breakdown is probably a fair representation of the interests of America's marketing academics, interests that become the thrust of the classroom teaching experience. It comes as no surprise to learn that today's marketing graduate, while quite expert in techniques of marketing research, quantitative decision making and consumer behavior, has very little feel for long-term competitive strategies. Moreover, the new MBA knows almost nothing about product strategy, design management, and the role of technological innovation. The graduate is a technician, not a strategist, and feels more at home playing with the elements of the marketing mix than developing bold new strategies with new products and new markets.

Similar problems beset other important areas of management education. For example, the finance educator appears to be going the route of the theoretical economist: production is no longer production, but operations research; and so on. We are educating a generation of number pushers and tacticians and calling them managers.

Behind this clear movement towards concentrating on theoretical trivia is the academic measurement system itself. The heart of academic research is the scientific method where everything can be assigned a number, measured, controlled, replicated, validated, and relied upon. So professors and others who aspire to academic advancement tend not to concern themselves with those areas where the scientific method is most difficult to apply. They search for problems that will yield the "correct" methodology rather than seeking new and better ways of looking at the major problem areas that beset managers. The academic evaluation system, then, is at the root of the problem.

The second force underlying the preoccupation with non-product tactics is the way managers themselves are evaluated. First, most performance measures are made over the short term. One year is about the maximum period over which performance is measured: this year's sales versus last year's; ROI for the year; and so on. And the best way to show "good results" in the short term is to gain or hold market share through tactical moves—advertising, promotion, selling—while cutting costs in the manufacture of the product, sometimes at the expense of product quality. The short-time horizon tends to discourage strategic development and significant product innovation, whose costs may be incurred today, but whose payoffs are years away. As one senior manager, in charge of product and business development of the multinational firm, said: "Our firm is committed to yesterday's bottom line; and managers are measured on the past, not future performance."

A second aspect of management evaluation is the way managers themselves evaluate investments and expenditures. Today the manager is provided with myriad evaluative tools to help in making decisions about resource allocation. Of course, the criteria used in these decisions are closely related to the ways used to evaluate individuals. And quantifiable measures, such as short-term profitability, are usually included in the measurement system. Uncertainty and the future are handled poorly by most quantitative evaluation techniques. For example, it is usually difficult to predict the sales that an innovative product may generate. Lacking certain sales data as an input to the usual IRR or ROI calculations tends to make the evaluation come out negative. The result is that the short-term projects with highly certain outcomes are favored at the expense of riskier, long-term expenditures or investments.

The kind of training managers receive today coupled with the way managers are evaluated, and how they, in turn, evaluate resource allocations are largely responsible for the shift from product strategy and technological innovation. Instead of genuine advances, we witness a tactical and short-term orientation, one where the focus is on cosmetic product changes, advertising and promotion, and cutting production costs.

THE SOLUTION: PRODUCT VALUE

The essence of business is to deliver a product which satisfies a need and whose market value exceeds its cost. In the transaction between buyer and seller, it is the product's value that the customer pays for. Thus *product value* is an important concept to business. According to the Concise Oxford Dictionary, the term "value" means "worth, desirability, utility." Price and cost are essentially concerned with money, while value is concerned with worth and desirability and is a subjective matter.[7] The marketplace provides a rough measure of the worth or value of a product: the price a product can command is a monetary measure the customer places on the product. Profits are thus the difference between a product's value (measured by its price) and the product's cost. The firm's task becomes the maximization of the spread between the value of a product and the cost to manufacture and deliver. The role of a business is the modulation of value, price, and cost of a product.

The ability to provide a product with superior value, but at competitive costs (or the same value at lower costs) is the key to long-run business success. A product has properties or attributes that can be translated into value. One such attribute is usefulness: a product may supplement or magnify a human effort, save time, or produce an otherwise unachievable result. Another value-inducing attribute is security: protection, safety, reliability. Availability is a third value-inducing attribute: people pay a premium for immediate delivery. Other value-inducing attributes include rarity (a Paris original or a limited edition); custom make (such as a made-to-measure suit); and original, creative work (a fine painting).

The manufacturer's task is to maximize the product's value for a given cost. He can do this by improving availability—fast delivery or more stock in inventory. Alternately, since

[7]Parts of this discussion are based on: L. Bruce Archer, *Design Awareness and Planned Creativity in Industry* (Department of Industry, Trade and Commerce, Ottawa, and Design Council of Great Britain, London, 1974).

value is in the eye of the beholder, often advertising and marketing communication will convince the buyer of the product's value. Advertising can actually increase the value of the product to the buyer by emphasizing certain desired attributes or by making existing attributes appear more important. But the product itself—its inherent attributes or properties—is by far the most important and enduring value-inducing element. Thus, the product should be the central or core element in the firm's competitive strategy. And the firm that strives to provide a higher value or "better" product has a more sound and longer-lasting base for prosperity. Even the auto makers are learning the lesson. For example, GM's new chairman, Roger B. Smith, notes that attention to product quality along with fuel economy will be GM's product strategy in the future.

The critical role of having a superior and unique product has been reinforced by studies about what makes a new product a success.[8] Marketing skills and resources were assets; so were production and technological skills. And being in a growth market was a positive factor. But the most important characteristics that separated the successes from the failures were uniqueness and superiority—a product that did a unique task; performed better; lasted longer; saved the customer time or money; and so on. The point seems an obvious one. But is it? An inspection of the sample of products studied reveals that most firms were not developing unique and superior products. Product extensions and incremental developments are the rule rather than the exception in today's product development game. Other investigations have shown similar results.

[8]Robert G. Cooper, "The Dimensions of Industrial New Product Success and Failure," *Journal of Marketing* (Summer 1979), pp. 93–103.

MUST BE BETTER THAN COMPETITORS

The focus of a firm's competitive strategy should be on product and product value. The proponent of the marketing concept is right when he says the product must meet a market need. Otherwise it would have no value. But product value implies a comparison. And so it must do more than merely satisfy a need; the product must meet the needs *better* than the competitors' products. It is this focus on "being better" that is missing in the marketing concept.

A better or more highly valued product is a function of its attributes. And these in turn depend on the technology that goes into the product, the design and engineering that shape the product, and the product's manufacture (which determines quality of workmanship and product reliability). Note that the factors that create the superior value are the resources of the firm—R&D, engineering, design, and production—and suggest an inward focus.

In contrast, a market-oriented philosophy urges us to look outward—to the marketplace— for new products and new opportunities. This may result in a product that meets a market need, but meeting a market need is a necessary but *not sufficient* condition for success. Being able to "do it better" is key— and here is where a focus on the firm's distinctive competencies and internal resources is required.

An example of the marketing concept taken to an extreme is the plight of certain universities and colleges in the U.S. Faced with declining enrollments, many colleges spotted new market needs, and in the tradition of a market orientation, developed new programs and courses. Continuing education was a favorite area. The trouble was that, in the case of many institutions, the expertise and material resources to deliver a good program in these new areas simply did not exist. And now many are in trouble, facing loss of accreditation. University administrators have learned what many businessmen now are experiencing: any astute organization can spot a market need; but only a minority can deliver a sound product for a particular need. Today the universities that focused on excellence rather than chasing market needs are in a sounder position.

It is time the firm stopped being so market driven and began turning its attention back to its own internal areas of excellence. Let the firm do what it does best; let it build on its areas of strength; and let a preoccupation with technological, design, and manufacturing excellence dominate the desire to cater solely to market whims.

THE ROUTE TO RECOVERY

How can American business recapture its former prowess? One way is to reflect on the attitudes and approaches that once made American business the envy of the world. We must go beyond the marketing concept. The answer lies not just in satisfying customer needs but in providing a product of superior value to the marketplace. We must adopt a product value concept (which is, of course, very different from a production concept):

The product value concept is a business orientation that recognizes that product value is the key to profits. It stresses competing on the basis of customer need satisfaction with superior, higher value products. Value depends on the customer's perception of the product attributes, which are largely a function of the firm's technological, design, and manufacturing strengths and skills.

The implication, then, is that for long-term success, the firm must build on what it does best with the objective of delivering a superior quality, high value product. We borrow a familiar military strategic premise and argue that "the firm should operate from a position of power; it should build in areas where it can utilize its existing strengths." If concentrating on what the firm does best is essential for long-term success, then the corporation must be reasonably clear about what it is good at. Texas Instruments' success has been based on its strong production resources and its abilities to move down the learning curve rapidly. Of course, it also had to market the products it produced. Procter & Gamble recognized its success was due to its marketing abilities. But it also had to have good products. On the rare occasions that its products were not superior—Rely tampons and Pringle's New Fangled Potato Chips—disaster or relative failure resulted.

Let us take a look at a company that shifted its focus away from what it does best. Massey Ferguson was a leader in the 1930s, 40s, and 50s in combine harvester technology and in other aspects of farm machinery design. Indeed, Massey Harris merged with Ferguson in 1953 in order to enhance this leadership by obtaining access to Ferguson's hydraulic technology.

From the mid-sixties on, however, management diverted its attention to other markets. It became more heavily involved in diesel engines and concentrated aggressively on earthmoving and construction equipment. An office equipment manufacturer was even acquired. Large investment was needed for the new businesses, and little top management time was left for the traditional business. Competitors, meanwhile, improved their products, fine-tuned their distribution systems, and began to leave Massey Ferguson behind. Larger, heavier, and more powerful farm equipment became available and Massey Ferguson began to find it difficult to compete.

In 1980, after several years of difficulties, it seemed the firm had reached a crisis. High interest rates and the recession proved damaging to a company that was highly leveraged and whose main lines were purchased by farmers on credit. The product line was not as strong competitively as it had been. And the dealer network was fraying. Management was trying to dispose of its peripheral businesses, begging money from government, and wondering what had happened to a proud old company.

What had happened was a failure to concentrate on providing a quality product in an area where it had leadership and expertise. Other aspects of the business took precedence. Massey Ferguson learned too late about building from a position of strength, about concentrating on what it did best.

The occasional company that has successfully moved into markets and products not based on traditional corporate resources has done so only after realizing the full implications of its move. IBM, for example, took three years after its decision to enter the computer field before it produced its first product. It hired a number of the available people with knowledge in the field during this period. And it built or acquired the necessary resources. To do this, of course, required top management commitment. As Tom Watson, Jr., IBM president said, "We realized we had to succeed at this or fail as a company."

This product orientation we propose leads to a view of the strategic planning process very different from the market driven approach accepted today. The strategic notions expressed in the famous 1960 article on marketing myopia represented an appealing but simplistic and one-sided solution. In today's complex world, the idea of building a business solely in terms of market needs does not necessarily work. According to this market-oriented strategic approach, the railroads should have seen themselves as providing transportation services to America (a market need); this would have taken them into trucking, airlines, and telecommunications, which are more viable businesses today. But the same logic would also have led them to car rentals, taxi fleets, and perhaps even the manufacture of transportation equipment or automobiles. These businesses are probably very wrong for railroads, simply because they do not build on the strengths and skills found in a railroad.

One very successful railroad in North America is Canadian Pacific. Now the world's largest privately-owned transportation firm, it was once just a transcontinental railroad. Following the "transportation concept," it expanded into trucking, airlines, ships, intermodal shipping, and telecommunications (including Telex). Note that this successful firm expanded only into areas that could build on its internal strengths. But the company was also successful in a number of non-transportation areas: mining operations, because lead and zinc were found on its land in the Rocky Mountains; hotels around the world, because it knew how to accommodate travelers; real estate development, partly because of its land holdings. These non-transportation areas are quite inconsistent with a market-oriented view of strategy, yet because they built on a resource the firm owned or some competence the firm possessed, these areas too were logical opportunities for exploitation.

A product orientation also focuses more attention on execution. Strategic choice—the right market and product concept—is only part of the battle. Being able to deliver the right product is the main issue. The emphasis here is on proper execution: sound technology, good industrial design, meticulous engineering, and workmanship and efficiency in production. Planning is important; but execution—"doing it right"—is equally critical, which brings us back to the necessity of basing strategy on what the firm does best.

Operationally, it is clear that changes are needed in a number of areas in order to achieve a product value orientation. In the field of management education:

☐ Marketers must place less emphasis on the marketing concept as the *only* business philosophy. Let us downplay the marketing concept in texts, courses, and seminars. Instead, a product orientation—delivering product value based on what firms do well— should be taught. In addition, more emphasis on product strategy, technological innovation, management of technology, and industrial design is needed in business school curricula.

☐ The technology push model must be reinvented as a viable route to new products in management courses. Typical management texts on new products sound as though market pull were the *only* model.

☐ Academic research must be reoriented to deal with the problems and issues facing industry. Relevance, as well as academic rigor, should be the key. Instead of trying to be just as theoretical and elegant as their learned colleagues in the pure sciences, business academics should recognize that management is a profession. The audience for academic research should be far more frequently the practitioner, and not solely other academics.

In the business firm itself, many changes are possible. Most must begin with a change in attitude and our approach to doing business. Hence, these changes must be initiated from the top of the company. We suggest that, for most firms:

☐ The product value concept—delivering the most product value efficiently—should become the corporate credo.

☐ A competitive strategy based on product quality, design, and technology should be the long-term approach to domestic and international competition.

☐ R&D should not be strictly market-oriented.

Extensions, modifications, and style changes in response to market wants will certainly be required. But a significant portion of R&D should be allocated to the long term: to the creation of innovative products, and even to scientific discovery, simply to keep the firm at the "state of the art."

☐ Performance measures for managers should be future-oriented and not stricly short term. Yesterday's bottom line should not be the only criterion of evaluation. Provision should be made in evaluation systems to encourage wise, but forward-looking, thinking.

☐ Evaluation techniques for resource allocations should recognize the need for a balance between the lower risk, ordinary ventures and the more adventurous projects with longer term, but less certain, pay-off. The usual ROI and discounted cash flow capital budgeting techniques need to be supplemented by evaluation approaches that permit subjective and nonquantitative inputs for these bolder projects.

☐ And above all, the firm must recognize what it does well. It must be aware of its distinctive competencies and unique resources. Having identified these areas of excellenece, the firm should use these in its task of producing a product of superior value.

Perhaps, in the 1950s and 60s, many firms, especially those in industrial markets, had to become more market-oriented. Management of that era was based on experiences of war and post-war shortages and a seller's market. A new outlook was needed.

By now, we have learned the lesson too well. In our efforts to cater to every whim of the consumer, we have become too concerned with the short term and the cosmetic. This attitude has been encouraged by academic institutions in their teaching and research activities. And it has been further reinforced by the essentially short-run nature of most corporate evaluation systems.

It is time for a new philosophy to emerge, based on the idea that product value is the key to success. Behind that concept lies the notion of providing superior products at competitive costs. Doing this requires the corporation to analyze its own skills and resources and to build from these positions of strength. While the firm cannot neglect market forces, the driving force must often come from elsewhere.

To achieve this change in philosophy will require a significant shift in attitudes and behavior. A good deal of what has been built up in recent years as a result of the marketing concept, our ideas of what constitutes good methodological research, and the control systems prevalent in most organizations today, will have to be reconsidered.

From the time of the introduction of the marketing concept in the late 1940s to its general acceptance in the early to mid-60s, fifteen years elapsed; many of its ramifications are still today working their way through corporate structures. For the sake of the economic health of America, we hope that the focus on product value occurs far more quickly.

4

Diagnosing the Product Portfolio

George S. Day

How to use scare cash and managerial resources for maximum long-run gains

The product portfolio approach to marketing strategy formulation has gained wide acceptance among mangers of diversified companies. They are first attracted by the intuitively appealing concept that long-run corporate performance is more than the sum of the contributions of individual profit centers or product strategies. Secondly a product portfolio analysis suggests specific marketing strategies to achieve a balanced mix of products that will produce the maximum long-run effects from scarce cash and managerial resources. Lastly the concept employs a simple matrix representation which is easy to communicate and comprehend. Thus it is a useful tool in a headquarters campaign to demonstrate that the strategic issues facing the firm justify more centralized control over the planning and resource allocation process.

With the growing acceptance of the basic approach has come an increasing sensitivity to the limitations of the present methods of portraying the product portfolio, and a recognition that the approach is not equally useful in all corporate circumstances. Indeed, the implications can sometimes be grossly misleading. Inappropriate and misleading applications will result when:

☐ The basic **assumptions** (especially those concerned with the value of market share dominance and the product life cycle) are violated,

☐ The **measurements** are wrong, or

☐ The **strategies** are not feasible.

This article identifies the critical assumptions and the measurement and application issues that may distort the strategic insights. A series of questions are posed that will aid planners

Reprinted with permission from *Journal of Marketing*, published by the American Marketing Association (April 1977), pp. 29–38.

and decision-makers to better understand this aid to strategic thinking, and thereby make better decisions.

WHAT IS THE PRODUCT PORTFOLIO?

Common to all portrayals of the product portfolio is the recognition that the competitive value of market share depends on the structure of competition and the stage of the product life cycle. Two examples of this approach have recently appeared in this journal.[1] However, the earliest, and most widely implemented is the cash quadrant or share/growth matrix developed by the Boston Consulting Group.[2] Each product is classified jointly by rate of present or forecast **market growth** (a proxy for stage in the produce life cycle) and a measure of **market share dominance**.

The arguments for the use of market share are familiar and well documented.[3] Their basis is the cumulation of evidence that market share is strongly and positively correlated with product profitability. This theme is varied somewhat in the BCG ap-

proach by the emphasis on relative share—measured by the ratio of the company's share of the market to the share of the largest competitor. This is reasonable since the strategic implications of a 20% share are quite different if the largest competitor's is 40% or if it is 5%. Profitability will also vary, since according to the experience curve concept the largest competitor will be the most profitable at the prevailing price level.[4]

The product life cycle is employed because it highlights the desirability of a variety of products or services with different present and prospective growth rates. More important, the concept has some direct implications for the cost of gaining and/or holding market share:

☐ During the **rapid growth stage**, purchase patterns and distribution channels are fluid. Market shares can be increased at "relatively" low cost by capturing a disproportionate share of incremental sales (especially where these sales come from new users of applications rather than heavier usage by existing users).

☐ By contrast, the key-note during the **maturity stage** swings to stability and inertia in distribution and purchasing relationships. A substantial growth in share by one competitor will come at the expense of another competitor's capacity utilization, and will be resisted vigorously. As a result, gains in share are both time-consuming and costly (unless accompanied by a breakthrough in product value or performance that cannot be easily matched by competition).

PRODUCT PORTFOLIO STRATEGIES

When the share and growth rate of each of the products sold by a firm are jointly considered, a new basis for strategy evaluation emerges.

[1] Bernard Catry and Michel Chevalier, "Market Share Strategy and the Product Life Cycle," *Journal of Marketing*, 38 No. 4 (October 1974), pp. 29-34; and Yoram Wind and Henry J. Claycamp, "Planning Product Line Strategy: A Matrix Approach," *Journal of Marketing*, 40 No. 1 (January 1976), pp. 2-9.

[2] Described in the following pamphlets in the *Perspectives* series, authored by Bruce D. Henderson, "The Product Portfolio" (1970), "Cash Traps" (1972), and "The Experience Curve Reviewed: The Growth-Share Matrix or the Product Portfolio" (Boston Consulting Group, 1973). By 1972 the approach had been employed in more than 100 companies. See "Mead's Technique to Sort Out the Losers," *Business Week* (March 11, 1972), pp. 124-30.

[3] Sidney Shoeffler, Robert D. Buzzell, and Donald F. Heany, "Impact of Strategic Planning on Profit Performance," *Harvard Business Review*, 52 (March-April 1974), pp. 137-45; and Robert D. Buzzell, Bradley T. Gale, and Ralph G. M. Sultan, "Market Share—A Key to Profitability," *Harvard Business Review*, 53 (January-February 1975), pp. 97-106.

[4] Boston Consulting Group, *Perspectives on Experience* (Boston: 1968 and 1970), and "Selling Business a Theory of Economics," *Business Week* (September 8, 1974), pp. 43-44.

EXHIBIT 1

The cash quadrant approach to describing the product portfolio[a]

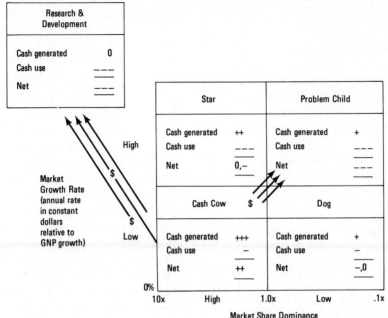

[a] Arrows indicate principal cash flows.

While there are many possible combinations, an arbitrary classification of products into four share/growth categories (as shown in Exhibit 1) is sufficient to illustrate the strategy implications.

Low Growth/Dominant Share (Cash Cows)

These profitable products usually generate more cash than is required to maintain share. All strategies should be directed toward maintaining market dominance—including investments in technological leadership. Pricing decisions should be made cautiously with an eye to maintaining price leadership. Pressure to over-invest through product proliferation and market expansion should be resisted unless prospects for expanding primary demand are unusually attractive.

Instead, excess cash should be used to support research activities and growth areas elsewhere in the company.

High Growth/Dominant Share (Stars)

Products that are market leaders, but also growing fast, will have substantial reported profits but need a lot of cash to finance the rate of growth. The appropriate strategies are designed primarily to protect the existing share level by reinvesting earnings in the form of price reductions, product improvement, better market coverage, production efficiency increases, etc. Particular attention must be given to obtaining a large share of the new users or new applications that are the source of growth in the market.

Low Growth/Subordinate Share (Dogs)

Since there usually can be only one market leader and because most markets are mature, the greatest number of products fall in this category. Such products are usually at a cost disadvantage and have few opportunities for growth at a reasonable cost. Their markets are not growing, so there is little new business to compete for, and market share gains will be resisted strenuously by the dominant competition.

The slower the growth (present or prospective) and the smaller the relative share, the greater the need for positive action. The possibilities include:

1. Focusing on a specialized segment of the market that can be dominated, and protected from competitive inroads.

2. Harvesting, which is a conscious cutback of all support costs to some minimum level which will maximize the cash flow over a foreseeable lifetime—which is usually short.

3. Divestment, usually involving a sale as a going concern.

4. Abandonment or deletion from the product line.

High Growth/Subordinate Share (Problem Children)

The combination of rapid growth and poor profit margins creates an enormous demand for cash. If the cash is not forthcoming, the product will become a "Dog" as growth inevitably slows. The basic strategy options are fairly clear-cut; either invest heavily to get a disproportionate share of the new sales or buy existing shares by acquiring competitors and thus move the product toward the "Star" category or get out of the business using some of the methods just described.

Consideration also should be given to a market segmentation strategy, but only if a defensible niche can be identified and resources are available to gain dominance.

This strategy is even more attractive if the segment can provide an entrée and experience base from which to push for dominance of the whole market.

OVERALL STRATEGY

The long-run health of the corporation depends on having some products that *generate* cash (and provide acceptable reported profits), and others that *use* cash to support growth. Among the indicators of overall health are the size and vulnerability of the "Cash Cows" (and the prospects for the "Stars," if any), and the number of "Problem Children" and "Dogs." Particular attention must be paid to those products with large cash appetites. Unless the company has abundant cash flow, it cannot afford to sponsor many such products at one time. If resources (including debt capacity) are spread too thin, the company simply will wind up with too many marginal products and suffer a reduced capacity to finance promising new product entries or acquisitions in the future.

The share/growth matrix displayed in Exhibit 2 shows how one company (actually a composite of a number of situations) might follow the strategic implications of the product portfolio to achieve a better balance of sources and uses of cash. The *present* position of each product is defined by the relative share and market growth rate during a representative time *period*. Since business results normally fluctuate, it is important to use a time period that is not distorted by rare events. The *future* position may be either (a) a momentum forecast of the results of continuing the present strategy or (b) a forecast of the consequences of a change in strategy. It is desirable to do both, and compare the results. The specific display of Exhibit 2 is a summary of the following strategic decisions.

☐ Aggressively **support** the newly introduced product A, to ensure dominance (but

EXHIBIT 2
Balancing the product portfolio

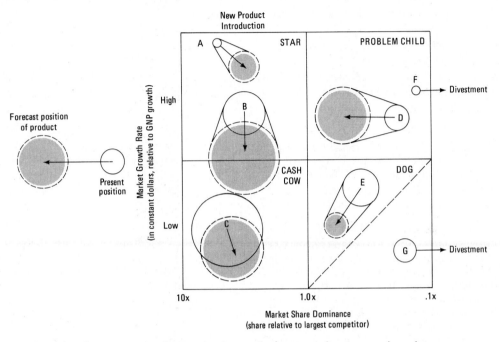

Diameter of circle is proportional to product's contribution to total company sales volume.

anticipate share declines due to new competitive entries).

☐ Continue present strategies of products B and C to ensure **maintenance** of market share.

☐ Gain share of market for product D by investing in **acquisitions**.

☐ Narrow and modify the range of models of product E to **focus** on one segment.

☐ **Divest** products F and G.

PITFALLS IN THE ASSUMPTIONS

The starting point in the decision to follow the implications of a product portfolio analysis is to ask whether the underlying assumptions make sense. The most fundamental assumptions relate to the role of market share in the businesses being portrayed in the portfolio. Even if the answers here are affirmative one may choose to not follow the implications if other objectives than balancing cash flows take priority, or there are barriers to implementing the indicated strategies.

What Is the Role of Market Share?

All the competitors are assumed to have the same overhead structures and experience curves, with their position on the experience curve corresponding to their market share position. Hence market share dominance is a proxy for the *relative* profit performance (e.g., GM vs. Chrysler). Other factors beyond market share may be influential in dictating *absolute, profit performance (e.g., calculators versus cosmetics)*.

The influence of market share is most apparent with high value-added products, where there are significant barriers to entry and the competition consists of a few, large, diversified corporations with the attendant large overheads (e.g., plastics, major appliances, automobiles, and semi-conductors). But even in these industrial environments there are distortions under conditions such as:

□   One competitor has a significant technological advantage which can be protected and used to establish a steeper cost reduction/ experience curve.

□   The principal component of the product is produced by a supplier who has an inherent cost advantage because of an integrated process. Thus DuPont was at a cost disadvantage with Cyclohexane vis-à-vis the oil companies because the manufacture of the product was so highly integrated with the operations of an oil refinery.[5]

□   Competitors can economically gain large amounts of experience through acquisitions or licensing, or shift to a lower (but parallel) cost curve by resorting to off-shore production or component sourcing.

□   Profitability is highly sensitive to the rate of capacity utilization, regardless of size of plant.

There are many situations where the positive profitability-and-share relationship becomes very tenuous, and perhaps unattainable. A recent illustration is the building industry, where large corporations—CNA with Larwin and ITT with Levitt—have suffered because of their inability to adequately offset their high overhead charges with a corresponding reduction in total costs.[6] Similar problems are also encountered in the service sector, and contribute to the many reasons why services which are highly labor-intensive and involve personal relationships must be approached with extreme caution in a product portfolio analysis.[7]

There is specific evidence from the Profit Impact of Market Strategies (PIMS) study[8] that the value of market share is not as significant for consumer goods as for industrial products. The reasons are not well understood, but probably reflect differences in buying behavior, the importance of product differentiation, and the tendency for proliferation of marginally different brands in these categories. The strategy of protecting a market position by introducing line extensions, flankers, and spin-offs from a successful core brand means that product class boundaries are very unclear. Hence shares are harder to estimate. The individual brand in a category like deodorants or powdered drinks may not be the proper basis for evaluation. A related consequence is that joint costing problems multiply. For example, Unilever in the U.K. has 20 detergent brands all sharing production facilities and marketing resources to some degree.

When Do Market Shares Stabilize?

The operating assumption is that shares tend toward stability during the maturity stage, as the dominant competitors concentrate on defending their existing position. An important corollary is that gains in share are easier and cheaper to achieve during the growth stage.

There is scattered empirical evidence,

[5] Robert B. Stobaugh and Philip L. Towsend, "Price Forecasting and Strategic Planning: The Case of Petrochemicals," *Journal of Marketing Research*, 12 (February 1975), pp. 19-29.

[6] Carol J. Loomis, "The Further Misadventures of Harold Geneen," *Fortune* (June 1975).

[7] There is incomplete but provocative evidence of significant share-profit relationships in the markets for auto rental, consumer finance, and retail securities brokerage.

[8] Schoeffler, Buzzell, and Heany, "Impact of Strategic Planning on Profit Performance," pp. 137-45; and Buzzell, Gale, and Sultan, "Market Share—A Key to Profitability," pp. 97-106.

including the results of the PIMS project, which supports these assumptions. Several qualifications must be made before the implications can be pursued in depth:

☐ While market share *gains* may be costly, it is possible to mismanage a dominant position. The examples of A&P in food retailing and British Leyland in the U.K. automobile market provide new benchmarks on the extent to which strong positions can erode unless vigorously defended.

☐ When the two largest competitors are of roughly equal size, the share positions may continue to be fluid until one is finally dominant.

☐ There are certain product categories, frequently high technology oriented, where a dominant full line/full service competitor is vulnerable if there are customer segments which do not require all the services, technical assistance, etc., that are provided. As markets mature this "sophisticated" segment usually grows. Thus, Digital Equipment Corp. has prospered in competition with IBM by simply selling basic hardware and depending on others to do the applications programming.[9] By contrast, IBM provides, for a price, a great deal of service backup and software for customers who are not self-sufficient. The dilemma for the dominant producer lies in the difficulty of serving both segments simultaneously.[10]

WHAT IS THE OBJECTIVE OF A PRODUCT PORTFOLIO STRATEGY?

The strategies emerging from a product portfolio analysis emphasize the balance of cash flows, by ensuring that there are products that use cash to sustain growth and others that supply cash.

[9] "A Minicomputer Tempest," *Business Week* (January 27, 1975), pp. 79–80.

[10] Some argue that the dilemma is very general, confronting all pioneering companies in mature markets. See Seymour Tilles, "Segmentation and Strategy," *Perspectives* (Boston: Boston Consulting Group, 1974).

Yet corporate objectives have many more dimensions that require consideration. This point was recognized by Seymour Tilles in one of the earliest discussions of the portfolio approach.[11] It is worth repeating to avoid a possible myopic focus on cash flow considerations. Tilles' point was that an investor pursues a balanced combination of risk, income, and growth when acquiring a portfolio of securities. He further argued that "the same basic concepts apply equally well to product planning." The problem with concentrating on cash flow to maximize income and growth is that strategies to balance risks are not explicitly considered.

What must be avoided is excessive exposure to a specific threat from one of the following areas of vulnerability:

☐ The economy (e.g., business downturns).

☐ Social, political, environmental pressures.

☐ Supply continuity.

☐ Technological change.

☐ Unions and related human factors.

It also follows that a firm should direct its new product search activities into several different opportunity areas, to avoid intensifying the degree of vulnerability. Thus, many companies in the power equipment market, such as Brown Boveri, are in a quandary over whether to meet the enormous resource demands of the nuclear power equipment market, because of the degree of vulnerability of this business compared to other possibilities such as household appliances.

The desire to reduce vulnerability is a possible reason for keeping, or even acquiring, a "Dog." Thus, firms may integrate backward to assure supply of highly leveraged

[11] Seymour Tilles, "Strategies for Allocating Funds," *Harvard Business Review*, 44 (January-February 1966), pp. 72–80.

materials.[12] If a "Dog" has a high percentage of captive business, it may not even belong as a separate entity in a portfolio analysis.

A similar argument could be used for products which have been acquired for intelligence reasons. For example, a large Italian knitwear manufacturer owns a high-fashion dress company selling only to boutiques to help follow and interpret fashion trends. Similarly, because of the complex nature of the distribution of lumber products, some suppliers have acquired lumber retailers to help learn about patterns of demand and changing end-user requirements. In both these cases the products/businesses were acquired for reasons outside the logic of the product portfolio, and should properly be excluded from the analysis.

Can the Strategies Be Implemented?

Not only does a product portfolio analysis provide insights into the long-run health of a company; it also implies the basic strategies that will strengthen the portfolio. Unfortunately, there are many situations where the risks of failure of these strategies are unacceptably high. Several of these risks were identified in a recent analysis of the dangers in the pursuit of market share.[13]

One danger is that the company's financial resources will not be adequate. The resulting problems are enormously compounded should the company find itself in a vulnerable financial position if the fight were stopped short for some reason. The funda-

mental question underlying such dangers is the likelihood that competitors will pursue the same strategy, because they follow the same logic in identifying and pursuing opportunities. As a result, there is a growing premium on the understanding of competitive responses, and especially the degree to which they will be discouraged by aggressive action.

An increasingly important question is whether government regulations will permit the corporation to follow the strategy it has chosen. Antitrust regulations—especially in the U.S.—now virtually preclude acquisitions undertaken by large companies in related areas. Thus the effort by ITT to acquire a "Cash Cow" in Hartford Fire and Indemnity Insurance was nearly aborted by a consent decree, and other moves by ITT into Avis, Canteen Corp., and Levitt have been divested by court order at enormous cost. Recent governmental actions—notably the *Rea-Lemon* case—may even make it desirable for companies with very large absolute market share to consider reducing that share.[14]

There is less recognition as yet that government involvement can cut both ways, making it difficult to get in *or out of* a business. Thus, because of national security considerations large defense contractors would have a difficult time exiting from the aerospace or defense businesses. The problems are most acute in countries like Britain and Italy where intervention policies include price controls, regional development directives, and employment maintenance which may prevent the replacement of outmoded plants. Unions in these two countries are sometimes so dedicated to protecting the employment status quo that a manager may

---

[12]This argument is compelling when $20,000 of Styrene Monomer can affect the production of $10,000,000 worth of formed polyester fiberglass parts.

[13]William E. Fruhan, "Pyrrhic Victories in Fights for Market Share," *Harvard Business Review*, 50 (September-October 1972), pp. 100–107.

[14]See Paul N. Bloom and Philip Kotler, "Strategies for High Market-Share Companies," *Harvard Business Review*, 53 (November-December 1975), pp. 63–72.

not even move employees from one product line to another without risking strike activity.

The last implementation question concerns the viability of a niche strategy, which appears at the outset to be an attractive way of coping with both "Dogs" and "Problem Children." The fundamental problem, of course, is whether a product or market niche can be isolated and protected against competitive inroads. But even if this can be achieved in the long-run, the strategy may not be attractive. The difficulties are most often encountered when a full or extensive product line is needed to support sales, service, and distribution facilities. One specialized product may simply not generate sufficient volume and gross margin to cover the minimum costs of participation in the market. This is very clearly an issue in the construction equipment business because of the importance of assured service.

PITFALLS IN THE MEASURES

The "Achilles' Heel" of a product portfolio analysis is the units of measure; for if the share of market and growth estimates are dubious, so are the interpretations. Skeptics recognize this quickly, and can rapidly confuse the analysis by attacking the meaningfulness and accuracy of these measures and offering alternative definitions. With the present state of the measurements there is often no adequate defense.

What Share of What Market?

This is not one, but several questions. Each is controversial because they influence the bases for resource allocation and evaluation within the firm:

- Should the definition of the product-market be broad (reflecting the generic need) or narrow?
- How much market segmentation?
- Should the focus be on the total product-market or a portion served by the company?
- Which level of geography: local versus national versus regio-centric markets?

The answers to these questions are complicated by the lack of defensible procedures for identifying product-market boundaries. For example, four-digit SIC categories are convenient and geographically available but may have little relevance to consumer perceptions of substitutability which will influence the long-run performance of the product. Furthermore, there is the pace of product development activity which is dedicated to combining, extending, or otherwise obscuring the boundaries.

Breadth of Product-Market Definition?

This is a pivotal question. Consider the following extremes in definitions:

- Intermediate builder chemicals for the detergent industry *or* Sodium Tri-polyphosphate.
- Time/information display devices *or* medium-priced digital-display alarm clocks.
- Main meal accompaniments *or* jellied cranberry.

Narrow definitions satisfy the short-run, tactical concerns of sales and product managers. Broader views, reflecting longer-run, strategic planning concerns, invariably reveal a larger market to account for (a) sales to untapped but potential markets, (b) changes in technology, price relationships, and supply which broaden the array of potential substitute products, and (c) the time required by present and prospective buyers to react to these changes.

Extent of Segmentation? In other words, when does it become meaningful to divide the total market into subgroups for the purpose of estimating shares? In the tire industry it is evident that the OEM and replacement markets are so dissimilar in behavior as to dictate totally different marketing mixes. But how much further should segmentation be pushed? The fact that a company has a large share of the high-income buyers of replacement tires is probably not strategically relevant.

In general the degree of segmentation for a portfolio analysis should be limited to grouping those buyers that share situational or behavioral characteristics that are strategically relevant. This means that different marketing mixes must be used to serve the segments that have been identified, which will be reflected in different cost and price structures. Other manifestations of a strategically important segment boundary would be a discontinuity in growth rates, share patterns, distribution patterns, and so forth when going from one segment to another.

These judgments are particularly hard to make for geographic boundaries. For example, what is meaningful for a manufacturer of industrial equipment facing dominant local competition in each of the national markets in the European Economic Community? Because the company is in each market, it has a 5% share of the total EEC market, while the largest regional competitor has 9%. In this case the choice of a regional rather than national market definition was dictated by the *trend* to similarity of product requirements throughout the EEC and the consequent feasibility of a single manufacturing facility to serve serveral countries.

The tendency for trade barriers to decline for countries within significant economic groupings will increasingly dictate regiocentric rather than nationally oriented bound-

aries. This, of course, will not happen where transportation costs or government efforts to protect sensitive industry categories (such as electric power generation equipment), by requiring local vendors, create other kinds of barriers.

Market Served versus Total Market?

Firms may elect to serve only just a part of the available market, such as retailers with central buying offices or utilities of a certain size. The share of the market served is an appropriate basis for tactical decisions. This share estimate may also be relevant for strategic decisions, especially if the market served corresponds to a distinct segment boundary. There is a risk that focusing only on the market served may mean overlooking a significant opportunity or competitive threat emerging from the unserved portion of the market. For example, a company serving the blank cassette tape market only through specialty audio outlets is vulnerable if buyers perceive that similar quality cassettes can be bought in general merchandise and discount outlets.

Another facet of the served market issue is the treatment of customers who have integrated backward and now satisfy their own needs from their own resources. Whether or not the captive volume is included in the estimate of total market size depends on how readily this captive volume can be displaced by outside suppliers. Recent analysis suggests that captive production—or in-feeding—is "remarkably resilient to attack by outside suppliers."[15]

[15]Aubrey Wilson and Bryan Atkin, "Exorcising the Ghosts in Marketing," *Harvard Business Review*, 54 (September-October 1976), pp. 117-27. See also, Ralph D. Kerkendall, "Customers as Competitors," *Perspectives* (Boston: Boston Consulting Group, 1975).

WHAT CAN BE DONE?

The value of a strategically relevant product-market definition lies in "stretching" the company's perceptions appropriately—far enough so that significant threats and opportunities are not missed, but not so far as to dissipate information gathering and analysis efforts on "long shots." This is a difficult balance to achieve, given the myriads of possibilities. The best procedure for coping is to employ several alternative definitions, varying specificity of product and market segments. There will inevitably be both points of contradiction and consistency in the insights gained from portfolios constructed at one level versus another. The process of resolution can be very revealing, both in terms of understanding the competitive position and suggesting strategy alternatives.[16]

Market Growth Rate

The product life cycle is justifiably regarded as one of the most difficult marketing concepts to measure—or forecast.

There is a strong tendency in a portfolio analysis to judge that a product is maturing when there is a forecast of a decline in growth rate below some specified cut-off. One difficulty is that the same cut-off level does not apply equally to all products or economic climates. As slow growth or level GNP becomes the reality, high absolute growth rates become harder to achieve for all products, mature or otherwise. Products with lengthy introductory periods, facing substantial barriers to adoption, may never exhibit high

growth rates, but may have an extended maturity stage. Other products may exhibit precisely the opposite life cycle pattern.

The focus in the product portfolio analysis should be on the long-run growth rate forecast. This becomes especially important with products which are sensitive to the business cycle, such as machine tools, or have potential substitutes with fluctuating prices. Thus the future growth of engineered plastics is entwined with the price of zinc, aluminum, copper, and steel; the sales of powdered breakfast beverages depends on the relative price of frozen orange juice concentrate.

These two examples also illustrate the problem of the self-fulfilling prophecy. A premature classification as a mature product may lead to the reduction of marketing resources to the level necessary to defend the share in order to maximize net cash flow. But if the product class sales are sensitive to market development activity (as in the case of engineered plastics) or advertising expenditures (as is the case with powdered breakfast drinks) and these budgets are reduced by the dominant firms, then, indeed, the product growth rate will slow down.

The growth rate is strongly influenced by the choice of product-market boundaries. A broad product type (cigarettes) will usually have a longer maturity stage than a more specific product form (plain filter cigarettes). In theory, the growth of the individual brand is irrelevant. Yet, it cannot be ignored that the attractiveness of a growth market, however defined, will be diminished by the entry of new competitors with the typical depressing effect on the sales, prices, and profits of the established firms. The extent of the reappraisal of the market will depend on the number, resources, and commitment of the new entrants. Are they likely to become what is known in the audio electronics industry as

[16]George S. Day and Allan D. Shocker, *Identifying Competitive Product-Market Boundaries: Strategic and Analytical Issues* (Boston: Marketing Science Institute, 1976).

"rabbits," which come racing into the market, litter it up, and die off quickly?

PITFALLS FROM UNANTICIPATED CONSEQUENCES

Managers are very effective at tailoring their behavior to the evaluation system, *as they perceive it*. Whenever market share is used to evaluate performance, there is a tendency for managers to manipulate the product-market boundaries to show a static or increasing share. The greater the degree of ambiguity or compromise in the definition of the boundaries, the more tempting these adjustments become. The risk is that the resulting narrow view of the market may mean overlooking threats from substitutes or the opportunities within emerging market segments.

These problems are compounded when share dominance is also perceived to be an important determinant of the allocation of resources and top management interest. The manager who doesn't like the implications of being associated with a "Dog" may try to redefine the market so he can point to a larger market share or a higher than average growth rate. Regardless of his success with the attempted redefinition, his awareness of how the business is regarded in the overall portfolio will ultimately affect his morale. Then his energies may turn to seeking a transfer or looking for another job, and perhaps another prophecy has been fulfilled.

The forecast of market growth rate is also likely to be manipulated, especially if the preferred route to advancement and needed additional resources is perceived to depend on association with a product that is classified as "Star." This may lead to wishful thinking about the future growth prospects of the product. Unfortunately the quality of the review procedures in most planning processes is not robust enough to challenge such distortions. Further dysfunctional consequences will result if ambitious managers of "Cash Cows" actually attempt to expand their products through unnecessary product proliferation and market segmentation without regard to the impact on profits.

The potential for dysfunctional consequences does not mean that profit center managers and their employees should not be aware of the basis for resource allocation decisions within the firm. A strong argument can be made to the effect that it is worse for managers to observe those decisions and suspect the worst. What will surely create problems is to have an inappropriate reward system. A formula-based system, relying on achievement of a target for return on investment or an index of profit measures, that does not recognize the differences in potential among business, will lead to short-run actions that conflict with the basic strategies that should be pursued.

ALTERNATIVE VIEWS OF THE PORTFOLIO

This analysis of the share/growth matrix portrayal of the product portfolio supports Bowman's contention that much of what now exists in the field of corporate or marketing strategy can be thought of as contingency theories. "The ideas, recommendations, or generalizations are rather dependent (contingent) for their truth and their relevance on the specific situational factors."[17] This means that in any specific analysis of the product portfolio there may be a number of factors beyond share and market growth with a much greater bearing on the attractiveness of a product-market or business; including:

[17]Edward H. Bowman, "Epistemology, Corporate Strategy, and Academe," *Sloan Management Review* (Winter 1974), pp. 35–50.

□   The contribution rate.

□   Barriers to entry.

□   Cyclicality of sales.

□   The rate of capacity utilization.

□   Sensitivity of sales to change in prices, promotional activities, service levels, etc.

□   The extent of "captive" business.

□   The nature of technology (maturity, volatility, and complexity).

□   Availability of production and process opportunities.

□   Social, legal, governmental and union pressures and opportunities.

Since these factors are situational, each company (or division) must develop its own ranking of their importance in determining attractiveness.[18] In practice these factors tend to be qualitatively combined into overall judgments of the attractiveness of the industry or market, and the company's position in that market. The resulting matrix for displaying the positions of each product is called a "nineblock" diagram or decision matrix.[19]

Although the implications of this version of the product portfolio are not as clear-cut, it does overcome many of the shortcomings of the share/growth matrix approach. Indeed the two approaches will likely yield different insights. But as the main purpose of the product portfolio analysis is to help guide—but not substitute for—strategic thinking, the process of reconciliation is useful in itself. Thus it is desirable to employ both approaches and compare results.

SUMMARY

The product portfolio concept provides a useful synthesis of the analyses and judgments during the preliminary steps of the planning process, and is a provocative source of strategy alternatives. If nothing else, it demonstrates the fallacy of treating all businesses or profit centers as alike, and all capital investment decisions as independent and additive events.

There are a number of pitfalls to be avoided to ensure the implications are not misleading. This is especially true for the cash quadrant or share/growth matrix approach to portraying the portfolio. In many situations the basic assumptions are not satisfied. Further complications stem from uncertainties in the definitions of product-markets and the extent and timing of competitive actions. One final pitfall is the unanticipated consequences of adopting a portfolio approach. These may or may not be undesirable depending on whether they are recognized at the outset.

Despite the potential pitfalls it is important to not lose sight of the concept; that is, to base strategies on the perception of a company as an interdependent group of products and services, each playing a distinctive and supportive role.

---

[18] The choice of factors and assessment of ranks is an important aspect of the design of a planning system. These issues are described in Peter Lorange, "Divisional Planning: Setting Effective Direction," *Sloan Management Review* (Fall 1975), pp. 77–91.

[19] William E. Rothschild, *Putting It All Together: A Guide to Strategic Thinking* (New York: AMACOM, 1976).

5

Key Options in Market Selection and Product Planning

E. Raymond Corey

Sound market and product selection decisions are vital to the success of industrial as well as consumer marketers. These decisions must be based on evaluations of market opportunities, corporate capabilities, industry technologies, competition, and other information.

In 1957 when John F. Connelly was elected president of Crown Cork & Seal Company, the company was on the verge of bankruptcy. A loss of $600,000 was reported in the first quarter of that year, a $2.5 million loan was being called by Bankers Trust, and an additional $4.5 million in short-term notes was due by the end of 1957. Only seven years later Crown Cork enjoyed a higher return on sales than its two largest competitors, as Exhibit 1 shows, and forces had been set in motion that led to rising sales volume and profitability throughout the 1960s and early 1970s.[1]

The main secret of the company's success—and Connelly's—was an understanding of marketing strategy. I believe the approach used by Crown Cork & Seal may prove valuable to other companies as well.

[1]For this and other facts on the company, see "Crown Cork and Seal Company and the Metal Container Industry," a Harvard Business School case study (ICCH No. 6-373-077), and the company's 1974 annual report.

But before abstracting and generalizing the concepts involved, let us look in more detail at the situation Connelly had to contend with.

Crown Cork & Seal was (and is) a major producer of metal cans, crowns (bottle caps), closures (screw caps and bottle lids), and filling machinery for beer and soft drink cans. With sales of $115 million in 1956, the company competed in an industry dominated by two giants, American Can (with sales of $772 million in 1956) and Continental Can (with sales of $1,010 million in that year).

The industry was and still is characterized by a high degree of technological change; glass, aluminum, fiberfoil, and the plastics have competed with tinplate to serve the packaging needs of more than 135 different industries. New and revolutionary concepts in packaging have emerged with developments such as the aerosol containers and the "pop-top" metal can. To compete

EXHIBIT 1

Sales and return on sales (after taxes) for three companies

YEAR	NET SALES (IN MILLIONS)			RETURN ON SALES (AFTER TAXES)		
	CROWN CORK & SEAL	CONTINENTAL CAN	AMERICAN CAN	CROWN CORK & SEAL	CONTINENTAL CAN	AMERICAN CAN
1964	$218	$1,198	$1,292	5.1%	4.1%	3.8%
1965	256	1,234	1,337	5.7	4.8	4.9
1966	280	1,339	1,449	6.0	5.3	5.2
1967	301	1,398	1,522	6.3	5.6	5.0
1968	337	1,508	1,636	6.2	5.5	4.8
1969	371	1,780	1,724	6.2	5.2	3.7
1970	414	2,037	1,838	6.2	4.6	3.6
1971	448	2,082	1,897	6.3	3.6	2.6
1972	489	2,193	2,016	6.4	3.7	2.7
1973	572	2,540	2,182	6.0	3.8	3.0
1974	766	3,087	2,658	5.2	3.9	3.6

SOURCE: Annual reports of the three companies.

in this industry companies must make large capital investments in can-making lines. In addition, the major can producers have found it necessary to invest large amounts in research and development.

A "fact of life" in the industry is the ever-present threat of self-manufacture by large users. For example, one of the largest manufacturers of cans in the United States is a user company, Campbell Soup. Another fact is the high cost of materials as a percenage of total manufacturing cost. When John Connelly assumed the presidency of Crown Cork, approximately 65% of the price to users of tinplate cans went to the tinplate producers. Thus value added by manufacture was only one-third of the value of shipments of metal cans.

Pressed on one side by rising material and labor costs, on another side by the threat of new low-cost materials, and on a third side by large, powerful customers and the threat of self-manufacture, companies in the metal container business have had to put up with typically low profit margins and prices.

The major manufacturers have responded to these conditions, first, by investing heavily in research on packaging materials, container design, and can manufac-

turing and using equipment. Second, they have diversified within the packaging field to provide a wide range of paper, plastics, glass, and aluminum as well as tinplate containers to a broad range of customers. Third, they have offered increased customer service in such areas as market studies, product planning, materials handling, and production lay-out and design.

UNIQUE STRATEGY

John Connelly's strategic response in 1957 was significantly different from that of his giant competitors. He elected to concentrate on two product/market segments. One was metal cans for such "hard-to-hold" products as beer and soft drinks, and the second was the emerging aerosol container market. Both markets were growing rapidly. Both called for high skills in container design and manufacturing, thus reducing the threat of self-manufacture. In both market segments it was likely that metal would be the dominant material—and Crown Cork had particularly high skills in metal forming and fabrication. In the canned beverage market, Crown Cork had a particular advantage, since its machinery division supplied 60% of all the filling equipment used by soft drink manufacturers and 90% of the filling equipment used in the brewing industry.

In spite of the fact that Crown Cork had captured 50% of the huge motor oil can business when it introduced the first aluminum one-quart oil can in 1958, its management decided *not* to continue to compete aggressively in this market. Fiberfoil was rapidly emerging as the dominant packaging material for motor oil containers, and management felt that the cost economics of the paper can would give the paper companies a significant advantage. Moreover, there was a high risk of self-manufacture of such cans because the technology was simple, the product was standardized, and the oil companies required large quantities of these containers.

Connelly's decision to stay essentially with metal containers, based on a judgment that long-run requirements in the beer, soft drink, and aerosol markets would favor metal, allowed him to conserve considerably on R&D expenses and to focus these efforts sharply.

Connelly did commit major capital investments to plant improvement and relocation. In particular, he embarked on a program of moving plants to places where there were large concentrations of customers in his chosen markets. He designed his plants to serve the full range of customer needs, including prompt delivery.

The new strategy paid off. As of 1974, Crown Cork had increased its sales to $766 million (see Exhibit 1). Consolidated net income was over $39 million in 1974, and earnings per share had grown from $0.01 (corrected for stock splits) in 1957 to $2.20 in 1974. As the exhibit indicates, Crown Cork outperformed its two larger competitors both in sales growth and in return on sales in the 1964–1974 period.

During this time American Can and Continental Can diversified widely. The former moved strongly into such customer items as Dixie cups and Butterick dress patterns, as well as chemicals, printing,

and biomedical items. The latter company stressed forest products in its diversification moves, operating woodlands and mills for making building products and corrugated containers. Continental Can also added such diversified items as cellulose casings for meats and soy protein products. But Crown Cork continued to build its strength in the beer and aerosol container markets. In 1973, for example, it invested $40 million in new plant, of which $27 million was for drawn and ironed steel can capacity in the United States.

The success of Crown Cork after 1956 can be attributed to a wide range of actions, including a changed organization structure, a modified control system, constant emphasis on overhead reduction, and top management leadership. At the heart of its success, however, are the choices management made with regard to markets and products. These choices might be divided into four categories. I shall describe these categories next, then return to Crown Cork.

KEY CONCEPTS

In problems of market selection and product planning, it is important to keep four key ideas in mind.

What Markets Should be Served?

The most important decisions in planning marketing strategy are those related to the choice of a market or markets to serve. All else follows. Choice of market is a choice of the customer and of the competitive, technical, political, and social environments in which one elects to compete. It is not an easily reversed decision; having made the choice, the company develops skills and resources around the markets it has elected to serve. It builds a set of relationships with customers that are at once a major source of strength and a major commitment. The commitment carries with it the responsibility to serve customers well, to stay in the technical and product-development race, and to grow in pace with growing market demand.

Such choices are not made in a vacuum. They are influenced by the company's background; by its marketing, manufacturing, and technical strengths; by the fabric of its relations with existing customers, the scientific community, and competitors; and by other considerations.

What Form Should the Product Take?

Products are planned and designed to serve markets. Marketing strategies should not be developed for products but for *markets*— the product is a variable, not a given, in the strategy. In theory, at least, market selection comes first, and the choice of product form follows. An aluminum manufacturer, for example, might elect to serve the residential housing market by supplying aluminum siding, shingles, gutters, and downspouts. Alternatively, it could supply aluminum sheet stock and coil to independent fabricators of these building components. Another option, conceivably, would be to make and sell certain types of housing, such as mobile homes.

The *market*, in this case, might be broadly defined as residential housing. The *product options* are semifabricated materials, building components, and end products. Other product choices may be whether to make a full line or narrow line in any given product area; whether to offer high, medium, or low quality; and whether to have a full range of sizes or to work across only part of the range.

What Should the Product Do for the User?

The "product" is what the product *does;* it is the total package of benefits the customer receives when he buys. This includes the functional utility of the goods, the product service that the manufacturer provides, the technical assistance he may give his cus-

tomers, and the assurance that the product will be delivered when and where it is needed and in the desired quantities. Another benefit might be the seller's brand name and reputation; these may help the buyer in his promotional activities.

Another benefit that the customer may gain has to do with the range of relationships, technical and personal, that may develop among people in the selling and buying organizations. Particularly in industrial marketing, such relationships are normally part of the "package of benefits" that the purchaser is likely to buy.

My point is that the product should not be conceived of narrowly in terms of its primary function. Even if it is nondifferentiable, in the most narrow sense, the supplier may differentiate it from competitive offerings through special service, distribution, or brand image.

For Whom Is the Product Most Important?

The product, in this broader sense, will have different meaning to different customers. It is strategically advantageous for a supplier to concentrate on those prospective customer groups that will value the product the most. If, for example, technical service is an important part of what the seller provides, a promising market may be smaller companies that have no research and development facilities of their own. Larger, technically sophisticated customers with extensive in-house research skills may place little or no value on that aspect of the product offering. Also, of course, a product generally commands the highest prices among the customers for whom it has the greatest utility.

MAKING PRODUCT/MARKET CHOICES

One observation that should emerge from this discussion is that product planning and market selection are integrally related.

Decisions in these two areas cannot be made independently. Accordingly, I shall use the term *product/market* to describe the choices and strategies that management is concerned with.

Strategic choices with regard to product/market strategy may be made along two dimensions, *horizontal* and *vertical*. On each dimension there are choices to be made with regard to customer subgroups, that is, the specific customers that the company will seek to cultivate. These types of choices might be differentiated as follows:

☐ Horizontally, industrial markets can be segmented in terms of end-use application. A manufacturer of air conditioning systems, for example, will distinguish among such market segments as residential tract builders, small "stick" builders, and commercial contractors.

☐ On the other hand, vertical product/market choices have to do with the market level at which the supplier sells. For instance, the aluminum producer serving the residential housing market may have a choice whether to sell raw materials, semifabricated materials, components, or end products.

☐ Customer subgroup choices relate to the selection of particular types of customers within a horizontal or vertical market segment. Generally, customer subgroups may be distinguished in terms of buyer-behavior characteristics. For instance, government agencies typically make their purchases differently than private companies do. Large companies typically have more sophisticated buying organizations and procurement processes than do small ones. Some companies tend to be innovative and are among the first to try new products, while others exhibit "follower" characteristics.

Now let us consider the horizontal and vertical dimensions of strategy in turn.

HORIZONTAL PRODUCT/MARKET SELECTION

Market selection, as noted earlier, is influenced considerably by the manufacturer's assessment of his own strengths and weaknesses. He may count his product design, possibly protected by patents, as an important asset. He may start with a technical innovation and seek the market segments and product forms that would give him a competitive advantage over products performing similar functions. He may perceive his established position and reputation with existing customers as his critical strength. He may regard his size, financial strength, and production resources as his strong suit. Limitations in any of these areas must be counted as weaknesses.

Over and against this assessment of strengths and weaknesses should be posited a list of feasible product/market opportunities, with an evaluation of buying behavior, market needs, and the competitive environment for each one. Market selection is then a matter of electing those product/market opportunities where the company has a meaningful edge and where its weaknesses will not be critical deterrents to success.

Crown Cork's Decision Analyzed

At Crown Cork & Seal, for example, management elected to concentrate on markets for aerosol cans and metal containers for beer and soft drinks. It did not commit itself to the large and growing markets for such applications as frozen citrus juices and motor oil. One might have matched corporate strengths and limitations against market needs and opportunities as follows.

Corporate Strengths

☐ Technical capability in the design, manufacture, and use of *metal* containers for "hard-to-hold" applications

☐ Good working relationships with major suppliers of metals

☐ A major position as a supplier of filling equipment for soft drink and beer cans

Corporate Limitations

☐ Much smaller market share than the two major companies in the industry

☐ Limited financial resources for supporting research and development

☐ Outmoded manufacturing plants not located near concentrations of potential customers

Market Needs, Opportunities, and Risks.
Beer, soft drink, and aerosol containers:

☐ High growth rate

☐ Need for high-strength containers (probably metal)

☐ Technical maturity of metal cans and relatively low needs for R&D (aerosol tops and pull-tops)

☐ Low risk of self-manufacture by user companies

☐ High service needs for delivery, for layout and operation of can-filling lines, and for lithographing container surfaces

☐ Customer desire for at least two sources of supply

Motor oil cans:

☐ Large market potential

☐ Rapid changes in packaging materials mean greater risk of self-manufacture by user companies and relatively low value added in fiberfoil containers

Having assessed the company's strengths and limitations against known market opportunities, Crown Cork's management made clear choices—and with considerable success. There was and is, of course, some risk attached to a dependency on a narrow market base. Crown Cork may be vulnerable to new materials or new forms of packaging for applications in which its metal cans are now used. But these risks seem a fair trade-off for the advantages of the strategy.

Diversifying into New Markets

In the situation where an industrial company is diversifying into new markets, four considerations are very important. They can be stated in the form of questions for managers to ask:

1. Does the market have high growth potential?

2. Is the market currently dominated by large and powerful competitors, or is it still possible to claim a large market share? Companies with large market shares generally enjoy higher returns on investment than their competitors with lower market shares. The competitor with the largest market share often enjoys a low unit cost position in manufacturing and marketing. He may be able to support the largest R&D effort. He may, in addition, be able to exercise some price leadership. In a study of a widely diversified sample of approximately 620 businesses in 57 different companies undertaken by the Marketing Science Institute, it was demonstrated that businesses with large market shares had much higher returns on investment than those businesses with relatively low market shares.[2]

3. Is the market easy or difficult for competitors to enter? Relative ease of entry depends on how high the required investments are in manufacturing plants, in R&D, and in field sales and service facilities. In many industries—basic chemicals, heavy electrical equipment, steel, aluminum, pharmaceuticals, aircraft, synthetic fibers, paper, and office equipment, among others —large investments in all three types of facilities are generally needed.

More important, a certain "critical mass" is needed for a producer to be efficient. To achieve low unit manufacturing costs, very large plants are needed. The "critical mass" concept is also relevant in such areas as R&D and field sales and service.

To support and justify such investments there may have to be the prospect of a significant market share. Yet the level of demand may support only a handful of suppliers—say, three to eight. Such considerations would make it difficult for new competitors to enter a market, thus provid-

[2]See Sidney Schoeffler, Robert D. Buzzell, and Donald F. Heany, "Impact of Strategic Planning on Profit Performance," *Harvard Business Review* (March–April 1974), p. 137.

ing a measure of protection for those who can afford the high stakes required.

4. How high is the value added by manufacture, or, conversely, how low is the ratio of the cost of materials and purchased parts to the selling price? Low value added tends to make the product/market opportunity less attractive. The manufacturer is vulnerable to rising costs of materials and equipments—costs that he may not be able to pass on to his customers in the form of higher prices. If, on the other hand, the value added is high relative to the selling price, the manufacturer controls a large portion of his costs and may usefully pursue cost-reduction programs to gain a competitive edge. Equally important, he probably has opportunities to develop unique skills through which he may differentiate his product from those of competitors, thus achieving a market advantage.

Product/Market Positioning

Very often selecting markets is a matter of identifying potential applications for some new product, possibly one that comes from a research laboratory. The problem then is one of product/market positioning.

After accurately defining the product's performance characteristics, management should determine what applications maximize its advantages and minimize its disadvantages. For instance, a plastic that has high tensile strength, dimensional stability, heat resistance, and machinability, but poor electrical properties (e.g., not fire-retardant), might be very useful for making certain appliance parts but not for making electrical components.

Engineers and marketers often seem to get carried away with new technical innovations and to be insufficiently objective in defining that "window" in the range of competing products where the innovation has its real place. Failing to establish a niche based on unique performance advantages, the strategists turn, usually un-

profitably, to fighting for the market survival of the product on a price basis.

Product-Line Proliferation

The extension of a product line to provide a range of sizes, models, or specifications, each designed for some particular market segment and end use, is a key competitive weapon in the fight for market share. For example, a synthetic fiber like Du Pont's nylon may be purchased in more than a thousand different "put-ups." Each fiber is tailored for use in a different end product, such as women's hosiery, parachutes, or nylon-reinforced rubber tires. Often, too, product-line proliferation comes through providing a range of optional equipment to meet the individual preferences of users.

Product-line growth may take the form of developing larger and larger units as technology permits and market needs grow —steam turbines for power plants, jet engines for aircraft, and so on. For the technical leader this kind of proliferation may be immensely useful as a means of achieving overall market leadership, preserving a dominant market share, and increasing profits.[3]

In still other cases, product-line proliferation may be forced by competitors. When this happens, the manufacturer who is defending his market position may be faced with a Hobson's choice: suffer a sharp drop in market share or add products to match competitive offerings and suffer a loss in profits. For example, with the rapid growth of markets for minicomputers, small computer manufacturers are threatening the large, integrated companies at one end of the product range. The logical response

---

[3]See Ralph G. M. Sultan, *Competition or Collusion: Economic and Legal Issues of Pricing in the Electrical Equipment Industry* (Boston, Mass.: Division of Research, Harvard Business School, 1974), for a detailed study of how General Electric has retained its long-term dominance in the market for turbine generators.

for the latter has been to develop and aggressively promote small computers, even though they may be less profitable to sell than the large machines.

VERTICAL PRODUCT/MARKET SELECTION

At what stage of manufacture should a company market its products? At issue here are management's willingness and ability to invest in the required manufacturing and marketing resources at different levels. The resource requirement varies considerably from one stage to another. In addition, of course, the market "environments" vary greatly from stage to stage along with customer characteristics. To illustrate:

Shortly after World War II the Aluminum Company of America (Alcoa) undertook the market introduction of an aluminum bearing for use in large diesel engines. The bearing was made from a special aluminum alloy called Alloy 750. Performance test indicated that bearings made from Alloy 750 were superior to conventional bearings in that they resisted corrosion better. Also, they dissipated heat more rapidly, minimizing the possibility of a bearing freezing on a crankshaft in the event of insufficient lubrication. Moreover, it was claimed that solid aluminum bearings would outwear conventional bearings many times over. Yet they cost much less to make than conventional bearings.

Alcoa managers had three options with regard to market level: (1) they could supply Alloy 750 to bearing manufacturers, (2) they could supply castings to bearing manufacturers and/or diesel engine builders, or (3) they could make and sell finished bearings to diesel engine builders and, as replacement parts, to diesel engine users.

Initially, an effort was made to supply castings. One reason was the importance of assuring product quality. Alloy 750 required special foundry techniques. If Alcoa did the casting, it could considerably minimize the risk of product failure due to poor casting quality. In addition, by making bearing castings rather than supplying aluminum ingots to foundries, Alcoa could realize higher sales and profit margins.

The company's field representatives worked with large diesel engine builders to generate interest in aluminum bearings. The representatives then referred these companies to bearing manufacturers as sources of supply for finished aluminum bearings. This approach was relatively unsuccessful because bearing manufacturers promoted their own conventional bearings, thus negating Alcoa's efforts to build a market for the new aluminum bearings. After ten years, annual sales of aluminum castings were only a small fraction of the potential that Alcoa managers had envisaged. The question that comes to mind, of course, is why Alcoa chose this particular marketing option.

Analyzing the Market-Level Choice

Let us put outselves in the position of Alcoa's management when it was choosing its market. What were the pros and cons of the different market levels?

First, let us begin with the question of customer receptivity:

☐ Diesel engine *users* could realize significant advantages from having long-life, trouble-free bearings. Not only might there be a saving in the cost of replacement bearings, but there could also be significant savings in downtime for engine maintenance.

☐ Diesel engine *builders* might realize some advantage in designing engines with Alloy 750 bearings if this feature could be given promotional significance in selling diesel engines. On the other hand, some diesel engine builders might be reluctant to experiment with new components, especially if they were advised against it by their regular bearing suppliers, the recognized experts in the field.

☐ Bearing *manufacturers* would have strong disincentives for adopting aluminum bearings. Such a move would make their facilities for producing conventional bearings obsolete. It would also sacrifice their position as manufacturers of proprietary products, with little or nothing by way of product differentiation to support claims to their respective market shares. Finally, aluminum bearings made from castings would mean less value added by manufacture.

In short, a compelling consideration is what market segment will benefit the most from adopting the product. In this case, diesel engine users would seem to have the most to gain.

What about the product quality question? Particularly in the early stages of market development, control of end-product quality is critically important. Poor quality and misapplications of the product can easily kill its potential. If Alcoa elected to make bearing castings, it could control one element of quality. If it chose to make finished bearings, it could assure itself of complete quality control. Moreover, it could become involved in direct working relationships with engine builders on diesel engine matters having to do with the use of aluminum bearings; this would mean opportunities to promote aluminum bearings through the company's technical service.

These three considerations—market receptivity to the product concept, ability to control end-product quality, and product promotability—argue for choosing a position in the finished bearings market. The major disadvantage would be the high cost of holding such a market position. It would probably be desirable to build a sales force at least as large as those of the major bearing manufacturers. It might be necessary to make and sell a full line of different types of bearings to support such a sales force and to serve the full range of customer needs. The prospective payoff from such commitments would have to be weighed against the anticipated gains and costs of other strategies.

To market bearing castings to the ten or so bearing manufacturers was undoubtedly the least-cost, lowest-commitment option.

In the long run, however, it was not likely to yield optimal results as measured in terms of sales volume and profits.

By making this choice, Alcoa's management indicated that it was unwilling, in view of other opportunities it might have had to increase sales of aluminum, to make the necessary resource commitments to manufacture and sell finished bearings. While it thus reduced its risk, it was less successful than it had hoped in developing a market for aluminum bearings.

The Alcoa case does not mean that a position at the end-product level is always to be preferred. It may be desirable to take a position as a materials or components producer because barriers to entry may be greater at the early stages in the manufacturing process, while profit margins may fall short at the end-product market level because of intensive competition among large numbers of sellers.

In addition, the product innovation may be less beneficial to end users than to prospective buyers at intermediate stages in the production process. One medium-sized chemical company, for example, undertook to develop a market for a siliceous mineral that could be used as a filler in making tiles, paints, and some plastic products. As a filler for tiles—and this was by far the largest potential use—the mineral could be used by tile manufacturers to reduce production costs significantly.

By contrast, the product had no benefits either structural or aesthetic for tile contractors, builders, or home owners. The product benefits all related to cost savings in tile manufacture, not to use. This was an important consideration in management's decision to function as a materials supplier rather than as a producer of ceramic tiles.

Questions for Managers to Ask

It is largely in connection with *vertical* product/market selection that management should remember that the product is a variable in marketing strategy. At what market level is the product concept most meaningful? Does it have the greatest value to end users (as in the case of the aluminum bearing), or is it most meaningful to end-product manufacturers (as in the case of the filler material)? Everything else being equal, industrial marketers should elect to sell the product at that market level where the product concept has the greatest meaning and in the form that that market can use.

As suggested earlier, the choice of product form (material, component, or end product) is influenced by the importance of controlling product quality and application. This is an especially important matter in developing markets for new products. The relevant questions to ask are these:

☐ Is there a possibility that market development may be aborted by poor product quality or by product misuse?

☐ At what points in the manufacturing chain do quality risks exist?

☐ Can the company minimize those risks by taking responsibility itself for that step in the manufacturing process?

Not infrequently, these considerations seem to dictate taking a product/market position at or close to the end-product level. But other reasons may favor the choice of some earlier stage. For instance, management may, for one of the following reasons, elect to serve as a supplier of materials or components:

☐ It is unwilling to commit itself to the extensive marketing and manufacturing investments that are required to compete in the end-product market. Alternative product/market opportunities may offer potentially higher returns on the funds available for investment.

☐ There may be higher profits and a more protected market position available if the company functions as a supplier of materials or components. The high plant and technical investments needed to enter the industry at these stages may seem prohibitive to would-be competitors.

☐ The company has traditionally taken a position as a marketer of materials or components to producers of end products and does not want to change its image. Executives may be concerned that if they start making end products, they will be perceived as competing with their customers.

If considerations such as the foregoing dictate taking a position at some early market level in the manufacturing chain, while the product concept is most meaningful at the end-product level, then another strategic option becomes attractive. The industrial marketer may manufacture and sell at the early level, but promote and seek to control quality at or near the end-product stage.

For example, when Dow Chemical was developing a market for polystyrene plastic, it worked with plastic molders in the design of the products made from Dow's polystyrene. If these products met Dow's design criteria, the molders were authorized to mark them with a Dow label. Dow then advertised approved products to retailers and to consumers. Thus, although the company chose to be a supplier of materials, it was also active in quality control and product promotion at the retail level.

This was what is called an industrial marketing "pull" strategy. It sought to put pressure on Dow's immediate customers, the plastic molders, to use Dow's polystyrene by creating demand at the end-user level. It can be a sound strategy indeed, but *only* if there are significant advantages for end-users in the product concept.

6

Strategic Windows

Derek F. Abell

Strategic market planning involves the management of any business unit in the dual tasks of *anticipating* and *responding* to changes which affect the marketplace for their products. This article discusses both of these tasks. Anticipation of change and its impact can be substantially improved if an organizing framework can be used to identify sources and directions of change in a systematic fashion. Appropriate responses to change require a clear understanding of the alternative strategic options available to management as a market evolves and change takes place.

DYNAMIC ANALYSIS

When changes in the market are only incremental, firms may successfully adapt themselves to the new situation by modifying current marketing or other functional programs. Frequently, however, market changes are so far reaching that the competence of the firm to continue to compete effectively is called into question. And it is in such situations that the concept of "strategic windows" is applicable.

The term "strategic window" is used here to focus attention on the fact that there are only limited periods during which the "fit" between the key requirements of a market and the particular competencies of a firm competing in that market is at an optimum. Investment in a product line or market area should be timed to coincide with periods in which such a strategic window is open. Conversely, disinvestment should be contemplated if what was once a good fit has been eroded—i.e., if changes in market requirements outstrip the firm's capability to adapt itself to them.

Among the most frequent questions

Reprinted with permission from *Journal of Marketing*, published by the American Marketing Association (July 1978), pp. 21–26.

which management has to deal with in this respect are:

☐ Should funds be committed to a proposed new market entry? Now? Later? Or not at all? If a commitment is to be made, how large should it be?

☐ Should expenditure of funds of plant and equipment or marketing to support existing product lines be expanded, continued at historical levels, or diminished?

☐ When should a decision be made to quit and throw in the towel for an unprofitable product line or business area?

Resource allocation decisions of this nature require a careful assessment of the future evolution of the market involved and an accurate appraisal of the firm's capability to successfully meet key market requirements. The "strategic window" concept encourages the analysis of these questions in a dynamic rather than a static framework, and forces marketing planners to be as specific as they can about these future patterns of market evolution and the firm's capability to adapt to them.

It is unfortunate that the heightened interest in product portfolio analysis evident in the last decade has failed to adequately encompass these issues. Many managers routinely classify their various activities as "cows," "dogs," "stars," or "question marks" based on a *static* analysis of the *current* position of the firm and its market environment.

Of key interest, however, is the question not only of where the firm is today, but of how well equipped it is to deal with *tomorrow*. Such a *dynamic* analysis may foretell nonincremental changes in the market which work to disqualify market leaders, provide opportunities for currently low share competitors, and sometimes even usher in a completely new cast of competitors into the marketplace. Familiar contemporary examples of this latter phenomenon include such products as digital watches, women's pantyhose, calculators, charter air travel, office copiers, and scientific instrumentation.

In all these cases existing competitors have been displaced by new contenders as these markets have evolved. In each case changing market requirements have resulted in a *closing* strategic window for incumbent competitors and an *opening* window for new entrants.

MARKET EVOLUTION

The evolution of a market usually embodies more far-reaching changes than the relatively systematic changes in customer behavior and marketing mix due to individual product life cycles. Four major categories of change stand out:

1. The development of new primary demand opportunities whose marketing requirements differ radically from those of existing market segments.

2. The advent of new competing technologies which cannibalize the existing ones.

3. Market redefinition caused by changes in the definition of the product itself and or changes in the product market strategies of competing firms.

4. Channel changes.

There may be other categories of change or variants in particular industries. That doesn't matter; understanding of how such changes may qualify or disqualify different types of competitors can still be derived from a closer look at examples within each of the four categories above.

New Primary Demand

In a primary demand growth phase, decisions have to be reached by existing competitors about whether to spend the majority of the resources fighting to protect and fortify market positions that have already been established, or whether to seek new development opportunities.

In some cases it is an original entrant who ploughs new territory—adjusting his approach to the emergent needs of the marketplace; in other cases it is a new entrant who, maybe basing his entry on expertise developed elsewhere, sees a "strategic window" and leapfrogs over the original market leader to take advantage of the new growth opportunity. Paradoxically, pioneering competitors who narrowly focus their activities in the early stages of growth may have the most difficulty in making the transition to new primary demand growth opportunities later. Emery Air Freight provides an example of a company that did face up to a challenge in such a situation.

Emery Air Freight.   This pioneer in the air freight forwarding business developed many of the early applications of air freight in the United States. In particular, Emery's efforts were focused on servicing the "emergency" segment of the market, which initially accounted for a substantial portion of all air freight business. Emery served this market via an extensive organization of regional and district offices. Among Emery's major assets in this market was a unique nationwide, and later worldwide, communications network; and the special competence of personnel located in the district offices in using scheduled carriers in the most efficient possible way to expedite deliveries.

As the market evolved, however, many new applications for air freight emerged. These included regular planned shipments of high value-low weight merchandise, shipments of perishables, "off-line" service to hard-to-reach locations, and what became known as the TCC (Total Cost Concept) market. Each of these new applications required a somewhat different approach than

that demanded by the original emergency business.

TCC applications, for example, required detailed logistics planning to assess the savings and benefits to be obtained via lower inventories, quicker deliveries, and fewer lost sales through the use of air freight. Customer decisions about whether or not to use air freight required substantially more analysis than had been the case for "emergency" use; furthermore, decisions which had originally been made by traffic managers now involved marketing personnel and often top management.

A decision to seek this kind of business thus implied a radical change in Emery's organization—the addition of capability to analyze complex logistics systems and to deal with upper echelons of management.

New Competing Technologies

When a fundamental change takes place in the basic technology of an industry, it again raises questions of the adaptability to new circumstances of existing firms using obsolete technology.

In many cases established competitors in an industry are challenged, not by another member of the same industry, but by a company which bases its approach on a technology developed outside that industry. Sometimes this results from forward integration of a firm that is eager to develop applications for a new component or raw material. Texas Instruments' entry into a wide variety of consumer electronic products from a base of semiconductor manufacture is a case in point. Sometimes it results from the application by firms of a technology developed in one market to opportunities in another. Or sometimes a breakthrough in either product or process technology may remove traditional barriers to entry in an industry and attract a completely new set of competitors. Consider the following examples:

□ Watchmakers have recently found that a new class of competitor is challenging their industry leadership—namely electronic firms who are seeking end market applications for their semiconductors, as well as a new breed of assemblers manufacturing digital watches.

□ Manufacturers of mechanical adjustable speed drive equipment found their markets eroded by electrical speed drives in the early 1900s. Electrical drives were based on rotating motor-generator sets and electronic controls. In the late 1950s, the advent of solid state electronics, in turn, virtually obsoleted rotating equipment. New independent competitors, basing their approach on the assembly of electronic components, joined the large electrical equipment manufacturers in the speed drive market. Today, yet another change is taking place, namely the advent of large computer controlled drive systems. This is ushering yet another class of competitors into the market—namely companies whose basic competence is in computers.

In each of these cases, recurrent waves of new technology fundamentally changed the nature of the market and usually ushered in an entirely new class of competitors. Many firms in most markets have a limited capability to master all the technologies which might ultimately cannibalize their business. The nature of technological innovation and diffusion is such that most *major* innovations will originate outside a particular industry and not within it.

In many cases, the upheaval is not only technological; indeed, the nature of competition may also change dramatically as technology changes. The advent of solid state electronics in the speed drive industry, for example, ushered in a number of small, low overhead, independent assemblers who based their approach primarily on low price. Prior to that, the market had been dominated by the large electrical equipment manufacturers basing their approach largely on applications engineering coupled with high prices and high margins.

The "strategic window" concept does not preclude adaption when it appears feasible, but rather suggests that certain firms may be better suited to compete in certain technological waves than in others. Often the cost and the difficulty of acquiring the new technology, as well as the sunk-cost commitment to the old, argue against adaption.

MARKET REDEFINITION

Frequently, as markets evolve, the fundamental definition of the market changes in ways which increasingly disqualify some competitors while providing opportunities for others. The trend towards marketing "systems" of products as opposed to individual pieces of equipment provides many examples of this phenomenon. The situation of Docutel illustrates this point.

Docutel. This manufacturer of automatic teller machines (ATMs) supplied virtually all the ATMs in use up to late 1974. In early 1975, Docutel found itself losing market share to large computer companies such as Burroughs, Honeywell, and IBM as these manufacturers began to look at the bank's total EFTS (Electronic Funds Transfer System) needs. They offered the bank a package of equipment representing a complete system of which the ATM was only one component. In essence their success may be attributed to the fact that they redefined the market in a way which increasingly appeared to disqualify Docutel as a potential supplier.

Market redefinition is not limited to the banking industry; similar trends are under way in scientific instrumentation, process control equipment, the machine tool industry, office equipment, and electric control gear, to name but a few. In each case, manufacturers basing their approach on the marketing of individual hardware items are seeing their "strategic window" closing as computer systems producers move in to take advantage of emerging opportunities.

CHANNEL CHANGES

Changes in the channels of distribution for both consumer and industrial goods can have far-reaching consequences for existing competitors and would-be entrants.

Changes take place in part because of product life cycle phenomena—the shift as the market matures to more intensive distribution, increasing convenience, and often lower levels of channel service. Changes also frequently take place as a result of new institutional development in the channels themselves. Few sectors of American industry have changed as fast as retail and wholesale distribution, with the result that completely new types of outlets may be employed by suppliers seeking to develop competitive advantage.

Whatever the origin of the change, the effect may be to provide an opportunity for a new entrant and to raise questions about the viability of existing competitors. Gillette's contemplated entry into the blank cassette tape market is a case in point.

Gillette.   As the market for cassettes evolved due to increased penetration and new uses of equipment for automotive, study, business, letter writing, and home entertainment, so did distribution channels broaden into an increasing number of drug chains, variety stores, and large discount stores.

Presumably it was recognition of a possible "strategic window" for Gillette that encouraged executives in the Safety Razor Division to look carefully at ways in which

Gillette might exploit the cassette market at this particular stage in its evolution. The question was whether Gillette's skill in marketing low-priced, frequently purchased package goods, along with its distribution channel resources, could be applied to marketing blank cassettes. Was there a place for a competitior in this market to offer a quality, branded product, broadly distributed and supported by heavy media advertising in much the same way that Gillette marketed razor blades?

Actually, Gillette decided against entry, apparently not because a "strategic window" did not exist, but because profit prospects were not favorable. They did, however, enter the cigarette lighter business based on similar analysis and reportedly have had considerable success with their *Cricket* brand.

PROBLEMS AND OPPORTUNITIES

What do all these examples indicate? *First*, they suggest that the "resource requirements" for success in a business—whether these be financial requirements, marketing requirements, engineering requirements, or whatever—may change radically with market evolution. *Second*, they appear to suggest that, by contrast, the firm's resources and key competencies often cannot be so easily adjusted. The result is a *predictable* change in the fit of the firm to its market—leading to defined periods during which a "strategic window" exists and can be exploited.

The "strategic window" concept can be useful to incumbent competitors as well as to would-be entrants into a market. For the former, it provides a way of relating future strategic moves to market evolution and of assessing how resources should be allocated to existing activities. For the latter, it provides a framework for diversification and growth.

Existing Businesses

Confronted with changes in the marketplace which potentially disqualify the firm from continued successful participation, several strategic options are available:

1. An attempt can be made to assemble the resources needed to close the gap between the new critical marketing requirements and the firm's competences.

2. The firm may shift its efforts to selected segments, where the "fit" between requirements and resources is still acceptable.

3. The firm may shift to a "low profile" approach—cutting back severely on all further allocation of capital and deliberately "milking" the business for short-run profit.

4. A decision may be taken to exit from that particular market either through liquidation or through sale.

All too frequently, however, because the "strategic window" phenomenon is not clearly recognized, these strategic choices are not clearly articulated. Instead, "old" approaches are continued long after the market has changed with the result that market position is lost and financial losses pile up. Or, often only half-hearted attempts are made to assemble the new resources required to compete effectively; or management is simply deluded into believing that it can adapt itself to the new situation even where this is actually out of the question.

The four basic strategic choices outlined above may be viewed hierarchically in terms of *resource commitment*, with No. 1 representing the highest level of commitment. Only the company itself can decide which position on the hierarchy it should adopt in particular situations, but the following guideline questions may be helpful:

☐ To what extent do the changes call for skills and resources completely outside the traditional competence of the firm? A careful analysis has to be made of the gap which may emerge between the evolving requirements of the market and the firm's profile.

☐ To what extent can changes be anticipated? Often it is easier to adapt through a series of minor adjustments—a stepping-stone approach to change—than it is to be confronted with a major and unexpected discontinuity in approach.

☐ How rapid are the changes which are taking place? Is there enough time to adjust without forfeiting a major share of the market which later may be difficult to regain?

☐ How long will realignment of the functional activities of the firm take? Is the need limited to only some functions, or are all the basic resources of the firm affected—e.g., technology, engineering, manufacturing, marketing, sales, and organization policies?

☐ What existing commitments—e.g., technical skills, distribution channels, manufacturing approaches, etc.—constrain adaption?

☐ Can the new resources and new approaches be developed internally or must they be acquired?

☐ Will the changes completely obsolete existing ways of doing business or will there be a chance for coexistence? In the case of new technologies intruding from outside industry, the decision often has to be made to "join-em rather than fight-em." Not to do so is to risk complete obsolescence. In other cases, coexistence may be possible.

☐ Are there segments of the market where the firm's existing resources can be effectively concentrated?

☐ How large is the firm's stake in the business? To the extent that the business represents a major source of revenues and profit, a greater commitment will probably need to be made to adapt to the changing circumstances.

☐ Will corporate management, in the event that this is a business unit within a multibusiness corporation, be willing to accept different goals for the business in the future than it has in the past? A decision not to adapt to changes may result in high short-run returns from that particular business. Looking at the problem from the position of corporate planners interested in the welfare of the total corporation, a periodic market-by-market analysis in the terms described above would appear to be imperative prior to setting goals, agreeing on strategies, and allocating resources.

New Entrants

The "strategic window" concept has been used implicitly by many new entrants to judge the direction, timing, and scale of new entry activities. Gillette's entry into cigarette lighters, major computer manufacturers, entry into ATMs, and Procter & Gamble's entry into many consumer markets *after* pioneers have laid the groundwork for a large scale, mass market approach to the specific product areas, all are familiar examples.

Such approaches to strategic market planning require two distinctly different types of analysis:

1. Careful assessment has to be made of the firm's strengths and weaknesses. This should include audits of all the key resources of the company as well as its various existing programs of activity.

2. Attention should be directed away from the narrow focus of familiar products and markets to a search for opportunities to put unique competencies to work. This requires a broader appreciation of overall environmental, technical, and market forces and knowledge of many more markets than is encountered in many firms today. It puts a particular burden on marketing managers, general managers, and business planners used to thinking in terms of existing activities.

Analysis of patterns of market evolution and diagnosis of critical market requirements in the future can also be of use to incumbent competitors as a forewarning of potential new entry. In such cases, adjustments in strategy can sometimes be made in advance, which will ultimately deter would-be new competitors. Even where this is not the case, resource commitments may be adjusted to reflect the future changes in structure of industrial supply.

CONCLUSION

The "strategic window" concept suggests that fundamental changes are needed in marketing management practice, and in particular in strategic market planning activities. At the heart of these changes is the need to base marketing planning around predictions of future patterns of market evolution and to make assessments of the firm's capabilities to deal with change. Such analyses require considerably greater strategic orientation than the sales forecasting activities which underpin much marketing planning today. Users of product portfolio chart analysis, in particular, should consider the dynamic as opposed to the static implications in designating a particular business.

Entry and exit from markets is likely to occur with greater rapidity than is often the case today, as firms search for opportunities where their resources can be deployed with maximum effectiveness. Short of entry and exit, the allocation of funds to markets should be timed to coincide with the period when the fit between the firm and the market is at its optimum. Entering a market in its early stages and evolving with it until maturity may, on closer analysis, turn out to be a serious management error.

It has been said that while the life of the product is limited, a market has greater longevity and as such can provide a business with a steady and growing stream of revenue and profit if management can avoid being myopic about change. This article suggests that as far as any one firm is concerned, a market also is a temporary vehicle for growth, a vehicle which should be used and abandoned as circumstances dictate—the reason being that the firm is often slower to evolve and change than is the market in which it competes.

REFERENCES

Ben M. Enis, Raymond LaGarce, and Arthur E. Prell, "Extending the Product Life Cycle," *Business Horizons* (June 1977), p. 46.

Nelson N. Foote, "Market Segmentation as a Competitive Strategy," presented at the Consumer Market Segmentation Conference, American Marketing Association, Chicago, February 24, 1967.

The Product Portfolio, Boston Consulting Group Perspective; see also, "A Note on the Boston Consulting Group Concept of Competitive Analysis and Corporate Strategy," Intercollegiate Case Clearing House No. 9-175-175; and George S. Day, "Diagnosing the Product Portfolio," *Journal of Marketing*, 41, No. 2 (April 1977), p. 29.

See the following cases: Emery Air Freight Corporation (B); Gillette Safety Razor Division: The Blank Cassette Project; and Docutel Corporation; Intercollegiate Case Clearing House Nos. 9-511-044, 9-574-058 and 9-578-073, respectively.

A. C. Cooper, E. DeMuzzio, K. Hatten, E. J. Hicks, and D. Tock, "Strategic Responses to Technological Threats," Proceedings of the Business Policy and Planning Division of the Academy of Management, Paper #2, Boston, Academy of Management, August 1974.

Derek F. Abell, "Competitive Market Strategies: Some Generalizations and Hypotheses," Marketing Science Institute, April 1975, Report No. 75-107.

Derek F. Abell, "Business Definition as an Element of the Strategic Decision," presented at the American Marketing Association/Marketing Science Institute Conference on Product and Market Planning, Pittsburgh, November 1977.

William E. Rothschild, *Putting It All Together: A Guide to Strategic Thinking* (New York: AMACOM, 1976), pp. 103–21.

Theodore Levitt, "Marketing Myopia," *Harvard Business Review* (September-October 1975), p. 26.

Analyzing Market Opportunities

One implication of the marketing concept is that marketing managers must continually look for opportunities in the marketplace. As a starting point, an on-going evaluation of environmental opportunities and threats to that organization is essential. Important environmental forces include economic, legal and political, social and cultural, and technological forces. From a marketing management viewpoint as seller, marketing managers need to understand buyer behavior. The understanding of consumer behavior and industrial buyer behavior is extremely important to marketing decision makers.

After reading this part, you should have a better understanding of:

1. The complex competitive forces in the environment.
2. The reasons why marketing managers need to be aware of and adaptive to the changing legal and political environment
3. The ways changing social and cultural values create both opportunities and threats for organizations.
4. The value of understanding buyer behavior, both at the industrial and consumer level.

7

Industry Structure and Competitive Strategy: Keys to Profitability

Michael E. Porter

The first step in structural analysis is an assessment of the competitive environment in which the company operates—the basic competitive forces and the strength of each in shaping industry structure. The second is an assessment of the company's own strategy—of how well it has positioned itself to prosper in this environment. Taken together, these steps are the key to forecasting a company's earning power.

The success of a company's competitive strategy depends on how it relates to its environment. Although the relevant environment is very broad, encompassing social as well as economic forces, the key aspect of the company's environment is the industry or industries in which it operates. Industry structure has a strong influence in defining the rules of the competitive game as well as the strategies potentially available to the company.

The intensity of competition in an industry is not a matter of luck. Rather, competition is rooted in underlying industry economics and goes well beyond the established competitors. Not all industries

At the time of this writing, Michael Porter was Associate Professor at the Harvard Business School.

have equal potential. They differ fundamentally in their ultimate profit potential as the collective strength of the forces of competition differs; the forces range from intense in industries like tires, paper, and steel, where no firm earns spectacular returns, to relatively mild in industries such as oil field equipment and services, cosmetics and toiletries, where high returns are common.

The essence of competitive strategy for a company is to find a position in its industry where it can best cope with these competitive forces or can influence them in its favor. Knowledge of the underlying sources of competitive pressure can reveal the basic attractiveness of an industry, highlight the critical strengths and weaknesses of a company, clarify the areas where strategic changes may yield the greatest payoff, and

Reprinted by permission of Michael E. Porter, *Competitive Strategy: Techniques for Analyzing Industries and Competitors* (New York: The Free Press, 1980).

pinpoint the industry trends that promise the greatest significance as either opportunities or threats.

STRUCTURAL DETERMINANTS OF COMPETITION

Competition in an industry continually works to drive down the rate of return on invested capital toward the competitive floor rate of return, or the return that would be earned by the economist's "perfectly competitive" industry. This competitive floor, or "free market," return is approximated by the yield on long-term government securities adjusted upward by the risk of capital loss. Investors will not tolerate returns below this rate for very long before switching their investment to other vehicles, and firms habitually earning less than this return will eventually go out of business.

The presence of rates of return higher than the adjusted free market return serves to stimulate the inflow of capital into an industry either through new entry or through additional investment by existing competitors. The strength of the competitive forces in an industry determines the degree to which this inflow of investment drives the return down to the free market level, hence the ability of firms to sustain above-average returns.

The state of competition in an industry depends on five basic competitive forces, illustrated in Exhibit 1. The collective strength of these forces determines the ultimate profit potential in the industry, where profit potential is measured in terms of return on invested capital. As Exhibit 1 demonstrates, competition extends well beyond the established players. Customers, suppliers, substitutes, and potential entrants are all competitors and may be more or less prominent depending on the particular circumstances.

All five competitive forces jointly determine the intensity of industry competition

EXHIBIT 1

Forces driving industry competition

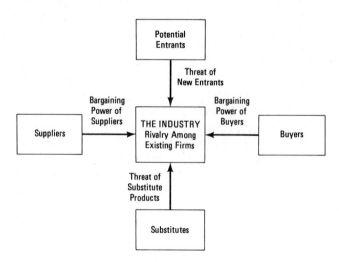

and profitability, but the strongest force or forces become crucial from the point of view of strategy formulation. For example, even a company with a very strong market position in an industry where potential entrants are no threat will earn low returns if it faces a superior, lower cost substitute. Even with no substitutes and blocked entry, intense rivalry between existing competitors will limit potential returns.

Different forces take on prominence, of course, in shaping competition in each industry. In the ocean-going tanker industry the key force is probably the buyers (the major oil companies), while in tires it is powerful original equipment market buyers coupled with tough competitors. In the steel industry, the key forces are rivalry with foreign competitors and substitute materials.

The underlying *structure* of an industry, reflected in the strength of its five competitive forces, should be distinguished from the many short-run factors that can affect competition and profitability in a transient way. Fluctuations in economic conditions over the business cycle can influence the short-run profitability of nearly all firms in an industry, as can material shortages, strikes, spurts in demand, and the like. While such factors have tactical significance, the focus of structural analysis is on identifying the stable, underlying characteristics of an industry—its economic and technological structure—that shape the arena in which competitive strategy must be set.

Industry structure can shift gradually over time, and firms will have unique strengths and weaknesses in dealing with structure. Yet understanding industry structure must be the starting point for strategy analysis. The key economic and technological characteristics critical to the strength of each competitive force are discussed below.

THREAT OF ENTRY

New entrants to an industry bring new capacity, the desire to gain market share, and often substantial resources. They can bid down prices or inflate costs, reducing profitability. Companies diversifying through acquisition into an industry from other markets often apply their resources to cause a shake-up, as Philip Morris did with Miller beer. Thus acquisition into an industry with intent to build position should probably be viewed as entry, even if it doesn't add a competitor in the literal sense.

Most often, the decision whether or not to enter or diversify into an industry will depend on the *entry deterring price*. The entry deterring price is that which, adjusted for product quality and service, just balances the potential rewards from entry (forecast by the potential entrant) against the expected costs. Of course, incumbent firms may eliminate the threat of entry by pricing below the hypothetical entry deterring price. If they price above it, gains in terms of profitability may be short-lived, since potential entrants will forecast above-average profits from entry, and will enter.

The cost of entry into an industry will depend in part on the *probable reaction from existing competitors*. If a potential entrant expects the incumbents to respond forcefully to make its stay in the industry a costly and unpleasant one, it may well decide not to enter. If the industry has a history of vigorous retaliation to entrants, if the incumbent firms have substantial resources to fight back (including excess cash and unused borrowing capacity, excess productive capacity, or great leverage with distribution channels or customers), or if the industry's growth is sufficiently slow that entry of a new competitor would depress the sales and financial performance of established firms, then potential entrants are likely to meet strong retaliation from incumbents.

The cost of entry will also depend importantly on *barriers to entry* into the industry. Entry barriers are features of an industry that give incumbents inherent advantages over potential entrants. A number of industry characteristics commonly lead to such barriers.

The *need to invest large financial resources in order to compete* creates a barrier to entry, whether those resources must be raised in the capital markets or not. While today's major corporations have the financial resources to enter almost any industry, the huge capital requirements in fields like computers and mineral extraction limit the pool of likely entrants. Capital may be required not only for production facilities, but also for things like customer credit, inventories, or covering start-up losses. Xerox created a major barrier to entry in copiers, for example, when it chose to rent copiers rather than sell them outright.

Potential entrants will generally be at a disadvantage in the *capital markets*. Unless a company is entering an industry through diversification, the newcomer is an inherently riskier position than the established firms, and this will be reflected in the risk premiums it will have to pay to attract capital.

A potential entrant will face barriers if the industry is characterized by *economies of scale* — declines in unit costs of a product (or operation or function that goes into producing a product) as the absolute volume produced per period increases.[1] Scale economies deter entry by forcing the entrant either to come in at large scale and risk strong reaction from existing firms or to accept a cost disadvantage, both undesirable options. Scale economies can be present in nearly every function of a business — production, research and development, marketing, service network, sales force utilization, or distribution. For example, scale economies in production, research, marketing, and service are probably the key barriers to entry in the mainframe computer industry, as Xerox and GE sadly discovered.

Scale economies may relate to an entire functional area, as in the case of a sales force, or they may stem from particular operations or activities. In television set manufacturing, economies of scale are large in color tube production but less significant in cabinet-making and set assembly. Each component of costs must be examined separately to determine the extent of economies of scale.

Scale economies may form a particularly significant entry barrier if the companies in an industry are generally diversified or vertically integrated. A company that is part of a multibusiness firm may be able to achieve scale economies if it is able to *share operations or functions* subject to economies of scale with other companies in the firm. Consider, for example, a company that manufactures small electric motors that go into industrial fans, hairdryers, and cooling systems for electronic equipment assembled by other divisions of the firm. If its economies of scale in motor manufacturing extend beyond the number of motors needed in any one market, it will reap economies in motor manufacturing that exceed those available if it only manufactured motors for use in, say, hairdryers. Thus related diversification around common operations or functions can remove restraints imposed by limited volume of a given market.[2] The prospective

---

[1]To avoid needless repetition, the term "product," rather than "product or service," is used throughout to refer to the output of an industry. The principles of structural analysis will apply equally to product and service businesses. They also apply to industry competition in any country or international market, although some of the institutional circumstances may differ.

[2]For this entry barrier to be significant, it is crucial that the shared operation or function be subject to economies of scale that extend beyond the size of any

entrant must be appropriately diversified or face a cost disadvantage.

The benefits of sharing are particularly potent when a company can incur *joint costs*. Joint costs occur where a firm producing product A (or an operation or function that is part of producing A) must inherently produce B. For example, technological constraints limit the amount of space airline passenger services can devote to passengers, but make available cargo space and payload capacity. Since it can spread the cost of putting the plane into the air over both passengers and freight, the firm that competes in both passenger and freight may have a substantial advantage over the firm competing in only one market. A similar advantage accrues to businesses whose manufacturing processes result in by-products. The entrant that cannot capture the highest incremental revenue from the by-products will face a disadvantage if incumbent firms can.

The potential entrant also faces the possibility of foreclosure of inputs or markets for its product if most established competitors in the industry are *integrated* (operate in successive stages of production or distribution). In such cases, incumbents purchase from in-house units or sell their inputs in-house. The unintegrated entrant will face a difficult time getting comparable prices and may get "squeezed" if integrated competitors offer it different terms from those offered their captive units.

Entry can be deterred by an entrant's need to secure *distribution channels* for its products. Existing competitors may have

---

one market. If this is not the case, cost savings of sharing can be illusory. A company may see its costs decline after entering a related business as overhead is spread, but this depends solely on the presence of excess capacity in the operation or function in the base business. Such economies are short-run, and once capacity is fully utilized the true cost of the shared operation will become apparent.

ties with channels based on long relations, high quality service, or even exclusive contracts whereby the channel is solely identified wth a particular manufacturer. To the extent that logical distribution channels for the product are served by established firms, the newcomer must persuade the channels to accept its product, using price breaks, co-operative advertising allowances, and other measures that generally cut into profits. A new food product, for example, must displace others from the fiercely competitive supermarket shelf via promotions, intense selling efforts, or heavy advertising to create consumer pull. Sometimes this barrier to entry is so high that, to surmount it, a new firm must create an entirely new distribution channel in order to get into the industry.

Newcomers will find it particularly difficult to compete with established firms for distribution channels and buyers if the industry is characterized by *product differentiation*. Product differentiation means that established firms have brand identification and customer loyalties stemming from past advertising, customer service, and product differences. Not infrequently, these firms can benefit from economies of scale as a result. The cost of creating a brand name, for instance, need only be borne once; the name may then be freely applied to other products of the company, subject only to any costs of modification. A newcomer, on the other hand, must spend heavily to overcome existing distributor and customer loyalties. Investments in building a brand name are particularly risky, since they are unrecoverable.

Product differentiation is perhaps the most important entry barrier in baby care products, over-the-counter drugs, cosmetics, investment banking, and public accounting. In the brewing industry, product differentiation is coupled with economies of scale in production, marketing, and distribution to create high barriers.

Entry can also be deterred if *switching costs* are high. Switching costs are one-time costs of switching brands or switching from one supplier's product to another's. Switching costs may include such things as employee retraining costs, the cost of new ancillary equipment, the cost and time needed to test or qualify a new source or to redesign a product, or even the psychic costs of severing a relationship. If such costs are high, the entrant must offer a major improvement in cost or performance to induce the buyer to switch. For example, suppliers of intravenous solutions and kits for use in hospitals have different procedures for attaching solutions to patients, and the hardware for hanging the solution bottles are not compatible. This industry is characterized by relatively high returns.

Government policy may also represent a substantial entry barrier in some industries. Government can consciously or unconsciously limit or even foreclose entry into industries, using such controls as licensing requirements or limits on access to raw materials (e.g., coal lands or mountains suitable for ski areas). Government regulation restricts entry to such industries as trucking, railroads, liquor retailing, broadcasting, and freight forwarding.

More subtle restrictions on entry can stem from government subsidies to incumbents or from governmental controls such as air and water pollution standards or product safety and efficacy regulations. Pollution control requirements can raise capital needed for entry and can increase required technological sophistication and even optimal scale of facilities. Standards for product testing, common in industries like food and other health-related products, can impose substantial lead times on getting into an industry, not only raising the cost of entry but giving established firms ample notice of impending entry and, sometimes, full knowledge of competitor products. Government policy in such areas certainly may have social benefits, but it often has second-order consequences for entry that go unrecognized.

While the barriers mentioned so far can perhaps be surmounted by entrants willing to invest the capital, established firms may have other *cost advantages* not replicable by potential entrants no matter what their size and attained economies of scale. For instance, some industries are characterized by *proprietary product technology*—know-how or techniques that are kept proprietary through patents or secrecy. In others, the established firms may have locked up the most *favorable raw material sources*, or tied up foreseeable raw material needs early at prices reflecting a lower demand for them than currently exists. For example, Frasch sulphur firms like Texas Gulf Sulphur gained control of some very favorable salt dome sulphur deposits many years ago, before mineral right holders were aware of their value as a result of the Frasch mining technology. Discoverers of sulphur deposits were often disappointed oil companies exploring for oil. Similarly, established firms in some industries may have cornered *favorable locations* before market forces bid up prices to capture their full value. Potential newcomers will enter at a permanent competitive disadvantage.

Experience Curve. Another important factor that creates cost advantages is the *experience curve*. In some businesses, unit costs tend to decline as the firm gains more cumulative experience in production. Experience is just a name for certain kinds of technological change. Workers become more efficient (the classic learning curve), layout improves, equipment and processes become specialized. Changes in product design techniques and operations control make manufacturing easier.

Cost declines with experience seem to be

most significant in businesses involving a high labor content and/or complex assembly operations (aircraft, shipbuilding). They are nearly always greatest in the early and growth phases of a product's development, diminishing in later phases.

In some ways, cost declines with experience operate in the same manner as scale economies. Experience can lower costs in marketing, distribution, and other areas as well as production or operations within production, and each component of costs must be examined for experience effects. Diversification can enhance cost declines due to experience, since diversified firms can share operations or functions subject to experience cost declines and units in diversified firms can benefit from the experience gained by other related units. In the case where an activity like raw material fabrication is shared by multiple business units, experience obviously accumulates faster than it would if the activity were used solely to meet the needs of one company.

Economies of scale are often cited as one of the reasons costs decline with experience. But economies of scale are dependent on volume per period, not cumulative volume, and are very different analytically from cost declines with experience. Economies of scale and experience also have very different properties as entry barriers. The presence of economies of scale *always* leads to cost advantage for the large-scale or properly diversified firm, presupposing that the large firm has the most efficient facilities, distribution systems, service organizations, and other functional units for its size.

Experience is a more ethereal entry barrier than scale. The mere presence of an experience curve does not ensure an entry barrier. The experience must be proprietary —i.e., not available to competitors and potential entrants through (1) copying, (2) hiring competitors' employees, or (3) purchasing the latest machinery from equip-

ment suppliers or the relevant know-how from consultants or others.

If the experience curve can be kept proprietary by established firms, then they can erect an entry barrier. Newly started firms, with no experience, will have inherently higher costs than established firms and will have to incur heavy start-up losses from below or near-cost pricing before they can gain the experience requisite to cost parity with established firms. Because of their lower costs, established firms (particularly the market share leader) will have higher cash flows to invest in new equipment and technique. New entrants will never catch up. A number of firms (notably Texas Instruments, Black and Decker, and Emerson Electric) have built successful strategies based on the experience curve through aggressive investments to build cumulative volume early in the development of their industries, often by pricing in anticipation of future cost declines.

Many times, however, experience cannot be kept proprietary. Even when it can, it may accumulate more rapidly for the second and third firms in the market than it did for the pioneer. The later firms can observe some aspects of the pioneer's operations. In situations where experience cannot be kept proprietary, new entrants may actually have an advantage if they can buy the latest equipment or adapt to new methods unencumbered by having operated the old way in the past.

An experience barrier can be nullified by product or process innovations leading to a substantially new technology that creates an entirely new experience curve.[3] New entrants can leapfrog the industry leaders and alight on the new experience curve, to which the

[3]For an example of this drawn from the history of the automobile industry, see William J. Abernathy and Kenneth Wayne, "The Limits of the Learning Curve," *Harvard Business Review* (September–October 1974), p. 109.

leaders may be poorly positioned to jump. Similarly, technological change may penalize the large-scale firm if facilities designed to reap economies of scale are specialized, hence less flexible in adapting to new technologies.

Commitment either to achieving scale economies or to reducing costs through experience has some potential risks. It may cloud the perception of new technological possibilities, or of other ways of competing less dependent on scale or experience. Emphasis on scale over other valuable entry barriers such as product differentiation may work against image or responsive service. Hewlett-Packard has erected substantial barriers based on technological progressiveness in industries like calculators and minicomputers, where other firms are following strategies based on experience and scale.

Properties of Entry Barriers. All entry barriers can and do change as conditions in the industry change. The expiration of Polaroid's basic patents on instant photography, for instance, greatly reduced its absolute cost entry barrier built by proprietary technology; it is not surprising that Kodak plunged into the market. Product differentiation in the magazine printing industry has all but disappeared, reducing barriers. Conversely, in the auto industry economies of scale increased enormously with post-war automation and vertical integration, virtually stopping successful new entry.

While entry barriers sometimes change for reasons largely outside a company's control, company strategic decisions can have a major impact on entry barriers. In the 1960s, many U.S. wine producers stepped up product introductions, raised advertising levels, and expanded distribution nationally, increasing entry barriers by raising economies of scale and product differentiation and making access to distribution channels more

difficult. Similarly, decisions by members of the recreational vehicle industry to integrate vertically have greatly increased the economies of scale there.

Finally, some firms may possess resources or skills that allow them to overcome entry barriers into an industry more cheaply than most other firms. Gillette, with well-developed distribution channels for razors and blades, faced lower costs of entry into disposable lighters than many other potential entrants would have faced.

RIVALRY BETWEEN EXISTING COMPETITORS

Rivalry between existing competitors takes the familiar form of jockeying for position—using tactics like price competition, advertising battles, product introductions, and increased customer service or warranties. Rivalry occurs because one or more competitors either feel pressured or see the opportunity to improve position. In most industries, competitive moves by one firm have noticeable effects on its competitors and thus may incite retaliation. Firms are consequently *mutually dependent.*

A sequence of actions and reactions may or may not leave the initiating firm and the industry as a whole better off. If moves and countermoves escalate, then all firms in the industry may suffer and be worse off than before. Some forms of competition (notably price competition) are highly unstable and likely to leave the entire industry worse off from a profitability standpoint. Price cuts are quickly and easily matched by rivals and, once matched, lower revenues for all firms unless industry price elasticity of demand is very great. Advertising battles, on the other hand, may well expand demand or raise the level of product differentiation in the industry, to the benefit of all firms.

Rivalry in some industries is characterized by such phrases as "warlike," "bitter," or "cut-throat," while in other industries it is termed "polite" or "gentlemanly." The intensity of rivalry can be traced to the presence of a number of interacting structural factors.

When the *competitors in an industry are numerous,* the likelihood of mavericks that will touch off rivalry is great, since some firms may believe they can make moves without being noticed. Even if there are relatively few firms, if they are *relatively balanced* in terms of the resources for sustained and vigorous retaliation, they may be prone to take each other on. On the other hand, when an industry is highly concentrated or dominated by one or a few firms, relative power will be stable and apparent to everyone, and the leader or leaders will be able to impose discipline through devices like price leadership.

Slow industry growth is generally a destabilizing force for rivalry, since it can turn competition into a market share game for firms seeking expansion. When industry growth is rapid, firms can improve results just by keeping up with the industry; in fact, all their financial and managerial resources may be consumed by expanding with the industry.

High fixed costs create strong pressures for all firms to fill capacity, which often leads to rapidly escalating price cutting. Many basic materials like paper and aluminum suffer from this problem. The key is fixed costs relative to value added, rather than the absolute level of fixed costs. Firms purchasing a high proportion of costs in outside inputs (low value added) may feel enormous pressures to fill capacity to break even, even if the absolute proportion of fixed costs is low. A similar situation faces industries whose products are very difficult or costly to store. Here firms will be vulnerable

to temptations to shade prices in order to ensure sales. This sort of pressure keeps profits low in lobster fishing and in industries that manufacture certain hazardous chemicals.

When the industry *product is perceived as a commodity or near-commodity,* buyer choice will largely be dictated by price and service, creating strong pressures for price and service competition. Differentiation, on the other hand, creates layers of insulation against competitive warfare because buyers have preferences and loyalties to particular sellers. Similar insulation against rivalry is provided by *switching costs* (defined earlier).

Rivalry is increased by pressures that lead to *chronic overcapacity.* For example, where economics dictate that capacity can be augmented only in large increments, capacity additions can be chronically disruptive to the industry supply-demand balance, particularly when there is a risk of bunching of capacity additions. The industry may face chronic periods of the kind of overcapacity and price cutting that afflict chlorine, vinyl chloride, and ammonium fertilizer.

Competitors that are diverse in strategies, origins, personalities, and relationships to their parent companies create volatile rivalry because they have differing goals and differing ideas about how to compete and are continually colliding head-on in the process. They have a hard time accurately reading each others' intentions and agreeing on the rules of the game for the industry. Strategic choices "right" for one competitor will be "wrong" for the others.

Foreign competitors often add a great deal of diversity to industries because of their differing circumstances and often differing goals. Owner-operators of small manufacturing or service firms may be willing to accept subnormal rates of return on their investment capital in exchange for independence; such low returns may appear unacceptable or irrational to a large publicly held competitor. In such an industry, the posture of the small firms may limit the profitability of the larger concern. Similarly, firms viewing a market as a dumping outlet for excess capacity will adopt policies contrary to those of firms that view the market as their main business.

Differences in the way companies competing in an industry relate to their corporate parents is another important source of diversity. A company that is one part of a vertical chain of businesses within its corporate organization may well adopt goals very different from those of a free-standing company competing in the same industry. A company that represents a "cash cow" in its parent company's portfolio of businesses will behave differently from one being developed for long-run growth.

Industry rivalry becomes even more volatile if a number of firms in the industry have *high stakes in achieving success*. For example, a diversified firm may place great importance on achieving success in a particular industry in order to further its overall corporate strategy. Or a foreign firm like Bosch, Sony, or Philips may perceive a strong need to establish a solid position in the U.S. market in order to build global prestige or technological credibility. Such firms may be willing to sacrifice profitability for the sake of expansion.

Finally, industry rivalry can be volatile when an industry faces high *exit barriers*— factors that keep companies competing in businesses even though they may be earning low or even negative returns on investment. Excess capacity does not leave the industry, and companies that lose the competitive battle do not give up. Rather, they hang on grimly and, because of their weakness, sometimes resort to extreme tactics that can destroy the profitability of the entire industry.

Exit barriers may be high when assets are highly specialized to a particular business or location, hence difficult to liquidate; when labor agreements, resettlement costs, or spare parts maintenance create fixed costs of exit; when interrelationships between one company and others in a multibusiness firm in terms of image, marketing ability, access to financial markets, shared facilities, and so on lend the business broader strategic importance; when government denies or discourages exit because of job loss and regional economic effects (particularly common outside the U.S.); or when managements are unwilling to make economically justified exit decisions because of loyalty to employees, fear of the consequences for their own careers, pride, or other emotional reasons.

While exit barriers and entry barriers are conceptually separate, their combination is an important aspect of the analysis of an industry. Exit and entry barriers often rise and fall together. The presence of substantial economies of scale in production, for example, usually implies specialized assets, as does the presence of proprietary technology. Exhibit 2 illustrates the possible combinations. The best case from the viewpoint of industry profits is where entry barriers are high but exit barriers are low. Here entry will be deterred and unsuccessful competitors will leave the industry. Where both entry and exit barriers are high, profit potential is high but is usually accompanied by more risk. Although

EXHIBIT 2

Exit and entry barriers combine

		EXIT BARRIERS	
		Low	High
ENTRY BARRIERS	Low	Low Returns	Worst Case
	High	Best Case	High Returns but Risky

entry is deterred, unsuccessful firms will stay and fight in the industry.

While the case of low entry and exit barriers is unexciting from a profitability standpoint, the worst case is where entry barriers are low and exit barriers are high. Here entrants will be attracted by upturns in economic conditions or other temporary windfalls. They will not leave the industry, however, when results deteriorate. As a result, industry capacity will stack up and profitability will usually be chronically poor.

Shifting Rivalry. Industry features that determine the intensity of competitive rivalry can and do change. As an industry matures, its growth rate declines, resulting in intensified rivalry, declining profits, and (often) a shakeout. In the booming recreational vehicle industry of the early 1970s, nearly every producer did well; but slow growth since then has eliminated the high returns to all except the strongest members. The same story has been played out in industry after industry—snowmobiles, aerosol packaging, and sports equipment, to name a few.

Rivalry can also shift when an acquisition introduces a very different personality into an industry. This has been the case with Philip Morris' acquisition of Miller Beer and Proctor & Gamble's acquisition of Charmin Paper Company. Also, technological innovation can boost the level of fixed costs in the production process and raise the volatility of rivalry, as it did in the shift from batch to continuous-line photofinishing in the 1960s.

While a company must live with many of the factors determining the intensity of industry rivalry that are built into industry economics, it may have some latitude to influence rivalry through its choice of strategy. A company may try to raise buyers' switching costs by designing its product into its customers' operations or by making its customers dependent for technical advice. A company can attempt to raise product differentiation through new kinds of service, marketing innovations, or product changes. Focusing selling efforts on the fastest growing segments of the industry or on market areas with the lowest fixed costs can reduce the impact of industry rivalry. If it is feasible, a company can try to avoid confrontation with competitors having high exit barriers, thus sidestepping involvement in bitter price cutting.

PRESSURE FROM SUBSTITUTE PRODUCTS

All firms in an industry are competing, in a broad sense, with industries producing substitute products. Substitutes limit the profit potential of an industry by placing a ceiling on the prices firms in the industry can charge. The more attractive the price-performance trade-off offered by substitutes, the tighter the lid on industry profits. Sugar producers confronted with the large-scale commercialization of high fructose corn syrup, a sugar substitute, are learning this lesson today, as are producers of acetylene and rayon, who face tough competition from lower cost alternatives.

Substitutes not only limit profits in normal times, but also reduce the bonanza an industry can reap in boom times. In 1978, the producers of fiberglass insulation enjoyed unprecedented demand as a result of high energy costs and severe winter weather. But the industry's ability to raise prices was tempered by the plethora of insulation substitutes, including cellulose, rock wool, and styrofoam. These substitutes are bound to become an even stronger force once the current round of plant additions by fiberglass insulation producers has boosted capacity enough to meet demand (and then some).

Identifying substitute products entails searching for other products that can perform the same *function* as the product of the industry. Sometimes this can be a subtle task, one that takes the analyst into businesses seemingly far removed from the industry in question. Securities, for example, face increasing competition from alternative investments such as real estate, insurance, and money market funds.

Government regulations, subsidies, and tax policies should also be considered in the search for substitutes. The U.S. government is currently promoting solar heating, for example, using tax incentives and research grants. Government decontrol of natural gas is quickly eliminating acetylene as a chemical feedstock. Safety and pollution standards also affect relative cost and quality of substitutes.

Attention should focus on substitute products that (a) are enjoying steady improvement in price-performance trade-off with the industry's product, (b) would entail minimal switching costs for prospective buyers, or (c) are produced by industries earning high profits. In the latter case, substitutes often come rapidly into play if some development increases competition in their industries and causes price reduction or performance improvement.

Effective defense against substitute products may require *collective industry action*. While advertising by one firm in an industry does little to bolster the industry's position against a substitute, heavy and sustained advertising by all industry participants may well improve the industry's collective position against the substitute. Similar arguments apply to collective industry response through industry groups and other means in areas such as product quality improvement, marketing efforts, and product distribution.

Trend analysis can be important in deciding whether company strategy should be directed toward heading off a substitute strategically or accepting the substitute as a key competitive force. Electronic alarm systems, for example, represent a potent substitute in the security guard industry. Electronic systems can only become more important as a substitute since labor-intensive guard services face inevitable cost escalation, while electronic systems are highly likely to improve in performance and decline in cost. Here the appropriate response of security guard firms is probably to offer packages of guards and electronic systems, with the security guard redefined as a skilled operator, rather than attempt to compete against electronic systems with a traditional guard service.

BARGAINING POWER OF BUYERS

Buyers represent a competitive force because they can bid down prices, demand higher quality or more services, and play competitors off against each other—all at the expense of industry profitability. The power of each important buyer group depends on a number of characteristics of its market situation and on the relative importance of its purchases from the industry compared with the industry's overall business.

A buyer group will be powerful if it *purchases large volumes relative to seller sales*, so that retaining its business is financially important to the seller. Large volume buyers are particularly potent forces if heavy fixed costs characterize the industry (as in corn refining and bulk chemicals) and raise the stakes to keep capacity occupied.

Buyer power is enhanced if the products purchased from the industry *represent a significant fraction of total purchases*. In this case, the buyer will be prone to expend the resources necessary to shop for a favorable price and to purchase selectively. If the product sold by the industry is a small fraction of the buyer's costs, the buyer will usually be much less price sensitive. Similarly, a buyer suffering from *low profits* has great incentive to lower purchasing costs. Suppliers to Chrysler, for example, are complaining that they are being pressed for superior terms. Highly profitable buyers are generally less price sensitive and more concerned about the long-run health of their suppliers (that is, unless the purchase represents a large fraction of their costs). Buyer power is also increased if buyers have a lot of *information* about market conditions, supplier costs, and offers to other buyers.

If buyers are either already partially integrated or *pose a strong threat of backward integration*, they are in a position to demand bargaining concessions. Major automobile producers like General Motors and Ford frequently use this bargaining lever. They engage in the practice of *tapered integration*, or producing some of their needs for a given component in-house and purchasing the rest from outside suppliers. Not only is their threat of further integration particularly credible, but partial manufacture in-house gives them detailed knowledge of costs, which is a great aid in negotiation. Buyer power can be partially neutralized when firms in the industry offer a threat of forward integration into the buyer's industry.

Finally, the *impact of the supplier's product* on the buyer's business will help determine the bargaining power of purchasers. If the quality of the buyer's product is very much affected by the quality of the industry's product, the buyer will generally be less price sensitive. In oil field equipment, for instance, a malfunction can lead to large losses (as witness the enormous cost of the recent failure of a blowout preventer in a Mexican offshore oil well); the quality of enclosures for electronic medical and test instruments can greatly influence the user's impression about the quality of the equipment inside.

Finally, *switching costs* (defined earlier) lock the buyer to particular sellers and mitigate buyer power. On the other hand, if the industry's products are standard or undifferentiated, buyers, sure that they can always find alternative suppliers, may play one company against another, as they do in aluminum extrusion.

Most sources of buyer power apply to consumer as well as to industrial and commercial buyers. For example, consumers tend to be more price sensitive if they are purchasing products that are undifferentiated or expensive relative to their incomes.

The power of wholesalers and retailers is determined by the same rules, with one important addition. Retailers can gain significant bargaining power over manufacturers if they can *influence consumer's purchasing decisions*, as they do in audio components, jewelry, appliances, and sporting goods. Similarly, wholesalers can gain bargaining power if they can influence the decisions of the retailers of other firms to which they sell.

Altering Buying Power. The power of buyers can rise or fall as the underlying factors creating buyer power change with time or as a result of a company's strategic decisions. In the ready-to-wear clothing industry, for example, the buyers (department stores and clothing stores) have become more concentrated and control has passed to large chains; as a result, the industry has come under increasing buyer pressure and suffered failing profit margins. So far the industry has been unable to differentiate its products or to engender switching costs that would lock its buyers in sufficiently to neutralize these trends.

A company's choice of the buyer group it sells to is a crucial strategic decision. A company can improve its strategic posture by finding buyers who possess the least power to influence it adversely—in other words by *buyer selection*. Rarely do all the buyer groups a company sells to enjoy equal power. Even if a company sells to a single industry, there are usually segments within that industry that exercise less power (and that are less price sensitive) than others. For example, the replacement market for most products is less price sensitive than the original equipment market.

BARGAINING POWER OF SUPPLIERS

Suppliers can exert a competitive force in an industry by raising prices or reducing the quality of the goods they sell. Such price increases can squeeze profitability out of an industry unable to recover costs increases in its own prices. By raising their prices, for example, chemical companies have contributed to the erosion of profitability of contract aerosol packagers because the packages, facing intense competition from self-manufacture by their customers, have limited freedom to raise their prices.

The conditions making suppliers powerful are largely the inverse of those making buyers powerful. If a supplier group is *dominated by a few companies and more concentrated than the industry it sells to*, it will be able to exert considerable influence on prices, quality, and terms. On the other hand, the power of even large powerful suppliers can be checked if they have to compete with *substitutes*. Industries producing alternative sweeteners, for example, compete sharply for many applications even though individual suppliers are large relative to individual customers.

If suppliers sell to a number of industries, so that one particular *industry does not* *represent a significant fraction of sales*, they will be much more prone to exert pricing pressure. If the industry is an important customer, suppliers' fortunes will be closely tied to the industry, and suppliers will want to protect the industry through reasonable pricing and assistance in activities like research and development and lobbying.

Differentiation and switching costs cut off buyers' options in playing one supplier off against another and raise supplier power. And a *credible threat of forward integration* provides a check against an industry's ability to improve the terms on which it purchases.

It is important to recognize *labor* as a supplier, and one that exerts great power in many industries. There is substantial empirical evidence that scarce, highly skilled employees (e.g., engineers and scientists) and/or tightly unionized labor can bargain away a significant fraction of potential profits in an industry. The features that determine the potential power of employees as a supplier include those outlined above plus labor's *degree of organization* and the ability of the supply of scarce varieties of employees to *expand*. Where labor is strongly organized and supply of scarce employees constrained from expansion they can be a factor in competition.

Government, which has been discussed primarily in terms of its possible impact on entry barriers, must also be recognized as a potentially powerful buyer and supplier. In these roles, government can often influence industry competition by the policies it adopts. Government plays a crucial role as a buyer of defense-related products and as a supplier of timber through the Forest Service's control of vast timber reserves in the western United States. Many times government's role as a supplier or buyer is determined more by political factors than by economic circumstances, and this is probably a fact of life.

The conditions determining supplier power are frequently beyond a company's control. However, as with buyer power, the firm can sometimes improve its situation through strategy. It can promote a threat of backward integration, seek to eliminate switching costs, and the like.

STRUCTURAL ANALYSIS AND COMPETITIVE STRATEGY

Once the forces affecting competition in an industry and their underlying causes have been diagnosed, a company is in a position to identify its strengths and weaknesses relative to the industry. The crucial strengths and weaknesses from the strategic standpoint are the company's posture vis à vis the underlying causes of each competitive force. Where does it stand against substitutes? Against the sources of entry barriers? In coping with rivalry from established competitors?

Competitive strategy is taking offensive or defensive action in order to strengthen a company's position in relation to the five competitive forces—positioning the company so that its capabilities provide the best defense against the existing array of competitive forces, influencing the balance of forces through strategic moves that improve the company's relative position or anticipating shifts in the factors underlying the forces, and responding so as to exploit change by choosing a strategy appropriate to the new competitive balance before rivals recognize it.

A *positioning strategy* takes the structure of the industry as given and matches the company's strengths and weaknesses to it, building defenses against the competitive forces or finding positions in the industry where the forces are weakest. Knowledge of the company's capabilities and of the causes of the competitive forces will highlight the areas where the company should confront competition and where it should avoid competition. If the company is a low-cost producer, for example, it may choose to confront powerful buyers while it takes care to sell them only products not vulnerable to competition from substitutes.

Alternatively, a company can take an offensive approach by developing *strategies designed to influence the balance of competitive forces*. Innovations in marketing can raise brand identification or otherwise differentiate the company's product. Capital investments in large-scale facilities or vertical integration can bolster entry barriers. Structural analysis can be used to identify the factors driving competition that will be most susceptible to strategic actions.

Industry evolution is important strategically because evolution can present opportunities to *exploit changes in the sources of competition*. In the familiar product life cycle pattern of industry development, for example, growth rates change as the business matures, advertising declines, and companies tend to integrate vertically.

These trends are not so important in themselves; what is critical is whether they affect the structural sources of competition. For example, extensive vertical integration, both in manufacturing and in software development, is taking place in the maturing minicomputer industry. This very significant trend has greatly increased economies of scale as well as the amount of capital necessary to compete in the industry. This in turn has raised entry barriers and threatens to drive some smaller competitors out of the industry.

Obviously, the trends carrying the highest priority from a strategic standpoint are those that affect the most important sources of competition in the industry and those that elevate new structural factors to the forefront. In contract aerosol packaging, for instance, the dominant trend toward less product differentiation has increased the power of buyers, lowered the barriers to entry, and intensified competition.

The task of structural analysis in the long run is to examine each competitive force, forecast the magnitude of each underlying cause, and construct a composite picture of the likely profit potential of the industry. Of course, this picture may differ considerably from present realities. Today, the solar heating business is populated by dozens and perhaps hundreds of companies, none with a major market position. Entry is easy and competitors are battling to establish solar heating as a superior substitute for conventional heating methods.

The potential of solar heating will depend largely on the shape of future barriers to entry, the improvement of the industry's position relative to substitutes, the ultimate intensity of competition, and the power that will be captured by buyers and suppliers. These characteristics will, in turn, be influenced by such factors as the establishment of brand identities, the creation of significant economies of scale or experience curves in equipment manufacture, the ultimate capital costs, and the eventual importance of fixed costs in production.

Of course, no structural analysis can be complete without a diagnosis of how present and future government policy, at all levels, may affect competitive conditions. For purposes of strategic analysis it is usually more illuminating to consider how government affects competition through the five competitive forces than to consider it as a force in and of itself. However, strategy may well involve treating government as a factor to be influenced.

STRUCTURAL ANALYSIS AND DIVERSIFICATION

The framework for analyzing industry competition is obviously useful in setting diversification strategy, since it provides a guide for answering the extremely difficult question inherent in diversification decisions. What is the potential of this business? The framework may allow a company to spot an industry with a good future before this potential is reflected in the prices of acquisition candidates. It will also help a company identify industries where its strengths will allow it to overcome entry barriers more cheaply than other firms. And the framework can help in identifying acquisitions that can take advantage of existing operations—for example, acquisitions that would allow a firm to overcome key entry barriers by providing shared functions or pre-existing relations with distribution channels.

8

The Legal Environment for Marketing

Dorothy Cohen

How will marketing decision making be affected by recent major legislative and regulatory activities?

Although businessmen acknowledge that the legal environment is a major influence in marketing decision making, they frequently lack the specific information needed to avoid excessive and costly legal complications. To help provide such information, the author reviews some of the significant changes in the legal environment for business since 1976 and discusses their implications for marketing decision-makers.

From the viewpoint of public policy makers, the major factors influencing the current design of the legal environment for business include concerns for maintaining (or increasing) competition, consumer protection, and ecological/environmental imperatives. From the businessman's perspective, the resulting legal climate since 1976 has featured somewhat greater control over marketing activities and potentially greater penalties for violations.

In 1976, Congress strengthened the anti-trust laws and curtailed the ability of the firm to set resale prices. Several products were banned from sale by regulatory agencies, and the Federal Trade Commission and the Department of Justice proceeded against alleged monopolists and price fixers. Though the penalties imposed against violators have not yet been particularly severe, the potential exists for extensive fines, lengthy prison terms, treble damages to competitors, and large restitutions to consumers. The possibility of compulsory trademark licensing also has been raised in an FTC complaint against monopolization.

Some freedoms were extended for marketing decision-makers, mostly by the Supreme Court, which declared that advertising has the protection of the First Amendment, and accordingly eliminated state restrictions on advertising of prescription drugs and legal services. The Court also overturned the *per se* illegality of vertical territorial restraints in distribution. How-

Reprinted with permission from Gerald Zaltman and Thomas Bonoma, eds., *Review of Marketing, 1978*, published by the American Marketing Association, pp. 389–412.

ever, in the area of antitrust, the Court followed the movement toward greater control by indicating that only strictly local companies could consider themselves immune from violation of the federal antitrust laws.

It is evident that the impact of the legal environment is becoming increasingly significant in marketing decisions. This article provides a review of some recent major legislative and regulatory activities and their implications for marketing decision making.

MERGERS AND MARKET POWER

Antitrust activities since 1976 suggest that large firms will find it increasingly difficult to engage in mergers, oligopolies will be the subject of anticompetitive investigations, and more businesses will come under the aegis of antitrust regulation, as efforts are made to "increase competition."

Dissatisfaction by public policy makers with antitrust proceedings led to the passage of the first major antitrust law since 1960. Some of the dissatisfaction arose out of the lengthy litigative process of antitrust actions. For example, an antitrust suit instituted against El Paso Natural Gas Co. in 1957 was not resolved until 1974.

The Hart-Scott-Rodino Act of 1976 strengthened the antitrust regulatory mechanism in three major ways: it provides for easier access to investigative information—to accelerate the litigative process; it requires premerger notification for very large mergers—in an effort to stop undesirable mergers before they occur; and authorizes *parens patriae* actions by state attorneys general—permitting a state attorney general to bring antitrust suits for damages suffered by citizens under certain circumstances.[1] Thus, a firm's merger decisions may now

be subject to prior scrutiny by both the Department of Justice and the Federal Trade Commission, and companies may be required to pay consumers for damages resulting from improper mergers.

Efforts to curb market power have been directed against industries designated as "shared monopolies." Antitrust treatment of shared monopolies (or structural oligopolies), which exhibit "conscious parallelism," is seen by some regulators as the most important unsolved question faced by antitrust enforcers.[2] Conscious parallelism implies that there has been no agreement but merely independent decisions to act in a parallel manner in the independent interest of each firm involved. According to the regulators, the results may be anticompetitive. The Federal Trade Commission is attempting to eliminate such alleged anticompetitive practices in cases against the energy industry[3] and the breakfast cereal industry.[4]

The monopolistic practices of the individual firm are also the focus of regulatory action. The FTC issued complaints against ITT-Continental Baking Co., Inc., for monopolization in the bread industry, and against General Foods Corporation, charging that company with monopolistic pricing and marketing practices in the sale of its Maxwell House brand coffee.[5]

In general, antitrust enforcement has been extended since 1976 so that fewer companies and industries are exempt from federal action. The one antitrust decision of major importance produced by the Supreme Court indicated that state regulators may not be immune to antitrust enforcement.[6] In another ruling, the Court in-

---

[1] The Hart-Scott-Rodino Antitrust Improvements Act of 1976, Public Law 94-435.

[2] *Trade Regulation Reports*, May 9, 1977 (Chicago: Commerce Clearing House, Inc.), p. 4.

[3] *Exxon, et al.*, FTC Dkt. 8934 (1976).

[4] *Kellogg Co., et al.*, FTC Dkt. 8883 (1974).

[5] *Annual Report of the Federal Trade Commission, 1976* (Washington, D.C.: U.S. Government Printing Office), p. 1.

[6] *Cantor* v. *Detroit Edison Co.*, 96 S.Ct. 3110 (1976).

dicated that only minor local businesses may be antitrust-proof.[7]

The issue of the immunity of utilities from federal antitrust laws has also been raised. In a landmark case currently before the courts, the government charged AT&T with monopolization of the telecommunications industry. AT&T argued that the regulation imposed by the Federal Communications Act and state regulatory schemes gives it implied immunity from antitrust liability. However, a district court declared that AT&T's operations are not expressly immunized from Sherman Act liability.[8]

PRICING DECISIONS

A major focus of business legislative activity since 1976 has been pricing practices. Congress repealed federal fair trade legislation, the Justice Department replaced mergers with price-fixing as its top-priority concern, and a comprehensive congressional review concluded that restraints on price discrimination as contained in the Robinson-Patman Act should not be weakened.

Resale Price Maintenance

With the repeal of federal legislation enabling states to enact fair trade laws,[9] methods used by manufacturers to maintain resale prices became hazardous. The Consumer Goods Pricing Act repealed the Miller-Tydings and McGuire Acts, making fair trade agreements again subject to the price-fixing prohibition of Section 1 of the Sherman Act.

This change does not indicate that all attempts to maintain resale prices are necessarily illegal. As far back as 1919, the Supreme Court held that a seller could unilaterally select customers, and could annouce conditions (such as maintenance of resale prices) which a distributor would have to meet in order to avoid termination.[10] However, strict limitations were applied to such practices in subsequent court decisions. In 1960, the Supreme Court stated that when a supplier goes one step beyond a mere announcement of a resale price maintenance policy and a simple refusal to deal, he has put together a combination in violation of the Sherman Act.[11]

Thus, the presence of any additional ("plus") factors besides the refusal to deal will bring about an antitrust violation. Among the "plus" factors often found are: obtaining assurances of compliance with pricing policies from dealers, monetary inducements, causing wholesalers to discipline discounting retailers, using coercive devices such as delayed shipments, withholding advertising allowances to induce adherence to prices, or establishing an elaborate policing system to assure compliance.[12] These earlier guidelines will be the standards by which resale price maintenance activities are judged now that the federal legislation enabling states to pass fair trade laws has been repealed.

For the manufacturer who wishes to maintain a minimum retail price for his merchandise, in an effort to avoid a discount image, for example, an appropriate strategy may be available. An analysis of a recent case suggests the following guidelines may comprise an acceptable policy for a manufacturer who wants to avoid discounting customers:[13]

---

[7]*Hospital Building Co.* v. *Trustees of Rex Hospital*, 96 S.Ct. 1848 (1976).

[8]*United States* v. *American Telephone and Telegraph Co.*, 5 *Trade Reg. Rep.*, CCH#61,163 (November 1976).

[9]Consumer Goods Pricing Act of 1975, Pub. Law 94-145, 89 Stat. 801.

[10]*United States* v. *Colgate & Co.*, 25 U.S. 300 (1919).

[11]*United States* v. *Parke, Davis & Co.*, 362 U.S. 29 (1960).

[12]Richard A. Givens and Laura P. Worsinger, "Vertical Restraints After Repeal of Fair Trade," *Fordham Law Review*, 45 (April 1977), p. 1094.

[13]*Garrett's Inc.* v. *Farah Manufacturing Co., Inc.*, 5 *Trade Reg. Rep.*, CCH #60,833 (April 1976).

1. Establish a policy of not dealing with discounters.

2. Use only the firm's own personnel to determine whether retailers are discounting its merchandise.

3. Do not attempt to persuade these retailers to change their policy.

4. Simply stop dealing with these retailers.

However, there is no certainty that a program embodying these guidelines will be immune from legal complaint.

Price-Fixing

Both the Department of Justice and the Federal Trade Commission have directed their efforts to the elimination of price-fixing. Although traditionally manufacturers were the subject of price-fixing investigations, such activities have been expanded to include collusive pricing among retailers and restraints on the pricing of professional services.

In 1975, several New York department stores signed consent decrees prohibiting the fixing of prices on ladies' garments and in 1976 provided refunds to past purchasers of the alleged price-fixed items. Investigations in the health care industries have increased significantly since the *Goldfarb* case, which declared that professional practitioners are not protected from antitrust regulation.[14] The FTC and the Justice Department have launched investigations of the pricing practices of physicians, lawyers, optometrists, and others who provide health care services.

Price-fixers are subject to severe penalties such as felony charges and treble damage suits. However, a recent Supreme Court decision placed limitations on such suits, at least temporarily. According to the Court's decision, only direct purchasers, not the indirect purchasers to whom the

high fixed prices may be passed, can sue price-fixers for such treble damages.[15] The State of Illinois had instituted suit against brick makers whose prices were fixed when they sold bricks to masonry contractors who were erecting buildings for the State. The Court denied the right of the State of Illinois to sue on the ground that antitrust legislation can be simplified if only direct purchasers can sue.

Dissatisfaction with the Supreme Court's decision that indirect purchasers of price-fixed products cannot sue the price-fixers for treble damages has led several congressmen to propose an amendment to the antitrust laws. The measure would amend the Clayton Act to state that each person "injured, in fact directly or indirectly," could recover antitrust damages.[16]

Price Discrimination

Despite the fact that there has been a decline in the initiation of price discrimination cases in recent years, the legislative policy concerning price discrimination apparently will continue to prevail. In recent years, the Robinson-Patman Act has been criticized. Some complaints have focused on the presumption that it causes price rigidity, and others on the fact that it does not appear to accomplish its objective of aiding small competitors. As a result of these criticisms, an evaluation of the effects of this Act was undertaken at the request of the Small Business Committee of the House of Representatives.[17] The report concluded that the Act should not be repealed, amended, or tampered with in any way.

[14]*Goldfarb,* 5 *Trade Reg. Rep.,* 1975-1 Trade Cases, CCH #60,355.

[15]*Illinois Brick Co.,* 5 *Trade Reg. Rep.,* CCH #61,460 (S.Ct., July 1977).

[16]A Bill to Restore Effective Enforcement to the Antitrust Laws, S. 1874 and H. 8359, introduced July 15, 1977.

[17]"Recent Efforts to Amend or Repeal the Robinson-Patman Act," House Report No. 94-1738, 94th Congress, 2nd Sess. (Washington, D.C.: U.S. Government Printing Office, 1976).

According to the committee's report, the evidence discredits allegations that enforcement of the Robinson-Patman Act is anticompetitive and promotes rigidity of pricing by prohibiting flexibility that would arise if sellers were permitted to make different prices to different customers. Other congressional committees have compiled extensive evidence to prove that discriminatory pricing practices actually destroy competition.

The major recommendation of the ad hoc committee was that no action be taken on proposals to weaken, emasculate, or repeal the Robinson-Patman Act or other provisions of federal laws against price discrimination practices which may injure, lessen, or destroy competition.[18] One of the primary reasons for this conclusion was the necessity of keeping small business as a viable and essential element of American society. Thus, marketers apparently will continue to be bound by the price discrimination provisions of the Robinson-Patman Act as they were in the past.

Furthermore, of particular significance to the business world, in view of the widespread revelations of its use, is a court decision which concluded that "commercial bribery" can be included within the Robinson-Patman Act prohibitions on kickbacks and commissions, and therefore can be subject to the same penalties as antitrust violations.[19]

DISTRIBUTION DECISIONS

Many businesses are engaged in multi-marketing, that is, they sell a variety of products through several channels and to various customers who may differ in type, in volume purchased, in location, and in other characteristics. This situation has given rise to legal problems in setting up channels of distribution.[20] In a decision that has a major impact on distribution decisions, the Supreme Court relaxed its decade-old ruling on the establishment of vertical territorial restraints in such channels. In 1967, in *United States* v. *Arnold Schwinn and Co.*,[21] the Court held that such restrictions were *per se* violations of antitrust laws, even if they were "reasonable," if title to the goods actually passed to the retailer. However, if the manufacturer retained title, such as in a consignment situation, there would not be a *per se* violation. The new Supreme Court decision modifies the *per se* violation implicit in vertical restrictions by applying the "rule of reason" and declaring the reasonableness of the manufacturer's restrictions should be considered.

The new ruling means that many restrictions imposed by manufacturers (these do not include setting the retail price) will not violate the law if they do not unreasonably restrain competition. Some of these potentially permissible restrictions include limiting sales of products to certain sites and prohibiting the sale by retailers of franchised items to nonfranchised retailers.

The case involved Continental TV, which held a Sylvania television set franchise.[22] Continental contended that a provision of the franchise agreement with Sylvania that restricted locations where the company could sell Sylvania television sets was a violation of antitrust laws, whether or not it was reasonable, because title to the TV sets had passed from Sylvania to Continental.

One of the considerations by the Supreme Court related to the fact that vertical restrictions may increase interbrand competition by decreasing intrabrand com-

[18]*Ibid.*, p. 123.

[19]*Grace* v. *E. J. Kozin Company*, 538 F.2d 170 (7th Cir., 1976).

[20]See, for example, Robert E. Weigand, "Fit Products and Channels to Your Markets," *Harvard Business Review* (January–February 1977), p. 95.

[21]388 U.S. 365 (1967).

[22]*Continental TV, Inc.* v. *GTE Sylvania, Inc.*, 45 U.S.L.W. 4828 (1977).

petition. This outcome may occur because the manufacturer may achieve efficiencies in his own distribution that enhance competition against other manufacturers. In the *Sylvania* case, for example, the company's national market share jumped to about 5% from about 2% after it limited the number of retailers and their locations.

The Court declared that the *Schwinn* distinction between the sale and nonsale transactions was unrelated to any relevant economic impact and indicated that it would return to the rule of reason that governed vertical restrictions prior to *Schwinn*. However, vertical restrictions that have a "pernicious effect on competition" or lack "any redeeming virtue" will be automatic violations of the antitrust laws.

This new ruling creates difficulty for antitrust prosecutors because the prior automatic violation rule merely required proof that the arrangements exist, rather than that the arrangements have an unreasonable impact on trade. Moreover, it indicates that the Court may tend to look at the economic impact of restrictions, rather than the social or political aspects of antitrust laws.

For the marketer, the *Sylvania* decision permits greater freedom in the establishment of vertical restrictions on retailers, distributors, and franchisees, as may be dictated by sound business reasons, which in turn, as the Court indicated, could lead to potentially greater efficiencies. However, these restrictions will still be subject to the test of unreasonableness. One negative aspect of the *Schwinn* decision, which this new ruling overcomes, was its tendency to generate greater power among the larger and stronger organizations. By permitting vertical restrictions by manufacturers who retained title, the *Schwinn* decision offered restrictive opportunities to those who had the financial and economic strength to engage in vertical integration. The *Sylvania* decision does not perpetuate the strength of the most powerful.

PRODUCT DECISIONS

Many of the product regulations since 1976 represent a continuing expression of concern for consumer protection and the environment. However, competitive considerations have influenced regulations involving the delivery of health care services and the use of trademarks.

Consumer Protection

Much of the current consumer protection regulation is designed to continue to ensure that unsafe or unhealthy products are eliminated and the consumers are provided with sufficient information to make informed choices. The following brief discussion covers relevant legislation.

Health and Safety. There is a growing concern for the carcinogenic properties of products sold in the marketplace. The Consumer Product Safety Commission banned the sale of children's nightwear treated with the flame retardant called "Tris" because of its presumed carcinogenicity.[23] The Food and Drug Administration banned the sale of saccharin as a food for similar reasons. However, Congress set that ban aside for 18 months after widespread complaints by consumers that the ban would cause hardships on diabetics and others, and permitted it to be sold temporarily as a nonprescription product in drugstores.

Other health and safety factors are under examination by regulators as exemplified by the establishment of safety standards for appliances and other consumer products by the Consumer Product Safety Commission, and the seizure by the Food and Drug Administration of numerous foods and drugs on charges of containing poisonous and deleterious substances and contamination.[24]

[23]"Tris—A Sleepwear Flame Retardant Banned," *Consumer Research Magazine* (June 1977), p. 4.

[24]*F.D.A. Consumer* (June 1977), p. 4.

Labeling. In recent years, there has been a strong movement toward requiring firms to provide more product information disclosures so that consumers can make informed choices. Some of the recent efforts are devoted to food labeling. Under current Food and Drug Administration regulations, any food to which a nutrient has been added, or any food for which a nutritional claim has been made, must have the nutritional content listed on the label. Additional requirements under consideration by the FDA relate to the mandatory stamping of a perishability date of contents.

Warranties. To enable consumers to make "valid and informed comparisons of warranties for similar products," the Magnuson-Moss Warranty Act of 1975 gave the FTC the power to promulgate rules affecting warranty practices for any product warranted in writing with an actual cost to the consumer exceeding five dollars. In 1976, the FTC established several sets of rules for product warranties.[25] For the firm that wishes to provide warranties, these rules require (1) the disclosure of written warranty terms, (2) availability of presale warranty terms, and (3) the establishment of informal dispute settlement mechanisms.

Environmental Considerations

There is widespread acknowledgment that environmental and ecological considerations should have high priority in the establishment of business regulations. In fact, an environmental impact statement must be submitted whenever a federal action is taken that has significant impact on the quality of the environment. This requirement has resulted in a delay in the imposition of some regulations. For example, the FTC's trade regulation rule requiring the posting of octane ratings on gasoline pumps has been delayed in the courts for several years.[26]

Technological and economic factors also impede environmental controls. As a result of such difficulties, the automobile industry was given an extension in the timetable proposed for meeting the antipollution standards of the Clean Air Act.

Nevertheless, efforts are continuing to maintain ecological balance and protect the quality of the environment. The Federal Trade Commission is devoting the largest portion of its antitrust efforts to the energy industries.[27] There is a movement against "horizontal diversification" in the energy industry to prevent companies from developing a variety of energy sources, such as oil and natural gas, coal, uranium, etc. The purpose is to require companies actively competing in these fields to restrict themselves to only one form of energy. This limitation is designed to encourage energy development and eliminate excessive controls by energy producers.

Continuing efforts are being made to restrict the excessive use of energy. The Energy Policy and Conservation Act was passed in 1976, charging the FTC with promulgating and enforcing trade regulation rules requiring disclosure of energy efficiency for designated products.

The U.S. Environmental Protection Agency is continuing its surveillance of potential pollutants. Recently, for example, the EPA ordered Ford Motor Company to recall 21,000 automobiles for not meeting air pollution standards.[28]

Environmental considerations, and particularly energy factors will continue to be important in the businessman's product development decisions.

[25]"Product Warranty Requirements Under FTC Rules," *Trade Reg. Rep.*, CCH #40,012-14 (January 1976).

[26]"Environmental Statement on Labeling Gasoline Pumps with Octane Ratings," 41 *Federal Register* 20, 017 (May 14, 1976).

[27]*Federal Trade Commission, Annual Report 1976*, p. 3.

[28]*Environmental News* (Boston: U.S. Environmental Protection Agency, July 1977), p. 5.

Health Care Services

The manner in which health care services can be "packaged" is given greater flexibility and is subject to fewer restrictions as a result of recent legal activities. Investigations of the pricing practices of health care industries have increased since the *Goldfarb* case, which declared professional practitioners are not protected from antitrust regulation.[29] This investigation has extended to the general delivery of health services, and the FTC has investigated use by physicians and their associations of codes of professional ethics and relative value scales. In some cases, consent orders have been obtained to discontinue these practices.

The FTC indicated it will investigate the licensing of physicians, artificial restraints on alternative health care systems, the denial of the use of hospitals to osteopaths and chiropractors, and the imposition of economic sanctions against physicians who practice on other than a fee-for-service basis. This area will also have high priority in actions by the Department of Justice which will be examining efforts of individuals or organizations to maintain excessive controls in the health care services market.

Trademarks

The Federal Trade Commission launched its first major challenge to the exclusivity of trademarks. The concept that creating brand loyalty through trademarks is an acceptable way to solidify a legitimate market position is being challenged in an initial decision by an administrative law judge of the FTC. In a case concerning Borden's maintenance of market power for ReaLemon, the judge found "that a monopoly results as the consequences of a defendant's conduct for business management."[30] Borden's conduct, according to the judge, was

to exercise trademark control, leading the judge to establish a precedent-setting attack against trademarks.

The remedy, according to the judge, was mandatory licensing of the Borden's ReaLemon trademark at a royalty of one-half of one percent of net sales made by any trademark licensee. The judge declared that this action will erode Borden's position, so that in 10 years Borden will no longer have monopoly power. This is only an initial decision and appeals are likely.

Although the ReaLemon case has not been decided, it is significant because it presents a relatively new regulatory notion that an influential trademark fosters a monopoly. Possibly this notion may survive regardless of the outcome of this particular case.

The potential effects of the remedy proposed, compulsory trademark licensing, have been viewed with alarm by many businessmen.[31] Members of the trademark bar generally suspect that such an action might prove a disservice rather than a service to the public.[32] They question the FTC's position that compulsory licensing will ease market entry and increase competition. They note the loss of the trademark's value as a means of identifying a manufacturer, and the consumers' resulting inability to exercise their rights of preference. In the short run, maintenance of product quality may be difficult and there are predictions that compulsory licensing will lead to a generic status for trademarks in the long run, and therefore lower incentives for controlling quality.

PROMOTIONAL DECISIONS

Two Supreme Court decisions in 1976 had significant impact in support of the right

---

[29]*Trade Reg. Rep.*, May 9, 1977, p. 12.

[30]*In re Bordon Inc.*, FTC Dkt. 8978 (August 1976).

[31]The *Journal of Marketing* featured this case in a "Call to Action" section of the October 1976 issue, p. 121.

[32]"Trademarks: ReaLemon Showdown Begins," *Product Marketing*, 8 (February 1977), p. 8.

to advertise, though at the same time the Federal Trade Commission's power to control unfair and deceptive promotional practices was strengthened. These two movements may raise conflicts in future promotional decisions.

Freedom of Speech

Of major significance to the field of advertising was a 1976 Supreme Court decision which declared that commercial speech had the protection of the First Amendment.[33] It overturned a doctrine that had existed for some 30 years to the effect that freedom of speech did not relate to commercial advertising.

The case involved restrictions on the advertising of prescription drugs, and the initial impact of the decision was to eliminate the ban on such advertising. The Court declared that in concluding that commercial speech is protected, it does not hold that it can never be regulated in any way. There can be restrictions related to the time, place, and manner of expression of advertising, as well as to advertising that is false and misleading. However, the old standard, that commercial speech is unprotected, is now replaced with a newer standard which calls for a "balancing of competing societal interests." Though the elements of this standard are not yet clearly delineated, one strong factor favoring First Amendment protection for an advertisement is "the customer's concern for the free flow of commercial information."

A subsequent Supreme Court decision extended First Amendment freedom to lawyer advertising, paving the way for the elimination of many restrictions on professional advertising.[34]

Corrective Advertising

At this time, the Federal Trade Commission appears to have the power to require corrective advertising. Although it has been using this remedy for several years, the FTC previously had issued corrective advertising orders only in consent decrees, that is, if the companies had consented to abide by a commission order.

The first time the commission imposed such a requirement was in a litigated case involving Warner Lambert's advertising for Listerine. Although still subject to a review by the Supreme Court, a recent Court of Appeals decision represents the first time the courts have declared that the FTC has the power to impose corrective advertising in a cease-and-desist order.[35] The court declared that the corrective advertising remedy was not an innovation and stated, "The label may be newly coined, but the concept is well established."

The court also held reasonable the requirement that the corrective statement must be run until the company has spent a sum equal to the average annual advertising budget for Listerine for a 10-year period (about $10 million). The corrective statement ordered by the FTC was to disclose, "Contrary to prior advertising, Listerine will not help prevent colds or sore throats or lessen their severity." However, the court ruled the "confessional preamble" to the corrective statement—"contrary to prior advertising"—was humiliating and not warranted in this case.

Warner Lambert has announced its intention to appeal the decision to the Supreme Court. If the Supreme Court refuses a review, the decision will be left standing, and the question of whether or not the Federal Trade Commission has the authority to impose corrective advertising will have been decided.

Still unanswered, however, are the ques-

[33]*Virginia State Board of Pharmacy* v. *Virginia Citizens Consumer Council, Inc.*, U.S. 96 S.Ct. 1817 (1976).

[34]*Bates* v. *State Bar of Arizona*, 45 U.S.L.W. 4895 (1977).

[35]*Warner Lambert Co.* v. *FTC*, 5 *Trade Reg. Rep.*, CCH #61,563 (August 1977).

tions related to the specific kinds of corrective statements that may be ordered and, in fact, their effectiveness. Recent court decisions indicate that the FTC cannot order the complete excision of a phrase ("Instant Tax Refund").[36] In the Listerine case, the court declared that a "humiliating" corrective statement was not warranted, but noted that it may be warranted in other circumstances.

There have been relatively few definitive findings in empirical research into the effectiveness of corrective advertising and its impact on the firm. One recent experimental study concluded that the FTC may have difficulty "correcting" well-established beliefs.[37] However, the potential for firms to be subject to this remedy has increased.

Case Law

A company engaging in deceptive practices may no longer have the benefits of litigative delays or of the FTC's need to approach each infraction on a case-by-case basis. The Magnuson-Moss Warranty-FTC Improvements Act provided the FTC with the authority to establish "case law." This new authority is designed to eliminate the extended administrative proceedings involved in litigating individual cases. If the commission has previously determined that certain practices are unlawful, it may now spell out requirements for prevention of such practices, and impose penalties for violations of these requirements.

Such case law rules were applied in 1976 to door-to-door sellers and to toy manufac-

turers.[38] The FTC sent letters to firms selected in these two industries notifying them of the potential penalty of $10,000 per violation for knowingly engaging in acts and practices which the commission had determined to be deceptive or unfair in prior proceedings.

Case law rules in door-to-door sales require that companies not misrepresent either the purpose of the salesman's visit, that customers have been specially selected to receive an offer, or that products will be received free or for almost no charge if certain acts are performed.

In the toy industry, case law rules focus on misrepresentations in advertising of the performance of children's toys, the use of over-sized containers, and pictures or written materials on containers that create a misleading impression of the contents.

Businessmen should take cognizance of the FTC's new case law powers which permit the commission to sue companies for penalties because they have violated rules developed in administrative litigation against other firms.

PENALTIES

For the businessman, the consequences of violation of marketing law are becoming increasingly severe. The potential for the imposition of penalties emerges from governmental institutions, competitors, and consumers.

Under a statute passed in 1974,[39] antitrust violations were raised from a misdemeanor to a felony and could elicit $500,000 maximum fine and a three-year jail sentence for individual defendants. In the past, it seems that a higher percentage

[36]*Beneficial Corp.* v. *FTC*, 5 *Trade Reg. Rep.*, CCH #61,066 (September 1976).

[37]Meryl Gardner, Andrew Mitchell, and Richard Staelin, "The Effects of Attacks and Innoculations in Public Policy Context: A Cognitive Structure Approach," *Contemporary Marketing Thought*, Proceedings of the Education Conference of the American Marketing Association, 1977, pp. 292-97.

[38]*In re Door-to-Door Sellers of Encyclopedias* and *In re Toy Manufacturers*, 3 *Trade Reg. Rep.*, CCH #50,258 (March 1976).

[39]Antitrust Procedures and Penalties Act of 1974.

of persons convicted of violating migratory bird laws were sentenced to prison, for longer terms, than of those who violated the antitrust laws.

The risk of prison for antitrust violators has now increased. In 1976, prison sentences of from 5 to 60 days were imposed on 15 executives of folding carton manufacturing concerns who pleaded "no contest" to price-fixing charges.[40] This case was decided under the earlier misdemeanor status of antitrust violations and, according to the sentencing judge, if the action had been brought under the new felony statute, he would have found prison indicated for all 40 defendants before him "except where such practical considerations such as ill health should intervene."

Economic penalties imposed by regulatory agencies have also increased. In part, this increase is due to an effort to eliminate the relegation of such payments to the company's "cost of doing business," and to reduce incentives for unfairness and deception. The Environmental Protection Agency required payment of $52,000 in penalties from Scott Paper Company for violation of emission standards for sulfur dioxide in one of its pulp mills.[41] In a case involving deceptive practices in selling land, the FTC issued one of its largest restitution requirements. A company agreed to pay almost $4 million in cash refunds and to spend up to $16 million over a 10-year period on various capital improvements for real estate that was sold.[42]

The Food and Drug Administration can invoke penalties through seizure of unsafe or mislabeled products and its ability to place a complete ban on selling a product such as saccharin as a food.

Competitor's Actions

Private damage litigation under antitrust is increasing.[43] Firms with large and well-entrenched market shares face legal actions from competitors as well as government regulators. Two major companies, blamed for the market failures of their competitors, are the object of antitrust suits instituted by these competitors. GAF announced that it was withdrawing from the consumer photography market, and was instituting suit against Kodak for engaging in market practices alleged to have caused GAF's failure. Heinz claims it was forced out of the canned soup market by Campbell Soup's marketing tactics.

These yet-to-be-resolved cases are significant because they represent a relatively unexplored legal area. Of particular interest is Heinz's allegation that Campbell has engaged in "advertising and promotional practices directly tied to retailers' allocation of additional shelf space" to foreclose entry of competitors.[44] These allegations parallel those used by the FTC in its still-undecided case against four major cereal manufacturers, which is based on the theory that certain promotional practices, such as brand proliferation and shelf-spacing tactics, could result in monopoly.

Should Heinz prevail in its suit against Campbell (or the FTC in its cereal case), manufacturers may have to change many traditional advertising and promotional practices, particularly in strongly competitive industries.

Heinz is asking Campbell for $105 million in damages for its product failures such as Great American and Happy soups. These payments could be trebled if a jury finds violation of federal antitrust laws.

[40]*United States* v. *Alton Box Board Co., et al.,* 5 *Trade Reg. Rep.,* CCH #61,190 (November 1976).

[41]*Environmental News* (Boston: U.S. Environmental Protection Agency, July 1977), p. 4.

[42]*In re Great Western United Corp.,* 3 *Trade Reg. Rep.,* CCH #21,261 (January 1977).

[43]Peter C. Carstensen, "Antitrust," *Chicago-Kent Law Review,* 53 (1976), p. 167.

[44]"Heinz vs. Campbell: More Than Meets the Eye," *Product Management,* 5, No. 12 (December 1976), p. 8.

However, there may be no damages awarded if the courts find that, although the alleged violations took place, they were merely incidental to more pertinent reasons for Heinz's decline in the marketplace, such as poor management, poor marketing, or a poor product.[45] In fact, recently Procter & Gamble was able to defend itself successfully against a treble damages suit on similar grounds.

Procter & Gamble, ordered to divest itself of Clorox several years ago, was able to defend itself against a treble damage suit by Purex by providing proof that P&G's marketing success during the merger period was due to superior market techniques. Purex, a competitor of Clorox, claimed that Clorox had been passive and benign toward competitors before its acquisition by Procter & Gamble, and became aggressive after the acquisition, increasing its market share at the expense of Purex. Despite the fact that Procter & Gamble had been required to divest itself of Clorox, a Federal District Court found that damages are not implicit in Section 7 violations because that section specifies the prediction of an effect ("...may be substantially to lessen competition, or tend to create a monopoly"), rather than accomplished facts. The implication of this finding is that the plaintiff must prove injury "by reason of the violation."[46]

Clorox was shown to have consistently done a better job of marketing liquid bleach than had Purex, and Purex's comparative inferiority in marketing liquid bleach was shown to have stemmed principally from the decisions of its own management.

Consumer Actions

The ability of consumers to sue for damages in product liability cases has been extended in past years. Under recent legislation (de-

noted as *parens patriae*), both the Department of Justice and the Federal Trade Commission can institute suits on behalf of consumers to secure restitution for deceptive practices and for antitrust activities as well. The ability of consumers to bring their own suits in such areas has been limited, in part by the stringent requirements set by the Court for class-action suits. Recently, however, the courts appear to be acknowledging the rights of consumers themselves to institute such class-action suits under the Federal Trade Commission Act and the Clayton Act. The Court declared that consumers could seek recovery from sellers of a freezer-food plan for sales practices that allegedly violated an FTC consent order against the seller's franchisor.[47] The Court stated that in view of the government's inability to act in more than a small fraction of cases of deceit, a private right of action is necessary.

CONCLUSION

One of the major complexities facing the business decision-maker is adapting to the legal environment. The public policy goals implicit in the legislative and regulatory design (maintaining competition, consumer protection, and maintaining the quality of the environment) are socially and economically acceptable, but may lead to conflicting regulations. Efforts to attain these goals frequently are conducted on an ad hoc basis, and thus give rise to legal complications.

The fact that there are no easy solutions should not deter efforts to find them. A holistic approach may reduce the conflicts as, for example, Grether's suggestion of "market structure" analysis.[48] This approach is recommended as a useful means

---

[45]*Ibid.*, p. 10.

[46]*Purex Corp., Ltd.* v. *Procter & Gamble Co., and the Clorox Co.*, 5 *Trade Reg. Rep.*, CCH #60,985 (July 1976).

[47]*Guernsey*, 5 *Trade Reg. Rep.*, CCH #60,740 (March 1976).

[48]E. T. Grether, "Marketing and Public Policy: A Contemporary View," *Journal of Marketing*, 38, No. 3 (July 1976), pp. 2-7.

of relating market competition to contemporary environmental-ecological-political forces.

A problem more specific to the businessman is that the regulatory mechanism pays little attention to the individual who is inundated by extensive marketing restrictions with which he is unfamiliar or who cannot afford expensive legal counsel in suits for unknowing violations. Some effort should be made to provide the marketing manager with a greater understanding of the legal framework, and the freedoms and restrictions under which he can operate.

9

Confronting the Crisis
in Mass Marketing

Stephen P. Arbeit

The changes which are facing the marketing profession today are so fundamental that in order to find an adequate metaphor, I have been forced to go back to the most fundamental of all equations: Einstein's $E = M$ or the equivalence between energy and mass.

We have heard a great deal about the energy crisis. . . a single-minded concentration on the left side of this equation. I think it is more important today that we concentrate on the right side of the equation, for we in marketing face a crisis in mass: we are losing access to mass markets, mass merchandising, and mass media.

The best model that I can draw of the marketing environment through the 1950s, 60s, and mid-70s would be the classical pyramid.

We can say that power always flows from the tip of the pyramid toward the base. At the peak of the pyramid, there would be a marketer or an advertiser and they would have a brand at the tip of the pyramid. They

knew that if they created a commercial about that brand that they could run it on the three networks, and they could pretty well be assured that, over time, everyone in the country would see their commercial and at least understand what that product was all about.

Then, further down the pyramid at the retail level, the marketer knew that if they could get their product on the shelves of the leading supermarkets in each area, they were pretty well guaranteed that, when someone came to shop for their product, they would find it and be able to take it home.

Down at the base of the pyramid, we would have the relatively homegeneous mass of consumers who would be identified as the brand's target audience.

But all of that has changed. The model has literally been flipped over on its head. What we are facing in the 80s is an inverted pyramid.

At the tip of that pyramid now is the

Reprinted with permission by *Viewpoint*, 1982. Published by Ogilvy and Mather Ad Agency.

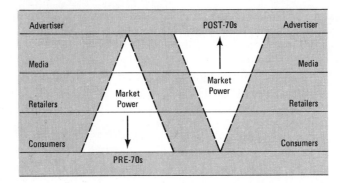

consumer, and power now flows from the consumer. Each consumer is basically his own individual target audience, his own market segment. I will elaborate on that a little later on. And, when that consumer goes into the marketplace, he no longer finds a homogeneous retailing environment. He finds a tremendous degree of diversification—a de-massification of the retailing function. And when he turns on his television set, he doesn't just have three networks and perhaps an independent as his options, but he has sixty, eighty, one hundred ten channels of programming choices.

Therefore, the base of the pyramid, which is now where the advertiser is, can no longer be occupied by one coherent brand image. But, rather, all advertisers will be forced to design products that fit with the multiplicity of channels, with a multiplicity of retail outlets, and with a multiplicity of discrete consumer target audiences.

What has accounted for this change? Why this fragmenting of the consumer audience into narrower and narrower segments? What we are witnessing is the expression in the market place of the most fundamental (to use that word again) of consumer behavior axioms—which is really very simple: *People will make for them-*

selves the decisions they feel capable of making. Those people who feel capable of making no decisions for themselves join cults. Those who need to be told what time to get up in the morning, join the Army. Those people who feel they can make the majority of decisions for themselves are active, exciting, contemporary consumers.

What has accounted for this sudden upsurge in consumer decision-making power, this perceived competence on the part of people to make their own choices? And how is this ability to make decisions expressing itself in the marketplace?

There are two things that go into giving the consumer the ability to make decisions. I call one "degrees of freedom" and the second is the availability of information.

Let's take a look at "degrees of freedom":

- Baby boom
- More households
- Fewer children
- More disposable income
- More women in labor force
- Higher levels of education
- More information workers
- Consumer learning curve

If we take a glance at the list of demographic and behavioral factors we are all so familiar with, we don't need to look at each one in individual detail. But we can see how each one contributes to the consumer's perception that he has the freedom and ability to make decisions. We have a greater proportion of adults in the population than ever before. Clearly, adults have greater decision-making capability and flexibility than the youth market or adolescents that previously made up the bulk of the population. We have more dual-income households with more disposable income. This opens up a continually expanding horizon of options. Thanks to ever increasing levels of education the consumer feels competent to deal with these options. Because they have fewer children, people now know that when they make a decision, they are making a decision that affects themselves and perhaps another adult, but not a large extended family group. Consider the presence of women in the workplace: besides the fact that this contributes to the dual-income households, it means that women are now exposed to the decision-making process so that, when they go out into the marketplace, they are more competent decision-makers than they were before.

We can also hypothesize something that I call the "consumer learning curve." The average supermarket now has twelve to fourteen thousand items on its shelves. Our consumers have been exposed to a greater amount of media information and a greater number of product choices than our parents ever were. They have *learned*—we have trained them—how to be consumers. Consumers are reclaiming their right to make decisions. All these demographic factors contribute to people's perceived ability to make decisions in the marketplace.

What evidence do we have that the consumer market is really fragmented, that the consumer is really making a whole new range of decisions for himself? We hav a lot of supporting evidence. We have *The Trend*

Report[1] and I am not going to go through all ten key trends in detail, but what they basically say is that America is restructuring itself. The reason this restructuring is taking place, I say, is because the consumer is making for himself the decisions he feels capable of making. For example, *The Trend Report* documents movement toward:

- *Decentralization:* power will no longer be centralized in the federal government, but is flowing back to the local community. The consumer no longer needs fireside chats to tell him where he ought to be going and what he ought to feel. He's saying, "I'm going to pick the issues that mean the most to me, and make those decisions, whether they're anti-abortion, or pro-ERA, or whatever. I want to make the choices for myself."

- *De-institutionalization:* the classic institutions that we trusted to be our intermediaries (hospitals, airlines, the media) are being reconceptualized—their legitimacy is being questioned. The consumer is able to find alternatives to take care of his needs in a more direct and efficient manner.

- *The movement north to south:* consumers are willing, as they always have been, to pack up and move to where the economy is growing.

  But what's growing in the South is not the industrial base that made this country strong, but the information society, the "high-tech" industries: semiconductors, communications, data processing, etc. These information industries foster decision-making competence in employees at all levels.

- *The move from organization man to entrepreneur:* The days of the corporate patriot are over. Individuals are saying, "I want to be my own boss and make decisions for myself," even within the structure of large corporations.

- *Biology as the dominant science:* replacing physics or chemistry as the basis of our

[1]*The Trend Report* is published by The Naisbitt Group. It is a social forecasting service based on a content analysis of local newspapers.

paradigms or metaphors. Biology is the science of information transfer. On a molecular level, DNA is simply a method of storing and transferring information; on the level of the organism, the body may be viewed as basically an information transmission, storage, and generation facility; on the level of ecology, the way that systems in communities interact is again on the basis of transfer of information. So that while biology is the dominant science because of the move to genetic engineering, etc., biology also provides us with the proper metaphors for an information-based age—a focus on inner space.

□ *Multiple options:* we have moved from a nation that valued conformity to a new tolerance for diversity, ambiguity, and change in life-styles, careers, and relationships. This is, of course, an expression of the increasing "degrees of freedom" in our lives.

□ *"High tech"/"high touch":* for every element of high technology we introduce, we find the need for a compensatory humanizing element. The consumer is actively shaping the new environment. Computers are finding their way into our homes because we can play games with them.

We have additional corroborating evidence in the Stanford Research Institute's VALS[2] study, which has defined two basic personality types—what they call "outer-directed" consumers who say, "The standard of reference for what's right and wrong in life is outside myself," and "inner-directed" consumers who say, "I am my own standard of reference." It is the "inner-directed" group that's growing. These are the people who have taken the decision-making power on themselves and say, "I know what's right in my life."

So we do have some outside objective evidence that the consumer is exercising a greater degree of decision-making power.

[2]*VALS* is published by SRI International, Menlo Park, California.

How does this new decision-making consumer affect retailing?

Let's go to the first step up the pyramid. Consumers are making two basic types of decisions for themselves. They are choosing outlets that are congruent with the decision they have to make. There are "high ego intensity" decisions: decisions in which the consumer is very personally involved (buying a car, buying a dress), and "low ego intensity" decisions: decisions in which the consumer needs little extra outside information, needs little comparison shopping, etc., like choosing a brand of toothpaste or a brand of rice. I could also call these decisions using Marshall McLuhan's terms: "hot decisions" and "cool decisions". A "hot decision" is one in which the consumer needs to participate very little, a "low ego intensity" decision. All the information is right up front versus a "cool decision," one in which the consumer wants to participate, in which he is needed to complete the picture. Or I could redefine the terms "high tech" and "high touch" and call them "high-tech" and "high-touch" decisions. A "high-tech" decision is one where everything is spelled out very explicitly, where the consumer needs to be involved very little, where technology replaces effort, versus a "high-touch" decision—one where the consumer needs the ego gratification, the personal attention, the personal involvement, in order to make a final choice.

Well, how has this affected retailing? Let's take a look at some of the conventional retailers who used to be all things to all people and we will see that they are losing their market in two directions: the marketplace is polarizing in a "high-tech" direction and in a "high-touch" direction.

The conventional supermarket today is faced with two new types of intense competition, and is losing market share. On

Polarization of retailing

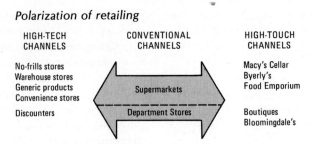

HIGH-TECH CHANNELS	CONVENTIONAL CHANNELS	HIGH-TOUCH CHANNELS
No-frills stores		Macy's Cellar
Warehouse stores		Byerly's
Generic products	Supermarkets	Food Emporium
Convenience stores		
Discounters	Department Stores	Boutiques
		Bloomingdale's

the "high-tech" side, the supermarket is losing business to box stores, warehouse stores, convenience stores, and generic products. These "high-tech" markets offer cartons of goods that are opened but not shelved; customers bag their own groceries; selection is limited to those brands the grocer could purchase at discount that week. That makes a lot of sense, because consumers are saying that, for the majority of categories in the typical supermarket, they feel capable of making the decisions for themselves. They don't need brand loyalty to make the decision for them, or brand names as a surrogate. For example, in Denver today, the largest selling brand of paper towels is not "Bounty," or "Viva," but rather it is labeled "paper towels." And that is significant because the consumer is saying, "I know that for this product category there is no significant brand advantage and, therefore, I am unwilling to pay a premium for the brand reassurance. I am willing to go out and take my chances and make my own decisions."

On the other hand, the supermarket is being faced by "high-touch" competition. Here, in Manhattan, Macy's Cellar is a good example, as is Byerly's out in the Midwest. These are prestige food retailers who are bringing sight, smell, touch, and sound, the festivity of the bazaar, the marketplace, back into food retailing.

The department stores, for example, are facing similar competition. The conventional department stores are losing business to discount mass merchandisers on the "high-tech" side, and on the "high-touch" side to boutiques and specialty stores. On the one hand the specialty stores are offering the intense personal service, design care, etc. On the other hand, the off-the-rack stores— the K-Marts—are offering a minimum amount of personal service for those items the consumer feels capable of choosing for himself. Bloomingdale's has been revitalized by becoming a collection of specialty stores under one roof.

What happened to both the supermarkets and the department stores is that over time they chose to become representatives of the vendors and not representatives of the consumer. What that means is that vendor brand names have become so powerful in many cases that they have overwhelmed the retailer's own identity; if I want to buy Jordache jeans or a Bill Blass dress, I don't have to buy it in Saks or in Bloomingdale's or in Macy's or in Gimbels. I can buy it anywhere. The conventional retailer has lost any significant role in the consumer's choice processes. The crisis affects all conventional retailers.

Banks, for example. The "high-tech" side of banking, of course, is the domain of automated tellers and bill-pay-by-phone; the banks are losing business on the "high-touch" side to the brokerage houses like

Merrill Lynch, to Shearson/American Express—those who bring a greater degree of personalized attention to the consumer's decision-making process. By focusing on "high-tech" remote intermediaries, the banks lose access to their customers' "high-touch" financial needs.

The retailers are losing their leverage and the marketplace is fragmenting into retail outlets that best fit the type of decision the consumer has to make. Each consumer generally shops in each type of channel depending on the mood he is in, the decision he has to make, the time he has to spend from his limited time budget in making that decision.

What's happening at the media level? We talked earlier about the fragmentation of network broadcasting. There are several different points I would like to make about cable to try to explain the changes that are going on in media.

We can take a look at QUBE, for example. The mose interesting thing to me about QUBE is not the fact that it is interactive. If you look at the QUBE handset, what you see are thirty channels of programming that are in Columbus, Ohio, today. And that is an old system. Thirty channels of programming available to the consumer. Seven movies going on simultaneously on a pay-per-view basis, including a channel of adult films, hard R or soft X, two 24-hour-a-day movie channels, 24-hour-a-day news channels, 24 hours a day of sports, 14 hours a day of children's programming, cultural channels, religious channels, as well as the networks.

What does all of this mean, for example, for the advertising business? Well, let's go back to a traditional household, where the networks are dominant and picture yourself sitting at home watching "Laverne and Shirley." On comes a commercial. Now you have several choices. You can turn the channel, but in that case you are going to come in on NBC's or CBS's commercials or in the middle of their sitcom, or you can go to the bathroom, or get something to eat, or talk to your spouse, or you can at least allow yourself to be exposed to the advertising. Now contrast that with driving along in your car, and you have got all the buttons on your car radio programmed to channels that you like. You are listening to your favorite rock channel and all of a sudden the DJ comes on, or some commercials come on and what do you do? You hit the button. Because the assurance you have of finding a channel with music that will be acceptable to you is pretty damn high. That's what's happening in cable TV homes right now—you are watching "Laverne and Shirley," and on comes the commercial, and you, the viewer, hit a button.

We can say that the audience level is here, and then there is a tremendous drop in audience level, and two minutes later the audience comes back. Because they can catch two minutes' worth of news, two minutes' worth of sports to see how the Yankees are doing, they can flip to the adult channels and try to catch the "good parts," like thumbing through a Harold Robbins' novel. But whatever it is, the consumer now has a diversity of choices available. There is no need to stay there and watch the advertising. What this means is that the real issue in advertising on cable is not a matter of lengths (three-minute commercials, info-

Slice of life phenomenon

mercials, etc.), the real issue is that we are going to have to *learn how to market advertising*.

The best definition of marketing I have ever heard is that marketing is the study of transactions. It says, "What do I have to give up of value to get something of value in return?" In the case of advertising, it is going to mean, "What do I have to give the consumer in return for his attention, his concentration, and perhaps his retention of my message?" We are going to have to find ways to get people to tune in and stay tuned to the advertising when there are a dozen and one places they would rather be.

The second issue is what's going to happen to the networks? You hear a great deal of talk that the networks will always be the dominant source of mass-audience programming and that the networks are here to stay. I don't believe it. I think that the proper analogy is that cable, as all media are, is just a channel of distribution for products called entertainment or information. And that, just like the conventional department stores, the conventional supermarkets, so, too, the networks are representatives of vendors and not of consumers. They are trying to be all things to all people and are carrying a broad, undifferentiated line of products.

The networks are going to be losing business on the "high-touch" side to specialty cable channels, to interactive programming—all of which do a better job of doing movies, doing sports, doing news or whatever, than the networks. And on the "high-tech" side, they are going to lose business to the Teletext, Videotext, informational channels where you can get your information right off the rack. It's packaged, ready-to-go information and the consumer can turn there for quick news or shopping information—so again, there will be no need to turn to the networks.

Now, what do I mean when I say that the networks have become representatives of the vendor instead of the consumer? Just as in the department stores, there are brand names on television. The brand names on television are Norman Lear and Tandem Productions, MTM Productions, Lee Rich and Lorimar Productions. There are the people who are responsible for the majority of the programming that the networks offer outside of sports and news.

Well, Norman Lear is going to be sitting there one of these days, and saying to himself, "'Why do I need CBS? I get hassled by the network censors, I've got the Moral Majority on my ass, where can I go to get away from those pressures? Second of all, I don't really strike it rich until I get into syndication. I'm Norman Lear. There was a time when I owned CBS, when in the course of a week more than half the country was tuned in to see 'All in the Family' or 'Maude' or 'Good Times' or 'The Jeffersons' or anything I put on. Well, I, Norman Lear, am going to create the Tandem Network. I am going to lease transponder space on one of the satellites, on the multiplicity of satellites that will be up there in the near future, and I am going to take my programming away from the networks and put it in an environment that I control. And, seven nights a week I am going to play the same five programs, changing them on a week-by-week basis. Over the course of the week, cumulatively, everyone in this country is going to see one of my programs at least once. And I'm going to go out and sell advertising time directly. That advertising revenue should accrue to me, Norman Lear."

Not only will Lear do that, but MTM will do that, Lorimar will do that, and if you think this is farfetched, if you think it's a little unrealistic to talk about the show's producers bypassing the networks, the same thing is going to happen in the movie

Polarization of media

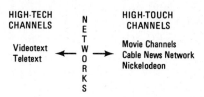

industry. In an interview with Steven Spielberg and George Lucas, following the release of "Raiders of the Lost Ark," Lucas said, and I think he is right, that the studio system is dead. The studio system was like the networks, like the department stores, like the supermarkets. They were choosing products en masse to satisfy their bottom-line needs and not really in the best interest of the consumer and certainly not in the best interest of the brand-name manufacturer. "Well, I don't need those guys," says Lucas. Lucas has already started Lucas Films, Steven Spielberg has withdrawn from the studio system, Francis Coppola experimented with Zoetrope Studios. These gentlemen are going to produce their own branded programming, their own branded movies.

Now, where's the money going to come from? The studios are very confident that they control the source of financing. Well, one of Zoetrope's movie productions was financed by Canadian venture capitalists. It is important to note that 48% of the U.S. GNP is now derived from communications and information-based industries.[3] It is only natural that the venture capitalists are looking to these growing areas to invest their money. They are going to put their money into program development, film development, and distribution.

How about distribution? At the end of that interview in *Newsweek*[4] with George Lucas, Lucas said, "I'm talking to my fi-

[3]*Wall Street Journal*, September 4, 1981.
[4]*Newsweek*, June 15, 1981.

nancial people about getting my own satellite." He doesn't need his own satellite. All he needs to do is rent transponder time. Because with the high-resolution TV broadcast technique and direct satellite broadcast, Lucas will be able to put together an ad hoc network of theaters to show his films outside the normal theater distribution system. He will be able to beam his show to the satellite, and down from the satellite to the theaters. There is not a theater in this country that wouldn't want to have an exclusive for a time period to show a George Lucas or a Steven Spielberg or a Francis Coppola movie. The intermediary system is changing drastically.

So I think that the networks as presently structured will be out of business. Because people who made the brand-name merchandise for the networks are going to abandon it. The networks only do two things themselves: sports and news. There already is ESPN, now in a venture with ABC, doing sports. Not to mention news networks like the new venture between NBC and Westinghouse doing news, so who will need the conventional networks? The networks must begin now to build distinct brand images through their selection of programming and promotion so that they will represent a meaningful choice among the dozens of channels soon to be available.

Now how about interactive programming? The real "high-touch" aspect. QUBE's interactive feature really is an amazing system. On a typical evening on "Columbus Alive" they had a consumer advocate featured. What the consumer advocate had done was to shop all the stores in Columbus, Ohio, where one could buy different types of Kodak film. The text then crawled up the screen telling you where he had shopped, and how much the film had cost. He then told you where he had taken the film to be developed, how much developing cost, and how much time it took—so that when he was done with his presentation the citizens of Columbus knew exactly where they could get the best prices on film, the fastest turnaround, and the best price for developing. That segment was followed by a debate between a very skilled moderator and two guests discussing U. S. participation in El Salvador, pro and con. They debated for a while and then the moderator said, "All right, you people at home, here are your options." And on the screen appeared five choices: send troops, send advisors only, send money only, try to get a resolution in the U. N., or do nothing. And the audience at home voted and the votes were tallied and appeared on the screen instantly. You saw that the majority of the people favored sending advisors only. The moderator turned to the more "right wing" of his guests and said, "Clearly, professor, you failed to convince the people at home that your argument is correct. What do you want to say that you think will change their minds?" The "high touch," the high participation, the real days of TV as a cool medium are here.

I think that it is as wrong to call cable *television* (to use the word "television") as it would have been to call television "radio with pictures." I think that if "the medium is the message," that cable TV is fundamentally a different medium from television as the term has been used up until now. And I think we need a new term, so that we can demystify cable, so that we can get ourselves to understand it properly and stop thinking of it in TV terms. What the new media has given the consumer is sovereignty over text: the ability to edit, to choose viewing time, viewing sequence, viewing pattern for himself. It is that same decision-making ability that we talked about down at the peak of the pyramid that the consumer is now exercising in media choice. And that is a very,

very important point and the last point I want to make about cable.

I've argued for a long time that *advertising is really the last step in the manufacturing process*. We're the ones who give the product its *branding*, give it a place in the consumer's vocabulary, in the consumer's mind and in the consumer's pantry. And, therefore, when the consumer sees that advertising on television, that's when the brand is made; that's the last step in the manufacturing process.

The characteristic mode of manufacturing in the U.S. up until the 60s and 70s was the assembly line. The worker stood at a given place and the work passed by him at a fixed, programmed, repetitive rate. And the worker was relatively passive in relationship to the work to be done. Certainly there was very little, if any, individual decision-making. That's how network television worked. Network television is the assembly line of information. The viewer sits passively in front of the television and the entertainment and information crawls by him at a fixed, steady, dependable, sequenced rate. Well, all that has changed in the workplace and at home.

We know that in the workplace two things have happened. Even in the traditional manufacturing jobs, workers are demanding participation in the manufacturing process. We have the Lordstown phenomenon, the Volvo concept of complete control by work groups over the product, the introduction of quality circles, the attention we are paying to the Japanese worker's involvement in the manufacturing process. But more importantly, 55% of the American workers are involved in information businesses. At any level of those businesses, you have worker participation and decision-making. You have the worker affecting what goes on. Well, just as work has changed, this loss of the assembly line, the growth of automation and the growth of worker participation have taken place in the home environment. The last step in the manufacturing process has been taken away from the assembly line. Because advertising now is in the environment of choice. The consumer will no longer sit there passively and allow us to program his evening for him. We no longer can expect him to expose himself to advertising because it flows along as part of the total programming mix. The consumer now is an active participant in his programming decision-making. Therefore, the entire way we construct media plans, the entire way we try to reach the consumer will have to change.

For example, in Dallas and Houston, we are going to have one hundred ten channels of programming. How are we going to be able to write coherent media plans? Are we going to roadblock on one hundred ten channels? Even if we know where consumer A is from 8 to 8:30, there is no way we can predict where he will be at 8:31. He may put on a videotape, video disc, or play with his computer. But, there is no reason any longer to assume that he will sit there and watch the next show to come on or tune to one of the other two networks.

It seems to me not farfetched that eventually we will have a page in *TV Guide* that says, "Brand X advertising may be seen on the following channels at the following times." And the consumer damn well better care about the message Brand X is bringing him, because we may have to ask him to tune in. Assuming that we can't do advertising that way, assuming that it's too much to ask the consumer to stay exposed or to tune in, we are going to have to encourage our clients to get back into programming—either by actually owning the program and having their product be an inherent part of the program (e.g., General Foods-sponsored cooking shows where the product is used),

or, perhaps, we'll have sponsor-related programs, such as American Express Travelogues, or sponsor-identified shows like "The Kraft Music Hall" where, while there is no immediate product identity, at least the consumer is tuning in and allowing himself to be exposed to traditional advertising. So we are going to have to fundamentally change the way we do business.

What we are facing in this fundamental revolution in the marketing environment is a tremendous heterogeneity of consumer groups, increasingly narrowed consumer segments, a tremendous diversification of retailing types, a plethora of media types and opportunities.

Now we are at the base of this inverted pyramid. What is a marketer supposed to do? How can it determine what its products should be when they have to be marketed through diverse media, diverse retailing channels, to narrow consumer segments?

As far as I know, the best example of a marketer who is really addressing this new marketing environment is McDonald's. And we can draw the McDonald's system on this inverted pyramid:

McDonald's marketing pyramid

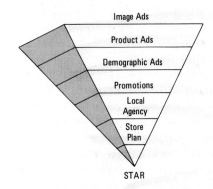

Up, at the base of this inverted pyramid, McDonald's has, of course, a layer of national advertising. After all, they do want to stand for something uniform to everyone in the country, since everyone is a potential customer. They had a national image-building campaign, for example, "You Deserve a Break Today." Below that campaign, McDonald's knows that they've got different people shopping for different products in their stores. So, first of all, they create product-specific advertising—fish fillets, Big Macs, etc. And they start to make that advertising available with different regional weightings because they understand that in different parts of the country there are different product preferences. For different groups of people, they do have a broad but segmented target audience, they produce Hispanic advertising and Black advertising through specialized agencies, they produce senior citizens' advertising, kids' advertising—all designed to speak specifically to people who come into the store for a special reason. And that advertising, again, is weighted differently, in different parts of the country, based on the demographic mix. And below that, while created at a national level but again made available at a regional level, McDonald's does an awful lot of promotion, because they understand that there always has to be something exciting going on in the store to justify a revisit. So, they create constant promotional excitement.

Now we really start to get down to the local level, because below this level of nationally devised promotions, McDonald's has seventy-two individual regional agencies. Each McDonald's co-op has its own advertising agency. These agencies understand the local consumers, their eating preferences, and the competitive situation more intimately than a national agency could. After all, southerners want different things from breakfast than Yankees do. When the

Egg McMuffin was introduced in the Southeast, the whole notion of an English muffin or eggs Benedict was really not familiar, and special advertising had to be done to create interest in the product offering. So, they have seventy-two regional agencies.

These agencies also do specialized promotion. They get McDonald's involved in the community—things like Ronald McDonald House, a charitable activity that takes part of what a consumer spends in the store for a product and diverts it to a well-known McDonald's brand-image building cause.

Below that level, McDonald's develops a marketing plan for each and every store. McDonald's says that the trading area of a store is a circle with a three-mile radius around that store. Within that three-mile radius, that operator has to develop a marketing plan that reflects an in-depth understanding of his community: travel and shopping patterns, competitive activity, purchase levels, demographics, dining habits, and on, and on, and on, so that he can develop store-specific promotions to involve the people in his territory.

And at the very point of the pyramid, McDonald's has what they call the "STAR" System—"Store Trading Area Representative." This is a man or woman assigned to "work the territory," to go to each local community institution and make them loyal McDonald's consumers. They can go to an old-age home, with McDonald's Golden Arches' Club cards, and give them out to everyone there—offering a significant discount on McDonald's food. They go to the local public school and offer to bring Ronald McDonald and his friends and put on a show on safety; they have local bands, local Boy Scout activities, local birthday parties. It is the responsibility of the STAR to really work the territory, and that's the real secret of McDonald's strength. McDonald's understands the great lesson of the 1980s—that marketing in the 80s is guerrilla warfare. You can no longer fly over in your network B-52s and drop coherent heavy messages, saturating communities with what you want to say, and hope for a response. Guerrilla warfare marketing in the 80s means that the battles for the heart and mind and pocketbook of the consumer will be won on a block-by-block, store-by-store, purchase-by-purchase basis. Because, as we said earlier, the consumer is now capable of making more decisions for himself than ever before and marketers must be there when those decisons are made.

What does this mean to conventional marketers? You can say, "Well, we're not in the fast-food business." But McDonald's lesson needs to be learned by all marketers. What is a packaged-goods marketer's obligation to the conventional supermarket that is now under attack? How can they help the supermarket to fight back, to understand its community? What kind of promotions should they run? The supermarket is the most unchanging, the most fossilized of distribution channels. For the majority of consumer-shopping activity, shopping can be recreation. You can go to Bloomingdale's and see the China exhibit, or go to Macy's and see cooking demonstrations. But the only thing that changes in the majority of supermarkets is the prices. Maybe it's up to marketers to help these retailers, to help the supermarkets respond. This need to help the supermarket is going to become more and more prevalent.

What the whole growth of generic products and the new competition is forcing supermarkets to do is to reconsider the value of every inch of shelf space, and the scanner and the computer programs enable them to do that. The supermarket is going to say to the manufacturer, "Look, let me tell you who can justify his right to my shelf space: the number one and number two brand in the category, the house brand or private label, and a generic. I don't need to stock every single item in depth. "Because what the warehouse stores and the box stores have proven is that if price or convenience is the issue, the consumer is willing to forego breadth and depth of stocking and settle for what is available at a given point in time. So, for example, here in New York, the grocer might say, "I'm going to stock Maxwell House and Folger's and my Safeway private label and a generic, and I'm going to get rid of Chase & Sanborn, Chock Full o'Nuts, Savarin, and all the other brands that I have always felt obliged to carry. I don't need to carry 12,000 individual items."

All across the country, warehouse stores are demonstrating the weakness in traditional brand loyalty. A typical warehouse store carries 5,000 products instead of 12,000, and has a far greater volume than the conventional supermarket. Now, what that means to the manufacturer of the number 3, number 4, or number 5 brand of products is the loss of shelf space in significant parts of the country. And once you lose shelf space the economies of scale that keep the sales force going are against you.

What does that mean for all the companies whose products aren't number 1 or 2 in the majority of the categories they compete in, in the majority of the country? These manufacturers, and even the leaders, need to find ways to help the supermarket, to help the retailer be more successful. Because the shift of power is now down to the consumer level. And since power flows from the point of the pyramid toward the base, we can now say that power is closer to the hands of the retailers, and then to the media, and only, lastly, to the hands of the advertisers.

Where do all the conventional retailers go? It is up to our clients, manufacturers of branded products, to help the retailers to help the consumers. It's an entire change in marketing philosophy.

What do these changes mean for new product development? Ted Levitt said that "a product is not something people buy, but a tool they use to solve their problems." What we called "brand loyalty" in the past was really consumer inertia—a willingness to keep buying a tool which adequately solved the problem. In this new environment, real brand loyalty will accrue to products explicitly designed to maximize the *fit* between the product category needs of ever smaller consumer segments, their chosen retail outlets, and their multifarious media mix. A "brand" will be the best *total* solution to the consumer's problem.

The inverted pyramid structure of the new marketplace will have to be acknowledged in all areas of marketing operations. Alan Zakon, BCG's chief executive, recently wrote that "the relationship between relative market share and profitability doesn't hold as much significance anymore. Almost every industry is beginning to form a V-curve. You can be successful with a low-cost product or a high-value-added product. It's getting tougher and tougher to live anywhere in between." (*Business Week,* 6/1/81.) What BCG is documenting is the new expression of consumer decision-making in the marketplace: low-cost products fit "high-tech" needs, channels, and media; high-value-added products fulfill "high-touch" requirements. The conventional middle is the new DMZ—the de-marketing zone.

What do the marketplace changes mean to those of us in the agency business? I was in the electronics business for five years and in those five years there was a complete revo-lution. When I got into the business, the discrete semiconductor was still dominant. That means that you could still open the back of your transistor radio and see a little can with a couple of wires and that was a transistor and another little can with a couple of wires and that was a diode. Within five years, all that changed. The integrated chip came into its own. And there was a whole generation of engineers who became obsolete overnight. Not because they couldn't understand the physics of integrated circuits, but because they didn't *think* integrated circuits. They didn't "feel it coming out of their fingertips." We could go to MIT and hire kids just coming out of school who were imbued with the philosophy, the understanding of integrated circuits, and replace these expensive, discrete semiconductor engineers.

The same thing is going to happen in the advertising business. Cable television represents the turning of our country into one large integrated circuit. One large, holistic, switching, relaying, information-flowing, transferring, storing system. And those who don't know how to work in it, who aren't out there in the streets watching retailing change every day, who aren't out there walking with and talking to consumers and seeing the way they shop, who aren't out there understanding that cable television is not television but is a fundamentally new medium of choice for a fundamentally new consumer—these people, and the agencies that employ them, are going to be obsolete.

We can go back to that equation $E = M$, because it is really very simple: When there is a tremendous fragmentation of mass on the right-hand side of the equation, you are going to have to put more energy into your marketing on the left-hand side of the equation to make it all balance.

10 What Do We Know About Consumer Behavior?

Robert Ferber

HOUSEHOLD DECISION MAKING

It is becoming increasingly apparent that the household (or family), not the individual, is the appropriate unit of study in consumer behavior. Many items are jointly consumed (housing, food, transportation); often one member shops for others; and many decisions of whether to buy and what to buy are either joint decisions or in part based on the wants and needs of others in the family. Relatively few products are purchased by an individual for his sole consumption. Although most research on consumer behavior continues to regard the decision maker as an individual, there is a growing body of research on household decision making, which is reviewed by Harry Davis and others.

Studies on who makes decisions on *frequently purchased items* have been carried out primarily on behalf of magazines (to attract advertisers). Repeatedly, it has been observed that although husbands do little actual shopping, they have a substantial influence on product and brand purchases. Davis cautions, however, that the husband's influence may be overstated. Consideration of the husband's preferences is the socially approved behavior of the "good wife" and may, in fact, occur less frequently than data suggest.

More frequently, research on family decision making has dealt with durable goods buying, probably because an item that costs a lot, lasts a long time, and is purchased infrequently and perhaps at the expense of other items would be likely to involve more family members in the purchase decision. Thus, studies of purchases of houses and autos find that wives play a more important role in house buying than in car buying, although their influence even in the latter increases as the decision moves from make to model to color of car.

A much smaller number of studies have been concerned with money management (who pays the bills, keeps the accounts,

Reprinted with permission from *Selected Aspects of Consumer Behavior*, National Science Foundation (1975), pp. 521–29.

decides on the budget), savings behavior (who decides how much to spend, how much to save), and asset management (what form do the savings take). Another area that has attracted increasing interest is family planning. Such programs have almost always been directed toward the women, in the belief that they were the strategic decision makers. But recent studies show that husbands may, in fact, play a more important role than the wives in the adoption of family planning practices.

Certain generalizations can be formulated from these purchase-influence studies:

1. Husband-wife involvement varies widely by product category.

2. Influence within product category varies by specific decisions and decision stages, e.g., there is less joint effort in the information search stage than in other decision stages.

3. For each type of consumer decision, family-member influence varies considerably among families.

Although little attention has been paid to the *way* in which families reach their decisions (as opposed to the *outcomes* of decision making), some characteristics of the process can be pointed out. There are two broad types of decision situations: "consensual" (unanimous agreement or equal consent is arrived at following discussion of the issues) and "accommodative" (since no one alternative is agreeable to all, a solution is achieved by bargaining, coercion, or other means).

From the limited research so far, it appears that family decision making is more accurately described by the bargaining, coercing model than the problem-solving model. Even where the goal appears to be shared by family members, in many cases the reasons for desiring it differ. Thus, one study on family planning showed that husbands saw the advantage of low fertility in terms of lower living costs and increased educational opportunities for children, while wives emphasized the reduction of their work loads.

The family arrives at its decision under circumstances that are anything but ideal. Thus, many decisions must be made when people are tired or irritable or when there are many distractions—demanding children, TV playing, etc. In addition, the family is an ongoing group, protective of its future as a group and threatened by conflict situations. Hence, there may be a tendency to fall back on "legitimate roles" and have decisions made by the person with the legitimate power, if not necessarily the expertise, in an effort to lessen conflict.

It is difficult for the researcher (and indeed often the family) to tell whether an observed conflict relates specifically to a given product or whether it reflects more general controversy over decision-making roles within the family. Nor is the family in a position to deal with a single problem in isolation from all others, as in a laboratory situation. Most families face several problems simultaneously. Problems will be pushed into the background because of disagreement about just what the problem is or because of the impact that solution of one problem may have on another. It has been suggested that families often become aware that a problem has existed only after its solution appears. For example, when a family moves to a house that permits children who formerly shared a bedroom to each have his own, there may be a marked reduction in general family tensions, which were not fully recognized before.

The family can utilize a variety of decision-making strategies. For instance, if family members agree on the goals sought, discussion may be lessened or eliminated by the designation of someone as the "specialist" in a certain area, with decision rights; or through infrequent meetings, a budget may be agreed on, which then becomes an impersonal arbitrator; or finally, the family may, through searching for information and discussing the matter, attempt to solve its decision problem jointly. The "multiple purchase" is an example of the problem-solving decision—having more than one car, TV, or telephone reduces the number of conflicts within the family over use of the product.

If there is no family agreement on goals, various techniques of persuasion and bargaining will be utilized, such as nagging, coercion, making "deals" between family members, or "impulse" buying to avoid prior discussion.

INTERNAL FACTORS THAT INFLUENCE THE CONSUMER

The discussion so far has shown that if we are really to understand consumer behavior, we must turn from the individual to whatever the appropriate unit of analysis happens to be for the particular situation. In some cases, the unit may be the whole family, or the husband and wife, or father and son, etc. But while consumers often interact in arriving at purchasing decisions, these decisions take place in individual minds. Hence, it is important to consider how the consumer processes the information received about a consumer product in arriving at a decision regarding purchase.

In the following section, we will consider how the individual absorbs information on the road to a decision—a psychologist's view of the various stages of "information processing." Next we will consider the relationships between consumer characteristics, such as personality traits, and purchasing behavior. This will lead into the broader types of analysis known as life-style research.

Stages of Information Processing

There are various ways in which to subdivide the act of human information processing. William McGuire suggests dividing the process into successive steps of exposure, perception, comprehension, agreement, retention, retrieval, decision making, and action.

For an item of information about a product or service to be effective in influencing eventual selection by consumers, it must first of all be heard of or seen by the consumers—they must be exposed to it.

But we are presented with so much information in our daily lives that we cannot possibly receive it all effectively. What information does get perceived depends both on our attention level and on what we selectively notice of the stimuli that are received by our senses. For instance, is the ad we hear while driving our car received as attentively as one we view on our TV at home? Does it matter if ads are placed at the beginning, the end, or the middle of a program? Does the kind of program have an effect on viewer receptivity to the advertising material?

How does the consumer deal with "sensory overload" (being presented with too much information about the product)? One uses procedures such as short-term storage of the information for later processing, alternating attention between aspects of the product, lumping information into general categories, diverting energy from other activities to concentrate on the product information, or noticing certain aspects of current sensory information and ignoring others. (For instance, the product price may be noticed, but not the nutritional value or package convenience.) This selectivity may be based on the consumer's own characteristics, such as needs and values, expectations, and past experiences; or the selectivity may be determined by product characteristics, such as distinctiveness, intensity, and novelty.

Once a message has been adequately perceived, it must be comprehended meaningfully or it will have no further effect. For the produce information to become meaningful to us, we must abstract and encode those aspects of the product that our already-formed mental categories can handle. This encoding can be in the form of images as well as words, so we can comprehend material that has not reached the conscious level. This means that consumers probably absorb, and then act on the basis of, much information that they are not aware they have.

The next step in processing information about a product, if that information is to affect the consumer's subsequent purchasing, is that the consumer accept it as true. This will depend, in part, on the believability of the message—Is the source considered trustworthy, expert, attractive? Is the content of the message convincing? The consumer's own characteristics also affect belief, credulity varying with such characteristics as age, education, ability, and personality. In contrast to the frequent depiction of the consumer as hard to sell, McGuire states that "research suggests that one's audience is generally favorably predisposed to accept what one has to say, although somewhat uninterested in paying much attention to it and a bit opaque about seeing its implications for their own decisions as consumers."

The study of memory, retention, forgetting, etc., is nearly as old and popular among psychologists as is the topic of "sensation." Most forgetting occurs soon after learning; then the rate of memory decay slows down, with less in absolute terms being forgotten in each successive time period. There is a long-standing argument over the basic nature of forgetting: Does it occur because of the subsequent learning of new interfering material, or is it simply decay over time? Interference is certainly at least a contributor to decreasing retention over time and becomes more of a problem as the consumer is asked to absorb more and more product information.

But information retained in one's memory doesn't just lie there untouched. It may be reworked, both at the conscious and unconscious levels, resulting in delayed-action effects, taking place hours, or even days, after hearing a persuasive message. And attitude changes that are induced remain with us for longer than does the memory of the information that was re-

sponsible for those changes. Thus, we may have forgotten that a former officemate was often complaining about his car, but the belief that that make of car is inferior, induced by his forgotten complaint, may remain.

If the relative effectiveness of different modes of presenting information about products is judged only by the immediate impact on attitude change, the results may be misleading because long-term attitude change may be quite different from immediate effects. Moreover, a message may, after a period of time, affect parts of the belief system beyond those directly addressed. For example, a communication about a whole class of products will eventually spread to specific types or brands of that product, or to related classes of products.

Let's return to our consumer who has to make a purchasing decision on the basis of numerous pieces of information retrieved from memory plus others presented by the current environment. The consumer must decide which considerations are important—how to weight and integrate the information available in order to make purchasing decisions. McGuire sees the consumer as "typically operating in a situation of uncertainty where information is lacking or ambiguous for many dimensions, and it is far from clear what optimal weightings need to be given to the various considerations." (Contrast this view with that of traditional economic theory. . . .*) The consumer seems to use problem-solving shortcuts that are economical and reasonably effective but that can introduce systematic biases under certain conditions. In fact, research has shown that people often arrive at a decision on bases other than those that they think they used.

It is also frustrating that, even given a consumer's attitudes and intentions, we cannot predict precisely what action will be

*This theory is discussed in Chapter 2 of *Selected Aspects of Consumer Behavior.*

taken, because behavior is often poorly correlated with measured attitude. The further back in this information-processing chain we go from actual purchase, the poorer is the prediction. For example, testing the effectiveness of communications to provide consumers with nutritional information in terms of how well these communications are comprehended may not provide a very good prediction of eventual purchase behavior. McGuire suggests that "the communicator should design the communications with components that maximize effective transmission through each of the necessary steps of information processing and that interfere with other steps as little as possible."

Consumer Characteristics and Behavior

An extensive literature deals with the relationship between the purchase of products or services and such general customer characteristics as income and personality traits. Despite these studies, however, prediction of individual consumer purchases remains an elusive goal. Following their review of this literature, Morris Holbrook and John Howard summarize the lack of conclusive results by saying, "The safest conclusion may be that *some* researchers have found *some* general customer characteristics that significantly predict *some* purchase criteria under *some* circumstances." Prediction is apparently more successful for those goods and services that are relatively more permanent, such as financial services (bank accounts and credit card usage) and products for which the consumer is brand-loyal.

The different results and contradictory conclusions that have resulted from this research can be partially explained by such technical matters as the varying statistical techniques used, different data bases, and different criteria for measuring the usefulness of the relationships found. But another important reason for these mixed results is that certain standard personality profiles used in this research bear little relation to an individual's purchasing behavior. The standardized personality and interest inventories measure traits not directly related to one's consumption activities.

However, when one considers other measures more directly related to consumer activities (such as shopping, budgeting, and leisure activities) as well as media exposure and relates them to the usual demographic questions (age, sex, occupation, etc.), certain correlations are discovered between purchases of products and living patterns. Thus "life-style" research has come into being. As quoted by William Wells and Stephen Cosmas, "Life styles refer to the distinctive modes of living of a whole society or any of its segments." People are grouped on the basis of how they choose to spend their time, money, and energy; and products and services are considered not as isolated items purchased by a consumer, but as items fitting into a larger pattern in the consumer's mind.

The notion of "life-style" has existed for centuries as a qualitative concept; but only recently has an attempt been made to quantify it and use it as a tool in studying consumer behavior. Two different approaches have been taken to divide consumer populations into relatively homogeneous groups—the product-specific approach and the more general approach.

The product-specific approach assembles numerous activity, interest, and opinion items closely related to the product or service under scrutiny (e.g., relating to cars and driving), then groups these and correlates them with purchases of products or services or with exposure to media. Such studies, with their resulting depictions of various types of consumers of a product or service, are useful in the areas of product planning and advertising strategy. An example of the sorts of classifications derived from this method is one researcher's breakdown of car buyers into the following groups: Speed Enthusiasts, Power Drivers, Apprehensive Motorists, and Pragmatists.

The other approach produces segments that are not specifically related to any particular product but that provide more general pictures of types of consumers, based on general activity, interest, and opinion item responses. For example, one researcher grouped male consumers into six segments: the "Active Achiever," the "Self-Indulgent Pleasure Seeker," the "Traditional Homebody," the "Blue-Collar Outdoorsman," the "Business Leader," and the "Successful Traditionalist."

Besides its application to buyer behavior, life-style analysis has been useful in making cross-cultural comparisons, that is, comparing the attitudes, opinions, needs, and values of national, regional, or ethnic groups in relation to the use of goods and services. It has also been used to add detail to certain familiar notions (such as "opinion leaders," "innovators," "private brand buyers," or the various social classes) and to describe the audience of various media (e.g., comparing the readers of *Playboy* with those of farm magazines).

EXTERNAL FACTORS THAT INFLUENCE THE CONSUMER

Having reviewed internal factors that influence consumer decisions, we now turn to external factors: mass media communication (from advertising, government agencies, or consumer groups), contacts with others (which will introduce the notions of reference groups and the diffusion of ideas), and direct experience with the product (including past experience and reactions to price of product as well as to other promotional methods).

Mass Media and Advertising

Billions of dollars are spent on mass media campaigns to influence our buying decisions, our political voting behavior, and, through public service messages, our health

practices. Much of the data on the effectiveness of these expenditures are unpublished proprietary reports, but the published data on advertising campaigns seldom show that there has been any sizable impact on sales. From data available in the political area, McGuire draws the surprising conclusion "that political campaigning produces little, if any, net effect and that, in fact, the more exposed one is to mass media political communications, the less likely one is to change one's voting preference during the campaign."

This conclusion suggests the difficulty in demonstrating any massive impact resulting from the huge investments in advertising and the possibility of similarly disappointing results of public service consumer information campaigns through mass communication. . . .*

Even though the mass media may not be accomplishing through advertising what is intended, McGuire feels that the media *are* having significant unintended and sometimes undesirable impacts on public behavior. Just as, in his view, the depiction of violence on television has a small but statistically significant impact on overt aggression in viewers, so do the programs (and even the ads) have an effect on the viewer in many other ways. In fact, he suggests that what is shown only incidentally or nonverbally may have more persuasive power than an explicit exhortation in an advertisement. For instance, he notes that daytime serials influence viewers in many ways, from styles of clothing and home decoration to attitudes regarding mortality and life-style.

Contacts with Others

We as consumers are not influenced just by messages deliberately aimed at us; we are also affected by our contacts with other

*A different point of view is considered in Chapter 2 of *Selected Aspects of Consumer Behavior.*

people and groups. Recognition of this fact has led to the development of two areas of study by social scientists that have relevance to consumer behavior: (1) the diffusion, or spread, of innovations and (2) reference group theory.

Research on the diffusion of innovations attempts to trace in what manner ideas (or practices or objects) perceived as new are communicated within a social system. For instance, a path-breaking study by Ryan and Gross in 1943 of the adoption of hybrid corn resulted in these findings (as summarized by Everett Rogers):

The first farmers to adopt (the innovators) were more cosmopolite (indicated by traveling more frequently to Des Moines) and of higher socioeconomic status than later adopters. The typical Iowa farmer first heard about the innovation from a seed corn salesman, but interpersonal communication with peers was the most frequent channel leading to persuasion. The innovation process from awareness/knowledge to final adoption averaged about nine years, indicating that considerable time was required for adoption to occur.

Numerous studies of family planning innovations have been carried out in the developing nations—following the progress of the program from the initial introduction of the idea and techniques to measurement of attitudes and adoption of the idea. These studies demonstrated a general desire in these countries for fewer children and for government programs of family planning. (They also demonstrated the need to use nonprofessionals to help overcome resistance to discussion of the general subject.)

A relatively new development in diffusion research is "network analysis," which attempts, by using data about the patterns of communication between persons, to identify how communication within a social system is structured. The units of analysis for this purpose are interpersonal relationships. The greater the communication link between all members of a social system and also between that system and

its environment, the more likely it is that new ideas will be introduced and adopted. Ideas are communicated effectively within a network of friends, but for *new* ideas to be introduced, there must be links *between* such networks.

To further our understanding of human behavior, it is necessary to study those "reference groups" that help to mold an individual's attitudes, values, and aspirations. A widely accepted definition of reference groups is that they are "those groups to which the individual relates himself as a part or to which he aspires to relate himself psychologically." James Stafford and Benton Cocanougher point out that of particular significance to consumer behavior is the importance to individuals of certain groups of which they are not even members (and which could even be nonexistent) in shaping attitudes and setting standards for their behavior.

The reference group might be an athletic team whose physical requirements can never be met by the individual, or it might be a group that existed only in the past. The group may be admired or despised, real or imaginary. For most people, there are numerous reference groups, not just one.

Why do these groups exert such a strong influence? The explanation lies partially in the functions performed by the group and partially in the particular needs of the individual. The reference group appears to serve two functions:

1. It sets certain standards, or group norms, and enforces those norms by meting out rewards or punishments.

2. It serves a comparative function, by providing a basis by which the individual can assess his relative standing and feel either more or less satisfied or deprived.

Often, the same group will serve both functions. The group in question may be either one of which the individual is a member or one to which he aspires to belong. The individual may actually be mistaken in his perception of the norms of a referent group, but that doesn't matter—the nonvalid standards will still influence his behavior.

However, not all people are equally susceptible to group influences. As mentioned earlier, some explanations for the importance of reference groups are to be found within the individual, and, of course, individuals differ in their personalities and needs.

For a group to become important to an individual, an attraction must be felt to the group members or to group activities. The influence of the group is correlated with a liking for group members as well as with the perception that economic or psychological benefits are to be received by conforming with group norms.

The personality of the individual, as common sense suggests, has some bearing on reference group acceptance. Those more apt to submit to authority, those who lack self-confidence, and those who feel that the desires and actions of others are more important than their own goals and standards are more apt to come under group influence. There is some indication, however, that those with *very* low self-confidence do not readily accept the reference group, possibly because of a fear of rejection. Other personality traits may have some bearing, but more research is needed before any conclusions can be drawn.

Another approach to summarizing the effects of our contacts with others, or face-to-face communication, is suggested by McGuire's classifying the various types of influence under four headings—suggestion, conformity, group discussion, and coercive persuasion.

1. Suggestion. One of the oldest notions is that "people tend to imitate examples or act in accordance with statements made by others, even where there is no pressure of any sort to do so." And so we have billboards, slogans, etc. There is little evidence of the effectiveness of suggestion below

the perceptual threshold (as in "subliminal advertising"), but no question about it above that threshold. It appears that suggestibility is greatest in children seven to ten years old, perhaps because younger persons are deficient in comprehension and older ones are less accepting of what they hear or see.

2. Conformity. These situations arise when to simple suggestion is added at least implicitly the idea that peers or authority figures expect the person to act as they do and that sanctions will be applied if the person does not comply. It has been found that three or four unanimous peers can be as effective as many times that number. On the other hand, a single defector is very effective in negating the influence of a majority.

Another issue is how the amount of change produced in the person is affected by the size of the discrepancy (or difference) between the person's initial position and what is being urged by the group members. Theoretical models suggest that intermediate levels of discrepancy will result in the most change in behavior and that large discrepancies (between existing beliefs and message) provoke hostility or incredulity and consequent rejection of the pressure rather than compliance. However, the empirical data generally show an increasing change in behavior up to discrepancies of extreme magnitude. This suggests that, for example, nutritional information will have the appropriate impact on the consumer even if it differs greatly from what the consumer initially thought.

3. Group Discussion. In these situations, arguments and information presentation tend to be tailored to the individual upon whom the behavior is being urged. People are more apt to be influenced by those very similar to themselves, probably because they come in contact most with such persons and because people are most attracted to those with a similar ideology.

4. Coercive Persuasion. This type of influence, which involves intensive indoctrination, has little implication for consumer behavior except as it applies in the "total institution" situation. This term is used to apply to such settings as the mental hospital, the army, etc., but it also has application to the family environment during childhood. In these "mini-environments," the stimulus situations, response options, and motivational and reward schedules presented to the individual are almost entirely under the control of the institution in question. Thus, behavior and thought patterns are shaped, often unconsciously, and patterns instilled in children will influence their style of consumer behavior as adults.

Direct Experience with the Product

Aspects of psychological research that have application to this question are the importance of a single experience, the effect of cumulative experiences, and the relationship between mere exposure to an object and liking for it.

First impressions are frequently assumed to be lasting and very difficult to overcome: this is known as the "primary effect." From this one might expect that the first experience with a product would be more influential than subsequent ones, but both theory and experimentation have indicated that the opposite, "recency effects," are at least as common as "primary effects."

Research on the effect of cumulated experiences has been conducted more on the subject of interethnic contacts than on familiarization with consumer products. Results indicate an intensification of initial attitudes, favorable or unfavorable, with a slight trend toward liking if the contact can be maintained for long enough and under the right conditions. Laboratory research has found a consistently positive relationship between frequency of exposure to an object and liking for it; this holds true whether the object in question is a person, a physical object, or a relatively meaningless stimulus. This appears to contradict common sense, other theoretical and empirical principles (desire for change), and the marketing axiom that products pass through a three-year life cycle. Yet, it may well be that resources are being wasted on constant product replacement and alteration dictated by an exaggerated assumption of consumer boredom.

Price of Product and Consumer Choice

The price of a product is obviously a major determinant of consumer behavior. Not so obvious is the complex manner in which price affects consumer behavior.

The term "price" itself involves much more than the amount of money exchanged for a product or service. It includes the quality and quantity of the product or service, the time and place of the exchange, the form of money, credit terms, guarantees, etc. Thus, the "true" price consists of a number of associated factors, and it changes whenever any of these factors changes.

Few empirical studies have reported on consumer consciousness of price. However, much unpublished private research as well as intuitive reasoning suggests that consumers are indeed aware of price and that it is important to them, although they do not possess that perfect knowledge of price which many economists assume. . . .*

If price is a stimulus, it must have a threshold value above which it stimulates a response and below which no response is forthcoming. In the case of price, it is hypothesized that there is an upper and a lower limit. If price is below the lower limit, the consumer suspects the product to be of poor quality; above the upper limit, the item would simply be too expensive.

*Chapter 2 of *Selected Aspects of Consumer Behavior* considers the economist's view of how price affects demand.

It appears that the consumer shops with an "acceptable" range of prices in mind rather than with a single figure firmly fixed in mind. Furthermore, these threshold prices are not constant and will vary with numerous factors, including the prices charged for similar products and the individual's evaluation of the usefulness or satisfaction to be derived from the product. It has been suggested that the individual has in mind a "fair" price or "reference" price for a particular product and that actual prices are perceived as high or low in terms of this reference price.

The most-studied psychological aspect of price is the price-quality relationship. It has been suggested that the consumer is usually unable to judge quality from the product itself and must use other information—such as financial success, trademark, and price—to make that judgment. To use price in this way implies a belief that the market forces of demand and supply interact rationally to determine price—that is, a belief that the product is worth its price.

David Gardner notes that when price is the only clue to possible quality differences between products, it significantly influences the perception of quality. In experimental studies, the higher-priced item was more frequently favored when products were thought to be dissimilar than when no differences were seen between products. Willingness to rely on price as an indicator of quality may be considered an attitudinal trait—a personality variable. Those who rely on price appear to see greater differences between products and greater risk in the choice.

But what happens when other cues—store information, brand name, physical qualities of the product—are added to price? In general, price becomes less important, and the other cues more important. However, when unknown brands are involved, price assumes greater importance as a clue to quality.

How does the posting of unit prices (price per standard unit of measure, such as ounces or pounds) affect the influence of price on consumer behavior? Studies show that unit pricing information is not used very much by consumers, that when used it definitely helps in picking out the lowest-priced alternatives (if that is the goal), and that it is used more for homogeneous products and especially for low-priced brands. Perhaps the low utilization of unit pricing information can be explained by its newness; shoppers have in the past had sufficient trouble making price comparisons that they have become accustomed to relying on information other than price in making their selections.

On the public policy level, one hears the argument that if more product information were available, the consumer would not rely so much on price as an indication of quality. But as Gardner notes, the literature reveals that consumers might not take advantage of the availability of more information but might prefer to continue relying on price and brand information.

Other Promotional Methods

The term "promotional methods" refers to a variety of methods used to bring a product to the favorable attention of the consumer. Although "advertising" comes immediately to mind, also included are in-store displays, sampling, dealing, packaging, publicity, and personal selling. Difficult as it is to believe, more money is currently being spent on sales promotion (all nonmedia techniques) than on advertising. Such devices as cents-off deals, contests, combination offers, etc., act to reduce price to the consumer or to enhance the product's value.

Research on other promotional methods points to the fact that consumers can be divided into those who are deal prone and those who are brand loyal. And there is some indication that advertising can have significant long-term effects on sales of a product, whereas a promotion has immediate visible effects, but these are not usually lasting.

SHOPPING PATTERNS

Do people shop around a lot before deciding on a purchase? Do they follow the same pattern for *all* purchases? How far do they travel on a shopping trip? Are there differences in shopping patterns between different economic or racial groups?

Studies of durable goods purchases reveal vast differences among individuals in the amount of search that precedes purchase. (Besides store visits, search activities include exposure to advertising, discussions with experts or acquaintances, and reading consumer publications.) Donald Granbois mentions one study that found that less than one-quarter of buyers were "very careful"; another concluded that 34 percent of furniture buyers and 65 percent of appliance buyers were "nonthorough." Numerous studies of durable goods purchases have substantiated that only one or two stores are visited by most purchasers.

Price appears to be directly related to the amount of search, whereas satisfaction with the product currently used appears to be related to decreased search. When such consumer characteristics as income and education have been studied as possible determinants of shopping behavior, mixed results have been obtained, although several studies point to a positive relation between income, education, and extent of search.

Numerous studies of "soft goods," such as clothing, fabrics, and household items, show that about three-quarters of such goods are purchased in the first store visited; the number of stores visited increases with item price and with items involving fashion and style. Unplanned purchases make up more than one-third of the total purchases of soft goods and appear to increase during sales and when the shopper is in the company of others.

The fact that people derive enjoyment from shopping, quite apart from the "search" and "exchange" functions of such an activity, makes prediction along the usual lines of search theory less reliable.

If motives such as diversion, recreation, physical exercise, sensory stimulation, and social communication affect shopping behavior, then the influence of, for example, price or purchase frequency will be only one of many factors that determine shopping patterns.

Food shopping, as one might expect, is the most frequent form of shopping; the average number of weekly food store trips is about three. A greater *regularity* of shopping is found, however, among families with relatively low demand and little disposable time.

To learn what information is absorbed by the consumer within the store, the researcher must either follow the shopper and try to make guesses about mental processes from observed behavior or interview the shopper as he or she enters the store, list the items planned for purchase, and then compare the purchases actually made. Study results show that a significant amount of in-store information gathering and decision making occurs. Indeed, according to one study, about half of all food purchases are unplanned.

Some forms of shopping can also be done at home, by telephone or mail order or by purchasing from door-to-door salesmen. Those with higher income, more education, children, and fashion consciousness appear to be greater users of such in-home shopping methods. Those items that can be clearly identified, or are standard or already tried items, are more apt to be purchased from home, because they entail less risk. There is more chance for disappointment in ordering clothes by mail, since they must fit and be the right color, than in ordering, for example, housewares by mail.

To learn how shopping patterns develop, new residents in a community are especially useful subjects. New residents choose a regular food store in 3–4 weeks, and many head first for a store known in their previous location. However, factors such as prices, quality of meat and produce, and selection of brands may lead to a change between the "first tried" store and the eventual "favorite" store.

Shopping Behavior of Disadvantaged Consumers

A new area of research which came into prominence in the 1960s is that of the low-income and minority consumer. Initial concern was directed at the suspicion that food chains deliberately discriminated against disadvantaged communities by charging higher prices and stocking poorer quality goods. These charges were found to be invalid. What did become clear, however, was that small independent food stores, and probably clothing and durable goods stores as well, did charge more than the large supermarkets.

It was anticipated that most shopping is done close to home, partly because of the poor consumer's psychological disposition, relative lack of access to transportation facilities, and desire to trade at minority-run stores. But empirical studies show that the subject is more complex than first thought. Several studies of low-income shoppers indicate a far greater usage of chain supermarkets than expected, as well as greater awareness of price differentials between stores. Mexican-Americans and Puerto Ricans are more likely than blacks to patronize the small independent neighborhood stores. Since the goods bought differ significantly from one group to another, and since the quality of food is frequently not comparable from store to store, it is difficult to generalize about prices paid by various groups.

A relatively high rate of durable goods ownership, combined with evidence that lower-income groups undertake less information search and may be subject to discriminatory price and credit practices on the part of retailers, has led to concern over the durable goods shopping behavior of lower-income households. Most empirical studies so far have concentrated on price and credit discrimination, with mixed results. In some, prices were found to be higher in ghetto stores, but there was no evidence of discrimination within stores by race of shopper, although credit charges were found to be discriminatory. Other studies did show price discrimination by race of customer.

There appear to be important cultural differences in shopping behavior among different low-income ethnic groups, such as the credit usage and durables ownership. The few studies to investigate soft goods shopping behavior by race have found some differences. For example, whites are more likely to order by mail or phone and to have department store credit cards. However, most of the differences could also be explained simply by income level differences, for within income levels, few differences by race were found.

Store Patronage

There is substantial evidence that shopper's evaluations of stores may be biased owing to mistaken perceptions about such store attributes as price and location. Price misperceptions are probably greater where price differences among stores are small and where the usual clues to price do not, in fact, hold. Thus, longer hours and extra services do not necessarily indicate higher prices; nor do heavy advertising and wide assortment necessarily indicate lower prices. As for location, it has been found that a better predictor of shopping frequencies at supermarkets is a person's *perception* of the distance from home rather than the actual distance.

11 A Model of Industrial Buyer Behavior

Jagdish N. Sheth

Although industrial market research has generated large data banks on organizational buyers, very little from the existing data seems helpful to management. What is needed before more data is collected is a realistic conceptualization and understanding of the process of industrial buying decisions. This article integrates existing knowledge into a descriptive model to aid in industrial market research.

The purpose of this article is to describe a model of industrial (organizational) buyer behavior. Considerable knowledge on organizational buyer behavior already exists[1] and can be classified into three categories. The first category includes a considerable amount of systematic empirical research on the buying policies and practices of purchasing agents and other organizational buyers.[2] The second includes industry reports and observations of industrial buyers.[3]

[1] For a comprehensive list of references, see Thomas A. Staudt and W. Lazer, *A Basic Bibliography on Industrial Marketing* (Chicago: American Marketing Association, 1963); and Donald E. Vinson, "Bibliography of Industrial Marketing," unpublished listing of references (University of Colorado, 1972).

[2] Richard M. Cyert, et al., "Observation of a Business Decision," *Journal of Business*, 29 (October 1956), pp. 237–48; John A. Howard and C. G. Moore, Jr., "A Descriptive Model of the Purchasing Agent," unpublished monograph (University of Pittsburgh, 1964); George Strauss, "Work Study of Purchasing Agents," *Human Organization*, 33 (September 1964), pp. 137–49; Theodore A. Levitt, *Industrial Purchasing Behavior* (Boston: Division of Research, Graduate School of Business, Harvard University, 1965); Ozanne B. Urban and Gilbert A. Churchill, "Adoption Research: Information Sources in the Industrial Purchasing Decision," and Richard N. Cardozo, "Segmenting the Industrial Market," in *Marketing and the New Science of Planning*, R. L. King, ed. (Chicago: American Marketing Association, 1968), pp. 352–59 and 433–40, respectively; Richard N. Cardozo and J. W. Cagley, "Experimental Study of Industrial Buyer Behavior," *Journal of Marketing Research*, 8 (August 1971), pp. 329–34; Thomas P. Copley and F. L. Callom, "Industrial Search Behavior and Perceived Risk," in *Proceedings of the Second Annual Conference, the Association for Consumer Research*, D. M. Gardner, ed. (College Park, Md.: Association for Consumer Research, 1971), pp. 208–31; and James R. McMillan, "Industrial Buying Behavior as Group Decision Making," paper presented at the Nineteenth International Meeting of the Institute of Management Sciences (April 1972).

[3] Robert F. Shoaf, ed., *Emotional Factors Underlying Industrial Purchasing* (Cleveland, Ohio: Penton Publishing Co., 1959); G. H. Haas, B. March, and E. M. Krech, *Purchasing Department Organization and Authority*, American Management Association Research Study No. 45 (New York, 1960); *Evaluation*

Reprinted with permission from *Journal of Marketing*, published by the American Marketing Association, 37 (October 1973), pp. 50–56.

Finally, the third category consists of books, monographs, and articles which analyze, theorize, model, and sometimes report on industrial buying activities.[4] What is now needed is a reconciliation and integration of existing knowledge into a realistic and comprehensive model of organizational buyer behavior.

It is hoped that the model described in this article will be useful in the following ways: first, to broaden the vision of research on organizational buyer behavior so that it includes the most salient elements and their interactions; second, to act as a catalyst for building marketing information systems from the viewpoint of the industrial buyer; and, third, to generate new hypotheses for future research on fundamental processes underlying organizational buyer behavior.

A DESCRIPTION OF
INDUSTRIAL BUYER BEHAVIOR

The model of industrial buyer behavior is summarized in Exhibit 1. Although this illustrative presentation looks complex due

of Supplier Performance (New York: National Association of Purchasing Agents, 1963); F. A. Hays and G. A. Renard, _Evaluating Purchasing Performance_, American Management Association Research Study No. 66 (New York, 1964); Hugh Buckner, _How British Industry Buys_ (London: Hutchison and Company, Ltd., 1967); _How Industry Buys/1970_ (New York: Scientific American, 1970). In addition, numerous articles published in trade journals such as _Purchasing and Industrial Marketing_ are cited in Vinson, _op. cit._, and Strauss, _op. cit._

   [4]Ralph S. Alexander, J. S. Cross, and R. M. Hill, _Industrial Marketing_, 3rd ed. (Homewood, Ill.: Richard D. Irwin, 1967); John H. Westing, I. V. Fine, and G. J. Zenz, _Purchasing Management_ (New York: John Wiley & Sons, 1969); Patrick J. Robinson, C. W. Farris, and Y. Wind, _Industrial Buying and Creative Marketing_ (Boston: Allyn & Bacon, 1967); Frederick E. Webster, Jr., "Modeling the Industrial Buying Process," _Journal of Marketing Research_, 2 (November 1965), pp. 370–76; and Frederick E. Webster, Jr., "Industrial Buying Behavior: A State-of-the-Art Appraisal," in _Marketing in a Changing World_, B. A. Morin, ed. (Chicago: American Marketing Association, 1969), p. 256.

to the large number of variables and complicated relationships among them, this is because it is a generic model which attempts to describe and explain all types of industrial buying decisions. One can, however, simplify the actual application of the model in a specific study in at least two ways. First, several variables are included as conditions to hold constant differences among types of products to be purchased (product-specific factors) and differences among types of purchasing organizations. These exogenous factors will not be necessary if the objective of a study is to describe the process of buying behavior for a specific product or service. Second, some of the decision-process variables can also be ignored if the interest is strictly to conduct a survey of static measurement of the psychology of the organizational buyers. For example, perceptual bias and active search variables may be eliminated if the interest is not in the process of communication to the organizational buyers.

This model is similar to the Howard-Sheth model of buyer behavior in format and classification of variables.[5] However, there are several significant differences. First, while the Howard-Sheth model is more general and probably more useful in consumer behavior, the model described in this article is limited to organizational buying alone. Second, the Howard-Sheth model is limited to the individual decision-making process, whereas this model explicitly describes the joint decision-making process. Finally, there are fewer variables in this model than in the Howard-Sheth model of buyer behavior.

Organizational buyer behavior consists of three distinct aspects. The first aspect is the psychological world of the individuals involved in organizational buying decisions. The second aspect relates to the conditions which precipitate joint decisions among these individuals. The final aspect

   [5]John A. Howard and J. N. Sheth, _The Theory of Buyer Behavior_ (New York: John Wiley & Sons, 1969).

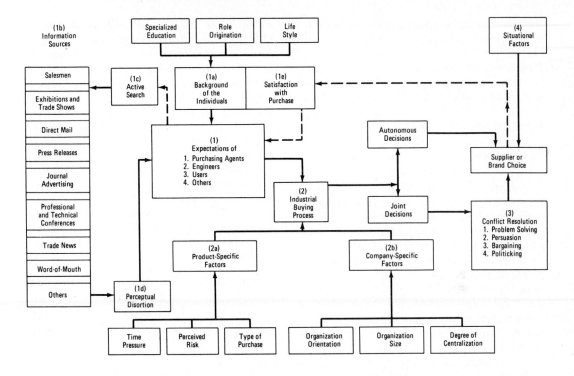

is the process of joint decision making with the inevitable conflict among the decision makers and its resolution by resorting to a variety of tactics.

PSYCHOLOGICAL WORLD OF THE DECISION MAKERS

Contrary to popular belief, many industrial buying decisions are not solely in the hands of purchasing agents.[6] Typically in an industrial setting, one finds that there are at least three departments whose members are continuously involved in different phases of the buying process. The most common are the personnel from the purchasing, quality control, and manufacturing departments. These individuals are identified in

[6]Howard and Moore, *op. cit.*; Strauss, *op. cit.*; McMillan, *op. cit.*; *How Industry Buys/1970*, *op. cit.*

the model as purchasing agents, engineers, and users, respectively. Several other individuals in the organization may be, but are typically not, involved in the buying process (for example, the president of the firm or the comptroller). There is considerable interaction among the individuals in the three departments continuously involved in the buying process and often they are asked to decide jointly. It is, therefore, critical to examine the similarities and differences in the psychological worlds of these individuals.

Based on research in consumer and social psychology, several different aspects of the psychology of the decision makers are included in the model. Primary among these are the *expectations* of the decision makers about suppliers and brands [(1) in Exhibit 1]. The present model specifies five different processes which create differential expectations among the individuals involved in the purchasing process: (1a) the *background of the individuals*, (1b) *information sources*, (1c) *active search*, (1d) *perceptual distortion*, and (1e) *satisfaction with past purchases*. These variables must be explained and operationally defined if they are to fully represent the psychological world of the organizational buyers.

Expectations

Expectations refer to the *perceived* potential of alternative suppliers and brands to satisfy a number of explicit and implicit objectives in any particular buying decision. The most common explicit objectives include, in order of relative importance, product quality, delivery time, quantity of supply, after-sale service where appropriate, and price.[7] However, a number of studies have pointed out the critical role of several implicit criteria such as reputation, size, location, and reciprocity relationship with the supplier; and personality, technical expertise, salesmanship, and even life-style of the sales representative.[8] In fact, with the standardized marketing mix among the suppliers in oligopolistic markets, the implicit criteria are becoming marginally more and more significant in the industrial buyer's decisions.

Expectations can be measured by obtaining a profile of each supplier or brand as to how satisfactory it is perceived to be in enabling the decision maker to achieve his explicit and implicit objectives. Almost all studies from past research indicate that expectations will substantially differ among the purchasing agents, engineers, and product users because each considers different criteria to be salient in judging the supplier or the brand. In general, it is found that product users look for prompt delivery, proper installation, and efficient serviceability; purchasing agents look for maxi-

mum price advantage and economy in shipping and forwarding; and engineers look for excellence in quality, standardization of the product, and engineering pretesting of the product. These differences in objectives and, consequently, expectations are often the root causes for constant conflict among these three types of individuals.[9]

Why are there substantial differences in expectations? While there is considerable speculation among researchers and observers of industrial buyer behavior on the number and nature of explanations, there is relatively little consensus. The five most salient processes which determine differential expectations, as specified in the model, are discussed below.

Background of Individuals. The first, and probably most significant, factor is the background and task orientation of each of the individuals involved in the buying process. The different educational backgrounds of the purchasing agents, engineers, and plant managers often generate substantially different professional goals and values. In addition, the task expectations also generate conflicting perceptions of one another's role in the organization. Finally, the personal life-styles of individual decision makers play an important role in developing differential expectations.[10]

It is relatively easy to gather information on this background factor. The educational and task differences are comparable to demographics in consumer behavior, and life-style differences can be assessed by psychographic scales on the individual's interests, activities, and values as a professional.

---

[7]Howard and Moore, *op. cit.*; *How Industry Buys/1970, op. cit.*; Hays and Renard, *op. cit.*

[8]Howard and Moore, *op. cit.*; Levitt, *op. cit.*; Westing, Fine, and Zenz, *op. cit.*; Shoaf, *op. cit.*

[9]Strauss, *op. cit.*

[10]For a general reading, see Robert T. Golembiewski, "Small Groups and Large Organizations," in *Handbook of Organizations*, J. G. March, ed. (Chicago: Rand McNally & Company, 1965), Chapter 3. For field studies related to this area, see Donald E. Porter, P. B. Applewhite, and M. J. Misshauk, eds., *Studies in Organizational Behavior and Management*, 2nd ed. (Scranton, Pa.: Intext Educational Publishers, 1971).

Information Sources and Active Search.
The second and third factors in creating
differential expectations are the source and
type of information each of the decision
makers is exposed to and his participation
in the active search. Purchasing agents receive disproportionately greater exposure
to commercial sources, and the information
is often partial and biased toward the supplier or the brand. In some companies, it
is even a common practice to discourage
sales representatives from talking directly
to the engineering or production personnel.
The engineering and production personnel
therefore, typically have less information
and what they have is obtained primarily
from professional meetings, trade reports,
and even word-of-mouth. In addition, the
active search for information is often relegated to the purchasing agents because it is
presumed to be their job responsibility.

It is not too difficult to assess differences among the three types of individuals
in their exposure to various sources and
types of information by standard survey
research methods.

Perceptual Distortion. A fourth factor is
the selective distortion and retention of
available information. Each individual
strives to make the objective information
consistent with his own prior knowledge
and expectations by systematically distort-
ing it. For example, since there are substantial differences in the goals and values
of purchasing agents, engineers, and production personnel, one should expect different interpretations of the same information
among them. Although no specific research
has been done on this tendency to percep-
tually distort information in the area of
industrial buyer behavior, a large body of
research does exist on cognitive consistency to explain its presence as a natural
human tendency.[11]

Perceptual distortion is probably the
most difficult variable to quantify by stan-

[11]Robert P. Abelson, et al., *Theories of Cognitive Consistency: A Source Book* (Chicago: Rand
McNally & Company, 1968).

dard survey research methods. One possible
approach is experimentation, but this is
costly. A more realistic alternative is to
utilize perceptual mapping techniques such
as multidimensional scaling or factor analysis and compare differences in the judgments of the purchasing agents, engineers,
and production personnel to a common list
of suppliers or brands.

Satisfaction with Past Purchases. The fifth
factor which creates differential expectations among the various individuals involved in the purchasing process is the satisfaction with past buying experiences
with a supplier or brand. Often it is not
possible for a supplier or brand to provide
equal satisfaction to the three parties because each one has different goals or criteria. For example, a supplier may be lower
in price but his delivery schedule may not
be satisfactory. Similarly, a product's quality may be excellent but its price may be
higher than others. The organization typically rewards each individual for excellent
performance in his specialized skills, so
the purchasing agent is rewarded for economy, the engineer for quality control, and
the production personnel for efficient scheduling. This often results in a different level
of satisfaction for each of the parties involved even though the chosen supplier or
brand may be the best feasible alternative
in terms of overall corporate goals.

Past experiences with a supplier or
brand, summarized in the satisfaction variable, directly influence the person's expectations toward that supplier or brand. It is
relatively easy to measure the satisfaction
variable by obtaining information on how
the supplier or brand is perceived by each
of the three parties.

DETERMINANTS OF JOINT VS. AUTONOMOUS DECISIONS

Not all industrial buying decisions are
made jointly by the various individuals

involved in the purchasing process. Sometimes the buying decisions are delegated to one party, which is not necessarily the purchasing agent. It is, therefore, important for the supplier to know whether a buying decision is joint or autonomous and, if it is the latter, to which party it is delegated. There are six primary factors which determine whether a specific buying decision will be joint or autonomous. Three of these factors are related to the characteristics of the product or service (2a) and the other three are related to the characteristics of the buyer company (2b).

Product-Specific Factors

The first product-specific variable is what Bauer calls *perceived risk* in buying decisions.[12] Perceived risk refers to the magnitude of adverse consequences felt by the decision maker if he makes a wrong choice, and the uncertainty under which he must decide. The greater the uncertainty in a buying situation, the greater the perceived risk. Although there is very little direct evidence, it is logical to hypothesize that the greater the perceived risk in a specific buying decision, the more likely it is that the purchase will be decided jointly by all parties concerned. The second product-specific factor is *type of purchase*. If it is the first purchase or a once-in-a-lifetime capital expenditure, one would expect greater joint decision making. On the other hand, if the purchase decision is repetitive and routine or is limited to maintenance products or services, the buying decision is likely to be delegated to one party. The third factor is *time pressure*. If the buying decision has to be made under a great deal of time pressure or on an emergency basis, it is likely to be

delegated to one party rather than decided jointly.

Company-Specific Factors

The three organization-specific factors are *company orientation, company size,* and *degree of centralization.* If the company is technology oriented, it is likely to be dominated by the engineering people and the buying decisions will, in essence, be made by them. Similarly, if the company is production oriented, the buying decisions will be made by the production personnel.[13]

Second, if the company is a large corporation, decision making will tend to be joint. Finally, the greater the degree of centralization, the less likely it is that the decisions will be joint. Thus, a privately-owned small company with technology or production orientation will tend toward autonomous decision making and a large-scale public corporation with considerable decentralization will tend to have greater joint decision making.

Even though there is considerable research evidence in organization behavior in general to support these six factors, empirical evidence in industrial buying decisions in particular is sketchy on them. Perhaps with more research it will be possible to verify the generalizations and deductive logic utilized in this aspect of the model.

PROCESS OF JOINT DECISION MAKING

The major thrust of the present model of industrial buying decisions is to investigate the process of joint decision making.

[12]Raymond A. Bauer, "Consumer Behavior as Risk Taking," in *Dynamic Marketing for a Changing World*, R. L. Hancock, ed. (Chicago: American Marketing Association, 1960), pp. 389–400. Applications of perceived risk in industrial buying can be found in *Levitt, op. cit.;* Copley and Callom, *op cit.;* McMillan, *op cit.*

[13]For some indirect evidence, see Strauss, *op. cit.* For a more general study, see Victor A. Thompson, "Hierarchy, Specialization and Organizational Conflict," *Administrative Science Quarterly*, 5 (March 1961), p. 513; and Henry A. Landsberger, "The Horizontal Dimension in Bureaucracy," *Administration Science Quarterly*, 6 (December 1961), pp. 299–332, for a thorough review of numerous theories.

This includes initiation of the decision to buy, gathering of information, evaluating alternative suppliers, and resolving conflict among the parties who must jointly decide.

The decision to buy is usually initiated by a continued need of supply or is the outcome of long-range planning. The formal initiation in the first case is typically from the production personnel by way of a requisition slip. The latter usually is a formal recommendation from the planning unit to an ad hoc committee consisting of the purchasing agent, the engineer, and the plant manager. The information-gathering function is typically relegated to the purchasing agent. If the purchase is a repetitive decision for standard items, there is very little information gathering. Usually the purchasing agent contacts the preferred supplier and orders the items on the requisition slip. However, considerable active search effort is manifested for capital expenditure items, especially those which are entirely new purchase experiences for the organization.[14]

The most important aspect of the joint decision-making process, however, is the assimilation of information, deliberations on it, and the consequent conflict which most joint decisions entail. According to March and Simon, conflict is present when there is a need to decide jointly among a group of people who have, at the same time, different goals and perceptions.[15] In view of the fact that the latter is invariably present among the various parties to industrial buying decisions, conflict becomes a common consequence of the joint decision-making process; the buying motives and expectations about brands and suppliers are considerably different for the engineer, the user, and the purchasing agent, partly due to different educational backgrounds and partly due to company policy of reward for specialized skills and viewpoints.

Interdepartmental conflict in itself is not necessarily bad. What matters most from the organization's viewpoint is *how* the conflict is resolved (3). If it is resolved in a rational manner, one very much hopes that the final joint decision will also tend to be rational. If, on the other hand, conflict resolution degenerates to what Strauss calls "tactics of lateral relationship,"[16] the organization will suffer from inefficiency and the joint decisions may be reduced to bargaining and politicking among the parties involved. Not only will the decision be based on irrational criteria, but the choice of a supplier may be to the detriment of the buying organization.

What types of conflict can be expected in industrial buying decisions? How are they likely to be resolved? These are some of the key questions in an understanding of industrial buyer behavior. If the interparty conflict is largely due to disagreements on expectations about the suppliers or their brands, it is likely that the conflict will be resolved in the *problem-solving* manner. The immediate consequence of this type of conflict is to actively search for more information, deliberate more on available information, and often to seek out other suppliers not seriously considered before. The additional information is then presented in a problem-solving fashion so that conflict tends to be minimized.

If the conflict among the parties is primarily due to disagreement on some specific criteria with which to evaluate suppliers—although there is an agreement on the buying goals or objectives at a more fundamental level—it is likely to be resolved by *persuasion*. An attempt is made, under this type of resolution, to persuade the dissenting member by pointing out the importance of overall corporate objectives and how his criterion is not likely to attain

[14]Strauss, *op. cit.*

[15]James G. March and H. A. Simon, *Organizations* (New York: John Wiley & Sons, 1958), Chapter 5; and Landsberger, *op. cit.*

[16]George Strauss, "Tactics of Lateral Relationship: The Purchasing Agent," *Administrative Science Quarterly*, 7 (September 1962), pp. 161–86.

these objectives. There is no attempt to gather more information. However, there results greater interaction and communication among the parties, and sometimes an outsider is brought in to reconcile the differences.

Both problem solving and persuasion are useful and rational methods of conflict resolution. The resulting joint decisions, therefore, also tend to be more rational. Thus, conflicts produced due to disagreements on expectations about the suppliers or on a specific criterion are healthy from the organization's viewpoint even though they may be time consuming. One is likely to find, however, that a more typical situation in which conflict arises is due to fundamental differences in buying goals or objectives among the various parties. This is especially true with respect to unique or new buying decisions related to capital expenditure items. The conflict is resolved not by changing the differences in relative importance of the buying goals or objectives of the individuals involved, but by the process of *bargaining*. The fundamental differences among the parties are implicitly conceded by all the members and the concept of distributive justice (tit for tat) is invoked as a part of bargaining. The most common outcome is to allow a single party to decide autonomously in this specific situation in return for some favor or promise of reciprocity in future decisions.

Finally, if the disagreement is not simply with respect to buying goals or objectives but also with respect to *style of decision making*, the conflict tends to be grave and borders on the mutual dislike of personalities among the individual decision makers. The resolution of this type of conflict is usually by *politicking* and backstabbing tactics. Such methods of conflict resolution are common in industrial buying decisions. The reader is referred to the sobering research of Strauss for further discussion.[17]

Both bargaining and politicking are

[17]*Ibid.*

nonrational and inefficient methods of conflict resolution; the buying organization suffers from these conflicts. Furthermore, the decision makers find themselves sinking below their professional, managerial role. The decisions are not only delayed but tend to be governed by factors other than achievement of corporate objectives.

CRITICAL ROLE OF SITUATIONAL FACTORS

The model described so far presumes that the choice of a supplier or brand is the outcome of a systematic decision-making process in the organizational setting. However, there is ample empirical evidence in the literature to suggest that at least some of the industrial buying decisions are determined by ad hoc *situational factors* (4) and not by any systematic decision-making process. In other words, similar to consumer behavior, the industrial buyers often decide on factors other than rational or realistic criteria.

It is difficult to prepare a list of ad hoc conditions which determine industrial buyer behavior without decision making. However, a number of situational factors which often intervene between the actual choice and any prior decision-making process can be isolated. These include: temporary economic conditions such as price controls, recession, or foreign trade; internal strikes, walkouts, machine breakdowns, and other production-related events; organizational changes such as merger or acquisition; and ad hoc changes in the marketplace, such as promotional efforts, new product introduction, price changes, and so on, in the supplier industries.

IMPLICATIONS FOR INDUSTRIAL MARKETING RESEARCH

The model of industrial buyer behavior described above suggests the following implications for marketing research.

First, in order to explain and predict supplier or brand choice in industrial buyer behavior, it is necessary to conduct research on the psychology of other individuals in the organization in addition to the purchasing agents. It is, perhaps, the unique nature of organizational structure and behavior which leads to a distinct separation of the consumer, the buyer, and the procurement agent, as well as others possibly involved in the decision-making process. In fact, it may not be an exaggeration to suggest that the purchasing agent is often a less critical member of the decision-making process in industrial buyer behavior.

Second, it is possible to operationalize and quantify most of the variables included as part of the model. While some are more difficult and indirect, sufficient psychometric skill in marketing research is currently available to quantify the psychology of the individuals.

Third, although considerable research has been done on the demographics of organizations in industrial market research—for example, on the turnover and size of the company, workflows, standard industrial classification, and profit ratios—demographic and life-style information on the individuals involved in industrial buying decisions is also needed.

Fourth, a systematic examination of the power positions of various individuals involved in industrial buying decisions is a necessary condition of the model. The sufficient conditions is to examine trade-offs among various objectives, both explicit and implicit, in order to create a satisfied customer.

Fifth, it is essential in building any market research information system for industrial goods and services that the process of conflict resolution among the parties and its impact on supplier or brand choice behavior is carefully included and simulated.

Finally, it is important to realize that not all industrial decisions are the outcomes of a systematic decision-making process. There are some industrial buying decisions which are based strictly on a set of situational factors for which theorizing or model building will not be relevant or useful. What is needed in these cases is a checklist of empirical observations of the ad hoc events which vitiate the neat relationship between the theory or the model and a specific buying decision.

Researching Target Markets

The marketing concept is meaningless unless marketing managers obtain information about relevant target markets. Researching these markets is a continuing process within marketing departments.

After reading this part you should have a better understanding of:

1. The value of decision support systems to marketing managers.
2. The ways secondary data can help in allocating marketing effort.
3. An awareness of marketing segmentation as an operational way of implementing the marketing concept.
4. The complex choices in segmenting industrial markets.

12 Decision Support Systems for Marketing Managers

John D. C. Little

In the past ten years, a new technology has emerged for assisting and improving marketing decision making. We define a marketing decision support system as a coordinated collection of data, models, analytic tools, and computing power by which an organization gathers information from the environment and turns it into a basis for action. Where such systems have taken root, they have grown and become increasingly productive for their organizations.

The combination of large potential pay-offs, highly motivated professional staffs, evolving OR/MS techniques, and rising computer power is making an impact on marketing management. A problem-solving technology is emerging that consists of people, knowledge, software, and hardware successfully wired into the management process. Following Gorry and Scott Morton (1971), we shall call the set of facilitating tools a decision support system or, more specifically a *Marketing Decision Support System* (MDSS). Intellectual contributions to MDSS have come from many disciplines: OR/MS, marketing research, computer science, behavioral science, and statistics, to name a few. We view the results collectively as an advance in management science or, more specifically marketing science. Our purpose is to define and illustrate the concept of an MDSS and show its effects on marketing practice.

WHAT IS IT? A BLACK BOX VIEW

A manager takes action with respect to an environment in order to achieve the objectives of his organization. To do this he must perceive and interpret the market, even if imperfectly. Then he must think up strategies, analyze them, and converge on one to put into practice. This process is conducted through a complicated system of people, paper, and machines. We call the inanimate part of this an MDSS. Exhibit 1, modified

Reprinted with permission from *Journal of Marketing*, published by the American Marketing Association (Summer 1979), pp. 9–26.

EXHIBIT 1

A manager uses a marketing decision support system (MDSS) to learn about the business environment and take action with respect to it

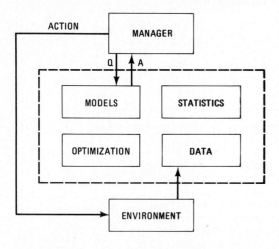

from Montgomery and Urban (1969), shows the MDSS and its components and traces their roles in interpreting and analyzing the environment.

Data Bank.   A stream of information comes into the organization from the world at large in many ways: from members of the organization; from talking to people; from reading *The Wall Street Journal;* from purchasing market research; and especially from distilling the multitude of individual transactions of the business—orders, shipments, purchases, records of internal action, and much more. The data are stored in varied forms; on paper, in people's heads, and, most relevant for our present purposes, in large chunks on machine readable media. The amount of data handled by a large company is staggering. Business runs on numbers. Sales alone have vast detail, and might, for example, be broken out by time period, market area, brand, package size, salesperson, and customer. How did people get along before computers? (Quite well,

thank you, but they missed many profit opportunities open to us now.)

Less obvious than the flood of data washing over companies is the information they do *not* have. Often they may have it in principle, but not in practice. For example, I recently asked a large and successful company for the following data, which they could not supply: product category sales by month and major market area, competitive advertising, and, even more surprising, the company's own promotional spending by market area. At another company, I once sought advertising expenditures by month, but they could only be provided in terms of when the bills were paid, not when the advertising was run. This was not too helpful for marketing analysis. Certain data are simply not gathered, others are aggregated and the original detail lost or prohibitively costly to recover. Competitive data usually comes from syndicated services as hard copy which is inadequate for any but the most aggregate analysis.

Clearly, a basic task of any MDSS is to capture major marketing variables such as sales, advertising, promotion, and price in reasonable detail and truly accessible form. Remarkably few companies do an adequate job today. The issue is cost and therefore value, since data for data's sake is a worthless luxury. It takes skillful analysis and effective coupling with management to provide the benefits that justify the cost, but the payback can be large.

Models.   Whenever a manager (or anybody else) looks at data, he or she has a preconceived idea of how the world works and therefore of what is interesting and worthwhile in the data. We shall call such ideas *models.* Even a person who is browsing through tables has a set of constructs in mind that signal when a particular number is important and worth further consideration. Thus, a manager or management scientist uses theories to determine what aggregations or manipulations are meaningful for the decision at hand. The data user may want to confirm or disprove a hypothesis, guide an action, or learn the magnitude of a past number so as to judge the reasonablenesss of a current one. Manipulation of the numbers may cause an old theory to be discarded and a new one created to conform better to the facts.

Some models remain in people's heads, but the ones of most interest here are those that find explicit mathematical and computational representation. These aid planning, decision making, and many less publicized supporting tasks required for understanding and analyzing the market.

Statistics. We shall call the process of relating models to data *statistics*. The most important statistical operation is addition. This makes big important numbers out of small, trivial ones. Many sophisticated techniques also are available for model and hypothesis testing and they often prove useful. However, it is not widely realized, except by those with their hands on the data, that the most frequent operations are basic ones like segregating numbers into groups, aggregating them, taking ratios, making comparisons, picking out exceptional cases, plotting, tabulating summaries, etc. These manipulations are required by such standard managerial models as pro forma profit and loss statements, budgeting, and forecasting, to say nothing of more complicated models for new product tracking, marketing-mix planning, and the like.

Optimization. A manager constantly seeks to improve the performance of his organization. Abstractly this is *optimization*. The most frequent operations are deceptively simple: calculating two numbers and seeing which is larger, ranking a set of numbers, or

sorting a set of alternatives into categories of effectiveness. In addition, there are many cases where formal OR/MS optimization methods such as linear programming and its extensions offer substantial payoffs.

Q/A. Finally, the manager and his or her staff must communicate with the system. Insofar as the required skills, talent, and information are distributed throughout the organization, communication involves the standard processes of meetings, studies, and reports. As the systems become formal and automated, some of the communication takes place through interactive time-shared computing. Individual tools are stored as computer programs. With the right software, data and files pass easily between analyses, and a management scientist or other person can perform a wide scope of analysis smoothly, quickly, and efficiently.

To summarize, a marketing decision support system is a coordinated collection of data, systems, tools, and techniques with supporting software and hardware by which an organization gathers and interprets relevant information from business and environment and turns it into a basis for marketing action.

THE CRITICS

We have described the concept, but what about the practice? Management science has its critics. Let's see what C. Jackson Grayson Jr. (1973) says in the *Harvard Business Review*. Grayson, a Harvard DBA, author of a book applying decision analysis to oil drilling decisions, former dean of a business school, and currently head of a productivity institute, writes:

Management Science has grown so remote from and unmindful of the conditions of "live" management that it has abdicated its usability.

We would like to dismiss this as an isolated complaint, not likely to be repeated. But wait, let's see what John D. C. Little (1970), professor of Operations Research and Management at M.I.T., says in *Management Science:*

The big problem with management science models is that managers practically never use them.

This situation must be serious! On close examination, however, Grayson's article and mine are quite different in content and tone. Grayson reports that in the most important administrative role of his career (Chairman of the U.S. Price Commission), he found no use for his management science training. He goes on to describe managers generally as confused and dissatisfied with management science activities in their organizations and admonishes management scientists and managers to build bridges to each other. One can hardly advocate that they should not, but this proposal seems patronizing at best and indicates an ignorance of a great deal of useful work that has gone on.

My own paper, written three years earlier, sought to draw on a variety of practical experiences to describe "how-to-do-it" in building useful models. By 1970 much had been learned, sometimes by painful trial and error, about doing OR/MS successfully in business and government. Regrettably, good applications often lie concealed because little incentive exists for their revelation and, worse yet, strong forces favor secrecy. Fortunately, studies are beginning to appear more regularly. (See for example, the prize paper issues of *Interfaces*, Nigam, 1975, 1976, 1977.)

OR/MS practitioners and marketing researchers have continued to learn what works and what does not. This paper tries to report some of this.

HOW AN MDSS WORKS: A TRUE STORY

The Marketing Manager, the Management Scientist, and the MBA

Once upon a time (1973), an MBA student took a summer job with a large food manufacturer. He reported to a management scientist in the principal division of the company. The MBA was assigned to put key marketing information, basically store audit data, on a time-shared computer. The goal was an easy-to-use retrieval system, essentially the DATA box of Exhibit 1.

O.K. He did this.

By the end of the summer, word of the system had reached the marketing manager of the major product of the division who asked for a demonstration and so the three met. The MBA and the management scientist showed the marketing manager how simple, Englishlike commands could retrieve data items: sales, share, price, distribution level, etc., each by brand, package size, and month.

The marketing manager was impressed. "You must be fantastically smart," he told the MBA. "The people downstairs in MIS have been trying to do this for years and they haven't gotten anywhere. You did it in a summer."

It was hard for the MBA to reject this assessment out of hand, but he did acknowledge, and this is a key point, that the software world had changed. There are now high level analytic languages available on time-sharing that make it easy to bring up data and start working on it right away.

The MBA and the management scientist, flushed with success, now said to the marketing manager: "O.K. Ask us anything!" (Famous last words.)

The marketing manager thought a minute and said: "I'd like to know how much the competition's introduction of a 40 oz. package in Los Angeles cut into the sales of our 16 oz. package."

The MBA and the management scientist looked at each other in dismay. What they realized right away, and what you might too if you think about it, is that there isn't going to be any number in the machine for sales that *didn't* occur. This isn't a *retrieval* question at all, it's an *analysis* question.

Here then is another point. The marketing manager had no idea the number would not be in the machine. To him it was just one more fact no different in his mind from other facts about the market. Notice also that the question is a reasonable one. One can visualize a whole string of managerial acts that might be triggered by the answer, possibly even culminating in the introduction of a new package by the company.

What is needed to answer the question is a *model*, probably a rather simple model. For example, one might extrapolate previous share and use it to estimate the sales that would have happened without the competitor's introduction. Then subtraction of actual sales would give the loss.

The three discussed possible assumptions for a few minutes and agreed on how to approach the problem. Then the management scientist typed in one line of high level commands. Out came the result, expressed in dollars, cases, and share points.

The marketing manager thought the answer was fine, a good demonstration. The MBA and the management scientist thought it was a miracle! They had responded to the question with a speed and accuracy unthinkable a few months earlier.

The story is simple but contains several important lessons. I see the same points coming up again and again in various organizations, although not always so neatly and concisely:

☐ *Managers ask for analysis not retrieval.* Sometimes retrieval questions come up of course, but most often the answers to important questions require nontrivial manipulation of stored data. Knowing this tells us much about the kind of software required for an MDSS. For example, a data base management system is not enough.

☐ *Good data are vital.* If you haven't done your homework and put key data on the system you are nowhere. Thus, a powerful analytic language alone is not enough.

☐ *You need models.* These are often simple, but not always. Some can be prepackaged. Many are ad hoc.

☐ *The management scientist is an intermediary.* He connects the manager to the MDSS. The manager does not use the system directly. The management scientist interprets questions, formulates problems in cooperation with the manager, creates models, and uses them to answer questions and analyze issues.

☐ *Quick, quick, quick.* If you can answer people's questions right away, you will affect their thinking. If you cannot, they will make their decisions without you and go on to something else.

☐ *Muscular software cuts out programmers.* New high level languages on time-sharing permit a management scientist or recently trained MBA to bring up systems and do analyses singlehandedly. This makes for efficient problem-solving. Furthermore, the problem-solver identifies with and deals directly with marketing management so that his understanding and motivation are high. Time-sharing costs more than batch processing, but an army of programmers is eliminated and, far more important, problems get solved on time.

DECISION SUPPORT FOR THE PRODUCT LIFE CYCLE: CRADLE TO GRAVE CARE

Let's look at marketing per se. Over the past 10 or 15 years and continuing unabated, there has evolved from diverse origins a series of tools and techniques for support of the product life cycle.

By product life cycle we mean a sequence of conveniently defined stages that describe the history of a product from conception to possible demise. We do not imply that every product goes through every stage or that any stage lasts some prescribed length of time.

The product life cycle is illustrated in Exhibit 2. A product starts as someone's bright *idea*, thereby identifying a category. The idea then goes through a stage of concept and product *development and evaluation,* leading to a detailed design and market position. Development and evaluation are closely linked; at various times during development, evaluations of greater or lesser

EXHIBIT 2

Marketing scientists have developed models and measurements to support almost every stage of the product life cycle

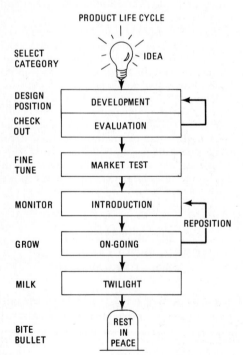

depth will be made and the results fed back to refocus development.

The next step is usually *test market,* although an industrial product will not ordinarily have this step. Then comes national *introduction.* In the *ongoing* stage, the product becomes, one hopes, an established and profitable business. From time to time a product may go through a revamping or "reintroduction." Many at some point go into a *twilight* of obsolescence (the slide rule and the mechanical watch seem headed this way). Finally many products including quite a few former household names, go out of existence entirely. The tombstone in Exhibit 2 might read: "Chrysler Imperial: 1926–1975, died at age 49 of sales starvation."

The mortality of new products has traditionally been notorious. For example, General Foods reported in *Business Week* (1973) a 15 year history in which 83% of new products did not get out of the idea stage. Of those that did, 60% never reached test market; of those entering test market, 59% failed; and even among those making it to national introduction, 25% were considered financial failures. At the same time, new product introduction is very expensive. For a typical package good of a major manufacturer, the development and evaluation stage might cost $150,000; a test market, $1 million; a national introduction, $5–10 million. A new industrial product would omit the test market expense, but might well spend an equivalent amount on development and evaluation.

Responding to the challenge of the heavy expenses and high profit aspirations of new products, marketing scientists have developed an array of methodologies and measurements to support decision making at various stages of the life cycle.

At the *idea and category selection* stage, systematic search procedures drawn from behavioral science supplement traditional inspiration. Focus groups (Cox, Higginbotham, and Burton, 1976) probe customer feelings about needs and perceptions. "Synectics" (Prince, 1972) is a technique whereby a group of people seek to solve a problem in an organized way, e.g., conceive of a product to meet a specified set of customers needs. As demonstrated by von Hippel (1978) customers themselves are an important source of industrial product ideas. Industrial and governmental data on potential markets suggest new product opportunities. Environmental scanning can turn up danger spots for existing products and needs for new ones.

The bulk of the new techniques, however, begins to come into play at the next stage: *development and evaluation*. Value-in-use analysis (Gross, 1977) looks at a product from the customer's point of view and asks: "What advantages are there to the customer from using this product? What cost savings? What time savings? What investment would be required to achieve this savings?" By answering such questions for each potential market segment, an aggregate picture of volume versus price can be synthesized.

A particularly well-articulated description of a formal new product design, development, and positioning methodology is that of Hauser and Urban (1977). Their normative design process envisages first finding out the customer's words for talking about the product category. This might be done through focus groups. Then, customer words are developed into psychometric scales. Potential customers use these scales to rate new and existing products in the category. As customers do this, they also express preferences among the products and so generate data that can be analyzed to identify the customers' key utility dimensions. Such information permits the calibration of a model of new product share and sales. A feedback

loop between model and manager facilitates the modification of the product and its market position.

Other tools fit in at this stage of the life cycle, some within the Hauser-Urban framework. These include mapping studies, conjoint measurement, and consumer choice models. Mapping is a general term to describe the visual representation of competitive products relative to each other in a space of consumer perceptual dimensions. Conjoint measurement (Green and Wind, 1975) presents alternative product features to customers in order to obtain their trade-offs and build new products with high market potential. Consumer choice models (Shocker and Srinivasan, 1977; Hauser, 1978) relate choice to consumer utility or preference.

A particularly successful blend of models, measurements, and statistical techniques has emerged for *pretest market evaluation*. The best example is Silk and Urban's ASSESSOR (1978). In their method, people passing through a shopping mall are invited to participate in a marketing study. They view competing advertising commercials including one for the new product under test, and then have an opportunity to select a brand from a shelf display containing the new product. Data are taken by questionnaire during the process and later a telephone call-back determines the customer's likelihood of repurchasing. This type of careful orchestration of psychometric scaling, consumer choice models, trial-repeat purchase models, and statistical calibration has proven extremely useful to marketers of package goods and holds the promise of extension to new areas, e.g., pharmaceuticals and small durables.

As we move on to *test marketing* and *national introduction*, the techniques change. The principal tools become trial-repeat models calibrated by store audits, ad hoc surveys, and consumer diary panels. The task is to follow the buildup of consumer trial and repurchase and project to future sales and share. Parfitt and Collins (1968) provide a simple model and Urban (1970) in SPRINTER a comprehensive model for doing this. As pretest market evaluations increasingly eliminate costly failures, test marketing becomes more of a fine-tuning for the marketing mix than a go/no-go test. Therefore, new product tracking models that contain major control variables become most useful.

At the *established brand stage*, the picture changes again. On-going brands frequently take a back seat as new products consume managerial attention. Yet for many companies, this is a mistake since major profit opportunities often lie with the old breadwinners. Market response analyses assisted by marketing-mix models like Little's (1975) BRANDAID or Bloom and Stewart's (1977) MAPLAMOD harness major control variables such as price, promotion, and advertising for strategy planning and permit tracking predicted versus actual sales. Discrepancies lead to diagnosis of market problems. Econometric analysis of historical data (Parsons and Schultz, 1976; Bass and Clarke, 1972) can help calibrate such models. Consumer panel analyses like those of Ehrenberg (1972) can detect customer purchase shifts. Individual models of price, promotion, and advertising are frequently useful for specific tactical problems.

The basic information sources are also different in the on-going stage since product management relies more heavily on continuing data: factory shipments; promotion reports; advertising expenses; and syndicated services such as store audits, warehouse withdrawals, and consumer panels. These services are well developed in consumer package goods, spotty in consumer durables, and almost absent in industrial markets.

The *twilight* or obsolescence stage also

has attracted effort. For example, Hess (1967) discusses the pricing of new and old products when the new is destined to supplant the old. The final phasing out of a product from a product line is studied as a part of product portfolio analyses (Day, 1977).

Thus every part of the product life cycle has generated marketing science activity. Some efforts are more extensive and more successful than others in affecting practice, but it is clear that changes are afoot.

MARKETING SCIENCE: WHO IS KIDDING WHOM?

I like to use the term "marketing science." However, the phrase makes some people flinch and others stir restlessly. Is what we have described an advance in fundamental understanding or is it merely a series of commercial fads? Can we sensibly talk about science in a flamboyant field where the motivation and funding are so far from the usual domain of the natural philosopher? I shall argue that we are indeed engaged in science.

First, it should be observed that most of the actors on the marketing stage are *not* scientists. Many are skillful performing artists and very successful, but not scientists any more than, say, a sculptor is. But when a sculptor hammers a chisel into a piece of marble, he initiates a process that is well described by the laws of physics. In marketing we are not so far along.

Are we anywhere? Natural science is concerned with understanding how the world works. This means models and measurements, the twin engines of scientific advance. Models provide structure for describing phenomena and permit knowledge to be more than an encyclopedia of facts. Measurements separate good models from bad and allow good ones to be calibrated for practical application. It seems obvious that you can make a scientific study of any observable phenomenon and that we are certainly doing that on many occasions in marketing.

Whereas understanding is the province of science, application is the domain of technology. Common usage expands science to cover both. (Thus: "Science put men on the moon, why can't it cure the common cold?") The dividing line is blurred and we shall follow the common usage, but identify understanding as the essential ingredient of science.

Two characteristics of marketing practice tend to obscure accomplishments in fundamental understanding. First, application regularly oversteps knowledge, a situation that makes for confusion, since truths are often proclaimed that are not true. I used to read articles in the business press about marketing successes and marvel that people knew so much more about their markets than I was able to discover by analysis. Eventually I realized that the authors were using different standards of knowing. What was being written reflected the fact that businessmen often make good decisions with relatively poor information. As part of the process, they usually make assertive statements whether or not they possess firm knowledge. In any case, businessmen much prefer to have knowledge and would like us to give it to them whenever possible.

The second point is that, because so much marketing data collection, analysis, and model building is bent toward specific decisions, underlying discoveries are frequently the spinoff of the application, rather than the reverse. On the way to solving a practical problem, people often develop new understanding. This certainly isn't novel in science—probability, for example, was born at the gaming tables. Not all marketing studies produce scientific knowledge—most are not done nearly carefully enough—but the potential is there and sometimes the realization. The marketing papers appearing in *Management Science, Operations Research,* and *Journal of Marketing Research* over the past 15 years demonstrate the quality of the work and the vitality of the field.

Thus, we view marketing science as real. It is an applications-driven subject that is building a base of understanding about marketing processes.

Measurements

Measurements are contact points with reality; they generate the excitement of new discovery and practical pay-off more often than models. Companies pay a great deal for measurements. Syndicated services in store audits, diary panels, media ratings, and the like constitute at least a $200 million industry per year in the United States. Ad hoc surveys, copy tests, etc., reach a comparable dollar magnitude.

Measurements motivated by theories and models are most valuable. For example, Exhibit 3 shows the results of an advertising test. Sales are plotted versus time before, during, and after a heavy-up of advertising.

The results are striking. Notice the rapid rise, leveling off, and slow decay. The data cry out for a theory—and more measurement. Why do sales go up quickly and down slowly? What would happen if the same test were repeated in the same areas a year later? Clearly Exhibit 3 has strong policy implications. It appears that much more profit was generated by removing the heavy advertising after six months than would have occurred by continuing it. This is because decay was so slow. However, to determine an optimal, or even a sensible, policy requires a theory of what is going on.

EXHIBIT 3

Sales went up quickly under increased advertising, but declined slowly after it was removed. Sales are measured as the ratio of sales in test areas to sales in control areas not receiving the heavy advertising

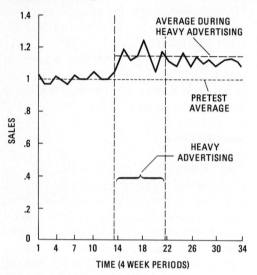

This will expose the assumptions that must be made to turn these measurements into decisions. Clearly, there is no shortage of practical and scientific questions here.

The experiment just described was a project within a marketing decision support operation of a large package goods company. Management asked for the experiment because of concern over advertising budget levels. The sales data used were captured routinely from external syndicated sources and internal company records. Company management scientists analyzed the results using a high level language and wielding a variety of standard and nonstandard statistical tools.

Whenever new measurement technologies appear, they create special opportunities for learning how the world works. Exhibit 4 shows data of the type that is becoming available through automated checkout equipment in grocery stores. Shown is *daily* market share of two brands of a pack-

EXHIBIT 4

Daily market shares of two national brands in a supermarket chain clearly show the effect of store specials. Data was collected on electronic checkout equipment

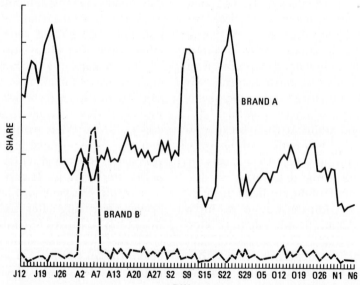

age good in a supermarket. The bumps are promotions. The speed and precision with which the promotion effect can be read is portentous. Here is an indicator of opportunities for new knowledge that will become possible in the near future.

Models

Models form the other half of the models and measurements team of natural science. They provide theories that seek to bring order to the chaos of collected facts. They are much less well understood by laypeople and, indeed, the word is used in enough different ways by professionals that its meaning is often unclear.

For present purposes, I shall define a model as a mathematical description of how something works. Once upon a time, in a simpler age, scientists thought they were discovering the laws of nature; thus in physics we find Ohm's law, Newton's laws, and the like. Unfortunately, as people subjected these laws to closer and closer examination, they often found unsettling imperfections. These frequently led not to outright rejection, but to deeper, more comprehensive theory. A famous example is Einstein's generalization of Newtonian mechanics through relativity. However, after enough incidents like this, physical scientists became more cautious and often described their theories as models. In more recent times, as social and management scientists have sought to develop mathematical understanding of their worlds, they have entertained few illusions about the exactness of their representations. Consequently, they have readily taken up the term.

There is an important practical advantage to the incompleteness implied by the word model. Consider the construction of a model to help solve a marketing problem. We would wish it to include all the important marketing phenomena required to analyze the problem, but, equally, we would wish it to exclude extraneous complication. This incompleteness is important and desirable. Managers, however, are sometimes nervous about it; they conceive that science is exact (even though science and especially engineering abounds with approximations). If a model is full of art, managers become wary. They say art is just what they were trying to get rid of by hiring expensive, overeducated terminal thumpers.

As something of a corroboration of this mind-set, we observe that consulting firms which say they have discovered "laws of marketing" have sometimes had remarkable success with high levels of management.

Managers use models all the time but without the name. Successful management scientists working with managers often de-emphasize the word, using models as required for the job but communicating the results as ideas and phenomena, going into detail as requested. One important development in this direction should be noted by those complainers who say models are not used in practice. Management scientists imbed models into problem-solving systems where the models themselves are relatively inconspicuous because they are only a part of the final product. Silk and Urban's (1978) ASSESSOR for evaluating new products is a good example. It employs high technology consumer choice models and statistical calibration, yet the manager-client focuses on the output and its message for his product. A similar situation arises in the models used for audience exposure analysis of advertising media schedules (research and frequency studies). In such cases the client company should, and frequently does, treat the analytic system like any other industrial product and perform a technical evaluation of it before using it routinely.

I would like to distinguish between *model* and *procedure*. If you allocate the advertising budget to major markets proportional to last year's sales in those markets, you have specified a procedure. Implicit in the procedure may or may not be a model. For example, if you hypothesize that advertising response is proportional to last year's sales times a suitably chosen function of advertising dollars, then you can construct a model of market response that will yield as the optimal budget allocation the same results as the described procedure.

Thus a *procedure is a way of calculating a result; a model is a set of assumptions about how something works.* Managers frequently use procedures, usually based in part on implicit intuitive models. Management scientists devise procedures directly, but often try to develop and calibrate explicit models which will generate good procedures.

In my simple world, I like to distinguish between two types of models: good and bad. Bad models include those that are simply wrong. For example, a model with a linear relationship between sales and advertising has to be incorrect. Other models are vacuous. The symbols may not really be defined or the model may merely be a formalistic way of saying something obvious that is better said simply. Still other models are so extraordinarily elaborate that they collapse of their own weight as data and calibration requirements become so enormous that testing and calibration are infeasible.

We have lived through many bad marketing models and, if we are to continue to progress, we will have to live through many more. At least we have good models, too. Fortunately, it is a characteristic of science that once you discover something worthwhile you can use it from then on and make it a building block for continued progress.

Three types of good models are: (1) small models offering insight and structure for thinking, (2) general structures permitting the synthesis of a variety of phenomena, and (3) models of new phenomena. Without trying to cover the whole field, I shall illustrate each of these types.

Small Models Offering Insight. The customer flow model displayed in Exhibit 5 has very much affected people's thinking about new products in the past 15 years. Here is the basic proposition: A new product has some intended set of customers, called its target market. Suppose we have developed an inexpensive gyrocompass for recreational vehicles. Recreational vehicle owners are the *target population.* Before any of them can possibly buy the product they have to be *aware* of it. A company can inform people about the existence of a new product by advertising and, in fact, any advertising agency can produce a reasonable estimate of how much money it will take to do this. For some number of millions of dollars, for example, you can teach 20% of the American public your brand name.

FIGURE 5

A simple customer flow model provides a mathematical structure for estimating future sales of a new product

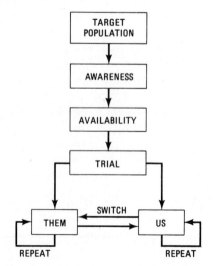

But people cannot buy the product unless it is available. This is a distribution problem. Assuming a company is marketing somewhat similar goods, it will know the appropriate distribution channels and will be able to tell what kind of availability can be achieved for the product.

Once a person in the target market is aware of the product and has a place to buy it, the next question is will that person *try* the product, i.e., buy it once? Involved here is the success of advertising in communicating the product's attributes to the prospective customer and how the customer evaluates the desirability of those attributes. Reasonable estimates can usually be made of trial probability. In some categories of package goods, historical norms are now available. You can also make more refined estimates by taking field measurements with the actual product. Note, however, that even without this, and long before the product has even been made, estimates based on historical norms or managerial judgments will permit useful market calculations.

Given that a person has tried the product, the next question is whether he or she will *repeat* the purchase the next time such a product is needed. Alternatively the customer may *switch* to another brand. Provided that reasonable estimates of switching and repeating probabilities can be made, we can calculate the share of purchases going to the new product among people who try it once.

A straightforward calculation puts together the whole sequence: the number of people in the target market *times* the fraction who become aware of the product *times* the fraction who find it available *times* the fraction of those who try it *times* the share of purchases that triers devote to the new brand *times* the sales rate for the product class, determines the sales rate of the new product.

The notion of awareness, availability, trial, repeat, and switching are fundamental. These processes are obviously going on. The model can be made very elaborate (see Urban, 1970), but the basic conceptual structure and the process described above for calculating long-run sales rate are exceedingly simple.

The quality of that calculation will depend on the quality of the inputs, but just using sensible numbers helps keep the new product manager from becoming a total dreamer. Every new product manager is a wild advocate for his or her product. Probably this is necessary since most new products fail and somebody has to be a believer to keep from giving up before starting. The prehistoric way to estimate new product sales was to declare a final number in one judgmental swoop. Amazingly, the number usually turned out to be exactly that value which would justify continuing the development. The discipline of putting plausible numbers into the above calculation restricts answers to a believable range. Then, as the company goes through the new product development sequence, increasing investments in field measurements narrows the uncertainty in the final sales.

Models for Synthesis. Another useful type of model provides a structure for assembling measurements and phenomena from a variety of sources to solve a given problem. An example is the marketing-mix model BRANDAID (Little, 1975). BRANDAID, when appropriately calibrated for a product of interest, relates brand sales and profit to major marketing control variables, competitive actions, and environmental influences. The structure is modular so that marketing effects can be added or deleted to suit the application. Each effect is a submodel which can be designed separately. Major control variables such as price, promotion, and advertising are premodeled, but custom versions can be substituted if desired. The number of geographic regions and competitors is flexible, from one to whatever patience will permit.

Model calibration makes the general structure specific to a particular application. Historical data, field experiments, econometric analysis, and whatever else may prove useful are used to develop values for model parameters so that the model becomes a suitable representation of a given market.

Usually a few key variables account for most of the effects on sales. Exhibits 6 and 7 show an application employing four submodels. The submodel outputs are plotted in Exhibit 6. These outputs multiply to-

gether to give the three-year retrospective tracking shown in Exhibit 7. Such a model is useful for brand planning and sometimes even more useful for generating an anticipated sales rate. This becomes a standard to be compared with actual sales. Discrepancies trigger diagnosis and feedback to management.

New Phenomena.   It is always exciting to discover a new phenomenon and build a model of it. This does not happen often and, because of commercial secrecy, the news sometimes spreads rather slowly. An example that originated a number of years ago, but continues to have ramifications, deals with concentration of retail outlets.

EXHIBIT 6

An application of the marketing-mix model BRANDAID. Historical company actions and environmental conditions fed into four submodels give the outputs shown

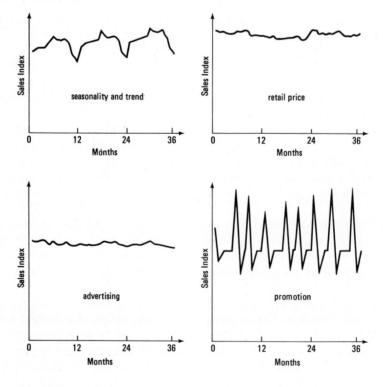

EXHIBIT 7

The BRANDAID submodels are combined to track historical sales

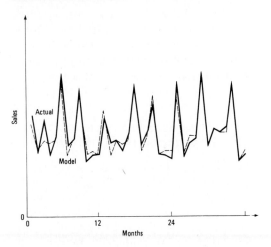

EXHIBIT 8

Surprisingly, as the number of service stations for a brand in a city increases, so does the gallonage per station

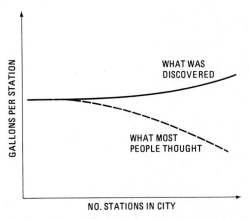

The original work was done on gasoline service stations. All the oil companies are familiar with it, but, as with many scientific phenomena, the principle is more general. In this case, it carries over into other franchise operations (e.g., branch banks and fast food outlets), and in these industries the idea is just beginning to take hold.

The phenomenon deals with competition between outlets in a given city. I recall sitting in the office of a marketing economist from a major oil company and discussing service station site location.

He said, "One thing you have to be careful about is putting two of our stations close together or putting too many stations in the same market. First of all, the dealers will scream, but, in addition, you start running into self-competition. If the company puts new stations in a market where it already has many, it is taking business away from itself."

This point of view is represented in Exhibit 8 by the curve marked "What people thought" and shows gallonage per sta-

tion decreasing with number of outlets in a city.

What Hartung and Fisher (1965) and later Naert and Bultez (1975) did was to collect data, analyze it, and build a theory. After filtering out a variety of variables that confused the situation, they found that the curve actually goes *up*. In other words, up to a certain point, stations actually reinforce each other; the more stations the company has, the greater the gallonage *per station*.

To me this is quite surprising, although, once a fact is known, it is easy to offer explanations. For example, stations are outdoor advertisements for the company; the more stations, the more people become aware of the brand. In addition, media advertising which is hardly worthwhile for one or two stations in a market becomes economical if there are many. Credit cards become more useful to a customer if the brand has many stations and therefore will enhance total brand sales in the market. Everything makes sense—once you know the answer.

Exhibit 9 sketches the station reinforce-

EXHIBIT 9

The resulting S-shaped relation between share of market and share of stations leads to strong regional brands

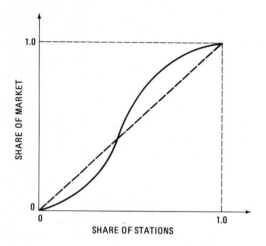

ment phenomenon as a plot of market share versus station share. If the effect did not exist, we would expect the diagonal straight line. With the effect, the company does worse than the straight line at low station share, then with increasing station share crosses over the diagonal, and finally bends over to unity as diminishing returns set in.

The strategy implications of the relationship are dramatic and quite opposite to the actions most oil companies were taking at the time. The curve tells a company to add stations where it is already strong, at least up to quite a high level, whereas most companies were trying to reach out geographically as fast as possible to become national companies with the widest possible markets. As we now see, this was not the best way to gain the most new business with new investment dollars. (Notice, incidentally, that the oil industry is characterized by strong regional marketers, a piece of empirical support for the underlying phenomenon.)

Later Lilien and Rao (1976) imbedded the reinforcement model into a financial model that takes into account laydown costs, competitive pricing conditions, building costs, total budget, etc. This provided marketing management with a tool to allocate service station investment dollars to maximize long-run return, thereby reaping the productivity of the basic discovery.

MDSS IN PRACTICE: THE BOTTOM LINE IS ON TOP

The best marketing decision support system I know of grew up over several years in the major division of a large package goods company. Although the first big data base came on stream in mid-1972, the system is still evolving. It has become an integral part of marketing operations and has materially affected management style in several ways.

A management science group of two or three professionals and a similar number of clerical and long-time company people run the activity. Their online data base contains internal company sales, records of marketing activities (e.g., advertising and promotion), and a sizeable block of syndicated data (e.g., panel and store audit information). As a rough estimate, 10^6 numbers are online and more can be available with a few days notice.

The system software is a high level, analytic language which offers not only data base management, but powerful manipulative and statistical capabilities. Gradually, many small and large analytic routines and models have been written and incorporated into the system. The computer is in constant use; one or two people are logged in virtually all the time and overnight batch runs ordered online during the day are common.

The bread and butter business of the MDSS consists of responding to a remarkable variety of small requests from brand managers and higher levels or marketing management. Rarely does raw data retrieval provide the answer. Almost always, data are manipulated and presented in a special way because of some issue at hand. Service is sufficiently good with such fast turn-around on short requests that, at one point, barriers had to be raised to reduce requests and maintain quality control on jobs performed. An important block of time goes into data base maintenance and updating.

Changes in Management Style

Two significant changes in marketing management style can be traced to the MDSS. Tendencies toward each had existed previously, but the MDSS permits them to emerge in a practical way.

The first is the growth of a "try and see" approach to new marketing programs. The marketing managers in the company are activists who want to introduce new ideas, but also want to know whether they really work. A miniexperiment program has evolved. The management science group has identified a bank of market areas appropriate for tests. The annual marketing plan includes a set of tests for the coming year. Extra tests can be put in the field quickly. Typical projects are new promotion ideas, packages, product line extensions, and changes in advertising media strategy, copy, or weight. The management science group has developed analytic routines for reading the results quickly and efficiently. The detail, flexibility, and rapid turnaround of the MDSS along with the experience and skill of professional people make the operation possible.

The miniexperiment program is the invention of marketing management, not management scientists. This has important consequences. In the first place, the tests are

sometimes not very precise. They are often done in single markets and, as any statistician will point out, it is difficult to estimate a standard error from one observation. Nevertheless, the program prospers. Although an individual test may be statistically weak, the whole collection screens a considerable number of new ideas. Real winners stand out. Run-of-the-mill improvements are hard to read but correspondingly less important. As has been shown by Gross (1972) in the case of advertising copy testing, significant gains accrue to creating multiple ideas and screening them, even if the precision is limited. It is doubtful that the management science department would ever have proposed the program on its own. The technical people would have proposed careful multiple market experiments that were more statistically defensible, but then costs would have prevented a really extensive program. As it is, marketing management, having invented the idea, is willing to absorb the uncertainties of the results.

Larger scale, multiple market experiments also are conducted. In fact, a carefully designed advertising weights test analyzed within the MDSS recently led to a major shift in advertising spending strategy.

The second managerial style change is a shift toward regional marketing. Anyone can think up regional strategies, but it is another matter to maintain management control over them and do follow-up evaluations. These are necessary to determine successes and failures and to adjust strategies to changing conditions. The MDSS has been critical in making this possible.

Market Response Reporting

Conventional reviews of brand and company performance stress *status* reporting, i.e., how things are. For example, what are sales, share, price, promotion, and advertising expenditures and what are their trends? Status reporting is characteristic both of standard market monitoring systems like SAMI and Nielsen and of internal company reporting.

A more action-oriented performance review is becoming possible with the evolution of MDSSs. This is market *response* reporting, i.e., how effective marketing actions are. For example, what is price elasticity, how do sales respond to promotion, and what effect will increased advertising have on sales?

The markets of this company have witnessed important competitive changes over the past few years. The historical events captured in company and syndicated data permit extensive analysis of various marketing tactics. Analytic methods have evolved not overnight, but over several years to permit estimates of market response to major changes in marketing actions. These response estimates are the subject of ongoing reviews similar to those conventionally made with static indicators and offer marketing management new and sharper information for decision making.

The market response information also permits projection of future performance by means of marketing-mix models. While this is done for certain purposes, a more important role of models has been in the historical analysis itself. A credible model of the effects of all major marketing variables is essential to performing the market response analysis.

Costs/Benefits

The cost of the MDSS in this company is large in dollars: several hundreds of thousands. As a fraction of sales, however, the cost of the system, the data, and the people who run it is small, perhaps 0.1%. This seems modest considering that marketing budgets run about 5% of sales and, more important, the decisions being affected influence sales and profit by much more. The cost of the system and its operation splits roughly equally among data, people, and computation.

The MDSS did not spring full blown from the marketing vice president's head nor did it evolve without controversy. Its growth has been incremental, moving from the first tentative beginnings and useful initial results, to further extensions, more results, and so on. This has brought certain inefficiencies ("If we'd known then, what we know now . . ."), but the idea of "best" at each evolutionary stage changes considerably by the time of the next one so that a flexible approach pays off.

The MDSS has used outside time-sharing services copiously and so has been a constant target for an inhouse data processing takeover. Yet the power, flexibility, and responsiveness of languages available on external time-sharing has not been duplicated inhouse. Marketing management has insisted on high and increasing levels of service which have only been available externally.

Some pay-offs have been explicit. An analysis of promotion led to a strategy change with a profit increase in seven figures. Such incidents are obviously helpful and may well be essential for survival. However, my own feeling is that the largest benefits have come simply by facilitating good management. Bold changes of direction in a company are infrequent (which is probably good). For the most part management deals with a series of adjustments to conditions, no one adjustment being particularly spectacular nor uniquely traceable to any specific piece of data or analysis. Yet the collection of analyses adds up to influence, decision, and improved profit.

Another usually unrecognized role is assistance in preventing disasters. The pressure for improvement in a company turns up fascinating proposals, some of which are bound to be bad. Analyses that lead to recommendations for inaction are not very exciting, but are sometimes more valuable than calls for revolution.

In summary, this particular company has developed an effective MDSS over a multiyear period. The process has been evolutionary with high costs, but higher benefits. Marketing management has become more innovative as it receives more and better feedback from "try and see" operations. The system has encouraged a shift from market status reporting to market response reporting. However, the main point to be made is that effective MDSSs are not "pie in the sky." They are here now.

PROBLEM-SOLVING WITH INTERACTIVE SYSTEMS: THE GREY FLANNEL ROBOT

In the early days of time-shared computers, many people realized that a marvelous invention was at hand. A person could have convenient access to huge computers from any place with a telephone. Without too much difficulty, a computer could interrogate the user in a semblance of natural language, using words and phrases to ask for input and deliver output.

What People Thought

Clearly time-sharing was a breakthrough and the imaginations of the visionaries were stimulated. A new world was forecast in which managers would sit at terminals and formulate their problems. With the help of easy-to-use commands, they would put key assumptions and judgments into the computer. These would be incorporated into models relevant to the issues to be examined. The managers would ask "what if" questions and evaluate various strategies. New ones would be stimulated by the analysis. Finally the managers would select their best alternatives and go off to take action.

What People Found

Managers do not like terminals. They are impatient and busy. They do not formulate problems in model terms because that is not the way they naturally think. They want to think about strategy, not analysis. They will propose actions to be analyzed, but they do not want to do it themselves.

Anecdotes to illustrate these points are many. I recall one excruciating incident in the early days of online models when the president of a very large corporation was invited to use the new toy hands-on. Unfortunately, he couldn't type—not even with a tolerable hunt and peck. The situation became embarrassing. Vice presidents fluttered about. Finally a data processing manager took over the keyboard. More fundamentally, however, managers do not go online because of their function and style. As Mintzberg (1973) has observed, the manager leads a high pressure, communications-intensive life which is much more try-and-see than think-and-analyze.

The notion of the hands-on manager is not dead, however. I have rather recently been told that a large computer manufacturer has sold an elaborate information system that will put video terminals on the desks of 10 bank vice presidents for constant use in running their departments. I am not optimistic about the ultimate level of use. We shall find an occasional top executive who is an avid hands-on analyst, but I feel quite confident the majority will not be for some time to come.

A New Role

All is not lost, however. Interactive systems are definitely the way to go. We need only recognize that managers work through human organizations in this as in most things they do. What we find happening is that individuals are emerging who can be described as *marketing science intermediaries*. They are typically OR/MS professionals or recent MBAs with good technical skills. They are first and foremost problem-solvers. They convert managers' questions into models and analyses. They enter into dialogue with managers and others in the organization about what the problems really are. They provide answers to managers' questions and respond to the new questions that the answers provoke. They build portfolios of data bases, models, and systems to solve recurring problems. They do the homework managers lack the time to do. They want the manager's jobs in a few years. For the present they are the organizers and internal consultants who build knowledge and systems to support marketing operations.

Typically, marketing science intermediaries program and use models and systems personally, or with small staffs. However, they are not computer scientists and do not report to MIS. What makes their role possible are powerful new computer languages available on time-sharing.

Hardware and Software: Ready-to-Wear

Computers are impossible to work with, but are getting better. Advances in hardware and software are pushing the evolution of decision support systems. Hardware manufacturing costs are dropping and prices are following at a respectful distance. Some people forecast that hardware costs will eventually become negligible. I am not sure

because we are so good at thinking up big new jobs for computers. However, it is fair to predict that hardware cost will become a negligible part of the computations we are doing today. Software, on the other hand, continues to be expensive but has undergone advances in ways particularly relevant to us here.

The philosophy behind contemporary software is to let the computer solve its own problems. Why should users have to go through elaborate contortions to move data from a statistical package to a marketing model to a report generator? They shouldn't. Good software systems can solve these and many other machine problems, leaving the users free to concentrate on the essence of the analysis. High level commands permit easy plotting, tabling, array arithmetic, statistical analysis, optimization, report generation, and model building, all on the same data base.

As a user, I am most appreciative of "default" options. Thus, if SALES is a defined data variable, I can give a command like PLOT SALES and out comes a plot. It fits on a 8½x11 inch page, the curve approximately fills the plot, the axes are labeled, a sensible grid has been selected that has round-number gradations, etc. The computer has finally become a moderately effective clerk. If I want something different from default specifications, I can override them, but most of the time, especially during exploratory work, the automated plot is fine. Furthermore, the same commands will work on a dozen different terminals; it is only necessary to tell the computer which one is being used.

High level analytic languages that embody many of these features are increasing in number and scope. An early one with the emphasis on a concise and powerful mathematical notation is APL. A commercial system with a strong business orientation is

EXPRESS. Somewhat similar are PROBE, TSAM, and XSIM. Some of the systems are easily extendable so that, for example, FORTRAN subroutines can be easily introduced as new commands. Why reinvent the wheel? Features and degree of power vary, but all these languages try to let the analyst work an order of magnitude faster than a FORTRAN programmer on a bare-bones, time-sharing system.

Most of the observations just made about interactive systems extend well beyond the context of marketing (see for example, Keen and Scott Morton, 1978).

IMPLEMENTATION: WHICH WAY IS UP?

Any attempt to install an MDSS has organizational ramifications. Will marketing management's antibodies reject the graft? Will the internal computer establishment gag?

Taking these issues in order, consider Argyris' view (1971) in *Management Science:*

If management information systems achieve their designers' highest aspirations, they will tend to create conditions where executives will experience: (1) reduction of space of free movement, (2) psychological failure and double bind, (3) leadership based more on competence than formal power, (4) decreased feelings of essentiality. These experiences will tend to create genuine resistance to MIS.

Another hand-wringer. I do not agree and will argue otherwise, but first let me give an anecdote to favor Argyris' view. A marketing vice president I know refused to conduct a field experiment which would have sought to measure the effect of advertising on sales. He had various reasons for his position, but I suspect the real reason was that he had negotiated an increased advertising budget with the president.

Therefore, if the experiment should confirm the increased budget, it would be redundant and, if not, he would look bad. So why do the experiment? To use Argyris' words, better information only restricted his space of free movement.

I believe that the executive was wrong and that by such actions his company could lose competitive advantage which would eventually reflect on him. However, this type of managerial reaction certainly exists. A better style, in my opinion, is to view the advertising increase as an opportunity for measurement and further adaptation to the market.

Such examples notwithstanding, my main observation is that it takes a first class marketing manager to bring an MDSS into being in the first place and such people are not about to let their systems run them. On the contrary it gives them a feeling of power to act on moderately reliable information for a change.

Lets check other commentators on the MIS scene. Gruber and Niles (1976) write:

Understanding what managers actually do and . . . organizing the information they currently use is the only way to build relevancy . . . the biggest mistake in . . . current . . . work is that it . . . builds . . . products that serve some assumed decision making process which real managers do not carry out.

I agree in part, but we have gone past this stage. To support their point, I recall a director of marketing who was very impressed with computer technology and decided he wanted instant retrieval. His idea was to have a video terminal on his desk so that, if he wanted to know sales last month in Buffalo, he could press a button and, presto, the data would appear.

We told him, "It's not really retrieval you want but models," and explained why.

He said, "OK, you people are the experts not me."

So we gave him models. It turned out that he wanted retrieval. We went back and gave him retrieval. Actually, what we gave him was retrieval plus analysis plus models, and even more important, he hired a marketing science intermediary. This particular marketing director was not about to push any buttons that did not have people on the other end of the wire.

Gruber and Niles' point about doing better and faster whatever is being done now is a good one and an excellent way to build credibility and support for an MDSS. However, we are well beyond that in many areas and have plenty of examples of new and useful analysis, measurements, and models. A variety of these have been discussed already.

A major issue for an MDSS is its relation to inhouse data processing and management information systems. The first 10 years of business applications of time-sharing have been dominated by external vendors. In this period, fixed costs of time-sharing have been high because of hardware, software, communication equipment, and marketing. Much of the marketing has really been low level applications consulting. The costs and required skills have deterred inhouse time-sharing in many organizations. Furthermore, inhouse data processing typically has had its hands full meeting its current operational commitments. As a result, most activities that look like MDSSs have been done on outside time-sharing. Yet, inhouse data processing departments, which typically live in an environment of repetitive batch jobs, frequently consider the cost of commercial time-sharing to be exorbitant. Marketing management, however, has not found the cost high relative to the value of the tasks performed and has preferred to pay an apparent premium rather than wait for specially programmed batch runs or, in some cases, deal with cumbersome, leanly serviced, inhouse time-sharing systems.

The scene continues to change with two rather different patterns now in evidence. On the one hand, central MIS is in some cases becoming a better time-sharing vendor, bringing in good operating systems and languages. It thus becomes a bigger supplier of computations, but one with less concern about the content of the computation, since the usage is decentralized. In our case, this would be done by a marketing science intermediary working for the marketing department.

Another and perhaps more significant development is the decentralization made possible by the increasing power of minicomputers. Small computers with high level analytic languages can be installed in the functional department and only interconnect with MIS to pick up or deposit data. Costs are moderate and technical support requirements manageable. If these machines and their software prove reasonably robust, the growth of decentralized MDSSs seems very likely.

SUMMARY: WHITHER DECISION SUPPORT?

The main thrust of this paper is to say that marketing management can, and should, obtain better analytic help for its planning and operations. This can be done by a marketing decision support system that puts the new technology of computers and marketing science to work on increasing marketing productivity. An MDSS means hiring people with marketing science skills, It means organizing data bases and putting them in usable form. It means building a portfolio of models and analytic techniques directed at important company issues. It means integrating problem-solving and problem-finding within the marketing function using the marketing science intermediary to facilitate the process. A strong system does not spring up overnight. It takes two or three years of evolution and development, but it can lead to new styles of marketing management.

Let's look ahead. In the next five to 10 years, I foresee:

☐ *An order of magnitude increase in the amount of marketing data used.* Through MDSS development, the internal data of a company will finally become accessible on a rather detailed basis: sales, advertising, promotion, etc. Automatically collected point-of-sale information from the marketplace (e.g., Universal Product Code data from supermarkets) will replace most current store audits. Much better longitudinal data on customers (e.g., panels) will be generally available and will include such currently missing information as media use. The monitoring of competitive advertising, promotion, and price will be vastly improved.

☐ *A similar tenfold increase in computer power available for marketing analysis.* The hardware is already built; it is out there and purchasable. The price is going to break. The only problem will be for marketing to absorb computer power in a useful way.

☐ *Widespread adoption of analytic computer languages.* These make data accessible and greatly facilitate analysis. Some exist now, more will be introduced, and all will improve.

☐ *A shift from market status reporting to market response reporting.* This is an important change. SAMI, Nielsen, and other market monitoring systems, including internal sales reporting, emphasize market status, i.e., how things are: what are sales, share, price, advertising, etc.?

Tomorrow's systems will report response, i.e., how things react: what's price elasticity, advertising response, promotional effectiveness, etc.? Companies will even do a reasonably good job of monitoring competitor's market response.

Much work lies ahead for marketing scientists in order for this to come to pass. We need well-designed data sources and many new tools. How do we handle eclectic data sources in developing and calibrating mod-

els? What are the best underlying models to represent marketing phenomena? We can expect a flowering of new work.

☐ *New methodology for supporting strategy development.* Marketing scientists will further advance our understanding of product-market boundaries. Better response measurements will expose more clearly the nature of competitive interaction and give rise to game theoretic strategy development.

And, finally, I foresee:

☐ *A shortage of marketing scientists.* You know what that means: higher salaries, more fun, exciting new toys. From this I conclude that marketing is the right field to be in.

REFERENCES

Argyris, Chris (1971), "Management Information Systems: The Challenge to Rationality and Emotionality," *Management Science*, 17 (February), B275-292.

Bass, F. M., and D. G. Clarke (1972), "Testing Distributive Lag Models of Advertising Effect," *Journal of Marketing Research*, 9 (August), pp. 298-308.

Bloom, D., and M. J. Stewart (1977), "An Integrated Marketing Planning System," *Proceedings of ESOMAR Conference* (February), pp. 168-86.

Business Week (1973), "Ten Year Experience at General Foods" (August 25), pp. 48-55.

Cox, K. K., J. B. Higginbotham, and J. Burton (1976), "Applications of Focus Group Interviews in Marketing," *Journal of Marketing*, 40 (January), pp. 77-80.

Day, George S. (1977), "Diagnosing the Product Portfolio," *Journal of Marketing*, 41 (April), pp. 29-38.

Ehrenberg, A. S. C. (1972), *Repeat Buying* (New York: American Elsevier).

Gorry, G. Anthony, and Michael S. Scott Morton (1971), "A Framework for Management Information Systems," *Sloan Management Review*, 13 (Fall), pp. 55-70.

Grayson, C. Jackson, Jr. (1973), "Management Science and Business Practice," *Harvard Business Review*, 51 (July-August), pp. 41-48.

Green, Paul E., and Yoram Wind (1975), "New Way to Measure Consumers' Judgments," *Harvard Business Review*, 53 (July-August), pp. 107-17.

Gross, Irwin (1972), "The Creative Aspects of Advertising," *Sloan Management Review*, 14 (Fall), pp. 83-109.

—— (1977), "The Value of 'Value-in-Use,' " unpublished note, (Wilmington, DE: DuPont Company).

Gruber, William H., and John S. Niles (1976), *The New Management* (New York: McGraw-Hill), pp. 138-39.

Hartung, Philip H., and James L. Fisher (1965), "Brand Switching and Mathematical Programming in Market Expansion," *Management Science*, 11 (August), B231-243.

Hauser, John R. (1978), 'Testing the Accuracy, Usefulness, and Significance of Probabilistic Choice Models: An Information Theoretic Approach," *Operations Research*, 26 (May-June), 406-21.

—— and Glen L. Urban (1977), "A Normative Methodology for Modeling Consumer Response in Innovation," *Operations Research*, 25 (July-August), pp. 576-619.

Hess, Sidney W. (1967), "The Use of Models in Marketing Timing Decisions," *Operations Research*, 15 (July-August), pp. 720-37.

von Hippel, Eric (1978), "Successful Industrial Products from Consumer Ideas," *Journal of Marketing*, 42 (January), pp. 39-49.

Keen, Peter G. W., and Michael S. Scott Morton (1978), *Decision Support Systems: An Organizational Perspective* (Reading, MA: Addison-Wesley).

Lilien, Gary L., and Ambar G. Rao (1976), "A Model for Allocating Retail Outlet Building Resources Across Market Areas," *Operations Research*, 24 (January-February), pp. 1-14.

Little, John D. C. (1970), "Models and Managers: The Concept of a Decision Calculus," *Management Science*, 16 (April), B466-485.

—— (1975), "BRANDAID: A Marketing-Mix Model, Parts 1 and 2," *Operations Research*, 23 (July-August), pp. 628-73.

Mintzberg, Henry (1973), *The Nature of Managerial Work* (New York: Harper and Row).

Montgomery, David B., and Glen L. Urban (1969), *Management Science in Marketing* (Englewood Cliffs, NJ: Prentice-Hall, Inc).

Naert, Phillippe A., and Alain V. Bultez (1975), "A Model of Distribution Network Aggregate Performance," *Management Science*, 21 (June), pp. 1102-12.

Nigam, A. K., ed. (1975, 76, 77), Special Issues on Practice, *Interfaces*, 6 (November), 7 (November), 8 (November), Part 2.

Parfitt, J. H., and B. J. K. Collins (1968), "Use of Consumer Panels for Brand-Share Prediction," *Journal of Marketing Research*, 5 (May), pp. 131-45.

Parsons, Leonard J., and Randall L. Schultz (1976), *Marketing Models and Econometric Research* (Amsterdam: North Holland).

Prince, George M. (1972), *The Practice of Creativity* (New York: Macmillan).

Silk, Alvin J., and Glen L. Urban (1978), "Pre-Test Market Evaluation of New Packaged Goods: A Model and Measurement Methodology," *Journal of Marketing Research*, 15 (May), pp. 171-91.

Shocker, A. D., and V. Srinivasan (1977), "Multiattribute Approaches for Concept Evaluation and Generation: A Critical Review," working paper no. 240 (October) (Pittsburgh: Graduate School of Business, University of Pittsburgh).

Urban, Glen L. (1970), "SPRINTER Mod III: A Model for the Analysis of New Frequently Purchased Consumer Products," *Operations Research*, 18 (September-October), pp. 805-54.

13

New Way to Measure
Consumers' Judgments

Paul E. Green
Yoram Wind

*Conjoint measurement can help the marketing manager
determine which of a product's or service's qualities
are most important to the consumer.*

Taking a jet plane for a business appointment in Paris? Which of the two flights described below would you choose?

☐ A B-707 flown by British Airways that will depart within two hours of the time you would like to leave and that is often late in arriving in Paris. The plane will make two intermediate stops, and it is anticipated that it will be 50% full. Flight attendants are "warm and friendly" and you would have a choice of two movies for entertainment.

☐ A B-747 flown by TWA that will depart within four hours of the time you would like to leave and that is almost never late in arriving in Paris. The flight is nonstop, and it is anticipated that the plane will be 90% full. Flight attendants are "cold and curt" and only magazines are provided for entertainment.

Are you looking for replacement tires for your two-year-old car? Suppose you want radial tires and have the following three options to choose from:

☐ Goodyear's, with a tread life of 30,000 miles at a price of $40 per tire; the store is a 10-minute drive from your home.

☐ Firestone's, with a tread life of 50,000 miles at a price of $85 per tire; the store is a 20-minute drive from your home.

☐ Or Sears's, with a tread life of 40,000 miles at a price of $55 per tire; the store is located about 10 minutes from your home.

How would you rank these alternatives in order of preference?

Both of these problems have a common structure that companies and their marketing managers frequently encounter in trying to figure out what a consumer really wants in a product or service. First the characteristics of the alternatives that the consumer must choose from fall along more than a single dimension—they are multiattribute. Second, the consumer must make an overall judgment about the relative value of those characteristics, or attributes; in short, he must order them according to some criterion. But doing this requires complex trade-offs, since it is likely that no alternative is clearly better than another on every dimension of interest.

In recent years, researchers have developed a new measurement technique from the fields of mathematical psychology and psychometrics that can aid the marketing manager in sorting out the relative importance of a product's multidimensional attributes.[1] This technique, called conjoint measurement, starts with the consumer's overall or global judgments about a set of complex alternatives. It then performs the rather remarkable job of decomposing his or her original evaluations into separate and compatible utility scales by which the original global judgments (or others involving new combinations of attributes) can be reconstituted.[2]

Being able to separate overall judgments into psychological components in this manner can provide a manager with valuable information about the relative importance of various attributes of a product. It can also provide information about the value of various levels of a single attribute. (For example, if price is the attribute under consideration, conjoint measurement can give the manager a good idea of how sensitive consumers would be to a price change from a level of, say, 85¢ to one of 75¢ or one of 95¢.) Indeed, some models can even estimate the psychological trade-offs consumers make when they evaluate several attributes together.

The advantages of this type of knowledge to the planning of marketing strategy are significant. The knowledge can be useful in modifying current products or services

and in designing new ones for selected buying publics.

In this article, we first show how conjoint measurement works from a numerical standpoint. We then discuss its application to a variety of marketing problems, and we demonstrate its use in strategic marketing simulations. The Appendix provides a brief description of how other research tools for measuring consumer judgments work, and how they relate to conjoint measurement.

HOW CONJOINT MEASUREMENT WORKS

In order to see how to apply conjoint measurement, suppose a company were interested in marketing a new spot remover for carpets and upholstery. The technical staff has developed a new product that is designed to handle tough, stubborn spots. Management interest centers on five attributes or factors that it expects will influence consumer preference: an applicator-type package design, brand name, price, a *Good Housekeeping* seal of endorsement, and a money-back guarantee.

Three package designs are under consideration and appear in the upper portion of Exhibit 1. There are three brand names under consideration: K2R, Glory, and Bissell. Of the three brand names used in the study, two are competitors' brand names already on the market, whereas one is the company's present brand name choice for its new product. Three alternative prices being considered are $1.19, $1.39, and $1.59. Since there are three alternatives for each of these factors, they are called three-level factors. The *Good Housekeeping* seal and money-back guarantee are two-level factors, since each is either present or not. Consequently, a total of $3 \times 3 \times 3 \times 2 \times 2 = 108$ alternatives would have to be tested if the researcher were to array all possible combinations of the five attributes.

Clearly, the cost of administering a consumer evaluation study of this magnitude—

---

[1]R. Duncan Luce and John W. Tukey, "Simultaneous Conjoint Measurement: A New Type of Fundamental Measurement," *Journal of Mathematical Psychology* (February 1964), p. 1.

[2]The first marketing-oriented paper on conjoint measurement was by Paul E. Green and Vithala R. Rao, "Conjoint Measurement for Quantifying Judgmental Data," *Journal of Marketing Research* (August 1971), p. 355.

EXHIBIT 1

Experimental design for evaluation of a carpet cleaner

Package Designs

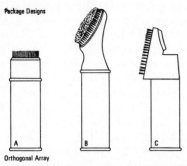

A   B   C

Orthogonal Array

Package design	Brand name	Price	Good Housekeeping seal?	Money-back guarantee?	Respondent's evaluation (rank number)
1	A	K2R	$1.19	No	No	13
2	A	Glory	1.39	No	Yes	11
3	A	Bissell| 1.59	Yes	No	17
4	B	K2R	1.39	Yes	Yes	2
5	B	Glory	1.59	No	No	14
6	B	Bissell| 1.19	No	No	3
7	C	K2R	1.59	No	Yes	12
8	C	Glory	1.19	Yes	No	7
9	C	Bissell| 1.39	No	No	9
10	A	K2R	1.59	Yes	No	18
11	A	Glory	1.19	No	Yes	8
12	A	Bissell| 1.39	No	No	15
13	B	K2R	1.19	No	No	4
14	B	Glory	1.39	Yes	No	6
15	B	Bissell| 1.59	No	Yes	5
16	C	K2R	1.39	No	No	10
17	C	Glory	1.59	No	No	16
18	C	Bissell| 1.19	Yes	Yes	1*

*Highest ranked

not to mention the respondents' confusion and fatigue—would be prohibitive. As an alternative, however, the researcher can take advantage of a special experimental design, called an _orthogonal_ array, in which the test combinations are selected so that the independent contributions of all five factors are balanced.[3] In this way each factor's

[3]A nontechnical discussion of this special class of designs appears in Paul E. Green, "On the Design of Experiments Involving Multiattribute Alternatives," *Journal of Consumer Research* (September 1974), p. 61.

weight is kept separate and is not confused with those of the other factors.

The lower portion of Exhibit 1 shows an orthogonal array that involves only 18 of the 108 possible combinations that the company wishes to test in this case. For the test the researcher makes up 18 cards. On each card appears an artist's sketch of the package design, A, B, or C, and verbal details regarding each of the other four factors: brand name, price, *Good Housekeeping* seal (or not), and money-back guarantee (or not). After describing the new product's functions and special features, he shows the respondents each of the 18 cards (see Exhibit 1 for the master design), and asks them to rank the cards in order of their likelihood of purchase.

The last column of Exhibit 1 shows one respondent's actual ranking of the 18 cards; rank number 1 denotes her highest evaluated concept. Note particularly that only *ranked* data need be obtained and, furthermore, that only 18 (out of 108) combinations are evaluated.

Computing the Utilities

Computation of the utility scales of each attribute, which determine how influential each is in the consumers' evaluations, is carried out by various computer programs.[4] The ranked data of a single respondent (or the composite ranks of a group of respondents) are entered in the program. The computer then searches for a set of scale values for each factor in the experimental design. The scale values for each level of each factor are chosen so that when they are added together the *total* utility of each combination will correspond to the original ranks as closely as possible.

Notice that two problems are involved here. First, as mentioned previously, the experimental design of Exhibit 1 shows only

[4]As an illustration, see Joseph B. Kruskal, "Analysis of Factorial Experiments by Estimating Monotone Transformations of the Data," *Journal of the Royal Statistical Society*, Series B (March 1965), p. 251.

EXHIBIT 2

Results of computer analysis of experimental data of Exhibit 1

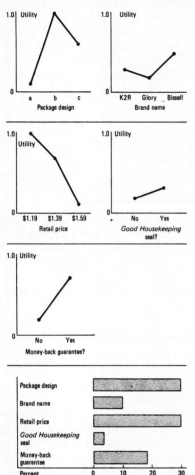

In general, more accurate solutions are obtained as the number of combinations being evaluated increases. Still, in the present case, with only 18 ranking-type judgments, the technique works well. Exhibit 2 shows the computer results.

As can be observed in Exhibit 2, the technique obtains a utility function for each level of each factor. For example, to find the utility for the first combination in Exhibit 1, we can read off the utilities of each factor level in the five charts of Exhibit 2: U (A) = 0.1; U (K2R) = 0.3; U ($1.19) = 1.0; U(No) = 0.2; U (No) = 0.2. Therefore the total utility is 1.8, the sum of the five separate utilities, for the first combination. Note that this combination was ranked only thirteenth by the respondent in Exhibit 1.

On the other hand, the utility of combination 18 is 3.1 (0.6 + 0.5 + 1.0 + 0.3 + 0.7), which is the respondent's highest evaluation of all 18 combinations listed.

However, as can be easily seen from Exhibit 2, if combination 18 is modified to include package Design B (in place of C), its utility is even higher. As a matter of fact, it then represents the highest possible utility, even though this specific combination did not appear among the original 18.

Importance of Attributes

By focusing attention on only the package design, the company's marketing researchers can see from Exhibit 2 that Design B displays highest utility. Moreover, all utility scales are expressed in a common unit (although their zero points are arbitrary). This means that we can compare utility ranges from factor to factor so as to get some idea of their relative importance.

In the case of the spot remover, as shown in Exhibit 2, the utility ranges are:

☐ Package design (1.0 − 0.1 = 0.9)
☐ Brand name (0.5 − 0.2 = 0.3)
☐ Price (1.0 − 0.1 = 0.9)
☐ *Good Housekeeping* seal (0.3 − 0.2 = 0.1)
☐ Money-back guarantee (0.7 − 0.2 = 0.5)

18 of 108 combinations. Second, only rank-order data are supplied to the algorithms. This means that the data themselves do not determine how much more influential one attribute is than another in the consumers' choices. However, despite these limitations, the algorithms are able to find a *numerical* representation of the utilities, thus providing an indication of each factor's relative importance.

How important is each attribute in relation to the others? The lower portion of
Exhibit 2 shows the relative size of the utility
ranges expressed in histogram form. As
noted, package design and price are the
most important factors, and together they
account for about two-thirds of the total
range in utility.

It should be mentioned that the relative
importance of a factor depends on the levels
that are included in the design. For example, had price ranged from $1.19 to a high
of $1.89, its relative importance could easily
exceed that for package design. Still, as a
crude indication of what factors to concentrate on, factor importance calculations
provide a useful by-product of the main
analysis regardless of such limitations.

Managerial Implications

From a marketing management point of
view the critical question is how these
results can be used in the design of a
product/marketing strategy for the spot
remover. Examination of Exhibit 2 suggests
a number of points for discussion:

☐ Excluding brand name, the most desirable
offering would be the one based on package
Design B with a money-back guarantee, a
Good-Housekeeping seal, and a retail price
of $1.19.

☐ The utility of a product with a price of
$1.39 would be 0.3 less than one with a price
of $1.19. A money-back guarantee which
involves an increment of 0.5 in utility
would more than offset the effect of the
higher price.

☐ The use of a *Good Housekeeping* seal of
approval is associated with a minor increase
in utility. Hence including it in the company's product will add little to the attractiveness of the spot remover's overall
offering.

☐ The utility of the three brand names provides the company with a quantitative
measure of the value of its own brand

name as well as the brand names of its
competitors.

Other questions can be answered as well by
comparing various composites made up
from the utilities shown in Exhibit 2.

The Air Carrier Study

What about the two Paris flights you had
to choose between? In that study, the sponsor was primarily interested in how air
travelers evaluated the B-707 versus the
B-747 in transatlantic travel, and whether
relative value differed by length of flight
and type of traveler—business versus vacation travelers. In this study all the respondents had flown across the Atlantic at least
once during the preceding 12 months.

Exhibit 3 shows one of the findings of
the study for air travelers (business and
vacation) flying to Paris. Without delving
into details it is quite apparent that the
utility difference between the B-707 and the
B-747 is very small. Rather, the main factors
are departure time, punctuality of arrival,
number of stops, and the attitudes of flight
attendants.

The importance of type of aircraft did
increase slightly with length of flight and
for business-oriented travelers versus vaca-
tioners. Still, its importance to overall
utility was never greater than 10%. It became abundantly clear that extensive replacement of older aircraft like the B-707
would not result in major shifts in consumer
demand. On the contrary, money might
better be spent on improving the scheduling
aspects of flights and the attitudes and
demeanor of flight personnel.

The air carrier study involved the preparation of some 27 different flight profiles
(only two of which appear at the beginning
of the article). Respondents simply rated
each flight description in terms of its
desirability on a seven-point scale. Only the
order properties of the ratings were used in

EXHIBIT 3
Utility functions for air travelers to Paris

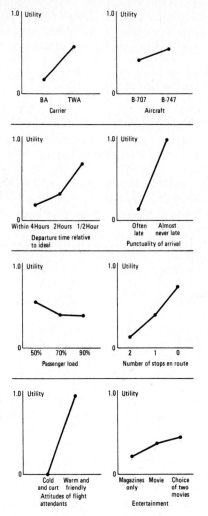

the computer run that resulted in the utility scales appearing in Exhibit 3.

The Replacement Tire Study

The conjoint measurement exercise in the replacement tire study was part of a larger study designed to pre-test several television commercials for the sponsor's brand of steel-belted radial tires. The sponsor was particularly interested in the utility functions of respondents who expressed interest in each of the test commercials.

The respondents considered tread mileage and price as quite important to their choice of tires. On the other hand, brand name did not play an important role (at least for the five brands included in the study). Not surprisingly, the most popular test commercial stressed tread mileage and good value for the money, characteristics of high appeal to this group. What was surprising was that this group represented 70% of the total sample.

This particular study involved the preparation of 25 profiles. Again, the researchers sorted cards into seven ordered categories. The 25 profiles, also constructed according to an orthogonal array, represented only one twenty-fifth of the 625 possible combinations.

POTENTIAL USES OF CONJOINT MEASUREMENT

The three preceding studies only scratch the surface of marketing problems in which conjoint measurement procedures can be used. For example, consumer evaluations can be obtained on:

☐ New product formulations involving changes in the physical or chemical characteristics of the product

☐ Package design, brand name, and promotional copy combinations

☐ Pricing and brand alternatives

☐ Verbalized descriptions of new products or services

☐ Alternative service designs

Moreover, while the three preceding examples emphasized preference or likelihood-of-purchase orderings, any explicit judgmental criterion can be used. For example, alternatives might be ordered by any of these criteria:

☐ Best value for the money
☐ Convenience of use
☐ Suitability for a specified type of consumer or for a specified end use
☐ Ruggedness, distinctiveness, conservativeness, and other "psychological images"

Designing Bar Soaps

In one recent study researchers related the psychological imagery of physical characteristics of actual bars of soap to end-use appropriateness; this study was conducted for the laboratory and marketing personnel of a diversified soap manufacturer.

While the designing of a bar of soap—by varying weight, size, shape, color, fragrance type and intensity, surface feel, and so on—may seem like a mundane exercise, the fact remains that a cleverly positioned bar soap (for example, Irish Spring) can rapidly become a multimillion-dollar enterprise. Still, the extent of knowledge about the importance of such imagery is woefully meager. The researchers formulated actual bars of soap in which color, type of fragrance, and intensity of fragrance were constructed according to a design in which all possible combinations of the experimental factors appeared. All the other characteristics of the soap were held constant.

Respondents examined the soaps and assigned each bar to the end use that they felt best matched its characteristics—moisturizing facial soap, deep-cleaning soap for oily skin, woman's deodorant soap, or man's deodorant soap. The data were then analyzed by conjoint measurement techniques, leading to a set of psychophysical functions for each of the characteristics.

The study showed that type of fragrance was the most important physical variable contributing to end-use appropriateness. Rather surprisingly, the type of fragrance (medicinal) and color (blue) that appeared best suited for a man's deodorant soap were also found to be best for the deep-cleaning soap, even though deep-cleaning soap had been previously classed for marketing purposes as a facial soap. On the other hand, fragrance intensity played a relatively minor role as a consumer cue for distinguishing among different end uses.

In brief, this study illustrated the feasibility of translating changes in various physical variables into changes in psychological variables. Eventually, more detailed knowledge of these psychological transformations could enable a laboratory technician to synthesize color, fragrance, shape, and so forth to obtain soaps that conjure up almost any desired imagery. Moreover, in other product classes—beers, coffees, soft drinks—it appears possible to develop a psychophysics of taste in which such elusive verbal descriptions as "full-bodied" and "robust" are given operational meaning in terms of variations in physical or chemical characteristics.

Verbalized Descriptions of New Concepts

In many product classes, such as automobiles, houses, office machines, and computers, the possible design factors are myriad and expensive to vary physically for evaluation by the buying public. In cases such as these, the researcher usually resorts to verbalized descriptions of the principal factors of interest.

To illustrate, one study conducted among car owners by Rogers National Research, Inc., employed the format shown in Exhibit 4. In this case the researchers were interested in the effects of gas mileage, price, country of manufacture, maximum speed, roominess, and length on consumer preferences for new automobiles. Consumers evaluated factor levels on a two-at-a-time basis, as illustrated in Exhibit 4.

EXHIBIT 4

A two-at-a-time factor evaluation procedure

What is more important to you?

There are times when we have to give up one thing to get something else. And, since different people have different desires and priorities, the automotive industry wants to know what things are most important to you.

We have a scale that will make it possible for you to tell us your preference in certain circumstances — for example, gas mileage vs. speed. Please read the example below which explains how the scale works — and then

tell us the order of your preference by writing in the numbers from 1 to 9 for each of the six questions that follow the example.

Example:
Warranty vs. price of car

Procedure:
Simply write the number 1 in the combination that represents your first choice. In one of the remaining blank squares, write

the number 2 for your second choice, and so on, from 1 to 9.

	Years of warranty		
Price of car	3	2	1
$3,000	1		
$3,200			
$3,400			

	Years of warranty		
Price of car	3	2	1
$3,000	1		
$3,200	2		
$3,400			

	Years of warranty		
Price of car	3	2	1
$3,000	1	3	
$3,200	2		
$3,400			

	Years of warranty		
Price of car	3	2	1
$3,000	1	3	6
$3,200	2	5	8
$3,400	4	7	9

Step 1 (Explanation)
You would rather pay the least ($3,000) and get the most (3 years). Your first choice (1) is in the box as shown.

Step 2
Your second choice is that you would rather pay $3,200 and have a 3-year warranty than pay $3,000 and get a 2-year warranty.

Step 3
Your third choice is that you would rather pay $3,000 and have a 2-year warranty than pay $3,400 and get a 3-year warranty.

Sample:
This shows a sample order of preference for all possible combinations. Of course, your preferences could be different.

For each of the six questions below, please write in the numbers from 1 to 9 to show your order of preference for your next new car.

	Miles per gallon		
Price of car	22	18	14
$3,000			
$3,200			
$3,400			

	Miles per gallon		
Maximum speed	22	18	14
80 mph			
70 mph			
60 mph			

	Miles per gallon		
Length	22	18	14
12 feet			
14 feet			
16 feet			

	Miles per gallon		
Roominess	22	18	14
6 passenger			
5 passenger			
4 passenger			

	Miles per gallon		
Made in	22	18	14
Germany			
U.S.			
Japan			

	Price of car		
Made in	$3,000	$3,200	$3,400
Germany			
U.S.			
Japan			

Market Facts, Inc., employs a similar data collection procedure.[5]

In the Rogers study it was found that consumer evaluations of attributes were

[5]Richard M. Johnson, "Trade-Off Analysis of Consumer Values," *Journal of Marketing Research* (May 1974), p. 121.

highly associated with the type of car currently owned and the type of car desired in the future. Not surprisingly, gas mileage and country of manufacture were highly important factors in respondent evaluations of car profiles. Somewhat surprising, however, was the fact that even large-car owners (and those contemplating the purchase of a large car) were more concerned with gas economy than owners of that type of car had been historically. Thus, while they fully expected to get fewer miles per gallon than they would in compact cars, they felt quite strongly that the car should be economical compared to others in its size class.

Organizations as Consumers

Nor is conjoint measurement's potential limited to consumer applications. Evaluations of supply alternatives by an organizational buyer are similar to benefits sought by the consumer. Thus, one can argue, these evaluations are among the most important inputs to industrial marketing strategy.

As an illustration, the management of a clinical laboratory was concerned with the problem of how to increase its share of laboratory test business. It had a study conducted to assess how physicians subjectively value various characteristics of a clinical laboratory in deciding where to send their tests.

Each physician in the study received 16 profiles of hypothetical laboratory services, each showing a different set of characteristics, such as reliability of test results, pick-up and delivery procedures, convenience of location, price range of services, billing procedures, and turn-around time. Utility functions were developed for each of these factors. On the basis of these results the management of the laboratory decided to change its promotion by emphasizing a number of convenience factors in addition to its previous focus on test reliability.

MARKETING STRATEGY SIMULATIONS

We have described a variety of applications of conjoint measurement, and still others, some in conjunction with the other techniques outlined in the Appendix, could be

mentioned.[6] What has not yet been discussed, and is more important, is the role that utility measurement can play in the design of strategic marketing simulators. This type of application is one of the principal uses of conjoint measurement.

As a case in point, a large-scale study of consumer evaluations of airline services was conducted in which consumer utilities were developed for some 25 different service factors such as on-ground services, in-flight services, decor of cabins and seats, scheduling, routing, and price. Moreover, each utility function was developed on a route (city-pair) and purpose-of-trip basis.

As might be expected, the utility function for each of the various types of airline service differed according to the length and purpose of the flight. However, in addition to obtaining consumers' evaluations of service profiles, the researchers also obtained information concerning their *perceptions* of each airline (that is, for the ones they were familiar with) on each of the service factors for which the consumers were given a choice.

These two major pieces of information provided the principal basis for developing a simulation of airline services over all major traffic routes. The purpose of the simulation was to estimate the effect on market share that a change in the service configuration of the sponsor's services would have, route by route, if competitors did not follow suit. Later, the sponsor used the simulator to examine the effect of assumed retaliatory actions by its competitors. It also was able to use it to see what might happen to market share if the utility functions themselves were to change.

Each new service configuration was evaluated against the base-period configuration. In addition, the simulator showed which competing airlines would lose business and which ones would gain business

[6]Paul E. Green and Yoram Wind, *Multiattribute Decisions in Marketing: A Measurement Approach* (Hinsdale, Ill.: Dryden Press, 1973).

under various changes in perceived service levels. Thus, in addition to single, ad hoc studies, conjoint measurement can be used in the ongoing monitoring (via simulation) of consumer imagery and evaluations over time.

PROSPECTS AND LIMITATIONS

Like any new set of techniques, conjoint measurement's potential is difficult to evaluate at the present stage of development and application. Relatively few companies have experimented with the approach so far. Capability for doing the research is still concentrated in a relatively few consulting firms and companies.

Conjoint measurement faces the same kinds of limitations that confront any type of survey, or laboratory-like, technique. First, while some successes have been reported in using conjoint measurement to predict actual sales and market share, the number of applications is still too small to establish a convincing track record at the present time.

Second, some products or services may involve utility functions and decision rules that are not adequately captured by the models of conjoint measurement. While the current emphasis on additive models (absence of interactions) can be shifted to more complex, interactive models, the number of combinations required to estimate the interactions rapidly mounts. Still, little is known about how good an approximation the simpler models are to the more elaborate ones.

Third, the essence of some products and services may just not be well captured by a decomposition approach that assumes that the researcher can describe an alternative in terms of its component parts. Television personalities, hit records, movies, or even styling aspects of cars may not lend themselves to this type of reductionist approach.

While the limitations of conjoint measurement are not inconsequential, early experience suggests some interesting prospects for measuring consumer trade-offs among various product or service characteristics. Perhaps what is most interesting about the technique is its flexibility in coping with a wide variety of management's understanding of consumers' problems that ultimately hinge on evaluations of complex alternatives that a choice among products presents them with.

APPENDIX:
OTHER TECHNIQUES FOR
QUANTIFYING CONSUMERS' JUDGMENTS

Conjoint measurement is the latest in an increasing family of techniques that psychometricians and others in the behavioral and statistical sciences have developed to measure persons' perceptions and preferences. Conjoint measurement can often be profitably used with one or more of the following:

Factor Analysis. Factor analysis in marketing research has been around since the 1940s. However, like all the techniques to be (briefly) described here, factor analysis did not reach any degree of sophistication or practicality until the advent of the computer made the extensive computations easy to carry out. A typical input to factor analysis consists of respondents' subjective ratings of brands or services on each of a set of attributes *provided by the researcher*. For example, a sample of computer systems personnel were asked to rate various computer manufacturers' equipment and services on each of the 15 attributes shown in Exhibit 5.

The objective of factor analysis is to examine the commonality across the various rating scales and find a geometric representation, or picture, of the objects (computers), as well as the attributes used in the rating task. As noted in Exhibit 5, International

EXHIBIT 5

Factor analysis of average respondent ratings of eight computer manufacturers' images on each of 15 attributes

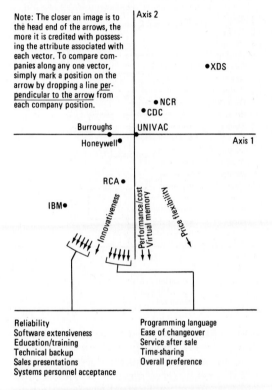

Note: The closer an image is to the head end of the arrows, the more it is credited with possessing the attribute associated with each vector. To compare companies along any one vector, simply mark a position on the arrow by dropping a line perpendicular to the arrow from each company position.

Reliability
Software extensiveness
Education/training
Technical backup
Sales presentations
Systems personnel acceptance

Programming language
Ease of changeover
Service after sale
Time-sharing
Overall preference

Business Machines (IBM) was ranked highest on virtually all attributes while Xerox (XDS), a comparatively new entrant at the time of the study, National Cash Register (NCR), and Central Data Corporation (CDC) were not perceived as highly as the others with regard to the various attributes of interest to computer users.

The tight grouping of the attribute vectors also suggests a strong "halo" effect in favor of IBM. Only in the case of price flexibility does IBM receive less than the highest rating, and even here it is rated a close second. Thus as Exhibit 5 shows, factor analysis enables the researcher to develop a picture of both the things being rated (the manufacturers) and the

attributes along which the ratings take place.

Perceptual Mapping. A somewhat more recent technique—also abetted by the availability of the computer—is perceptual mapping. Perceptual mapping techniques take consumer judgments of *overall* similarity or preference and find literally a picture in which objects that are judged to be similar psychologically plot near each other in geometric space (see Exhibit 6). However, in perceptual mapping the respondent is free to choose *his own* frame of reference rather than to respond to explicitly stated attributes.

EXHIBIT 6

Perceptual mapping of respondents' judgments of the relative similarity of 11 cars and two respondents' preference orderings

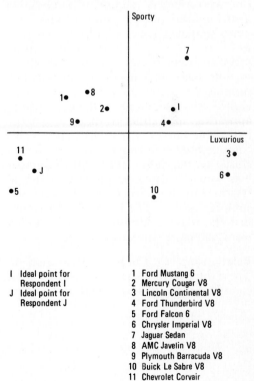

I Ideal point for Respondent I
J Ideal point for Respondent J

1 Ford Mustang 6
2 Mercury Cougar V8
3 Lincoln Continental V8
4 Ford Thunderbird V8
5 Ford Falcon 6
6 Chrysler Imperial V8
7 Jaguar Sedan
8 AMC Javelin V8
9 Plymouth Barracuda V8
10 Buick Le Sabre V8
11 Chevrolet Corvair

The perceptual map of the 11 automobiles shown was developed from consumers' judgments about the relative similarity of the 55 distinct pairs of cars that can be made up from the 11 cars listed. The dimension labels of *luxurious* and *sporty* do *not* come from the technique but rather from further analysis of the map, once it is obtained from the computer. Ideal points I and J are shown for two illustrative respondents and are fitted into the perceptual map from the respondents' preference judgments. Car points near a respondent's ideal point are preferred to those farther away. Thus respondent I most likes Ford Thunderbird, while respondent J most likes Chevrolet Corvair. In practice, data for several hundred respondents might be used to find regions of high density for ideal points.

Cluster Analysis. Still another way to portray consumers' judgments is in terms of a hierarchical tree structure in which the more similar a set of objects is perceived to be, the more quickly the objects group together as one moves from left to right in the tree diagram. Thus the words *body* and *fullness* are perceived to be the two most closely associated of all of the descriptions appearing in Exhibit 7 that characterize hair. Note further that smaller clusters become embedded in larger ones until the last cluster on the right includes all 19 phrases. The words in this example were based on respondents' free associations to a set of 8 stimulus words. The researchers assumed that the more a stimulus evoked another word, the more similar they were.

Relationship to Conjoint Measurement. These three methods are best noted for their complementarities—both with each other

EXHIBIT 7

Hierarchical cluster analysis of 19 phrases evoked in a free association task involving women's hair shampoos

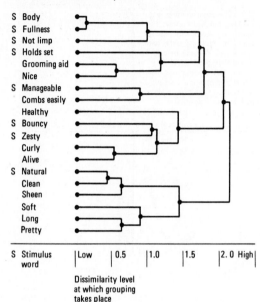

and with conjoint measurement. Factor analysis and perceptual mapping can be used to measure consumers' perceptions of various products or services, while conjoint measurement can be used to quantify how consumers trade off some of one attribute to get more of another. Cluster analysis can be used in a variety of ways, either as a comparison technique for portraying the similarities of various objects or as a basis for grouping people with common perceptions or preferences. In short, all these techniques can—and frequently are—applied in the *same* study. As such, their combined use can heighten different aspects of the same general types of input data.

14 Putting the Four to Work

SM's Big Four, Briefly Described

These are the four statistical issues published annually by Sales Management:

Survey of Selling Costs (SSC)—published in January; covers compensation, training, transportation, lodging, meals, and related selling expenses.
Survey of Industrial Purchasing Power (SIPP)—published in April; lists the number of plants and volume of shipments for counties throughout the U.S.
Survey of Buying Power (SBP)—published in July; contains population, Effective Buying Income, and retail sales data for metro areas, states, counties, and cities.
Survey of Buying Power—Part II (SBP—II)—published in October; details TV, radio, and newspaper markets, as well as metro area projections for the U.S. and Canada.

Frank Phillips is sales manager for Southwest Label, based in Dallas. The company sells office labelling equipment in the East South Central (Alabama, Kentucky, Mississippi, Tennessee) and West South Central (Arkansas, Louisiana, Oklahoma, Texas) areas of the U.S. Most office equipment sales are made in metropolitan areas, which have large concentrations of office workers. Southwest Label also has a line of industrial labelling equipment, sales of which are usually made to large machinery plants.

This year, the company introduced its first consumer product, an indelible labelling system for appliances, home entertainment units, and the like, to help prevent thefts.

Phillips has nine salesmen, each of whom sells the complete line of labelling products. Advertising is done in regional editions of industry magazines, local business publications, and newspapers. Sales for 1974 are running at a $30 million annual rate—$24 million from office equipment, $5 million from industrial products, and $1

EXHIBIT 1

Southwest Label's original sales territory; circles show where salesmen are based

million from the new consumer product, which is being test marketed in the Dallas-Fort Worth metro area.

For 1975, Phillip's top management wants to expand operations into the West North Central states (Iowa, Kansas, Missouri, Nebraska, North Dakota, South Dakota) and roll out the consumer product into the entire marketing area. Phillips's task is to evaluate the effectiveness of his own sales force, map out sales territories for the new region, and plan the ad budget. Fortunately, as a loyal SM reader, he has all four *Surveys* to help him.

His first step is to evaluate the performance of his existing sales personnel. Historically, his company has found that the Effective Buying Income (EBI) total in the *Survey of Buying Power* (*SBP*) is a fairly reliable guide to office equipment expendi-

tures. Therefore, in the company's present market area, its salesmen are based in the nine metro areas with the largest EBIs. (See Exhibit 1.) Salesmen will go into adjoining states to complete coverage of a metro area. For example, his Nashville man, who is responsible for metro Chattanooga, will sell in Catoosa, Dade, and Walker counties in Georgia.

Exhibit 2 is SM's EBI ranking from the *SBP*, with the nine richest metros in Phillips's marketing region marked →. When Phillips maps out territories and chooses sales office sites, it will help you to refer to this table. Phillips will use it in gauging sales potential for office equipment.

Sales quotas are based on each territory's percentage of EBI for all the metro areas in the region, with Phillips making an adjustment to reflect the industrial sales

EXHIBIT 2

SM metro market ranking: Effective Buying Income (EBI)

AREA	($000)	RANK	TERRITORY
New York	50,404,907	1	
Chicago	36,481,890	2	
Los Angeles-Long Beach ...	34,491,000	3	
Detroit	22,982,445	4	
Philadelphia	22,173,291	5	
Washington	17,278,071	6	
San Francisco-Oakland	17,009,766	7	
Boston	15,708,661	8	
Nassau-Suffolk	13,718,426	9	
→ Dallas-Fort Worth	11,575,069	10	Northeast Texas
Newark, N.J.	11,031,027	11	
St. Louis	10,496,828	12	
Pittsburgh	10,364,631	13	
Cleveland	9,880,934	14	
→ Houston	9,775,470	15	Southeast Texas and Western Louisiana
Minneapolis-St. Paul	9,540,701	16	
Baltimore	8,911,795	17	
Atlanta	7,750,040	18	
Anaheim-Santa Ana-Garden Grove	7,725,720	19	
Kansas City	6,675,275	20	
San Diego	6,650,789	21	
Seattle-Everett	6,647,517	22	
Denver-Boulder	6,502,330	23	
Milwaukee	6,373,502	24	
Miami	6,212,590	25	
Cincinnati	6,093,351	26	
San Jose	5,880,009	27	
Buffalo	5,782,384	28	
Indianapolis	5,272,082	29	
Tampa-St. Petersburg	4,962,356	30	
Phoenix	4,859,112	31	
Bridgeport-Stamford-Norwalk-Danbury	4,851,746	32	
Columbus, Ohio	4,698,234	33	
Riverside-San Bernardino-Ontario	4,646,671	34	
Portland, Ore.	4,630,644	35	
Hartford-New Britain-Bristol	4,480,026	36	
Rochester, N.Y.	4,410,467	37	
→ New Orleans	4,389,805	38	Eastern Louisiana and Mississippi
Dayton	4,037,117	39	
→ Louisville	3,950,092	40	Kentucky
Providence-Warwick-Pawtucket	3,704,936	41	
Sacramento	3,664,122	42	
Toledo	3,636,289	43	
Fort Lauderdale-Hollywood.	3,636,100	44	

EXHIBIT 2 (cont.)

AREA	($000)	RANK	TERRITORY
Albany-Schenectady-Troy ..	3,570,118	45	
New Haven-Waterbury- Meriden	3,433,371	46	
⟶ Memphis	3,339,165	47	Metro Memphis and Arkansas
⟶ San Antonio	3,330,554	48	Western Texas
⟶ Oklahoma City	3,193,773	49	Oklahoma
Honolulu	3,120,767	50	
Total Top 50	473,935,966		
Akron	3,110,462	51	
Greensboro-Winston-Salem- High Point	3,104,603	52	
⟶ Birmingham	2,999,829	53	Alabama
⟶ Nashville-Davidson	2,948,710	54	Tennessee, except Memphis
Salt Lake City-Ogden	2,896,053	55	
New Brunswick-Perth Amboy-Sayerville	2,796,291	56	
Gary-Hammond-East Chicago	2,778,878	57	
Allentown-Bethlehem- Easton	2,743,216	58	
Omaha	2,661,393	59	
Worcester-Fitchburg- Leominster	2,660,085	60	
Norfolk-Virginia Beach- Portsmouth	2,657,614	61	
Flint	2,651,349	62	
Syracuse	2,644,060	63	
Jersey City	2,560,883	64	
Charlotte-Gastonia	2,549,900	65	
Springfield-Chicopee- Holyoke	2,498,881	66	
Wilmington, Del.	2,472,765	67	
Richmond	2,441,860	68	
Jacksonville	2,423,403	69	
Youngstown-Warren	2,374,313	70	
Tulsa	2,348,053	71	
Northeast Pennsylvania	2,302,863	72	
Long Beach-Asbury Park ...	2,296,907	73	
Orlando	2,291,454	74	
Grand Rapids	2,285,330	75	
Paterson-Clifton-Passaic	2,184,808	76	
Lansing-East Lansing	2,115,278	77	
West Palm Beach-Boca Raton	2,003,811	78	
Greenville-Spartanburg	1,916,790	79	
Harrisburg	1,909,834	80	
Raleigh-Durham	1,856,081	81	
New Bedford-Fall River- Taunton	1,816,323	82	
Oxnard-Simi Valley-Ventura	1,728,712	83	

EXHIBIT 2 (cont.)

AREA	($000)	RANK	TERRITORY
Wichita	1,678,190	84	
Tucson	1,665,700	85	
Peoria	1,649,484	86	
Tacoma	1,639,845	87	
Des Moines	1,637,580	88	
Fort Wayne	1,637,285	89	
Davenport-Rock Island- Moline	1,632,627	90	
Canton	1,627,230	91	
Knoxville	1,615,706	92	
Trenton	1,595,774	93	
Fresno	1,532,194	94	
Brockton	1,499,556	95	
York	1,488,102	96	

The metro areas marked with an →, the nine largest in EBI in Southwest Label's sales territory, are the areas where the nine salesmen are based.

opportunities in each area. From the *SBP*, he compiles the following total metro EBI:

STATE	METRO EBI ($BIL.)
Alabama	7.7
Arkansas	3.1
Kentucky	6.4
Louisiana	8.8
Mississippi	2.5
Oklahoma	6.1
Tennessee	10.8
Texas	37.7
Total	**82.7**

Clarksville [Tenn.]-Hopkinsville (Ky.) and Texarkana metro EBIs have been deducted from Kentucky and Arkansas, respectively, to avoid double counting.

For example, Kentucky's share of the total is 7.7%, and Phillips had been pleased that his man in Louisville had accounted for 9% of company sales so far in 1974. But last April, when SM introduced its *Survey of Industrial Purchasing Power (SIPP)*, Phillips was given a more accurate gauge of industrial sales potential. From his own sales records, he knows that most of his industrial customers are large plants (100 employees or more) that fall into the SIC 3500 and SIC 3600 categories. From the

SIPP, he finds that such plants in his market area account for $4 billion worth of shipments:

STATE	LARGE MACHINERY PLANTS	SHIPMENTS ($MIL.)
Alabama	8	110.0
Arkansas	8	450.6
Kentucky	16	1,500.3
Louisiana	1	60.3
Mississippi	1	48.6
Oklahoma	26	517.5
Tennessee	8	533.6
Texas	79	787.5
Total	**147**	**4,008.4**

From that calculation, he sees that Kentucky should be his best industrial market, especially Jefferson County (part of metro Louisville), which has $1 billion worth of large machinery plant shipments itself. Exhibit 3 shows those data.

Therefore, his Kentucky man should be bringing in 7.7% of office equipment sales, the percentage of metro EBI in the territory, but 37.4% of industrial sales, especially with such a heavy concentration of key customers close to home. Because office equipment sales represent 80% of corporate sales ($24 million of $30 million), Phillips

EXHIBIT 3

STATE COUNTY SIC	INDUSTRY	NUMBER OF PLANTS		TOTAL SHIPMENTS $MIL.	% OF U.S.	% IN LARGE PLANTS
		TOTAL PLANTS	LARGE PLANTS			
KENTUCKY (cont.)						
Carroll	All mfg	9	6	70.9	.0112	96
Carter	All mfg	5	2	13.5	.0021	80
Casey	All mfg	5	1	5.0	.0008	32
Christian	All mfg	22	10	118.4	.0188	80
Clark	All mfg	14	6	151.9	.0241	93
Clay	All mfg	1		.6	.0001	
Clinton	All mfg	2	2	10.7	.0017	100
Crittenden	All mfg	5	2	25.6	.0041	81
Cumberland	All mfg	1	1	2.9	.0005	100
Daviess	All mfg	36	17	375.2	.0595	91
2085	Dist & blended liquors	3	3	158.0		100
3671	TV rec electron tubes	1	1	42.3		100
Edmonson	All mfg	1	1	9.5	.0015	100
Elliott	All mfg	1	1	1.9	.0003	100
Estill	All mfg	1		1.4	.0002	
Fayette	All mfg	74	23	758.2	.1202	85
3572	Typewriters	1	1	335.1		100
3613	Switchgear & switchbds	1	1	56.0		100
Fleming	All mfg	2	2	13.2	.0021	100
Floyd	All mfg	8	3	16.4	.0026	35
Franklin	All mfg	14	9	187.7	.0298	96
2085	Dist & blended liquors	4	4	151.4		100
Fulton	All mfg	8	3	23.3	.0037	54
Gallatin	All mfg	2		3.3	.0005	
Garrard	All mfg	3	1	6.6	.0010	63
Grant	All mfg	1	1	5.4	.0009	100
Graves	All mfg	11	5	87.8	.0139	93
2311	Men's, boys' suits, coats	3	2	30.8		95
Grayson	All mfg	8	3	18.2	.0029	56
Green	All mfg	9		20.9	.0033	
Greenup	All mfg	5	1	21.4	.0034	32
Hancock	All mfg	7	5	28.2	.0045	83
Hardin	All mfg	13	5	54.5	.0086	83
Harlan	All mfg	8		8.8	.0014	
Harrison	All mfg	14	2	43.6	.0069	25
Hart	All mfg	6	2	8.6	.0014	56
Henderson	All mfg	30	11	62.3	.0099	56
Henry	All mfg	6	2	13.9	.0022	71
Hickman	All mfg	4	1	16.7	.0026	45
Hopkins	All mfg	17	5	33.7	.0053	51
Jackson	All mfg	1		1.0	.0002	
Jefferson	All mfg	404	124	5,022.5	.7965	89
1911	Guns, howitzers, mortar	1	1	53.3		100
2011	Meat packing plants	4	3	353.9		99
2085	Dist & blended liquors	7	5	300.6		96

EXHIBIT 3 (cont.)

STATE COUNTY SIC	INDUSTRY	NUMBER OF PLANTS		TOTAL SHIPMENTS $MIL.	% OF U.S.	% IN LARGE PLANTS
		TOTAL PLANTS	LARGE PLANTS			
2111	Cigarettes	3	3	1,214.8		100
2511	Wood furn not upholst	6	3	17.1		87
2711	Newspapers	3	1	25.0		95
2751	Printing letterpress	12	4	21.9		66
2822	Synthetic rubber	3	3	113.1		100
2851	Paints & varnishes	14	4	58.3		68
3352	Alum rolling & drawing	9	7	84.0		95
3432	Plumbing fittings brass	1	1	40.8		100
3494	Valves & pipe fittings	4	2	61.5		97
3522	Farm mach & equip	3	2	268.3		99
3535	Conveyors	7	3	30.7		72
3564	Blowers & fans	4	2	57.6		94
3585	Refrigeration machinery	2	1	85.3		98
3632	Household refrigerators	1	1	334.0		100
3633	Household laundry eqp	1	1	191.9		100
3639	Household appliances	4	2	85.2		97
3717	Motor vehicles & parts	3	1	210.5		95
Jessamine	All mfg	5	4	50.2	.0080	98
Johnson	All mfg	2		1.0	.0002	
Kenton	All mfg	42	9	90.0	.0143	47
Knox	All mfg	5	2	13.8	.0022	75
Larue	All mfg	2	1	13.3	.0021	18

NOTE: **Total Plants:** 20 or more employees; **Large Plants:** 100 or more employees. **SIC Industry Descriptions:** Space limitations bar use of complete SIC industry name, but sufficient wording is retained to permit easy identification of the four-digit industry.

The Kentucky section of the *Survey of Industrial Purchasing Power* shows Phillips that Jefferson County is an excellent market for him.

makes up a weighted formula, eight parts EBI to two parts plant shipments, to get an overall quota:

$$8 \times 7.7 = 61.6$$
$$2 \times 37.4 = 74.8$$
$$61.6 + 74.8 = 136.4$$
$$136.4 \div 10 = 13.6$$

From that calculation, he sees that his salesman in Louisville should produce 13.6% of corporate sales, not 9%. Phillips makes a note to talk to the man to discuss ways to increase industrial penetration.

Similarly, Phillips goes through the rest of his territory, checking the *SIPP* figures against the *SBP*. He discovers that Dallas-Fort Worth offers greater industrial opportunities than Houston; that explains

why his Dallas salesman is consistently a point or two above the Houston man. He also finds that Alabama, Louisiana, and Mississippi are practically devoid of large machinery plants; so he decides to have his men in New Orleans and Birmingham drop that part of the line to concentrate more on office equipment and possibly consumer product sales.

Finally, he notes that Sebastian County, in Arkansas, has two large machinery plants, with $198.7 million in total shipments. A check with the *SBP* shows that Sebastian County is in the Fort Smith metro area, on the Oklahoma state line. Sales records show that his Oklahoma City man, with 24 large plants in Oklahoma and Tulsa counties to call upon, has a better industrial

EXHIBIT 4

Section III: metro sales costs—selling costs in major markets

METRO AREA	LODGING (DAILY)	MEALS (MEDIAN)	PER DIEM TOTAL	PER DIEM INCREASE 1972–73	PER DIEM INDEX	COST OF TWO DRINKS	AIRPORT TO DOWNTOWN	AUTO RENTAL
Norfolk-Virginia Beach-Portsmouth, Va.	Average $14.50 Range $14.00–$18.00	B—$1.95 L—$3.50 D—$7.80	$27.75	.8%	92	$2.50	Limo: $2.00 Taxi: $5.10 Dist.: 8 mi. Time: 25 min.	$15/day 15¢/mi.
New Orleans, La.	Average $18.50 Range $14.00–$24.50	B—$1.95 L—$3.15 D—$8.40	$32.00	.4%	106	$2.80	Limo: $3.00 Taxi: $7.90 Dist.: 15 mi. Time: 30 min.	$16/day 17¢/mi.
Oklahoma City, Okla.	Average $15.00 Range $14.00–$20.00	B—$1.95 L—$2.80 D—$6.10	$25.85	9.4%	86	No sale by drink permitted	Limo: $2.00 Taxi: $6.20 Dist.: 10 mi. Time: 30 min.	$16/day 17¢/mi.

EXHIBIT 5

U.S. metropolitan area projections

STATE METRO AREA	COUNTY	POPULATION 1973 (THOUS.)	POPULATION 1978 (THOUS.)	% CHANGE 1973–78	1978 HOUSEHOLDS (THOUS.)	% CHANGE 1973–78
ALABAMA						
ANNISTON	Calhoun	102.6	100.3	2.2	34.8	7.7
BIRMINGHAM..................		779.2	782.9	.5	288.5	10.8
	Jefferson	646.9	640.6	–1.0	238.1	9.3
	St. Clair	30.1	32.0	6.3	11.0	17.0
	Shelby	41.2	44.5	8.0	15.2	18.8
	Walker	61.0	65.8	7.9	24.2	19.2
FLORENCE		123.6	129.1	4.4	46.2	15.2
	Colbert	49.4	48.4	–2.0	17.3	8.1
	Lauderdale	74.2	80.7	8.8	28.9	19.9
GADSDEN	Etowah	95.2	95.6	.4	35.7	10.5
HUNTSVILLE		289.6	294.8	1.8	100.2	12.2
	Limestone	46.0	50.6	10.0	17.0	21.4
	Madison	190.5	193.1	1.4	64.6	12.0
	Marshall	53.1	51.1	–3.8	18.6	5.7
MOBILE		391.4	404.1	3.2	136.2	14.0
	Baldwin	63.9	68.5	7.2	24.0	18.2
	Mobile	327.5	335.6	2.5	112.2	13.1
MONTGOMERY		237.7	248.6	4.6	86.3	15.4
	Autauga	25.4	26.1	2.8	8.4	13.5
	Elmore	36.3	39.1	7.7	13.3	18.8
	Montgomery ..	176.0	183.4	4.2	64.6	14.9
TUSCALOOSA ..	Tuscaloosa	123.7	131.7	6.5	43.0	17.2
Metro Totals		2,143.0	2,187.1	2.1	770.9	12.5
State Totals		3,555.1	3,638.3	2.3	1,277.4	12.9

sales record than the Memphis man. So Phillips decides to add the Fort Smith metro, and the two machinery plants, to the Oklahoma City territory.

Phillips also uses the *Survey of Selling Costs (SSC)*, which SM introduced last year, to check how his men are doing on their expenses. In the metro sales costs section, he finds the per diem index numbers for the cities in which his salesmen are based, figuring that's a pretty good barometer of total selling costs. He discovers that the range is from Houston's 107 and New Orleans' 106 down to 92 in Birmingham and Memphis and 86 in Oklahoma City.

Everything seems to be in order, except for the Oklahoma City man, whose expense

accounts rival those coming out of the French Quarter. Almost all his business, Phillips sees from our *Surveys*, as well as the salesman's call reports, is done in Oklahoma City and Tulsa (per diem index: 91); so Phillips makes a note to query him a little more closely about his expenses. (See Exhibit 4.)

Next, Phillips establishes sales quotas for 1975. Instead of arbitrarily assigning a 10% or 15% increase to each man, he consults the Metropolitan Market Projections table in *SBP—II*, paying special attention to the EBI estimates as well as the *SBP*. In his Alabama territory, for example, he looks up the 1973 total EBI for that state's metro areas in the *SBP;* the amount is

EFFECTIVE BUYING INCOME				RETAIL SALES		
1978 EBI ($000)	% of U.S.		1978 AVG. HSLD. EBI	1978 ($000)	% CHANGE 1973–78	1978 BUYING POWER INDEX
	1973	1978				
575,000	.0384	.0398	16,523	382,433	87.4	.0414
5,207,556	.3406	.3607	18,050	3,722,451	91.0	.3719
4,481,994	.2964	.3105	18,824	3,223,002	89.1	.3177
147,587	.0093	.0102	13,417	83,711	97.7	.0107
263,036	.0155	.0182	17,305	123,601	112.6	.0172
314,939	.0194	.0218	13,014	292,137	102.7	.0263
705,941	.0459	.0489	15,280	512,801	92.3	.0528
282,267	.0186	.0196	16,316	218,136	89.6	.0213
423,674	.0273	.0293	14,660	294,665	94.3	.0315
497,515	.0350	.0345	13,936	386,370	77.8	.0385
1,922,654	.1271	.1331	19,188	1,495,707	93.4	.1417
269,161	.0158	.0186	15,833	164,942	112.7	.0193
1,254,467	.0896	.0869	19,419	860,313	75.0	.0888
399,026	.0217	.0276	21,453	470,452	130.2	.0336
1,976,883	.1386	.1370	14,515	1,529,400	77.2	.1548
386,448	.0234	.0268	16,102	240,989	106.3	.0275
1,590,435	.1152	.1102	14,175	1,288,411	72.6	.1273
1,709,719	.1001	.1184	19,811	1,417,344	113.7	.1277
132,250	.0085	.0092	15,744	98,645	95.2	.0102
218,479	.0125	.0151	16,427	100,500	118.9	.0144
1,358,990	.0791	.0941	21,037	1,218,199	114.9	.1031
730,871	.0446	.0506	16,997	498,015	104.7	.0534
→ 13,326,139	.8703	.9230	17,286	9,944,521	92.0	.9822
20,190,779	1.3108	1.3983	15,806	14,498,898	92.9	1.4998

$7.66 billion. Then, from *SBP—II*, he sees that 1978 EBI is projected at $13.33 billion (Exhibit 5).

A little deft calculation puts the expected annual increase in EBI at 14.8%; combining that with reports from the field (new machinery plants coming on-stream, any extraordinary office building development), Phillips comes up with a sales forecast for the Alabama territory for 1975. Using similar methods, he works out sales goals for his other salesmen as well. (The effects of the new consumer product will be factored in later.)

SM's statistical issues are often used to monitor sales force performance. If he uses them like that, however, the sales executive must get his men to make the necessary adjustments, whether it's cutting back on sales expenses or increasing penetration in a particular market.

With that out of the way, Phillips turns to the West North Central states, the area into which Southwest Label is scheduled to expand (Exhibit 6). He starts out by compiling regional totals for EBI and machinery plant shipments from the *SBP* and *SIPP*:

STATE	METRO EBI ($BIL.)	LARGE MACHINERY PLANTS	SHIPMENTS ($MIL.)
Iowa	5.7	32	2,081.0*
Kansas	2.8	4	124.4
Minnesota	11.3	43	1,265.3
Missouri	18.9	28	767.8
Nebraska	3.4	3	296.1
North Dakota	1.0	0	0
South Dakota	.8	0	0
Total	44.0	110	4,534.6

Fargo [D.D.]-Moorehead [Minn.] was excluded from Minnesota to avoid double counting.
*The Iowa total includes Rock Island County, Ill., part of the Davenport-Rock Island-Moline metro area.

Immediately, Phillips notices that North and South Dakota have no large machinery plants listed, and few metropolitan areas. Therefore, he decides that that area will not be profitable enough to support a company salesman; he decides to try to find a manufacturer's rep to work the territory for him on a straight commission basis.

For the rest of the territory, total metro EBI is $42.2 billion, 51% of the comparable figure for the existing original region, which indicates that Phillips can expect it to produce $12 million worth of office equipment sales. But shipments here are larger ($4.5 billion vs. $4 billion), causing him to forecast $6 million worth of industrial sales. Including the new consumer product, a tentative sales figure for the coming year is $20 million in the new region, or two-thirds the volume in the old region. Therefore, Phillips decides he'll need two-thirds as many salesmen, or six men.

The three largest metro areas—St. Louis, Minneapolis-St. Paul, and Kansas City—are logical places for new sales offices. The next two largest—Omaha and Wichita—also fall into place easily. But now Phillips has to decide whether to place the sixth man, who'll cover Iowa, in Davenport or Des Moines. They're virtually equal in EBI ($1.638 billion vs. $1.633 billion); Davenport is on the state's eastern border and Des Moines is in the center.

However, a study of the *SIPP* tells Phillips that the Davenport metro has 13 large machinery plants (including some in Rock Island County, Ill.) that account for $1.2 billion worth of shipments. The three in Des Moines account for only $262 million. The selling costs index in the *SSC* shows no great differences between the two metro areas; so Phillips decides to locate the man in Davenport, to get the most out of his industrial sales effort.

Armed with the *SBP*, *SIPP*, and a map, Phillips sits down to plot sales territories. He wants to make them fairly even in sales potential, yet as compact as possible.

He discovers that his men in St. Louis (metro EBI: $10.5 billion), Minneapolis-St.

EXHIBIT 6

Area into which Southwest Label plans to expand in 1975

Paul ($9.5 billion), and Kansas City ($6.7 billion) each have a sizable sales potential right at home; a check with the *SIPP* confirms that there are industrial buyers in all three areas as well. However, Kansas has only two metro areas, Wichita and Topeka, with a total EBI of $2.8 billion, and Nebraska has Omaha and Lincoln, with $3.4 billion worth of EBI. Both states have a few large machinery plants.

Therefore, Phillips decides to assign the Columbia, Joplin, and Springfield metros in Missouri to his man in Wichita. Travelling distance will not be excessive, and his men in St. Louis and Kansas City will be able to spend more time working on key local customers. Using the same reasoning, he assigns St. Joseph, Mo., and Sioux City and Des Moines, Iowa, to his man in Omaha. True, that cuts down a bit on his Davenport man's territory, but he'll still have the more urbanized eastern half of

Iowa (Cedar Rapids, Dubuque, Iowa City, Waterloo), as well as those large machinery plants we noted earlier.

In addition, Phillips decides to give his Davenport salesman responsibility for Rochester, Minn. He wants his man in the Twin Cities, with the second largest EBI and the heaviest concentration of large machinery plants in the region, to stick close to home. Upstate Minnesota can also go to a manufacturer's rep (Exhibit 7).

With his territories set, Phillips can compute goals for each salesman. As we noted earlier, he expects the West North Central territory to produce $18 million in office equipment and industrial sales next year. Now he must decide how much of that each man should produce.

For example, he learns from the *SBP* that 25% of the total EBI of the region's metro areas is in St. Louis; the *SIPP* tells him that 10% of the shipments from large

EXHIBIT 7

Southwest Label's new region, with sales territories marked off; circles show where salesmen will be based

machinery plants originate there. Using a weighted formula (two parts EBI to one part plant shipments, because he expects industrial sales to be more important in the new region than in the old one), he finds that 20% of the $18 million should come from his man in St. Louis. Similarly, Minneapolis-St. Paul, with 22.5% of metro EBI and 27% of large machinery plant shipments, should account for 24% of the total. He does that for the other salesmen as well.

However, before arriving at a final figure, he checks the metro projections in

SBP—II. There he finds that EBI is expected to grow more rapidly in the Twin Cities than in St. Louis; so he uses those forecasts as a final refinement in arriving at sales goals for the coming year.

Next, he must make up a sales budget for the year. The per diem index numbers in the *SSC*, which range from 111 in Kansas City to 83 in Wichita, tell him that sales costs in the new region will be roughly comparable to the old one, with the men in the three larger metro areas expected to turn in the more exotic expense accounts.

EXHIBIT 8

Automobile standard allowances: 1974 vs. 1973

COST AREA NUMBER	OWNERSHIP PER DAY		OPERATING PER MILE		COST AREA NUMBER	OWNERSHIP PER DAY		OPERATING PER MILE	
	1974	1973	1974	1973		1974	1973	1974	1973
1	$5.13	$5.03	5.8¢	4.9¢	16	$3.66	$3.88	5.6¢	4.8¢
2	4.38	4.22	5.9	5.3	17	3.67	3.72	5.3	4.4
3	4.27	4.13	6.0	5.2	18	3.87	3.81	5.7	5.0
4	4.01	3.95	5.9	5.0	19	4.08	4.02	5.8	5.0
5	4.04	3.97	5.8	5.0	20	3.93	3.86	5.8	4.9
6	3.93	4.04	5.9	5.0	21	4.86	4.70	5.6	4.7
7	3.66	3.83	5.6	4.8	22	4.36	4.35	5.3	4.5
8	3.65	3.59	5.3	4.6	23	3.58	3.52	5.7	4.9
9	4.04	3.93	5.2	4.3	24	3.79	3.51	5.2	4.6
10	3.81	3.75	5.1	4.4	25	4.31	4.24	5.7	4.9
11	3.92	3.88	5.5	4.7	26	3.80	3.97	5.2	4.5
12	3.88	3.77	4.9	4.2	27	5.30	5.10	8.0	6.8
13	4.26	4.19	5.7	4.8	28	5.13	4.93	7.2	6.1
14	3.84	3.80	5.2	4.4	29	4.19	4.13	6.0	5.4
15	4.10	4.03	5.3	4.5					

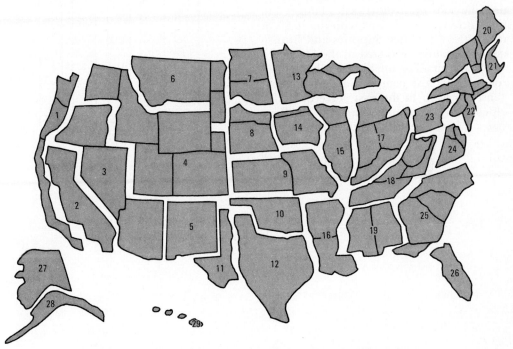

On the above map, areas 8, 9, 13, and 14 apply to the new territory.

That should be somewhat tempered, however, because those salesmen will stay close to home while the Omaha, Wichita, and Davenport men put on the mileage. By using SM's Runzheimer figures in *SSC* (Exhibit 8), he finds that men driving in Missouri, Kansas, and Minnesota will have higher expenses than those in Nebraska and Iowa. Once again, Phillips uses that information and adjusts his mileage allowances accordingly. The auto-leasing table in the *SSC* is another handy tool.

He also finds the *SSC* useful for recruiting. His company has already decided to hire experienced salesmen, but by using the tables on senior salesmen's compensation, he knows how much he'll have to offer to hire good men (Exhibit 9).

Using SM and various corporate figures, he adds up his total sales budget and finds it fairly well in line with the 10.9% of total sales for Office Supplies and Equipment companies, as listed in the *SSC*.

While making up his sales budget, of course, he must compute advertising expenses as well. In the past, advertising for office equipment and industrial labelling systems has been in local publications, in-

cluding newspapers, with spending roughly in proportion to the area's EBI. But this year, he can see by the *SIPP* that Louisville, Davenport, and Minneapolis-St. Paul have industrial sales potential beyond their percentage of EBI; so he decides to step up advertising in those markets, on the theory that it will have a better chance of reaching decision makers at the local large machinery plants.

EXHIBIT 9
Senior salesman

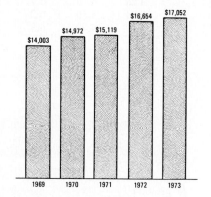

15 Market Segmentation: A Strategic Management Tool

Richard M. Johnson

In the past, marketing research has largely been restricted to tactical questions. However, with the advent of new techniques, marketing research can contribute directly to the development of strategic alternatives to current product marketing plans.

Like motivation research in the late 1950s, market segmentation is receiving much attention in research circles. Although this term evokes the idea of cutting up a market into little pieces, the real role of such research is more basic and potentially more valuable. In this discussion *market segmentation analysis* refers to examination of the structure of a market as perceived by consumers, preferably using a geometric spatial model, and to forecasting the intensity of demand for a potential product positioned anywhere in the space.

The purpose of such a study, as seen by a marketing manager, might be:

1. To learn how the brands or products in a class are perceived with respect to strengths, weaknesses, similarities, etc.

2. To learn about consumers' desires, and how these are satisfied or unsatisfied by the current market.

3. To integrate these findings strategically, determining the greatest opportunities for new

brands or products and how a product or its image should be modified to produce the greatest sales gain.

From the position of a marketing research technician, each of these three goals translates into a separate technical problem:

1. To construct a product space, a geometric representation of consumers' perceptions of products or brands in a category.

2. To obtain a density distribution by positioning consumers' ideal points in the same space.

3. To construct a model which predicts preferences of groups of consumers toward new or modified products.

This discussion will focus on each of these three problems in turn, suggesting solutions now available. Solutions to the first two problems can be illustrated with actual data, although currently solutions for the third problem are more tentative. This will not be an exhaustive catalog of tech-

Reprinted with permission from *Journal of Marketing Reseach*, published by the American Marketing Association, 8 (February 1971), pp. 13–18.

niques, nor is this the only way of structuring the general problem of forecasting consumer demand for new or modified products.

CONSTRUCTING THE PRODUCT SPACE

A spatial representation or map of a product category provides the foundation on which other aspects of the solution are built. Many equally useful techniques are available for constructing product spaces which require different assumptions and possess different properties. The following is a list of useful properties of product spaces which may be used to evaluate alternative techniques

1. *Metric:* distances between products in space should relate to perceived similarity between them.

2. *Identification:* directions in the space should correspond to identified product attributes.

3. *Uniqueness/reliability:* similar procedures applied to similar data should yield similar answers.

4. *Robustness/foolproofness:* procedures should work every time. It should not be necessary to switch techniques or make basic changes in order to cope with each new set of data.

5. *Freedom from improper assumptions:* other things being equal, a procedure that requires fewer assumptions is preferred.

One basic distinction has to do with the kinds of data to be analyzed. Three kinds of data are frequently used.

Similarity/Dissimilarity Data

Here a respondent is not concerned in any obvious way with dimensions or attributes which describe the products judged. He makes global judgments of relative similarity among products, with the theoretical advantage that there is no burden on the researcher to determine in advance the important attributes or dimensions within a product category. Examples of such data might be: (1) to present triples of products and ask which two are most or least similar, (2) to present pairs of products and ask which pair is most similar, or (3) to rank order k-1 products in terms of similarity with the kth.

Preference Data

Preference data can be used to construct a product space, given assumptions relating preference to distances. For instance, a frequent assumption is that an individual has ideal points in the same space and that product preference is related in some systematic way to distances from his ideal points to his perception of products' locations. As with similarity/dissimilarity data, preference data place no burden on the researcher to determine salient product attributes in advance. Examples of preference data which might lead to a product space are: (1) paired comparison data, (2) rank orders of preference, or (3) generalized overall ratings (as on a 1 to 9 scale).

Attribute Data

If the researcher knows in advance important product attributes by which consumers discriminate among products, or with which they form preferences, then he may ask respondents to describe products on scales relating to each attribute. For instance, they may use rating scales describing brands of beer with respect to price vs. quality, heaviness vs. lightness, or smoothness vs. bitterness.

In addition to these three kinds of data, *procedures* can be *metric* or *nonmetric*. Metric procedures make assumptions about the properties of data, as when in computing a mean one assumes that the difference between ratings of values one and two is the same as that between two and three, etc. Nonmetric procedures make fewer assumptions about the nature of the data; these are usually techniques in which the only operations on data are comparisons such as "greater than" or "less than." Nonmetric procedures are typically used with data from rank order or paired comparison methods.

Another issue is whether or not a *single product space* will adequately represent all respondents' perceptions. At the extreme, each respondent might require a unique product space to account for aspects of his perceptions. However, one of the main reasons for product spaces' utility is that they summarize a large amount of information in unusually tangible and compact form. Allowing a totally different product space for each respondent would certainly destroy much of the illustrative value of the result. A compromise would be to recognize that respondents might fall naturally into a relatively small number of subgroups with different product perceptions. In this case, a separate product space could be constructed for each subgroup.

Frequently a single product space is assumed to be adequate to account for important aspects of all respondent's *perceptions*. Differences in *preference* are then taken into account by considering each respondent's ideal product to have a unique location in the common product space, and by recognizing that different respondents may weight dimensions uniquely. This was the approach taken in the examples to follow.

Techniques which have received a great deal of use in constructing product spaces include nonmetric multidimensional scaling [3, 7, 8, 12], factor analysis [11], and multiple discriminant analysis [4]. Factor analysis has been available for this purpose for many years, and multidimensional scaling was discussed as early as 1938 [13]. *Nonmetric* multidimensional scaling, a comparatively recent development, has achieved great popularity because of the invention of ingenious computing methods requiring only the most minimal assumptions regarding the nature of the data. Discriminant analysis requires assumptions about the metric properties of data, but it appears to be particularly robust and foolproof in application.

These techniques produce similar results in most practical applications. The technique of multiple discriminant analysis will be illustrated here.

EXAMPLES OF PRODUCT SPACES

Imagine settling on a number of attributes which together account for all of the important ways in which products in a set are seen to differ from each other. Suppose that each product has been rated on each attribute by several people, although each person has not necessarily described more than one product.

Given such data, multiple discriminant analysis is a powerful technique for constructing a spatial model of the product category. First, it finds the weighted combination of attributes which discriminates most among products, maximizing an F-ratio of between-product to within-product variance. Then second and subsequent weighted combinations are found which discriminate maximally among products, within the constraint that they all be uncorrelated with one another. Having determined as many discriminating dimensions as possible, average scores can be used to plot products on each dimension. Distances between pairs of products in this space reflect the amount of discrimination between them.[1]

Exhibit 1 shows such a space for the Chicago beer market as perceived by members of Market Facts' Consumer Mail Panels in a pilot study, September 1968. Approxi-

[1]McKeon [10] has shown that multiple discriminant analysis produces the same results as classic (metric) multidimensional scaling of Mahalanobis' distances based on the same data.

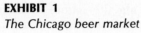

EXHIBIT 1
The Chicago beer market

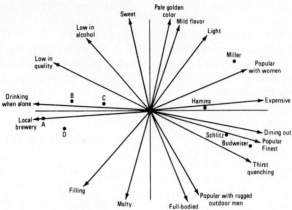

mately 500 male beer drinkers described 8 brands of beer on each of 35 attributes. The data indicated that a third sizable dimension also existed, but the two dimensions pictured here account for approximately 90% of discrimination among images of these 8 products.

The location of each brand is indicated on these two major dimensions. The horizontal dimension contrasts premium quality on the right with popular price on the left. The vertical dimension reflects relative lightness. In addition, the mean rating of each product on each of the attributes is shown by relative position on each attribute vector. For instance, Miller is perceived as being most popular with women, followed by Budweiser, Schlitz, Hamms, and four unnamed, popularly priced beers.

As a second example, the same technique was applied to political data. During the weeks immediately preceding the 1968 presidential election, a questionnaire was sent to 1,000 Consumer Mail Panels households. Respondents were asked to agree or disagree with each of 35 political statements on a four-point scale. Topics were Vietnam, law and order, welfare, and other issues felt to be germane to current politics. Respondents also described two preselected politi-

cal figures, according to their perceptions of each figure's stand on each issue. Discriminant analysis indicated two major dimensions accounting for 86% of the discrimination among 14 political figures.

The liberal vs. conservative dimension is apparent in the data, as shown in Exhibit 2. The remaining dimension apparently reflects perceived favorability of attitude toward government involvement in domestic and international matters. As in the beer space, it is only necessary to erect perpendiculars to each vector to observe each political figure's relative position on each of the 35 issues. Additional details are in [5].

Multiple discriminant analysis is a major competitor of nonmetric multidimensional scaling in constructing product spaces. The principal assumptions which the former requires are that: (1) perceptions be homogeneous across respondents, (2) attribute data be scaled at the interval level (equal intervals on rating scales), (3) attributes be linearly related to one another, and (4) amount of disagreement (error covariance matrix) be the same for each product.

Only the first of these assumptions is required by most nonmetric methods, and some even relax that assumption. However,

EXHIBIT 2

The political space, 1968

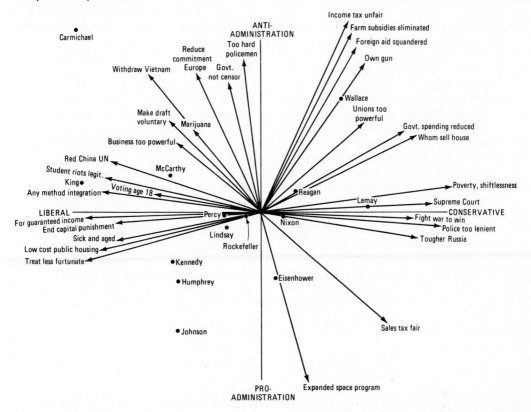

the space provided by multiple discriminant analysis has the following useful properties:

1. Given customary assumptions of multivariate normality, there is a test of significance for distance (dissimilarity) between any two products.

2. Unlike nonmetric procedures, distances estimated among a collection of products do not depend upon whether or not additional products are included in the analysis. Any of the brands of beer or political figures could have been deleted from the examples and the remaining object locations would have had the same relationships to one another and to the attribute vectors.

3. The technique is reliable and well known, and solutions are unique, since the technique cannot be misled by any local optimum.

OBTAINING THE DISTRIBUTION OF CONSUMERS' IDEAL POINTS

After constructing a product space, the next concern is estimating consumer demand for a product located at any particular point. The demand function over such a space is desired and can be approximated by one of several general approaches.

The first is to locate each person's ideal point in the region of the space implied by his rank-ordered preferences. His ideal point would be closest to the product he likes best, second closest to the product he likes second best, etc. There are several procedures which show promise using this approach [2, 3, 7, 8, 12], although difficulties remain in practical execution. This approach has

trouble dealing with individuals who behave in a manner contrary to the basic assumptions of the model, as when one
chooses products first on the far left side of
the space, second on the far right side, and
third in the center. Most individuals giving
rank orders of preference do display such
nonmonotonicity to some extent, understandably producing problems for the application of these techniques.

The second approach involves deducing
the number of ideal points at each region
in space by using data on whether a product has too much or too little of each attribute. This procedure has not yet been fully
explored, but at present seems to be appropriate to the multidimensional case only
when strong assumptions about the shape
of the ideal point distribution are given.

The third approach is to have each person describe his ideal product, with the
same attributes and rating scales as for existing products. If multiple discriminant analysis has been used to obtain a product space,
each person's ideal product can then be in-
serted in the same space.

There are considerable differences between an ideal point location inferred from
a rank order preference and one obtained
directly from an attribute rating. To clarify
matters, consider a single dimension,
heaviness vs. lightness in beer. If a previous
mapping has shown that Brands A, B, C,
and D are equally spaced on this one dimension, and if a respondent ranks his
preferences as B, C, A, and D, then his ideal
must lie closer to B than to A or C and closer
to C than to A. This narrows the feasible
region for his ideal point down to the area
indicated in Exhibit 3. Had he stated a preference for A, with D second, there would be

no logically corresponding position for his
ideal point in the space.

However, suppose these products have
already been given the following scale
positions on a heavy/light dimension:
A = 1.0, B = 2.0, C = 3.0, and D = 4.0. If a respondent unambiguously specifies his ideal
on this scale at 2.25, his ideal can be put
directly on the scale, with no complexities.
Of course, it does not follow *necessarily*
that his stated rank order of preference will
be predictable from the location of his ideal
point.

There is no logical reason why individuals must be clustered into market segments.
Mathematically, one can cope with the case
where hundreds or thousands of individual
ideal points are each located in the space.
However, it is much easier to approximate
such distributions by clustering respondents
into groups. Cluster analysis [6] has been
used with the present data to put individuals into a few groups with relatively similar
product desires (beer) or points of view
(politics).

Exhibit 4 shows an approximation to
the density distribution of consumers' ideal
points in the Chicago beer market, a "poor
man's contour map." Ideal points tended
somewhat to group themselves (circles) into
clusters. It is not implied that all ideal
points lie within the circles, since they are
really distributed to some extent throughout
the entire space. Circle sizes indicate the
relative sizes of clusters, and the center of
each is located at the center of its circle.

EXHIBIT 4

Distribution of ideal points in product space

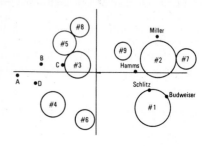

EXHIBIT 3

A one-dimensional product space

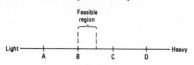

A representation such as this contains much potentially useful marketing information. For instance, if people can be assumed to prefer products closer to their ideal points, there may be a ready market for a new brand on the lower or "heavy" side of the space, approximately neutral in price/quality. Likewise, there may be opportunities for new brands in the upper middle region, decidedly light and neutral in price/quality. Perhaps popularly priced Brand A will have marketing problems, since this brand is closest to no cluster.

Exhibit 5 shows a similar representation for the political space, where circles represent concentrations of voters' points. These are not ideal points, but rather personally held positions on political issues. Clusters on the left side of the space intended to vote mostly for Humphrey and those on the right for Nixon in the 1968 election. Throughout the space, the percentage voting Republican increases generally from left to right.

It may be surprising that the center of the ideal points lies considerably to the right of that of the political figures. One possible explanation is that this study dealt solely with positions on *issues*, so matters of style or personality did not enter the definition of the space. It is entirely possible that members of clusters one and eight, the most liberal, found Nixon's position on issues approximately as attractive as Humphrey's, but they voted for Humphrey on the basis of preference for style, personality, or political party. Likewise, members of cluster two might have voted strongly for Wallace, given his position, but he received only 14% of this cluster's vote. He may have been rejected on the basis of other qualities. The clusters are described in more detail in [5].

A small experiment was undertaken to test the validity of this model. Responses from a class of sociology students in a western state university showed them to be more liberal and more for decreasing govern-

EXHIBIT 5

Voter segment positions relative to political figures

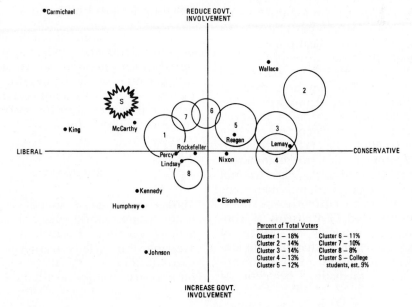

Percent of Total Voters	
Cluster 1 – 18%	Cluster 6 – 11%
Cluster 2 – 14%	Cluster 7 – 10%
Cluster 3 – 14%	Cluster 8 – 8%
Cluster 4 – 13%	Cluster S – College
Cluster 5 – 12%	students, est. 9%

ment involvement internationally than any of the eight voter clusters. Their position is close to McCarthy's, indicated by an "S."

STRATEGIC INTEGRATION OF FINDINGS

Having determined the position of products in a space and seen where consumer ideal points are located, how can such findings be integrated to determine appropriate product strategy? A product's market share should be increased by repositioning: (1) closer to ideal points of sizable segments of the market, (2) farther from other products with which it must compete, and (3) on dimensions weighted heavily in consumers' preferences. Even these broad guidelines provide some basis for marketing strategy. For instance, in Exhibit 4, Brand A is clearly farthest from all clusters and should be repositioned.

In Exhibit 5, Humphrey, Kennedy, and Johnson could have increased their acceptance with this respondent sample by moving upwards and to the right, modifying their perceived position. Presumably, endorsement of any issue in the upper right quadrant or a negative position on any issue in the lower left quadrant of Exhibit 2 would have helped move Humphrey closer to the concentration of voters' ideal points.

Although the broad outlines of marketing strategy are suggested by spaces such as these, it would be desirable to make more precise quantitative forecasts of the effect of modifying a product's position. Unfortunately, the problem of constructing a model to explain product choice behavior based on locations of ideal points and products in a multidimensional space has not yet been completely solved, although some useful approaches are currently available.

As the first step, it is useful to concentrate on the behavior of clusters of respondents rather than that of individuals, especially if clusters are truly homogeneous. Data predicting behavior of groups are much smoother and results for a few groups are far more communicable to marketing management than findings stated in terms of large numbers of individual respondents.

If preference data are available for a collection of products, one can analyze the extent to which respondents' preferences are related to distances in the space. Using regression analysis, one can estimate a set of importance weights for each cluster or, if desired, for each respondent, to be applied to the dimensions of the product space. Weights would be chosen providing the best explanation of cluster or individual respondent preferences in terms of weighted distances between ideal points and each product's perceived location. If clusters, rather than individuals, are used, it may be desirable to first calculate preference scale values or utilities for each cluster [1, 9]. Importance weights can then be obtained using multiple regression to predict these values from distances. If explanations of product preference can be made for *existing products*, which depend only on locations in space, then the same approach should permit *predictions* of preference levels for new or modified products to be positioned at specific locations in the space.

Models of choice behavior clearly deserve more attention. Although the problem of constructing the product space has received much attention, we are denied the full potential of these powerful solutions unless we are able to quantify relationships between distances in such a space and consumer choice behavior.

SUMMARY

Market segmentation studies can produce results which indicate desirable marketing action. Techniques which are presently available can: (1) construct a product space, (2) discover the shape of the distribution of consumers' ideal points throughout such a space, and (3) identify likely opportunities for new or modified products.

In the past, marketing research has often been restricted to *tactical* questions such as package design or pricing levels. However, with the advent of new techniques, marketing research can contribute directly to the development of *strategic* alternatives to current product marketing plans. There remains a need for improved technology, particularly in the development of models for explaining and predicting preferential choice behavior. The general problem has great practical significance, and provides a wealth of opportunity for development of new techniques and models.

REFERENCES

1. BRADLEY, M. E., and R. A. TERRY. "Rank Analysis of Incomplete Block Designs: The Method of Paired Comparisons," *Biometrika*, 39 (1952), pp. 324–45.

2. CARROLL, J. D. "Individual Differences and Multidimensional Scaling," Murray Hill, N.J.: Bell Telephone Laboratories, 1969.

3. GUTTMAN, LOUIS. "A General Nonmetric Technique for Finding the Smallest Space for a Configuration of Points," *Psychometrika*, 33 (December 1968), pp. 469–506.

4. JOHNSON, RICHARD M. "Multiple Discriminant Analysis," unpublished paper, Workshop on Multivariate Methods in Marketing, University of Chicago, 1970.

5. ———. "Political Segmentation," paper presented at Spring Conference on Research Methodology, American Marketing Association, New York, 1969.

6. JOHNSON, STEPHEN C. "Hierarchial Clustering Schemes," *Psychometrika*, 32 (September 1967), pp. 241–54.

7. KRUSKAL, JOSEPH B. "Multidimensional Scaling by Optimizing Goodness of Fit to a Nonmetric Hypothesis," *Psychometrika*, 29 (March 1964), pp. 1–27.

8. ———. "Nonmetric Multidimensional Scaling: A Numerical Method," *Psychometrika*, 29 (June 1964), pp. 115–29.

9. LUCE, R. D. "A Choice Theory Analysis of Similarity Judgments," *Psychometrika*, 26 (September 1961), pp. 325–32.

10. MCKEON, JAMES J. "Canonical Analysis," *Psychometric Monographs*, 13.

11. TUCKER, LEDYARD. "Dimensions of Preference," Research Memorandum RM-60-7, Princeton, N.J.: Educational Testing Service, 1960.

12. YOUNG, F. W. "TORSCA, An IBM Program for Nonmetric Multidimensional Scaling," *Journal of Marketing Research*, 5 (August 1968), pp. 319–21.

13. YOUNG, G., and A. S. HOUSEHOLDER. "Discussion of a Set of Points in Terms of Their Mutual Distances," *Psychometrika*, 3 (March 1938), pp. 19–22.

16

Industrial Market Segmentation

Yoram Wind
Richard Cardozo

The purpose of this paper is to outline theoretically sound segmentation strategies, to explore the current market segmentation practices among manufacturers of industrial goods and services, and finally to contrast theoretically-derived strategies with current practice. It is our hope that understanding and questioning the current industrial segmentation practices in light of an "ideal" model may help identify promising areas for further study and encourage such explorations. The "ideal" model described here has been developed from the literature on market segmentation (which is primarily concerned with consumer markets), combined with pertinent literature on industrial buyer behavior.

The concept of market segmentation is a logical outgrowth of the marketing concept and economic theory, and is at least conceptually as applicable in industrial marketing as it is for the marketing of consumer goods. Daniel Yankelovich (1964) showed examples of the usefulness of segmentation in industrial markets. Knowledge of the size

At the time of writing Yoram Wind was a professor of marketing at the Wharton School, University of Pennsylvania.

Richard N. Cardozo was professor and director of the Center for Experimental Studies in Business in the Graduate School of Business Administration at the University of Minnesota.

and heterogeneity of market segments may be essential to organizing for effective industrial marketing (Ames, 1971).

Recent texts and articles on industrial marketing (Alexander *et al.*, 1967; Rowe and Alexander, 1968; Wilson, 1968; and Dodge, 1970) include, however, no more than brief mention of market segmentation, and only cursory attention to the nature and behavior of the industrial buying decision-making units. Given our initial statement that the concept of segmentation is conceptually a relevant (and even a crucial) ingredient in the design of industrial marketing strategies, the neglect of market segmentation in the industrial marketing literature can be explained if industrial firms do not follow a strategy of market segmentation, or, alternatively, if the introductory statement is wrong.

Our research indicates that industrial marketers by no means use market segmentation strategies as widely of effectively as they might. Segmentation appears to be largely an after-the-fact explanation of why a marketing program did or did not work, rather than a carefully thought-out foundation for marketing programs. Yet two examples which will be described make it clear that market segmentation can indeed be a profitable strategy for industrial marketers.

THE CONCEPT AND IMPORTANCE OF MARKET SEGMENTATION[1]

A market segment is simply a group of present or potential customers with some common characteristic which is relevant in explaining (and predicting) their response to a supplier's marketing stimuli. For example, a market segment may consist of all firms whose annual purchases of steel exceed $5 million, but are less than $10 million. Buyers of noise-muffling equipment may be divided between those whose applications will be visible, in which appearance is important, and those in whose applications appearance is inconsequential. Buyers of many products may usefully be segmented into two groups: repeat buyers and first-time buyers, which differ with respect to the communications strategy which a prospective supplier might employ (Robinson and Faris, 1967).

[1]Portions of this section are drawn from Frank *et al.*, 1972.

As a marketing strategy, market segmentation involves first identifying particular segments, and then developing differentiated marketing programs for each of those segments. These programs may differ with respect to product design, communication or distribution channels used, and advertising and selling messages. To be useful to marketers, segments must be sufficiently large (and profitable) to make such tailoring or marketing programs worthwhile. Segments must also be accessible through specific communication and distribution channels. This accessibility may be, however, either via the media and distribution outlets reaching the segment (controlled strategy), via the message design (self-selection strategy), or in the most desirable case via both the media and message strategies (Frank *et al.*, 1972). Sometimes identification may be very difficult or economically unfeasible, in which case the industrial marketer faces essentially one undifferentiated set of buyers. At the other extreme, each individual customer might conceivably constitute a segment. Unless the customers were few in number and each economically significant, the marketer would face an array of virtually unmanageable variety. The art of employing market segmentation, then, involves appropriate grouping of individual customers into a manageable and efficient (in a cost/benefit sense) number of market segments, for each of which a different marketing strategy is feasible and likely profitable.

Conceptually, the choice of segmentation as a marketing strategy for industrial goods and services is predicated on the same assumption and criteria as segmentation for consumer goods. The only differences, therefore, between consumer and industrial market segmentation involve the specific bases used for segmentation.

EXHIBIT 1

An approach to segmentation of organizational markets

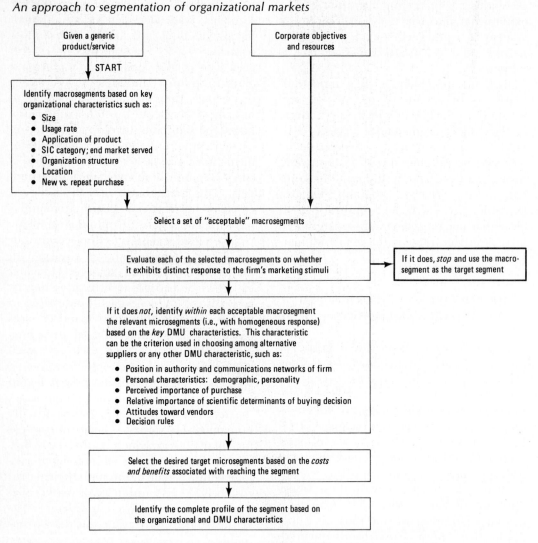

An "Ideal" Segmentation Model. Because some of these bases differ, we propose that industrial markets be segmented in two stages. The first stage involves formation of macrosegments, based on characteristics of the buying organization and the buying situation. The second stage involves dividing those macrosegments into microseg-ments, based on characteristics of decision-making units (DMUs). A flow chart which outlines this approach appears in Exhibit 1.

This hierarchical approach enables an initial screening of organizations and selection of those macrosegments which, on the basis of organizational characteristics, provide potentially attractive market opportunities. Organizations which may have no use for the given product or service can be eliminated. Starting with the grouping of organizations into homogeneous macrosegments also provides a reduction in the total research effort and cost. Instead of examining detailed buying patterns and attempting to identify the characteristics of the decision-making units in each organization individually, such analysis is limited only to those macrosegments which passed the initial screening. Furthermore, since most of the data for the initial screening can be drawn from available secondary sources (e.g., company files) and the screening procedure can be largely programmed, the research phase is relatively cheap and can be standardized as part of the firm's marketing information system.

In this first stage, a marketer may use a variety of bases, singly or in combination, to form macrosegments. Size of buying firm and rate of use of the particular product for which the marketer is planning can provide an estimate of potential sales.

Once the marketer has formed a set of acceptable macrosegments, he may divide each of them into microsegments, or small groups of firms, on the bases of similarities and differences among DMUs within each macrosegment. Information for this second stage of segmentation will come primarily from the sales force, based on salesmen's analyses of situations in particular firms, or from specially-designed market segmentation studies.

DMUs may differ with respect to the composition and position within a firm, and with respect to their decision-making behavior. Composition of the DMU may affect its position in the authority and communications networks of a firm. A DMU composed of relative newcomers to a buying firm, no one of which occupies a top or second-level position in his department, is likely to have little power to press its recommendations on others, and may not be fully integrated into the "informal organization" which may frequently be the network necessary to obtain acceptance of new concepts, products, or procedures. Clearly, such a DMU presents a more difficult task for a marketer with a novel offering than one composed of senior established corporate officials who have close contacts throughout the organization.

DMUs may differ with respect to the importance they attach to the purchase of a particular item; the relative weight they attach to such purchase variables as price, quality, and service; their attitudes toward particular types of vendors; and the specific rules they employ to seek out and evaluate alternative offerings. DMUs which consider a specific product important, require prompt delivery and perhaps technical assistance, wish to deal with well-known vendors and seek a bid first from a supplier with which they have dealt previously, constitute a microsegment of considerable promise to a highly visible supplier with ability to meet delivery and service requirements, who has done business with firms in this micro-segment. Such a supplier would have distinct advantage over a competitor who sought to enter this microsegment with a low-service, low-price product.

The output from this segmentation model should include (1) a key dependent variable on which firms can be assigned to segments, i.e., the *bases* for segmentation, and (2) a set of independent variables which allow a marketer to predict where along the key dependent variable a particular group of potential customers may lie as well as provide greater insight into the key characteristics of the segment, i.e., the *descriptors* of the segment. For example, a key dependent variable might be "criteria used to evaluate alternative suppliers." In one situation, a marketer found that "prompt periodic delivery of lots with less than five percent defects" was the paramount consideration used by some firms in choosing among suppliers for a particular component part. That same component was purchased by other firms almost entirely on a "lowest cost per thousand units" basis. After some investigation, the marketer discovered that three independent variables differentiated these two types of buyers, or segments: (1) size of firm, measured in number of employees; (2) SIC category; and (3) the type of individual most influential in the buying decision. Customers who insisted on adherence to delivery and quality standards were typically large firms in three SIC codes. Within these firms the most powerful member of the DMU was a quality controlman or a purchasing agent with engineering training. In contrast, customers who bought on price were typically smaller firms, in half a dozen SIC codes, only one of which overlapped that of the first type of customer. Principal buying influences in these firms included purchasing agents without technical backgrounds, and production management personnel.

Selection of appropriate dependent variables should be based on the particular marketing problem the manager wishes to solve. In the preceding example, the problem was to reach new customers with a product which they had previously not purchased in appreciable quantities from any vendor. As users' requirements increase, they solicited numerous bids and began to set standards for reviewing those bids. Consequently, knowledge of those standards became the variable of key importance to the marketer. In another situation, knowledge of buyers' "switching rules" was of central importance. The marketer had lost a few

previously loyal customers to competitors, and wished to know why. The key dependent variable of interest to him was "buyers' sensitivity to changes in competitors' offerings." He discovered that some buyers would switch for a price reduction of less than five percent, while others were reluctant to change suppliers until the price differential on this particular product exceeded 20 percent.

The art of market segmentation involves choosing the appropriate bases for segmenting industrial markets. The bases mentioned here have appeared in the marketing literature (Cardozo, 1968; Feldman and Cardozo, 1969; Frank et al., 1972), and are presented as illustrative but by no means exhaustive of the bases which could be used. Because a marketer may choose key segmentation variables from an array of several dozen (or more), research to identify the most appropriate of those variables may be well worthwhile. Furthermore, because customers' needs and competitors' activities are constantly changing, a marketer must review his segmentation strategy periodically.

After identifying appropriate target segments the marketer must analyze the profitability of differentiating his marketing program to reach multiple target segments. A first approximation of this cost/benefit analysis may often be make before detailed segmentation analysis is begun.

Relevant costs typically include those associated with product modification, selling, and advertising. Although costs of making initial modifications of a particular product may be modest, the marketer will incur costs in carrying an additional product or line in inventory, and may incur hidden costs through confusion or misunderstanding on the part of salesmen and distributors. During the last several years many firms have proliferated their product lines to reach customers with highly individualized requirements. Today, many of those same firms look at product deletion (and not only new product introduction) as a source for increased profitability, hence eliminating the highly specialized and unprofitable offshoots of their principal products.

Sometimes an especially intensive selling effort may be required to reach a particular market segment. If this effort transfers salesmen from their routine calls, there will likely be a cost in terms of sales delayed or lost entirely. If headquarters personnel, in addition to field sales staff, are involved, the costs may be much greater. Because these costs typically involve no internal budget transfers and only modest out-of-pocket expenditures, marketing managers frequently overlook them.

The costs of advertising to reach a particular market segment ordinarily include preparation of separate copy and perhaps illustrations, as well as media costs. Because both types of charges may be highly visible, many firms underutilize differentiated advertising as a tool in a marketing segmentation strategy.

The Payoff from Segmentation. Two examples illustrate the potential payoff from following a marketing segmentation strategy. The first example describes a situation in which a fairly simple, single-stage segmentation strategy yielded substantial profits. The second example describes a case in which the second stage of segmentation contributed to a substantial increase in profit.

Single-Stage Segmentation—A marketer of spray painting and finishing equipment who had a new system to offer divided his markets into macrosegments on the bases of SIC category, size of buying firm, and lo-

cation. The marketer developed two distinct strategies: one for large firms in a particular SIC category, all of which were located within four states; another for smaller firms located both in those and in other states. The SIC categories of firms in the second segment overlapped, but were not identical with, those in the first segment. The marketer had observed that decision-making practices for capital equipment differed between the two segments. The large firms were receptive to cost-saving innovations in equipment, tested new equipment extensively, and willingly switched to new equipment which had proved its value in operating tests and benefit-cost analyses. Firms in the second segment were notably resistant to change, and historically had adopted new capital equipment innovations only after large firms—like those in the first segment—had done so.

Accordingly, the marketer concentrated his efforts on the first segment. Field salesmen, supported by headquarters staff, diverted their activities from smaller firms to concentrate almost exclusively on the larger ones. The marketer provided equipment for testing, and set up and helped to supervise test lines in plants of the largest manufacturers. Later, as this effort became successful, the field sales force reapplied its efforts to the smaller firms, without, however, entirely discontinuing contact with the larger ones. These selling efforts to the smaller, more dispersed firms were supported with an advertising campaign which described installations in selected large firms and included endorsements by executives in these firms, but did not include provisions for extensive testing.

Results of this segmentation strategy included penetration of both segments, which had previously been dominated entirely by competitors. Company executives attributed their success to a good product and to following this segmentation strategy, citing instances in which other cost-effective innovations had not been accepted in these markets.

Two-Stage Segmentation—In the preceding example, single-stage segmentation sufficed, because decision-making behavior was correlated closely and positively with size, SIC category, and location. In the following example, decision-making behavior appeared not to be related to size of firm. Consequently, two-stage segmentation was necessary.

A small manufacturer of high quality metal components had traditionally segmented the geographically concentrated market which it served on the bases of SIC category and size of buying firm. The company concentrated its sales and sales support activities more on some SIC categories than on others, and followed a form of "key account" planning, which led to emphasis on customers with large potential volumes. Because sales potentials were frequently not attained, company officials and salesmen attempted to differentiate those customers which gave the company a high proportion of their business from those which gave the company only a small portion of their business. Results from this analysis indicated that the company enjoyed considerable success among customers who purchased its particular type of product simply by telephoning previous suppliers and placing the order with the first one which could meet product and delivery requirements ("satisficers"). The company fared poorly with customers which solicited bids, reviewed them, and finally chose a supplier for this particular type of product ("optimizers").

These differences in "purchasing strategy," which crossed size and SIC categories, suggested a basis for forming micro-

segments within each SIC category. The company directed its sales and support efforts primarily at the first segment ("satisficers"), with which it had historically been more successful, and reduced its frequency of calls and sales support activities toward the second segment ("optimizers"). As a result, the company experienced an increase in profits of more than 20 percent. Company officials attributed the increase almost wholly to the new market segmentation strategy.

These examples support the theoretical arguments for market segmentation strategy. With this initial empirical support for our belief that market segmentation was an economically viable approach for industrial marketers, we undertook an exploratory study to determine the extent to which market segmentation was employed by industrial marketers and the various ways in which segmentation was used.

INDUSTRIAL SEGMENTATION: SOME CURRENT PRACTICES

Data.   To access the extent and nature of industrial market segmentation, we first conducted a series of unstructured interviews with marketing managers of five Philadelphia-based industrial companies. Following these unstructured interviews we conducted structured interviews with marketing managers of 25 companies within the Minneapolis metropolitan area. The reporting units in the final sample included both operating divisions of large, decentralized corporations and independent firms. In sales volume, the size of these reporting units ranged from $3 million to more that $2 billion. More than 25 SIC codes were represented.

The interview schedule included questions about the use of different strategies in selling to different customers; the nature of the differentiated strategy; the bases used to segment one's market; the importance of the various bases for segmentation; and company background data.

Methodology. The unstructured interviews and open ended questions of the structured interview were content analyzed. The structured parts of the questionnaire were then subjected to cross classification and multidimensional scaling analyses. This latter procedure was utilized to illustrate graphically the marketing managers' evaluation of the various bases for segmentation.

Results. The results of this study indicate that industrial marketers do differentiate their marketing programs among customers. But the differentiation appears less a conscious, explicit strategy of market segmentation, and more an explanation or concept applied *after* the fact to explain differences in the success of particular marketing programs. Detailed results are grouped under six research questions.

1. *To what extent is segmentation strategy used by industrial firms?*

All the firms participating in the study indicated that they do use different strategies in selling to different customers. This overwhelming subscription to a policy of differentiation implies acceptance of—or at least lip service to—the concept of market segmentation. Nevertheless, examination of the specific examples given by the respondents suggests that segmentation is used primarily to describe ex-post events, and not as an explicit strategy which provides the foundation for the industrial marketing program.

2. *What is the nature of a segmentation-based industrial marketing strategy?*

Industrial firms which differentiate their marketing offerings, to appeal to and reach different market segments, only rarely try to differentiate all their marketing variables. Nevertheless, more than half of the firms differentiated at least one of their marketing variables. Of the various ways in which a company can vary its marketing strategies to meet the needs of its target markets, elements reported as most important were the product and service mix (72%) followed by price (18%) and only in very few cases by promotion (5%) and distribution (5%).

Most of the respondents modify or adapt their products to meet the requirements of particular customers. Product changes vary considerably and include technical as well as symbolic (e.g., changes from manufacturer to private brand) alterations. Quite frequently a firm's product strategy is supplemented or replaced by service strategy— training, maintenance, warranties, and technical information.

In addition to different products and services most of the firms offered a variety of pricing options to their customers. The reasons for such a policy were primarily volume and specific customer requirements.

The majority of respondents indicated that they emphasize different appeals (product benefits) to different customers. Yet, the examples presented suggest that such differentiation is accomplished "intuitively" by field salesmen, or that differentiation is an after-the-fact explanation of marketing activity, rather than a carefully designed strategy aimed at emphasizing for each segment the appropriate product benefits and usage situations. About 80 percent of the firms used a variety of promotional tactics— especially different media (trade magazines, direct mail, newspapers, general magazines, TV, radio, and displays)—to reach their markets. No evidence exists, however, that the media selection or the message design decisions were based on an explicit analysis and understanding of the target market segments and the nature of the decision-making units.

More than two-thirds of the firms used different channels of distribution in selling to different customers. The selection of the specific channel was based primarily on the nature of the customer (especially government vs. nongovernment clients), the nature of the products (components vs. systems), the geographical location of the buyers, and the availability of particular channels.

3. *What are the bases used to segment industrial markets?*

Organizational "demographics" such as size, SIC category, end use of product, and geographical location were the most frequently used bases for segmentation. End use was generally thought to vary directly with the type of business in which the business firm is engaged.

Other bases used—considerably less frequently—by the responding firms to segment their markets were personal characteristics of the decision-making units, such as the function of the buying unit, and the DMU's degree of source loyalty.

4. *How do industrial marketers evaluate various bases of segmentation?*

Marketers group bases of segmentation into three clusters, which they evaluate on two different sets of criteria. The three clusters of bases for segmentation are (1) organizational characteristics, (2) product characteristics, and (3) DMU characteristics. Organizational characteristics include type of industry, size of firm, and geographic location. Product characteristics include usage rates, end use, and product specifications. DMU characteristics include buyers' job title and personality, and pattern of source loyalty. The three clusters are displayed in a two-dimensional map in Exhibit 2. There were no clear differences in clusters (or in eval-

uation) among the different types of firms represented in our sample.

Marketers used two sets of criteria to evaluate these clusters. The first set included three criteria: (1) cost of identifying segments and differentiating marketing programs, (2) acceptance of bases of segmenting by marketing personnel, and (3) ease of identifying segments and differentiating marketing programs. Of these three, cost was clearly the most important. The other set included one criterion—appropriateness—which respondents construed as a global evaluation, one which had normative futuristic implications.

The two sets of criteria correspond to the two dimensions in Exhibit 2. The vertical dimension can be viewed as the "difficulty of implementing" set of criteria. Given the grouping of the bases into three clusters, within each cluster the vertical spread of the bases reflects their perceived difficulty of implementing. For example, within the cluster of DMU characteristics the buyer's identity is the easiest to identify, the cheapest, and the most acceptable of the three bases. The buyer's personality, on the other hand, is viewed as the most difficult to identify, most expensive, and least acceptable to marketing management.

The horizontal dimension can be interpreted, consistently with the second set of criteria, as the "appropriateness" dimension with the DMU characteristics as the most appropriate followed by organizational characteristics and the product characteristics perceived as the least appropriate.

The two sets of criteria result, therefore, in quite different evaluations of the three clusters. Marketers evidently now use inexpensive and acceptable means of segmentation, which they consider much less appropriate than what they'd like to use. For examples, DMU characteristics are seen as very appropriate, yet are not currently used

EXHIBIT 2

Two-dimensional configuration of nine bases of segmentation

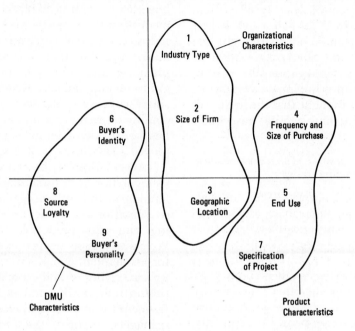

as bases of segmentation. Product characteristics, now used in some circumstances, are considered least appropriate as bases for segmentation. Organizational characteristics appear to be used more widely now than may be appropriate. Respondents' evaluations of the two sets of criteria with respect to their appropriateness and frequency of usage are summarized in Exhibit 3.

5. Which bases for segmentation may be used in the future?

More than 80 percent of the respondents thought that differences of industry type, geographic location, end use of the product, and specification of product (including cost and delivery) would continue to be important determinants of customer requirements

EXHIBIT 3

Evaluation of bases of segmentation

CRITERIA	BASES OF SEGMENTATION		
	ORGANIZATIONAL CHARACTERISTICS	PRODUCT CHARACTERISTICS	DMU CHARACTERISTICS
Set 1: Cost Acceptability Ease	Frequently used	Sometimes used	Not used
Set 2: Appropriateness	Some are appropriate	Least appropriate	Very appropriate

and useful bases for segmentation. About 70 percent indicated source or brand loyalty as important factors, while only 62 percent mentioned the size of the firm. Slightly over 50 percent of the respondents thought that the identity of the buyer (e.g., engineer, purchasing agent) and the buyer's personality would be of some importance, while only 42 percent thought that the frequency and size of purchase would have some importance.

6. *What criteria are used to* evaluate *segmentation-based marketing strategies?*

Sales volume (33%), profits (23%), and market share (11%) are the primary criteria used by marketing managers to evaluate their marketing strategies. Growth (10%), image (5%), length of relationship with customers (5%), ability to meet customers' needs (5%), and cost (8%) were the other criteria used. These measures are not, however, applied separately to each segment. Consequently, marketing segmentation is not employed as a control strategy.

In summary, this study indicates that, while the concept of marketing strategy differentiation is widely accepted among industrial firms, there is little evidence to suggest that firms do follow a conscious segmentation strategy to plan or control their marketing activities. Although marketing managers are aware of the concept of segmentation, they appear not to articulate fully the concept of segmentation or to use the variety of possible bases for segmentation.

CONCLUSIONS

The concept of marketing segmentation has been one of major focuses of consumer research since the early sixties. The concept has had a great impact on the thought and practice of marketing of consumer goods. These developments have had less impact, however, on industrial marketing management. Results from this study indicate that industrial marketers typically fail to employ market segmentation as a foundation for planning and control of marketing programs. At best, industrial marketers use only single-stage segmentation, and by no means employ or even examine some of the other bases of segmentation which might be employed profitably.

Articulation of the concept of market segmentation may by itself provide a basis for more precise marketing planning and for coordination of product development, selling, and sales support activities. A marketer who accepts segmentation as the basis for his marketing strategy will have a basis for conceiving of and estimating potential profits from specific product modifications. Segmenting markets will enable field sales managers to direct their resources more efficiently at particular target firms or groups of firms in their geographic areas. At the same time, sales support materials and activities—including advertising—can be tailored to suit economically viable market segments.

We believe that industrial marketers who do not follow explicit segmentation strategies, planned in advance, either treat all customers alike or treat each customer differently. In the first case, marketers are losing opportunities for profit and laying themselves open to competitive inroads. In the second case, marketers undoubtedly are practicing unprofitable—and uncontrolled—segmentation in many instances. Interestingly, those marketers who permit sales (and sales support) men to treat each customer differently typically believe and state that they treat all customers alike. Those marketers generally lack adequate marketing planning and control techniques, they do not provide their sales force adequate support and typically have not thought about differences among their present and prospective customers.

Research into segmentation, therefore, is an essential precondition for intelligent marketing planning. Such research is feasible, and can readily be integrated with other marketing research projects. Once the marketing plan is fully developed, marketing operations may be controlled on a segment-by-segment basis. Such a control mechanism is more precise than most in use today and may be more responsive in changing environment.

Once segmentation is accepted and articulated as a useful way of looking at markets, marketers can address the discrepancy, revealed in this study, between bases of segmentation which are considered appropriate, but too costly to implement, and those which are inexpensive but not always appropriate. One way to deal with this problem is to identify new, less costly bases of segmentation, perhaps by indentifying particular types of behavior and their correlates. Another way is to develop advertising (media and message) and sales management plans, for example, which fit appropriate segments in particular markets. As a marketer gains experience in devising such policies, cost of differentiating marketing programs should decrease.

REFERENCES

Alexander, Ralph S., Cross, James S., and Hill, Richard M., *Industrial Marketing* (Homewood, Ill.: Richard D. Irwin, 1967).

Ames, Charles B., "Dilemma of Product/Market Management," *Harvard Business Review*, 49 (March-April, 1971), pp. 66–74.

Cardozo, Richard N., "Segmenting the Industrial Market," in R. L. King (ed.), *Marketing and the New Science of Planning* (Chicago: The American Marketing Association, 1968).

Dodge, Robert H., *Industrial Marketing* (New York: McGraw-Hill, 1970).

Feldman, Wallace, and Cardozo, Richard N., "The 'Industrial' Revolution and Models of Buyer Behavior," *Journal of Purchasing*, 5, No. 4 (November 1969).

Frank, Ronald E., Massy, William F., and Wind, Yoram, *Market Segmentation* (Englewood Cliffs, N.J.: Prentice-Hall, 1972).

Robinson, Patrick J., and Faris, Charles W., *Industrial Buying and Creative Marketing* (Boston: Allyn & Bacon, 1967).

Rowe, David, and Alexander, Ivan, *Selling Industrial Products* (London: Hutchinson & Co., 1968).

Webster, Frederick E., Jr., and Wind, Yoram, *Organizational Buying Behavior* (Englewood Cliffs, N.J.: Prentice-Hall, 1972).

Wilson, Aubrey (ed.), *The Marketing of Industrial Products* (London: Hutchinson & Co., 1965).

Yankelovich, Daniel "New Criteria for Market Segmentation," *Harvard Business Review*, 42 (March-April, 1964), pp. 83-90.

IV Developing Marketing Strategies

This part covers various aspects of developing marketing strategy. Marketing strategy sets the direction for the detailed development of the marketing mix programs. Three specific topics covered include the development of the marketing plan, new products development, and various aspects of the product life cycle.

After reading this part, you should have a better understanding of:

1. The value of marketing planning.
2. The process of developing new products.
3. The ways marketing strategy can be adapted to various stages of the product life cycle.

17 Planning Gains in Market Share

C. Davis Fogg

A comprehensive approach to the process and problems of planning share gains.

Gaining market share is a key factor in reaching a leadership or number one position in any industry. It is particularly important to the achievement of a high volume of profits that can be used to expand a firm's business and pay dividends to stockholders, and to the attainment of leadership profit performance as measured by return on sales and return on investment. It is well documented that the higher a firm's market share, the larger its cumulative production of a product, the lower its costs, and the higher its profitability.[1]

However, gaining significant share requires careful planning, thoughtful well-executed market strategies, and specific

[1] See the Boston Consulting Group, *Perspectives on Experience* (Boston, Mass.: Boston Consulting Group, 1968). Additional unpublished work by the Boston Consulting Group concerning the automotive, brewing, aluminum, cosmetics, and mobile home industries, and using public data, conclude that the higher a firm's market share, the higher its profitability, and that the leader in market share in an industry is usually the most profitable.

account-by-account tactical plans. It requires a comprehensive, well-thought-out, and well-planned program. The purpose of this article is to present such a comprehensive program for gaining market share: to examine ways of increasing share, the key steps in planning market share gains, and the pitfalls that must be anticipated in implementing such a program.

WHEN TO PLAN MARKET SHARE GAINS

Typical situations where a business manager should seriously consider a plan to gain market share include: *poor market position*—share must be gained to increase profitability and profit volume; *new products* are being launched head-on against competition; significant *losses in share* have been suffered at the hands of competitors; a *new acquisition* is justified only if sales, profits, and market share can be sig-

Reprinted with permission from *Journal of Marketing*, published by the American Marketing Association, 38 (July 1974), pp. 30–38.

nificantly increased; *competition becomes vulnerable* by virtue of a strike, poor customer service, product shortage, financial difficulties, and the like.

WHEN SHARE GAINS ARE DIFFICULT

It should be noted, based on the author's experience, that gains in market share are particularly difficult under several key circumstances. One such situation would be when a firm has low share, is coming from behind, and is attempting to take share away from the leaders. It's easier to grow with the market than take share away from someone who "owns" it. Secondly, it's more difficult to gain share in a commodity market where there is little or no opportunity for a unique product and significant product differentiation. Finally and obviously, share gains are tougher when there is significant competition—competition with an adequate product offering and good distribution channels and methods.

MEANS OF INCREASING MARKET SHARE

The author has found the following five key strategies to be most important for gaining market share in an industrial market.

1. *Price*—lower prices below competitive levels to take business away from competition among price-conscious customers.

2. *New Products*—introduce product modifications or significant innovations that meet customer needs better and displace existing products or expand the total market by meeting and stimulating new needs.

3. *Service*—offer more rapid delivery than competition to service-conscious customers; improve the type and timeliness of information that customers need from the service organization, information such as items in stock, delivery promise dates, invoice and shipment data, and the like.

4. *Strength and Quality of Marketing*—field a larger, better-trained, higher-quality sales force targeted at customers who are not getting adequate quality or quantity of attention from competition; build a larger or more effective distribution network.

5. *Advertising and Sales Promotion*—increase advertising and sales promotion of superior product, service, or price benefits to underpenetrated or untapped customers; advertise new or improved benefits to all customers.

Competitive price, new products, and service are all tangible benefits that are needed by, and can be evaluated by, customers. The marketing organization is a means of both communicating benefits and facilitating service. Advertising and sales promotion are means of communicating benefits to customers and increasing their awareness of a particular manufacturer's product line.

In addition to the five key strategies for gaining share, there are a number of lesser strategies that may be important in select markets and can be considered. These strategies include improving product quality, expanding engineering assistance offered customers, offering special product testing facilities, broadening the product line to offer a more complete range of products, improving the general corporate image, offering the facilities to build special designs quickly, and establishing inventories dedicated to serving one customer.

There are several key considerations that should be taken into account in using these methods to gain market share. First, one or more of these methods should be used only when significant (to the customer) distinct product, price, or service advantages over specific competitors can be found. The advantage must be sustainable for a sufficient period of time to gain targeted share and significant enough to cause target customers to shift their business from a competitor to the firm attempting the market share gain. If a distinct sustainable advantage cannot be found or if competition is extremely competent, aggressive, and expected to counter any attempt to gain share, then the cost of gaining share may far exceed the benefits. Under the circumstances, a firm should look for another business or product line in which to invest for share gain. Second, gains in market share will not only increase sales and profit volume, but will incur significant costs—the "cost" of decreased gross margins as prices are lowered, the cost of developing new products, the cost of new plant capacity to permit decreased delivery time, and the like.

Finally, the time that it takes to implement each method varies from strategy to strategy. Pricing changes can be quickly implemented. Improving delivery may take six to eighteen months if new plant capacity must be added. Strengthening, upgrading, and training of the sales force may take six to twelve months, and developing and launching a new product may take one or more years depending upon the extent and difficulty of technical innovation required. A plan to gain share may, therefore, involve a number of different moves over a relatively long period of time.

Exhibit 1 summarizes the circumstances under which each strategy can be used, how the strategy is applied in the marketplace, and the detailed cost implications of each strategy.

EXHIBIT 1

Strategies for gaining market share

STRATEGY	WHEN USE	HOW APPLY IN MARKETPLACE	COST IMPLICATIONS
1. Price	To gain share in a product line (a) where there is room for growth; (b) in launching a new product, preferably in a growth market	A. Set general market price level below average ("catch share generally" strategy)	☐ Will lower gross margin by decreasing spread between cost and price for a period of time
		B. Lower prices at specific target customer accounts where reduced prices will capture high volume accounts and where competition is vulnerable on a price basis; lower prices enough to keep the business	☐ Will lower cost as cumulative volume increases and costs move down the experience curve
		C. Lower prices against specific competitors who will not or cannot react effectively	
2. New product	When a new product need (cost or performance) can be uncovered and a new product will (a) displace existing products on a cost or performance basis, or (b) expand the market for a class of product by tapping previously unsatisfied demand	A. Develop and launch the new product, generally	☐ Cost of R&D necessary to develop product
		B. Target specific customers and market segments where the need for the product is strongest and competition most vulnerable, and immediate large gains in share can be obtained	☐ Capital expenditures on plant to manufacture the product
			☐ Start-up operating losses
			☐ Promotion costs of launching the new product

EXHIBIT 1 (cont.)

STRATEGY	WHEN USE	HOW APPLY IN MARKETPLACE	COST IMPLICATIONS
3. Service	To gain share for specific product lines when competitive service levels do not meet customer requirements	A. Improve service generally beyond competitive levels by increasing capacity for specified product lines B. Target specific accounts where improved service will gain share and the need for superior service is high C. Offer additional services required in general or at specific customers— information, engineering advice, etc. D. Expand distribution system by adding more distribution points	☐ Cost of adding capacity and/or bolstering service systems ☐ Cost of expanding the distribution system, including additional inventories required
4. Quality/ strength of marketing	When a market segment or specific customers are getting inadequate sales force coverage (too few calls/month) or inferior quality of coverage (poor salesmen or insufficient information conveyed by salesmen)	A. Add salesmen or sales representatives to improve call frequency above competitive levels in target territories or at target accounts B. Sales training programs to improve existing sales skills, product knowledge, and territorial and customer management abilities C. Sales incentive program with rewards based on share increases at target customers or in target markets or products	☐ Salary and overhead cost of additional salesmen or representatives ☐ Cost of training or retraining ☐ Cost of incentive program
5. Advertising and sales promotion	(a) When a market segment or specific customers are getting inadequate exposure to product, service, or price benefits compared to competition (b) A change in the benefits offered is made and needs to be communicated	A. Select appropriate media to reach target customer groups B. Set level and frequency of exposure of target customers high enough to create adequate awareness of benefits and counter level of competitive efforts	☐ Cost of creative work to create campaign ☐ Production and media costs

THE PROCESS OF PLANNING SHARE INCREASES

There are eight key steps in the process of planning share increases. They are:

1. *Information Collection*—collect critical market and competitive information necessary to establish market share goals and strategies for reaching them.

2. *Competitive Analysis*—define which competitors are vulnerable to specific strategies, why, and what their likely reaction will be to attempts to gain share by different methods.

3. *Product Line Segmentation*—divide current (or proposed) product lines into groups where there is room for: (a) no gain in share; (b) share gain using nonproduct strategies—such as price, service, or strengthened marketing; and (c) new product and product innovations to gain share.

4. *Establish Overall Share-Gain Goals and Strategies* for each product line marketed.

5. *Key Account Analysis*—identify where competition is particularly vulnerable at specific key accounts; establish key account goals and share-gain policies, particularly if they deviate from general policies applied nationally throughout the market.

6. *Cost/Benefit Analysis*—calculate the expected share and profit gains, the costs of achieving these gains; judge whether or not the cost/benefit ratio is satisfactory; repeat steps 1 through 6 until the cost/benefit ratio is acceptable.

7. *Execute the Plan.*

8. *Monitor Results* and modify goals and action, if necessary, to combat competitive reaction or to react effectively to changes in the marketplace.

Exhibit 2 graphically depicts the planning process. The remainder of the article is devoted to methods of obtaining and analyzing information necessary to implement the process of planning share gains.

Information Collection

The two types of information required to properly plan share gains are: "bottom-up" information typically obtained from salesmen, sales representatives, and industrial distributors; and "top-down" information typically obtained by market research and competitive intelligence activities.

Bottom-up research will accomplish three objectives. First, it will establish overall national competitive practices and patterns, including competitive pricing policies, product line strengths and weaknesses, sales force type, strength and quality, strength of distribution, market penetration, and the like. Second, it will define how vulnerable each key competitor is to moves against him and the extent to which share can be taken away for each distinct product line. Third, it will identify key large volume accounts where business is held by competition, and estimate how much business can be taken away from competition by what means.

In a bottom-up survey, salesmen basically are asked what they feel is needed in price, service, nonproduct benefits, or new products to gain and maintain share in their district or territory. This information can be effectively obtained—either by drawing on the salesman's prior knowledge of, or having him conduct a direct field survey of, a specified sample of accounts. The survey sample normally will include all key large accounts and distributors and a random sample of moderate to small accounts. Salesmen are then asked to identify what each competitor's share is, at which key accounts, what strategies can be effective in taking share away and keeping it for each product line, and how much (for example, in price) is necessary to effect a change in share. They are also asked, based on previous experience or speculation, to predict what each competitor's probable reaction will be to specified moves such as price cuts, new products, increased field sales coverage, and the like. Such surveys require excellent sample design, a good information-processing system, and careful design of questionnaires to be administered to salesmen in the field and to be administered by salesmen to sample accounts. The number of accounts to be sampled and the

EXHIBIT 2

Schematic diagram of the process of planning market share gains

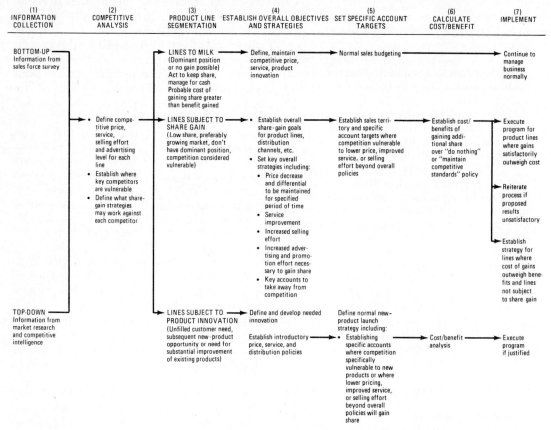

(1) INFORMATION COLLECTION	(2) COMPETITIVE ANALYSIS	(3) PRODUCT LINE SEGMENTATION	(4) ESTABLISH OVERALL OBJECTIVES AND STRATEGIES	(5) SET SPECIFIC ACCOUNT TARGETS	(6) CALCULATE COST/BENEFIT	(7) IMPLEMENT
BOTTOM-UP Information from sales force survey		LINES TO MILK (Dominant position or no gain possible) Act to keep share, manage for cash Probable cost of gaining share greater than benefit gained	Define, maintain competitive price, service, product innovation	Normal sales budgeting		Continue to manage business normally
	• Define competitive price, service, selling effort and advertising level for each line • Establish where key competitors are vulnerable • Define what share-gain strategies may work against each competitor	LINES SUBJECT TO SHARE GAIN (Low share, preferably growing market, don't have dominant position, competition considered vulnerable)	• Establish overall share-gain goals for product lines, distribution channels, etc. • Set key overall strategies including: • Price decrease and differential to be maintained for specified period of time • Service improvement • Increased selling effort • Increased advertising and promotion effort necessary to gain share • Key accounts to take away from competition	Establish sales territory and specific account targets where competition vulnerable to lower price, improved service, or selling effort beyond overall policies	Establish cost/benefits of gaining additional share over "do nothing" or "maintain competitive standards" policy	Execute program for product lines where gains satisfactorily outweigh cost ◆ Reiterate process if proposed results unsatisfactory ◆ Establish strategy for lines where cost of gains outweigh benefits and lines not subject to share gain
TOP-DOWN Information from market research and competitive intelligence		LINES SUBJECT TO PRODUCT INNOVATION (Unfilled customer need, subsequent new-product opportunity or need for substantial improvement of existing products)	Define and develop needed innovation Establish introductory price, service, and distribution policies	Define normal new-product launch strategy including: • Establishing specific accounts where competition specifically vulnerable to new products or where lower pricing, improved service, or selling effort beyond overall policies will gain share	Cost/benefit analysis	Execute program if justified

amount of information requested must be kept small to avoid overburdening the sales force with information collection.

Top-down research is also important. Professionally conducted surveys of select customers, distributors, and key salesmen can both identify key new product concepts that can be developed and used against competition and confirm or expand on findings from the bottom-up survey. Normal competitive intelligence activities can monitor a competitor's financial condition and ability to respond to an attack on his market, his probable new product policy, and his probable reaction, based on historical information, to each type of share-gain move being contemplated.

Competitive Analysis

An in-depth analysis of competition based on survey results is required to identify those product lines where share gain is thought possible and pinpoint where and how much each competitor is vulnerable to specific share-gain strategies. Exhibit 3 provides a simplified example of such an analysis and the key conclusions derived from the data.

Product Line Segmentation

Management judgment based on the competitive analysis should tentatively divide

EXHIBIT 3
Simplified competitive analysis

COMPETITIVE DIMENSIONS	Market Size	Growth Per Year	US	A	B	C	COMMENTS ON DATA
				Market Share			
1. Product Position							
Line 1	$15MM	0%	65%	20%	10%	5%	1. Not subject to share gain, manage for cash.
2	30MM	10	25	40	15	20	2. Subject to share gain, A most vulnerable, B, C less so.
3	20MM	15	10	25	30	35	3. Subject to share gain, A, B, C equally vulnerable. Substantial unfilled need for a new product.
2. Pricing Strategy							
H = Price with margin	Line 1		C	C	C	H	B and C will be easiest to take share away from on price, and it will be least expensive to maintain share taken away. A is more competitive, will require larger price differentials to gain and maintain share, and it is therefore more costly to take share away.
C = Price with market	2		C	L	C	C	
L = Price leader or very aggressive	3		C	L	C	C	
3. New Product Policy							
L = Leader	Line 1		L	L	F	F	Expect new products first from A, monitor market carefully to identify what they're working on—expect A to imitate earliest any new products introduced.
F = Follower	2		F	L	F	F	
	3		L	L	L	F	
4. Overall Marketing Strength							
No. Representatives	Line 1		5	10	15	15	A strongest and equal to us. B and C vulnerable to more intensive selling effort offered by us.
No. Distributors	2		40	35	30	30	
No. Salesmen	3		25	20	10	7	
5. Geographic Strength							
No. Salesmen and Reps							We may be weak in district G and should consider adding salesmen, otherwise are equal or superior to competition.
Territory E			9	7	7	6	
F			7	7	6	6	
G			5	8	7	6	
H			9	8	6	4	
6. Distributor Strength							
No. Distributors							A approximately equal in strength. B and C weaker and definitely vulnerable.
Territory E			12	10	8	7	
F			10	9	7	8	
G			10	9	7	7	
H			8	7	6	6	

COMPETITORS

EXHIBIT 3 (cont.)

7. *Delivery Norm (Weeks)*

Product					Delivery improvements necessary in 1, 2 to be competitive. Improvement beyond competitive levels will not gain share. Improvement in line 3 will gain advantage against A, B, and C according to sales force survey.
1	6	6	4	7	
2	6	3	4	4	
3	6	6	7	9	

8. *Penetration by Account Size (%)*

$ Market—all products

40 Large	40%	30%	15%	15%	We're weak in medium and small accounts, need program to improve penetration and coverage there.
15 Medium	15	30	25	30	
10 Small	10	30	20	40	
$65MM					

9. *Probable Reaction to:*

Lower price	A—Immediate retaliation, continued price reduction to gain share back.	Cost in taking share away from A on price will be high. B and C more vulnerable.
	B, C—Weaker response. Will try to hold large accounts.	
New product	A—Will immediately match new product offering.	B and to some extent C vulnerable to new product offering.
	C—May match immediately.	
	B—Eventually match.	
Increased sales coverage	A—Will match.	B and C vulnerable in some measure to sales coverage, particularly if a new product is launched.
	B, C—Some increase	

KEY STRATEGIC CONCLUSIONS:

1. *Product Policy:* Focus on lines 2 and 3 where gain is possible by increased penetration and growth with the market and product modification for product 3.
2. *Competitive Strategy:* Focus on taking share away from B and C, who are vulnerable to lower pricing and a new product innovation requested by salesmen. Selectively take business away from competitor A—only up to the point where expensive price retaliation is expected.
3. *Marketing Strategy:* Add three salesmen to territory G and one to F to build strength against key targets—B and C. Shift call pattern and develop mktg. programs for medium to small accounts where penetration is poor. Develop distributor promotion program to capitalize on advantage over B and C.
4. *Service:* Invest in capacity to lower delivery time in product 2 to level competitive with B and C. Maintain competitive standards in other lines.

230

product lines into three basic categories—
product lines where there is:

☐ No room for share gain
☐ Room for product innovation and subse-
    quent share gain
☐ No room for product innovation but room
    for gain share with existing products

In general, there is *little room for share gain* when competition is highly compe-
tent—is equal or superior in strength and ability to penetrate the market and has significant or dominant market share. There is often little room for gain when a firm has achieved dominant stable market share (usually 35% to 70% of the market) or the market for a product line is stable or de-
clining. In each of these circumstances, the cost of gaining market share will probably outweigh the additional benefits provided by a gain in share. The principal strategy under these circumstances is to manage the product line to produce cash: price only to maintain market share and make only the minimum required investments in product changes, plant and equipment, and marketing. If there is some doubt that a product line falls into this category it should be treated as a product where share gain is possible, and a detailed plan and calcula-
tions should be prepared to substantiate whether or not share gains are worth the cost.

There is room to gain share by *product innovation* where significant unfilled needs can be identified in the market, where it is technically feasible to develop a product to meet those needs, and where the product advantage in the market is sufficient to gain substantial share. In this case, the strategy is to undertake prototype product development and prove that the product is technically feasible before developing a plan to launch the product and gain share.

Finally, there is generally *room for a share gain* when a firm has less than dominant share and survey information indi-
cates that a competitive advantage can be obtained in price, service, or selling and distribution methods and systems. This is particularly true where the product market is rapidly growing and competition is weak, fragmented, or known to be sluggish in reaction to aggressive moves by competitors. In this instance, a detailed plan for gaining share is called for as outlined below.

Establishing Share-Gain Goals and Strategies

The competitive analysis will permit es-
tablishment of overall share-gain goals and the strategies to be implemented in general in the marketplace and against each key competitor.

After preliminary overall strategies have been established, the two most difficult subsequent tasks are to establish how much change must be made (in price and service, for example) to gain share and approxi-
mately how much share gain a given change will produce. Estimates of the sensitivity of market share to proposed changes can be obtained in several ways. First, historical records document share changes based on previous moves by or against competition. Second, and perhaps best, salesmen can estimate the sensitivity of share in their territories and indicate the amount of change necessary to take business away at specified key accounts. Finally, knowledge of competitors, judgment of their probable reactions, and the percentage of share they will permit to be taken away before retaliation should put a limit on expected share gains.

How much share a competitor will allow to be taken away is a function of several factors. The first is his financial con-
dition and ability to retaliate by building additional capacity or investing cash in other means of gaining back share. Second is his business philosophy concerning the product lines in question: does he want profits and incoming cash now, or is he

willing to defer current financial return for future, larger returns resulting from maintained or increased share? Finally, the importance of the product line under attack to the firm's total business will influence a competitor's reaction. If the product is of minor importance in the competitor's business, attempts to maintain share are less likely than if the product line constitutes a major portion of his business.

It is important, in addition, to realize that all of the share initially gained during an assault on competition probably cannot be maintained indefinitely and a portion of

the share may have to be "given back" to stabilize the market.

Exhibit 4 is a typical objective and strategy matrix showing overall share-gain goals by product line and detailed strategies by type of product for products sold direct to original equipment manufacturers. Each cell in a strategy matrix will normally include:

☐ Share (or sales) to be taken away from competition

☐ Specific accounts where share is to be gained

☐ Key strategies—price, product, promotions, change in call patterns, and the like

EXHIBIT 4

Competitive matrix for products sold direct to original equipment manufacturers*

PRODUCT	COMPETITOR A	COMPETITOR B	COMPETITOR C	OVERALL GOALS
1	No change	No change	No change	Maintain 65% share, competitive pricing. Manage for cash. Improve service to competitive levels.
2	—Take away 3% —Focus on accounts X, Y, and Z with below average pricing	—Take away 6% —Focus on accounts L, M, and N with below average pricing	—Take away 6% —Focus on accounts Q, R, and S	Increase share from 25%–40% by: ☐ Establishing competitive service and capacity ☐ Price 3%–7% lower than market
3	—Take away 5% —Focus on accounts X and Y where need for product modification great	—Take away 10% —Focus on accounts L, M, N, and X with lowered pricing on conventional product	—Take away 10% —Focus on accounts Q, R, S, and M with mix of modified product and low price on conventional product	Increase share from 10%–35% by: ☐ Product modification ☐ Cutting price on established product 3%–7% ☐ New plant with superior service

OVERALL STRATEGIES FOR ALL PRODUCTS
1. Add salesmen to territories F and G where weak.
2. Shift call patterns to call on more medium to small size accounts.
3. Increase overall advertising level 25% during share-gain period.
4. Maintain competitive service in all lines.

*The same type of matrix could also be used for products sold through different distribution channels.

The simple product line vs. competition matrix in Exhibit 4 assumes that strategy will vary only by competitor and product line. A more complex analysis will be necessary when share-gain strategy is expected to vary along other dimensions such as size of customer, customer's end market (industrial, consumer, computer, etc.), different distribution channels, and the like.

Territory Goals. Specific goals are then set for each territory and for key accounts that salesmen have targeted for share gain. The potential share gains are totaled and discounted to factor in probability of success to see if reasonable account and territory goals add up to the overall share-gain goals

established in the previous step. These goals become territory and account action steps if the share-gain program is accepted.

Cost Evaluation and Analysis. Once program goals are established, the costs and benefits of the proposed plan must be carefully evaluated. Exhibit 5 is a simplified flow diagram for calculating the incremental costs, benefits, cash flow, and return on investment (ROI) for a firm intending to gain share by a combination of lowered prices on existing products, introduction of a new product, additional field sales coverage, and improved service. The chart lists most of the key items that will have a positive or negative effect on cash

EXHIBIT 5

Schematic flow of calculation to compute ROI and cash flow of a share-gain plan

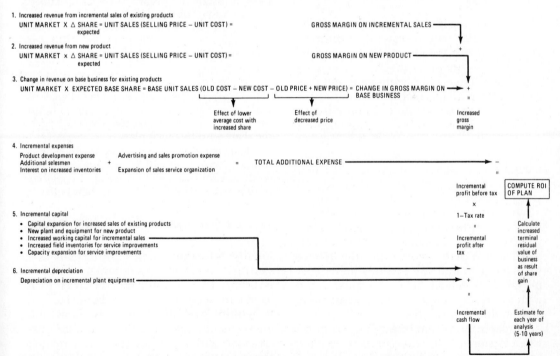

NOTE: See the Boston Consulting Group, *Perspectives on Experience* (Boston: Boston Consulting Group, 1968), for a method of calculating the present value of market share gains accounting for the effects of decreasing prices, decreasing unit costs, and increasing unit volume.

flow. The analysis isolates both the gain in profits from newly acquired share and the change in profitability of the base business—that business that would have been obtained without a share-gain plan—as a result of decreased prices and lowered costs as production costs move down the experience curve with increased cumulative volume. This type of analysis is easily adapted for computer calculation.

Assessing Risk. A "source of sales analysis" is useful in assessing the risk and realism of a share-gain plan. In general, the higher the portion of a firm's five- to ten-year cumulative sales expected to come from disruptive moves against competition—lowered price, improved service, and new products—the higher the risk of the plan and the greater the advantage over competitors necessary to succeed.

Monitoring and Follow-up. An intricate share-gain plan requires careful monitoring and control if it is to be effective. It is particularly important to insure that key account sales targets are being met, and that cost goals are on target and new product introductions are on schedule. Timing is also important. Once implementation begins, competitors will be aware of the threat to their market share; rapid, timely implementation of share-gain plans can catch competitors unaware, and share gain can take place before competitive retaliation.

It is also important to monitor competitive reaction to moves to gain share. Competitive moves should have been anticipated in the plan, figured into the market share targets, and calculations and plans prepared to defend held or gained share with continued price and cost reductions and product innovation.

Finally, it is important to recognize when attempts to stabilize competitive market shares should take place. When it is apparent that goals have been met, and/or the costs of gaining additional share obviously outweigh the benefits, it is important to attempt to stabilize shares by reverting to competitive—not aggressive—price, product, and service policies.

PITFALLS

There are five key pitfalls in implementing a plan to gain share. They are:

1. *Moving Too Slowly* and giving competition time to regroup and retaliate. Pricing, product, and service moves must be made quickly.

2. *Not Doing Enough* and being timid and conservative in moves against competition. Price cuts must be more than adequate, product advantage great and clear, and so on. It does not pay to do "just a little bit" to see if it works.

3. *No Follow Through*—neglecting the tools necessary to sustain share once gained, such as sustained cost reduction and ability to lower price or sustain excellent service or develop new products. One must be willing to stick with the battle to gain share over a long period of time.

4. *Underestimating Competition* and their ability to react, resulting in higher than forecast costs of gaining share; forgetting to figure the costs of combating competitive reaction in the share-gain financial plan.

5. *Don't Know When to Quit*—sometimes competitive reacton will be too strong; it is too costly to gain share, and giving up and concentrating on another business is the best policy.

LEGAL IMPLICATIONS OF MARKET SHARE

Finally, before planning significant market share gain and seeking a dominant industry position, plans should be reviewed with legal counsel to insure that planned action is within established antitrust laws and government guidelines. In general, the government will not challenge high market share if it is attained by internal growth and legal competitive activity in the marketplace. The government may challenge market dominance if it is thought to significantly lessen competition in the industry in question or if significant share gains are obtained by acquisition rather than by internal growth.

If one attains a dominant position in a given market, the strategies appropriate to maintain or augment that position must be carefully scrutinized from the legal point of view. Aggressive, competitive action permissible for a firm seeking to improve its position in a fragmented market may be viewed quite differently by the Justice Department if undertaken by a dominant firm seeking to augment or merely defend its position in a concentrated market. A firm that dominantes must guard against the possibility that in defending its dominant position, it is accused of predatory conduct that constitutes an abuse of an alleged monopoly position.

SUMMARY

Gaining and keeping significant market share is considered by many to be the single most important key to high, long-term profitability and substantial profit volume. Market share gains must be carefully planned. The vulnerability of competition to changes in price, product, service, marketing and distribution methods, and advertising must be assessed. Potential advantages vis-à-vis competition must be identified and the costs and potential benefits of a plan to gain share carefully evaluated. Overall share-gain goals and strategies must then be translated into sales territory and individual sales account goals for implementation. Although the process of planning share gains is time consuming and costly, the profit rewards can be substantial.

18

Make Your Annual Marketing Plan Must Reading

F. Beaven Ennis

Management's decisions on your product will be based on this key administrative document. Here's how to get your points across clearly and concisely.

The annual marketing plan is the most important of all administrative documents in the marketing field, and one of the most difficult for many product managers to master.

The plan presents basic objectives and strategies, no more, no less. Its sole purpose is to help decision making, not to inform management of every fact and supposition about a brand.

Obviously then, a readable, orderly, to-the-point format is essential. Such a format is presented on the following pages. No single format can accommodate all situations, of course; revisions and adaptations will be needed for your individual needs. Just remember, however, that your goal is to present information on which decisions can be made, not to organize miscellaneous data simply for a format requirement. In preparing your annual report, keep this in mind:

1. Limit your report to six to eight standard size pages typed single space. Product managers often are not sure how much detail is needed to support their plan so they load the report with nonessentials that contribute nothing but bulk. Management does not have time to wade through unedited odds and ends that serve only to obscure the main issue.

2. Be concise and avoid editorializing. A simple but meaningful outline indicates to management that the product group knows what's going on and can be counted on to deliver. Such an impression brings fast and positive decisions from management.

3. If information isn't available to complete a given section in the format, include the section's title and explain why the information is missing. From a management standpoint, it's as important to know what information is lacking as it is to know what is available. The absence of critical data should be pointed out so management can assess whether it significantly increases the risks which are inherent in all decision making.

4. Show actual numbers whenever they can be substituted for editorial comments. Numbers can tell a marketing story better than words, with text used only to emphasize or explain numerical data.

Reprinted with permission from *Product Management* (February 1976).

A variety of numerical exhibits are usually attached to the annual marketing plan. In the following format, only a profit and loss statement has been included (all figures are hypothetical). You may want to add more tabular exhibits such as price and profit structure, media allocation schedule, and promotion spread sheet.

The price and profit structure exhibit is probably the least used tool in marketing management, although one of the more essential ones. While retail prices are usually set by pricing practices in the market, this exhibit reveals the effect of the brand's price structure on such issues as: whether production and/or formula costs are too high relative to profits being delivered; whether the profit margin on each size is compatible with company norms; which size generates the largest profit return (which sug-

gests where the brand's promotion efforts might be concentrated); whether it is economically practical for the company to continue selling all sizes in the line.

Another advantage is that the P&P structure tells production and purchasing what marketing expects to sell by package size, thereby enabling them to better estimate their own operation costs.

5. Be prepared to answer all questions management may raise at the annual plan's presentation. Nothing is more frustrating to management than to have questions unanswered or answers delayed while facts are being retrieved. During the presentation, have on hand detailed records of the brand's past performance; the effect of merchandising activities; a summary of all relevant market research and information on competitive brands.

I CURRENT YEAR PERFORMANCE

One or two short paragraphs summarizing performance vs. objectives; any significant variations from plan; factors affecting the market. About ¼ page in length.

Hypothetical (HP) bar soap is expected to achieve its target objective this year of 1.8 million cases, representing $35.0 million in sales and $10.6 million in gross profits.

Of major significance is the continued unique position of HP soap. Market figures indicate that 50 percent of consumers use complexion bar soap; 40 percent deodorant soap; 10 percent detergent. Our brand, combining certain features of each plus its floating characteristic, has succeeded in a short period because of its broad base family appeal. However, we should be aware that several imitations are being tested by major marketers and revisions of the plan may be necessary as the marketing thrust becomes more evident.

II RECOMMENDATIONS

Two or three sentences stating next year's objective in total shipping units and sales value; expenditures to support the brand and its share objective.

The 1976 objective of HP bar soap is to obtain a 5.9 percent share of the bar soap retail market, representing shipments of 2.0 million cases and factory sales of $39.0 million. To achieve this objective, the brand will spend $3.5 million in advertising and $3.8 million in promotion.

III BACKGROUND

Short paragraphs describing market in units and/or volume and growth rate. Competitive brands and share position vs. company brand.

Size. The total retail value of the bar soap market is approximately $650 million. The category continues to maintain a growth rate of about 4 percent a year, keyed roughly to the population growth. Competition comes largely from four long-established companies with about three-quarters of the complexion-deodorant market. Strong individual brands ordinarily command about 5 to 7 percent market shares, with Dial commanding a 20 percent, Ivory bar about a 14 percent share.

Buyer. The housewife is the primary buyer; consumers include all members of the family. Men and teen-agers are the primary users of deodorant soaps while women ages 18–39 are the primary users of complexion bars. Although consumption is universal among all socio-economic groups, it is 50 percent greater in larger households. Geographically, this category is strong in all sections, but price weakens premium brands in depressed metropolitan and rural areas.

Brief profile of buyer and consumer demographics; any geographic variations.

Pricing. The price for bar soap varies depending on type and quality. Average prices are:

A brief table, preferably without comment, showing competitive retail price structures.

	DEODORANT	COMPLEXION
Premium price brands	.39/5 oz.	.37/3.75 oz.
Regular price brands	.47/7.75 oz.	.33/5 oz.
HP bar soap	.42/5 oz.	

Competitive Spending. The market is characterized by heavy advertising spending for major brands and heavy promotion spending by minor brands:

Resumé of media and promotional spending by competition. Estimates of promotion costs should include only regional and national promotions, not tests. If needed, provide table breaking out expenditures in six month periods.

	JAN.–JUNE		JULY–DEC.	
	(IN MILLIONS)			
	ADV.	PROM.	ADV.	PROM.
Brand A	$2.9	$1.0	$2.0	$ .4
Brand B	2.0	.7	2.4	1.2
Brand X	.6	1.1	.9	1.0
Brand Y	.7	.9	.8	1.1

Television is the basic medium used in advertising bar soap, with promotion funds being channeled primarily into trade allowances in order to obtain price features.

Seasonality. There is a seasonal increase in deodorant soaps during June, July, August, and September which accounts for almost 40 percent of this category's total volume.

The Product. HP is a complexion-deodorant soap that floats, the first of its kind marketed nationally. Additionally, the brand has a chemical property which enables it to last longer in usage than any other brand on the market.

Manufacturing. Production confirms that plant capacity is adequate for next year's sales objectives, but additional capacity will be required if growth rate continues. Estimates are being prepared on cost and timing of the new capacity and will be available at quarterly review.

Product Research. Blind product tests conducted in September 1975 reveal HP is significantly preferred over major competitors:

PREFERENCE	RESPONSE	REASONS FOR PREFERENCE	RESPONSE
HP	59%	Purity	50%
Other brands	30	Long-lasting	63
No opinion	11	Floats	33
		Unique combination	30

Market Research. Research indicates some areas of consumer resistance: 33 percent doubted one soap could perform two functions; 16 percent complained of poor soap consistency after use; 32 percent stated the brand doesn't lather as much as Dial or Ivory.

IV OPPORTUNITIES AND PROBLEMS

List why you expect to achieve gains or market objectives as cited in your plan.

Opportunities. Continued growth is anticipated for these reasons: (1) A steady increase in brand share over three years with increasing product acceptance by trade and consumers. (2) A unique combination of product attributes which consumers prefer over major established brands. (3) An exceptionally high awareness and recall of the brand's award-winning advertising campaign. (4) Trade preference and a trade margin that any challenging brand will have difficulty in matching.

Similarly, outline factors that might jeopardize the brand's ability to achieve goals. Explain what steps have been taken to minimize these risks.

Problems. (1) Completion of test market activities by Company Z on similar product with national expansion of their product anticipated within the next six months. (2) Continued inability of technical research to improve HP's lathering properties during use. (3) Economic factors which are eroding sales of some premium priced brands. We are preparing a supplemental ad/promotion budget for the first eventuality plus new trade incentives. Technical research will soon test a new bar designed to improve lathering, and progress is expected in this area before the end of the year.

V STRATEGIES

Concisely state the brand's basic objectives and strategy. The length of this section will vary but should not exceed half a page.

Marketing. The objective of HP is to achieve a 5.9 percent share of the market, representing an 11 percent increase in case shipments. To achieve this objective, the brand's basic marketing strategy is to position HP as a high quality soap whose price is offset by the fact it performs the functions of two ordinary soaps and lasts longer.

This section is optional. Primarily intended for brands with heavy ad expenditures which may vary greatly according to sales areas or opportunities.

Spending. We will spend in advertising and promotion at an A to S ratio of 19 percent to continue to build distribution and trial nationally and to accelerate the brand's development in weak market areas prior to the expansion of Company Z's brand. Spending during warmer months will be slightly heavier to capture new users during period of increased soap usage.

Copy. The objective of HP advertising will be to convince housewives that all members of their families will be able to use HP for all cleansing purposes and affect an overall economy. To achieve this, copy will show HP used by housewives for skin care and the entire family for deodorant protection. Continued emphasis will be placed on the brand's unique "last longer" demonstration, and its inherent mildness to the skin. Equal weight will be given to the housewives and family campaigns except during the summer when the family campaign will run at twice the frequency as our housewife commercials. While the prime objective is to stress HP's long-term economy, copy will also attempt to overcome skepticism about our product's three-in-one characteristics by presenting it in real-life situations.

Media. HP's media objective is to reach housewives ages 18 to 39 as frequently as possible. Television will continue as the brand's major medium because it delivers efficient messages with broad coverage and good frequency, provides good cumulative line frequency against primary market (housewives), and permits a high degree of visualization of the brand's unique demonstration. Network daytime television will be used for year-round reach and frequency at maximum efficiency; spot TV will be concentrated in leadership areas as well as markets of low brand development; women's magazines will be used during the summer months, a period of peak consumption. (Note: in some cases, a breakdown of media spending by major sales regions may be appropriate; list in terms of volume, media dollars, and media dollars per case. In each instance, figures should be supplied for current year and next year. Any significant differences from previous years should be explained.)

Copy section should be three brief statements: objective, strategy to achieve objective, and the brand's TV/print pool or rotation policy.

Give objective and strategy to achieve objective; be as specific as possible in terms of coverage, frequency, and geographic weight.

Again, objectives and strategy to achieve them; keep under a page.

Promotion. HP's basic promotion objective is to maximize trade features and price reductions during the brand's four major drive periods. To achieve this, we will: (1) maintain trade margins generally above that of regular brands by responding instantly with case allowances to match any introductions by competition; (2) offer four cooperative merchandising allowances to the trade in our four major drive periods; (3) conduct two major national consumer-oriented promotions in peak consumption periods involving high value premiums; (4) offer special distribution allowances in weak market areas. (Note: a breakdown of allocations by major sales regions may be necessary, as in the case of media.)

VI TESTS/RESEARCH

Briefly list media or promotion tests, product tests, packaging research, etc., planned for next year. Give only nature, purpose, and cost of each.

1. Blind product test of new consistency formula, $45,000;

2. Sales district test of multi-pack to build in-home inventories, $20,000;

3. District test of coupons for free bar of soap to accelerate brand development in weak market areas, $35,000.

Hypothetical (HP) bar soap profit and loss statement 1976 budget (000)

	PREVIOUS YEAR	(PERCENT SALES)	CURRENT YEAR	(PERCENT SALES)	NEW YEAR	(PERCENT SALES)
1. TOTAL MARKET:						
Value	$600.0		$625.8		$652.7	
Percent Increase	4.0%		4.3%		4.3%	
2. BRAND SHARE	5.0%		5.5%		5.9%	
3. BRAND SHIPMENTS:						
Value	$ 30.0	100%	$ 35.0	100%	$ 39.0	100%
Cases	1.6		1.8		2.0	
Percent Increase/Cases	11.0%		13.0%		11.0%	
4. COST OF GOODS	$ 12.0	40%	$ 14.0	40%	$ 15.6	40%
5. GROSS MARGIN	$ 18.0	60%	$ 21.0	60%	$ 23.4	60%
6. MARKETING EXPENSES:						
Media/Production	$ 2.9	10%	$ 3.6	10%	$ 3.5	9%
Advertising Reserve	0.3	1%	0.1	—	0.2	—
Sampling/Couponing	1.3	4%	1.2	4%	0.0	—
Trade Allowance	1.2	4%	1.6	5%	1.8	5%
Other Promotions	0.3	1%	0.5	1%	2.0	5%
Total Marketing Expenses	$ 6.0	20%	$ 7.0	20%	$ 7.5	19%
7. OTHER EXPENSES:						
Market Research	$ 0.1	—	$ 0.1	—	$ 0.2	
Sales Force Cost	1.1	4%	1.5	5%	1.6	4%
Distribution Cost	1.0	4%	1.2	3%	1.2	3%
Administration	0.4	1%	0.6	2%	0.6	2%
Total Other Expenses	$ 2.6	9%	$ 3.4	10%	$ 3.6	9%
8. PROFIT CONTRIBUTION:	$ 9.4	31%	$ 10.6	30%	$ 12.3	32%
Increase	10.4%		12.8%		16.0%	

19 New Products Management for the 1980s

Booz, Allen & Hamilton, Inc.

THE NEW PRODUCT MANAGEMENT CHALLENGE

During the 1980s, managers in all industries expect new products to fuel industry sales and profit growth. Indeed, the contribution made by new products to sales growth is expected to increase by one-third, while the portion of total company profits generated by new products is expected to increase by 40 percent over the next 5 years. These higher expectations exist in all industries, including the information processing industry, which had over the last 5 years the highest profit contribution from new products of all industry groups surveyed.

To support these new product targets, companies expect to double the number of new products introduced over the next 5 years. From 1976 to 1981, the companies we surveyed introduced from zero to over 100 new products; the median number of new products introduced was 5. Over the next 5 years, that number is expected to double.

This trend towards increased development and introduction of new products is supported by a number of factors. Technology advances, changing market requirements, and world market competition are expected to increase the number of new products introduced over the next 5 years. On the other hand, several factors could impede new product development in the coming decade. The increased cost of capital, in particular, is expected to have a negative impact on the number of new products introduced over the next 5 years.

A short-term orientation by management is viewed as the principal *internal* obstacle to successful new product development. Inadequate market research, delays in decision-making, lack of a new product

Reprinted with permission by Booz, Allen & Hamilton, 1982.

strategy, and ineffective communication between functions and departments are other major internal obstacles.

Despite these obstacles, many new products will be selected for development and brought to the marketplace by the mid-1980s. How well-prepared U.S. companies are to meet the challenge is suggested by our major survey findings:

Most companies use a formal new product process, usually beginning with identifying the new product strategy. According to our survey results, companies that have successfully launched new products are more likely to have had a formal new product process in place for a longer period of time. They are also more likely to have a strategic plan, and be committed to growing through internally developed new products.

The new product strategy links corporate objectives to the new product effort, and provides direction for the new product process. The step identifies the strategic roles to be played by new products—roles that depend on the type of product itself and the industry. It also helps set the formal financial criteria to be used in measuring new product performance and in screening and evaluating new product ideas.

The more sophisticated new product process has dramatically reduced the number of new product ideas considered for every successful new product introduced—from an average of 58 in 1968 to 7 in 1981. Again, our survey results indicate that companies with a strong record of successful new product introductions consider fewer ideas per successful new launch, and do more and better screening of ideas.

More management attention and more financial resources are given to the early steps in the new product process than was the case a decade ago. In 1968, roughly one-half of all new product expenditures was made during the commercialization stage. Today, commercialization accounts for only one-fourth of all new product expenditures. Conversely, the portion of expenditures in the first three steps more than doubled during the same period, from 10 percent in 1968 to 21 percent in 1981.

The percent of total new product expenditures allocated to products that are ultimately successful has increased—from 30 percent in 1968 to 54 percent today. The probable causes are the reduction in the number of ideas considered and the increase in resource allocations to early process steps.

Almost half the companies surveyed use more than one type of organization structure to guide new product programs. Over three-fourths of these companies tie the choice of structure used to product-specific requirements.

Experience in introducing new products enables companies to improve new product performance. With increased new product experience, companies improve profitability by reducing the cost per introduction. For the 13,000 new product introductions between 1976 and 1981 in the 700 companies we surveyed, at each doubling of the number of new products introduced, the cost of each introduction declined by 29 percent.

Two-thirds of all companies surveyed formally measure new product performance. The three most commonly used criteria are profit contribution, return on investment, and sales volume.

The success rate of commercialized new products has not improved, on average, over the last two decades. In the period from 1963 to 1968, 67 percent of all new products introduced were successful—that is, they met company-specific financial and strategic criteria. From 1976 to 1981, a 65 percent rate of success was achieved.

The dichotomy of the major findings is obvious. More companies are using a more sophisticated new product process, thereby reducing the number of new ideas needed to generate a successful product and increasing the portion of total resources spent on market "winners." And more companies are fitting the organizational structures used to their product-specific requirements. Yet, there has been virtually no change in the *rate* of successful introductions.

New product managers are thus faced with the important challenge in the coming decade of improving new product performance to meet their higher new product objectives. To that end, and based on our findings from the survey and our in-depth interviews with new product executives, Booz·Allen concludes:

□ A company-specific, implementation-oriented approach is the key to improving new product performance.

□ A well-defined new product strategy should be at the core of the company-specific approach.

□ The new product effort should be guided by a formal, seven-step process.

□ Consistent management commitment to new product development for extended periods of time allows a company to accumulate the new product experience crucial to achieving and maintaining competitive advantage.

□ The entire new product program should be carried out in an environment conducive to achieving company-specific new product and corporate objectives.

These summary results and their implications for new product management in the 1980s are expanded on in the following sections.

CURRENT PRACTICES AND TRENDS

Our analysis of the survey findings identified four key new product practices and trends. They relate to: (1) the mix of new products introduced; (2) changes in the new product process; (3) the types of organization structures used to guide new product programs; and (4) the impact of improved new product processes on new product development.

Mix of New Product Introductions

In our survey, we identified six categories of new products in terms of their newness to the company and to the marketplace.

□ *New-to-the-world products:* New products that create an entirely new market (10 percent of total new introductions).

□ *New product lines:* New products that, for the first time, allow a company to enter an established market (20 percent of total).

□ *Additions to existing product lines:* New products that supplement a company's established product lines (26 percent of total).

□ *Improvements in/revisions to existing products:* New products that provide improved performance or greater perceived value, and replace existing products (26 percent of total).

□ *Repositionings:* Existing products that are targeted to new markets or market segments (7 percent of total).

□ *Cost reductions:* New products that provide similar performance at lower cost (11 percent of total).

The results of the survey indicate that, typically, a company's new product program includes a mix of these new products. Additions to existing product lines and improvements in or revisions to existing products have accounted for 52 percent of all new product introductions over the last 5 years. Another 30 percent of introductions are new-to-the-world products and new product lines, which often become a firm's most successful new products. Indeed, they account for 60 percent of new products viewed as most successful.

Despite the obvious attractiveness of these two new product categories, many new product managers are reluctant to introduce these types of new products because their variability of return is greater. As a result, over 50 percent of the companies surveyed introduced *no* new-to-the-world products over the last 5 years, and 25 percent of the companies introduced *no* new product lines, thus supporting the notion that few innovative new products were introduced over the 5-year period.

This broad mix of new product introductions is consistent across all industries, although rapidly changing technology has fostered more truly innovative new products in high technology or growth industries. For example, although only 10 percent of all new products introduced over the last 5 years were new-to-the-world products, advances in electronics technology prompted a larger percentage of new-to-the-world product introductions in the information processing industry (over 20 percent of total) and in the instruments and controls industry (15 percent).

Changes in New Product Process

The new products introduced over the last 5 years have been selected for development through a seven-step new product process. [Exhibit 1.] A new step, developing an explicit new product strategy, is the major addition to the process developed by Booz· Allen in the 1950s, with 77 percent of the companies surveyed using it in their new product process.

The addition of this step has changed the nature of the beginning of the process. The first three steps—developing a new product strategy, generating ideas and concepts, and screening and evaluating those ideas and concepts—are now more closely linked to each other and have become more iterative. The new product strategy development step provides a focus for the idea-generation step in that the ideas and concepts

EXHIBIT 1
New product process in the 1980s

generated are developed to meet strategic objectives. In addition, screening criteria used during the screening and evaluation step are tied to the same strategic objectives.

The purpose of the step to develop new product strategy is to identify the strategic business requirements that new products should satisfy. The requirements, which can be both market and company driven, determine the roles to be played by new products. For example, over the last 5 years, defending a market share position and maintaining position as a product innovator were the two most common new product roles. As a consumer nondurable company executive told us: "We have different uses and roles for new products. Some are developed to meet earnings growth objectives; others are introduced to maintain distribution leverage or to combat a competitive entry."

The roles played by new products are influenced by individual industry needs. For example, industrial goods companies are more likely to have developed their most successful new products to satisfy technological objectives, while consumer nondurable companies are more likely to have developed their most successful new products to satisfy market requirements.

The strategic role played by a new product is linked also to the *type* of new product. To maintain a position as a product innovator or to exploit technology in a new way, for example, more companies develop a new-to-the-world product than any other type. To defend a market share position, more companies introduce an addition to an existing line or a revision of an existing product.

Once a new product strategy has been developed and new product ideas selected on the basis of the roles they can play in achieving strategic objectives, financial performance criteria can be established. Nearly two-thirds of the companies surveyed formally measure new product performance, using, on the average, more than one performance criterion. The three most commonly used are profit contribution, sales volume, and return on investment.

A consumer packaged goods company illustrates how performance criteria are tied to the strategic roles played by new products. This company set a higher return-on-investment threshold for products used to enter a new geographic market (25 percent) than for products designed to increase (15 percent). The higher performance standard in the former situation reflects the higher investment level and higher probability of failure associated with entering a new geographic market.

The increased attention given new product strategy development reflects a general increase in management attention to the early steps in the new product process. Companies that have excellent records of successful new product introductions are more likely to develop specific new product strategies. They conduct more analyses early in the process and focus their idea and concept generation. And they conduct more rigorous

screening and evaluation of the ideas generated. However, in comparing product development in the United States with that in Japan, we found that the Japanese invest even more time in and give more attention to these early steps in the new product process. In particular, the Japanese carry out extensive analyses and more carefully define the roles of their new products in corporate strategy.

Over the last decade, U.S. companies also have increased the share of total new product expenditures spent on analysis, screening, and development, and have reduced the share of the total expended on commercialization. In 1968, roughly one-half of all new product expenditures was made during the commercialization stage. Today, commercialization accounts for only one-fourth.

Consistent with reduced commercialization expenditures and the reality of the high cost of capital, capital expenditures in support of new product projects declined from 46 percent of total new product expenditures in 1968 to 26 percent today.

The steps up to and including development benefited most from this reapportionment of new product dollars. Expenditures during the development step increased from 28 percent of total in 1968 to 37 percent today. The portion of expenditures in the first three steps more than doubled during the same period, from 10 percent in 1968 to 21 percent in 1981.

Although the early steps in the process of developing new products are generally viewed as the most critical, different industries emphasize different steps, depending on industry dynamics. Industries with rapidly changing markets, such as information processing, instruments and controls, consumer nondurables, and textiles, place greater emphasis on developing a new product strategy. Companies in industries with more stable markets, like chemicals, industrial machinery, OEM components, and power-generating equipment, focus more on business analysis.

Types of New Product Organization and Management

The organization structures used to guide new product programs fall into two general categories: free-standing or autonomous units, like interdisciplinary teams, separate new product departments, and venture groups; and functionally based units that are part of existing planning, marketing, R&D, or engineering departments.

Almost half the companies surveyed use *more* than one type of structure, and over three-fourths of these companies tie the choice of organization structure used to product-specific requirements. For example, a manager in an information processing company told us: "New products related to one of our existing businesses are developed within an existing division. New products that represent a shift in direction for the company are developed by a separate venture group."

Heading these new product units are managers who need and use a range of general and functional management skills to develop new products. Almost half the companies surveyed encourage "product champions" to promote and shepherd new product concepts through the development process.

The tenure of senior new product managers, who usually are functional department heads, increased from 2.5 years to 8.0 years over the last 15 years, suggesting top management is providing for greater continuity in new product development.

There are no standard compensation practices for new product executives. Fifty-seven percent of all companies surveyed tie compensation for new product managers to general performance. Thirty-eight percent use base salary alone. Only 5 percent tie compensation *directly* to new product performance. But the results of our interviews suggest compensation for new product managers is an important and unresolved issue within many companies. As an industrial components company executive told us: "Compensation for new product managers is one of the hottest issues within our company. This year, for the first time, we have implemented a bonus system tied to long-term new product objectives."

Impact of Refined Process on New Product Development

The more sophisticated new product process has had a profound effect on the number of ideas considered in developing one successful new product. The "mortality curve" for new product ideas has changed dramatically. In 1968, on average, 58 new product ideas were considered for every successful new product. Today, only seven ideas are required to generate one successful new product.

However, there are variations by industry. Consumer nondurable companies consider more than twice as many new product ideas to generate one successful new product as industrial or consumer durable manufacturers.

Companies have reduced the number of new ideas needed to produce one successful new product, in part, by increasing their attention to the market and to potential new applications of available technologies. A consumer durable company executive told us: "One thing that has changed is the level of sophistication in segmenting the market. Ideas generated today are more clearly defined and better focused that they were 5 to 10 years ago." And a high-technology company executive told us: "In our company, technology advances drive idea generation, limiting new product concepts to the application of these technologies."

Industries also differ in the allocation of time to the various steps in the new product process. Industrial goods companies devote 47 percent of their total time to the development step, compared with 30 percent spent by consumer nondurable companies and 36 percent spent by consumer durable companies. On the other hand, consumer durable and nondurable companies devote a higher percentage of total time to commercialization—26 percent and 29 percent, respectively, versus 18 percent for industrial goods companies.

The net result of the improved process has been better expenditure allocations. By reducing the number of ideas considered to develop one successful new product, companies have been able to increase the portion of total new product expenditures going to products that are ultimately successful. Thus, the overall percentage of new product expenditures attributable to successful products increased from 30 percent in 1968 to 54 percent today.

But despite the increased sophistication of the process and improved effectiveness of allocations, there has been, as we have cited, no improvement in the percentage of successful new product introductions. It remains at about 65 percent. This suggests greater process sophistication does not necessarily lead to improved new product performance. Rather, various other factors are also at work.

KEY FACTORS IN IMPROVING
NEW PRODUCT PERFORMANCE

To determine the keys to improved new product performance, we examined successful new product introductions as well as companies that had successfully launched new products. We learned that the two most important factors in successful new product introductions are how well the product fits market needs and the functional strengths of the company. *However*, the relative importance of the several factors cited varies significantly by industry and by type of product being introduced.

In addition, successful companies appear to have developed a corporate philosophy, a strategic approach, and a management style that encourage successful new product development. In particular, they maintain commitment to growing through internally developed new products, and select management styles that foster the kind of environment needed to satisfy company-specific new product objectives.

Factors Contributing to the Introduction of Successful New Products

The two most important factors in successful new product introductions are the fit of the product with market needs and with internal functional strengths. Having a technologically superior product, receiving support from top management, and using a multiple-step new product process are additional factors contributing to new product success.

The relative importance of each factor does vary, however, by industry. Although fit of the product with market needs is cited as the most important factor by the sample as a whole, technological superiority is considered more important by industrial goods companies, and top-management support is more important in consumer durable and nondurable companies.

Factor importance varies also by the type of new product being developed. Overall, as in the industry rankings of factors responsible for successful new product introductions, the fit of the product with market needs is the most important factor for every type of product being introduced. Technological superiority of the product is important in developing new-to-the-world products. As an executive of a major chemicals company told us: "We are trying to develop innovations that will reach the market in 5-10 years. Our new product development executives understand today's marketplace, but they emphasize technology to generate new product ideas since they have no mechanism to identify the market requirements 5-10 years from now."

In the development of new product lines and additions to existing lines, how well the product fits with internal functional strengths is important. In developing this type of product, a company is trying to enter existing markets in which production, distribution, and selling requirements are known and can be assessed relative to company capabilities. In the development of improvements to/revisions in existing products, technological superiority is important because in this case a company is trying to improve its position within an existing market, which depends more on developing a technologically-based competitive advantage. And top-management support is cited as one of the three most important factors to the successful introduction of new product lines and of additions to existing lines.

Characteristics of Companies with Successful New Products

To determine the existence of common characteristics in companies that had successfully launched new products, we divided our sample into two groups: companies achieving greater than 90 percent success in all new product introductions (i.e., 90 percent of all new product introductions met company-set performance criteria); and companies achieving less than 50 percent success for their new products.

In many ways, companies successful in new product introductions look like their less successful counterparts. They introduce about the same mix of new products. They spend about the same amount of money (as a percent of sales) on R&D and promotion in support of new products. Both groups are as likely to use a formal new product process or formally measure new product performance. And both groups spend about the same proportion of total time and expense on the various steps in the new product process. These similarities strongly suggest that successful new product management is a delicate and subtle process, not subject to broad generalizations or universal guidelines.

Important differences as well as similarities exist between the two groups. These differences are related to operating philosophy, organization structures, extent of experience with new product introductions, and management styles.

Operating Philosophy. Successful companies in our survey are more committed to growth through new products developed internally. They are more likely to have a formal new product process in place for a longer period of time. They are more likely to have a strategic plan that includes a certain portion of company growth from new products. They are also more likely to prescreen new product ideas thoroughly, considering almost 10 times fewer new product ideas per successful new product as unsuccessful companies.

Probably as a result of this philosophy and commitment, successful companies report fewer major obstacles to successful new product development. Short-term-oriented management, lack of a new product strategy, and organizational issues are considered less of an obstacle by successful companies than by unsuccessful ones.

Organization Structures. From an organizational standpoint, successful companies are more likely to house the new product organization in R&D or engineering, and are more likely to allow the marketing and R&D functions to have greater influence on the new product process. They are also more likely to keep the senior new product executive in place for a longer period of time.

The Experience Effect.   We also found that experience in introducing products enables companies to improve new product performance. Specifically, with increased new product experience, companies improve new product profitability by reducing the cost per introduction.

The concept at work is the experience curve—that is, the more you do something, the more efficient you become at doing it. More precisely, in this situation, with each doubling of the number of new product introductions, the cost of each introduction declines at a predictable and constant rate.

New product development costs conform to this concept. For the 13,000 new product introductions between 1976 and 1981 in the 700 companies we surveyed, the experience effect yields a 71 percent cost curve. At each doubling of the number of new products introduced, the cost of each introduction declines by 29 percent.

Companies that adroitly exploit the benefits of experience can achieve competitive advantage. For example, if Company A and Company B introduce two new products and are equally effective in managing them, they incur the same cost per introduction. But if Company B continues to devote resources to the introduction of new products and thus gains greater experience than Company A, Company B will achieve a sizable and sustainable advantage in the cost per new product introduction.

Much of the advantage stems from having acquired a knowledge of the market and of the steps required to develop a new product. This knowledge, accumulated over time, enables the experienced company to move more efficiently through the development process.

The positive effects of accumulated experience do not imply, however, that companies should introduce as many new products as possible for the sole purpose of gaining experience. Maintaining competitive advantage requires a consistent commitment to new product development. Theoretically, a firm that cuts back on its new product program may put itself at a competitive disadvantage from which it may never recover. As an executive of a consumer durable company stated: "While our company has been successful in new products over the last 10 years, top management has recently narrowed the new product pipeline due to current business pressure. What will it take to get back up to speed once the valve is turned on again?" In actual practice, our survey results show that successful companies remain committed to new product efforts for extended periods of time, thereby improving effectiveness and reducing the cost per introduction.

Management Styles.   Successful companies appear not only to select a management style appropriate to immediate new product development needs, but also to revise and tailor that approach to *changing* new product opportunities. For example, a major instruments and controls company that historically had used an entrepreneurial management approach to new product development is moving to a more structured, top-down managerial style as it finds some of its high-technology market segments maturing. A major industrial components company is moving to a less structured, more entrepreneurial style as it positions itself to enter emerging high-technology growth segments. Both companies report these management style changes are enabling them to meet new product objectives more effectively.

In general, the companies we surveyed use some form of one to three approaches to managing new product development:

☐ An entrepreneurial approach, associated primarily with developing new-to-the-world products.

☐ A collegial approach, associated primarily with entering new businesses and adding products to existing product lines.

☐ A managerial approach, most closely associated with developing new products that are closely linked to existing businesses.

In the entrepreneurial approach, an autonomous new product group is established, reporting to a general manager. It consists of an interdisciplinary venture team, headed by an entrepreneurial new product manager capable of integrating diverse functional skills. Top management is strongly committed to and involved in the effort to develop new products. But less attention is paid to formal business planning than in either of the other two approaches, and there is less dependence on formal financial criteria to evaluate new product opportunities.

This less restrictive approach supports entrepreneurial behavior, thus creating a positive environment for risk-taking. Moreover, new product managers in this environment enjoy incentive systems that reward success. As a result, they want to remain in the new product development function, which provides greater continuity and accumulation of new product experience.

The collegial approach is characterized by strong senior management participation in new product decision-making, strong top-management support of risk-taking, commitment to and support for a new product effort, and a formal new product process to guide the effort and ensure discipline. It is characterized also by a clear commitment across functional lines to provide whatever is necessary for success and to make decisions quickly.

The managerial approach is characterized by a hierarchical management structure that involves many levels of management and provides strong top-down direction to new product efforts. Such companies stress functional leadership, have a strong business planning orientation, use a formal and often inflexible new product process, and rely heavily on formal financial criteria to evaluate new product opportunities.

This approach is suitable for managing ongoing businesses because it rewards successful new product managers with quick promotions. However, it tends to restrict new product endeavors to variations on existing products, and provides less continuity than in the other two approaches because new product managers are promoted to other functions.

A "BEST PRACTICES" PRESCRIPTION FOR MANAGING NEW PRODUCTS IN THE 1980s

New product management will not be easy in the 1980s. In the rapidly changing and financially constrained environment envisioned, companies will be increasingly challenged to improve new product performance.

Although the similarities among successful companies may seem to imply a set of common factors for success, the differences suggest that effective management of new product development is very complex and highly company-specific.

Based on our survey results, the companies most likely to meet this challenge successfully will be those that develop new products internally as their primary means of growth, that have well-defined new product efforts, and that consistently commit the necessary resources to these efforts. They have in place and in use overall approaches carefully tailored to the specific goals and needs of their respective companies. In particular, at the core of their company-specific approaches are clearly defined new product strategies that allow management to generate and select new products that fulfill specific internal strategic and external market needs. They focus on opportunities for which they have the requisite internal strengths, and in which they enjoy competitive advantage, either cost or effectiveness, gained through cumulative experience. Finally, successful companies in the turbulent decade ahead will be those that tailor their organizational structures and management styles to the type of new product opportunities they pursue.

Making the Long-Term Commitment

Between the end of World War II and the late 1970s, U.S. business and industry enjoyed almost uninterrupted overall success in new product introductions both at home and abroad. Our management expertise, our technological know-how, and our design, production, and distribution superiority allowed us to introduce and market new products almost at will. At home, we found ready markets in an expanding economy characterized by stable, low inflation rates. Abroad, we marketed a range of mass-produced quality goods eagerly sought after by a world recovering from the devastation of a worldwide conflict.

Today, U.S. business faces a far different set of circumstances. The major industrial nations of the world have regained their footing not only at home but also in the United States and in many of the growth markets elsewhere. The competition is now world-scale competition. Technology

advances occur more rapidly, with high-technology products or their components enjoying ever-shortening life cycles. And the increased cost of capital in this country has escalated the cost of every new product introduced, whether or not it is successful.

In such an environment, companies cannot be satisfied with an average performance. Rather, they must commit themselves to achieving and sustaining outstanding results.

They must look inward for their future product opportunities, and be committed to internal development of new products as the major means of growth. They must be willing to mount well-defined new product efforts that are driven by corporate objectives and strategies, and that conclude with the development and introduction of specific new products that fulfill internal strategic and external market needs. They must support these efforts with consistent commitments of the necessary funds and of the requisite managerial and technical know-how. In short, successful corporate practitioners will be those who marry corporate needs to customer needs, and pledge the resources necessary to a successful marriage.

Developing a New Product Strategy

At the core of a company-specific approach to a sound new product program is a well-defined new product strategy. [Exhibit 2.] A new product strategy links the new product process to company objectives, and provides focus for idea/concept generation and guidelines for establishing appropriate screening criteria.

The purpose of developing a new product strategy is to identify the strategic roles new products will play to fulfill corporate objectives.

That identification is a complex analytical process in which the role new products will play in the company's growth de-

EXHIBIT 2

Strategic approach to new product planning

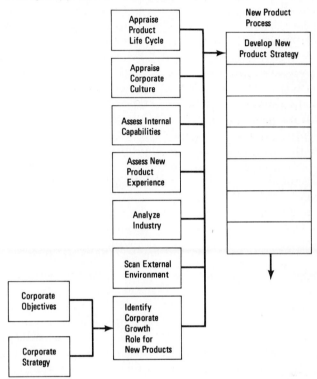

termines the level of new product activity. In the analytical process, industries are evaluated to determine the growth potential of existing markets, and the external environment is scrutinized to identify emerging product opportunities. Internal capabilities are assessed to identify relevant company strengths and weaknesses, and existing management style and new product experience are evaluated to determine their impact on the new product effort.

The outcome of this analysis is a set of strategic roles, used *not* to generate specific new product ideas, but to help identify markets for which new products will be developed. These market opportunities provide the set of product and market requirements from which new product ideas are generated. In addition, strategic roles provide guidelines for new product performance measurement criteria. Performance thresholds tied to strategic roles provide a more precise means of screening new product ideas.

Capitalizing on the Experience Advantage

As part of the new product effort, internal capabilities are assessed to determine specific strengths and weaknesses vis à vis the strategic goals to be accomplished and the competitors in the marketplace. One of the capabilities most closely scrutinized is the depth of experience a company enjoys in new product introductions, as new product performance can be improved with experience by reducing the cost per introduction.

Companies that refuse to recognize

or choose to ignore the importance of the experience effect in long-term success run the risk of placing themselves at a serious, perhaps fatal, competitive disadvantage. Winning companies in the 80s, however, will take a very hard look at their own—and their competition's—pluses and minuses, and ruthlessly weed out those new product ideas that, while popular, glamorous, or ego-satisfying, offer little if any real potential for success for their corporations. They will foucs, instead, on those opportunities in which they enjoy, by reason of solid, cumulative experience, a premier position or a competitive advantage. Chronic failure to "see things as they really are," and not as we would like them to be can, and all too often does, lead to debilitating failures.

Establishing an Appropriate Environment

Any new product program should be carried out in an environment conducive to achieving both new product and corporate objectives.

Once the types of new products required to meet strategic objectives have been identified, an environment must be created to support the development of these products. The elements of this environment are organization structure, management style, management responsibility, and top-management support.

In creating this supportive environment, the important consideration is matching the new product opportunities to these various elements. For example, in general, riskier ventures or those with a longer payback period, such as the development and launching of new product lines or new-to-the-world products, require a relatively unstructured, entrepreneurial management approach. A highly creative venture team headed by a general manager eager to take substantial risks and strongly supported by top management, is one such approach.

However, new product opportunities change over time, and many companies fail to change their environments accordingly. To avoid the problems that will inevitably result from the mismatch, companies must periodically and systematically evaluate the new product process environment, and tailor their approaches to support emerging new product objectives. Sensitivity and appropriate response to the need for change produce environments that directly support new product programs—programs that will allow companies and corporations to realize their goals rather than merely to fantasize about them.

American business and industry will face serious challenges from within and without in the coming decade. One of the most serious is the need to improve new product performance. Consequently, new product managers of ability, vision, and conviction are needed now, perhaps more than ever before. They must be able to confront the issues vital to corporate growth, profitability, and survival; seize the appropriate and promising opportunities; and solve the problems that impede progress toward achieving long-term corporate and strategic goals. To these ends, they must implement the requisite techniques, such as the seven-step new product process, and they must capitalize on whatever experience advantage they enjoy. For corporate management's part, it must be obviously committed to creating a corporate environment conducive to carrying out the tasks at hand successfully, and it must be willing to pledge the resources needed for the length of time required. Without this total commitment, we risk giving up the industrial leadership role we have played around the world for the past several decades.

20

The Importance of the Product Life Cycle to the Industrial Marketer

Chester R. Wasson

Different types of industrial product life cycles must be anticipated relative to existing use systems, maintaining a leadership position and strategy changes over time.

Business literature has been full of references to "the" product life cycle in recent years, as though there were only one kind of product life cycle, and that the term applied equally to really new products and to minor brand differentiations. Much of this is due to the blinkered eyes of many writers, who are aware of marketing solely in the context of low-priced consumer goods among which the difference is packaging, labeling, or mere perception of market position. Differentiation between industrial producers, however, is usually far more substantive, with the result that the marketer must be aware of the real differences in rapidity of market acceptance and of the consequent differences in product life cycles.

At the time of this writing Chester R. Wasson was chairman of the Business and Economics program at St. Xavier College, Chicago.

Most discussions of the product life cycle deal with heavily advertised consumer goods like beer, breakfast cereals, and soap. Far too many confuse brand life cycles (like that for Winston cigarettes) or minor product variants (as for menthol cigarettes or filter tips) with the much more basic product form cycles (like smoking products in general, or for cigarettes as a group). The result is a too simplistic concept of the product life cycle to be of any real planning value for marketing. As a result, many aspects of product acceptance of importance to industrial marketers are overlooked. With few exceptions, discussion has ignored the easily observed wide differences in initial introduction patterns, with the divergences in production planning, financing, and planning of marketing strategy that these differences imply. Confusion is added by analyzing what is new entirely in physical terms and judging the degree of revolutionary content in terms of engineering advances rather than that of buyer-perceived performance.

Yet even if we did not have some solid research evidence (which we do), a simple analysis of everyday observation would force us to recognize at least four different kinds of product life cycles, and a number of combinations of these four: slow acceptance cycles, mushrooming acceptance, fashion cycles, and fads. We would quickly realize that the differences are so great that the introductory marketing strategies must also differ in type as well as degree, and perceive that we must find some way to predict probable market acceptance patterns well in advance of market introduction. Fortunately, once we define product offerings in consumer terms, we find a key to such prediction in established knowledge of consumer behavior.

Even with a well-planned launch, a firm can lose its initial advantage if it does not plan to keep ahead of competition and change strategy to parallel changes in consumer habits and perceptions with changes in the phases of the cycle. Pricing and product development strategy can help minimize the intensity of the swarm of competition which will come with accelerating market growth and insure survival of the shakeout which comes with the diminution of the rate of market growth. When the saturation of the mature market is reached, with the resulting stability of competitive positions, the temptation to slack off on the search for product improvements can lose opportunities to start new growth periods by broadening demand, or lead to an earlier than necessary loss of markets to newly developed substitutes. The period of decline always raises the question of when to get out, but the best time for a given firm may even be much earlier.

THE DIFFERENT TYPES OF INDUSTRIAL PRODUCT LIFE CYCLES

The most cursory observation shows that the introductory phase of product life cycles differs radically. Thirty years passed between the initial development of the first man-made fiber—imitation silk, known as rayon today—and the first real spurt in market penetration in the 1920s. By contrast, the first real synthetic fiber, nylon, took off with a bang when it hit the women's hosiery market just before the United States entry into World War II. Likewise, electric typewriters needed over two decades of market development, from initial introduction in 1926, until they began to achieve significant acceptance in the late 1940s, while desk-top and hand-held electronic calculators replaced their mechanical predecessors so fast that the makers of the latter lost their market before they could see the threat coming. In the agricultural industry, hybrid corn took more than 10 years to get well-established, chlorinated pesticides, starting with DDT, rocketed to heavy use within little more than a year. Monochromatic television had an almost vertical growth, color TV growth scraped bottom for eight very costly years for RCA.

Quite clearly, some ultimately successful product forms require prolonged market development effort and costs before they take off, others attract a mushrooming demand almost from the first. If we take the standard simplistic description of "the" product life cycle as gospel, we will be misled in our plans. That description generally divides the market life cycle into five major phases, as shown in Exhibit 1:

1. *Introduction, or Market Development*—generally a phase of low growth and deficit investment in sales and promotion.

2. *Rapid Growth*—a period of rapidly accelerating sales, at increasing unit profit.

3. *Decelerating Growth, or Market Turbu-*

EXHIBIT 1

Dynamic competitive strategy and the market life cycle

	MARKET DEVELOPMENT (Introductory period for high learning products only)	RAPID GROWTH (Normal introductory pattern for a very low learning product)	COMPETITIVE TURBULENCE	SATURATION (MATURITY)	DECLINE
STRATEGY OBJECTIVE	Minimize learning requirements, locate and remedy offering defects quickly, develop widespread awareness of benefits, and gain trial by early adopters	To establish a strong brand market and distribution niche as quickly as possible	To maintain and strengthen the market niche achieved through dealer and consumer loyalty	To defend brand position against competing brands and product category against other potential products, through constant attention to product improvement opportunities and fresh promotional and distribution approaches	To milk the offering dry of all possible profit
OUTLOOK FOR COMPETITION	None is likely to be attracted in the early, unprofitable stages	Early entrance of numerous aggressive emulators	Price and distribution squeeze on the industry, shaking out the weaker entrants	Competition stabilized, with few or no new entrants and market shares not subject to substantial change in the absence of a substantial perceived improvement in some brand	Similar competition declining and dropping out because of decrease in consumer interest
PRODUCT DESIGN OBJECTIVE	Limited number of models with physical product and offering designs both focused on minimizing learning requirements. Designs cost- and use-engineered to appeal to most receptive segment. Utmost attention to quality control and quick elimination of market-revealed defects in design	Modular design to facilitate flexible addition of variants to appeal to every new segment and new use-system as fast as discovered	Intensified attention to product improvement, tightening up of line to eliminate unnecessary specialties with little market appeal	A constant alert for market pyramiding opportunities through either bold cost- and price-penetration of new markets or major product changes. Introduction of flanker products. Constant attention to possibilities for product improvement and cost cutting. Reexamination of necessity of design compromises	Constant pruning of line to eliminate any items not returning a direct profit
PRICING OBJECTIVE	To impose the minimum of value: perception learning and to match the value reference perception of the most receptive segments. High trade discounts and sampling advisable	A price line for every taste, from low-end to premium models. Customary trade discounts. Aggressive promotional pricing, with prices cut as fast as costs decline due to accumulated production experience. Intensification of sampling	Increased attention to market-broadening and promotional pricing opportunities	Defensive pricing to preserve product category franchise. Search for incremental pricing opportunities, including private label contracts, to boost volume and gain an experience advantage	Maintenance of profit level pricing with complete disregard of any effect on market share
PROMOTIONAL GUIDELINES Communications objectives	a) Create widespread awareness and understanding of offering benefits b) Gain trial by early adopters	Create and strengthen brand preference among trade and final users Stimulate general trial	Maintain consumer franchise and strengthen dealer ties	Maintain consumer and trade loyalty, with strong emphasis on dealers and distributors. Promotion of greater use frequency.	Phase out, keeping just enough to maintain profitable distribution
Most valuable media mix	In order of value Publicity Personal sales Mass communications	Mass media Personal sales Sales promotion, including sampling Publicity	Mass media Dealer promotions Personal selling to dealers Sales promotions Publicity	Mass media Dealer-oriented promotions	Cut down all media to the bone—use no sales promotions of any kind
DISTRIBUTION POLICY	Exclusive or selective, with distributor margins high enough to justify heavy promotional spending	Intensive and extensive, with dealer margins just high enough to keep them interested. Close attention to rapid resupply of distributor stocks and heavy inventories at all levels	Intensive and extensive, and a strong emphasis on keeping dealer well supplied, but with minimum inventory cost to him	Intensive and extensive, with strong emphasis on keeping dealer well supplied, but at minimum inventory cost to him	Phase out outlets as they become marginal
INTELLIGENCE FOCUS	To identify actual developing use-systems and to uncover any product weakness	Detailed attention to brand position, to gaps in model and market coverage, and to opportunities for market segmentation	Close attention to product improvement needs, to market-broadening chances, and to possible fresh promotion themes	Intensified attention to possible product improvements. Sharp alert for potential new inter-product competition and for signs of beginning product decline	Information helping to identify the point at which the product should be phased out

Copyright © 1974 by Chester R. Wasson. Based on Wasson, *Dynamic Competitive Strategy and Product Life Cycles*, Challenge Books, St. Charles, Il., 1974.

lence—unit profits decline and the large number of competitors who have entered during the boom period scramble for a solid niche in the market, with the weakest or least committed shaken out.

    4. *Maturity, or Saturation*—a period of relatively stable per capita sales, characterized by a relatively viscous industry structure.

    5. *Decline* in total market size as some new substitute proves to do a better job of satisfying customers.

As the exhibit hints, however, some product forms labeled "low learning" do not pass through any prolonged market development phase. Sales rise rapidly almost from the day of introduction, as happened with nylon stockings, electronic calculators, and DDT. When this occurs, the introducer must run fast to keep ahead of swarms of competitors slavering over the obvious lush profits (unless a really tight patent bars them). On the other hand, when initial sales are slow, and initial customers must be hunted down, the problem is not competition, but financing the heavy sales and promotional costs, and getting a few select aggressive distributors. As Exhibit 1 indicates, the fast-start product must be treated from the first with the strategy for the period of rapid growth and this strategy is at odds on almost every point from that for a market development product. Indeed, even the target specifications for the R&D must be different, so as to minimize the learning problem insofar as possible. Since this is so, we need some means of predicting the acceptance climate for any projected product at the concept stage, before any R&D targets are decided upon. We need especially to understand why products which appear to be physically analogous, as do rayon and nylon, electric typewriters and electronic calculators for instance, meet such different market receptions.

    Attention to physical similarities leaves us confused. Both rayon and nylon were introduced as continuous fibers, as substitutes for silk. Electric typewriters and desktop calculators both had at least a superficial resemblance to their predecessors, did similar tasks, and were operated in much the same ways. From an engineering point of view, the electric typewriter was a mere evolutionary change, the electronic calculator, a revolutionary one. Both rayon and nylon were, for their days, revolutionary advances, although rayon turned out to be quite similar to a fiber at whose market it was not initially aimed (cotton).

    The fog begins to dissipate, however, when we consider these and other seemingly contradictory pairs of introductions from the standpoint of the buyer, when we consider what they promised to do for him and to him. To the potential buyer, any offering or any sort is merely a promise that he can gain fulfillment of a bundle of felt needs—it is merely a set of performance characteristics fitting into some kind of total use-system which is the real source of need satisfaction. Whether the buyer is a housewife purchasing a box of laundry detergent or an industrial organization deciding on a raw material, manufacturing equipment, or an office machine, the proffered item is simply a possible key component of some specific use-system. The purchase decision will be based on how well the satisfaction bundle offered meets a corresponding desire-set, and on what changes must be made in his habits of action and thought involved in the use-system in order to gain the promised performance bundle.

PRODUCTS AS PARTS OF USE SYSTEMS

Spinners and weavers are not seeking textile fibers. They simply want some way, preferably a familiar one, to produce a finished textile desired by converters and garment makers who buy later on. The latter desire a profitable means of producing dresses, shirts, stockings, and other garments which are attractive to final customers in terms of their own standards of protection and decoration.

At every stage in the purchase chain, the item purchased produces the result desired only in conjunction with an habitual system of procedures, and usually in the context of an habitual intellectual system of thought about the way things are done. The physical use systems usually involve other products, often other persons (in industry, nearly always), and always a developed system of habitual skills. Accompanying most such systems are one or more of three systems of intellectual perceptual habits: perceptions of the expected satisfaction sources, perceptions of the social role of the user in relation to the product, and perceptions of the value of a given kind of satisfaction.

Psychological experiments long ago demonstrated what we all know—habit systems take time and energy to develop. The change in any habit sequence is a frustrating, effort-consuming process. Anyone who has ever made even a minor change of switching over from a car with a 3-speed transmission to one with a 4-speed shift can sympathize with the rats in a psychological experiment now 50 years old. They needed more than twice as many trials to learn a simple switch in the location of food in the arms of a T-maze than they needed to learn the original location. The old habit had to be broken before the new one could be perfected.

We should thus expect that introductions which require changes in accepted habits of either use or perceptual habits will be adopted reluctantly. And we would expect to find that products which are accepted with enthusiasm to be those which fit neatly into established systems of use and

perception and also promise a substantially better level of performance in some way. Such indeed proves to be a key to understanding the different receptions in the product pairs cited above, and to all other new product experiences the author has been able to analyze.

Consider the cases of rayon and nylon. Rayon was first intended to be a truly man-made silk (the inventor used mulberry leaves as his raw material), and for about 40 years was sold only in continuous filament form, largely for knitted goods. But although labeled initially as artificial silk, it was not really like silk, either to manufacture or use. It felt different to the hand, handled differently in processing and dyeing. It began to build a market only when given its own name, rayon, in the early 1920s, then given the needed heavy promotional backing, with strong technical assistance to processors. The big gains came with a physical change in the product—the introduction of staple (cut) fiber, adaptable to cotton processes. Ironically, it then displaced silk in a major use—women's better dresses. In the Sears' 1929 catalogue for example, all of the better dresses were silk. In the 1939 edition all of them were made of rayon.

Nylon, on the other hand, was not released for sale until processing problems were solved, and then backed up with strong technical assistance and promoted for use in a product making the greatest use of its major tensile strength and wear characteristics—women's hosiery. Since the appearance qualities were at least as good as those of silk stockings, and the durability greater, and since the intervening processors had little trouble adapting, it was an instant smash success (interrupted by the wartime diversion of the fiber to more critical substitute uses in parachutes and other military needs).

The electric typewriter may not, at first

glance, seem to pose any major habit change problem. The keyboard was the same, and operated in a similar manner. In fact, however, it required the typist to change the positioning of her hands. Any trained typist had developed the habit of resting her fingers on the middle alphabetical row. With the electric, she had to keep all fingers off all keys until ready to strike. The merest brushing of a key in passing would actuate it. The result was that the best of typists had to go through a substantial period of spoiled copy until she broke her old hand positioning habit—usually an average of two months. Since speed and accuracy were key items in her skill, this was a completely unacceptable price except for the few to whom the small extra uniformity of copy was of very high value. The market share of the electrics was minor until typists began to be taught initially on the electrics, then had problems changing to the heavier feel of typing on the manual machines.

The desk top calculator is a subsidiary tool for most users, and skill and speed in its use not a basic element in the job success. What minor operational differences the electronic versions posed relative to their mechanical predecessors were not significant, and would not disturb well-ingrained habits. Thus, performance-wise, they were simply an improvement in portability and in computational flexibility, even though they were completely revolutionary in terms of the mechanism under the housing. Thus they gained ready acceptance.

Likewise, hybrid corn was really a very minor innovation in terms of the product (dating back, in fact, to the early Indian practice of maintaining several separate strains). But from the farmer's point of view, it changed operation and financing habits drastically. Before he had simply saved some of the previous crop and used it for the next year's planting. But now he had to dispose of

the entire crop and buy new seed at a per-unit cost several times the per bushel price he received for his crop. DDT, on the other hand, was simply another chemical used in much the same way as those he had bought and used before, but more efficient.

Clearly, we must look beyond the physical product itself to make a critical prediction of what a proposed introduction does to user habits if we are to plan a successful introductory market strategy, or even set the correct targets for R&D.

All of the examples used above involved a change in physical procedures, and these can be predicted rather well by the use of simple flow diagrams comparing the step-by-step procedures required in the use-system of the old way of gaining the end desired and the new way required by the proposed introduction. However, products may also involve intellectual habits of valuation of benefits, such as understanding that a more expensive product may be cheaper in use, or accepting a changed role in the production process. Computer typesetting, for example, was certain of a very hostile reception from the lithographers because it downgraded their role in printing. It made original headway best in new enterprises outside union jurisdiction.[1]

GAINING AND HOLDING FIRST PLACE

As the figure indicates, competition is not the main problem to be met during the introductory phase of a high learning product. The initiator usually has the market to himself, in fact. Whether or not others enter at this point, the crucial problems are appropriate design for initial customer needs,

---

[1]For a discussion of methods of predicting the learning requirement, see Wasson, C. R., *Dynamic Competitive Strategy and Product Life Cycles*, pp. 199-207, Challenge Books, St. Charles, Il., 1974.

especially reliability and freedom from annoying defects, and education of the potential market.

With low-earning products, vigorous competition must be expected early, and every aspect of planning focussed on keeping well ahead of any newcomers. The first on the market has an advantage in terms of the learning curve, but can easily lose it. Bowmar had the initial advantage in the hand-held electronic computer market, only to lose it through lack of production expertise and economies when aggressive integrated producers came in. IBM was the second maker of computers, not the first, but took over the market because it perceived the need for software libraries and technical assistance as part of the bundle offered. None of the original labels on the automobile market survived the first phase of market growth, and Ford, who introduced the first low-priced utility design lost the market dominance he attained when he refused to follow the emerging market segmentation of the rapid growth phase in the second and third decades, with design variations.

Competitors can enter at any stage except possibly the one that does not matter—the decline phase. They will succeed to the extent that those already established leave open some areas of unfulfilled customer demand. The pattern of demand changes with changes in market maturity, so that every element of strategy must be constantly planned in advance to leave as few openings as possible for competition.

STRATEGY MUST CHANGE WITH THE CYCLE

During the rapid growth stage, pricing, product design, and distribution service are all critical. By this time, accumulated production experience will begin to cut unit costs substantially, and burgeoning demand will also cut into per-unit promotional costs and even the necessary distribution margins. Too many firms tend to let price cuts lag decreases in cost during this period, offering a luscious bait that will attract competitors from far and near. If prices are allowed to fall in concert with costs, experience has shown that added competition will be much less strong. Any weakness in distributive availability will cause distributors to encourage the entrance of new suppliers in order to promote their own profits. During this period, also, market demand tends to become differentiated, with both low end and premium segments becoming developed, as well as the need for other kinds of design variations. Even in the absence of a too high profit expectation, some alert enterprisers will find these potential market niches and develop them.

All of these forces tend to create a tendency for the industry as a whole to build capacity which cannot be fully utilized once growth begins to slow down, and some competitors must be shaken out. Those who survive will be those who have developed the strongest relations with final customers and distributors.

By the time the market shakes down into its saturation or maturity stage, the niche of each of the remaining suppliers has become fairly stable. Buyers' perceptions and expectations of each have become fairly well fixed. The core elements of each market segment have found offerings coming very close to their desire-sets and so are neither searching for new suppliers nor paying much attention to promotion of other offerings. Promotion should be primarily aimed at maintaining distribution, at keeping current market segments satisfied, and, of course, attracting the attention of any new buyers coming onto the market. Market entry and market share change become costly simply because customers have no incentive to seek new sources. Nevertheless, market entrance and market share gains, at a profit, are possible to whoever can develop an offering really perceived by buyers as a very substantially greater value to some segment of the market.

If it is to hope for success, any new entry into a saturated market must be perceived by some major market segment as a really substantial improvement in value of some kind over existing offerings; either a substantial gain in the perceived benefit content of the offering as compared to those currently available, a substantial gain in the ratio of those benefits desired to price, or a benefit in terms of purchase ease and availability. Except when the promotion causes buyers to perceive substantial new benefits, added promotional pressure alone is seldom effective.

The most certain route to market entry or market share gains during maturity is that of making a perceived major improvement in the offering. No product is ever likely to do everything the customer desires, at a price he feels worth paying. Furthermore, the market segment attracted by every offering always has fringe buyers who find nothing on the market very close to their desire set. Thus there is nearly always a potential new market niche which can be brought into being by designing an offering that nibbles off the edges of several segments. Changes in consumer desires over time as well as changes in the state of the art open possibilities of winning over large segments. Indeed, the decline of every life cycle is brought about by the revolutionary changes in the state of the art which create better substitute offerings. The corollary of this fact is that R&D focussed on diminution of the natural defects in the offering can raise the barriers to substitute offerings. The steel industry would not have lost as much container business to aluminum, paper, and plastics in the 1960s had the industry worked as hard to develop thinner tinplate, before the substitute came in, as they did afterward. Customers would have had less incentive to change their habitual processes. It should be noted that such customer habits give the established source of supply a very substantial protection. Copper cable, for example, had lost only one-third of its utility market by the time aluminum had dropped to less than two-thirds the cost of an equivalent copper capacity cable. But none of the utilities which went through the effort of changing their procedures ever changed back.

Changes in the benefit/cost ratio, provided they are truly perceived as really substantial, can always win substantial market segments. This, after all, is the basic principal behind every merchant's sales promotions. Some of this may be achieved, where production costs permit, by a substantial permanent cut in the price level of a product with an established market position. (But let it be noted that a new entrant, without the established reputation, which offers only a lower price, is very likely to be perceived as simply a lower-end quality.)

Changes in the customers' evaluation of components of the offering, which may come with the maturation of the market itself may open up such opportunities to offer a better benefit/cost ratio for the new desire sets of major market segments in the case of products which needed substantial elements of sales and market services in the introductory stage. Once the consumer is well educated on the product, he may have no further interest in such costly services and be open to a supplier who eliminates them from the offering bundle at an appropriate cost savings.

Such seems to have been the situation when the life cycle of polyethylene resins reached saturation. While the original producers maintained their technical research staffs, and the accompanying costs, sellers whose sales operation consisted of only a price list and a telephone captured a substantial market share at prices below the costs of the product-plus-service package the major producers were still offering. By this time, many buyers no longer had need for new know-how, and many had developed some special technical knowledge they did not care to make available to suppliers who might pass it on to competitors. Such experiences make it obvious that sellers must keep in touch with the changing nature of customer desire-sets at every stage of the cycle, and be prepared to adjust the offering accordingly.

Distribution availability is an important part of the value of any offering, industrial or consumer, but often of more crucial importance to the industrial buyer than to the consumer to whom many nearly identical substitutes are often freely available. A mere advantage in availability may win customers. In the crowded industrial fastener market, one small producer used this means to win a profitable share. His sales force consisted of nothing more than his telephone and a monthly newsletter and price list of readily available items. But in addition, he kept himself available by telephone, day or night, and in the case of emergency, would go immediately to the factory floor, change over machines to any special set-up necessary, and get a critical shipment out by plane the next morning if necessary. He gained a substantial volume from customers of the largest suppliers.

Sometimes the distributor himself can be the critical element of added value needed for market penetration, if he has an established reputation for quality and dependability. This is one reason an established seller of a line of products can often succeed

with another item new only to him, and also a reason that the quality of the distributors used can be critical in gaining a strong niche during the growth phase of the market. For instance when a maker of oil seals, with a strong distributive position, decided that the market for O-rings was becoming attractive, it discovered that an established maker of high quality rings had a weak distributive acceptance, and simply made an agreement to take over the latter's marketing operation instead of going into production. Because of the seal makers' reputation, the first order alone paid for his cataloguing of the item, to the advantage of both firms.

THE DANGERS OF GOING TO SLEEP

The relative stability of the mature market tends to induce a dangerous degree of somnolence on the part of the established firms. There is a dangerous reluctance to "obsolete our own product," with a coincident slackening of attention to possible new improvements in the state of the art which could create new pyramided growth phases by broadening or changing the nature of the demand. Whenever the established firms do this, they leave themselves vulnerable to competition which does not have their commitment to the status quo.

Good examples are the effects of the development of transistors and their more complicated successors on the established makers of electronic appliances, later on the makers of office calculators, and most recently on the watch industry. Bell Lab's development of the original transistors was initially ignored by both the major makers of radios and television sets, and even by the military in the United States. The result was the dominance of Japanese firms who had no vested interest in tube electronics. When integrated circuit chips made the compact hand-held calculator possible, the makers of mechanical devices left the R&D and the market to outsiders. At the moment, the major producers of mechanical watches seem to have made the same mistake.

Eventually, of course, the progress of knowledge will lead to some means of obsoleting any product, and decline will set in. At this point, some decision must be made as to when and how to quit.

WHEN TO GET OUT

Any product whose market is declining is an obvious candidate for elimination. But the exact timing of that exit will depend on the situation of the individual firm, and the market exit may be advisable at some earlier point in the cycle, for some firms. The only general rule is that the firm should withdraw from the market whenever the resources employed would earn a better opportunity profit in some alternate line of activity. For some, this will mean dropping out even before the product is launched on the market, preferably by selling the rights to someone better equipped to develop that market. This is, after all, the choice of most book authors, and it enables them to draw an income before there are any profits, or even

when some never come. Even the largest of firms may so choose if the product does not fit their capabilities, they lack the patience to wait out a development period, or lack the aggressive promotional skills to survive the mushrooming growth of the market for a low-learning product. At the other end of the life cycle, there is often room for a well-situated firm to profit from the residual demand from those reluctant to adopt the product's successor. There is still profit to be made by small firms in selling buggies to the Amish, for example.

Whatever the timing decision, the resources devoted to a declining product can and should be minimized. Promotional effort is almost completely ineffective, so marketing costs can be very low. Sometimes, of course, what is obsolete in one market may be what another requires. In the field of processing machinery, batch process equipment which is out-of-date in an advanced country may be best adapted to the needs of one in an earlier stage of technological development.

At every stage in the cycle, market opportunities and profits are functions of consumer habits and needs at that time and in that place. The changes in these which come inexorably with every turn of a calendar page require corresponding changes in market strategy.

21 The Search for Special Niches

Buffeted by persistently volatile interest rates, continued government regulation, and formidable nonbank competition, America's banks have finally concluded that their long-range salvation lies within themselves. Although banks still control the largest single chunk of the nation's financial assets, they worry about being pushed off their commanding heights. So they are designing strategies aimed at finding specialties and market niches in which they can compete vigorously and grow profitably. The first tangible signs are now appearing:

- BankAmerica Corp. is buying discount broker Charles Schwab & Co.
- Chemical New York Corp. is trying to buy an interest in a medium-size Florida banking institution.
- First Interstate Bancorp. is planning to franchise its name and services nationwide.

The nation's commercial banks, numbering 14,744 at year end, have long been viewed as fairly homogeneous. Be it globe-girdling Citibank or First National on innumerable Main Streets, the basic functions of each—to take in deposits and make commercial loans—remain identical and define each as a bank, legally and in the public mind.

This perceived similarity among banks is a severe handicap, which they finally are challenging, but amid considerable skepticism from corporate customers in particular. "I don't give the banks high marks for looking forward," asserts Robert S. Einzig, vice-president and treasurer at San Francisco-based Transamerica Corp. To convince Einzig and others, bankers must do much more to differentiate their institutions in what is essentially an undifferentiated service industry.

Increasingly, the quality of service will be crucial. And most banks, lacking the financial clout and geographic scope to serve all markets equally well, will elect to serve fewer markets. By upgrading some functions and downgrading or eliminating others, those that survive the intensifying competition and accelerating deregulation in the 1980s will emerge as specialty institutions. Only a handful can hope to be financial supermarkets.

The process of reevaluation and repositioning has already begun, but it is an arduous task involving hard choices that few bankers are willing to make as yet. Strategic planning "is not happening fast enough," warns Donald C. Waite III, partner at the consulting firm McKinsey & Co. Despite the realization that markets must be segmented and businesses refined, notes Waite, "there is still a great tradition of general banking."

To overcome that tradition and emerge winners in the battle for consumer and corporate dollars, bankers must:

☐ Create innovative products to set each bank apart from the competition.

☐ Focus on fewer lending and nonlending areas, thereby rejecting some customer groups.

☐ Project an image that registers clearly with corporate treasurers and consumers alike.

☐ Develop much more sophisticated marketing and operational skills.

☐ Anticipate and react to change by consorting with such enemies as money market funds, brokerage firms, and insurance companies and by emphasizing fee-generating services to offset narrowed lending margins.

The boldest innovations lately have been the entry by two California banking institutions into the discount brokerage business—bold because the National Banking Act of 1933, also known as the Glass-Steagall Act, prohibits banks from underwriting or dealing in corporate securities. Yet BankAmerica Corp., parent of Bank of America, and Security Pacific National Bank, which is the 10th largest, last No-

vember disclosed two very different schemes to offer discount brokering anyway.

Both stressed that their plans were legal, since they were merely going to execute buy and sell orders—as banks have long done for customers of their trust departments—at the lower transaction rates offered by discount brokers, and not "underwrite or deal in" securities. But both institutions clearly were laying the groundwork for the day when Glass-Steagall restrictions would be lifted. In the interim, they would stand to gain new customers and a new source of income.

Security Pacific's plan is already up and running because, unlike BankAmerica's, it does not involve an acquisition needing action by regulators. Through an arrangement with Boston-based Fidelity Brokerage Services, Inc., the Los Angeles bank now can execute securities transactions for any customer who walks into one of the bank's 640 branches in California. Security Pacific hopes the service will break even within a year and believes it will "cement relations" with existing customers and attract new ones, says Frank V. Cahouet, vice-chairman of Security Pacific.

BankAmerica's plan is to purchase Schwab, the San Francisco-based discount broker with more than 40 offices in 19 states, for $53 million in stock. The holding company acquisition, which awaits Federal Reserve Board approval, is the more daring because it would provide BankAmerica with a piece of the action. Moreover, the brokerage network could be upgraded to full service status if and when the law permits.

Stephen T. McLin, senior vice-president for strategic planning at BankAmerica, says that providing good execution of stock transactions at a reasonable price "will be an important part of the banking industry's pursuit of the upscale market." He estimates that more than 500,000 of Bank America's customers are potential Schwab customers, while virtually all of Schwab's 250,000 existing customers would be likely prospects for the bank.

SOUL-SEARCHING

The BankAmerica move is but one result of the extensive soul-searching that is now going on at the San Francisco-based giant. Although it is humbled by a 33% decline in earnings last year and reeling from the high cost of maintaining consumer deposits, BankAmerica—$121.1 billion in assets at year end ranked it No. 1—is simply too huge to narrow its product lines and market reach severely. It can, however, refine its business strategy. McLin says BofA will "accelerate" its developing specialty in lending to high-technology companies and has targeted the wine industry as a promising field for building on its role as the nation's biggest private lender to agriculture.

Too many bank executives, Waite of McKinsey & Co. charges, focus on setting budgets and growth targets for the near term and shun strategic planning for the long haul. Those bankers who do recognize the need for a redefinition of their institutions' business strategy hesitate to implement change for fear of causing "organizational disruptions."

But some halting steps are being taken, especially among the bigger banks. In Minnesota, the two leading bank holding companies, First Bank System, Inc. (FBS) and Northwest Bancorporation (Banco), are following similar paths to break out of a stagnant lending environment. Both built their portfolios by lending to the major food processing, grain trading, and technology companies in the region—companies that today borrow almost exclusively, and at less cost, in the commercial paper market.

The initial response was to go after the middle market—those companies with annual sales of $5 million to $100 million—but in this FBS and Banco bumped up against aggressive New York and Chicago banks. "We're going back to square one to define what businesses we're in," says E. Peter Gillette, chairman and chief executive officer of Northwestern Bank of Minneapolis, Banco's lead bank. "Once we define them, we are going to have to decide whether we're going to grow them, maintain them, or get out of them."

The newest tack has been to identify niches in the middle market, mainly in the energy, agricultural, and technology areas. Both have opened banking offices in Wisconsin, have expanded their international divisions, and are battling for the Iowa market. Banco last year purchased Iowa-based Dial Corp., a major consumer finance company, and FBS is trying to buy an interest in Banks of Iowa. Both are also trying to capitalize on their agricultural expertise by offering new services and more flexible financing to lure farmers away from smaller banks. "We're trying to find areas not served by the big banks," says Larry Buegler, chairman and chief executive officer of Northwestern Bank of St. Paul.

For many banks, specialization has been the by-product of location. The large Texas banks have always been heavy hitters in energy, which on average still accounts for more than a third of their commercial loans. The wisdom of putting so many eggs in one basket is in question now by investors worried about the oil glut (*BW*, Mar. 29). But there is some diversity even among Texas banks. The two Houston-based giants, Texas Commerce Bancshares Inc. and First City Bancorporation of Texas Inc., are emphasizing very different market sectors. TCB, always oriented toward the commercial, or wholesale, lending market, has been purchasing banks around the state with a similar focus, while First City is promoting consumer, or retail, banking.

Consumer deposits are no longer a very

cheap funding source, "but they're still less costly than other sources," and consumers offer "a balance against being completely in the commercial business," says First City President Nat S. Rogers. Despite its commitment to the retail market, however, First City still has about the same ratio of retail deposits to commercial deposits as does Texas Commerce. On the retail lending side, though, First City has more loans outstanding than Texas Commerce because of its credit card business.

And some Texas institutions are diversifying still further. Mercantile Texas, based in Dallas, has built up its data processing subsidiary, Affiliated Computer Systems Inc., and the income from fees is streaming in. The subsidiary now does extensive data processing work for other banks, and two years ago it launched a shared automated teller machine network, known as MPACT (*BW*, Oct. 12). Affiliated expects to bring in $50 million in revenues this year, with 80% coming from providing services for other financial institutions.

Meanwhile, banks from other parts of the country have been rushing pell-mell into the Texans' specialty of energy. Some have done so without adequate planning, figuring that financing energy offered limitless profits. "Energy is a real buzzword these days," comments one Midwestern banker. "Bankers follow each other around like sheep."

But a handful from outside Texas do have a strong reputation in this lending area. Continental Illinois today employs about 100 persons in its 25-year-old oil and gas lending unit. That staff includes 12 petroleum engineers who help "control the risks" of lending against oil reserves, says Gerald K. Bergman, an executive vice-president. The Chicago bank was one of the first, in the early 1970s, to offer revolving credits to independent producers, whose borrowing limits could be raised every six months as proven reserves grew.

Another facet of its energy emphasis is a subsidiary, Continental Illinois Energy Development Corp., recently opened in Houston. It will tailor deals for the smaller companies unable to qualify for conventional bank loans and will take an equity position in the form of overriding royalty interests, warrants, or stocks.

Through a department set up in 1977, Continental has arranged about 25 mergers and acquisitions for all types of industrial companies, with a total transaction value "well over $1 billion," says Caren L. Reed, an executive vice-president. Such deals generally are arranged by investment bankers, but the commercial banks do them at lower fees for smaller companies and can provide the money themselves.

For the large New York, Chicago, and California banks, the middle market has become a much-coveted specialty. Larger corporations have bargained down lending margins, and they increasingly turn to the commercial paper market for their short-term financing needs. In fact, the banks themselves did much to wean large corporations away from their dependence on the banking system: They gave corporations sophisticated cash-management tools and offered backup lines of credit to paper issuers, thereby enabling corporate giants to look elsewhere for cheaper funds.

Now bankers hope to fill that void with small and medium-size borrowers. These borrowers, as potentially higher-risk credits, usually pay more than the prime lending rate. But intense competition has pushed margins down even in this market, and now some regional banks believe they can outperform the big banks with small local companies.

Provident National Corp. in Philadelphia numbers among its middle-market customers numerous businesses owned or run by families, including paper company P. H. Glatfelter Co. and New Jersey-based Inductotherm Industries Inc., which manufactures induction furnaces. Similarly, Cleveland-based Ameritrust Corp. is planning to focus on lending to machine tool companies in the Midwest, building on what it believes to be special knowledge of the industry.

WOOING THE MIDDLE MARKET

European American Bank, dwarfed by other New York banks, has earmarked $1 billion to extend credit to small and medium-size businesses and has a promotional campaign to attract them. EAB, owned by six European banks, assumed the failed Franklin National Bank's branch network in New York City and Long Island eight years ago and has built a steady retail business. Now it hopes to capture more commercial business in the region by promising customers "speed of communications" and quicker loan approvals than the larger New York City banks can provide, says Senior Vice-President Robert Previdi.

But simply selecting a special niche will not assure banks the lucrative business they seek. An individual bank will have to convey a distinct and readily identifiable image, one that will provide an umbrella theme to all its businesses. And this will require not only sophisticated marketing skills but also solid operational backup. For it is ultimately the quality of service, be it a simple line of credit or a complex cash-management program, on which banking relationships depend. And the cleverest image can become an embarrassment if the back office fouls up. By the same token, if a bank does not capitalize on its state-of-the-art technology and services, it has lost a key marketing battle.

By and large, marketing is "a tool bankers don't know quite how to pick up and use," says David Flegal, senior vice-president at the market research firm of Oxtoby-Smith Inc. Although the top 200 banks have recognized the need, marketing managers are often frustrated by the paltry budgets and limited power granted them by financially oriented managers. Furthermore, the very fact that banks have traditionally served so many markets and failed to specialize has meant that advertising and marketing must cover a host of themes. The result, says Flegal, is that many banks, "in their attempts to appeal to all, are remembered by none."

The defense widely mounted by banks is that government-mandated interest rate ceilings have in effect designed the banks' consumer products for them, leaving them little room for creativity. As deregulation moves forward, banks "are going to have to figure out what products to offer consumers, rather than wait for the government to give them the next instrument," says Allan F. Paro, national advertising manager for the American Bankers Assn., trade association for more than 13,000 of the nation's commercial banks. But critics point out that other regulated or formerly regulated industries, such as airlines and liquor, have managed to create demand and distinct images.

Clearly, a number of large banks have secured a strong image, either by concentrating on the blue-chip wholesale banking market and carriage trade, as Morgan Guaranty Trust Co. has done for decades, or by a drastic strategy change, as when Bankers Trust New York Corp. six years ago shed its retail operations. Chemical New York, with rigorous self-evaluation, is currently trying to sharpen its fuzzy image and pinpoint certain businesses while curtailing or eliminating others (*BW*, Mar. 15). Right now, says Alan H. Fishman, chief financial officer at Chemical, the major bank competitors are "more alike than we're different." But Chemical has demonstrated uncharacteristic aggressiveness in battling for an interest in Florida National Banks of Florida Inc.

And a number of others have chosen to change their images by changing their names, as when Western Bancorporation last year applied the First Interstate label to itself and its 21 "grandfathered" banks in 11 states. The Los Angeles-based company went even further in March with plans to franchise its name and sell its services to other banks, especially in the states bordering its territory (*BW*, Apr. 5).

Superior technology is a highly marketable asset in the banking industry today, and numerous banks have been selling their operational capability not only to corporate customers and other banks but also to such rivals as money market funds, brokerage firms, and insurance companies. The resultant fee income is a small but rapidly growing portion of overall bank earnings today. "Over time, what will really differentiate banks will be operating services . . . . A customer will be able to buy credit as a commodity anywhere," says Leo F. Mullin, senior vice-president for corporate planning at First Chicago Corp. With this in mind, First Chicago is hoping to build a reputation as an "operating bank" over the next two or three years, and it has 817 performance charts to evaluate success in marketing and delivering 40 different operations products.

Close observers of the banking industry believe that the real money to be made from technological excellence will come not from the retail side of the business but rather from the corporate side. For many companies, it is the quality of operating service that makes or breaks a banking relationship. As competition escalates, corporate treasurers will "get a better product at a better price," says

Richard C. O'Sullivan, senior vice-president for finance at Allegheny Ludlum Steel Corp. Increasingly, banks are using operating services as a selling point to win over corporate clients for a broader array of services and loans.

Foremost among those selling data processing services is Mellon National Bank, the nation's 15th largest. Its Data center serves 200 institutions in 11 states and last year garnered Mellon $20.5 million in fees, which amounted to a healthy 17.6% of operating revenues. Mellon's entire data processing system has more than 10,000 terminals on line, processing an average 1.2 million transactions daily, and has allowed Mellon to move into new markets far afield of its Pittsburgh location. This nationwide marketing prompts one local company treasurer to assert that "Mellon has ignored its backyard completely," but the bank gets high marks from other local customers.

Making a niche for itself in selling fee-based investment management service is medium-size Provident National in Philadelphia. Roger S. Hillas, chairman of the $3.3 billion (assets) company, asserts that Provident is "playing in the big leagues" in this field. Of the trust division's $15.9 billion in assets under management, $4 billion is accounted for by Shearson/American Express' Temporary Investment Fund and $5.7 billion by Paine Webber's CashFund. Fees from managing those two funds alone netted $15 million for Provident last year. Provident will soon be the sponsoring, clearing, and lending bank for a number of asset management accounts offered to wealthy individuals by firms that include E. F. Hutton, Shearson/Amex, and Bache, and it is seeking insurance companies to sign on, too.

Columbus-based Banc One Corp. was the first to offer such services. It acts as processor and Visa card issuer for Merrill Lynch's revolutionary Cash Management Account, does similar processing work for seven other brokerage firms, and is negotiating with insurance companies and real estate firms to start a program that would permit customers to borrow against the equity in their homes and life insurance policies via bank cards. "The trend is toward a total assets account," says John G. Alexander, vice-president for financial services at Banc One.

High on the list of banks doing a volume business in processing mutual funds is State Street Bank & Trust Co. of Boston, which handles about 30% of the assets of all mutual funds. Also a major player is the Bank of New York, which handles processing for more than 100 mutual funds, including 33 money market mutual funds. This processing business helped boost trust department fees at the Bank of New York 30% to $93.4 million last year. Although Bank of New York is the 18th largest bank holding company in the country, it ranks No. 3 in trust income.

Now the bank has parlayed its expertise in serving the mutual fund industry into a popular new cash-management program. "We were looking for ways to exploit our position in serving the funds," says Richard Freimuth, vice-president at the Bank of New York. Under the program, dubbed Check-Invest, companies with less than $10 million in sales and nonprofit organizations with small amounts of idle cash can have their deposit balances above $7,500 "swept" daily and automatically into one of 13 money market funds. This vehicle produces high investment yields for small firms lacking the time or expertise to manage their own money and unable to afford a standard bank cash-management program.

For most major banks, the pursuit of fees takes them along the similar routes of acquiring subsidiaries in consumer and business finance, mortgages, and leasing— activities that rarely convey uniqueness to customers.

With so many banks rushing after similar markets and not focusing their energies, says Chemical's Fishman, there is an "overcapacity problem" in the industry. As banking deregulation proceeds, Fishman predicts, that capacity will be brought in line with demand, "and you'll see changes and patterns developing among banks."

PUSHING NONCREDIT SERVICES

Difficult as it may be, banking institutions must exploit their established credit market niches by conjuring up closely related noncredit services. EAB, for instance, has done just that with its "Eurabank" data base originally designed for its six foreign bank owners. Today Eurabank provides data on 2,100 foreign banks in 118 countries, and its users range from banks to federal banking agencies to insurance companies. "We want to be thought of as the place to go when people have a question about foreign bank analysis," says Jan D. Slee, assistant vice-president.

Seeking out specialties is not all a matter of expanding into new services, however. The toughest part for bankers may well be living up to their increasingly common refrain that they "cannot be all things to all people," for few find it in character to walk away from their customers. The most that some banks will own up to now is the need to retrench in European operations, a process already far along at some institutions. Designing a disposable branch that can be converted easily into a pizza parlor, as First Interstate has done, may be easier than turning away a corporate borrower for purely strategic reasons. As the industry begins to consolidate and specialize, outright rejection of customers will be, in the words of one astute observer, "one of the last things to change."

22 Management and Consumers in an Era of Stagflation

Avraham Shama

The effects of stagflation on marketing management and consumers, with specific recommendations for marketing management.

The nature and quality of the interactions between marketing management and consumers have changed drastically since the start of the current economic stagflation in 1973. A stagnant economy in a period of inflation, stagflation, may be experienced in different forms and to different degrees. Yet all forms and degrees of stagflation are totally new, and their effects on both marketing management and the consumers are quite drastic.

The primary objectives of this article are: (1) to discuss the effects of stagflation on business and its consumers; (2) to point out the resulting changes in the marketing mix and in consumers' attitudes and choices; and (3) to derive recommendations for marketing management. To achieve these goals, I conducted two related surveys designed to

The author would like to thank Prof. Conrad Berenson and Prof. David Rachman of Baruch College for their comments on earlier drafts of this article.

measure the impact of, and adjustments to, stagflation on the part of marketing management and consumers.

GROWTH VS. STAGFLATION

As long as changes in the economic environment follow a definable trend and are relatively easy to predict, both management and consumers can easily adjust to them and often take advantage of them. Such was the case between the end of World War II and 1973. The economy enjoyed rapid and meaningful growth, and the rates of inflation and unemployment were rather low (3%-5% annually). Marketing management enjoyed real and rapid growth in terms of sales, profits, and expansion, and thus became accustomed to a rapid and positive pace. Consumers too enjoyed real and rapid growth in terms of disposable income, consumption, and product selection.

Reprinted with permission from *Journal of Marketing*, published by the American Marketing Association (July 1978), pp. 43-52.

However, beginning with the oil shortage of 1973, stagflation—a radically different and less predictable economic state—took place. This left both marketing management and consumers uncertain as to how to respond. Yet, by now, many of them have indeed adjusted their marketing and buying practices.

Interactive Relationships

Exhibit 1 presents a conceptual framework of the relationships among the economic environment, marketing management, and the consumers. As depicted, changes in the economic environment such as shortages, inflation, recession, and various types of stagflation (Box I) affect both marketing management (Box II) and consumers (Box III).

As a result of such influences, marketing management develops new strategies and tactics to cope with the new economic climates (Box IV); so do consumers (Box V). Thus, for example, in an era of shortage marketing management may utilize a demarketing strategy, while in a climate of recession it may utilize a strategy designed to stimulate demand. Similarly, consumers facing shortages may start hoarding, and

EXHIBIT 1

A conceptual framework of the relationship among the economic environment, business, and the consumers

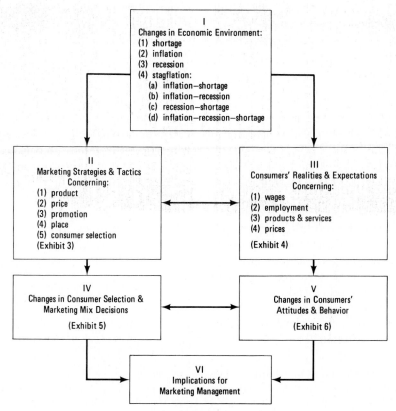

they may save less when they experience inflation.

The new result of such adjustments on the part of marketing management and consumers is a net change in the relationships between them in terms of prices, products, and product assortment, credit conditions, promotional appeals, and places of selling and purchasing. In turn, this change in the business-consumer relationship represents new and possibly more profitable opportunities to marketing management (Box VI).

CHANGES IN THE ECONOMIC ENVIRONMENT

The basic change in the economic environment popularly known as stagflation actually represents any *combination* of these three factors: shortage, inflation, recession.

Shortage

Shortage is both an economic and a psychological state, which occurs when demand is larger than supply at the existing (or administered) price level. In contrast to inflation, it usually applies to specific products or materials, rather than to the general economy.

Both businesses as users of raw materials and consumers of final products have experienced various degrees of shortage throughout the past five years. Consider such shortages—real or contrived—as occurred with coffee, natural gas, oil, aluminum, cement, copper, textiles, and lumber.

Here is a striking example of adjustment to a scarcity situation:

As consumers turned away from coffee when scarcity caused its prices to rise skyhigh, the major coffee roasters and packers turned to a cheaper substitute, chicory, and offered blends of coffee containing that ingredient.

Inflation

Inflation represents a process of rising prices of raw materials and final products and services caused by other factors than shortages and affecting virtually all products.

Depending on what triggers such a process, economic theory normally distinguishes between two types of inflation: (1) demand-push inflation characterized by "too much money chasing too few goods and services," and full employment; and (2) cost-pull inflation characterized by rising costs of raw materials, production channels, and marketing, usually resulting in weakened demand leading to various degrees of production overcapacity and unemployment.

The difference between these two types of inflation is important since they affect consumers and business differently, thus resulting in different adjustment measures. Nevertheless, the various degrees of inflation experienced in the past five years represent almost indistinguishable mixes of the two types of inflation. Accordingly, for the purposes of this article, inflation is defined as a process of escalating prices triggered by either demand-push or cost-pull.

Here is how one company changed its marketing mix, or more particularly its product mix, in pursuit of profitability in a period of inflation:

Sun Oil's division of Lubrication and Metalworking materials has cut its metalworking oils from 1,150 grades to 92, its lubes from 1,000 grades to 200, and its greases from 225 grades to 29. This product-line pruning has increased productivity by 20%-30%, as it drastically reduced kettle-cleaning time in the plant.[1]

[1]"The Squeeze on the Product Mix," *Business Week* (January 5, 1974), pp. 50-55.

Recession

Recession is a process of decreasing demand for raw materials, products, and services, including labor. A lower demand for labor means a smaller disposable income, which, in turn, further decreases demand. In essence, recession is a demand-push inflation in *reverse:* decreasing demand and generally a slow moving or contracting economy.

Such an environment normally calls for strategies to stimulate consumer demand, but at the same time results in some belt-tightening on the part of consumers.

The housing industry of 1975 is a good example of marketing management action in a recession period:

Faced with growing uncertainty and slow-growing disposable income, on the one hand, and the rising cost of private homes, on the other, many potential buyers left the housing market. To cope with this situation of radically declining demand, many builders adjusted their marketing mix by offering smaller, cheaper houses. Miami-based Deltona, for example, downgraded its entire product line in 1975—from a range of $30,000-$56,000 to a range of $17,800-$30,000.[2]

Adaptive strategies and tactics in periods of shortages, inflation, and recession are shown in Exhibit 2.

Stagflation

Though stagflation is defined as a stagnant economy experiencing inflation, one can distinguish among four types of stagflation: (1) inflation-shortage, (2) inflation-recession, (3) recession-shortage, and (4) inflation-recession-shortage. Each of these types of stagflation represents a cross-pressure environment, often calling for contradictory measures of adjustment.

[2]"Marketing When Growth Slows," *Business Week* (April 14, 1975), pp. 44-50.

Inflation-shortage. Alone of all four types of stagflation, this one includes components which to some degree reinforce each other. The occurrence of shortage in a period of inflation may further increase the gap between supply and demand and push prices up.

Therefore, this type of stagflation may be treated as inflation which affects those industries and consumers experiencing shortage more severely. A company affected by this type of stagflation will want to assess the relative impact of inflation and shortage, and proceed to develop adaptive strategies designed to reduce or regulate demand and/or to redefine the company's target groups. Fortunately, whatever strategy is chosen will also have some effectiveness in meeting both situations.

Thus, to meet consumer demand for fuel economy in a scarcity situation and to overcome price resistance:

General Motors has recently stripped down nine of its small car models—eliminating, among other things, four-speed transmissions and steel belted tires from the list of standard equipment. These product changes made it possible for GM to chop as much as 8% off the list price.[3]

Inflation-recession. An economic environment experiencing both inflation and recession is paradoxical in that inflation and recession call for diametrically opposing adjustment strategies and marketing-mix tactics. Thus, while inflation calls for a strategy and marketing mix designed to *reduce* total demand, recession calls for a strategy and marketing mix designed to *increase* total demand. A company confronted with inflation-recession is therefore confronted with the need for a trade-off between anti-inflation and anti-recession measures. The more the company employs

[3]*Ibid.*

EXHIBIT 2

Adaptive strategies and tactics in periods of shortages, inflation, and recession

	STRATEGY/TACTICS: SHORTAGE DEMAND REDUCTION IN THE SHORT-RUN, AND DEMAND ADJUSTMENT IN THE LONG-RUN	INFLATION DEMAND REDUCTION	RECESSION DEMAND INCREASE
PRODUCT	1. Narrow product line. 2. Offer cheaper, more functional products. 3. Purchase shortage materials more carefully and strategically. 4. Make shortage material go further. 5. Invest in researching substitute materials. 6. Introduce substitute products. 7. Avoid quantity discounts.	1. Narrow product line. 2. Offer cheaper, more functional products. 3. Purchase raw materials more carefully and strategically. 4. Use less expensive (or lower-grade) material in production. 5. Invest in researching substitute materials. 6. Avoid quantity discounts.	1. Narrow product line. 2. Offer cheaper, more functional products, and/or 3. Cut top of product line. 4. Use less raw materials in production. 5. Offer quantity discounts.
PRICE	8. Raise prices. 9. Adjust prices periodically (upward). 10. Change price differential among products in the line to decrease demand for shortage goods. 11. Stop price discounting practices. 12. Tighten credit. 13. Centralize price decisions.	7. Raise prices. 8. Adjust prices frequently (upward). 9. Change price differential among products in the line to decrease total demand. 10. Stop price discounting practices. 11. Tighten credit. 12. Centralize price decisions.	6. Lower prices whenever possible. 7. Change price differential to increase total demand. 8. Offer price discounts. 9. Loosen credit. 10. Centralize price decisions.
PROMOTION	14. Demarket through promotion. 15. Decrease promotion of shortage goods. 16. Increase promotion of more readily available products.	13. Demarket through promotion. 14. Decrease promotion via advertising and personal selling. 15. Push the more profitable products.	11. Remarket through promotion. 12. Increase promotion to stimulate demand. 13. Cultivate every potential account and territory. 14. Motivate sales force to sell more.
PLACE	17. Limit quantity per customer. 18. Limit distribution to make products less available.	16. Limit quantity per customer. 17. Limit distribution to make product less available. 18. Utilize a higher price to achieve product differentiation.	15. Increase distribution outlets. 16. Motivate middlemen to buy more of your product and push it. 17. Offer products directly to consumers.
CONSUMER	19. Study how consumers and potential consumers are affected. 20. Drop marginal accounts whenever possible. 21. Selective treatment of consumers to maximize loyalty.	19. Study how consumers and potential consumers are affected. 20. Drop marginal accounts whenever possible. 21. Selective treatment of consumers to maximize loyalty.	18. Study how consumers and potential consumers are affected. 19. Cultivate even marginally profitable accounts. 20. Selective treatment of consumers to maximize sales.
OTHER	22. Innovate. 23. Increase productivity. 24. Diversify.	22. Innovate. 23. Increase productivity. 24. Diversify.	21. Innovate. 22. Increase productivity. 23. Diversify.

anti-inflation measures, the more severe become the effects of recession.

The anti-inflation and anti-recession trade-off mix is determined by many factors, such as:

□ *The relative impact of inflation and recession.* The greater the impact of one (e.g., recession), the more drastic the strategy and tactics which can be employed to minimize its negative effects without great intensification of the negative effects of the other (e.g., inflation).

□ *The elasticity of the demand for the company's product.* Relatively inelastic demand may allow the company to utilize an adjustment mix containing relatively more anti-inflation tactics (e.g., demarketing), as one may assume only a marginal influence of the recession on the demand.

□ *The elasticity of the supply of the product.* An elastic supply curve makes it more possible for the company to include a greater portion of anti-recession measures in its adjustment mix.

□ *The degree of competition.* Stiffer competition tends to treat the inflation-recession environment relatively more in terms of anti-recession measures, and this tends to influence the company to follow suit so as not to lose its competitive position in the market. This may mean an increased demand but lower profitability since the costs of production and promotion have been going up.

□ *Consumer perceptions, attitudes, and expectations.* Consumers who perceive the situation basically as inflationary and expect it to continue as such suggest that management utilize a greater anti-inflation measure in the mix, and the contrary when consumers perceive the climate as mainly a recessionary climate. However, because consumer realities, sentiments, and uncertainties change quite rapidly, management may be required to utilize a very flexible anti-inflation-recession mix.

Quantifying the rate of exchange between anti-inflation and anti-recession measures is extremely difficult. Consequently, one may resort to the construction and evaluation of different anti-inflation-recession packages. For example, one package might include a 10% price increase and a narrower product line, while another package might include a 5% price reduction and product downgrading, and so on. After such packages are constructed, one can proceed to evaluate their performance along whatever criteria chosen by the company (e.g., profits, competition, company's image, etc.)—an analytical procedure that is likely to be more accurate when carried out product-by-product.

Steel, aluminum, and synthetic fibers are three major industries trying to deal with an inflation-recession environment.

In the last three years, the steel industry has been operating under conditions of (1) very weak demand because the major consumers of steel (the automobile industry and the appliances and housing industries) decreased their demand as they faced demand reduction for their own products; and (2) rising costs—an increase of about 30% in the cost of producing sheet and strip, but only a 12% increase in price.

Although the market was very weak, the steel industry increased its list prices 6% in September 1976. However, because of the weak market and strong competition, many companies were willing to sell at the old price. Thus, the attempt to make an anti-inflation adjustment, in a market which was experiencing recessionary pressures as well, failed because the recessionary pressures appeared to be stronger than the inflationary pressures.

However, as production costs have continued to go up, the steel companies again declared a price increase of 6% in December 1976. This time the price increase held up. Then, apparently experiencing or perceiving stronger inflationary pressures than recessionary pressures, major steel companies once more increased their list price of various items (6% or more) in May 1977, and once again in July 1977.

Later, governmental action was needed to help this industry.

Similarly, Reynolds has recently increased the price of aluminum (6%), and duPont increased the price of man-made fibers (10%). Whether these price increases will hold or not depends on the relative impact of the inflation-recession mix on these industries.[4]

Recession-shortage. Recession and shortage, again, call for opposing measures aimed at reducing and increasing demand at the same time. And, once again, the company is confronted with a trade-off between anti-recession and anti-shortage measures. Thus: in the travel industry, most major airlines offered cheaper products (charter flights) and fewer scheduled flights. On the other hand, Samsonite decided to change its product concept, market segmentation, and promotion strategies: women were to be offered fashionable, lightweight luggage, while men were to be offered durability and capacity.[5]

Inflation-recession-shortage. Stagflation characterized by simultaneous pressures of inflation, recession, and shortage is an economic climate experiencing the most contradictory pressures of all types of stagflation. Any measure taken by the company (e.g., an anti-recession measure) may increase the negative impact of the company's other environments (e.g., inflation and shortage). Consequently, the optimal mix among the anti-inflation, recession, and shortage measures is one representing a minimax solution—a solution designed to minimize the negative effects of the economic environment and maximize the positive.

Here again, because quantification of the trade-off among the various adaptive measures is virtually impossible, the construction and evaluation of various marketing mix adjustment packages may be an alternative. And, here too, the result may be that a company will adopt different adjustment mixes for different products or product lines. For example:

A case in point is General Mills. To cope with shortages and rising costs and to get a tighter grip on its markets in a slow-moving economy, General Mills has been increasing its research expenditures on consumer studies. To understand how consumers are reacting to their total life situation, General Mills hired Yankelovich, Skelly and White to conduct a rather large-scale consumer study. The result, among other things, was *Breakfast Squares*—a new instant breakfast commanding 30% of the market.[6]

A second case in point is Rohr Industries, Inc. Up to 1975 Rohr drew all its sales from aerospace. However, because of (1) shortages of basic raw materials such as aluminum, nickel, and copper, (2) soaring cost of energy, and (3) weak demand in an overall slow-moving economy, Rohr decided to adjust its product mix. As a result, Rohr has been shifting toward energy-conserving transportation systems such as mass transit.[7]

While the theoretical distinctions among the various types of stagflation are fairly clear, sensitive operational measures facilitating such distinctions among them in reality are yet to be devised. This is because (1) manifestation of one type of economic climate (e.g., shortage) can often be interpreted as a manifestation of another (e.g., inflation); and, more importantly, (2) due to economic interdependencies, a manifestation of one type of economic climate (e.g., recession) might have actually been triggered by another climate (e.g., shortage).

[4]"Some Steel Customers See Level Demand For Flat-rolled Items Over Near Term," *Wall Street Journal*, December 2, 1976, p. 4; "U.S. Steel Undercuts Price Boosts Announced by Republic and Lukens," *Wall Street Journal*, May 10, 1977, p. 3; and "Angry Steel Buyer Says Prices are Going Up in a Weak Market," and "DuPont Increases Fiber Prices," *New York Times*, December 1, 1976, p. D1.

[5]"The Travel Strategy of Samsonite," *Business Week* (June 15, 1975), pp. 73-74.

[6]"The Hard Road of Food Processors," *Business Week* (March 8, 1976), pp. 50-54.

[7]"Marketing When Growth Slows," *Business Week* (April 14, 1975), pp. 44-50.

In the remainder of this article stagflation is conceived of as any combination of inflation, recession, and shortage.

THE EFFECTS OF STAGFLATION

Literature and data dealing with the various effects of stagflation on marketing management and the consumer are rather scarce and fragmented, but nevertheless suggest that the effects of stagflation have been extreme.[8]

The purpose of the two complementary surveys I conducted was to obtain more systematic knowledge about the effects of stagflation on marketing management and the consumer and the adjustment measures taken in view of such effects.

The first survey questionnaire measured the effects of stagflation on marketing management, and then proceeded to measure subsequent changes in strategies and tactics. The population frame used for this study was "Fortune 500" companies. Of the systematic sample drawn from the Fortune 500 sample, 104 companies responded. All questionnaires were addressed to the vice president of marketing; all items were rated on five-point Likert scales. Items were state-

---

[8]See for example: David W. Cravens, "Marketing Management in an Era of Shortages," *Business Horizons*, 17 (February 1974), pp. 79-85; Philip Kotler, "Marketing During Periods of Shortage," *Journal of Marketing*, 38, No. 3 (July 1974), pp. 20-29; Philip Kotler, "The Major Tasks of Marketing Management," *Journal of Marketing*, 37, No.4 (October 1973), pp. 42-49; David Cullwick, "Positioning Demarketing Strategy," *Journal of Marketing*, 39, No. 2 (April 1975), p. 51; "The Squeeze on Product Mix," *Business Week* (January 5, 1974), pp. 50-55; "Consumer Research Goes to Work in Energy Shortage," *Advertising Age* (February 4, 1974), pp. 30-31; "Pricing Strategy in an Inflation Economy," *Business Week* (April 6, 1974), pp. 42-46; "The Two-Way Squeeze on New Products," *Business Week* (August 10, 1974), p. 130; Eugene J. Kelley and L. Rusty Scheewe, "Buyer Behavior in a Stagflation/Shortages Economy," *Journal of Marketing*, 39, No. 2 (April 1975), pp. 44-50.

ments concerning the effects of the economic environment on the various components of the marketing mix, or concerning the different adjustment measures, and asked respondents to point out the degree to which such effects and adjustments were experienced by their company.

Likewise, the second survey measured the effects of the economic stagflation on consumers, and the subsequent adjustments they made. The population frame utilized in this survey was the five boroughs of New York City; the sample drawn was a quota sample using age, sex, and race as control variables. Altogether 969 consumers responded. All data for the consumer survey were collected by the author and specially trained graduate and undergraduate students. All questionnaire items were close-ended and Likert in nature.

So juxtapositioning marketing management vis-à-vis consumers in terms of the effects of, and the adjustments to, the economic environment is an innovation in that it conceives and treats the relationships as dynamic, and makes it easier and more accurate to derive realistic and profitable implications for marketing management.

. . . On Marketing Management

The economic stagflation has drastically influenced marketing management. As can be seen from Exhibit 3, all marketing management decisions concerning target consumers, product, price, promotion, and location were drastically affected, but not equally. Taking the "very much" and "much" columns to indicate drastic effects, the resulting rank order was: *price* (highest), *product, consumers, promotion,* and *location* (lowest).

The possible reasons for such extreme effects on price decisions are (1) that the very nature of stagflation expresses itself in dol-

EXHIBIT 3

Degrees of stagflation effects on marketing management decisions (n = 104)

DECISION AREA AFFECTED	VERY MUCH	MUCH	SOMEWHAT	LITTLE	NO EFFECT	N/A
PRICE:						
Pricing Policy	36.5%	46.2%	11.5%	3.8%	1.9%	---
Consumer Credit	12.5%	25.0%	24.0%	20.2%	10.6%	7.7%
PRODUCT:						
Product Line	10.6%	23.1%	31.7%	22.1%	12.5%	---
Product Elimination	14.4%	18.3%	36.5%	18.3%	12.5%	---
R&D	5.8%	19.2%	24.0%	34.6%	15.4%	1.0%
CONSUMERS:						
Consumer Selection	6.7%	19.2%	32.7%	24.0%	13.5%	3.8%
Consumer Services	6.7%	10.6%	24.0%	31.7%	20.2%	6.7%
PROMOTION:						
Promotion Budget	7.7%	22.1%	40.4%	23.1%	5.8%	1.0%
Media Selection	4.8%	14.4%	36.5%	26.0%	17.3%	1.0%
Promotion Appeal	3.8%	13.5%	37.5%	27.9%	14.4%	2.9%
Personal Selling	4.8%	17.3%	39.4%	26.9%	11.5%	---
Public Relations	2.9%	17.3%	28.8%	29.8%	21.3%	---
PLACE:						
Channels of Distribution	3.8%	7.7%	20.2%	35.6%	32.7%	---

lars and cents, and (2) that the influence of stagflation on price decision is more immediate, while the same influence on the other elements of the marketing mix takes more time to emerge.

. . . On the Consumer

Consistent with the effects on marketing management, the effects of stagflation were drastic on consumers too. Of the 969 consumers surveyed, only 3.3% stated that economic stagflation did not have any affect on them; and, of the 937 consumers who were affected, 70.2% reported negative effects. Exhibit 4 presents consumers' perceptions of, and expectations concerning, the marketing mix offered to them in a stagflation economy.

Note that stagflation means that (1) it is harder to make ends meet (90.9%); (2) it is harder to make financial plans (83.5%); (3) one has to work harder to keep his/her present life-style (64.1%); and (4) *as a consumer,* most of the respondents (75.4%) feel frustrated; but (5) *as a person,* only 41.4% are less happy.

A comparison between Exhibits 3 and 4 shows a very interesting parallel—namely, that stagflation has influenced both marketing management and consumers along similarly *ranked* factors: *price, product, promotion,* and *location.* Both marketing management and the consumers have been most affected by price variables, and least affected by location variables. This lends support to a previous suggestion that the very nature of stagflation influences price more than it influences other components of the marketing mix. It can also be argued that as a result of the effect on prices, product offerings were the next in line to change, followed by changes in promotion and place decisions.

EXHIBIT 4
The meaning of stagflation to consumers (n = 969)

STAGFLATION MEANS . . .	STRONGLY AGREE n/%	AGREE n/%	SOMEWHAT AGREE n/%	SOMEWHAT DISAGREE n/%	DISAGREE n/%	STRONGLY DISAGREE n/%	N/A DON'T KNOW n/%
PRICE:							
Paying higher prices for products	568	308	75	5	6	4	3
and services.	58.7%	31.8%	7.7%	0.5%	0.6%	0.4%	0.3%
Prices will be a lot higher in	268	388	232	42	28	1	10
the future.	27.7%	40.0%	24.0%	4.3%	2.9%	0.1%	1.0%
PRODUCT:							
There are more low quality	268	276	188	99	89	23	26
products in the market.	27.7%	28.4%	19.4%	10.2%	9.2%	2.4%	2.7%
There are more new products	97	328	207	145	112	45	34
in the market.	10.0%	33.8%	21.4%	15.1%	11.6%	4.6%	3.5%
Product variety is decreasing.	65	95	132	206	361	85	25
	6.7%	9.8%	13.6%	21.3%	37.2%	8.8%	2.6%
Must buy less of everything.	122	221	233	163	179	29	22
	12.6%	22.8%	24.0%	16.7%	18.5%	3.0%	2.3%
Must delay purchase of							
durable goods.	157	243	262	101	124	23	59
	16.3%	25.1%	27.0%	10.4%	12.8%	2.4%	6.1%
PROMOTION:							
There is more advertising on	97	279	208	318	19	9	39
television.	10.0%	28.8%	21.5%	32.8%	2.0%	0.9%	4.0%
There are more cents-off coupons	167	189	159	388	47	12	8
in newspapers.	17.2%	19.6%	16.4%	40.0%	4.8%	1.2%	0.8%
PLACE:							
Spend more time (on the average)	133	263	200	90	181	52	50
shopping.	13.7%	27.1%	20.6%	9.3%	18.8%	5.4%	5.2%
Buy more products through	127	224	194	119	190	46	70
wholesale outlets.	13.1%	23.1%	20.0%	12.3%	19.6%	4.7%	7.2%
OTHER:							
It's harder to make ends meet.	340	341	200	40	18	22	8
	35.1%	35.2%	20.6%	4.1%	1.9%	2.3%	0.8%
It's harder to make financial plans.	256	339	215	69	51	7	32
	26.3%	35.0%	22.2%	7.1%	5.3%	0.7%	3.3%
I must work harder to be able to	195	246	180	86	135	28	99
afford my present way of life.	20.0%	25.4%	18.6%	8.9%	13.9%	2.9%	10.2%
As a consumer, I am more frus-	218	247	264	95	94	25	26
trated than I used to be.	22.6%	25.5%	27.3%	9.8%	9.7%	2.6%	2.7%
As a person, I am less happy	95	132	174	113	247	106	102
than I used to be.	9.8%	13.6%	18.0%	11.7%	25.5%	10.9%	10.5%

ADJUSTMENTS TO STAGFLATION

. . . By Marketing Management

Exhibit 5 presents adjustment measures and the degree to which they were adopted by the sample. As can be seen in Exhibit 5, most drastic adjustments were made in the area of pricing and least in the areas of promotion and location. This is congruent with the findings reported in Exhibit 2 concerning the perceived degree of stagflation effects on the marketing mix. In addition, even within each component of the marketing mix, different degrees of adjustment measures were adopted. For example, while 30.8% of the companies surveyed shifted (very much) to frequent price adjustments, only 11.5% who did so changed to stricter credit policies.

Note that only a few companies, eleven

EXHIBIT 5
Marketing management adjustments to stagflation (n = 104)

MARKETING MIX	DEGREE OF ADJUSTMENT					
	VERY MUCH n/%	MUCH n/%	SOMEWHAT n/%	LITTLE n/%	NONE n/%	N/A n/%
PRICE:						
Frequent price adjustments	31	40	20	10	2	---
	30.8%	38.5%	19.2%	9.6%	1.9%	---
Stronger emphasis on profit margin	27	38	20	11	6	2
	26.0%	36.5%	19.2%	10.6%	5.8%	1.9%
Competitive pricing	8	30	27	28	8	3
	7.7%	28.8%	26.0%	26.9%	7.7%	2.9%
Stricter credit	12	49	27	13	3	---
	11.5%	47.1%	26.0%	12.5%	2.9%	---
Extra services to justify higher prices	2	8	32	38	22	2
	1.9%	7.7%	30.8%	36.5%	21.2%	1.9%
CONSUMERS:						
Avoiding marginal accounts	11	46	25	14	7	1
	10.6%	44.2%	24.0%	13.5%	6.7%	1.0%
Better servicing of faithful accounts	13	39	29	10	11	2
	12.5%	37.5%	27.9%	9.6%	10.6%	1.9%
Consumer research	6	19	18	26	34	1
	5.8%	18.3%	17.3%	25.0%	32.7%	1.0%
Carrying even marginally profitable products to satisfy consumers	4	18	29	34	16	3
	3.8%	17.3%	27.9%	32.7%	15.4%	2.9%
Capitalizing on new markets	3	9	32	29	29	2
	2.9%	8.7%	30.8%	27.9%	27.9%	1.9%
PRODUCT:						
Product line reduction	14	26	39	16	9	---
	13.5%	25.0%	37.5%	15.4%	8.7%	---
Increased research and development	7	33	28	25	11	---
	6.7%	31.7%	26.9%	24.0%	10.6%	---
Developing alternative raw materials	10	26	30	28	9	1
	9.6%	25.0%	28.8%	26.9%	8.7%	1.0%
PROMOTION:						
Discounted slow-moving products	22	31	29	17	5	---
	21.2%	29.8%	27.9%	16.3%	4.8%	---
Increased use of coupons	16	34	23	18	12	1
	15.4%	32.7%	22.1%	17.3%	11.5%	1.0%
Increased promotion budget	5	12	33	29	25	---
	4.8%	11.5%	31.7%	27.9%	24.0%	---
Broadened sales force responsibilities	1	16	50	24	13	---
	1.0%	15.4%	48.1%	23.1%	12.5%	---
PLACE:						
Reexamining distribution channels	8	36	25	17	16	2
	7.7%	34.6%	24.0%	16.3%	15.4%	1.9%
Receptiveness to selling wholesale to consumers	1	5	12	18	66	2
	1.0%	4.8%	11.5%	17.3%	63.5%	1.9%

EXHIBIT 6
Consumer adjustments to stagflation (n= 969)

ADJUSTMENTS	STRONGLY AGREE n/%	AGREE n/%	SOMEWHAT AGREE n/%	SOMEWHAT DISAGREE n/%	DISAGREE n/%	STRONGLY DISAGREE n/%	N/A DON'T KNOW n/%
GENERAL:							
As a consumer, I have changed my	119	242	276	119	156	38	19
habits and preferences.	12.3%	25.0%	28.6%	12.3%	16.0%	3.9%	2.0%
I judge products and services in a	163	328	264	76	91	20	27
new way.	16.8%	33.8%	27.2%	7.8%	9.4%	2.1%	2.8%
Became more of a comparative	310	348	205	32	57	7	10
shopper.	32.0%	35.8%	21.1%	3.3%	5.8%	0.7%	1.0%
Became less wasteful.	260	375	205	47	51	11	20
	26.8%	38.7%	21.2%	4.9%	5.3%	1.1%	2.0%
Became more energy conscious.	220	328	227	74	82	9	29
	22.7%	33.8%	23.4%	7.6%	8.5%	0.9%	3.0%
Weigh purchase decisions with my	140	180	141	66	77	18	347
spouse more than I used to.	14.4%	18.6%	14.6%	6.8%	7.9%	1.9%	35.9%
Argue about financial matters.	78	136	209	126	238	87	95
	8.0%	14.0%	21.6%	13.0%	24.6%	9.0%	9.8%
Became insecure about my job.	92	103	154	106	259	99	156
	9.5%	10.6%	15.9%	10.9%	26.7%	10.2%	16.1%
PRICE:							
Am more careful with money.	283	359	215	55	38	8	11
	29.2%	37.0%	22.2%	5.7%	3.9%	0.8%	1.1%
Shop for "specials" and bargains	289	271	245	62	61	20	21
more than I used to.	29.7%	28.0%	25.3%	6.4%	6.3%	2.1%	2.2%
Use more credit.	94	133	152	95	234	151	110
	9.7%	13.7%	15.7%	9.8%	24.1%	15.6%	11.6%
Save less.	270	254	178	78	116	41	32
	27.9%	26.2%	18.4%	8.0%	12.0%	4.2%	3.3%
PRODUCT:							
Look for more durability when	274	380	189	32	50	13	31
shopping for durable goods.	28.3%	39.2%	19.5%	3.3%	5.2%	1.3%	3.2%
Look for cheaper products	141	205	245	128	169	49	32
(e.g. private labels).	14.5%	21.1%	25.3	13.2%	17.4%	5.1%	3.3%
Became a do-it-yourself person.	151	243	225	100	144	49	57
	15.6%	25.1%	23.2%	10.3%	14.9%	5.0%	5.9%
PLACE:							
Looking for wholesale outlets more	315	268	190	84	56	33	23
than before.	32.5%	27.6%	19.6%	8.7%	5.8%	3.4%	2.4%
Shopping at cut-rate stores	199	233	215	102	142	49	29
more than before.	20.5%	24.0%	22.2%	10.5%	14.7%	5.1%	3.0%
PROMOTION:							
Believe advertising claims	23	124	100	261	242	160	58
less than I used to.	2.4%	12.8%	10.4%	27.0%	25.0%	16.5%	6.0%

altogether, strongly capitalized on new markets created by stagflation. The balance took strictly defensive measures.

... By Consumers

Exhibit 6 presents consumers' adjustments to stagflation. Particularly striking is the way consumers in general adjusted to a stagflation economy. They either *strongly agree, agree,* or *somewhat agree* that as a result of stagflation, they . . .

☐ Have changed their habits and preferences (65.9%).

☐ Judge products and services in a new way (77.8%).

□   Have become more comparative shoppers (88.9%).

□   Have become less wasteful (86.7%).

□   Have become more energy-conscious (79.9%).

□   Weigh purchase decisions with spouse more than before (47.6%).

□   Argue about financial matters (63.6%).

□   Have become insecure about their jobs (36.0%).

The net result seems to be a new breed of consumers, whose reactions to the marketing mix may be utterly different from pre-stagflation consumers. And, once again, a comparison of Exhibits 5 and 6 shows that marketing management and consumers adjusted themselves along similarly ranked factors, placing price and product ahead of promotion and location.

IMPLICATIONS FOR MARKETING MANAGEMENT

Perhaps the most important implication for marketing management is the fact that consumers have changed drastically. As a result, rules of thumb which many corporations have developed about their target groups may have become less accurate; and decisions based on such outdated rules of thumb may be very costly. Consequently, consumer research becomes more imperative than ever before. Such research may result in (1) redefinition of target group or groups; (2) different degrees of product and product line modification due to the fact that the benefits derived from product features or components have changed as a

result of stagflation; and (3) changes in distribution, promotion budget, and advertising appeal.

SUMMARY AND CONCLUSIONS

The essence of modern marketing is to achieve business goals through consumer satisfaction. Therefore, juxtapositioning marketing management and consumers in a stagflation economy, as done in this article, becomes increasingly important if this marketing concept is to be practiced effectively.

Admittedly, the article indicates mostly general trends or changes, and more stagflation research is needed. Further avenues for such research are:

a. Developing clear and acceptable criteria to determine, and differentiate among inflation, recession, and shortage.

b. Studies designed to quantify the trade-offs among the various components of the various types of stagflation.

c. Specific case histories of industries and companies depicting how various types of stagflation were dealt with.

d. Longitudinal studies of the impact of stagflation on consumers and business management.

In addition, while stagflation was analyzed mainly from marketing management's point of view, its broader implications to other business functions are important as well. Even more basic, and thus more far-reaching, are the societal implications of stagflation in terms of life-style, priorities, and expectations.

23 Japan Plants a New U.S. Crop

With the first wave of Japanese products to hit the U.S., beginning in the early 1960s and unofficially ending with the recent international trade bargaining sessions, Japan took control of America's motorcycle and 35mm camera markets, snatched one-quarter of the car market, reshaped the watch industry, and positioned itself as a leader in the new video and electronic technologies. Now there are indications that a second wave of consumer products from Japan is rolling in.

Much of the press and government attention of late has focused on such areas as steel and high technologies, which have had a significant impact on our $10 billion balance of trade deficit with Japan for the first half of this year. And few observers expect Japan to repeat its earlier performance in consumer goods. Yet, any marketing push by such a formidable competitor bears watching, as it is likely to shake up the industries concerned.

In the photo field, Canon U.S.A., the 35mm camera leader, has decided to knock heads with Kodak in the much larger snapshot camera market. With its new Snappy models backed by $40 million in advertising over the next four years, Canon expects to grab 15-20% of the market by 1984. And little Fuji Photo Film U.S.A. recently outbid Kodak for the right to bill itself as the "official film of the 1984 Olympics," part of its plan to double its current 7% share of the U.S. Film market. Earlier this year, Fuji sponsored the World Cup soccer championship, carried in this country on network television for the first time.

In other areas, Nippon Electric Corp. (NEC), with 40% of Japan's personal computer market, is more than doubling its U.S. sales network to 500 dealers this year, and has set a goal of 5-7% of the market by 1985. Benihana of Tokyo, whose 50 "hibachi table" steak restaurants pull in over $60 mil-

Reprinted with permission from *Ad Forum* (September 1982).

287

lion a year, has teamed with the Las Vegas Hilton to build Benihana Village in Las Vegas. Kirin (beer), Suntory (liquor), Kikkoman (soy sauce), Bridgestone (tires), and Shiseido (cosmetics) are just a few of the Japanese companies that have been ambling along in the U.S. for nearly two decades but have recently upped their marketing efforts.

Securities analysts and other industry observers find it all too easy to downplay this activity. The Japanese selection of personal computers is "lame," "brings nothing new to the pantry," "shows no understanding of software." Kirin beer, the world's second best-selling brand after Budweiser, is "not worth mentioning," "not on the map," "insignificant." Japanese bike makers now hold 10% of the U.S. market, primarily with high-end models, but "can never enter the mass market—it's impossible." And Shiseido, the world's second largest cosmetics concern after Avon and the leader in department stores worldwide, is "not aggressive" and "doesn't sample or promote enough."

These disparaging comments bring to mind the remark made by a Swiss watch executive when little-known Seiko first advertised its watches on U.S. TV in 1968: "Seiko is a pimple on an elephant's ass." Seiko has since overtaken the Swiss to become the leader in sales of moderately priced high-quality watches. Seiko, it might also be remembered, first entered the U.S. in 1956 under the corporate banner of Okies (Seiko spelled backwards) and ran in the red for 20 years before hitting its stride in 1976.

Those Japanese companies now just teething in the U.S. can be expected to show the same patience and perseverance. Suntory International, which claims to be the world's leading whiskey seller, has spent a good 10 years in the U.S. without any visible success until now. "But we didn't turn tail when we weren't selling," notes Ron Kline, advertising manager.

The Japanese first penetrated the U.S. market at a time when many consumers were becoming disillusioned with American business and American products. Japan's success in the 1970s was based on offering innovative and high-quality durables that answered consumers' needs. The second wave promises similar product and marketing innovations, but in some ways its approach to the U.S. market is taking on different outlines.

Some companies that have already established themselves in the U.S. with high-end lines, such as Canon, now are focusing on the mass market. K. Hattori & Co., parent of Seiko Time Corp., plans a fall introduction of its Lorus line, priced at $13 to $60. Advertising for the watches, which run head-to-head with Timex, identifies Lorus as "The People's Watch—it's everything but expensive."

Other companies with established brand names in one field are extending them to new products. Yamaha markets tennis racquets, musical instruments, and motorcycles. Panasonic and Bridgestone sell bicycles as well as their better known video equipment and tires. Sony just introduced a personal computer, for the industrial market. Hitachi and Toshiba, known for consumer electronics, are also selling appliances. Both offer microwave ovens, and Toshiba also sells automatic coffee makers, vacuum cleaners, and food processors.

Another characteristic of the second wave is an emphasis on soft goods, as exemplified by Fuji's film drive. Like many of its fellow Japanese companies, Fuji has saturated its home market and is eager to expand internationally. Many of these firms established their outposts in the huge U.S. market during the 1960s, but have yet to become significant forces.

For example, Shiseido Co., a cosmetics concern specializing in skin-care products, came here in 1968 but virtually disappeared in the late 1970s. "They withdrew and left only a few people behind," says Alan Mottus, a cosmetics industry consultant. Now, however, Shiseido has a manufacturing plant in New Jersey that should make it more price competitive with department store leaders Clinique and Estee Lauder. Shiseido is in the midst of a drive to broaden its department store distribution from 400 to 1,000 stores, and expects sales to increase 60% by 1985.

Bridgestone tires ride into the U.S. as original equipment on half the Japanese import cars but have had trouble cracking the replacement market (only a 1% share). The trucking industry, however, has taken to Bridgestone tires manufactured with a high-quality casing that allows for more "recaps." With a 12% share of the truck tire market, the company has a base from which to promote its passenger tires in a national consumer magazine campaign. Last year Bridgestone aired its first network TV campaign, with golfer Lee Trevino speaking for SuperFiller radials.

Whatever the product category, the marketing strategies of the new wave are likely to be familiar. Finding and filling a consumer need with a high-quality product has become a Japanese trademark. Honda did it with a lightweight motorcycle in the early '60s. The automakers did it with fuel-efficient economy cars in the mid '70s. Canon is trying it now with the world's first 35mm snapshot camera, which reportedly provides clearer pictures. And Toshiba's My Cafe automatic coffeemaker, the only one to both grind beans and brew coffee, has been selling out in specialty and gourmet stores.

While many Japanese companies may spend years giving only minimal support to their products, they use that period to study the mechanics of their particular markets, with an eye to gaining distribution. This patience, which is often misinterpreted as a lack of aggression or of marketing skills, may be what prompts analysts to downplay the still fledgling efforts. But once distribution has been achieved, Japanese companies have shown a tendency to back their products with heavy advertising and promotion over the long term—building market share and brand awareness first, and profits later.

Richard Meidenfauer, advertising manager for consumer products at Toshiba, summarizes the traditional approach when he says, "We're crawling before we walk, and we'll walk before we run. But if things go well we'll be a major consumer advertiser in a few years."

Such was Seiko's approach to the watch market. It cracked the distribution problem by contracting with regional distributors known to the jewelry trade, in Timex fashion, rather than following the Swiss tradition by developing its own national sales force. Once having gained distribution in key markets, Seiko put almost all of its meager $75,000 ad budget into spot TV. Seiko was the first watch advertiser to add jewelry store tags to commercials on local stations. This later evolved into a network campaign.

In 1976, at about the time Seiko's strategy was beginning to pay off, Canon became the first 35mm camera marketer to use network TV. Its "easy to use" campaign for the AEI camera helped expand the entire category by 40% the following year, and solidified Canon's position as the market leader.

Suntory, which holds over 70% of Japan's hugh whiskey market and produces whiskey in Brazil and Mexico, as well as having bottling arrangements in other countries, took a back-door approach to national distribution in the U.S. Its first major move was not a strong push for its flagship whiskey brands. Rather, in 1978, it introduced a new product designed for the American market. Midori melon liqueur, with a distinctive light green color, was a new flavor in the fast-growing liqueur category that quickly gained national distribution. It has since attracted several imitators, according to Ben Corrado, a leading liquor industry analyst.

On the basis of its track record with Midori, Suntory is rolling out its Banzai vodka and expanding distribution of its whiskey in five major markets. Suntory backs its products with heavy magazine advertising and outdoor signage. Last May, Suntory distributed its recipe booklet, "What to Make of Midori," to 8 million consumers via inserts in *Bon Appetit, Travel & Leisure,* and *Metropolitan Home.*

Other major elements of its marketing strategy are innovative packaging and point-of-purchase displays. "Suntory believes strongly in packaging," says Rick Bland, national marketing manager. "Our graphics and point-of-purchase materials are on a par with or better than those of most American companies. And, like most Japanese companies, Suntory is willing to spend heavily upfront and keep spending, rather than backing off quickly for the profit kill."

A company that has wasted no time in gaining distribution is Mizuno Corp., the leading sporting goods marketer in Japan. Mizuno entered the U.S. in 1979 and now claims to rank third in sales of baseball gloves behind Rawlings and Wilson.

Mizuno has achieved rapid success largely through identification with major league baseball. Mizuno craftsmen tour spring training camps and hand-craft custom gloves for major league players. With 20% of the pros wearing Mizuno gloves, and an endorsement from Pete Rose, one of the game's household names, Mizuno has been able to approach the trade from a position of strength.

Mizuno is using similar promotional tactics to sell its line of Easton aluminum baseball and softball bats. A new ad campaign is being developed to celebrate its claim that 99 of 100 batters in this year's College World Series used Easton bats. All this is just preparation for the "demands of the 21st Century sports world," by which time Mizuno expects to be a "global enterprise that creates sports culture." Experimental products for the future include electronic bases and see-through plastic baseball gloves that shield the fielder's eyes from the sun.

While many of the products coming out of Japan fit neatly into the parameters of traditional U.S. culture, some are capitalizing on a growing fascination with ancient and contemporary Japanese culture. Films based on Japanese history and folklore have developed a cult following in several major cities. Stars of the Grand Kabuki Theatre achieved critical and box office success in recent performances at New York's Lincoln Center for the Performing Arts, and are now on national tour.

Japanese foods and fashions also have gained in popularity. Coverage of this year's fall fashions from Tokyo included favorable mentions alongside those from Paris, Milan, and New York. Imports of Japanese apparel, both high-end designer wear and moderately priced traditional garb, rose 60% last year, to $156 million. And in the first three months of 1982, imports were up 52%.

Some 50 to 100 Japanese restaurants open in the U.S. each year, according to the Japanese Restaurant Association. Even the conservative Harvard Club of New York has added a luncheon sushi bar to its traditional Continental menu. Sushi is becoming popular elsewhere as a high-protein, non-fatting meal. Benihana of Tokyo is market testing sushi bars in Atlanta and Los Angeles.

Other marketers that stand to gain from the new interest in Japanese cuisine are the likes of Kikkoman International and the Kirin Brewery Co. Kikkoman came to the

U.S. in 1961 and has since made its soy sauce bottles a fixture in Oriental restaurants. With 1981 U.S. sales of $27 million for soy and teriyaki steak sauces, Kikkoman has upped its ad budget and is airing a TV commercial that compares the quality of its soy sauce with that of a fine wine.

Sales of Kirin beer rose 27% last year and it now ranks third among imports in the New York market, behind Heineken and Beck's. Half of Kirin's distribution is in restaurants in major markets. But the company is slowly moving more product into retail outlets. Kirin Light, the only imported low-calorie beer in the U.S. besides Amstel Light, is now in test markets.

While Kirin still has only $3 million in sales in the U.S., it certainly has the resources to expand. Sales of its soda, food products, and beer, which is sold in 20 countries, totaled nearly $22 billion last year. In contrast, Anheuser-Busch, the leading U.S. and world brewer, had 1981 sales of $4.4 billion.

For all the advantages the Japanese enjoy, and their impressive track record to date, there are several forces that could work against them in their latest endeavors. Most important of these is a new vigilance at American companies. Kodak, which holds over 90% of the U.S. film market (and 20% of Japan's), vows that it won't take the same kind of beating the U.S. auto companies took from the Japanese. And General Electric's new chairman, John F. Welch, Jr., acknowledging the buffeting G.E. appliances have taken from foreign competition, is adopting the enemy's cloak. He has instructed his managers to concentrate more on market share than on quarterly profits until the company ranks first or second in all its businesses.

The new combative stance against the Japanese also can be seen in the recent spate of bad press surrounding their business dealings. G.E. has sued Sony for infringing on a G.E. patent on plastic used in casings for Sony's videocassette recorders. Mitsui pleaded guilty to dumping steel on the U.S. market and paid an unprecedented $11.2 million fine. Mitsubishi and Hitachi agents have been indicted by the F.B.I. for stealing I.B.M. computer secrets. While Japanese products generally enjoy a reputation for quality, such incidents could filter down to affect consumer attitudes.

But the Japanese have not been totally insensitive to the trade tensions between our two countries. The car makers agreed to a voluntary ceiling on imports last year. And several companies have or are establishing manufacturing or assembly plants here. Shiseido built a plant in New Jersey, and Datsun and Honda are building plants in Tennessee and Ohio, respectively. Tennessee is also the source of Toshiba's microwave ovens and color TV sets, and Bridgestone acquired a Firestone truck tire plant there. The company does not rule out the possibility of a passenger tire plant in the U.S.

Some observers question the wisdom of recent moves by the Japanese because of the poor health of the markets they are addressing. The recession and declining car sales have hurt the tire market where Bridgestone is making its push. All Japanese bike makers—Panasonic, Fuji, Bridgestone, Miyata—sell high-end touring bikes, a category that has lost much of its mid 1970s lustre. With the U.S. the low-cost producer, some analysts doubt the Japanese can compete in the somewhat more promising mass market. Suntory's lifeblood, whiskey, is looking for a foothold in the slowly eroding brown spirits category. Its vodka is fighting stiff competition in the small (less than 2%) imported category.

Yet, being the new entry in a soft market need not be a liability, as the leaders often are vulnerable. One liquor analyst makes that point when he says: "Even in categories that are down, such as blends and vodkas, new introductions have worked well. That's because many old liquor brands are stodgy and never try new promotions, packaging or pricing. There is room to maneuver, but they are frozen into a pattern." His reasoning holds true for almost any product category.

The question is whether U.S. firms can exhibit the resolve evidenced by so many of the Japanese companies. As a Kirin ad says: "Our success, like our beer, is the product of great patience." Underestimating the force of patience has damaged American industries in the past.

While the second wave may be but a trickle now, it shows every intention of washing over this land. A look at the crossroads of America and mecca of outdoor advertising, New York City's Times Square, through which 30 million people pass each month, provides telling evidence. Once the showplace of major U.S. cigarette, liquor, and soft drink brands, its billboards are now lit with such names as Aiwa, Canon, Casio, Citizen, Fuji, Panasonic, Maxell, Sony, Suntory, TDK . . .

V Planning Marketing Tactics

Once the marketing strategy is established or revised, the various parts of the marketing mix are developed by marketing management. This is the tactical stage of decision making within the marketing discipline. The major decision areas are product, pricing, distribution, and promotion.

After reading this part, you should have a better understanding of:

1. The ways marketing a service differs from marketing a product.
2. Various pricing alternatives available to management.
3. The complexities of distribution decisions.
4. Choices in measuring advertising effectiveness.
5. The role of salespeople and sales management.

24

No-Frills Food:
New Power for the Supermarkets

The president of King Soopers, Inc., the biggest supermarket chain in Denver, boasts that the largest-selling paper towel in his city is not Bounty, the national market leader, but his chain's three-year-old product labeled simply "Paper Towels." The president of Loblaws Ltd., a Toronto grocery chain, appears in a television ad describing the 25% saving on generic disposable diapers, which outsell even Pampers in his stores. And in Marlow Heights, Md., Grand Union Co. last March converted a $60,000-a-week supermarket into a stripped-down outlet that cuts prices 20% by eliminating the variety of brands and most of the other amenities of a modern food store. Yet the converted outlet consistently grosses more than $500,000 per week.

To bewildered supermarket and food company executives, such no-frills merchandising coups are no longer isolated events. As they multiply, they are producing anxious moments for packaged food and household product brand managers. Their primary distributors—the nation's 33,000 supermarkets—are posing their first serious threat to brand marketing by perfecting new forms of retailing that appeal to the consumer's basic instinct: price.

THE BALANCE SHIFTS

Starting from nearly zero in 1977, no-frills operators have grabbed 5% of the $200 billion grocery market, either with generic products or through high-volume supermarkets that cut prices by drastically reducing the services and the variety of brands they offer. Many observers predict these new forms of food retailing could capture up to 25% of the market during the 1980s. Such

---

growth is forcing conventional supermarkets to consider adopting some of the efficiencies of the no-frills operators. It is also shifting the balance of power in grocery marketing toward a supermarket trade that had been subservient to manufacturers with big ad budgets and reams of market data to justify their products' place on the grocery shelves.

No-frills supermarkets have already taught all food retailers one simple but critical lesson: They do not need to stock half a dozen brands in each category in order to attract customers. And that could leave the producers of the No. 3 or No. 4 brands out in the cold.

"Previously, retailers displayed the whole array of products that manufacturers wanted displayed," says Chairman Byron E. Allumbaugh of Ralphs Grocery Co. of Federated Department Stores Inc. "Now products are going to be in our stores because the customer wants them there." Concedes William V. Costello, U.S. sales vice-president at H. J. Heinz Co.: "Food retailers are trying to control their own destiny, and that means manufacturers have less influence."

This loss of influence will have the biggest impact on those food producers that fail to develop new products that meet real needs and are not simply line extensions. As a result, the winners in the supermarkets of the 1980s are likely to be companies such as Procter & Gamble, General Foods, Pillsbury, and Heinz, all of which have strong brands as well as the marketing and technical expertise to spot new needs and develop innovative products to serve them. The losers may well be those such as Lever Bros., Borden, Carnation, and Beatrice, which have weaker brands or brands in commodity areas and which are considered to lack the skills now needed to develop successful new products.

The food retailers, facing a grocery market that has ceased growing, labor costs that are rising sharply, and margins that have languished at dangerously low levels for a decade, lately have been desperate enough to try any new merchandising schemes in the hope that they will avoid the fate of Food Fair Inc., Allied Supermarkets Inc., and other operators forced into Chapter 11 in recent years. In the last five years the grocery market's real annual growth rate has sunk to a mere 0.3%, and the food retailing industry's net margins, consistently above 1% in the 1960s, made it above 1% only once in the 1970s.

Understandably, the moment one no-frills retailing concept shows promise, there is an immediate response to it. The chain reaction started quietly five years ago when Germany's Albrecht Group opened its first Aldi store in the Midwest. A stark contrast to the typical supermarket, crammed with 12,000 varieties of items, the new store stocked only one brand and size of product in only 500 categories, and it did away with bagging, item pricing, check cashing, and even the energy-intensive meat and produce sections. But it offered a 20% break on prices, and it attracted a crowd. Within months, Chicago-based Jewel Cos. responded by rolling out the nation's first line of generic products selling even below Aldi's prices.

TRADING-DOWN PRESSURE

What began as an experiment in no-frills merchandising has blossomed into a marketing revolution that for the first time is segmenting the historically homogeneous supermarket business. "One format doesn't seem to work for all of America anymore," observes Timothy M. Hammonds, senior vice-president of the Food Marketing Institute.

The new no-frills segment of the grocery market is now exploding as shoppers trade down on food in a manner undreamed of a few years ago. One key reason is two consecutive years of major declines in the average consumer's real income, with the shrinking standard of living this has brought (*BW*, Jan. 28, 1980). The supermarket has always been the primary area for trading down in hard times, but now the practice is spreading to shoppers who normally resist it. "For the first time we are seeing the emergence of a group—maybe 20% of up-scale shoppers—who are cutting back not because they have to now, but because they believe a constantly improving standard of living is no longer realistic," notes Florence R. Skelly, executive vice-president of Yankelovich, Skelly & White, market researchers. "Once it starts, that thinking spreads."

That prospect is chilling to manufacturers of branded products that are already losing market share to generics or losing distribution because of the growth of limited-assortment stores. "This is a consumer-driven phenomenon that is a clear and present danger to all branded manufacturers," says C. Gordon Wade, president of Cincinnati Consulting Group, a consumer product consulting firm. "Consumers are concluding that more and more brands in the supermarket are not providing sufficient value to justify their extra price."

That pressure is prompting food manufacturers to discount grocery product prices to an unprecedented degree, and the result is eroded margins on scores of consumer food and household products. For weaker brands, the long-term outlook is especially bleak: Some experts who track no-frills retailing predict that one-quarter of all brands in the supermarket will be eliminated in the 1980s. Many believe that supermarkets will ultimately carry no more than the top two brands in a category plus a private label and a generic. "Pity the manufacturer who has been lulled into thinking that his No. 3 brand is a steady profit contributor and who

hasn't been watching what is happening in the marketplace," says Raymond Asp, executive vice-president of Geo. A. Hormel & Co.

The failure of weaker brands will obviously enhance the market position of the leaders. But their manufacturers could still lose market power if, as some believe, the U.S. supermarket business is taking its first steps toward the European model. In Europe, the retail chains dominate the food business, and partly because of this they obtain much higher margins than food manufacturers—the very opposite of the relationship in the U.S.

U.S. food chains are a long way from being that powerful; the country's largest chain, Safeway Stores Inc., controls only 7% of the national market. But many changes being fashioned in the American supermarket show a European hand at work. Roughly 15% of the U.S. supermarket industry in recent years has come under European ownership through such acquisitions as Tengelmann Group's purchase of a controlling interest in Great Atlantic & Pacific Tea Co. and the purchase of Grand Union by Britain's Cavenham Ltd. The Aldi stores, which may have initiated the no-frills movement, were copied directly from stores that Albrecht runs in West Germany, and when Jewel Cos. introduced generics, it borrowed the idea from France's Carrefour chain.

None of the new supermarket techniques has been so badly underestimated as generics. When they were introduced in 1977, food company executives predicted that they would not take hold. When they did, the prediction was that they were peaking, even though research shows that most generics are still gaining share in stores that have had them for two years. "Brand guys keep saying that generics will pass, but they now account for 15% of our sales, and I can see them reaching one-third," says David A. Nichol, president of the Loblaw chain. "It reminds me of how Detroit kept saying that compacts would never get a large share of the auto market."

Some no-name items can now be found in half of the nation's supermarkets, but chains such as Pathmark, Ralphs, and King Soopers are selling more than 250 separate generic products—and none is planning to stop there. Overall, generics have won 1.5% of total U.S. grocery sales in just three years, but in many high-volume, commodity categories they easily exceed 5% of the market, having taken share even from the market leaders as well as weaker brands.

Generics, which essentially are lower-quality store brands, have also taken share from regular store brands, but their net effect has been to expand the supermarkets' private-label share for the first time in years. According to Selling Areas-Marketing Inc., a Time Inc. subsidiary, the private-label share of total grocery shipments grew to a record 15.4% in the fourth quarter of 1980, two points above the pregeneric level.

In many ways, generics provide the best evidence of the supermarkets' new marketing power. Until now private-label products virtually copied national brands but sold for 15% below them because of marketing efficiencies. With generics, stores have to create new products that are of acceptable quality but can be priced 30% lower than national brands because they involve less packaging, less processing, or cheaper ingredients.

Generic tea bags, for example, do not have tags or individual wrappers and are stuffed into plastic pouches. Jellies use lower-grade fruit and less sugar. And generic cooking oils are not put through the added processing steps that give branded products greater stability and purity.

But part of the savings comes from the stores' muscling of private-label manufacturers into accepting gross margins on generics that are often only half those on regular private-label products. Marginal manufacturers accept such deals because generics may well be the only thing keeping their plants running. But many more efficient manufacturers may accept such lower-margin work because they fear the chains will take their regular private-label business elsewhere if they refuse. Reportedly, this has already happened in a few cases. So, even though generics are giving private-label producers their first real sales growth in years, the producers are not too happy, notes Donald Addy, president of Home Brands Inc., a Minneapolis-based producer of private-label jellies.

The real rub is that many leading branded manufacturers now feel compelled to produce lower-margin generics, too, because either the market has grown too big to ignore or the inroads of generics have left them with idle capacity. As a result, Borden, the No. 2 maker of coffee creamers (Cremora); Scott paper, which markets the No. 2 paper towel (Viva); and Union Carbide, which owns the leading household-bag brand (Glad), are all making lower-margin generics that compete against their own brands. Making generics uses the 25% excess production capacity that was stifling Borden's Cremora operations, but the company is hardly proud of that. "Making private label is a cancer," grumbles Executive Vice-President Marvin J. Herb. "The better you do it the worse things get, because you erode your own brand's share."

Such moves by even the giants among consumer goods producers reveal that brand loyalty is showing an alarming weakness. Consumer researcher Skelly argues that the changing role of women is the underlying reason for this. "It used to be status among women to know the best brands in the supermarket, but that's not an arena for Brownie points anymore," she says.

The broad-based weakening of brand loyalty obviously explains the rise of generics, but curiously it is also credited with the sudden popularity of no-frills stores, even though they usually concentrate on selling national brands rather than private-label products. No-frills stores cut their costs by rejecting a previously unquestioned axiom in the industry that supermarkets must carry all major brands to be competitive. In addition to cutting back services, the new outlets carry a sharply reduced number of brands, and even these may change from week to week because no-frills retailers focus on merchandise they can buy on deals—the 10% wholesale discounts that branded manufacturers periodically offer to the trade.

The enthusiasm for no-frills stores began with the 500-item Aldi format, but these outlets have lately been overshadowed by more powerful no-frills units known as warehouse stores. Unlike the Aldi-type outlets, warehouse stores stock products in all grocery categories and feature complete meat and produce sections, too. But because they carry only one or two items in each category they still keep their total item count to about 5,000—less than half that of the average supermarket.

Despite the limited selection they offer, no-frills stores attract bargain-conscious shoppers by offering them an average 15% saving on food. According to Willard Bishop, a Barrington (Ill.) supermarket consultant, there are 1,800 no-frills supermarkets in the U.S.—most of which have opened since 1977. They have won 3.5% of the national grocery market, but they have taken 12% to 15% of the market away from conventional food retailers in such cities as Boston, Milwaukee, Kansas City, and St. Louis, and many in the industry now expect their market share to reach those levels nationally by the mid-1980s.

That alone is a scary prospect for producers of national brands. But the indirect impact is more threatening. The weakness in brand loyalty that the warehouse stores have exposed is prompting food retailers to get serious about cutting back drastically on the variety of packaged goods in their stores.

Supermarket chains that have no intention of cutting other services now are confidently chopping away at brand variety in the grocery section. When Giant Food Inc. responded late last year to competition from no-frills stores by opening four "hybrid" stores, it kept the deli, bakery, floral shop, and all the other services of its other huge stores that dominate the Washington (D.C.) market. But in its hybrid stores it cut in half the number of packaged foods and household goods items, mainly by stocking only the brand leaders and its own private label.

Yet another sign of this intention to cut product variety is the sudden explosion of demand for the $180,000 scanning systems that record supermarket sales by optically reading an item's universal product code and then transmitting that data to an in-store computer. Although the systems, first introduced in the early 1970s, were very slow to take off, demand for them is now outstripping supply. Last year the number of stores equipped with scanning doubled to 3,000 outlets, which account for 15% of supermarket volume. Well over half of all supermarket sales may be scanned by the mid-1980s.

There is already evidence of the role that the new equipment can play in eliminating the excessive variety of brands. Even as Ralphs installed a generic aisle in the last two years, it made a net reduction of 2,000 items in its Los Angeles stores. The cutback was simplified because the chain is one of only four that are totally equipped with scanners. "It's a great tool to analyze what is moving and what is not," explains Chairman Allumbaugh. Now some chains are preparing computer programs that will determine each product's profit contribution to the store, based on the investment in space and labor required to stock it. Schnuck

Markets Inc., the largest chain in St. Louis, will begin implementing such a program soon after scanners are installed in all of the chain's 54 stores this month. "It will identify all items not paying their way, and we'll decide either to merchandise them differently or to eliminate them," says President Donald O. Schnuck.

Even now, food manufacturers are beginning to act as if their sole purpose is to ensure that their brands are not among those dropped by the food chains. Responding to the wave of no-frills retailing, food and household product producers in the last year have shifted their marketing budgets sharply toward price promotion and away from advertising, the method they normally prefer.

Veterans of the supermarket business cannot recall a time when price dealing by producers was as pervasive as it is now. Observers suggest that the volume of discounts offered by manufacturers to supermarkets and to consumers in the form of coupons has roughly doubled since no-frills stores arrived on the scene. As a result, says Hercules A. Segalas, an analyst with Drexel Burnham Lambert Inc., household-products companies have probably shifted their marketing mix from 50-50 advertising and promotion two years ago to 40-60 in favor of price promotion today.

A SQUEEZE ON ADVERTISING

Such trends are having a decidedly negative impact on network television and women's magazines, which historically have benefitted from huge advertising outlays plugging food and household products. Since 1977 growth in network advertising for food products and household cleaners, the two major groups that use supermarkets as their primary distributors, has trailed overall growth in network advertising revenues. The seven leading women's magazines have been hit even harder. Their advertising growth slowed dramatically in 1978, and their total annual advertising pages have declined 10% since then.

So far, the price promotion fury has not reduced overall margins of the highly diversified food processing industry. Yet dozens of major brands in the last year have suffered severe margin erosion in those commodity-type areas where generics have made substantial inroads and where no-frills stores have shown their greatest determination to buy only on deal. Net margins of such household product giants as Procter & Gamble Co. and Colgate-Palmolive Co. tumbled last year. Analyst Segalas estimates that in paper towels and tissues, P&G's profits dropped 15%, partly because such normally stalwart brands as Bounty, Charmin, and Puffs lost share to generics. In canned goods, Castle & Cooke and R. J. Reynolds Industries' Del Monte Corp. also suffered margin setbacks in 1980.

Price promotion has become so pervasive that some big manufacturers are trying to restore some discipline to their markets. In what is widely regarded as a futile effort to put an end to the warehouse stores' practice of buying only on deal, P&G last year reportedly began enforcing a policy of offering discounts only to those supermarkets that purchase products on a regular basis. This policy has been challenged in a complaint to the Federal Trade Commisssion. Others, including Del Monte, are trying to price products to recover all cost increases, even if this means losing market share. "With the way everyone is dealing right now, we all must be kamikaze pilots," says F. R. Gumucio, a vice-president at Del Monte's U.S. Grocery Products Div.

But tinkering with prices is no long-term answer to the problem, and some companies are trying strategic responses. In the last two years, Colgate has concentrated its advertising on its top 11 brands, while it has eliminated or sharply reduced ad spending on such weaker brands as Ajax laundry detergent, once promoted by ubiquitous White Knight commercials. "We want to make sure that our bellwether brands earn their place in the supermarkets," says John Watkins, the company's marketing vice-president.

To help sell their weaker brands, Colgate and other companies are trying to turn the trading-down habit to their advantage. Colgate has grouped its weaker products, including such erstwhile leaders as Cashmere Bouquet soap, under a marketing umbrella called "Colgate Value Brands." These are not advertised anymore, but they sell for 20% less than other national brands.

Food producers are also finding that they can protect weaker brands by regionalizing them—marketing them where they are strong enough to remain on supermarket shelves but abandoning promotion efforts where they have difficulty commanding shelf space. Lately, Heinz has done this with its mustard—which ranks far behind the market leader, French's—by dropping marketing efforts in the West and putting all its promotional spending for the product into the Midwest and the East. Similarly, Beatrice Foods Co., which has a stable of brands that are weak nationally but dominant in certain regions, avoids expanding prematurely its marketing efforts for such products beyond their areas of strength.

STRATEGIES OF RESPONSE

Still other companies are responding to the generics and no-frills shopping by spending heavily to upgrade existing brands in the hope of convincing increasingly skeptical consumers that they are worth the extra price. While Union Carbide Corp., for example, began making generic trash bags as a defensive measure, it also last year spent $15 million to add another ply to its Glad Bags, which dominate the $900 million supermarket segment of the plastic bag business. Now the company is in the middle of a $20 million advertising and promotion campaign for the new three-ply bag. Like a new generation of commercials coming from Colgate and P&G, the ad for the new Glad bag compares its performance with generics. In one commercial, which a Glad brand manager says "goes for the throat," a generic bag is shown rupturing and spilling garbage everywhere.

Other major food companies such as Pillsbury Co. and General Mills Inc. are betting heavily on new products to keep them a step ahead. But the new-product challenge is sure to be tougher now than in the 1970s when easily half of the product introductions involved nothing more than extensions of existing lines. If the changes in supermarkets do nothing more, they will stop this kind of product proliferation cold.

In fact, no-frills products and supermarkets may be totally changing the skills a food products company needs to succeed. Clever marketing and promotion of cosmetic differences in products may have worked in the past, but such talents appear less important now. "As the consumer views more products as commodities, it makes it harder for companies to establish a meaningful point of difference for their products," observes consultant Wade. "As a result, technology—never considered as providing much leverage in food business before—suddenly has a premium on it."

25 Services Marketing Is Different

Leonard L. Berry

Services are relatively intangible, produced and consumed simultaneously, and often less standardized than goods. These unique characteristics of services will therefore present special challenges to the services marketer.

In 1978 $600 billion was spent by Americans for services—for airline tickets, electricity, rent, medical care, college tuition, sports entertainment, automobile repair, and so forth. Today, in excess of 45% of the average family's budget is spent on services.[1]

Despite the importance of the services sector in the American economy, services marketing has only recently attracted the attention of academic marketers. As a result, far more research has been done on how to market goods than on how to market services. This would not really matter if the problems encountered in services marketing were identical to those encountered in goods marketing, but such is not the case. This article examines some of the special characteristics of services and suggests some of the marketing strategy implications that arise from them.

CHARACTERISTICS OF SERVICES

Although service industries are themselves quite heterogeneous (ranging from beauty salons to electric utilities), there are some characteristics of services about which it is useful to generalize. Three of the most important of these characteristics are discussed here.

More Intangible Than Tangible. A good is an object, a device, a thing; a service is a deed, a performance, an effort. When a good is purchased, something tangible is acquired; something that can be seen, touched, perhaps smelled or worn or placed on a mantel. When a service is purchased, there is generally nothing tangible to show for it.

---

[1]Fabian Linden, "Service, Please," *Across the Board* (August 1978), p. 42.

Reprinted with permission from *Business* (May-June 1980), published by Georgia State University, pp. 24–28.

Money has been spent, but there are no additional clothes to hang in the closet and nothing to place on the mantel.

Services are consumed but not possessed. Although the performance of most services is supported by tangibles—for instance, the automobile in the case of a taxi service—the essence of what is being bought is a performance rendered by one party for another.

Most market offerings are a combination of tangible and intangible elements.[2] It is whether the essence of what is being bought is tangible or intangible that determines its classification as a good or a service. In a restaurant the acquisition of supplies, the preparation and serving of meals, and the after-meal cleanup (or some combination thereof) is performed for the consumer by another party. Hence, we think of the restaurant industry as a service industry. This is so even though there are tangibles involved—for example, the building, interior decor, kitchen equipment, and food.

The concept of intangibility has two meanings, both of which present challenges for marketing—

☐ That which cannot be touched, impalpable.
☐ That which cannot be easily defined, formulated, or grasped mentally.[3]

Addressing the marketing problems that intangibility presents is generally a matter of far more concern to the services marketer than to the goods marketer.

Simultaneous Production and Consumption. Services are generally produced and consumed in the same time frame. The college professor produces an educational service while the student consumes it. The telephone company produces telephone service

while the telephone user consumes it. The babysitter produces a babysitting service while the children and parents consume it.

Generally, goods are produced, then sold, then consumed. Services on the other hand are usually sold first, then produced and consumed simultaneously.

Simultaneous production and consumption means that the service provider is often physically present when consumption takes place. Whereas a washing machine might be manufactured in Michigan and consumed in Virginia, the dentist is present when examining a patient; the singer is present when performing a concert; the airline stewardess is present when serving an in-flight meal.

What is important to recognize about the presence of the service provider is that the "how" of service distribution becomes important. In the marketing discipline, great stress is placed on distributing goods where and when customer-prospects desire them to be distributed—that is, to the "right place" and at the "right time." With services, it often is important to distribute them in the "right way" as well. How automobile mechanics, physicians, lawyers, teachers, and bank tellers conduct themselves in the presence of the customer can influence future patronage decisions. Washing machines can't be rude or careless or thoughtless, but people providing services can be and sometimes are. And when they are, the result may be a search for a new service supplier.

Less Standardized and Uniform. Service industries tend to differ on the extent to which they are "people-based" or "equipment-based."[4] That is, there is a larger human component involved in performing

---

[2]For a good discussion of this point see G. Lynn Shostack, "Breaking Free From Product Marketing," *Journal of Marketing* (April 1977), pp. 73-80.

[3]*New World Dictionary of the American Language* (1974), p. 731.

[4]Dan R. E. Thomas, "Strategy Is Different in Service Businesses," *Harvard Business Review* (July-August 1978), pp. 158-65.

some services (for example, plumbing) than others (for example, telephone communications). One of the implications of this distinction is that the "outcomes" of people-based service operations tend to be less standardized and uniform than the outcomes of equipment-based service- or goods-producing operations. Stated differently, the extensive involvement of people in the production of a service introduces a degree of variability in the outcome that is not present when machines dominate. This is an important consideration, given the vast number of service industries that are labor-intensive.

The ever-present potential for variability in a labor-intensive service situation is well known in the marketplace. Whereas consumers expect their favorite breakfast cereal to always taste the same, and to almost always hear a dial tone when picking up a telephone receiver, expectations are far less certain on the occasion of getting a haircut. This is why consumers look at their hair in a mirror before the hair-cutting service is concluded. The outcome is uncertain and more service production may be needed, even when the barber or beautician has had long experience with the consumer.

The growing use of automatic-teller machines (ATMs) by the financial-services industry makes the point. The net effect of the ATM is to transform the delivery of certain traditional banking services from a human delivery mode to a machine delivery mode. This transformation does not mean that all consumers will like or use these machines. It does mean, however, that those who do use ATMs will find far less variability in the services rendered than if human tellers were used. A banker can paint a smile on an ATM and call it Tillie; except when not working properly, the machine will perform uniformly for all customers regardless of how these customers are dressed, the time of day, or the length of the queue waiting for ser-

vice. Such is not the case with the human teller who may have a bad day, get tired, or become angry with a supervisor, co-worker, or customer. Moreover, human tellers differ among themselves in their customer-relation and technical skills, their personalities, and their attitudes toward their work. In short, bankers cannot paint a smile on a human being.

MARKETING SERVICES

The special characteristics of services present a number of implications concerning their marketing. Although many marketing concepts and tools are applicable to both goods and services, the relative importance of these concepts and tools, and how they are used, are often different. This section suggests a number of strategic marketing opportunities of particular importance to the service industries.

Internal Marketing

In what Richard Chase calls "high-contact" service businesses, the quality of the service is inseparable from the quality of the service provider.[5] High-contact businesses are ones in which there is considerable contact between the service provider and the customer, e.g., health care, financial services, and restaurants. Human performance materially shapes the service outcome and hence becomes part of the "product."

Just as goods marketers need to be concerned with product quality, so do services marketers need to be concerned with service quality, which means—in labor-intensive situations—special attention to employee quality and performance. It follows that in

---

[5]Richard B. Chase, "Where Does the Customer Fit in a Service Operation?" *Harvard Business Review* (November-December 1978), pp. 137-42.

high-contact service industries, marketers need to be concerned with internal, not just external, marketing.

Internal marketing means applying the philosophy and practices of marketing to the people that serve the external customer so that (1) the best possible people can be employed and retained and (2) they will do the best possible work. (Technically the phrase "internal marketing" can be applied to any form of marketing inside an organization, for example, marketing an idea to a superior. In this article, the phrase concerns marketing to employees.) More specifically, internal marketing is viewing employees as internal customers, viewing jobs as internal products, and (just as with external marketing) endeavoring to design these products to better meet the needs of these customers.[6]

Although most executives are not accustomed to thinking of marketing in this way, the fact is that people do buy jobs from employers, and employers can and do use marketing to sell these jobs on an initial and ongoing basis. To the extent that high-contact service firms use the concepts and tools of marketing to offer better, more satisfying jobs, they upgrade their capabilities for being more effective service marketers.

The relevance of marketing thinking to personnel management is very real. The banks and insurance companies (among others) adopting flexible working hours are redesigning jobs to better accommodate individual differences, which is market segmentation.[7] The Marriott Corporation is

noted for its commitment to employee attitude monitoring, but what it really is doing is marketing research.[8] Indiana National Bank's recent "Person-to-Person" advertising campaign featuring its own personnel was designed to motivate employees as well as external customers and prospects. Aggressive investment in behalf of employee quality and performance is a hallmark of many of America's most successful service companies, including Delta Airlines,[9] Bank of America,[10] and Walt Disney.[11]

Importantly, the crucial matter is not that the phrase "internal marketing" come into widespread use, but that the implication of the phrase be understood; i.e., by satisfying the needs of its internal customers, an organization upgrades its capability for satisfying the needs of its external customers. This is true for most organizations and is certainly true for high-contact service organizations. As one recent article pointed out, "the successful service company must first sell the job to employees before it can sell its services to customers."[12]

Customizing Service

The simultaneous production and consumption characteristic of services frequently provides opportunities to "customize" service. Some service organizations take

---

[6]Thomas W. Thompson, Leonard L. Berry, and Phillip H. Davidson, *Banking Tomorrow—Managing Markets Through Planning* (New York: Van Nostrand Reinhold, 1978), p. 243.

[7]See, for example, Warren Magoon and Larry Schnicker, "Flexible Hours at State Street Bank of Boston: A Case Study," *Personnel Administrator* (October 1977), pp. 34-37; and Charles A. Cottrell and J. Mark Walker, "Flexible Work Days: Philosophy and Bank Implementation," *Journal of Retail Banking* (December 1979), pp. 72-80.

[8]See G. M. Hostage, "Quality Control in a Service Business," *Harvard Business Review* (July-August 1975), pp. 104-05.

[9]See "Delta's Flying Money Machine," *Business Week* (May 9, 1977), pp. 84-89.

[10]See "Listening and Responding to Employee Concerns—An Interview with A. W. Clausen," *Harvard Business Review* (January-February 1980), pp. 101-14.

[11]See N. W. Pope, "Mickey Mouse Marketing," *American Banker* (July 25, 1979), pp. 4 and 14; and N. W. Pope, "More Mickey Mouse Marketing," *American Banker* (September 12, 1979), pp. 4-14.

[12]W. Earl Sasser and Stephen P. Arbeit, "Selling Jobs in the Service Sector," *Business Horizons* (June 1976), p. 64.

full advantage of this opportunity within the boundary of productivity requirements, but many do not.

Since a fundamental marketing objective is to effect a good fit between what the customer-prospect wants to buy and what the organization has to sell, the potential for tailoring service to meet the precise desires of individual customers should not be taken lightly. The possibilities for service customization are far greater than first meet the eye. Free Spirit Travel Agency, headquartered in Boulder, Colorado, completes information forms for first-time customers indicating travel patterns and preferences. The marketing potential of such a customer-information system is significant—for example, automatically sending notices on travel specials to Japan to those customers expressing an interest in that country. Automotive Systems, a Decatur, Georgia, automotive repair and maintenance firm, provides explicit notes on its customer bills indicating what still needs to be done with the car and the degree of priority. A growing number of financial institutions have implemented training and incentive programs to encourage tellers to refer to customers by name during transactions. Wendy's designed its hamburger production line to accommodate individual preferences in the makeup of a hamburger and, in the process, to capitalize on the limited flexibility of the McDonald's system.

One of the key strategic issues for many service marketers is to determine the circumstances under which customization should apply and the circumstances under which standardization should apply. This issue is at the heart of an interesting trend in the banking industry toward the use of "personal bankers." Banks fully implementing personal banking assign to each retail customer a specific banker who opens new accounts and compiles information for future reference, makes loans and provides financial consultation, cuts red tape when problems arise, and in general is available when service of a nonroutine neature is needed. In short, personal bankers function on a client basis in much the same way as public accountants or attorneys function.[13]

Banks that have adopted a personal-banker mode of organization have, in effect, established a system in which customers can on appropriate occasions get individualized service from a trained banker with whom they have dealt before. For routine transactions, the customer continues to use the teller station or ATMs that provide more standardized services. Although neither inexpensive nor easy to implement, personal banking is growing because it facilitates the custom packaging and hence the cross-selling of financial services; because it helps banks attract more affluent customers who value personalized and competent service; and because it is a way for larger institutions—a Wachovia, Harris Bank, or Irving Trust, for example—to *credibly* position themselves in the market as personalized institutions.[14]

Managing Evidence

Because goods are tangible and can be seen and touched, they are generally easier to evaluate than services. The intangibility of services prompts customer-prospects to be attentive to tangibles associated with the service for clues of the service's nature and quality.

A prime responsibility for the service marketer is to manage these tangibles so

[13]Leonard L. Berry, "The Personal Banker," *Bankers Magazine* (January-February 1978), pp. 54-55.

[14]See Thomas J. Stanley, Leonard L. Berry, and William D. Danko, "Personal Service Versus Convenience: Perceptions of the High-Income Customer," *Journal of Retail Banking* (June 1979), pp. 54-61.

that the proper signals are conveyed about the service. As one author convincingly writes on this subject:

Product marketing tends to give first emphasis to creating *abstract* associations. *Service* marketers, on the other hand, should be focused on enhancing and differentiating "realities" through manipulation of *tangible* clues. The management of evidence comes first for service marketers.[15]

There are a number of ways service marketers can manage evidence, as the following sections indicate.

Physical Services Environment. The physical environment in which services are purchased generally provides an important opportunity to tell the "right" story about a given service. Fortunately, service marketers are frequently in a position to shape the environment to their specifications because they distribute the service they produce.

There are many examples of service marketers capitalizing on this opportunity to manage evidence. A Richmond, Virginia, pediatrician decorated his office with bright, multicolored carpeting, pictures of Disney characters on the walls, a huge balloon Superman suspended from the ceiling in one of the examining rooms, a play area in a corner of the waiting room, and an after-visit toybox from which each child could select an inexpensive toy to take home. Braniff Airlines not only painted the exteriors of its planes a variety of bright colors but also furnished the interior with leather seats and wall murals. Hyatt with its daring hotel designs, Walt Disney with its spectacular theme parks, and TransAmerica with its pyramid-like headquarters building are three service companies that have succeeded notably in making architecture a centerpiece of their marketing strategy.

[15]Shostack, "Breaking Free From Product Marketing," p. 78.

Appearance of Service Providers. The appearance of service providers is another tangible that can be managed. Fitness consultants at Cosmopolitan Health Spas often wear white "doctor" smocks and are rarely flabby. The Richmond pediatrician referred to earlier wore bright shirts and oversized bow ties rather than the traditional smock, which would have signaled "doctor" to the child. Braniff stewardesses wear designer outfits to complement the striking decor of the planes. Disney goes to great lengths to assure that theme park employees appear "freshly scrubbed," neatly groomed, and unfailingly cheerful.

Service Pricing. The tendency for customer-prospects to use the price of a product as an indicator of its quality is well known. Some researchers suggest that this tendency is even more pronounced for services. They argue that the relative absence of material data with which to appraise services makes price a potentially important index of quality.[16]

It follows that setting the right price is especially critical in circumstances where there is reason to expect differences in service quality from one supplier to another, and where the personal risk of buying a lower quality service is high. Lawyers, accountants, investment counselors, consultants, convention speakers, and even hair stylists can contradict signals they wish to communicate about quality by setting their prices too low. In short, price can be a confidence builder; price is a clue.

Tying Services Marketing to Goods Marketing. Sometimes increased credibility concerning a service's quality can be gained by distributing it through a goods-market-

[16]Pierre Eiglier and Eric Langeard, "A New Approach to Service Marketing," in Eiglier, et al., *Marketing Consumer Services: New Insights* (Cambridge, Mass.: Marketing Science Institute, 1977), p. 41.

ing organization that already has credibility. The automotive-service and insurance business lines at Sears have undoubtedly benefited greatly from the association with the Sears' name and reputation.

A recent paper illustrates the potential benefits of tying services marketing into a goods-marketing organization with a hypothetical scenario involving an established department store adding a health spa:

The store's strengths include a loyal market of middle age, upper middle class, upper income customers . . . a reputation for quality; and an image of progressive merchandising. . . . The health spa industry, in general, has a poor image which includes high pressure selling tactics, poor quality personnel, and inattention once the sale has been made. The new offering's intangibility allows the store to use its positive image to reduce the uncertainty and perceived risks for potential users of the spa. In addition to revenues generated from the spa services, there are many possibilities for cross-selling other store lines such as sporting goods, sportswear, and health food products.[17]

Interestingly, the process can work the other way with well-known and well-regarded service companies moving into goods marketing. The key of course is where the credibility and access to the customer-prospect lies. In the preceding scenario, it lies with the department store. In the case of service enterprises like American Express and TWA, it lies with them.

Making the Service Tangible

Earlier it was indicated that intangibility has two meanings: that which cannot be touched; that which cannot be easily grasped mentally. Marketing advantage usually is to be gained if the service can be made more "touchable" and more easily

grasped mentally. This involves attempting to make the service more tangible.[18]

Sometimes it is possible to make a service more palpable by creating a tangible representation of it. This is what has occurred with the development of the bank credit card. By representing the service with a specially encoded plastic card that, when used, triggers the service, Visa and others have been able to overcome many of the handicaps normally associated with marketing an intangible. The existence of the plastic card has allowed Visa to physically differentiate the service through color and graphics and to build and even extend a potent brand name, e.g., Visa travelers checks. Moreover, institutions distributing bank charge cards can extend their trading areas because once the card is obtained by consumers (often by mail), credit purchases can be made without going to the bank.

Just as service marketers should consider whether there are opportunities to develop a tangible representation of the service, so should they look for opportunities to make the service more easily grasped mentally. For example, the insurance industry has made it easier for consumers to perceive what is being sold by associating the intangible of insurance with relevant tangible objects. Consider the following:

- "You are in good *hands* with Allstate."
- "I've got a piece of the *rock*."
- "Under the Traveler's *umbrella*."
- "The Nationwide *blanket* of protection."

Hands, rocks, umbrellas, and blankets are used to more effectively communicate what insurance can provide people; they are de-

---

[17]William R. George, "The Retailing of Services— A Challenging Future," *Journal of Retailing* (Fall 1977), pp. 88-89.

[18]This section draws heavily from James H. Donnelly, Jr., "Service Delivery Strategies in the 1980s—Academic Perspective," in Leonard L. Berry and James H. Donnelly, Jr., eds., *Financial Institution Marketing: Strategies in the 1980s* (Washington, D.C.: Consumer Banker Association, 1980), pp. 143-50.

vices used to make the service more easily grasped mentally.

Synchronizing Supply and Demand

Because services are performances, they cannot be inventoried. This is a significant fact of life in a service business because demand peaks cannot be accommodated simply by taking goods off a shelf. If an airline has 40 more flight-reservation requests than capacity permits, some business will likely be lost. Conversely, if an airliner takes off with 40 empty seats, the revenue that those 40 seats could have produced, had they been filled, is lost forever. One of the crucial challenges in many service industries is to find ways to better synchronize supply and demand as an alternative to recurring conditions of severe overdemand and underdemand. This is easier said than done. Demand peaks can occur during certain times of the day (airlines, restaurants), during certain days of the week (movies, hair styling), and during certain months of the year (income tax services, beach resorts).[19]

The service marketer interested in better synchronizing supply and demand may attempt to reshape demand and/or supply patterns for the service.[20]

Reshaping Demand. All elements of the marketing mix are potentially available to help bring demand more in line with supply constraints. Delta Airlines, for example, has used pricing incentives to encourage travelers to fly during the early morning hours ("Early Bird" flights) and late evening hours ("Owly Bird" flights). Differential pricing to encourage demand during nonpeak periods is also commonly used by rental-car companies, movie theatres, and bars, among

others. Through intensive promotion, the U.S. Postal Service has persuaded many customers that it is beneficial to them and their addressees to mail Christmas cards and packages early.[21] By adding a breakfast product line, McDonald's and other fast-food companies have been able to make productive use of previously underutilized facilities. Many banks have been able to lessen lobby traffic during peak hours by the use of automatic teller machines.

Importantly, demand-altering marketing actions can only have an impact when customer-prospects have control over their demand patterns. One recent article discusses the failure of the Boston bus system to attract significant numbers of new riders between 10:00 A.M. and 2:00 P.M. by reducing the normal $.25 fare to $.10 (promoted as "Dime Time"). A key problem was that most rush-hour riders were commuting to and from work and had little control over work schedules. More recent efforts by the bus system have centered on helping area employers understand the benefits of staggered and flexible working hours and how to implement them.[22]

Reshaping Supply. Another option available to the service marketer is to attempt to alter supply capacities to better match demand patterns. The possibilities are many and include the following

☐ Using part-time employees and performing only essential tasks during peak demand periods.

☐ Training employees to perform multiple jobs so they can switch from one to another as demand dictates.

☐ Using paraprofessionals so that professionals can concentrate on duties requiring their expertise, e.g., parabankers who do legwork,

---

[19]W. Earl Sasser, "Match Supply and Demand in Service Industries," *Harvard Business Review* (November-December 1976), p. 138.

[20]*Ibid.*, pp. 137–40.

[21]Christopher H. Lovelock and Robert F. Young, "Look to Consumers to Increase Productivity," *Harvard Business Review* (May-June 1979), p. 176.

[22]*Ibid.*, p. 173.

solve routine problems, and handle clerical duties.

☐ Substituting equipment for human labor to make the service system more productive, e.g., automated car washes and computer-prepared income tax returns.

Obviously there are limits to how much supply capacity can be modified to fit demand requirements. The use of part-time personnel may be a variable cost, but the space they use when they come to work is a fixed cost. Nevertheless, the bottom-line potential from finding new ways to mesh supply capacity with demand is significant, and we can expect considerable innovation in this area during the 1980s. The same should be true for demand management as well. Indeed, America's best-managed service firms can be expected to vigorously work both sides of the street by seeking ways to reshape demand *and* supply patterns.

SUMMARY

Services differ from goods in some very important ways, and these differences present special challenges to the services marketer. The importance of the services sector in the American economy suggests the advisability of learning more about these differences and their marketing implications.

Services are more intangible than tangible, are produced and consumed simultaneously, and in many cases are less standardized and uniform than goods. These characteristics heighten the importance of certain marketing approaches that are usually not considered priorities or even applicable in goods marketing. These important services-marketing approaches include internal marketing, service customization, managing evidence, making the service tangible, and synchronizing supply and demand patterns.

In the academic discipline, services marketing has long been a stepchild to goods marketing, although progress has been made in recent years. It is time to do some serious catching up in terms of marketing thought. Perhaps the 1980s will be the decade in which this occurs.

26

A Decision-Making Structure for Price Decisions

Alfred R. Oxenfeldt

Pricing practice remains largely intuitive and routine. To gain insight as to why, the author examines critically some of the trends and gaps in the literature and practice. A comprehensive and systematic guide to successful price setting is offered.

Until recently, almost all pricing decisions have either been highly intuitive, as in the case of new product introductions, or based on routine procedures, as in cost-plus or imitative pricing. The proportion of price decisions representing these extreme approaches seems to have declined substantially; yet, many business executives have not altered their pricing methods substantially.[1]

Research continues on how businesses should set prices. Most of these studies attempt to uncover the best methods rather than those in current practice. No researcher has completely overcome the enormous difficulties of learning the basis on which group decisions are made and the "sensitive" reasons underlying many price decisions.[2] This article examines some trends in pricing and the apparent gulf between pricing theory and practice. A pricing framework is presented to aid practitioners structure their important pricing decisions.

THE GAP BETWEEN PRICING THEORY AND APPLICATION

The current pricing literature has produced few new insights or exciting new ap-

[1] Professor F. E. Gillis writes in 1969, "Joel Dean opines that cost-plus pricing is the most common technique in the United States. The statement is too weak; it is almost universal." See his *Managerial Economics* (Reading, Mass.: Addison-Wesley, 1969), p. 254.

[2] A. A. Fitzpatrick, *Pricing Methods of Industry* (Boulder, Colo: Pruett Press, Inc., 1964); *Decision Making in Marketing—A Description of Decision Making Processes and Its Application to Pricing*, 1971, Report No. 525, National Industrial Conference Board; Kaplan, Dirlam, and Lanzilotti, *Pricing in Big Business* (Washington, D.C.: The Brookings Institution, 1958); B. Fog, *Industrial Pricing Policies* (Amsterdam, Holland: North Holland Publishing Co., 1960); W. W. Haynes, *Pricing Decisions in Small Business* (Lexington, Ky.: University of Kentucky Press, 1962); and J. Fred Weston has been reported as directing a major study of this subject. See "The Myths and Realities of Corporate Pricing," *Fortune*, 85 (April 1972), p. 85.

Reprinted with permission from *Journal of Marketing*, published by the American Marketing Association, 37 (January 1973), pp. 48–53.

proaches that would interest most business-men enough to change their present methods. Those executives who follow the business literature have no doubt broadened their viewpoint and become more explicit and systematic about their pricing decisions; however, few, if any, actually employ new and different goals, concepts, or techniques.

The gap between pricing literature and practice may exist because the authors lack extensive personal experience with the practical problems facing executives in a highly competitive and complex business environment. Other explanatory factors include: the number of products for which executives are responsible, the lack of reliable information on product demand, the dynamic nature of technology, and the unpredictable responses from competitors. Because of the large number of highly uncertain and variable factors, executives responsible for pricing closely adhere to methods that they have found to be effective in the past. Economists and practitioners have long recognized that price is a dangerously explosive and complex marketing variable.

This discussion does not suggest that those responsible for pricing should always adhere to traditional methods of setting price, or that those writing about pricing have contributed little of value. The point is that a significant gap exists between two areas and that this gap must be closed if pricing is to continue to develop as a crucially important area of marketing theory and practice. Pricing specialists have suggested many helpful methods that have not been implemented in practice even after they have demonstrated to be valid.

LITERATURE TRENDS: A CRITIQUE

The field of pricing remains largely the domain of economic theorists who discuss price primarily in relation to the analyses of specific market structures.

Much of the pricing literature deals with tactics and stratagems for particular kinds of firms—wholesalers, manufacturers, franchisees, or joblot shops. Special corporate situations such as new product introductions, inflation, declining products, product-line pricing, price-structure problems, and price-cutting are also popular topics in the pricing literature.[3] The current literature on pricing, like that in most other areas of marketing, draws heavily on the behavioral sciences, quantitative tools, and detailed empirical research. Present-day writers employ simulation techniques and other computer applications much more than in the past, and are often concerned with cost computation and demand estimation. Pricing receives far more attention from marketing specialists today than it did when managerial economists such as Joel Dean, Jules Bachman, Arthur R. Burns, Donald Wallace, Edward Mason, Edwin Nourse, Walton Hamilton, Walter Adams, and Morris A. Adelman were the chief contributors to the field.

Recently, pricing specialists have channeled much of their research efforts into the development of approaches designed to aid the accuracy and efficiency of the decision-maker. The most promising methods are: use of the computer;[4] simula-

[3]The best of these writings are to be found in several collections of articles and talks about pricing. These are: Elizabeth Marting, ed., *Creative Pricing* (New York: American Marketing Association, 1968); Almarin Phillips and O. E. Williamson, eds., *Prices: Issues in Theory, Practice and Public Policy* (Philadelphia: University of Pennsylvania Press, 1967); D. F. Mulvihill and S. Paranka, eds., *Price Policies and Practices: A Source Book of Readings* (New York: John Wiley, 1967); American Management Association, *Competitive Pricing: Policies, Practices and Legal Considerations*, Management Report No. 17 (1958); American Management Association, *Pricing: The Critical Decision*, Management Report No. 66 (1961); Donald Watson, ed., *Price Theory in Action: A Book of Readings* (Boston: Houghton Mifflin, 1965); and B. Taylor and G. Wills, eds., *Pricing Strategy* (London: 1969).

[4]R. E. Good, "Using the Computer in Pricing," in *Creative Pricing*, Elizabeth Marting, ed. (New York: American Marketing Association, 1968), pp. 182–94.

tion as a method for anticipating the effect of price changes on sales and for testing complex strategies;[5] research techniques for obtaining more reliable information about prospective customer responses to price change;[6] and the nature and determinants of price perception.[7]

Nevertheless, large gaps still remain in the pricing literature. Very little is said about reconciling the various price-optima; i.e., the prices that are best vis-à-vis costs, the ultimate customer, resellers, and rivals. Most authors deal with pricing problems unidimensionally, whereas businessmen must generally deal with price as one element in a multidimensional marketing program. Price is often dealt with as if it were completely separated from the other elements in the marketing mix. These authors tend to concentrate on the effect of price on immediate marketwide sales without adequately considering long-run or individual market effects. The writers dealing with pricing decisions typically identify variables that are sometimes not considered and suggest conceptual errors that are commonly made, but they typically treat only small, isolated parts of the problem faced by a business executive. Little has been written on innovative approaches to pricing —approaches designed to *increase* demand, rather than *adapt to existing* demand. This failing has been most common in writings

that employ quantitative techniques. A price-setter must not merely view his responsibility as that of determining the various demand elasticities (price, promotion, assortment, quality, design, and place) and finding the price that best adapts to them. Attention must be given to measures that alter these elasticities in his firm's favor.

The setting of any price involves: (1) values that particular segments of customers place on a firm's offering; (2) consumer responses to price changes of the product; (3) competitive responses to any price changes; and (4) resellers' sensitivity to price changes. No one has yet developed a completely reliable method to measure the price elasticity of demand for a particular brand. Similarly, little is known about resellers' responses to margin changes or the sales support a brand will receive from distributors and retailers. The specific responses of competitors to both price and nonprice actions is still a matter of great uncertainty in almost all industries.

Pricing should be regarded as a field where the essential elements are quite clear and well known and where the concepts that need to be applied also are widely recognized and within reach of all executives. Practitioners face the problem of measuring a multitude of factors in many different specific situations; that is, they must attempt to quantify the response functions (elasticities) so they can be compared. One of the major problems in pricing is obtaining the data required to measure each of these response functions in different market contexts. Pricing specialists have made very few contributions to the solution of this problem.

[5] Arnold E. Amstutz, *Computer Simulation of Competitive Market Response* (Cambridge, Mass.: M.I.T. Press, 1967); and D. Kollat, R. Blackwell, and J. Robeson, *Strategic Marketing* (New York: Holt, Rinehart and Winston, 1972), Chapter 19.

[6] A. Gabor and C. W. J. Granger, "On the Price Consciousness of Consumers," *Applied Statistics*, 10 (1961), pp. 170–88; Gabor and Granger, "Price as an Indicator of Quality: Report on an Enquiry," *Economica*, 33 (1966), pp. 43–70; and Gabor and Granger, "The Pricing of New Products," *Scientific Business*, 3 (1965), pp. 141–50.

[7] Nystrom, *Retail Pricing: An Integrated Economic and Psychological Approach* (Stockholm: Economic Research Institute of Stockholm School of Economics, 1970), especially Chapters 7 and 8; Brown and Oxenfeldt, *Misperceptions of Economic Phenomena* (New York: Sperr and Douth, 1972).

CONSTRAINTS ON PRICING DECISIONS

Many vital price-related decisions made by top management deal with the following issues: Are we willing to drive competitors from business if we can? Should we inflict serious injury upon them when they have been struck by misfortune? Are we willing to violate the spirit or letter of the law to increase sales? At a different level of concern, pricing decisions are related to price strategy and general competitive policy by questions such as: Should we seek price leadership for ourselves or foster a pattern of price leadership with some other firm as leader? Should we try to shake out the weak firms in the industry to achieve price stability and higher profitability? Should we foster a spirit of cooperativeness among rivals by an avoidance of price competition?

These decisions are properly made by top executives and do not require a frequent revision. When they are not made explicitly, the executive responsible for pricing decision implicitly makes many of these decisions by default. A complete discussion of these constraints goes beyond the scope of this article.

To manage the complex nature of price-setting, practitioners need an effective, multidimensional model to guide their analysis. Such a pricing model would not only explicitly encourage systemized thinking, but also underscore the differential advantage available to the firm which strategically sets the prices of all of its products.

A FRAMEWORK FOR PRICING DECISIONS

The following discussion of price decisions employs a decision-making framework which identifies the following stages:

1. *Recognize the need for a pricing decision.*
2. *Price determination.*
3. *Develop a model.*
4. *Identify and anticipate pricing problems.*
5. *Develop feasible courses of action.*
6. *Forecast the outcome of each alternative.*
7. *Monitor and review the outcome of each action.*

These seven stages overlap somewhat and are not strictly sequential.

Recognize the Need for a Pricing Decision

A firm's pricing difficulties and opportunities are related to its overall objectives. Only when a firm is explicit in defining its corporate objectives can the executive specifically evaluate the obstacles and opportunities confronting him. Exhibit 1 provides a partial list of feasible pricing objectives. It is important to note that the objectives of profitability and growth constitute only a small part of this list. The pricing objectives of many different firms are listed below; however, *each firm* must evaluate and determine the priority of these objectives as they relate to the individual firm.

From this list of objectives, some of the

EXHIBIT 1
Potential pricing objectives

1. Maximum long-run profits
2. Maximum short-run profits
3. Growth
4. Stabilize market
5. Desensitize customers to price
6. Maintain price-leadership arrangement
7. Discourage entrants
8. Speed exit of marginal firms
9. Avoid government investigation and control
10. Maintain loyalty of middlemen and get their sales support
11. Avoid demands for "more" from suppliers— labor in particular
12. Enhance image of firm and its offerings
13. Be regarded as "fair" by customers (ultimate)
14. Create interest and excitement about the item
15. Be considered trustworthy and reliable by rivals
16. Help in the sale of weak items in the line
17. Discourage others from cutting prices
18. Make a product "visible"
19. "Spoil market" to obtain high price for sale of business
20. Build traffic

pricing problems that firms face can readily be inferred. Among the more important are:

1. A decline in sales.

2. Prices are too high—relative to those charged by rivals, relative to the benefits of the product. (Prices might be too high in a few regional markets and very appropriate elsewhere.)

3. Price is too low, again in certain markets and not in others.

4. The company is regarded as exploitative of customers and not to be trusted.

5. The firm places excessive financial burdens on its resellers.

6. The price deferentials among items in the line are objectionable or unintelligible.

7. Its price changes are too frequent—or do not take account of major changes in market circumstances.

8. The firm's price reflects negatively on itself and on its products.

9. The price is unstabilizing the market which had finally become stabilized after great difficulty.

10. The first is offering its customers too many price choices and confusing its customers and resellers.

11. The firm's prices seem higher to customers than they really are.

12. The firm's price policy attracts undesirable kinds of customers which have no loyalty to any seller.

13. The firm's pricing behavior makes customers unduly price sensitive and unappreciative of quality differences.

14. The company has fostered a decline in market discipline among sellers in the industry.

The list of pricing objectives in Exhibit 1 and the illustrative list of pricing difficulties above suggest that prices and price changes do not simply affect current sales, but have more far-reaching effects.

To identify the problems listed, a firm requires a monitoring system or a means of empirically determining the existence of potential problems and opportunities. Exhibit 2 presents indicators a firm might use to suggest the existence of pricing problems.

EXHIBIT 2

Data that might be used to design a price monitoring system

1. Sales—in units and in dollars
   a. Previous year comparisons
   b. Different markets/channels comparisons
2. Rivals' prices
3. Inquiries from potential customers about the line
4. Company's sales at "off list" price
   a. Measured as a % of total sales
   b. Revenue as % of sales at full price
5. Types of customers getting the most and largest price reductions
6. Market shares—in individual markets
7. Marketing costs; production cost; production costs at nearly output
8. Price complaints
   a. From customers
   b. From salesmen
9. Inventories of finished goods at different levels
10. Customers' attitudes toward firm, prices, etc.
11. Number of lost customers (brand-switching)
12. Inquiries—and subsequent purchases
13. Marketing costs

It is evident that some of these indicators are very difficult to measure with accuracy.

Price Determination

A warning system will detect pricing problems and allow the manager to decide how much attention to give to each potential price problem and to whom to assign it. In assigning a problem for study, a decision-maker must determine whether to use his own staff or call upon outside resources. Some price problems are self-correcting, in which case the price setter should ignore the warning.

Develop a Model

The primary question that must be addressed here is: What models would help businessmen to best cope with pricing responsibilities? Models developed by economic theorists rarely direct a pricing executive's attention to the key variables. Behavioral science offers far more insight into the factors that determine how price changes will be perceived and reacted to by consumers. The influence of price extends far beyond current sales figures, and behavioral science helps us more fully understand the extensive effect of price decisions.

Some mathematical models deserve a brief mention, even though they are not widely used in practice. The multiple regression model is familiar to most economists and marketing specialists. Based on historical data, this technique determines a linear functional relationship between sales and factors such as price, advertising, personal selling, relative product quality, product design, distribution arrangements, and customer services.

Another technique is the experimental approach to pricing strategy. One type of experimental approach, which may be based on regression analysis, is simulation. Such models allow the pricing specialist to combine wide varieties of inputs (including price) to achieve desired results such as short- and long-run sales together with the costs incurred. The relative merits of different factor combinations can be tested and compared.

A third type of mathematical model emphasizes the situation-specific parameters of a strategy. This approach is referred to as adaptive modeling and combines historical analysis with different environmental situations. A given input mix may have widely divergent results for each situation. This type of approach is particularly helpful in assessing the merits of market expansion, segmentation analysis, and other decisions where contextual analysis is important.

These last two models deal with some fundamental characteristics of price. First, the interdependence and synergy of related model components become key issues in their effective use. Second, the proper mix of variables will differ from occasion to occasion, even for the same product or brand. Third, the outcome of any combination of marketing actions may be perceived differently by different consumers.

To completely understand how and when price works, an executive must understand how potential customers perceive, interpret, and evaluate price changes in making their purchase decisions. These decisions vary with the individual; therefore, an executive must also consider different market segments.

Identify and Anticipate Pricing Problems

When a firm encounters a pricing problem, its manifestations are generally not subtle and obscure; however, executives still have difficulty obtaining information that identifies the source of the problem. Information about customer reactions to a product are extremely difficult to interpret because the responses must be related to their particular market segments. A seller primarily seeks the opinions of those customer segments he wishes to serve, rather than of all prospective customers. Most research data, however, do not match customer responses with the corresponding market segment to which they belong.

Price-setters require an information system to monitor the effects of their pricing arrangements and thus to help make prompt and specific adaptive action in a fast changing market environment. Salesmen's reports, current sales experience, and individual favorite customers are the primary sources of information available to most firms.

Develop Feasible Courses of Action

Traditionally, price setters have considered only a very limited number of alternatives when faced with pricing difficulties. If their price seemed high, they would lower it, and if it was too low, they would simply raise it. Much more complex behaviors are available to most pricers which provide opportunities for novel approaches. In addition to varying the price level, the executive responsible for pricing may also change the following factors: (1) the timing of the price change; (2) the number of price changes (he is not limited to a single change); (3) the time interval to which the price change applies; and (4) the number of items whose price he changes (he could raise some prices while lowering others). In addition, the executive can combine a price change with other marketing actions. For example, he might change the product's package, advertising, quality, appearance, or the after-sale customer service. Even more important, he can change price in some markets and not in others, or change them in different ways. The price-setter may even modify his discount arrangements in such a way as to increase the effectiveness of the price change.

A price-setter must not regard his actions as simply shifting prices on individual product offerings. He must recognize that his firm sells a line of products in a wide variety of geographic markets, and that its offerings embrace many benefits of varying importance to customers. Price is only one of those consumer benefits. A firm rarely makes its very best reaction to a pricing problem or opportunity by simply altering price.

Forecast the Outcome of Each Alternative Action

Once a price-setter has selected the most feasible actions available, he must forecast their consequences to determine which will best achieve his goals. At this stage, the price-setter must be as specific as possible about the expected short- and long-term consequences of his decision.

Successful management of pricing information requires an understanding of the possible consequences of price changes.

The more important of these include the effect of price changes on: the customer's ability to buy; the brand image and customers' evaluations of a product's quality; the value of inventories held by resellers; the willingness of resellers to hold inventory; the attitude of ultimate customers and resellers who recently purchased the product at a different price; the company's cash flow; and the need to borrow capital. Price changes can also disrupt or improve market discipline; foster or retard the growth and power of a trade association; instill the trust or suspicion of competitors in the integrity of one's business practices; or increase or reduce the probability of government investigation and criminal prosecution.

The effects of most business actions are extremely difficult to forecast, but an executive must attempt to forecast them. Before selecting an alternative, the executive should consciously consider all possible effects.

If the concept of price elasticity of demand has any value to price-setters, it is in forecasting the effect of price changes. Therefore, the following questions should be asked: Can price elasticity of demand be measured accurately? How much do such measurements cost? How long are such measurements valid? Does price elasticity apply to all geographic markets or only represent an average of all regions? Do elasticity measurements apply equally to all items in a firm's line of products? Is the elasticity of demand the same for all brands of the same product? The emphatic answer is that it is impossible to measure accurately the price elasticity of demand for any brand or product. However, executives responsible for pricing must continue to improve their understanding of the effects of price changes on sales.

Can a measure of demand be developed that is a better indicator than the price elasticity of demand? As implied above, past experience is an unreliable guide to present relationships. Rather than seek a quantitative measure of price elasticity, perhaps a different concept is needed. Businessmen will rarely change price alone, but ordinarily adopt a marketing program coordinated around the proposed price change. A marketing executive wishes to forecast the effects of the total marketing program, rather than the effect of price change alone.

Since most markets are highly dynamic and extremely complex, one cannot expect to develop reliable quantitative measures of the effects of different marketing programs on unit sales. How can a marketing executive forecast the results of alternative price strategies and marketing programs? He must intuitively estimate the effects of the program; however, he will rarely find precisely comparable circumstances in either his own firm's experience or in that of other firms. Specifically, the executive should consider the extent to which his price change will be perceived; the possible interpretations that customers and resellers can attribute to his price change; and the effects of customers' reactions to the price changes.

Select Among Alternative Outcomes

When a price-setter forecasts the outcomes of alternative actions, he selects that alternative which best achieves his objectives. As indicated earlier, an executive actually pursues many objectives; therefore, the selection among alternatives is quite diffi-

cult in practice, although it is simple in principle. An index should be developed to indicate the extent to which any set of outcomes achieves the executive's multiple goals—weighing each one according to its importance. Various outcomes of each feasible course of action can then be forecast by assigning probabilities to each one. The action selected should represent the alternative that best realizes product, department, and corporate goals, while reflecting an acceptable amount of risk.

SUMMARY

Pricing involves far more than arriving at a dollar and cents figure for a single product. A price-setter is responsible for managing a complex function, even though pricing involves relatively little effort for the implementation of decisions. To manage the pricing function, a firm must develop a detailed hierarchy of objectives; a monitor system; explicit mathematical models; and, most importantly, new approaches to pricing management.

The corporate pricing function within a decision-making structure is a very complex process. Many components must be integrated and managed as a unit if the firm is quickly to capitalize on its pricing opportunities.

27 Flexible Pricing

Industry's new strategy to hold market share changes the rules for economic decision making.

Scissored between soaring costs and sluggish demand at home and under intense competitive pressure from abroad, U.S. companies are overhauling ancient formulas for setting prices:

☐ To fight Japanese inroads, Ford Motor Co. and General Motors Corp., in an unprecedented move, are charging less for their 1978 subcompacts on the West Coast than elsewhere in the country.

☐ In a challenge to the industry's traditional price leaders, Armco Steel Co. last month announced plans to cut prices on four stainless steel products by an average of 5%.

☐ In an industry long sheltered by government regulation of competition, airlines have been slashing prices to hold on to market shares.

☐ In almost every consumer goods industry where producers had long believed that strong brand identification insulated their products from competition from cheaper makes, scores of famous names—Zenith, RCA, Singer, and even Sony Corp. of America—are being propelled headlong into a new world of fierce price competition.

The upshot is little short of a revolution in pricing practices that will have ramifications for capital spending, the inflation rate, industrial concentration, and the application of existing antitrust laws. Above all, though, an ability to adapt to the new pricing environment will characterize those companies that succeed in competing over the next decade.

The chief characteristics of the new price strategy are flexibility and a willingness to cut prices aggressively to hold market shares. On the way out the window are many of the pricing traditions of the U.S. industrial giants. Companies no longer try to hang on to fixed markups over cost through thick and thin. The strong no longer hold the umbrella of high prices firmly over weaker competitors. And in many industries, customary price leadership—where competitors passively follow a big company that sets the price for all—is on its way out.

The new practices differ radically from the old in aim and concept. The traditional model for pricing by large industrial corporations was codified in the management system introduced at General Motors by Alfred P. Sloan in the 1920s. Pricing was essentially static. Companies set a price that they believed would provide a desired long-run "target rate of return" at a given production volume. Although management was obviously forced to deviate from this pricing ideal by competition, the aim nevertheless was to create a pricing structure that was programmed to change gradually and predictably and to stick to it. Price changes to meet competition were regarded as the exception rather than the rule. The list price on steel mill products, for example, rose less than 4% from 1950 to 1965; aluminum by about 3%. The prices of industrial commodities and crude materials fluctuated only slightly over these years (chart, page [232]). Even though price-cutting occurred at the fringes of the market, the corporate establishment looked on it with disdain as "chiseling" and sometimes disciplined the offender, as happened in steel in 1968, when several small companies tried to undercut the industry price.

Although this may seem like a strategy better suited to industrial pachyderms than the modern managers that Sloan was supposed to have inspired, it was, in fact, well-suited to the climate produced by the rapid growth of the first 2½ decades following World War II. To set a price that will be consistent with meeting profit targets over the long run, companies must be able to count on generally high levels of capacity utilization and predictability in the future course of costs and product demand. Although there were four recessions between 1945 and the end of the 1960s, companies in general found themselves in an atmosphere in which it made sense to gear business decisions, including pricing decisions,

to long-run aims. Sloan-style pricing was an integral element in a business environment where companies confidently told securities analysts that they were aiming to iron out earnings fluctuations and were attempting to meet high and steady targets—such as Citicorp's famed 15% per year—for earnings growth.

THE NEW FLEXIBILITY

But in this decade, two recessions in five years, price controls introduced by a Republican Administration, and double-digit inflation have undermined the predictability and stability of growth as planning assumptions. And the restrictive policy reaction to inflationary forces—particularly in quadrupling of oil prices in 1974—sealed the doom of the old price strategy by producing slow growth and excess industrial capacity around the world.

The initial business response was a confused attempt to pass on cost increases in an unthinking way—an effort to retain target rates of return but in an atmosphere requiring higher and higher prices. But with unused capacity around the world, there was just too little demand and too much competition to allow target return pricing to work. Indeed, 1975 and 1976 were marked by repeated retreats from announced industrywide price boosts in steel, paper, aluminum, and chemicals.

"Target pricing just does not prove to be as viable as it once was," says Robert F. Lanzillotti, dean of the University of Florida School of Business and a member of the commission that administered Phase II of President Nixon's price control program. "Firms are becoming much more flexible in their price thinking now." Businessmen acknowledge that the days of complacent attitudes toward pricing are over. "We were fat, dumb, and happy back in the 1960s," says a top executive of a major chemical company, "but now most companies have been so badly burned that it will be a long time before they commit themselves to a long-run pricing strategy."

Instead, companies throughout the U.S. economy, from mammoth chemical companies to small computer time-sharing complexes, are turning to a pricing strategy that is flexible in every respect. It is a strategy, says Norma Pace, chief economist at the American Paper Institute, that stresses pricing "product by product instead of the whole glob." While companies have always shown some willingness to adjust prices, or profit margins, on specific products as market conditions varied, this kind of flexibility is being carried to the state of a high art.

Long-term contracts that passed on cost increases from sellers to buyers flourished in the 1950s and 1960s. But they are now breaking down in a wide range of industries, including chemicals, where they have been a way of life, in favor of short-lived and more flexible—but far less predictable—arrangements.

Companies are taking several major steps to make their price policies bob and weave like a well-trained boxer dodging the blows of his opponent. They are juggling prices among products—raising some, lowering others—to get the maximum mix of sales and profits.

MARKETING AUTOS

In the automobile industry, for example, companies are "doing a balancing act in pricing that is highly dynamic," says an economist at one of the Big Three auto manufacturers. "And this means a more sensitive effort to assess the competitive relationship of products and the costs of making them." GM still dominates auto pricing and it uses long-range profit targets as a guide. Nevertheless, the auto industry is an excellent example of how a confluence of forces—government-man-

dated product standards, foreign competition, and worries over slow growth—is generating a new pricing strategy.

For auto makers, a special impetus to be flexible comes in part from an attempt to produce and market a product mix that will maximize profits while on average meeting federal gas mileage requirements. But equally important have been the squeeze from foreign competition and a general industry expectation of slower growth in car sales in the long run. Low-cost subcompact models, especially from Japan, such as Hondas, Toyotas, and Datsuns, have been taking an increasing share of the domestic market—the total import share had grown from less than 15% in 1976 to over 20% last September. Moreover, many auto economists say the market is near saturation with one car for every two Americans.

After raising prices last year on small cars, GM this year has slashed the price of its subcompact Chevrolet Chevette to head off foreign competition. More striking, though, is that GM and Ford have begun to price by geography, with geographic differences in prices exceeding traditional transportation cost differentials. Subcompact models—such as the Ford Pinto—were reduced 10% on the West Coast, where Japanese competition is the stiffest, and 6% in the rest of the country.

To offset the lowest profit margins on lower-price, small cars, the industry is already raising the prices of large-size cars. The Cadillac Seville and Lincoln Versailles now sell for more than $14,000—four times the price of the lowest-price model. Ten years ago the top of the line was three times as costly as the lowest-price car. And some industry experts think this trend toward a wider pricing spread will intensify. "GM will be selling a $30,000 Cadillac by 1985," says Eugene F. Jennings, professor of management at Michigan State University.

Of course, such a pricing strategy is be-

Wholesale prices have become far more volatile

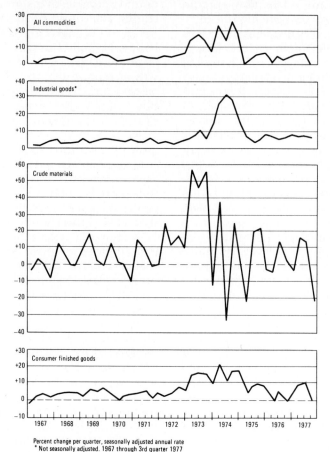

Percent change per quarter, seasonally adjusted annual rate
* Not seasonally adjusted. 1967 through 3rd quarter 1977

Data: Labor Dept.

yond the means of American Motors Corp., which does not build large-sized luxury cars. "I'm sure that GM, in its approach to small-car pricing, is awful damn glad it's got Cadillac Sevilles," says AMC Chairman Roy D. Chapin Jr.

In line with the new flexibility, manufacturers are now trying to build models in the low, medium, and high price ranges into each car size—small, intermediate, and full. By adding luxury appointments and optional equipment, companies are able to charge more, even for smaller-size cars.

Chrysler Corp.'s intermediate-size Volaré, for example, now has stripped-down and luxury models as well as several special models, such as the high-performance Volaré Road Runner.

The airline industry has plunged into fierce competition as carriers break away from federally regulated, industry-wide fares and initiate flexible pricing to maximize the use of seat space and airliners. Last summer Trans World Airlines Inc. began offering no-frills service on its Chicago to Los Angeles route, with discounts up to

43% off standard fare. Now the three other major airlines on that route—American, Continental, and United—have matched TWA's price cut. Flexible and more competitive pricing on domestic and international routes is fast becoming widespread.

THE END OF PRICE LEADERSHIP

Sharply rising energy costs, too, can impel companies to price flexibly. In the paper industry, for example, "companies now price selectively to protect profit margins," says economist Pace. The industry is the economy's second-largest industrial consumer of energy. In contrast, prior to the 1973 oil embargo, paper companies were able simply "to price across the board in reaction to overall changes in the economy," says Pace.

The new environment is forcing companies into what would have been regarded as an act of corporate sacrilege only a few years ago: they are violating the price leader-price follower pattern. "The worst thing a company can do now is price identically to its competitors," says Gerard Badler, director of service programs at the Strategy Planning Institute, a nonprofit research center in Cambridge, Mass. "It should either price above or below the competition—anything to set itself apart—but it should never price equally."

Under target return pricing, the price for the industry was set by the industry leader—usually the company with the largest market share such as a U.S. Steel Corp. or an International Business Machines Corp. Then the smaller companies fell in behind with identical prices. The system was designed to stave off price wars and "predatory" competition, which would force down prices and hurt all parties. Companies that deviated from this norm were chastised by discounting or shaving by the leaders. Price deviation was quickly disciplined. In the steel industry, for example,

price discipline was so stringent "that in 1968 Bethlehem Steel came on as the price enforcer," says Eugene J. Frank, vice president of Shearson Hayden Stone Inc. in Pittsburgh. In this case, Bethlehem announced formal price cuts. Within three months prices were raised back to the accepted industrywide level.

Now, however, smaller companies are taking bold steps to undercut the price leader. For example, while list prices of steel display a semblance of cooperation, companies are discounting prices of steel products more than ever. According to government sources, there is strong evidence that steel companies are offering substantial discounts under pressure from surging steel imports, which now account for nearly 20% of the total domestic market. "When this year's operating results are out, you're going to see that discounts of as much as 15% have been offered," says steel analyst Frank. "They are much bigger than expected." According to Frank, the large discounts have been offered in the Great Lakes market, where foreign imports have jumped by 73% this year.

Steel discounting does not always take the form of pure price reductions but often shows up in the elimination of inventory and freight charges or the knocking down of so-called "extra" charges for special cutting and treating of steel that normally are added to list prices. This kind of surreptitious price-shaving has gone on before, but now it is more intense than ever.

The only company that has publicly admitted to discounting is Armco Steel. Its big structural steel mill in Houston has taken a pounding from Gulf Coast imports, which now account for about 50% of the regional market. Last November the company announced a "foreign fighter" pricing campaign, shaving 20% off list prices and launching a splashy media effort against imported steel. Although the company suspended the discounts in the spring because the Japanese were still undercutting its prices, Armco revived the program this fall and recently announced that it would keep it running through next January. Now other steelmakers reluctantly admit that they are meeting the Armco discount. Further, Armco last month announced actual price cuts on four stainless products—an average decrease of about 5% that will put pressure on its competitors to break their price rigidity.

Domestic steel companies are hoping that the so-called "reference pricing" system now being drawn up by the Treasury Dept. will protect them from Japanese competition. The reference price sets a minimum price below which Japanese steelmakers—who account for 50% of all steel imports—cannot sell products in the U.S. market. But reference pricing will help U.S. steelmakers only if the price is set near the current list price for steel. If it is set substantially lower, domestic companies will be forced to either cut prices or continue to lose business to the Japanese competition.

Even if reference pricing succeeds in protecting domestic steel companies from foreign price competition, it still may be too late to resuscitate price discipline. It is widely held that in the past companies would announce to the press their desire to stop price discounting as a way of signaling to the other companies to restore industrywide pricing. Right now industry executives admit they are having problems with such signals because companies have become so accustomed to the competitive environment.

In the chemical industry, price leadership is breaking down under pressure from several forces. Competition from foreign chemical companies, such as West Germany's giant Bayer, is growing steadily, and global demand is flagging. The result has been "a rash of temporary allowances on prices that breaks the industry discipline," says a chemical industry analyst.

Traditional patterns of price leadership also are breaking down in the glass container industry, with smaller companies moving to the fore in pricing. Last year, for example, Owens-Illinois Inc.—which is larger than its next five competitors combined—increased its list prices by 4½%. Fearing that the increase would hurt sales to brewing companies that were just beginning to switch to glass bottles, the smaller companies broke ranks and offered huge discounts. The action not only negated O-I's increase but served notice that the smaller companies were after O-I's market share. "In effect, the smaller companies became the price leaders in order to entice the brewers," says William A. Kerr, president of Kerr Glass Mfg. Corp. in Los Angeles.

REVISING THE RULES

Indeed, it is often a desperate financial condition that drives many small companies to break the follow-the-leader rule. "The small firms are always the first to feel a dwindling cash flow," says one economist, "so it comes as no surprise that they aren't afraid to go for the jugular."

Price decisions and product decisions are obviously interconnected. In the new environment, companies more than ever either are trying to carve out a niche where they can raise prices without sacrificing sales or cut prices and try to gain a larger market share with aggressive pricing. "We now find that loss of volume has profit implications as significant as price markups on each unit," says John J. Nevin, chairman of Zenith Radio Corp. Zenith was badly burned by Japanese competition in the TV-set market because it insisted on keeping prices up to protect profit margins. "We're making a more aggressive bid to make the maximum use of price to catch up with imports," says Nevin.

The key to securing a niche is for companies to distinguish their product from others on the market. Says the financial vice president of the large data-processing company: "Because we can no longer depend on forward pricing, we try to find a proprietary enclave where our product has a unique application. This offers us a competitive alternative and helps protect our revenue stream from fluctuations." For this company, the solution lies in tailoring its data-processing services to customers' particular in-house computer requirements—such as inventory and production control. "We look harder now to find services that others just don't yet provide," says the vice president.

Selecting the proper market segment has led many companies to centralize pricing decisions in corporate headquarters, taking the authority out of the hands of division heads and sales representatives. For example, at U.S. Elevator Corp., a subsidiary of Cubic Corp., top management now allows its salesmen to bid only on jobs priced under $100,000. All other bidding is handled by a headquarters "estimating group" that has doubled its staff in the last two years.

And to avoid cutthroat competition in the sluggish construction industry, says U.S. Elevator President George C. Tweed, "we try to find something to sell where we have a unique edge. Then pricing isn't quite so traumatic." Tweed has increased his service business by 40% in the last year and is now emphasizing so-called "special projects" such as shipboard elevators and nuclear-plant elevators. "The secret is seeking out business that nobody else wants," says Tweed.

ALONG THE "LEARNING CURVE"

The best example of a successful "market niche" pricing strategy is provided by the Hewlett-Packard Co. In the highly competitive pocket calculator market, where price-cutting is rampant, H-P has been able to thrive by offering high-priced products for a select segment of the market. H-P equips its products with special features and then offers its calculators at an average price higher than the industry average. To stay in the market with this strategy, H-P must continually vary its product line and offer new models as the competition rushes in to undercut H-P's price. So far, the strategy has been successful: H-P's pretax income has grown by a staggering 400% since 1967.

While H-P follows the market niche strategy, its major competitor follows a market share strategy. Texas Instruments Inc. employs a pricing system based on high sales volume for a limited product line. It is called "design-to-cost" planning and relies on the concept of the learning or experience curve. The concept holds that production costs will decline as output rises, partly because of economies of scale, but—more important—because machines and workers "learn" with time how to produce standard products faster. TI prices along its learning curve, which means steadily lower prices at higher levels of output for a relatively unchanging product. "We perform a careful study of the market to see how it expands as the price of the product is lowered," says Charles H. Phipps, TI's head of strategic planning and corporate development.

Pricing along the learning curve to maximize market share "has been a strategy of the Japanese for years in gaining a hold on U.S. markets," says Harvard Business School professor Steven C. Wheelwright. "They have used it in everything from steel, to textiles, to electronics." Now, U.S. companies are finally using this aggressive price strategy against the Japanese in the burgeoning new market for TV-set tape recorders. RCA Corp. made the first major price move in August when it set a suggested price of $1,000. Last month Zenith cut its suggested price to $995 from $1,295. Under pressure from these price cuts, Sony recently announced it would lower the price of its Betamax model by $200, to $1,095. However, most analysts agree that Sony will have to lower its price further to stay in the market.

Basic processing industries such as steel and chemicals have been the slowest to learn the market share strategy. But these are the industries that need it the most, according to marketing expert Bruce D. Henderson of Boston Consulting Group Inc. "These companies have been too concerned with earnings and short-term cash flow," he argues. "They have to be willing to give up short-run profits to gain market share."

Contending that "once market share shifts, it rarely shifts back," Henderson says that companies in these industries must build capacity faster than their competitors. "Once capacity is in place, the competition can't enter the market at the same price," says Henderson.

The problem, he says, is that companies in the past have followed a "pricing mythology," attempting to predict costs and pass them through to the consumer no matter how high they go. He cites the case of U.S. Steel, which "kept prices high enough to allow 10 to 12 smaller companies to take a substantial share of the market." As a result, Big Steel has watched its market share dwindle from 48% in 1910 to 34% in the mid-1950s and to 23% today.

Dow Chemical Co. offers the contrasting example of a mammoth company that prices aggressively. "This company is trying to price on a flexible basis, while U.S. Steel is trying to be the industry statesman and hold prices steady in good times and bad," says Henderson. Unlike U.S. Steel, Dow will not hesitate to slash prices when and where demand is slack and raise them as high as possible when and where demand is strong, he says.

According to the Strategy Planning Institute (SPI), market share is a major determinant of profitability. SPI's computer analyses show that companies with larger market shares tend to have bigger profit margins. The reason, says SPI's Badler, is that "companies with larger market share realize economies of scale and are more clearly identified by customers."

PROFITS AND COST CONTROL

With financial support from 150 major corporations, including General Electric Co. and Control Data Corp., SPI has developed a computerized system, called profit impact of market strategy (PIMS), that pinpoints a company's market position. Then, depending on that position, SPI recommends an appropriate pricing strategy.

If excess capacity in the U.S. has contributed to the new price strategy, excess capacity abroad is making it vital to survival. Demand has been weak at home, but it has been moribund elsewhere in the industrialized West and in Japan. Growth rates in West Germany and Japan, for example, have slowed dramatically since the mid-1960s. The upshot is even more excess capacity in these countries than in the U.S. and intensification of industrial competition. Because the U.S. is the least unhealthy of these economies, foreign companies are rushing to capture ever-larger shares of its market.

Sustained periods of excess capacity have occurred before, most notably during the Depression of the 1930s. Then, in a highly protectionist atmosphere, the only real option that seemed open to industrial companies was to try to preserve what was left of profit margins by rigid adherence to target return pricing enforced by static follow-the-leader pricing patterns. While a huge deflation took place in agricultural, raw material, and service prices, industrial prices were characterized by a rigidity that was often noted and that was described in the voluminous report of the Temporary National Economic Committee.

But something new has been added to the pricing scene—if not to antitrust attitudes—since the 1930s. The growing sophistication of computer technology has provided the means for flexible pricing. Using computers, companies are now able to continuously monitor costs of inputs such as labor, raw materials, and energy across a wide range of product lines. In fact, computerized cost review has spread so fast that virtually all moderate-size companies use some kind of data-processing system for this purpose. U.S. Elevator, for example, initiated a cost-monitoring system earlier this year that follows daily and monthly cost fluctuations. The purchase price of every component or raw material is compared with its last purchase price and entered into a price book that the company president reviews daily. Every month a computer prints out how prices look in terms of 30-day periods.

And 18 months ago, International Telephone & Telegraph Corp. began a system of cost review that provides the company's controller at New York headquarters with monthly cost monitoring for each of the company's divisions. The system tracks deviations of actual from budgeted production costs.

THE IMPACT ON FEDERAL POLICY

The new pricing strategy is almost certain to change the structure of U.S. business and force changes in government policy designed to foster competition, such as antitrust policy.

A giant company following a flexible price strategy aimed at effective competition with foreign producers can no longer be counted on to hold a high-price safety net under its weaker domestic competitors. In the past, says economist Lanzillotti, the giants in such industries as automobiles and steel preferred target return prices partly because these companies feared antitrust action if price-cutting forced smaller companies out of business. Now, as flexible prices gain steam, "it will make

the positions of marginal companies like American Motors all the more precarious," he says. Indeed, AMC is already weakening under the new competitive pressure, even though the auto market in general has remained strong. The industry's smallest domestic producer recently announced the shutdown of its assembly plant in Kenosha, Wis., for one week because of declining sales. At the same time, both Ford and General Motors were working double shifts at their production plants.

What is happening in the auto industry is suggestive of what is almost bound to become a new trend toward more industrial concentration. As the U.S. industrial giants begin to price more efficiently to meet competition from the foreign industrial giants, it seems almost inevitable that the weaker, high-cost domestic producers will either fall by the wayside or be gobbled up in mergers. In effect, U.S. industry is being asked to choose between competing more effectively in a world of industrial giants, or hanging on to old price practices that allowed efficient and inefficient producers to coexist comfortably using price strategies that did not rile the antitrust enforcers.

In the case of the steel industry, economist Hendrik Houthakker, a former member of President Nixon's Council of Economic Advisers, says that the Justice Dept. may have to fundamentally change the way in which it approaches antitrust activity so that U.S. companies will be able to "achieve the economies of scale necessary to match the foreign competition."

Most companies appear to have decided to compete instead of coexist. And this could mean that the giants will soon be running into new battles with the Justice Dept. and the Federal Trade Commission, unless these agencies change their posture in a way that recognizes what life is really like in an internationally competitive world.

The new price strategy also appears to

have some implications for policies designed to stabilize the economy. It is true that "profits inflation"—inflation caused by business attempts to push up profit margins in periods of declining demand—is less likely under flexible than under target rate of return pricing. But flexible pricing also means that any surge in demand is likely to lead to quicker and bigger price boosts than it has in the past, while lower demand will result in quicker price cuts. This strongly suggests that a flexible price economy is likely to be a relatively unstable economy.

But it is also likely to be a more vigorous economy. Companies that use flexible pricing to build market shares are apt to be more willing to undertake new capital spending projects, despite the presence of excess capacity, than are companies that are wedded to achieving hard and fast target rates of return. "Pricing feeds back into investment decisions in a powerful way,"

says Henderson of the Boston Consulting Group. "And the company with foresight to expand will gain the benefits of added market share."

The move to a flexible pricing may eventually shake business investment out of the catatonic state it has been in for the past 2½ years.

The new competitiveness also makes business far riskier. Profits will be much more dependent on nimble decision making than in the past. Companies in the same industry are much more likely to show diverse profit performance than any time during the past 25 years. It has been fashionable for commentators and economists to argue that U.S. executives have become averse to taking risks. This may still be a correct assessment of their psychology. But the new competitive atmosphere is likely to force companies that wish to be successful to take more risks, like it or not.

28

A Frame of Reference
for Improving Productivity
in Distribution

Bert C. McCammon, Jr.
William L. Hammer

New strategies will have to be developed in response to consumerism, safety codes, and the changes which the next decade will bring. This paper discusses the outlook, acknowledging the need to accommodate social demands with an adequate rate of return on shareholders' equity.

INTRODUCTION

The service sector of the American economy is undergoing rapid expansion. Over the decade ahead, service industries will provide 86 percent of all new jobs created. Furthermore, by 1985, service workers will outnumber manufacturing employees by more than three to one.[1]

Unfortunately, many service industries, including retailing and wholesaling, tend to be labor-intensive. These industries have traditionally experienced severe productivity problems and have therefore been a major source of inflation. Between 1958 and 1972, for example, labor-intensive service industries accounted for 71 percent of total U.S. inflation while producing only 50 percent of the nation's output [1]. Clearly, this historical pattern must be reversed if inflationary pressures are to be contained during the decade ahead.

Improving productivity is much more

[1]For a careful analysis of these trends, see [2].

than inflation-fighting exercise, however. As Robert C. Scrivener points out, higher rates of productivity are required both to improve the quality of life and to compete more effectively in world markets [6]. In short, productivity is the cornerstone of continued economic and social development.

The balance of this report examines productivity developments in retail and wholesale trade. Many of the approaches and concepts discussed, however, can be applied in other service industries; thus, the analysis that follows should be of use to nondistribution executives.

THE PRODUCTIVITY CHALLENGE IN DISTRIBUTION

Labor Productivity Trends

In recent years, output per manhour in distribution has risen much less rapidly than

Reprinted with permission from Ronald C. Curhan, ed., *1974 Combined Proceedings*, published by the American Marketing Association, pp. 455–60.

EXHIBIT 1

ECONOMIC SECTOR	AVERAGE ANNUAL INCREASE IN REAL OUTPUT PER MANHOUR (1968–1972)
Agriculture	4.5%
Mining	3.9
Manufacturing	2.3
Wholesaling	1.7
Retailing	.8
Total economy	1.9%

SOURCE: U.S. Department of Labor, U.S. Department of Commerce, and authors' calculations.

in other sectors of the economy. Retailers, for example, increased their output per manhour at a rate of only .8 percent per year between 1968 and 1972, and wholesalers did only slightly better [Exhibit 1].

As a result of lagging productivity (and rising wages), retailing and wholesaling companies experienced sharp increases in their unit labor costs between 1968 and 1972. Consider the following labor cost comparisons between retailing, wholesaling, and manufacturing enterprises [Exhibit 2].

This pattern of rising unit labor costs had significant impact on profit margins. IRS data indicate that retail profit margins declined from 1.4 percent of sales in 1968 to 1.0 percent of sales in 1972. Wholesale profit margins fell from 1.2 to 1.0 percent of sales during the same periods [3]. In summary, low rates of productivity, accompanied by upward wage pressures, exerted a major influence on retail and wholesale profits over the past five years.

EXHIBIT 2

ECONOMIC SECTOR	AVERAGE ANNUAL INCREASE IN UNIT LABOR COSTS (1968–1972)
Manufacturing	3.0%
Wholesaling	5.1
Retailing	6.2

SOURCE: U.S. Department of Labor, U.S. Department of Commerce, and authors' calculations.

EXHIBIT 3

ECONOMIC SECTOR	AVERAGE HOURLY WAGE RATE FOR OPERATING EMPLOYEES		
	1968	1972	AVERAGE ANNUAL INCREASE
Manufacturing	$3.01	$3.81	6.1%
Retailing	2.16	2.70	5.7
Wage gap	$ .85	$1.11	6.9%

SOURCE: U.S. Department of Labor.

The Wage Gap Cycle

Lagging productivity can result in a vicious, regenerative cycle. Lagging productivity, at some point in time, inevitably results in lagging wages. Lagging wages, in turn, eventually result in the recruitment of marginal personnel, which further depresses productivity. The ultimate consequence of this iterative process is a stagnant and depressed industry.

Recent trends suggest that retailers are already confronted by a wage gap problem. Consider the following comparison between manufacturing and retailing wage rates [Exhibit 3]. If the gap between manufacturing and retailing wages continues to widen, retailers will find it increasingly difficult to attract and retain productive personnel.

Capital Productivity Trends

Retailers and wholesalers have also experienced difficulty in improving their capital productivity ratios over the past five years. This trend is documented in Exhibit 4.

EXHIBIT 4

ECONOMIC SECTOR	NET SALES TO TOTAL ASSETS (TIMES)	
	1968	1972
Wholesaling	2.9	2.8
Retailing	2.6	2.6

SOURCE: Internal Revenue Service and authors' calculations.

EXHIBIT 5

		$\left(\dfrac{\text{NET PROFITS}}{\text{NET SALES}}\right)$	×	$\left(\dfrac{\text{NET SALES}}{\text{TOTAL ASSETS}}\right)$	×	$\left(\dfrac{\text{TOTAL ASSETS}}{\text{NET WORTH}}\right)$	=	$\left(\dfrac{\text{NET PROFITS}}{\text{NET WORTH}}\right)$
Wholesaling	1968	1.2%	×	2.9X	×	2.4X	=	8.6%
corporations	1972	1.0%	×	2.8X	×	2.6X	=	7.3%
Retailing	1968	1.4%	×	2.6X	×	2.3X	=	8.8%
corporations	1972	1.0%	×	2.6X	×	2.5X	=	6.5%

The stagnant rates of asset turnover that prevail in the field of distribution acquire additional significance when viewed in the context of the strategic profit model. Such a model involves multiplying a company's profit margin by its rate of asset turnover and its leverage ratio to obtain its rate of return on net worth. Thus, the model combines the principal elements of a company's operating statement and balance sheet into a single profit planning equation.

As indicated, retailers and wholesalers achieved inadequate rates of return on net worth between 1968 and 1972. Since both types of organizations are already highly leveraged, improved results are most likely to be achieved by companies that simultaneously increase both their profit margins *and* their rates of asset turnover.

Managerial Implications

The performance mandate is clear. Retailers and wholesalers must significantly improve their labor and capital productivity ratios in the 1970s. In many cases, labor productivity increases of 6 to 8 percent a year will be required to offset rising wages and to improve profit margins.

Capital productivity ratios must be increased at a comparable rate, primarily through better management of inventories and through more intensive use of both equipment and physical facilities. In short, there must be a concerted attack on the productivity problem in distribution.

A FRAME OF REFERENCE FOR IMPROVING PRODUCTIVITY IN DISTRIBUTION

The total performance model is a new frame of reference for improving productivity in distribution. As specified in the model, management is the process by which strategic, administrative, and operating decisions are coordinated to achieve target re-

EXHIBIT 6
The total performance model

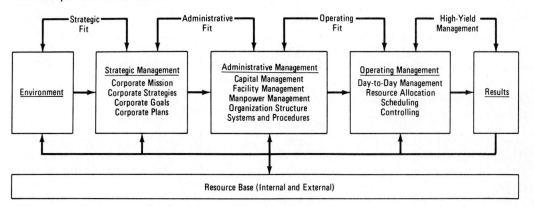

sults on a programmed and predictable basis. [See Exhibit 6.]

Executives and management scientists have traditionally focused on improving administrative and operating efficiency with significant results. Consider, for example, the following vignettes in the field of distribution.

☐ John Wanamaker, a leading department store in Philadelphia, used short interval scheduling techniques to increase the productivity of sales personnel by 19.8 percent over a two-year period [4].

☐ A. T. Kearney developed a truck scheduling model that produced delivery savings of 32 percent in the linen supply field [7].

☐ Early adopters of COSMOS report that their direct product profits increased by 15 percent after this sophisticated inventory management and space allocation system was installed. They also reduced their out-of-stock ratios by 25 percent during the same period [5].

☐ A computer simulation model in the department store field increased a staple department's gross margin return on inventory investment (GMROI) by 11.8 percent [8].

Clearly, continued emphasis should be placed on management science programs in the field of distribution. In a growing number of cases, however, *strategic* breakthroughs will be required to achieve adequate results.

MAINSTREAM STRATEGIES FOR IMPROVING PRODUCTIVITY IN DISTRIBUTION

Retailers and wholesalers are currently employing *five* major strategies to improve productivity and profitability in distribution. The results achieved by U.S., Canadian, and European companies employing these strategies are shown in the Appendix.

The strategies themselves may be described as follows.

Warehouse Retailing

Warehouse retailers have combined the economics of wholesaling and retailing to create a new low-cost form of distribution. Specifically, warehouse retailers achieve operating economies by occupying low-cost facilities, by utilizing vertical space intensively, and by employing modern materials handling and data processing techniques. In addition, they "escape" certain costs by shifting selected functions backward to suppliers or forward to consumers. As a result, warehouse retailers are able to underprice conventional merchants by 10 to 30 percent, which enables them to achieve unusually high sales per employee and per square foot of selling area.

The principal types of warehouse outlets currently in operation are furniture warehouse showrooms (Levitz, Leon's, Pascal, and Wickes); appliance and TV warehouse showrooms (Kennedy and Cohen, Luskin's, and Silo); catalog showrooms (Best Products, Consumers Distributing, and Service Merchandise); and hypermarches (Carrefour, Oshawa, and Wertkauf). Apparel, food, and sporting goods warehouses have also begun to appear in numerous metropolitan markets.

As indicated in the Appendix, warehouse retailers expanded rapidly between 1969 and 1973. They also achieved unusually high rates of return on investment. As a result, many analysts contend that warehouse retailing will be to the 1970s what discount department stores were to the 1960s.

Supermarket Retailing

The supermarket concept is being used extensively to improve productivity in distribution. Toys 'R' Us and Oshman's currently operate toy supermarkets; Beaver Lumber, Builder's Emporium, and Handy Dan are vigorous proponents of the self-service, home improvement center concept; and both Long's and Skagg's operate massive superdrugstores. Like their warehouse retailing counterparts, these merchants have achieved significant productivity breakthroughs.

Direct Marketing

Analysts agree that direct marketing could be the next revolution in retailing. Certainly, there are a sufficient number of prototypes to suggest that this could be the wave of the future. Beeline and Tupperware have been conspicuously successful in the party plan field; Avon and Shaklee are formidable direct selling organizations, and Fingerhut and New Process have achieved rapid rates of growth through catalog selling. Among the new arrivals on the direct marketing scene are Call-a-Mart, K-Tel, and Unity Buying Service.

Though the data are fragmentary, it is apparent that many forms of direct marketing are expanding two or three times more rapidly than total retail sales. This trend will undoubtedly accelerate in the 1980s when CATV retailing becomes a competitive reality.

Vertical Marketing Systems

Retailers affiliated with cooperative groups, voluntary groups, and franchise networks currently account for over 40 percent of total retail sales. Corporate chains represent another 32 percent of total retail sales. . . . If present trends continue, contractual groups and corporate chains could account for 85 percent of total retail sales by 1980.

More important, these vertical networks are becoming increasingly rationalized as productivity and profitability pressures intensify. Thus, they are still a viable strategy for improving results in the field of distribution.

Corporate Diversification

Finally, a growing number of companies have diversified in recent years to improve their overall results. A recent analysis of Value Line data indicates that diversified retailers performed much better than their conventional counterparts between 1968 and 1973. Jewell, Lucky, Malone & Hyde, Melville, and Zale are among the leading proponents of diversified distribution. All have achieved superior performance in the marketplace.

CONCLUSIONS

Retailers and wholesalers are currently confronted by *major* productivity and profitability problems. Over the decade ahead, they must improve their performance in both of these areas to fully satisfy stockholder expectations.

In addition, distribution organizations will be increasingly confronted by rising social pressures. Consumerism will become a more important force; product and environmental safety codes will proliferate; and zoning ordinances will become more restrictive. In this complex milieu, corporate acceptance of the new technology of management will become a prerequisite to survival. But, more important, new *strategies* must be devised to simultaneously respond to new social demands while maintaining an adequate rate of return on shareholders' equity.

REFERENCES

1. "Expanding Service Economy," *Quarterly Review of Economic Prospects,* 72-4 Part 2 (February 1973), p. 12-3.

2. Fuchs, Victor R. *The Service Economy.* New York: National Bureau of Economic Research, Inc., 1968.

3. Internal Revenue Service. *Corporation Income Tax Returns*, 1968 and 1969 editions, and authors' calculations.

4. Lubinski, Stephen R. "A Program for Improving Productivity," *Retail Control*, 42 (September 1973), pp. 10-21.

5. "Manufacturers Ponder COSMOS Data," *Grocery Manufacturer* (September 1971), pp. 1-4.

6. Schrivener, Robert C. "Productivity in a Modern Economy," *The Canadian Business Review* (Winter 1974), pp. 18-20.

7. "Successful Savings with CARD," *Linen Supply News* (September 1973), pp. 60-70.

8. Sweeney, Daniel J. "Improving the Profitability of Retail Merchandising Decisions," *Journal of Marketing*, 37 (January 1973), pp. 60-68.

APPENDIX

Mainstream strategies for improving productivity in distribution

STRATEGIC THRUST	COMPANY	CORPORATE PROFILE	STRATEGIC PROFIT MODEL RATIOS (1973)				COMPOUND ANNUAL GROWTH RATES (1969–1973)		
			NET PROFITS TO NET SALES	NET SALES TO TOTAL ASSETS	TOTAL ASSETS TO NET WORTH	NET PROFITS TO NET WORTH	NET SALES	NET PROFITS	EARNINGS PER SHARE
Warehouse retailing	Carrefour	Carrefour is the leading hypermarche chain in Western Europe. In fiscal 1973, the company operated on a gross margin of 16.4 percent, which enabled it to underprice conventional retailers by *at least* 10.0 percent. As a result of its underpricing strategy, Carrefour generates unusually high sales per employee and per square foot of selling area. In 1973, Carrefour announced that it plans to enter the North American market on a joint venture basis.	3.0	5.0	2.0	30.0	53.6	54.2	52.6
	Levitz	Levitz pioneered the furniture warehouse showroom concept in North America. Available data suggest that the company underprices conventional furniture stores by 13.3 percent. In 1974, Levitz added carpets, consumer electronics, and major appliances to its merchandise mix by signing leased department agreements with Allen Carpet and Kennedy and Cohen respectively.	3.7	2.5	1.9	17.8	69.6	64.4	53.4
	Consumers Distributing	Consumers Distributing is the major catalog showroom chain in Canada. In 1973, the company signed a joint venture agreement with May Department Stores to enter the U.S. market.	5.7	2.0	2.2	25.9	42.4	42.1	38.9

APPENDIX (cont.)

STRATEGIC THRUST	COMPANY	CORPORATE PROFILE	STRATEGIC PROFIT MODEL RATIOS (1973)				COMPOUND ANNUAL GROWTH RATES (1969–1973)		
			NET PROFITS TO NET SALES	NET SALES TO TOTAL ASSETS	NET ASSETS TO NET WORTH	NET PROFITS TO NET WORTH	NET SALES	NET PROFITS	EARNINGS PER SHARE
Supermarket retailing	Handy Dan	Handy Dan operates 52 home improvement centers in six states. A typical center generates $1.8 million in annual sales, contains over 40,000 square feet of space, and carries an inventory of 30,000 items.	2.9	2.8	2.3	18.4	35.9	40.7	23.6
	Standard Brands Paint	Standard Brands operates paint and decorating supermarkets in California and other Western states. At the present time, the company obtains 41 percent of its merchandise requirements from captive manufacturing facilities.	7.6	1.8	1.3	17.2	19.5	20.9	19.7
	Child World	Child World is a leading operator of toy supermarkets. A typical Child World unit contains 25,000 square feet of space and carries over 20,000 items in inventory.	3.4	2.9	1.5	14.8	35.4	37.6	15.7
Direct marketing	Unity Buying Service	Unity Buying Service operates a unique direct mail program. Through the company's Factory Buying Club, consumers purchase merchandise from a 10,000 item catalog. The consumer's purchase price is factory cost plus a 6 percent service fee, taxes where applicable, and shipping costs. As of September 1973, the Club's active membership consisted of 781,000 consumers.	4.5	3.1	2.0	27.5	26.1	42.3	40.9

	K-Tel	K-Tel is one of the leading direct response marketing organizations in North America. The company markets records and other specialty products through saturation TV campaigns. The products are distributed through 20,000 retail outlets on a consignment basis.	7.6	2.1	2.1	33.5	66.8	47.6	48.2
Vertical marketing systems	Koffler Stores	Koffler is the largest franchiser of drugstores in North America. In 1972, the company signed a joint venture agreement with Steinberg's to open franchise stores in Quebec.	2.1	3.2	2.2	14.3	41.0	32.2	20.3
	Canadian Tire	Canadian Tire is a large voluntary group wholesaler that supplies affiliated stores with a variety of lines, including automotive parts and accessories, hardware, housewares, small appliances, and sporting goods. A typical Canadian Tire outlet contains approximately 25,000 square feet of space and carries over 20,000 items in inventory.	5.2	1.9	1.6	16.2	19.5	27.4	25.1
Corporate diversification	Malone & Hyde	Malone & Hyde is a large voluntary group wholesaler in the food field. The company has pursued a vigorous diversification policy in recent years and currently obtains 34 percent of its earnings from company-owned stores and related ventures.	1.3	6.5	1.9	16.3	13.1	13.9	13.0
	Lucky Stores	Lucky Stores is the 8th largest food chain in the United States. The company also operates 115 discount department stores, 39 membership department stores, 39 home and auto stores, 29 drugstores, and 4 sporting goods stores.	1.5	4.2	3.0	19.7	17.9	20.6	14.8

29 The Role of the Industrial Distributor in Marketing Strategy

Frederick E. Webster, Jr.

*The industrial distributor and his role in the
manufacturer's marketing strategy are changing—slowly.*

The industrial distributor is an important institution in the American marketing system, yet he has received little attention from researchers. Trade association surveys have generally yielded small responses and have often been designed primarily to promote the image of the industrial distributor. Changing census definitions of this position and conflicting definitions used by different trade associations have made it virtually impossible to analyze trends in industry sales volume, degrees of specialization, firm size, and the like.

Yet manufacturers who sell to other manufacturers, and the industrial distributor himself, have a vital interest in the pressures and trends affecting this marketing channel. This is especially true in the current environment of materials shortages, depressed industrial production, tight money, and rising costs, since the industrial distributor may offer the manufacturer major opportunities for improved marketing effectiveness and physical distribution efficiency.

In an attempt to get an in-depth look at the industrial distributor, a field study of distributors and manufacturers was conducted in the summer of 1975. This article discusses that study in light of what is currently known about industrial distributors. Special attention is given to the results of the survey, which produced several insights into both the role of the industrial distributor in manufacturers' marketing strategies and how the distributor and his relationship to his suppliers are changing. Some highlights of the findings are:

1. For manufacturers who have been using industrial distributors, there has been a trend toward increased reliance on the distributor for a larger portion of total sales and a broader variety of marketing functions.

2. The average size of the distributor appears to be increasing, and there is a trend toward greater product specialization in distributor operations.

3. Basically, however, the typical industrial distributor remains a small, independent busi-

Reprinted with permission from *Journal of Marketing*, published by the American Marketing Association, 40 (July 1976), pp. 10–16.

ness, owner-managed, with limited management competence and little or no long-range planning.

4. In some product areas where specialized distributors have become strong, the industrial distributor has gained more control of the marketing channel.

5. There is no single marketing strategy characteristic of those firms that rely heavily on industrial distributors. Some stress market coverage and product availability; others stress high product quality and technical service; there are both high-price and low-price strategies; and so on. However, the nature of the distributor organization and the relationship between distributor and supplier will reflect the manufacturer's marketing strategy.

6. As firms have increased their reliance on industrial distributors, they have also tended to increase the amount of support given the distributor in the form of sales training (both product knowledge and salesmanship training), technical support, advertising and sales promotion assistance, and, in several cases, increased margins.

7. Industrial distributors are generally of little or no use to their suppliers as sources of market information.

8. Among the most common issues in the distributor-supplier relationship are how to handle large accounts, required inventory stocking levels for the distributor, the quality of distributor management, overlapping distributor territories, size of distributor margins, and the philosophical question of whether the distributor's primary obligations and loyalty are to the customer or to the supplier.

THE INDUSTRIAL DISTRIBUTOR

The industrial distributor is a specific type of agent middleman who sells primarily to manufacturers. He stocks the products that he sells, has at least one outside salesperson as well as an inside telephone and/or counter salesperson, and performs a broad variety of marketing channel functions, including customer contact, credit, stocking, delivery, and providing a full product assortment. The products stocked include: *maintenance, repair, and operating* supplies (MRO items); *original equipment* (OEM) supplies, such as fasteners, power transmission components, fluid power equipment, and small rubber parts, which become part of the manufacturer's finished product; *equipment* used in the operation of the business, such as hand tools, power tools, and conveyers; and *machinery* used to make raw materials and semifinished goods into finished products.

There are three types of industrial distributors. *General-line distributors,* or "mill supply houses," stock a broad range of products and are often referred to as "the supermarkets of industry." *Specialist firms* carry a narrow line of related products such as bearings, power transmission equipment and supplies, or abrasives and cutting tools. The *combination house* is engaged in other forms of wholesaling in addition to industrial distribution; an example is the electrical distributor who sells to the construction industry and manufacturers as well as to retailers and institutions. The distinction between the first two types of industrial distributor has been blurred in recent years by a growing trend for general-line houses to develop specialist departments. Less common but also found is the situation where a specialist firm broadens its product offerings in order to provide more complete service to customers; for example, bearing specialists may move into the broader field of power transmission.

Although available data are, as noted, somewhat limited, the total volume of sales through industrial distributors was estimated at \$23.5 billion for 1974.[1] A reasonable estimate of the total number of industrial distributors would be between 11,000 and 12,000, for an average firm with sales volume of around \$2,000,000. General-line distributors are, on the average, slightly larger than specialists in terms of sales volume. General-line distributors also maintain somewhat larger inventories than specialists, roughly \$500,000 as compared with

[1]*Industrial Distribution* (March 1975), pp. 31-38.

$375,000. The total volume of sales through industrial distributors has been growing slightly faster than GNP for several years, and the total number of distributors has been decreasing slightly, so average distributor size has been increasing.

There has been a trend toward branching and chaining in recent years, but the typical firm is still independently owned, owner-managed, and operates from a single location. Although average annual sales volume per firm is increasing, the typical firm continues to serve a rather small geographic area, from a 25-mile radius or even less in areas of industrial concentration to 100 or 150 miles in sparsely populated areas. The size of the average order would be in the neighborhood of $120.

Each data source has a somewhat different method for categorizing the types of products handled by industrial distributors. A 1970 publication listed fifteen major product categories for industrial distributors; these ranged in size from 5,505 distributors of mechanics and power tools (and accessories) to 2,184 distributors of ferrous and nonferrous metals.[2] More recently, the American Supply & Machinery Manufacturers' Association (ASMMA) used the following twelve-category product classification in its survey of members' 1973 sales:

1. Abrasives
2. Cutting tools
3. Saws and files
4. Hand tools
5. Power tools and accessories
6. Threaded products
7. Wire rope, chain, and fittings
8. Fluid power systems and accessories
9. Power transmission equipment and supplies
10. Industrial rubber goods
11. Material handling equipment
12. All other

[2]*Facts about Industrial Distribution*, a pamphlet copyrighted 1970 by *Industrial Distribution* magazine.

Since this classification was the latest available at the time the fieldwork for this study was planned, it was used as the basis for the sample selection. The ASMMA survey of 1974 sales, released in mid-1975, had a new Class 1, "chemicals including aerosols and lubricants; paints; tape; brushes," and abrasives had been absorbed into the "all other" category.

RESEARCH DESIGN

After extensive library research involving both academic marketing studies on the industrial distributor[3] and the trade literature, a field study was designed. This study was guided by four objectives:

1. To understand the role of the industrial distributor in manufacturers' marketing strategies and how this role is changing
2. To identify the major forces shaping the evolution of industrial distribution
3. To define the key issues in management of the distributor-supplier relationship, as seen by both parties
4. To define opportunities for enhancing the effectiveness of the distributor in marketing strategy and for improving the distributor-supplier relationship.

The initial stage of fieldwork involved a series of unstructured interviews with a convenience sample of eight industrial distributors in Vermont, New Hampshire, Rhode Island, Massachusetts, and Connecticut. The purpose of these interviews was to develop an understanding of the nature of distributor operations, to learn first-hand how the distributor views his

[3]Two of the most important studies are: Robert D. Buzzell, *Value Added by Industrial Distributors and Their Productivity*, Bureau of Business Research Monograph 96 (Columbus: Ohio State University, 1959); and William M. Diamond, *Distribution Channels for Industrial Goods*, Bureau of Business Research Monograph 114 (Columbus: Ohio State University, 1963).

relationship with his suppliers, and to further analyze the trends and pressures shaping industrial distribution as an industry.

When the distributor interviews were completed and analyzed, an interview guide was developed to direct field interviews with manufacturers. Constrained by the costs of travel and respondent availability, we selected a sample of 31 manufacturers to assure representativeness by product category, geographic location, and firm size and market position. These manufacturer respondents included the leading firms in each of the product categories and among them account for a major portion of the sales of most industrial distributors. Respondents were given the usual guarantee of anonymity, but it can be stated that the firms interviewed included those whose distributor policies are generally regarded as exerting major influence on the trade.

Interviews were conducted with one or more executives (titles included vice president of marketing and sales, product manager, sales manager, and the like) responsible for distribution in companies in all the ASMMA product categories. Generally, three or four companies from each category participated, and an attempt was made to interview both firms who were market leaders and firms who were not dominant in the markets under investigation. Respondents' sales volumes in the product categories considered varied from $3 million to $420 million, market shares varied from 2% to 75%, and the volume of sales through distributors varied between 15% and 100%. Manufacturer interviews were conducted in four states: Massachusetts, Connecticut, New York, and Ohio. The sample is believed to be both broad and representative of firms selling through industrial distributors.

When manufacturer interviews had been completed, two specialist distributors, in bearings and fasteners, were interviewed to deepen our awareness of the specialist firm. So the total sample was ten distributors and 31 manufacturers in eight states, representing all ASMMA product categories.

THE DISTRIBUTOR'S ROLE IN MARKETING STRATEGY

The study found no single marketing strategy that characterized those manufacturing firms that depend heavily on the industrial distributor. Furthermore, the distributor's role varied as a function of several interrelated factors, including:

1. The manufacturer's marketing strategy and especially the basis on which he attempts to achieve a unique competitive advantage: quality, price, availability, applications, engineering and technical service, full line, technical product leadership, and the like

2. The strength of the manufacturer's market position, that is, whether he is a market leader or a minor brand

3. The technical characteristics of the product, especially the presence of strongly differentiating product features among brands and the need to make technical judgments about the best response to customer requirements

4. The importance of immediate product availability to the customer or, conversely, the extent to which requirements can be forecasted and planned for

All of the products involved, however, are established products with broad and large demand. Industrial distributors generally lack the ability to aggressively develop markets for new products or to serve narrow market segments with specialized product needs. Even the specialist distributor in such product areas as bearings, power transmission equipment, or fasteners serves customers from a broad range of manufacturing industries.

It was also apparent that all companies using industrial distributors must maintain their own field sales forces as well. Typically, the salesperson's major function is to solicit orders from the distributor organization and to service and support it. This may involve frequent customer calls with distributors' salespeople, especially for technical service. In other cases, the manufacturer's salespeople are responsible for customer contact and order generation, with the distributor performing primarily a physical distribution function. Not uncommonly, the manufacturer's salespeople are responsible both for working with the distributor on most accounts and for giving direct service to large accounts.

Several major functions tended, in varying degrees depending on the market circumstances of the manufacturer, to characterize the role of the industrial distributor in the manufacturer's marketing strategy. These included: market coverage and product availability, market development and account solicitation, technical advice and service, and market information.

Market Coverage and Product Availability

The industrial distributor's key responsibility in all cases is to contact present and potential customers and to make the product available—with the necessary supporting services such as delivery, credit, technical advice—as quickly as economically feasible. In some product areas, such as abrasives, market coverage and availability require that the manufacturer use as many as 1,000 general-line distributors. In other areas, such as fluid power equipment, 25 to 30 distributors may be adequate. The number of distributors required to cover the market and insure availability was seen to depend on several variables, most notably:

1. Total market potential and its geographic concentration

2. The manufacturer's current market share and the intensity of competition

3. Frequency of purchase and whether the product is an MRO item or an OEM item

4. Whether lack of availability could interrupt the customer's production process

5. Amount of technical knowledge required to sell or service the product

6. Extent of product differentiation, determining how important immediate availability is as a competitive variable

Market Development and Account Solicitation

Although in most cases the distributor was responsible primarily for servicing existing demand, in some he also had major responsibility for soliciting new accounts and expanding the size of the market. For example, a manufacturer of saw blades depended on his distributors to solicit new business from potential customers whom the manufacturer had identified, after thorough and expensive market studies, in the distributor's assigned territory. Similarly, a manufacturer of pop rivets expected his distributors to aggressively solicit customers away from sheet metal screw manufacturers.

When the distributor takes on major responsibility for promoting the product line, it is likely to be a line that provides a large share of his total volume. In such circumstances, this responsibility often extends to sales promotion (especially direct mail) and advertising, in addition to field sales coverage.

Technical Advice and Service

Technical expertise is important for many products handled by industrial distributors. Even for product categories where the technology is rather stable, such as grinding wheels, the technical nature of the item is usually such that many customers need advice in determining optimum product specifications for a given application. Thus, the distributor's salespeople must have adequate product knowledge to render necessary assistance. In the case of grinding wheels, for example, minor differences in wheel composition can produce major cost differences in the grinding operation.

Market Information

The large majority of manufacturers interviewed reported that their distributors were of virtually no help as a source of market information. Notable exceptions were cases where a technical product was distributed mainly through specialists and where the manufacturer's line was over 50% of the distributor's volume. In such cases, the distributor's market scope is narrow enough to encourage development of some expertise and there is real incentive to be a true partner with the manufacturer in market development.

While the desire to protect competitively valuable information might have been a consideration for some distributors, in most cases the distributor did not have current or complete market data. Even where the distributor used electronic data processing (estimated to apply to less than one-third of all cases), the market analysis and planning function was virtually nonexistent.

ISSUES IN THE RELATIONSHIP

Direct Accounts

A perennial source of tension in the supplier-distributor relationship is the direct account issue. This issue usually arises when a major customer, often with multiple buying locations, threatens to do business with another manufacturer unless he receives a lower price than the manufacturer can provide through a distributor. In other cases, the customer may demand direct coverage to obtain better technical advice or because he wants the presumed recognition and higher service level of dealing direct.

Since such powerful accounts are often a major portion of the distributor's volume, the solution is usually a difficult one. Complicated commission or fee arrangements for the distributor's service on direct accounts may be negotiated, or the supplier may arbitrarily withdraw the account from the distributor. Only a minority of manufacturers have been able to steadfastly refuse to deal direct with major, national accounts.

Distributor Management

The owner-manager is not often a well-trained, professional manager. As a successful small businessman he may reach a point where he has little interest in opening new territories, soliciting new accounts, or developing new product lines. The distributor's lack of growth motivation was mentioned frequently as a source of frustration to the manufacturer who wished to improve his competitive position.

A related issue is the problem of management succession. The distributor owner-manager often is a one-man management show, and his retirement or death can seriously reduce the effectiveness of the distributorship. Suppliers attempt to deal with this issue by working with the distributor to assure smooth transitions and by having contract provisions for terminating the relationship if there is a change in ownership.

In general, the quality of distributor management is a pervasive issue. Lack of planning, inadequate financing, poor managerial and administrative control systems, cash flow problems, and haphazard inventory policies remain as common symptoms of inefficient management. Distributors often have inadequate information to determine product line profitability, order-processing costs, or optimum stocking levels.

Inventory Levels

It usually takes considerable persuasion to get distributors to increase inventory levels, a move that the manufacturer often sees as essential to effective customer service. One solution is to give increased profit margins; it is common for manufacturers to attempt to be among the most profitable lines stocked by their distributors. Reflecting the distributor's characteristically strained financial condition, the manufacturer may find it necessary to finance distributor inventory expansion by delayed billing, consignment sale, or even a cash loan. Often, the manufacturer's salesperson can demonstrate how larger inventories can improve the distributor's profitability.

Second Lines

Manufacturers cannot legally prohibit their distributors from carrying competing product lines. And most distributors want a second line in order to have a broader price range or to get a wider variety of product types. Quantity discounts for distributor purchases are one incentive used to encourage the distributor to concentrate his purchases in a single line. Some manufacturers compete for available distributors by positioning themselves as a second-line supplier, although this may lead to a "catch as catch can" distributor organization and leaves the distributor in control of the relationship.

The presence of second lines is especially annoying to those firms that make major investments in their distributors, as with training programs, market development expenses, and the like. Such commitments are made in an attempt to become the distributor's single most important and profitable line; second lines frustrate the achievement of those objectives.

Adding Distributors and Overlapping Territories

As markets and distributors change, existing distributor coverage patterns may prove inadequate. When it is determined that the existing distributor is incapable of covering

his assigned territory, he may be replaced or a new distributor may be added. Since distributors seldom have uniform geographical limits to what they regard as *their* territories, overlapping territories may result. This may, in fact, be the conscious intention of the supplier if he determines that different distributors have strengths in different market segments.

Obviously, such arrangements can lead to considerable controversy, and most distributors will seek to avoid them. The manufacturer who persists in this practice clearly runs the risk of losing the older distributor, but it is a risk he often intentionally takes.

HOW THE RELATIONSHIP IS CHANGING

No dramatic shifts appear to be occurring in the nature of industrial distribution, but a number of trends are quite evident. Perhaps the most important trend is the development of specialist distributors in such product areas as bearings and fasteners. Related to this is the development of *chains* of distributors with common name and ownership doing business in multiple locations. In these cases, the presence of strong distributor organizations, combined with relatively undifferentiated products and greater technical expertise (as a result of product specialization), has led to increased market power and channel control for the distributor.

Some distributors are strengthening their relationships with end-user customers by offering systems purchasing contracts, subassembly and submanufacturing, and a variety of inventory- and purchasing-related services. These services can produce significant cost savings for the customer, while they improve the distributor's attractiveness to both the manufacturer and the end-user.

A number of forces are combining to improve the quality of distributor management. Distributors are becoming larger. The owner-manager is being joined by professional managers, especially in larger, publicly owned firms. Distributor associations and suppliers are offering a broad variety of programs aimed at improving distributor management. Some manufacturers believe that the specialist firms are likely to be more marketing oriented, not just selling oriented, in order to achieve the market penetration necessary to succeed with a reduced product range. There is a stronger profit orientation and a greater concern for the profitability of individual product lines.

Many manufacturers have actively reviewed their distributor policies and organizations in recent years. On balance, there is a clear trend toward *greater reliance on fewer, larger, and better-managed distributors.* The result is a weeding out of the weak, marginal distributor firms. A variety of market-related and economic forces have stimulated this process. Manufacturers faced with tight money, increased competition (often price competitors from overseas), and rapidly increasing transportation costs are forced to search hard for ways to increase physical distribution system efficiency and marketing program effectiveness.

Most manufacturers have developed a variety of training programs and supporting services to make the distributor as effective as possible, thus strengthening the distributor and the commitment to him. There is also greater emphasis on the distributor's market development and account solicitation functions. Thus, it appears that the trend will sustain itself for some years to come, producing larger, more effective, better-managed industrial distributors, who will perform a broader variety of functions for their suppliers. For the typical manufacturer, it will mean fewer but better distributors to work with and a stronger, more effective partnership. It will also be that much harder for firms who wish to move from direct sales and service coverage to find available and qualified distributors,

since there will be fewer distributors and these will have stronger commitments to existing suppliers.

A final word of caution is in order. Even though the industrial distributor is becoming stronger and more effective, he still depends heavily on the manufacturer for his strength and effectiveness. The idea of *partnership* remains essential; when the manufacturer turns to the distributor for added help, he does not give up his own responsibility for effective marketing, nor can he expect the distributor to respond positively to all suggestions. Rather, he assumes new responsibilities for making the distributor more effective—through programs of product development, careful pricing, promotional support, technical assistance, and order servicing, and through training programs for distributor salespeople and management. This places increased responsibility on the manufacturer to make sure that *his* salespeople are well trained to implement these programs for the distributor organization. Developing and maintaining an effective relationship with the distributor should be regarded as the salesperson's primary responsibility.

CONCLUSION: DEVELOPING EFFECTIVE INDUSTRIAL DISTRIBUTORS

From this study, a number of guidelines emerge for marketing managers who wish to strengthen their relationships with their industrial distributors.

First, it is impossible to define the distributor's role in marketing strategy if the marketing strategy is not clearly developed. The initial step in developing effective distributors must be a careful statement of the role of customer service, product availability, technical support, and price in the total product-market positioning of the firm. Then, the role of the distributor can be more carefully defined in terms of the functions he will be expected to perform and for which he will be compensated.

As this study has indicated, the role of the industrial distributor is likely to become more important for most suppliers in the future. However, the findings have also suggested that distributors are not generally effective as a source of market information or in aggressively marketing new products. Likewise, specific steps must be taken to insure distributor cooperation in any program of new account development.

Assuming that the supplier company already has an established distributor network, the second step is an assessment of the capabilities of those distributors for fulfilling their role. This "situation analysis" must be matched with the planned role of the industrial distributor, and specific programs must be developed for improving defined areas of weakness. In this analysis, the supplier should be especially sensitive to the role that his salespeople must play as the linking pin between marketing strategy and distributor effectiveness. Rather than bemoan the characteristic shortcomings of the industrial distributor (limited managerial competence and growth motivation, excessive customer orientation, etc.), the manufacturer should think in terms of a distributor-salesperson team. The salesperson's first function is to serve and strengthen the distributor, but he must also be able to supplement the distributor's competence in technical support, new account development, and so on. The trend toward distributor specialization may alleviate the need for technical support, but that should not be taken for granted.

Third, the supplier must assess the appropriateness of various policies guiding his relationship with distributors. Recent development suggest that it may be desirable to help distributors finance higher levels of inventory. Special compensation arrangements may be necessary to encourage new account development. There may be an opportunity here to offset losses to the distributor caused by the supplier's need to recapture certain major customers as direct accounts. This latter problem area may also be treated by developing special commission arrangements to compensate distributors for their willingness to continue to provide service to these direct accounts and to otherwise compensate them for the loss in revenue.

To summarize, greater reliance on distributors of increased size and importance will require that suppliers commit resources to programs for enhancing the distributor's role and improving his effectiveness. The key concept here is that of a partnership where the supplier tries to strengthen his distributors as independent businesses while at the same time supplementing their weaknesses with a strong "missionary" sales organization.

30 A Remedy for Maldistribution

Stephen B. Oresman
Charles D. Scudder

Physical distribution, the function of moving products from manufacturing into the hands of the customer, is big business and getting bigger rapidly. During the past year, the top 500 industrial companies in the United States spent an estimated $69 billion moving their products to market. This compares with $40 billion for the same function ten years ago, and this upward trend will almost certainly continue and may even accelerate.

The trend can be accounted for by the increase in unit costs of physical distribution. Freight rates have increased more than 40 percent during the past five years. As mail service has deteriorated, companies' ability to receive orders promptly and reliably from customers has declined; to fill the gap, manufacturers have resorted to increasingly sophisticated and more expensive telecommunications systems. As wage costs have increased, particularly in overhead areas where productivity gains are small, distribution labor costs have risen.

The net effect of these factors has been a significant increase in unit costs—with no relief in sight.

Equally important in this rise in costs are the increased service demands that have been placed on companies' distribution activities. As the business environment becomes more competitive, customers place an increasing premium on fast delivery and reliable customer service. This steps up the demands made on manufacturers' distribution capabilities, increasing the need for the use of premium transportation and escalating distribution inventories as marketing and sales managers put pressure on their factories and warehouses to gain a competitive edge.

The combined result of these costs and service factors has been significant. Today, we estimate the average manufacturer spends about 13 percent of each sales dollar on physical distribution, up from 11 percent five years ago. While it is not surprising that unit costs have gone up, it is significant that spending for physical distribution has risen in proportion to the other costs of doing business. As a result, physical distribution is properly receiving increasing attention from top management in an effort to reduce costs and improve competitive effectiveness.

WHAT IS MALDISTRIBUTION?

Physical distribution encompasses numerous and varied functions, including order entry, customer service, warehousing, traffic, shipping, finished goods inventory control, and private fleet operations. An effective system requires the coordination of these functions to form the principal connecting link between the manufacturer and his customers, as shown in Exhibit 1. Physical distribution operations make up a system that is both an information flow (from the customer to the manufacturer) and a product flow (from the manufacturer to the customer). The purpose of these activities is to provide service to customers by promptly delivering ordered goods. As has been pointed out, the costs of operating this system are high and are directly related to the level of service provided.

Manufacturers may measure customer service in many different ways, but the relevant measure is how the customers think their supplier is meeting their needs. Since information and product flows that make up physical distribution are the principal day-to-day contact between the manufacturer and his customer, the customer's overall rating of his supplier is strongly colored by the job the supplier is doing in physical distribution. Distribution is, therefore, frequently second in importance only to the personal contact of the sales force in

EXHIBIT 1
Simplified materials and paper flow in physical distribution

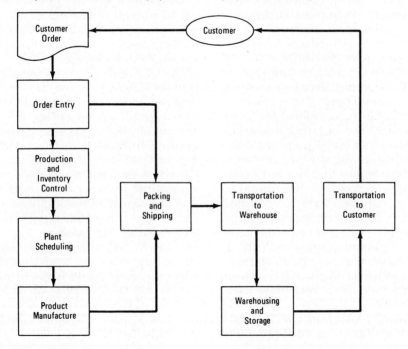

building a working relationship between supplier and customer.

Just as service is the customer's way of measuring the effectiveness of distribution, so is cost one of the manufacturer's principal measures of the performance of his physical distribution activities. There are two major kinds of costs associated with physical distribution:

Visible costs include those operating costs associated with warehousing, transportation, and handling. These costs are typically reported on company expense statements as "distribution expense." They are easy to identify and usually can be measured without difficulty.

Visible costs also include other indirect costs associated with inventory investment, property taxes, and inventory obsolescence and spoilage. All go into company profit-and-loss statements and hence directly affect profits but are rarely identified as distribution related costs.

Hidden costs consist principally of lost profit opportunities due to failure to ship the product on time, cancelled orders, and customer dissatisfaction. These costs never appear on the profit-and-loss statement but can have a significant impact on profits, particularly in the long run.

Customer service and these costs are logically interdependent. Improving the service provided by a distribution system should increase costs, and meaningful cost reduction should lower service performance. From this relationship, it appears that the principal problem in effectively managing distribution is to determine the appropriate service level for the business, and then run the distribution as efficiently as possible to achieve that level of service.

Unfortunately, our experience shows that this is frequently not the case. Many manufacturers are not doing an effective job in physical distribution because fundamental flaws in their distribution systems create inefficiencies. These inefficiencies can greatly distort the cost/service relationship. Experience shows that companies with comparatively high distribution costs frequently provide poorer service than some

of their competitors who have lower distribution costs, even though they are providing essentially the same products to identical markets.

Because this problem occurs again and again in companies of different sizes and across a wide variety of industries, it merits a name—maldistribution. Many companies are not getting full value in terms of service for their dollar expenditures in physical distribution. While no precise estimates are possible, maldistribution probably costs manufacturers several billion dollars per year; if the authors' experience can be extended validly across U.S. industry, the annual cost could be as high as $10 billion. This article explains why traditional approaches have failed to solve the problem and suggests a method of avoiding maldistribution.

TRADITIONAL APPROACHES

Because distribution is expensive and maintaining competitive customer service is important to company profitability, top management is periodically concerned about improving distribution operations. In almost every manufacturing company, improving distribution becomes a task of high priority. Because of this high interest level, considerable work has been done to develop approaches and techniques to solve distribution problems. There is now an extensive literature and a number of specialized techniques are available, including canned computer programs, mathematical modeling, statistical decision rules, and sophisticasted telecommunications and information display hardware.

Because so much information is available, it is difficult to choose the correct approach when management needs to make changes in physical distribution. Moreover, these specialized techniques generally focus on a single aspect of the problem or treat distribution in isolation from other parts of company operations. Overreliance on particular techniques is a major cause of maldistribution. Our experience in a variety of companies indicates that these traditional approaches to solving distribution problems come up with partial solutions at best. The following cases are illustrative.

A Cosmetic Company's Problem

A growing cosmetic company selling to both wholesalers and retailers experienced increasing difficulty with its distribution system. Over the years, the basic nature of the business changed from a primarily wholesale business into a predominantly retail business. As the nature of the customers changed, average shipment sizes decreased, and customer service requirements became more exacting. The consequences of late delivery were more serious to the company since the wholesaler's inventory was increasingly unavailable to back up the retailer supply. Because of these changing demands on this company's distribution system, freight charges mounted and service declined to the point where management decided that a reevaluation of their approach to physical distribution was needed.

This company chose to develop a computer model to establish the optimum system. This approach, which has become a classic, uses a linear programming model to determine the optimum number and location of warehouses in the distribution system. Such a model balances the costs of transportation, warehousing, and inventory carrying at various customer service levels to establish the appropriate cost/ service mix. This approach led this company to conclude that adding five warehouses to their current two-warehouse system would reduce LTL (less than truckload lot) freight, increase customer service to the desired levels, and result in a new increase in service with lower overall costs.

Guided by the computer model analysis, the company opened five more warehouses. The results were far below expectations. While freight costs from warehouse to customer were reduced because the warehouses were closer to the customer, these savings were offset by the need for more air freight and other premium transportation. While the time for delivery from warehouse to customer decreased, this improvement in service was offset by a marked increase in stockouts and backorders. Because of these disappointing results, the new distribution system was deemed a costly failure.

A Food Company's Problem

Another frequently used approach to solving distribution and service problems is to find ways to speed up the flow of information on which distribution decisions are based. For example, teleprocessing equipment can be used to get customer orders in from the branch warehouses, and on-line real time inventory systems can be installed to keep track of inventory balances. This approach presumes that if changes in sales rates, the occurrence of stockouts, and the location of all inventory are known instantaneously, then the corrective action can be taken sooner, thereby improving service.

This was the approach adopted by a large food manufacturer, unhappy with the system of thirty-five field warehouses which were supplied from six manufacturing plants. Many of this company's products had highly seasonal demand patterns, and delivery problems were acute in the peak selling season. In addition, about one out of every eight orders could not be filled completely, while competitive service demanded that no more than one out of every twenty orders be incomplete.

Analysis indicated that the sales forecasts used to determine the amount of inventory at each warehouse were inaccurate and that the stockouts that caused incomplete orders were primarily a local problem, since inventory was usually on hand in nearby warehouses. Because of the large number of warehouses in the system, additional stock was almost always available within a few hundred miles. As a result, the company revised its forecasting methods and installed a telecommunications system which provided on-line inventory balances in each warehouse. The basic idea was to make shipments out of the nearest warehouse with available stock if inventory was not available from the primary location serving that district.

The results were disappointing. Six months after new systems were installed, it was discovered that forecasts were more accurate but the increased accuracy did not improve service nearly as much as had been anticipated. A large number of orders had to be filled with product shipped from alternate warehouses and, while the telecommunications system enabled the company to fill more orders, freight costs increased significantly. The new distribution system increased service slightly at a substantial increase in costs.

A Building Materials Company's Problem

Statistical inventory management has come into its own with the widespread availability of computers capable of handling the large number of calculations required to make these techniques work. The basic idea is to protect against the uncertainty of the size and location of demand by distributing stock strategically, using statistical probabilities. This approach gets the maximum mileage from whatever inventory is available and, when used to establish inventory levels, accurately provides predetermined customer service levels.

A company which manufactures building materials had previously planned its production schedule based on an overall forecast of sales. The breadth of the product line and large variations in demand for individual products caused continual service problems. With an average order ranging from twenty to forty items, virtually no orders were shipped complete. Late and split shipments from the company's five field warehouses significantly increased freight, handling, and order processing costs.

Analysis indicated that a modern statistical inventory control system using safety stocks based on forecast error would improve service and reduce shipping and related costs. Such a system was installed at the warehouses, and stock replenishment orders were automatically written and placed at the plants. The results were disturbing. Although the warehouse inventory control system responded rapidly to variations in demand, raising and lowering safety stocks and reorder points from month to month, the plants were unable to respond effectively. As a result, a large number of stockouts occurred at the plants, and shipments could no longer be made to the warehouses in full truckload quantities. Freight costs increased dramatically. A later attempt to get more truckload shipments from the plants by holding up the trucks until the shortages were alleviated produced a sharp decline in the quality of customer service from the warehouses. The company was back in the same position it was in before the new system was installed.

What Went Wrong?

If there is a common thread in these three examples, it is that the approach followed was originally technique or equipment oriented and sought to deal with distribution in isolation from other company functions. Although the specific problem addressed such as inaccurate sales forecasts or the lack of timely inventory information was adequately solved, the changes re-

EXHIBIT 2

The balancing of conflicting objectives

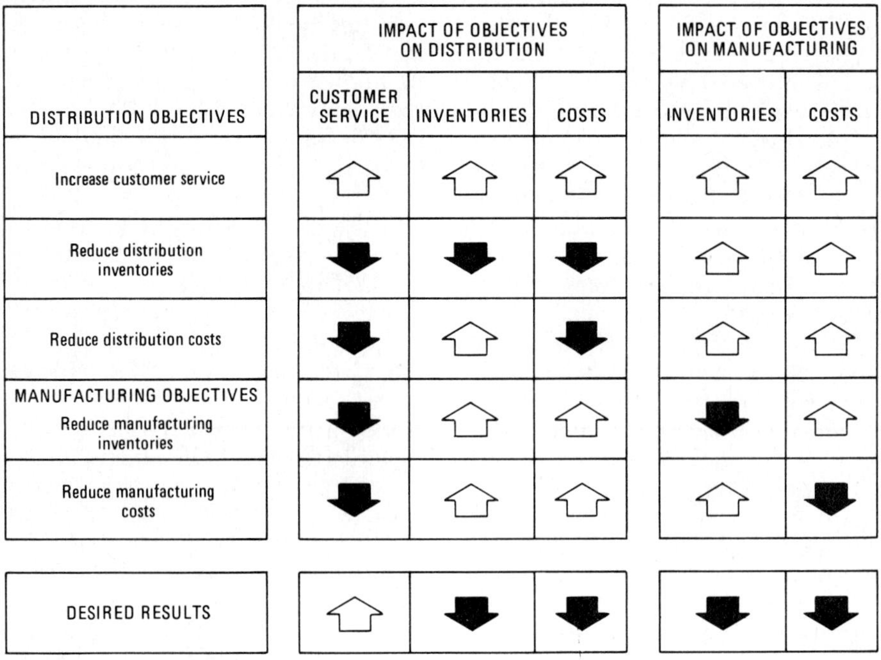

DISTRIBUTION OBJECTIVES	IMPACT OF OBJECTIVES ON DISTRIBUTION			IMPACT OF OBJECTIVES ON MANUFACTURING	
	CUSTOMER SERVICE	INVENTORIES	COSTS	INVENTORIES	COSTS
Increase customer service	⇧	⇧	⇧	⇧	⇧
Reduce distribution inventories	⬇	⬇	⬇	⇧	⇧
Reduce distribution costs	⬇	⇧	⬇	⇧	⇧
MANUFACTURING OBJECTIVES Reduce manufacturing inventories	⬇	⇧	⇧	⬇	⇧
Reduce manufacturing costs	⬇	⇧	⇧	⇧	⬇
DESIRED RESULTS	⇧	⬇	⬇	⬇	⬇

quired to implement those solutions created new unexpected problems that generally outweighed the improvements achieved.

Because distribution is closely related to other company operations, particularly manufacturing, the objectives of distribution are frequently in conflict with these other areas. Some of the more important conflicts between manufacturing and distribution are shown in Exhibit 2. Failure to recognize these conflicts and make carefully calculated trade-offs leads to problems of maldistribution encountered in the three case histories just discussed.

In practice, the more popular distribution techniques are only aids in solving the broad and complex problems frequently encountered. What is required is a method of organizing and attacking the complex interdisciplinary analysis needed to avoid maldistribution. The following case history illustrates how this can be done.

AN APPROACH THAT WORKS

A Successful Case History

A large manufacturer of consumer goods was faced with escalating inventories and declining customer service. Over a three-year period, sales had leveled after a decade of explosive growth, yet inventories had continued to climb an additional 30 percent. Customer service had deteriorated over this same period from the traditional 99 percent to less than 96 percent; customer complaints were at an all-time high; and salesmen's morale was seriously affected by the service problem.

Company management had previously made several piecemeal attempts to solve this problem. A linear programming computer model had been developed which had indicated that two more warehouses were needed, an on-line inventory control system had been designed and installed, and various organization changes had been made to focus attention on service and inventories. None of these efforts perceptibly slowed the increase in inventories or decline in customer service. As a result, top management decided that a more innovative approach was required.

The first step taken was to frame the basic question, "How much inventory should we have to provide a competitive level of service, and how can we assure that we achieve that level of service?" With this definition of the scope of the undertaking, a project team was formed consisting of four members: the manager responsible for customer service and warehousing, a line manufacturing manager responsible for production scheduling, a manufacturing systems specialist, and the manager of production and inventory control. This task force was assigned full time to the project, assisted by outside consultants, and made responsible to a steering committee to top management.

While the project team approach is certainly not new, there were several noteworthy elements in the charter, organization, and function of this team. The basic charter of the project was not framed in terms of a functional area, technique, or probable solution; instead, the team was assigned to determine the appropriate relationship between the parts of the problem and the method for arriving at the solution. This broad framing of the task force charter gave the team the understanding that they were dealing with a management problem of significant stature to challenge their capabilities. All of the disciplines that were involved in the solution were represented by key managers able and willing to speak and

act knowledgeably for their areas. The assignment of key managers full time to the team clearly demonstrated management's commitment and assured that adequate attention would be given to the problem. The managers' jobs were filled by temporary reassignment of subordinates, which caused an unexpectedly small number of operating problems.

The newly organized task force spent its first three months collecting and analyzing operating data and interviewing other company managers to accurately define the problem. Over the three-month data collection and analysis phase, a large number of projects were carried out. In most cases, they were performed by team members themselves, and the tendency to write a computer program to do the work was actively resisted. Most of the work was done with calculators and slide rules.

The following projects are representative of those carried out in the data collection and analysis phase of the project:

☐ A statistical analysis of warehouse shipments by line item measured warehouse variability of demand. The results of this analysis were in turn used to calculate the theoretical inventories required to give 99 percent service. This calculation showed that warehouse inventories were 50 percent higher than required in total, but significantly too low on a handful of products.

☐ A detailed analysis of customer service was based on a sample of invoices and backorders. Although a service problem was clearly recognized, the company had no way of measuring the extent of the problem quantitatively. The results of this analysis showed that over a three-year period service had declined from 99 percent to less than 96 percent. In dollar terms, backorders had risen from an average of $10,000 to more than $500,000.

☐ Manufacturing inventory replenishment was based on the policy of maintaining safety stocks of at least two months' sales. A comparison of actual stock levels with forecasts showed a variance of from one-half to six months instead of the expected two months. This discrepancy prompted further examination which revealed that there were at least two different forecasts for each item—one prepared by the sales and marketing department and another prepared by manufacturing.

☐ An analysis of manufacturing schedules showed that in the company's peak summer months only 20 percent of orders were made on time and that the principal component of lead times was waiting time rather than working time.

At the conclusion of the data collection and analysis phase, a number of major problems were identified:

☐ Inconsistent and inaccurate sales forecasts. In addition to the sales and manufacturing forecasts, a third distribution forecast was also uncovered.

☐ Inappropriate inventory levels. The two-month safety stocks policy led to insufficient protection on some items and excesses on others.

☐ Demand on the field warehouses was much more regular and predictable than demand on the plant after the warehouses had translated customer demand into reorders.

☐ The replenishment policy concentrated on freight costs and ignored inventory and storage costs and, as a result, overall costs were increased $100,000 annually.

☐ Capacity was severely overloaded during peak months. The scheduling system did not load by manufacturing departments and lead times were excessive because the scheduling system allowed for large queues of work before each operation.

Of particular significance in this step was the team's concentration on analysis rather than on techniques. The effort was concentrated on causes rather than on determining if various proposed approaches were desirable. Further, since the managers got into the details themselves, they were forced to discard preconceived notions and thus became aware of preconceptions on the part of others, including top management.

Finally, as they all worked together in the same room on various points of the same problem, they developed a strong feeling for the interrelationships among their various functions.

Once the key problem areas had been sharply defined, the specialists on and supporting the team could go to work designing solutions. To correct the problem of multiple inaccurate forecasts, the marketing team member and an operations research specialist developed a sales forecasting system. This system used computerized linear regression techniques to develop a statistical sales forecast, which was then modified by the responsible product manager. The modified forecast was divided by the computer into forecasts for each warehouse to be used in the distribution system and then reassembled by plant to be used in the manufacturing inventory control system.

The manufacturing and inventory control members of the team developed a statistical safety stock system based on the forecast to cover each item in each warehouse. A similar safety stock was calculated for the central warehouses and used in overall inventory control to take advantage of the fact that the variability of demand at the plants would be less than the sum of variability at the warehouses. The problem of lumpy demands from the warehouses was approached by reducing lot sizes of shipments to conform more closely to actual sales demand and by scheduling regular shipments so that freight costs would not increase.

To test the validity of these system design changes, a computer simulation model was constructed to prove that the various elements were truly integrated and that the predicted inventory and service levels were achievable. It was only at this fairly advanced step that emphasis changed to techniques and systems design. Operations research and inventory control techniques were used but only as methods for treating clearly identified problems, not as overall solutions.

The work of the task force did not stop with the development of the solution to the distribution inventory and service problem. Previous analysis had shown that the manufacturing systems could not support even the smoothed demand from the warehouses at certain periods of the year. A new manufacturing and planning system was designed to shorten lead times and to plan capacity on an overall basis so that inventory could be built during slack periods in anticipation of peak demand.

It is obviously essential that manufacturing and distribution work from the same information, but in this step the concept of integrated operations was carried further to raise the question of whether the manufacturing operations could provide the product after they had the proper information. If this last step had not been considered and a new capacity planning and scheduling system designed, much of the previous work would have been for naught.

The changes recommended by the task force were implemented over a period of about one year. The work during the implementation included programming and testing of new computer systems, training of users, and parallel testing of new systems along with old. The impact of the changes was dramatic. Inventories were reduced by 15 percent or almost $8 million. Backorders were reduced from a peak of $500,000 to a more normal level of $10,000 to $20,000. Customer complaints dropped substantially, and operating costs were reduced by more than $300,000 per year, excluding the savings from reduced inventories and improved service.

Why This Approach Works

A careful comparison of the preceding successful case history with the first three examples that resulted in maldistribution shows that the successful solution of distribution problems is based on close attention to four key concepts.

In Analyzing a Distribution Problem, Distribution is Closely Tied to Other Areas of the Company. Distribution is closely related to marketing, manufacturing, and finance in a number of different ways. Thus, for example, the marketing forecast and the error in that forecast are key determinants of the amount of inventory that must be carried in the warehouses to achieve a given level of customer service. Another example is the cost of money, a financial variable which has an important impact on inventory carrying costs and is one of the controlling factors in developing a satisfactory warehouse replenishment policy. Because distribution is closely tied to other areas of the company, an understanding of these interrelationships is essential to the effective solution of distribution related problems. One way of identifying these interrelationships is by means of the task force approach, used in the preceding case example.

The failure to properly handle one important interrelationship was the root of the problem in the case of the cosmetic company, the first failure discussed. The difficulty in this example had nothing to do with the number of warehouses, which was in fact properly determined by using the linear programming approach. The real problem was that the warehouses and manufacturing were running from different sales forecasts, with the warehouses assuming the factory had an infinite capacity for immediate delivery. The failure of this company to tie distribution and manufacturing together with a single forecast led to frequent field stockouts. Increasing the number of warehouses from two to seven without treating the underlying difficulty only exacerbated the service problem, causing a dramatic increase in air freight costs and a decline in inventory service to customers. The additional costs of coping with these problems more than outweighed the cost savings of the new warehouses.

Beware of Simplistic Solutions Since the Interrelationships Between Distribution and Other Functions Are Complex and Multi-leveled. A further consequence of the close interrelationship between distribution and other areas of the company is that distribution problems frequently have long and deep roots. A single problem may surface in different guises in different functional areas. Thus a customer service problem in sales may be the result of an inventory problem in distribution, which may, in turn, be the consequence of a scheduling problem in manufacturing. Solving the service problem in sales may not be possible without getting to the root scheduling problem in manufacturing.

Failure to seek out several important related problems outside the distribution area was a principal cause of trouble in the second example of failure discussed, the food company's service problem. In this example, product sales were seasonal and exceeded the plant's capacity to manufacture in peak selling periods. To assure product availability in these peak seasons, the factory had to produce more than the sales forecast in the slack season to build up stocks to carry it through the higher volume months. There was no mechanism in the distribution system to accomplish this and, as a result, steps to increase forecast accuracy and get better stock records did not address the real problem.

Adopt Specialized Techniques With an Appreciation of Their Limitations. A large number of specialized techniques are available to assist in solving distribution problems; linear programming, Monte Carlo simulations, statistical forecasting, and network analysis are examples of currently popular approaches. Each of these techniques was originally developed to apply

in specific types of situations, and their popularity is usually based on some well-deserved successes. But selection of an approach because it is popular or failure to recognize its inherent limitations frequently leads to trouble.

The case history of the building materials supplier is a good example of the misapplication of an excellent technique. In this situation, fluctuations in monthly sales of low volume items made it difficult to provide good inventory service on these items. Since an average order contained from twenty to forty line items, practically no orders were being shipped complete. The problem was diagnosed as arising in inventory management, and a statistical inventory control system was installed. This system, however, passed the erratic demand back to the plants, which were incapable of responding within the required lead times. As a result, the benefits of the statistical system could not be attained, and the overall system quickly became costly and unworkable.

Assure That the Interrelationships Recognized in the Analysis Are Carried Over into the System Design. In solving a distribution problem, it is frequently necessary to make significant changes in company operations. Thus, for example, warehouses may be opened or closed, different transportation modes utilized, stock levels increased or decreased, or a new order entry system installed. Unless the impacts of these changes on other company operations are carefully evaluated and prepared for, they can negate the positive impact of the overall program. Because of the close interrelationship between distribution and these other areas of the company and because of the conflicts and trade-offs previously shown in Exhibit 2, these impacts may not always be obvious.

Careful attention to this concept was one of the key factors responsible for the success achieved by the consumer products company in the last example discussed. In this instance, the impact of the new distribution system on manufacturing was carefully examined and evaluated. As a result, a new scheduling and capacity planning system was required to make the distribution system work. Without this key step, the new distribution system would undoubtedly have been a failure.

The results achieved with this four-step approach have been significant in every case where it has been applied. In the three earlier examples, where the first attempts at solving distribution problems resulted in failure, this approach fared considerably better. The specific results were as follows:

☐ In the cosmetics company, the more complex distribution network required support from a common sales forecasting system in order to be fully effective. Once this was done, freight charges were reduced by $50,000 per year, distribution inventories were reduced by 40 percent, and customer service was substantially improved.

☐ At the food company, the seasonal sales demand required a mechanism to build inventories in anticipation of demand. Once

this step was accomplished, service increased to a competitive 96 percent, and freight costs fell to the original levels. The telecommunications network originally installed proved expensive and unnecessary and was discontinued.

☐ Artificially induced erratic demand at the building materials plant largely offset the advantages of the statistical inventory control system in distribution. Once this demand was dampened down in view of the factories' ability to respond, service gradually improved and freight savings of $400,000 per year were achieved.

The results in each of these cases stem from the application of the concepts outlined above. Consider distribution a broad interdisciplinary problem and organize appropriately to work on it. Give the project team top management support and sufficient time to identify the causes of problems before suggesting solutions. Be wary of techniques that promise rapid solutions, but draw upon the wide range of proven techniques once the problem is identified. Finally, assure that distribution and other company operations, particularly manufacturing, are carefully integrated.

31

An Attitudinal Framework for Advertising Strategy

Harper W. Boyd, Jr.
Michael L. Ray
Edward C. Strong

Is it realistic to consider advertising strategy in terms of more than just levels on a "hierarchy of effect"? The authors report that it is. They present a five-alternative framework for advertising strategy based on attitude research which relates product and brand perceptions to consumer preferences.

Advertising and marketing researchers have developed a variety of new techniques for defining and measuring attitude and attitudinal change. These techniques have added much to the understanding of the communications process, but seldom have they been used in a comprehensive form to structure advertising strategies and tactics.[1] This article focuses on the nature of advertising objectives from an attitudinal perspective.

The proposed framework facilitates the formulation of a strategy of consumer attitudinal change and suggests that basically five advertising strategy alternatives are available to the decision maker. The nature of each of these strategy alternatives is discussed, but the framework also holds promise for meeting other marketing problems such as market segmentation and the development of product features and new products.

ATTITUDES AS ADVERTISING OBJECTIVES

The specification of advertising objectives is of critical significance for the formulation of advertising strategy. Therefore, it is important to select objectives that can be affected by advertising and that allow for efficient and continuous testing and evaluation.

The issue of objectives had been somewhat neglected in the advertising field until 1961 when the Association of National Advertisers published Colley's *Defining Advertising Goals for Measured Advertising Results*.[2] This book, and a subsequent

---

[1]Lee Adler and Irving Crespi, eds., *Attitude Research at Sea* (Chicago: American Marketing Association, 1966) and *Attitude Research on the Rocks* (1968); Allan Greenberg, "Is Communication Research Really Worthwhile?" *Journal of Marketing*, 31 (January 1967), pp. 48–50; and Charles K. Ramond, "Must Advertising Communicate to Sell?" *Harvard Business Review*, 43 (September–October 1965), pp. 148–61.

[2]Russell Colley, *Defining Advertising Goals for Measured Advertising Results* (New York: Association of National Advertisers, 1961).

Reprinted with permission from *Journal of Marketing,* published by the American Marketing Association, 36 (April 1972), pp. 27–33.

monograph, suggested that the goals of advertising are most often goals of communication rather than those pertaining to sales.[3] These and similar publications essentially conceptualized the advertising process as a "hierarchy of effect."[4] Their view was that advertising's purpose was to affect some level of the hierarchy—such as awareness, comprehension, or conviction—and that this effect, combined with the effects of other variables in the marketing mix, would lead to the ultimate goals of sales and profits.

This "hierarchy" view was criticized on two fronts. First, quantitatively oriented researchers and managers argued that inasmuch as sales are the ultimate outcome of advertising efforts, sales should be measured.[5] Second, certain behavioral scientists contended that little evidence supported the hierarchy of effects itself; that is, learning does not necessarily lead to attitudinal change, nor does attitudinal change necessarily lead to behavioral change.[6] Thus, advertising goals formed on the basis of changes in intermediate variables—such as recall or comprehension—may be of questionable value.

Fortunately, this controversy about objectives created some insight and raised a number of significant issues. For example, one of the recent key developments in marketing research has been that of techniques for measuring attitude as a predispositional response—one that is indicative of future behavior.[7] Richard Reiser, executive director of the market research department of Grey Advertising, has commented:

Our reason for selecting attitudes as our basic way of looking at a market is based on more than the fact that one function of advertising is to affect attitudes. There is considerable evidence to show that the way a person thinks and feels about a brand—his attitudinal set—determines how he will behave. His reasons for wanting a product determine his selection: we have always found a close relationship between opinion towards a product and probability of purchase.[8]

Maloney also concluded that consumer attitudes do relate to sales. He offers considerable evidence that ". . . consumer attitude data can become a focal point for defining marketing problems and determining marketing goals."[9]

Defining advertising goals in relation to attitudes and attitudinal change has considerable appeal. Attitudes have the operationally desirable quality of being measur-

---

[3]Harry Deane Wolfe, James K. Brown, and G. Clark Thompson, *Measuring Advertising Results* (New York: National Industrial Conference Board, 1962).

[4]See for example, Rosser Reeves, *Reality in Advertising* (New York: Alfred A. Knopf, 1961); Darrell Blaine Lucas and Steuart Henderson Britt, *Measuring Advertising Effectiveness* (New York: McGraw-Hill, 1963); and Robert J. Lavidge and Gary A. Steiner, "A Model for Predictive Measurements of Advertising Effectiveness," *Journal of Marketing*, 25 (October 1961), pp. 59-62.

[5]Kristian S. Palda, "The Hypothesis of Hierarchy of Effects: A Partial Evaluation," *Journal of Marketing Research*, 3 (February 1966), pp. 13-24; Ramond, *op. cit.*; and Ambar G. Rao, *Quantitative Theories in Advertising* (New York: John Wiley & Sons, 1970).

[6]Leon Festinger, "Behavioral Support for Opinion Change," *Public Opinion Quarterly*, 28 (Fall 1964), pp. 404-17; Jack B. Haskins, "Factual Recall as a Measure of Advertising Effectiveness," *Journal of Advertising Research*, 4 (March 1964), pp. 2-8; and Herbert E. Krugman, "The Impact of Television Advertising: Learning Without Involvement," *Public Opinion Quarterly*, 29 (Fall 1965), pp. 349-56.

[7]Alvin A. Achenbaum, "An Answer to One of the Unanswered Questions About the Measurement of Advertising Effectiveness," in *Proceedings of the 12th Annual Meeting of the Advertising Research Foundation* (New York: Advertising Research Foundation, 1966), pp. 24-32; George S. Day, "Using Attitude Measures to Evaluate New Product Introductions," *Journal of Marketing Research*, 7 (November 1970), pp. 474-82; and John C. Maloney, "Attitude Measurement and Formation," paper presented at the AMA Test Marketing Workshop (Chicago: American Marketing Association, 1966), mimeo.

[8]As quoted in *Advertising Age* (December 19, 1966), p. 1.

[9]Maloney, *op. cit.*

able, albeit with difficulty and some lack of precision. Attitudes also have long been the object of investigation by behavioral scientists, and a considerable body of knowledge has resulted from their studies and models. Today's psychologists believe that attitude includes both perceptual and preferential components; i.e., attitude is an inferred construct. When one refers to an attitude he means that a person's past experiences predispose him to respond in certain ways on the basis of certain perceptions. Attitude, therefore, may be viewed as a variable which links psychological and behavioral components.[10]

Since attitudes reflect perceptions, they inevitably indicate predispositions. Thus, they permit advertising strategists to design advertising inputs which will affect perceptions and thereby change predispositions to respond or behave. This process is the foundation of the strategy suggestions contained in the following sections.

AN EMERGING FRAMEWORK

The possibility of linking perceptions and preferences in formulating advertising strategy has only recently occurred, because strategists and researchers have emphasized either perceptions or preferences to the exclusion of the other. Some have emphasized brand image with only vague regard to response; others have emphasized brand loyalty with little regard to the perception that led to that loyalty.[11]

Now, however, marketing has witnessed an active integration of research on the perceptual and the preference aspects of attitude. The Colley-DAGMAR and NICB books hinted at this integration.[12] Maloney suggested using both perceptions and preferences with his CAPP (Continuous Advertising Planning Program) research.[13] Smith described General Motors' advertising evaluation program as including measurement of consumer perceptions of automobile characteristics and the relating of these characteristics to automobile preferences or likelihood of purchase.[14]

Even more recently, technical advances have been made in marketing that further allow managers to link perceptions and preferences in order to make advertising plans. These technical advances have come from two areas. One is the area of research for new product developments which is typified by the market structure studies pioneered by Stefflre and others.[15] The other area is that of consumer behavior models. These models typically examine the nature of the changes in the perceptions and preferences of consumers as they move toward a buying decision. Although a number of such models exist, they are typified by Amstutz's microsimulation model which posits that consumers move through four major stages in the purchase process: development of perceived need, decision to shop, purchase, and post-purchase. While moving through these stages, consumers can experience alterations in attitudinal

[10]See Martin Fishbein, ed., *Readings in Attitude Theory and Measurement* (New York: John Wiley & Sons, 1967); Marie Jahoda and Neil Warren, eds., *Attitudes* (Baltimore: Penguin Books, 1966); and Gene F. Summers, ed., *Attitude Measurement* (Chicago: Rand McNally, 1970).

[11]Summers, *ibid.*, pp. 227-34 and pp. 149-58; and Jacob Jacoby, "A Model of Multi-Brand Loyalty," *Journal of Advertising Research*, 11 (June 1971), pp. 25-31.

[12]Colley, *op. cit.*; and Wolfe, et al., *op. cit.*

[13]Maloney, *op. cit.*

[14]Gail Smith, "How G.M. Measures Ad Effectiveness," *Printer's Ink* (May 14, 1965), pp. 19-29.

[15]Volney Stefflre, "Market Structure Studies: New Products for Old Markets and New Markets (Foreign) for Old Products," in *Applications of the Sciences in Marketing Management* (New York: John Wiley & Sons, 1968), pp. 251-68; and Alvin J. Silk, "The Use of Preference and Perception Measures in New Product Development: An Exposition and Review," *Industrial Management Review*, 11 (Fall 1969), pp. 21-37.

structure.[16] His concept is the primary basis for the framework for advertising strategy suggested in this article.

Amstutz assumes that the consumer's attitudinal structure for any product class consists of a set of salient product class characteristics (choice criteria) and a set of brand perceptions regarding each of the salient product characteristics. That is, for a particular product class an individual considers a number of product characteristics to be salient. He also has a perception about what the ideal brand of this product would be like with respect to each of these characteristics or dimensions.

The consumer's choice criteria reflects his needs, values, prior product experience, and so on. In the case of mature products, the choice criteria are reasonably well defined. Such is not the case with many new products; therefore, the seller has the opportunity to play an important role in the building of attitudes toward the product class.

More specifically, the consumer is asked to indicate the extent to which each product characteristic is salient using a scale, say, of 0-10. The result is an attitudinal set which forms the consumer's choice criteria against which the individual brands belonging to the product class are evaluated. The consumer is then asked to rate the same product characteristics for each relevant brand again on a scale of 0-10. Conceptually, the consumer chooses a particular brand by comparing his ratings toward each brand with his ratings of the ideal brand. The brand which compares most

favorably with the "ideal" has the highest probability of being chosen. This is the link between perception and preference.

For example, a housewife who did not believe that nutrition was a highly salient product characteristic for a ready-to-eat cereal would, of course, be unlikely to buy such a cereal type. On the other hand, the following product characteristics might be salient to a housewife who is considering the purchase of such a cereal type: protein, minerals, vitamins, and the absence of sugar. Assume that a housewife is asked for her ideal saliency ratings on these four product characteristics using a scale of 0-10. Further assume that the same consumer is asked to rate brands A and B in the same fashion with the results shown in Exhibit 1.

Based on such an attitudinal set the consumer would probably buy brand A over brand B. It should be stated that predictions of behavior based on such ratings are essentially probabilistic.

The above described perceptual structure holds considerable promise as a framework for advertising strategy formulation. Rather than assume that advertising's function is to affect sales directly or to have an effect on a level of the hierarchy, it would seem more functional to assume that advertising can maintain or shift attitudes with respect to salient product characteristics and their ratings. If such can be accomplished, it will lead to preference which affects sales and profits.

If advertising's overriding goal is to influence attitudinal structures such as

[16]Arnold E. Amstutz, *Computer Simulation of Competitive Market Response* (Cambridge, Mass.: M.I.T. Press, 1967). For other microtype consumer behavior models see John A. Howard and Jagdish N. Sheth, *The Theory of Buyer Behavior* (New York: John Wiley & Sons, 1964); Francesco M. Nicosia, *Consumer Decision Processes* (Englewood Cliffs, N.J.: Prentice-Hall, 1966), pp. 155–91; and James F. Engel, David T. Kollat, and Roger D. Blackwell, *Consumer Behavior* (New York: Holt, Rinehart & Winston, 1968).

EXHIBIT 1

Hypothetical example of Amstutz-type attitude structure for nutritional ready-to-eat cereals

SALIENT PRODUCT CHARACTERISTICS	PRODUCT CATEGORY	RATINGS	
		BRAND A	BRAND B
Protein	8	9	5
Minerals	5	7	5
Vitamins	9	8	4
Absence of sugar	4	3	6

those suggested in Exhibit 1, then a manager can choose from among five broad strategy alternatives. He can seek to:

1. Affect those forces which influence strongly the choice criteria used for evaluating brands belonging to the product class;

2. Add characteristic(s) to those considered salient for the product class;

3. Increase/decrease the rating for a salient product class characteristic;

4. Change perception of the company's brand with regard to some particular salient product characteristic; or

5. Change perception of competitive brands with regard to some particular salient product characteristic.

The remainder of this article discusses these strategies.

Strategy One: Affect Product Class Linkages to Goals and Events

This strategy relates to the formulation of advertising which attempts to stimulate primary demand. Such a strategy would seek to enhance the saliency rating given one product class versus others with respect to obtaining certain goals. The framework is similar to that presented earlier in that the consumer has choice criteria which he uses to rate alternative product classes with respect to obtaining his goals.

If the advertiser knows (1) the goals of a given market segment with respect to (2) the choice criteria (salient product characteristics) used to evaluate the alternative product classes considered as ways of achieving the goals, and (3) the perceptions regarding each product class, he can better decide what action to take to stimulate demand for his product class. Inevitably he must link his product class to the relevant goals. But he must also seek to change the consumer's rating of his product class versus others with respect to the choice criteria involved.

The advertiser could seek to change the saliency of the consumer's goals and thus increase the demand for his product class. However, most of the change associated with goals comes about through environmental factors operating over long periods of time, although advertising can, no doubt, accelerate the trends.

Thus far no distinction has been made between "goals" and "needs." In the final analysis, products are judged on the basis of their function or role in helping the individual to attain some goal or in meeting a need. In the case of nutritional ready-to-eat cereal, the goal of many consumers is to maintain or improve health while not gaining (or losing) weight. Still other consumers might wish to achieve the goal of caring for their loved ones by ensuring that they receive their daily quota of minerals and vitamins. Many other goals could be outlined, but their importance lies, first, in that the goal(s) will partly determine what product class characteristics are salient (as well as how salient), and second, that the goal(s) will ultimately be reflected in the individual's attitudes toward alternative brands of the product. Thus, if goals are known—however imprecisely—they help to explain attitudinal ratings, or if salient product characteristics and ratings are known, goals may be deduced.

After the advertiser has differentiated individuals on the basis of goals and translated this differentiation into preference for one product class over another via saliency ratings, he now could try to alter these saliency ratings or product class choice criteria in the hope of attracting more consumers to *his* product class and ultimately to his brand. In the nutritional cereal example, at least one advertiser attempted to do this by making the appeal: "What's a mother to do . . . about vitamins? . . . Serve _____ the only leading cereal with a whole day's vitamin supply. . . . Feel vitamin-safe all day." Another advertiser perceived another goal as instrumental and advertised: "Charge Up, Sleek Down . . . Feel Like a Healthy Animal." The first advertiser tied goals to product class choice criteria, while the latter simply stressed the goal to be obtained.

Other examples of attempting to change, influence, or create additional goals as they relate to the use of product classes or brands are safety in automobiles, health protection by eliminating oral bacteria, and germs through the frequent use of a mouthwash, easing problems of mild insomnia by taking aspirin, reducing the financial burden of decentralized inventories through the regularized use of air freight, and the reduction in air pollution through the use of low-lead gasoline.

Once goals are set, the consumer will proceed to select products which will help him obtain his objectives. But there is an intervening consideration since most products are consumed as part of an "event"— that is, it is part of a situation which occurs at certain places at certain times and often involves the presence of more than one individual. The situation may be socially or work-oriented and often involves more than one product. The event is, of course, tied to the goal and is prescribed and constrained accordingly.

The possibility presented for strategy formulation at this level is the use of advertising to change the individual's attitude toward the use of a product class *within* a particular event. In other words, the salient product characteristics of alternative product classes will be judged according to how well they "fit" with the event to be pursued. The event itself is perceived by the individual as being associated with certain salient product class characteristics, and the decision process is similar to the notion of perception and brand choice. The advertiser seeks to change or modify the attitudes toward salient product class characteristics that the individual associates

with the event, in order to increase the probability that the product class of interest will be chosen.

It is at the event level of demand that social or group influence on the individual's choice of brand becomes more apparent. This is only natural, because social encounter is viewed as an "event" by individuals, whether people gather for some jointly agreed purpose (specific goal-related activities) or merely meet "by chance." Frequently, a modification or influence of attitude sets at the event level entails changing attitudes of the group or at least changing the individual's perception of attitudes held by the group. A prominent example of such attempted influence involves the social acceptability of women smoking small cigars in public. Others include the serving of margarine to guests, the serving of wine at family meals to bring greater enjoyment to a commonplace affair, and the drinking of milk after strenuous exercise to reduce body temperature.

The first broad strategy alternative is a complex one, and this article can only hint at how the strategy can be implemented. Nevertheless, goals and events are important to consider since they affect the way each product class is perceived and thus help to explain consumer response to the product class. Further, they provide the most appropriate communication setting in which the appeals are embedded and thus enhance their acceptability.

THE TWO PRODUCT CLASS STRATEGIES

The strategist who observes that his brand does not "fit" the ideal product class characteristics is faced with the alternative of either changing consumer attitudes toward his brand or changing consumer attitudes concerning the "ideal." These two approaches are discussed below.

Adding a Salient Characteristic— Strategy Two

Through advertising, a firm can make consumers aware of an attribute of a product class which has previously not been considered salient or which may not even have existed. Examples of this strategy's application include the use of additives to gasoline, the adding of fluorides to toothpaste, the adding of minerals to cereals, and the incorporation of light meters into cameras.

This type of strategy is most often attempted when a product is at the mature stages in its life cycle since by this time consumer attitudes pertaining to choice criteria have been well established. The advertising change is frequently combined with a product modification, although this may not be necessary. Clearly, research must show that the new characteristic has the potential of becoming salient; further, the advertiser must believe that his brand can attain a high relative rating on the new characteristic. Ideally, he would like to appropriate it so that competitors who followed would reinforce the claims made for his brand while simultaneously building the saliency of the product characteristics.

Altering the Perception of Existing Product Characteristics—Strategy Three

Increasing Salience. The advertiser who observes that his brand rates well on a product class characteristic which consumers do not consider too salient may wish to try to effect an increase in its salience. This strategy is an extension of the previous one and requires careful research to determine how the advertiser's brand and competitive brands are positioned by market segment. This kind of comparative examination is important since research has indicated that changing the importance of a product class characteristic will not affect preference for it unless one brand rates high and competitive brands are low with respect to that characteristic.[17] For example, an airline company which noted that "on schedule" was not given a high saliency rating might seek to increase the rating of this product class characteristic provided that it felt that its "on schedule" performance was better than that of its competitors.

Changing the Optimal Range. Underlying much of the above is an assumption of how advertising relates to brand and product perceptions and the way these relate to brand preference. Specifically, the purchase probability of any particular brand is the sum of the salient characteristics ratings multiplied by the brand ratings across all characteristics considered by a segment. In other words, the assumption is that the higher the brand is rated across all ideal characteristics, the more likely it is to be preferred and purchased.

This assumption probably holds true in only a few markets because, in order for it to be correct, consumers would have to desire an unlimited amount of any characteristic. More realistically, however, there may be optimal ratings below or beyond which preferences fall off. For in-

[17]For further discussion of this subject see Joel B. Cohen and Michael Houston, "The Structure of Consumer Attitudes: The Use of Attribute Possession and Importance Scores," Faculty Working Paper Number 2 (University of Illinois at Urbana, 1971); Martin Fishbein, "A Behavior Theory Approach to the Relations between Beliefs about an Object and Attitude Toward that Object," and "Attitudes and the Prediction of Behavior," in *Readings in Attitude Theory and Measurement*, Martin Fishbein, ed. (New York: John Wiley & Sons, 1967), pp. 382–89 and pp, 447–91; Jagdish N. Sheth and Wayne W. Talarzyk, "Relative Contribution of Perceived Instrumentality and Value Importance Components in Determining Attitudes," paper presented at the Fall Meetings of the American Marketing Association, Boston, 1970.

stance, in the nutritional cereal example shown earlier, it is likely that for the characteristics "protein," "minerals," and "vitamins," the more a brand is perceived as having the characteristic, the more a consumer is likely to buy the brand. But, for the characteristic "absence of sugar," a point probably exists beyond which the consumer is not willing to go; that is, a cereal could have too little sugar. Possibly the relationships are also somewhat different on either side of the optimal point. In the case of the cereal example in Exhibit 1, any deviation above the "4" ideal point on the characteristic "absence of sugar" may be enough to reject the brand. On the other hand, deviations below "4," however, may still be within the acceptable range.

These relationships can vary across the ideal characteristics within any given market. For instance, when price is considered as a variable, the ideal product rating usually represents a maximum level above which the consumer may not move and below which the consumer would happily go. For "quality," on the other hand, the ideal rating is usually a minimum level with higher rated brands acceptable and lower rated brands not acceptable. Moreover, interactions between characteristics often occur; e.g., consumers will accept infinite drops in price so long as no clearly perceptible quality decrease occurs. A price drop in some instances will affect the consumer's perception of the product's quality.[18]

Consequently, a manager must consider the optimal product rating not only with regard to its relation to brand perception and preference, but also with regard to (a)

the distribution of that relationship around the ideal point, and (b) the relationships between distributions for all of the characteristics considered to be important by consumers. While this may appear to be extremely complex, the process is simplified by the fact that few product characteristics seem to be utilized in any single product purchase decision.[19] Also, the characteristics by which products are identified and conceptualized are fairly stable over time. Further, managers have demonstrated their ability to understand and predict very well with the use of a few simple variables.[20]

Once the meaning of the saliency of product class characteristics is established, it is possible to consider the process which entails an attempt to change the nature of the acceptable distribution around the ideal point for a characteristic. If an advertiser is selling a higher priced product than his competitors, for instance, he may not be able to change the ideal rating a segment would give for price. But he may be able to get consumers to consider a range of prices *above* the ideal rating by affecting the price-quality relationship which is perceived by many. He could point out the quality that is possible only with the higher-priced product.

Similar strategy examples could be cited for all the negative relationships discussed above. Thus, for example, one could attempt to deal with the potential negative relationship between the perception of sweetness and nutrition for cereals, initial cost and upkeep for machinery, horsepower and safety for cars, taste and the effectiveness of mouthwashes, and so on. The goal of advertising is to change

[18]See Alfred Oxenfeldt, David Miller, Abraham Schuchman, and Charles Winick, *Insights Into Pricing* (Belmont, Calif.: Wadsworth Publishing Company, 1961), Chapter 4; and Joseph M. Kamen and Robert J. Toman "Psychographics of Pricing," *Journal of Marketing Research*, 7 (February 1970), pp. 27-35.

[19]Same references as footnote 15. Also see David Klahr, "A Study of Consumers' Cognitive Structure for Cigarette Brands," paper presented at the meetings of the Institute of Management Sciences, May 1968.

[20]David B. Montgomery, "Initial Distribution: A Gate Keeping Analysis of Supermarket Buyer Divisions," paper presented at the Institute of Management Sciences fall meetings, Detroit, 1971.

the nature of the range around the ideal point. Typically, this is done with advertising using two or more of the product characteristics.

A substantial amount of research has been conducted by psychologists on latitudes of acceptance and rejection in attitude.[21] This article does not discuss such research, but it will suffice to emphasize that the research indicates the significant value of considering strategies not only in terms of points but also in terms of the distribution around the points.

TWO BRAND-LEVEL STRATEGIES

Changing Perceptions of Advertiser's Brand—Strategy Four

Whereas strategies 2 and 3 were concerned with changing consumer perceptions of the ideal brand, the present strategy focuses on changing consumer perceptions of an advertiser's brand. In both cases, the strategy objective is to develop a better "fit" between the "ideal" brand and the advertiser's brand.

Little can be said about this strategy that has not been said already. Several significant suggestions, however, come from recent attitudinal research. An obvious one is that advertisers should not attempt to change perceptions for their brand when the brand itself does not possess an adequate quantity of the characteristic in question. The basic assumption of the Stefflre product development system, for instance, is that the purpose of advertising is to communicate the characteristics which the brand actually has.[22]

The framework suggested here provides a clear and measurable set of criteria for selecting the particular brand perceptions to be emphasized. Analysis of the optimal points and ranges for the salient product characteristics can indicate those characteristics that are most crucial in their effect on preference—and can do so by segments. Indeed such a process would appear to be at the very core of any segmentation scheme. Within this set of characteristics, the advertiser should seek to emphasize those for which he has the most relative advantage. Ideally, these would be characteristics for which both he and his competitors have low brand perceptions. These characteristics provide an opportunity for a profitable change in brand perception. This is especially true for those characteristics that the brand possesses and which will be difficult for competition to copy.

These conditions—high salience of a characteristic and exclusive possession of it by one brand—occur so seldom in marketing that their presence constitutes good reason to believe that there is a substantial opportunity for product development. Much of the criticism that is leveled against advertising has to do with the use of trivial claims; i.e., those which the consumer cannot link to any salient product class characteristics.

Changing Perceptions of Competing Brands—Strategy Five

Under some conditions, success may be achieved by altering perceptions for a brand with regard to salient characteristics that are perceived as being possessed to a greater extent by a competitive brand. There are techniques which boost the advertiser's brand while pointing out the fallibility of

---

[21]Carolyn W. Sherif, Muzafer Sherif, and Richard Nebergall, *Attitude and Attitude Change* (Philadelphia: W. B. Saunders, 1965); and George S. Day, "Theories of Attitude Structure and Change," in *Consumer Behavior: Theoretical Sources*, Scott Ward and Thomas S. Robertson, eds. (Englewood Cliffs, N.J.: Prentice-Hall, 1973).

[22]Stefflre, *op. cit.*, p. 262.

competitive claims. Specifically, two-sided and refutational messages provide a vehicle for fairly presenting both sides of an issue while at the same time improving the perceptions of the brand being advertised.[23]

Examples are Avis and Hertz advertising dealing with the advantages of first or second position in the rental car industry; Volkswagen's refutation of the small and ugly car counterclaims; Bayer Aspirin's counterattacks against other forms of headache remedy; and, in the political arena, Mayor John Lindsay's messages which refuted claims of his alleged mishandling of New York City's affairs. The strategy of dealing with competitive claims also occurs in industrial selling through the presentation of comparative cost data or competitive laboratory findings.

Once again, however, these techniques must be used carefully. Some evidence suggests that if they are not, the advertising can boomerang by giving support to competitive brands and claims.[24] Further evidence indicates that, unless the audience is relatively sophisticated and highly involved with the product, they are unlikely to comprehend two-sided messages fully. And if the audience is sophisticated and involved, their attitudes may be quite difficult to change with any kind of message.

CONCLUSION

For many years controversy has arisen concerning the determination of appropriateness of advertising effectiveness measures. No single measure suggested, however, has provided a basis for the formulation of advertising strategy, which has remained more art than science. Also, over the last several years, several theories of consumer behavior have made the marketing community sharply aware of the need to consider consumer behavior as a complete system. Few of these models specify the linkages between components of consumer behavior in sufficient detail to be managerially useful except for broad conceptual relationship. This article has taken a perspective of consumer brand choice from the model developed by Amstutz and extended it to various levels of demand. The resulting framework serves as a useful tool for advertising decision makers in developing comprehensive strategies of attitudinal change.

[23]Carl I. Hovland, Irving Janis, and Harold H. Kelley, *Communication and Persuasion* (New Haven, Conn.: Yale University Press, 1953); William J. McGuire, "Inducing Resistance to Persuasion: Some Contemporary Approaches," *Advances in Experimental Social Psychology*, 1 (1964), pp. 192-231; Percy H. Tannenbaum, "The Congruity Principle Revisited: Studies in the Reduction, Induction, and Generalization of Persuasion," *Advances in Experimental Social Psychology*, 3 (1967), pp. 272-320; and Michael L. Ray, "Biases in Selection of Messages Designed to Induce Resistance to Persuasion," *Journal of Personality and Social Psychology*, 9 (August 1968), pp. 335-39.

[24]Michael L. Ray, Alan G. Sawyer, and Edward C. Strong, "Frequency Effects Revisited," *Journal of Advertising Research*, 11 (February 1971), pp. 14-20; and Michael L. Ray and Alan G. Sawyer, "Behavioral Measurement for Marketing Models: Empirical Estimates of Advertising Repetition for Media Planning," *Management Science: Applications*, 17 (December 1971), Part II, pp. 73-89.

32 Advertising Research at Anheuser-Busch, Inc. (1963–68)*

Russell L. Ackoff
James R. Emshoff

The association with Anheuser-Busch, Inc. (A-B) that is described here began in 1959. Over the last fifteen years research has been carried out on almost every aspect of A-B's operations and planning. The company's view of this association has appeared in several articles.[1] *Business Week* and *Fortune*[2] have described aspects of this work and some of the theoretical output has also appeared.[3] This article, however, is the first case study to be published. It provides an account of a sequence of investigations involving advertising of the company's principal product, Budweiser beer.

*The authors acknowledge the major roles of Drs. Eli S. Marks and Maurice Sasieni in the work reported in this article.

[1] See Busch [2] and Vogel [6].

[2] See "Computers Can't Solve Everything" [3], "Wharton Analyzes the Beer Drinker" [8], and "While Big Brewers Quaff, the Little Ones Thirst" [9].

[3] See Ackoff and Emery [1], Curtis [4], and Rao [5].

BACKGROUND

A-B's original contact was made by E. H. Vogel, Jr., then manager of business planning. Work over the first few years was devoted to determining when new breweries would be required, where they should be located, and what size they should be. Facility plans were developed to cover a ten-year period. Capital requirements for these facilities were estimated and a financial model of the firm was developed and used to predict capital availability. The model showed that not quite enough capital would have been available to finance the building program without increasing the company's traditional debt to debt-equity ratio. Research then turned to ways of making more capital available when needed.

Production operations involving scheduling and allocation of demand to breweries already had been studied and modified to yield much of the potential savings.

Reprinted from *Sloan Management Review* (Winter 1975), pp. 1–15. Reprinted by permission.

Marketing, which involved a major share of the company's expenditures, had not yet been analyzed. An initial examination into this area revealed that the largest category of marketing cost involved advertising. Therefore, in 1961 we first recommended research into it. The proposal was turned down because of the widespread satisfaction with the company's advertising. Responsible managers were unwilling to evaluate and modify a successful program. Research turned instead to distribution and inventories.

ADVERTISING EXPENDITURES

Just before mid-1961 August A. Busch, Jr., then president and chairman of the board, asked us if we would evaluate an advertising decision he was about to make. In that year Budweiser was budgeted to receive about $15,000,000 worth of advertising. Mr. Busch has been approached by the vice president of marketing with a request for an additional $1,200,000 to be spent on advertising in twelve of the 198 areas into which the company divided its national market. The vice president had defended his proposal on the basis of the projected increase in sales that he believed would result. Mr. Busch explained that he was confronted with such a proposal every year and that he always had accepted it. He intended to do the same again, but he asked, "Is there any way I can find out at the end of the year whether I got what I paid for?" We said we would think about it and make some suggestions.

The proposal we presented to Mr. Busch shortly thereafter consisted of allowing the Marketing Department to select any six of the twelve areas initially proposed and giving it $600,000 for additional advertising. The remaining six areas would not be touched and would be used as controls. This biased selection procedure was intended to overcome some of the opposition that the Marketing Department felt toward any effort to evaluate its proposal.

Earlier we had developed an equation for forecasting monthly sales in each market area. Our plan now was to measure the deviation of actual monthly sales from the forecast for each market area in the test. Using the statistical characteristics of the forecasts we estimated that we had a 95 percent chance of detecting a 4 percent increase in sales in the areas with additional advertising. Since the increase predicted by the Marketing Department was in excess of this amount, Mr. Busch authorized the test and it was initiated.

The test was conducted over the last six months of 1961, yielding 72 (12 × 6) observations. The analysis of these data failed to reveal a significant difference between the test and control areas. Nevertheless, the control areas did better on average than was forecast. Therefore, we assumed that all the sales above those forecasted were attributable to the increased advertising and evaluated the results accordingly. Even under this assumption the increased amount of advertising was *not* justified by the deliberately overestimated increase in sales attributed to it.

Encouraged by these results, Mr. Busch asked us to design research directed at determining what amount should be spent on advertising. However, he wanted to proceed with caution, because he believed that much of the success of Budweiser, which was leading the beer market with a share of 8.14 percent in 1962, was due to its quality and the effectiveness with which this was communicated through its advertising. When we suggested research involving experimentation with market areas he authorized use of fifteen such areas provided they did not include any of the company's major markets.

Constrained in this way we sought an experimental design that would maximize learning about advertising expenditures. Our design effort was guided by two methodological principles. First, we knew that the company advertised for only one reason: *to increase sales.* Therefore, we were determined to measure the effect of advertising *on sales* and not on more easily measured intervening variables such as recall of messages or attitudes toward the product. For this reason we decided to continue to use deviations of actual from forecast sales as the variable to be observed. This allowed us to cancel out much of the effect on sales due to factors other than advertising. Accordingly, efforts to improve forecasting of monthly market-area sales were continuous.

Secondly, we were committed to an attempt to *explain* the causal effect of advertising on consumer purchases and not merely to find statistical correlations between them. Our search of the marketing literature for such an explanation was futile; it only revealed correlations and regressions between advertising and sales. These usually showed that increases (or decreases) in the former were associated with increases (or decreases) in the latter. From such associations it was almost universally inferred, and incorrectly, that increases in advertising yield increases in sales almost without limit. We believed that what these analyses really showed was that most companies forecast next year's sales quite accurately and then set their advertising budgets as a fixed percentage of predicted sales. In other words, forecasts of increased sales produce increased advertising.

Our commitment to experimentation derived from a determination to find a causal connection between advertising and sales, not merely an association between them, and to develop an ability to manipulate advertising so as to produce desired effects on sales that could be observed.

Since we knew of no tested theory, we fabricated our own. Our hunch was that advertising could be considered to be a stimulus and sales a response to it. Much is known about the general nature of stimulus-response functions. They usually take the

EXHIBIT 1
A typical stimulus-response function

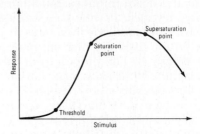

form shown in Exhibit 1. Therefore, we formulated the following hypotheses:

A small amount of advertising has virtually no effect on sales but as the amount is increased it pushes the response through a *threshold* after which it produces an increasing effect. This effect decreases and flattens out once the respondents are *saturated;* that is, they either turn off further exposure to the stimulus or are consuming up to their capabilities or capacities. Response to further increases in advertising remains relatively unchanged until the respondents reach *supersaturation,* a point beyond which they respond negatively.

In an earlier study conducted for the Lamp Division of the General Electric Company[4] we had found such a relationship between frequency of sales calls (stimulus) and purchases (response). In the sales-call context the idea of supersaturation is not as shocking as it is in advertising. Clearly, there is an amount of a salesman's presence that is intolerable to a buyer. Beyond this one would expect the buyer to try to get rid of the salesman by discontinuing his purchases. Similarly, we felt reasonably sure that, for example, if all television advertising were for only one product, the public would react negatively.

The First Experiment

A minimal experiment would have involved applying the same percentage change in

[4]See Waid, Clark, and Ackoff [7].

advertising expenditure to each of the fifteen market areas allotted to us and comparing the results obtained from them with those obtained from an equal number of control areas. But we needed only nine areas to obtain the level of accuracy set as our target: to be able to detect a 2 percent difference in sales 95 percent of the time. The introduction of two different treatments, one involving an increase and the other a decrease in advertising expenditures, required eighteen test areas, three more than were available to us. However, even an experiment with two different treatments would yield only three points: the average effect of each treatment and that of the control group. The difficulty this presented derived from the fact that every configuration of three points except one, V-shaped, could be fitted to the relationship (Exhibit 1) that we wanted to test. Therefore, there was a very low probability that even a three-level experiment would disprove our hypothetical relationship; hence, it was a very poor test of the validity of this relationship.

For these reasons we decided to ask for three different treatments and a control group even though this would require twenty-seven markets plus nine under control. Four experimental points could disprove our theory as easily as it could confirm it and, therefore, would have provided a reasonable test of it.

We had nothing to go on but our intuition in selecting the experimental treatment levels: a 50 percent reduction, and 50 and 100 percent increases in budgeted levels of advertising. We wanted to make changes large enough to produce observable effects on sales, assuming such changes had any such effect, and large enough so that if there were no observable effects this fact could not be dismissed because the changes were believed to be too small. Two increases rather than decreases were selected to make the experiment more palatable to the Marketing Department.

When this four-level design was presented it was rejected because it involved the use of too many market areas. However, Mr. Busch agreed to our use of eighteen rather than fifteen areas provided that we change the reduction in advertising we had proposed from 50 to 25 percent. He felt that a 50 percent reduction might irreparably damage the areas so treated. This left us with a three-level experiment: −25%, 0%, and +50% changes from budget.

Although we were not completely happy with this outcome because it did not provide an adequate test of our theory, we were pleased that we had the opportunity to conduct even a limited experiment. We were reasonably sure that if it produced interesting results, restrictions on future experiments would be lifted.

A 3 × 3 × 3 factorially designed experiment was prepared in which two other important marketing variables were explicitly controlled: *the amount spent on sales effort* (salesmen) and *the amount spent on point-of-sales displays and signs*. We also would have liked to control pricing but this was precluded. This design is illustrated in Exhibit 2.

Market areas were selected randomly from the "permissible list" and randomly assigned to the twenty-seven treatments. Use

EXHIBIT 2

The 3 × 3 × 3 experiment

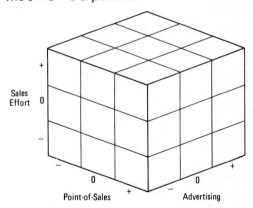

of the "permissible list" could obviously bias our results but again our hope was that the results would justify further experimentation and that it would not be so restricted.

The experiment was carried out over the calendar year 1962, thereby yielding twelve observations of each market area. We were able to reach a conclusion at the end of six months, but the experiment was continued to build up confidence in the results. The results, however, attracted little confidence; they were too much at variance with expectations within the company and its advertising agency. The three points shown in Exhibit 3 fell into the only configuration, V-shaped, that was inconsistent with our theory because the relationship being tested (Exhibit 1) had no V in it. In addition, we found no significant interaction between advertising, sales effort, and point-of-sales expenditures, a surprising but not an unacceptable result, and the results indicated that current levels of sales effort and point-of-sales expenditures were close to optimal. This last result was readily accepted.

No one found much difficulty in believing that a 50 percent increase in advertising produced a 7 percent increase in sales, but only Mr. Busch and Mr. Vogel were willing to consider seriously the possibility that a 25 percent reduction of advertising could

produce a 14 percent increase in sales. Even they were not ready to act on this finding but they did want to analyze the situation further. Therefore, they asked us to design another experiment that would check these results and that would be more convincing to others.

We had to revise our theory before designing the next experiment. On the surface it appeared necessary to reject the theory but we had grown very fond of it. Therefore, we sought a modification of the theory that would make it consistent with the experimental results.

It occurred to us that there might be two or more distinct consuming populations in each market area with a response curve like the one we had assumed but that these might be separated along the horizontal scale (see Exhibit 4). The aggregated response curve would then have a V in it. When this possibility was presented to Mr. Vogel, he thought it quite reasonable and suggested that the markets might be segmented into three parts: heavy, moderate, and light beer drinkers. This made sense to us. One would expect heavy users of a product to be more sensitive to its advertising than moderate users, and moderate users more sensitive than light users. We looked for some way of testing this assumption and we found one.

It would have been very time-consuming and costly to determine how many beer drinkers of each type there were in each

EXHIBIT 3

Results of first experiment (1962)

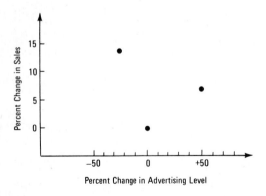

EXHIBIT 4

Response function of segmented population

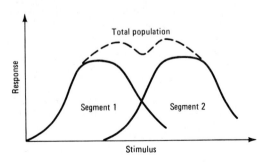

market area. We had neither the time nor the money required to do so. But we did know from previous studies that beer consumption correlated positively with discretionary income within the range of such income in which most beer drinkers fall. Therefore, we determined the average discretionary income in each market area that had been used in the previous experiment and compared it with the average deviations from forecasted sales in each area. There was a positive correlation between these deviations and average discretionary income, thereby lending some credence to the user-level segmentation assumption.

We revised our theory to incorporate three response functions for each market area. This meant that the aggregated response functions for markets as a whole could differ significantly because of different proportions of heavy, moderate, and light beer drinkers.

The Second Experiment

In order to test the revised theory we decided that we needed seven different advertising treatments. We wanted to repeat the earlier experiment and add treatments further out on both ends of the scale. Seven treatments were selected: −100% (no advertising), −50%, −25%, 0%, +50%, +100%, and +200%. Because of improvements in our forecasting methods only six areas were required for each treatment. This design was accepted with only slight modification: the number of test areas in the two extreme treatments was reduced.

The experiment was conducted over twelve months in 1963 and 1964. Again data were collected monthly. The results obtained confirmed the findings of the first experiment. When plotted, the seven points fell on a curve such as is shown in Exhibit 5. There were two deviations from our expectations. First, only two, not three, peaks appeared. But this was not serious because the points out on the right were so far apart that there could well be a third hump con-

EXHIBIT 5

Results of second advertising-level experiment (1963)

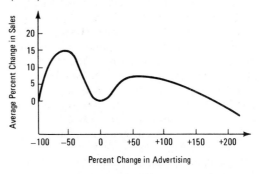

cealed by the interpolation between the points. It was harder to explain the finding that the areas in which all advertising had been eliminated (−100%) survived the year with no significant difference in performance from the control areas (0%). Hardly anyone believed this result. Those who did attributed it to the long history, strength, and exposure of Budweiser in the marketplace. We suggested further tests of the effect of complete elimination of advertising.

Although a willingness to act on our findings had not yet developed, there was growing agreement on the desirability of continuing the research. The 1963–64 experiment was continued with particular attention given to the areas from which all advertising had been removed. The objective was to determine how long it would take before any deterioration of sales could be detected, at what rate it would take place, and how easily lost sales could subsequently be recaptured. We also initiated some research into the relative effectiveness of different media. While this research was going on, the first opportunity to apply the results already obtained presented itself.

Application of Results

In mid-1964 Mr. Busch wanted to make more cash available to meet some commitments he had made. He asked Mr. Vogel and us if this could be done. We jointly proposed that advertising be reduced by 15 percent in twenty-five of the smallest markets. The smallest markets were chosen in order to minimize any possible long-run harmful effects. The proposed change was capable of yielding more than the amount Mr. Busch asked for. We also pointed out that we could maintain very close watch over the areas affected and report immediately on any reduction of sales that might occur in them. We predicted, however, that the proposed decrease in advertising would produce about a 5 percent increase in sales. Mr. Busch decided to go ahead.

The predicted results were obtained by the end of the year. As a consequence, the number of reduction areas was increased to fifty and the amount of the reductions was increased to 25 percent. From then on more and more areas were similarly treated and the reductions were gradually increased until the advertising expenditure per barrel was $0.80 in contrast to $1.89 which it had been when the research was initiated. During this period (1962–68) sales of Budweiser increased from approximately 7.5 million to 14.5 million barrels and its market share increased from 8.14 to 12.94 percent.

TIMING OF ADVERTISING

Returning to the experiment involving complete deprivation of advertising, the areas thus deprived showed no response until more than a year and a half later. From then on a small decline was noted each month. This was allowed to continue only long enough to provide good estimates of the deterioration rate. Moves to correct these markets were then made. They were restored to their normal growth rate in about six months with only their normal amount of advertising.

These results led to a new line of speculation. Would it not be possible to *pulse*

EXHIBIT 6

Pulsing patterns

	I	II	III	IV
Spring	X	X	O	X
Summer	X	O	X	X
Autumn	X	X	O	O
Winter	X	O	X	O

advertising, using an on-and-off pattern, and obtain the same effectiveness that is obtained by continuous advertising? We came to think of advertising as a motion picture which, of course, is really a sequence of motionless pictures. If sixteen still photographs are taken and projected per second, the appearance of motion is created because images are retained in the retina between exposures. We felt the same should be true of advertising.

Two types of pulsing were considered. In one, advertising expenditures in all media are on or off together. In the other, only one medium is used at any time but the media are alternated. We designed an experiment to test the first of these types of pulse. It involved four treatments: one control (I) and three pulsing patterns (II, III, and IV) shown in Exhibit 6. In addition, the level of expenditure in each was varied as is shown in Exhibit 7. The market areas used in this experiment were classified by median income and growth rates.

One of the pulsing patterns was found to be significantly better than the others and slightly better than normal advertising when accompanied by a high level of expenditure. Another pattern was found to be

EXHIBIT 7

Percent of local budget spent by pulsing pattern and advertising level

ADVERTISING LEVEL	PULSING PATTERN			
	I	II	III	IV
High	150%	100%	100%	100%
Low	100%	50%	50%	50%

best when accompanied by a low level of expenditure. In addition, the pulsing patterns were found to interact significantly with median income level and the growth rate of the market area. Subsequent experimentation revealed no significant difference between time-pulsing and media-pulsing. Media-pulsing, however, was easier to administer.

These results were cautiously incorporated into small reductions of advertising expenditures that were made in series. It was only after one change was demonstrated to have the predicted effect that the next change was made. Regular monthly checks on the performance of each market area were initiated and continue to this day.

MEDIA SELECTION

In the early experiments on advertising expenditures, the budgets for experimental areas were set by the research team but the way in which additional moneys were allocated or reductions were made was left entirely in the hands of the advertising agency. Five media were involved: billboards, magazines, newspapers, radio, and television. We examined the relationship between the actual changes in media allocations and changes in sales. This preliminary analysis indicated no significant difference in effectiveness between magazines, newspapers, and radio, but it suggested that television was slightly superior and that billboards were substantially inferior.

An experiment was designed to test these tentative findings (see Exhibit 8).

EXHIBIT 8

Media experiment (1967–68): number and treatment of market areas

	LOCAL TV	BILL-BOARD	RADIO	NEWS-PAPER
No National TV	5	5	5	5
National TV	5	5	5	5

Magazines were not included in this experiment because they could not be controlled within small areas. A distinction was made between *local* and *national* television. In each of twenty areas only one medium was used; in another twenty each medium was combined with national television. The results showed that national television was slightly superior to any local medium. Local television (with or without national television) and radio were more effective than newspapers or billboards. Billboards were the least effective.

To explain the poor showing of billboards, a number of observations were made to determine how much information could be conveyed by a billboard. We found that little more than the product name and a slogan could be communicated. This meant that billboards can do little more than remind one of the existence of an already familiar product; they cannot convey much, if any, new information about it. A second set of observations showed that the typical urban dweller in the United States saw but did not necessarily notice the word "Budweiser" on signs, displays, or beer containers almost ten times per day. He hardly needed additional reminding of its existence. On the basis of these findings virtually all billboard advertising was discontinued. The company had been spending about 20 percent of its advertising budget through this medium.

CONCLUSION

To summarize the results obtained by 1968, we note that volume had approximately doubled, market share had increased from 8.14 to 12.94 percent, and advertising expenditures were reduced from \$1.89 to \$0.80 per barrel, a 58 percent reduction. It would be foolish, of course, to claim that this improvement in performance was due entirely to changes in advertising. Other types of changes, some based on research and some not, were also made during this period. But one thing is clear: the changes induced by the research described here did not hurt Anheuser-Busch.

The strength of the opposition to the results of our early experiments is less surprising in retrospect than it was at the time. These results contradicted the strong beliefs of people who had good reason to believe they understood advertising and who had the success of the products involved to prove it. Furthermore, these people did not understand the logic of experimental design and the statistical analysis of the data yielded by experiments. They were convinced that sales were affected by a large number of completely interacting and inherently qualitative variables and, therefore, that the effect of any one of these on sales could not be isolated or measured.

The greatest resistance came from those managers who had direct responsibility for the decisions to which the research was addressed and from the advertising agency people who were attached to the account. It was clear that the agency people felt that our research cast doubt on their competence and creativity. It also threatened the agency's income.

For these reasons it became apparent to us that three things had to be done if we were to gain acceptance, let alone support, of our efforts. First, we would have to bring those who had to deal with the research results to an understanding of the logic of experimental design and statistical analysis. Second, we would have to involve them actively in the design of the experiments and in the analysis and interpretation of their results. Finally, we would have to try to change the method of compensating the advertising agency so that its fee was not decreased as the efficiency of advertising was increased.

The process of education and involvement took time. It was carried out both informally and formally in sessions conducted specifically for this purpose. Managers at the highest levels were generally the first to approve of experimentation. They sometimes became impatient with their subordinates and tried to force early research results on them. Such pressure slowed acceptance at the lower levels. But in general, when top managers felt compelled to act, as Mr. Busch did on the first reduction of advertising expenditures, they worked hard to make the implementation itself experimental and to carry it out as gradually and nondisruptively as possible. In all, it took about three years (1962–65) for the educational efforts to begin to pay off.

These efforts were facilitated by two other important changes. First, we proposed that the basis for the agency's compensation be changed so that it would benefit financially when the company did. As long as the agency was paid a percentage of A-B's expenditures on advertising, it naturally resisted research that had the potential of reducing its earnings. Therefore, we suggested a scheme by which the agency's fee was increased if either sales increased with no increase in advertising or advertising expenditures decreased with no decrease in sales. The agency was persuaded to try this scheme for a year with assurances that it would receive no less in fees during the trial year than it had in the previous year. In the trial year advertising expenditures decreased but since sales increased the agency's compensation also increased. The scheme was continued for another year with repetition of this outcome and then became permanent. Because of it the agency became increasingly interested in research, strengthened its research department, and encouraged it to collaborate with us. This was done to our mutual benefit. By 1968 the difficulties with agency acceptance of research results were largely a thing of the past. The agency has since initiated such a compensation scheme with other clients.

Acceptance of research as an instrument of management was greatly facilitated by the establishment of two very competent in-house groups, one in marketing and the other in corporate planning. Leon Pritzker, who was the initial director of the group in marketing, had a major role in the later phases of the research reported here. August A. Busch, III, then executive vice president but now president, observed: "The University and company units work together very closely. . . ."[5] E. H. Vogel, Jr., continued: "Today we hardly make any decision of any consequence that does not involve our researchers in one way or another. This blending of research and management did not occur overnight. It developed slowly under careful guidance."[6]

Research results were built up slowly but accumulatively. The results of each piece of research were integrated with previous results where they were consistent. Where they were not, a more general explanation was sought, one that made integration possible, and then the integrating principle was thoroughly tested. No result was ever taken to be true for all time. As Mr. Vogel observed:

We did not try to impose [research-based] recommendations as though we had suddenly gained possession of ultimate truth. We usually initiated the application of recommendations on a small scale with close controls imposed on them. As confidence in results developed, we extended applications.

No matter how generally management accepted a research result it was never applied without a well-designed control system to tell us whether the recommendations worked as expected. We have learned as much from the feed-back such control provided as we have from the research that produced the initial recommendations.

[5]See Busch [2].
[6]See Vogel [6], p. 24.

More important, perhaps, is that we now design controls for evaluating decisions which management reaches without the benefit of research. This enables us to learn more rapidly and accurately from experience, and it has indoctrinated management with an experimental approach to decision making.[7]

REFERENCES

1. Ackoff, R. L., and F. E. Emery. *On Purposeful Systems* (Chicago: Aldine-Atherton, 1972), Chapter 8.

2. Busch, A. A., III. "The Essentials of Corporate Growth." Address given to Charles Coolige Parlin Marketing Award Banquet, May 9, 1973.

3. "Computers Can't Solve Everything," *Fortune* (October 1969), p. 126 ff.

4. Curtis, K. P. *The Modelling of Consumer Purchase Behavior*, unpublished Ph.D. dissertation (University of Pennsylvania, 1969).

5. Rao, A. G. *Quantitative Theories in Advertising* (New York: John Wiley & Sons, 1970).

6. Vogel, E. H., Jr. "Creative Marketing and Management Science," *Management Decision* (Spring 1969), pp. 21-25.

7. Waid, C., D. F. Clark, and R. L. Ackoff. "Allocation of Sales Effort in the Lamp Division of the General Electric Company," *Operations Research*, 4 (1956), pp. 629-47.

8. "Wharton Analyzes the Beer Drinker," *Business Week* (March 24, 1973), p. 44.

9. "While Big Brewers Quaff, the Little Ones Thirst," *Fortune* (November 1972), p. 130 ff.

[7]See Vogel [6], pp. 24-25.

33 12 Basic Promotion Techniques: Their Advantages—and Pitfalls

William A. Robinson

It's been said that all the world's great promotion ideas can be traced to 12 basic and fairly simple techniques. And it's from these 12 that we fashion the programs that make or break the P&Ls that are the sole measure of the success of our thinking.

The 12 techniques are:

1. Sampling.
2. Coupons.
3. Trade coupons.
4. Trade allowances.
5. Price-offs.
6. In, on, or near-packs.
7. Free-in-the-mail premiums.
8. Self-liquidating premiums.
9. Contests and sweepstakes.
10. Refund offers.
11. Bonus packs.
12. Stamp and continuity plans.

Those are the building blocks of the craft. That's *all* you have to work with. But before you despair of coming up with something new for the coming quarter, consider the fact that these 12 can be combined 845,059,745 different ways. And that doesn't begin to count the varieties of headlines, copy, and layouts that can apply to each of these combinations.

If sometimes the choices seem tough, you now know why. But the job of selecting, combining, and timing may not be so difficult if we can agree on standards that will help us make the decisions.

Every move we can make in promotion has reasonably well defined strengths and weaknesses. In recent years, marketers have developed their ability to put strengths together and compensate for weaknesses in what we might call hybred promotions. These combinations of techniques often give us better results than any one of the techniques might give us alone.

For example, we know that a sweep-

Reprinted with permission of the publisher, *Advertising Age* (January 10, 1977).

stakes can build ad readership. So, if we're planning a couponing program, we're likely to get a higher rate of redemption and increased trial of our product if we include the coupon offer in an ad that also offers the opportunity to enter a sweeps. That's synergism, I believe.

We also know that retailers are more likely to buy more of your product, build their inventories, and give you off-shelf displays when you're couponing. Add a trade contest to your couponing program and you'll probably build sales volume still further.

The trick, of course, is to get all the elements to work together. And that calls for the same kind of creative excellence that goes into putting any major advertising program together; and *that* calls for a thorough understanding of the creative marketing techniques we have at our disposal.

SAMPLING

This is the one you've got to consider when you want to reach new users—either at the introduction of a new product or product improvement *or* in opening new markets (geographic or demographic) for an established product.

Generally, sampling is more effective than other techniques when your product's feature or benefits (for example, flavor or aroma) can't be fully conveyed in advertising.

Obviously, these are the reasons why cigaret people use sampling. New packs need to be tested, and the best way to do that is to get a sample pack in a potential customer's hands.

The same reasons led McCormick/Schilling to distribute spaghetti sauce and seasoned salt samples, along with a batch of 7¢ (the magic number) coupons, via full-color newspaper inserts in Chicago and several West Coast cities.

Nestle's took a somewhat different sampling-via-couponing route in introducing its new Cookie Mix line. Instead of putting the samples directly into the consumers' hands, they ran a coupon good for a free package "at your store . . . no strings."

Limitations of sampling: It's expensive. It can lack precision. It's said to be less efficient than couponing in converting triers to regular users.

COUPONING

The popularity of couponing sometimes makes the technique look like the magic elixir for dealing with all marketing ills. You can use it to produce trial, to convert triers to regular users, to reach large numbers of prospects (more economically than sampling), to load regular users or trade them up to larger sizes, to increase usage by present users, to hold current users against competitive activity, to increase trade buy-ins, etc.

Limitations of couponing: The method of distribution limits the kind of response you get. For example, in-pack coupons get you few new triers even when heavily advertised. (Their purpose, of course, is to reward and hold present users.)

Coupons work best with older, better educated, urban, and married consumers and less well with young, single, and/or less educated (less affluent?) consumers. The great number of variables—face value, timing, brand share, distributions, creative, etc.—makes results and the advertiser's financial jeopardy hard to predict.

The flood of couponing continues to grow—up 8% in 74; up almost 20% in 75. And it's still rising. The variety of coupons—direct mail, in-ad, hard goods as well as foods and perishables—continues to swell. And the creative combinations swell with the attention paid to the category: coupons with refund offers, coupons with premiums, coupons with premiums and continuity programs. Which combination best suits your next objective?

TRADE COUPONS

Trade coupons are the ones the stores run in their own ads. You'll want to consider the technique when your goal is trial on a geographic basis, or when you want to gain trade cooperation in getting off-shelf displays and price features.

Other uses for trade coupons are to help build distribution, to reduce trade inventories on a market-by-market basis and to increase the percentage of coupon redemptions. From the viewpoints of some advertisers, trade couponing has another somewhat subtle advantage in that couponing by a "third party" doesn't seem to directly affect brand image (the store gives the deal, not the brand).

Limitations of trade coupons: You've got to expect a lot of misredemption (primarily by the trade), and it's hard to really estimate what you're going to spend. To avoid the budgeting problem, several companies—Colgate-Palmolive among them—have a pre-redeemed coupon allowance. They agree in advance with the retailer on the number of coupons they will pay for when the retailer runs the coupons. Another economy in this arrangement is that coupons don't have to go through a clearing house.

TRADE ALLOWANCES

You don't read much about these in *Advertising Age*. But trade allowances are essential when you're thinking about gaining distribution, getting off-shelf display, encouraging price features and building up inventories. It's almost impossible to get a new product into distribution without a special introductory allowance.

Limitations of trade allowances: They're abused. The trade frequently doesn't want to hear about performance standards. And there's a lot of laxness about passing on savings to consumers. Also, there's a lack of direct consumer involvement—unless you accept the fact that the most desirable involvement centers around displays and advertising features. Trade allowances truly fit the vicious circle category: You'd like to get along without them, but you can't.

PRICE-OFFS

Here's another less-than-sparkling category that doesn't always grab the creative limelight. But think about price-offs we must if we propose to reward and load present users, head off competition by taking consumers out of the market, establish purchase patterns after initial trial, enforce pass-through of savings to the consumer, create on-shelf attention (with a package flag), get off-shelf display (when combined with trade allowances), accelerate upward sales trends and, finally, merely give the sales force some extra ammunition to load the trade.

Limitations of price-offs: Don't expect miracles. Price-offs can give sales a bump, but can't reverse a downward sales trend. They can't produce loyal new users. (Price conscious buyers go right back to private labels when price-offs are not available.)

Price-offs produce only a temporary increase in market share—and repeated use degrades the perceived value of the product while giving progressively smaller "bumps" in market share.

What else? To have any real effect, prices must be cut 15% to 20%—and the smaller the brand's share, the larger the price break's got to be. And, if it's trial you're after, don't opt for price-offs; they give you less trial than on-pack premiums, couponing, or sampling.

IN, ON, AND NEAR-PACKS

Reusable containers fall in this category. Like the glasses the fast-food chains have been featuring. Notable users of on-packs are the cigaret companies, *e.g.*, Virginia Slims' "Book of Days" and Winston's free beer stein holding five packs. The most consistent users of in-packs are the ready-to-eat cereal manufacturers.

What's good about the category? Well, pack-premiums can help increase product usage if the premium is directly related to the way the product is used (coffee cups for coffee, lighters for cigarets, etc.). On-packs that don't fit easily on the shelf can be used to force off-shelf display—but it's a dangerous way to go for weak brands that just might get thrown off the shelf and out of the store.

Pack premiums do give consumers greater perceived value than you can give them for the same amount spent for price-offs or coupons. Properly used, the technique can produce premiums that extend the advertising and the image of the brand to point of sale.

Limitations of pack premiums: Watch out. A bad one can actually reduce sales, and the trade resists premiums that compete with products they can sell for a profit. (Give some thought to custom pack-ons if your budget can take it.) Also: Pilferage can be a problem, but it's not as bad a problem as it's painted.

FREE-IN-THE-MAIL PREMIUMS

Steel yourself to the fact that sales increases are seldom measurable—and offers are seldom picked up by more than 1% of the media circulation. Also, offers that require multiple proofs of purchase will not attract new users . . . or even triers.

Prestone's radiator cap offer strikes me as the perfect reward for using the product and a great way to get the Prestone brand name on the radiator. 9-Lives' T-shirt and calendar offers worry not at all about our advice on multiple proofs. If you want the calendar for free, you cough up 20 labels, and if it's the T-shirt you crave, the ante goes up to 30. Maybe 9-Lives is relying on Morris-mania to upset the rules. More likely, they want to guard against low brand loyalty—cat food users who tend to switch brands to keep the menu "fresh" for the legendary "finicky" cat.

SELF-LIQUIDATING PREMIUMS

Once used when you couldn't think of anything else to do, liquidators today seem better understood and marketers seem to be using the techniques more sensibly.

Self-liquidating premiums can extend brand image, reinforce advertising and increase ad readership by as much as 50%. They also give you something to talk about to the trade. And the self-liquidator can serve as a not-too-disguised dealer loader.

Limitations of self-liquidators: Face it.

They're no good for building trial. Less than 10% of households have ever sent for a premium. And redemption is less than 1% of circulation.

Conventional wisdom used to keep the price of self-liquidators under a buck. Then they began creeping up. Kool showed us you could move a whopping number of sailboats—20,000, I believe—for close to $100. Currently, the Kool Catamaran is being offered at an eye-popping $699. The name of the game, of course, is image and interest; the number of items moved is only a secondary measure of success.

CONTESTS AND SWEEPSTAKES

If you're looking for something that will get your advertising read, extend and reinforce your product's image (should it be so lucky as to have one), provide a reason (when combined with others) for getting off the shelf and on-the-floor display space, if you want a change of pace in your advertising, plus a chance to lure new triers through a unique method of entering a contest or sweeps, and if you can afford to give it the kind of support it deserves, then this technique is for you.

Limitations of contests or sweepstakes: Remember these things when you budget your precious dollars. Contests and sweeps won't produce mass trial (barely 20% of the population has ever sent in an entry), over 75% of entries are accompanied by facsimilies—not proofs-of-purchase, and you'll always be entertaining a lot of professional entrants with your program.

Some imaginative uses of sweeps in the past year: Muriel cigars' "Vote for Miss Muriel"—a sexy and good-natured extension of their advertising; Chuck Wagon dog food's "Win your dog's weight in gold"; Coke's "Deni-machine"; and Newport's "Win Box Seats Every Week for a Year"—a local program that we uncovered in the *New York Times Magazine*. The latter, apparently an exercise in market segmentation, offers five winners the chance "to see a different show or event every week for 52 weeks."

REFUND OFFERS

This is one of the basics—like trade allowances and price-offs. Refunds create excitement at fairly modest cost. They provide the sales force with something to talk about and give you a chance to flag your package. And the ploy is a good one for reinforcing brand loyalty—especially when multiple purchase is required.

Limitations of refunds: Don't look for a lot of consumer interest. Refunds don't generate trial; they're slow . . . and results are hard to measure. The trade would usually rather see store coupons.

In states where it's legal, refund offers have recently popped up on spirits and wines. In the Lauder's Scotch offer, the $2 refund is split: $1 goes to MDA (Muscular Dystrophy Association) and $1 to the buyer. Skippy dog food takes a common route for pet food marketers, offering 10¢ per label, with "no limit on the amount of money you can get." We like the direct headline: "You send us labels, we'll send you cash."

The introduction of the $2 bill inspired some refund offers during 76. General Foods offered the $2 bill—for Sanka labels—as if it were a free-in-the-mail premium; Lysol—either deliberately or thoughtlessly—glossed right over the opportunity to make anything out of a similar offer.

BONUS PACKS

A favorite of the vitamin people, bonus packs are useful in converting triers to users. It's a good technique for making something happen at the shelf. Offered on the right display (sometimes a pre-pack), it can get you off the shelf. All this and it gives you an advertisable event, too.

Limitations of bonus packs: They don't get trial, do nothing for brand image, and they can be abused by the trade. Branded packs, for example, can be ripped apart for separate sale.

STAMP PLANS, CONTINUITY PREMIUMS

These come in a variety of shapes and sizes. Campbell has had a successful "Labels for Education" program going for some time; Post has followed up with a similar "Fun 'n Fitness" equipment program for schools; Domino sugar, I believe, has always had a teaspoon offer going; some companies have subscribed to co-op (bonus gift) stamp programs originated and administrated by outside promotion firms; and Raleigh, Bel Air, and Alpine are probably the last cigaret brands basing their marketing on on-pack coupons.

This is a strategy that can be used to get steady users and create differences in parity products. Perhaps it can best be thought of as a small part of a larger program or a low-cost substitute for higher-budget brand-image building.

Limitations of stamp plans and continuity premiums: They appeal to small segments of buyers; they don't interest the retailer or do anything to boost sales to the trade; and they won't get you off-shelf display (although one of the co-op stamp plans did try a joint point of sale effort). If you overemphasize them in your programming, you find you're advertising premiums in place of your brand's features and image.

34 The New Supersalesmen: Wired for Success

Supersalespeople: no longer are they glad-hand order takers. Instead they are vital elements of a carefully engineered selling system that takes a lot of money and time to develop.

If you want to rile Herbert D. Eagle, just slide a copy of *Webster's New Collegiate Dictionary* in front of him. "Have you ever read the definition of 'sell'?" fumes Eagle, vice president of marketing for Transamerica Corp. "Things like 'betray' and 'cheat' are capitalized, and there are phrases such as 'to deliver up or give up in violation of duty, trust, or loyalty.' I've been carrying on a running battle with G. & C. Merriam Co. to change that definition."

If anyone can sell Merriam on a new definition, it is 54-year-old Herb Eagle. As marketing vice president for giant, fast-growing Transamerica Corp. ($1.6 billion in sales last year), Eagle coordinates the marketing and sales strategies for 42 companies that field more than 6,000 internal salesmen and handle everything from insurance and financial services to car rentals. Eagle also doubles as president of Sales & Marketing Executives International, a professional society of 25,000 members scattered through 49 countries. As the official pick of his peers and thus the closest thing to industry's top salesman, Eagle is a drumbeater in the cause of supersalesmanship and the enormous change that is coming over that fine, old American institution: personal selling.

"A few years back," says Eagle, "it was usually the salesman out there alone, pitting his wits against the resistance of a single corporate purchasing agent. Now, more and more companies are selling on many different levels, interlocking their research, engineering, marketing, and upper management with those of their customers. This way, today's salesman becomes a kind of committee chairman within his company. Some manufacturers call them 'account managers.' Either way, his job is to exploit the resources of his company in serving the customer."

As industries consolidate and larger corporations continue to swallow up the small fry, a growing number of companies are also "preselling" their products through massive promotion, advertising, and improved communications between buyer and seller. The result is that the average salesman's prime responsibility is no longer selling, so much as clinching a sale that has already been set in motion even before he makes his first spiel.

MORE SALES PRODUCTIVITY

At the consumer level, this shows up in the cutback of retail sales help and the huge expansion of self-service merchandising. At the industry level, it shows up in a whole new function for the industrial salesman. No longer is he simply a pitchman or prescriber of his company's products. Now he must go beyond that and become a diagnostician.

"If a supplier's job is to service the customer, then the role of the salesman becomes one of problem-identifier first, problem-solver second, and prescriber third," says Charles S. Goodman, professor of marketing at the University of Pennsylvania's Wharton School. "I don't say this is common today. But as the economy becomes more consumer-oriented"—and thus open to greater challenge on product performance—"it's got to go that way."

An even greater goad is today's spiraling cost of selling, which demands that industry get far more out of its sales dollar. Rex Chainbelt, Inc., for instance, spends $5,000 to $20,000 to train a salesman and $30,000 to $35,000 a year to keep him on the road. That averages out to $52.80 per sales call, double the figure of 10 years ago. What is more, as product lines proliferate and product technology gets more complex, manufacturers and wholesalers have gradually boosted their number of internal salesmen to more than 1 million. And some experts claim that the demand for salesmen will grow by another 250,000 jobs a year over the next few years, not including replacements. "Obviously," as Transamerica's Eagle notes, "something has to give."

To cut costs and raise sales efficiency, more and more companies are reexamining the ways that they recruit, train, pay, equip, and manage their salesmen. Many companies are reorganizing their selling structures. Some are experimenting with new compensation and incentive programs. Nearly all are moving away from the old straight commission system to salary-plus-bonus.

"This is primarily the product of looking upon salesmen as account managers," says William E. Cox, professor of marketing at Case Western Reserve University. "You begin asking him to take on a lot of additional duties other than just simply writing an order. He becomes the company's broader marketing representative."

Industry is also drawing on a whole new battery of selling tools, ranging from audio/visual cassettes and special slide projectors to remote portable terminals that can plug the salesman straight into his home-office computer. The computer itself, of course, has become one of selling's biggest tools of all. It can lay out sales territories, budget the salesman's time by customer and product, and keep track of sales costs, time use, itineraries, payables and receivables, expenses, orders, inquiries, and overall performance.

"Fifteen years ago when I first started selling," says Frederick H. Stephens, Jr., sales vice president for Gillette Co.'s Safety Razor Div., "we couldn't tell at any point how much volume we did on promotional items, for instance, compared with open stock. Now we have monthly IBM printouts that tell our salesmen how much business he's doing with promotions compared to open stock and total business, how much business is being done in his territory, and how much each customer bought of each item. We used to tell a salesman, 'You're up 4.6% this year, that's pretty good.' Now we can say, 'You're up 4.6% but down 1.6% in discount stores and up only 2.1% over your territory.' And we have the information to get him back in the ballgame."

IDENTIFYING CUSTOMER NEEDS

Unfortunately, most salesmen are still somewhere between the locker room and the playing field. "Selling is very, very inefficient compared to what it could be," says Edward J. Feeney, vice president of the Systems Performance Div. of Emery Air Freight Corp. "Most salesmen," Feeney claims, "are sitting in lobbies. They're calling on wrong accounts. They're calling on accounts that give them all the business that they can. They're calling on people they think can make the buying decision when, in fact, they do not or cannot make much of it at all. They are efficient in talking about what they do—what their company provides—but not in how it fills the customer's need, because they haven't probed to find out what those needs are."

Those needs usually go far beyond the purchase of any one supplier's equipment or services. Hugh Hoffman, chairman of Opinion Research Corp., cites the experience of one of his company's clients, a major chemical producer. "Its salesmen told us," he says, "that if they're trying to sell plastic film to a packager who has several million dollars' worth of packaging equipment designed to use some other material, they must now know how to unload the present equipment, purchase new equipment, and work out the intricacies of amortization. Without that background, they cannot persuade the customer to accept delivery of a single carload of plastic film."

This is because today's major competitor is no longer one broom salesman against another. It is alternate uses of money. "And the modern salesman," says John R. Robertson, sales manager for the Business Systems Markets Div. of Eastman Kodak Co., "must be able to convince his customer that spending money on the salesman's product is a better investment than spending it elsewhere."

Above all, the supersalesman tries to build more than the old-style buyer-seller relationship. A top marketing executive at International Business Machines Corp., which is one of the companies that has spearheaded the development of superselling, claims that today's salesman must develop a "long-range partnership" with his clients. "The installation of a data-processing system," he emphasizes, "is only the beginning, not the end, of IBM's marketing effort."

To serve their customers better, IBM salesmen not only specialize by product and market. They now specialize by function: installation, equipment protection or maintenance, and upgrading of systems. To sharpen the focus of its salesmen even more, IBM—like most consumer-goods companies—is "segmenting" or targeting its markets. "The costs of developing new accounts by the cold-call approach," says the IBM marketer, "have risen so drastically that we are moving toward far more selective prospecting"—including a special computer experiment for picking only "high-potential prospects."

Among the other special qualities that set off the supersalesman:

Universality

"Ten years ago when I hired a salesman," says James Schlinkert, Pittsburgh-area branch manager for Olivetti Corp. of America, "I was looking for someone who would make a lot of calls and, through sheer effort and exposure, be reasonably successful. Now I want someone more versed in things unrelated to our business. Today's salesman must be able to talk on any and all current subjects—from the economy to world affairs—because these often affect his business." Not too many years ago, adds the marketing vice president for a major information-systems company, "you'd hire somebody with personality that you thought would wear well, and you'd point him out the door." Now it takes more. "A top manager's time is very precious," he says, "and we have to give him a meaningful message when we meet with him."

Patience

Because product technology has become more complex and salesmen are interrelating more products and moving deeper into systems selling, the time that it takes to close a sale has stretched out. "There are no quick sales today," says Anthony E. Schiavone, an assistant development manager for Rohm & Haas Co. "It may take a year just to get to know a new customer and his problems." Philip Rosell, Western regional sales manager for Singer's Business Machines Group, claims that he was on the verge of quitting Singer two years ago after he had gone his first full year without writing an order. "You have to gear yourself psychologically for a long haul," he says.

Persistence

With growing cost-consciousness, upper management is increasingly involved in major buying decisions. So the supersalesman often tries to go beyond the first level of decision making. "This is not usually the best-paid or most creative guy around anyway," says one Boston salesman. "It's when you go beyond this level that you can sell the extras. And it's not true that the top guy nevers sees salesmen. You can often enlist the aid of your own top people and set up a meeting."

More Work, Less Play

Lavish wining and dining of buyers is out. In fact, Don H. Hartmann, president of Crutcher Resources Corp., calls this "prob-ably the biggest thrust of all—the trend away from the massive entertainment of a few years ago." One top Eastern salesman adds, of his relations with his customers: "We're no longer a bunch of drinking buddies. I never have lunch with a man I haven't met before, and I never hesitate to talk business at lunch. After all, our relationship is business and not personal."

RESTRUCTURING THE TERRITORIES

Whether he is selling insurance, computers, catalytic crackers, or wholesale cosmetics, today's supersalesman has two big things going for him: improved transportation and communications. This allows him to cover more territory faster and to draw closer to his markets. As the president of a Houston industrial-goods company describes his ideal salesman: "He starts his day flying out nonstop from North Carolina to Chicago, then gets a midafternoon plane to Los Angeles to make two or three calls, and catches a night plane to Dallas. It's a fast-moving situation today. Five years ago, because of aircraft and flight scheduling, we couldn't do this."

Yet how much territory is too much? As far back as 10 years ago, adman and marketing seer E. B. Weiss, a senior vice president at Doyle Dane Bernbach, was calling for a whole new approach to the organization of sales territories and to the basic corporate selling structure. Then, as now, the problem was to minimize unproductive calls and contacts and to get close to the prospects who had both the need and purchasing authority to buy a given product or service. "The sales organization," Weiss wrote, "must be reorganized so as to be able to open up its channels of communication to those who make buying decisions, rather than to limit itself primarily to buyers who make merely buying motions. This calls for new sales organizational blueprints."

Those changes are finally beginning to come. Today's three basic levels of selling—manufacturing, wholesaling, and consumer and industrial services—are spawning dozens of highly-specialized subcategories aimed at shortening the lines of communication between buyer and seller. IBM is even experimenting with administrative specialists who help its sales specialists handle order preparation, scheduling, collections, and other paperwork. Along the way, more and more companies are organizing against markets, rather than products. For maximum productivity, a few are even organizing against profits.

"Historically," says Gennaro A. Filice, Jr., vice president of U.S. marketing for Del Monte Corp., "most food companies have been case-volume-oriented. As long as we could push out a lot of volume, we let the profits take care of themselves. That's no longer true. As products multiply and the competition for shelf space increases, salesmen have to be far more sophisticated in their approach to product management, and the company has to learn to identify those with the most profit potential."

To help pinpoint that potential, Del Monte recently restructured its entire field sales force, expanding from nine regional divisions to 21. "As our emphasis shifted away from case sales," says Filice, "and as the chains got bigger and more dominant, it became more difficult for a salesman to write an order. This restructuring was also designed to get us as close to the customer as possible."

Under Del Monte's new system, the actual selling is handled by an "account representative." He makes the direct calls on retailers and writes up the orders. Then one level below him is the sales representative. He is the junior type who works with store managers on shelf management, restocking, display, and other merchandising chores. Sales representatives are also information-gatherers. Using a new computerized system called "Key Facts," which

the company plans to expand nationwide next spring, Del Monte's California salesmen fill out a form during each store visit, listing shelf position, pricing, advertising support, and other basic marketing data. This is fed into the computer and later compared against actual product performance to arrive at maximum profitability.

WOMEN IN THE SALES FORCE

Hunt-Wesson Foods, Gillette, Allied Chemical, and several other companies have found another productivity booster for their field organizations: part-time female workers. Gillette maintains an auxiliary force of 150 middle-aged housewives who operate one rung below the individual store salesmen. The women work 24 hours a week for $3 an hour plus expenses, and handle retail displays, distribution, and stock replenishment.

"In 1958, when I started selling," says one sales executive at Gillette, "I spent 30% of my time calling on direct customers and 70% calling on local stores to work on display and distribution, and writing up turnover orders"—orders passed on to wholesalers to replenish out-of-stock items. "Today, our salesmen spend 85% of their time on direct accounts and only about 15% of their time at local stores on display and distribution."

Along with tightening the focus of their field forces, more and more companies are also creating broader "account executives," whose job is to crack that tricky, old marketing problem: how to deal with the big chains or a large, diversified company with a variety of product needs. Some suppliers, of course, simply send a battalion of salesmen swarming into such companies at all levels. Now a growing number are creating account executives who oversee all product needs of a single customer, often at the headquarters level. This way, the big customer has one sales contact that can satisfy and interrelate all its needs.

Over the last few years, Dow Chemical Co. has created 14 corporate account managers who operate one notch above the salesman and handle all 1,200 Dow products for a given customer. "There are no firm rules about how big an account must be before a corporate account manager takes over," says M. C. Carpenter, Dow's director of marketing communications. "But they are basically potential multi-million-dollar customers."

At the same time, Dow is trying to crack another problem that comes with the bigness of a customer: the difficulty of getting a territorial fix on where a sale actually occurs. In the past, Dow credited a sale to the office in the territory where the customer was located. Thus, any sale in the Houston area was chalked up to the Houston office, even though the key initiative may have come in New York. Now each sale is credited to the office where the sale originates. "That makes the accounting more complicated and subjective," Carpenter concedes. "But it gives sales managers a better idea of what's really going on in the field. We find out where the key marketing man is."

As sales organizations grow bigger and more complex, the challenge, of course, is to avoid costly duplication of sales effort. Hewlett-Packard Co. ran into this problem. It started out with a highly centralized organization that did most of its selling through outside manufacturers' representatives. By 1963, the company's product line had become so broad and complicated that Hewlett-Packard decided to acquire most of its reps and turn them into a corporate sales staff. "We stayed with reps longer than most companies," says Robert L. Boniface, marketing vice president. "We felt that it was important to have the sales force represent the customer's viewpoint as much as Hewlett-Packard's. By acquiring them rather than

cutting them off, we kept all their experience and momentum."

As Hewlett-Packard moved into medical instruments, calculators, electronic components, and other diverse new markets, the company split its sales staff into eight organizations. "Right away, we developed overlaps," says Alfred P. Oliverio, marketing manager for the Electronic Products Group. "We didn't want two salesmen calling on one customer if the product was not really all that different."

In Hewlett-Packard's most recent shift, the old product-oriented structure gave way to a combined product/market-oriented system. In electronic products, for instance, separate sales groups now concentrate on electrical manufacturing, aerospace, communications, and transportation equipment. Within each group, Hewlett-Packard tries to build a cadre of salesmen, application engineers, and software specialists. "We probably have better than one support person for every salesman," says Oliverio.

SELLING THE "DREAM LIST"

Hans G. Moser, field director for Northwestern Mutual Life Insurance Co. and a chartered life underwriter, sold $4.5 million worth of life insurance last year. That makes him 29th out of the company's 2,900 agents. Moser's distinctive selling approach is typical of how today's supersalesman tackles his customer.

Like a consumer-goods maker who targets his market, Moser ignores "run-of-the-mill types" and zeroes in on prospects who can either afford heavy insurance now or who are obviously on the way up and will be able to in the future. Moser adopted this tactic when he broke into the insurance business in 1960. "Many of my earlier customers," he says, "are now in a position to set up trust accounts, dabble with stocks, and deal with other sophisticated methods of estate planning. And, of course, I am right in there, making a pitch for life insurance and other securities."

Moser keeps two lists of prospects: one made up of day-to-day business that he expects to close within a month, and the other composed of "dream cases"—each ranging anywhere from $100,000 to $500,000 or more of coverage—that may take three months to a year to close. His goal is to add a new dream case every month and maintain a working inventory of at least 10 or 12 such cases. This way, he closes one every four to six weeks. As part of the same goal, Moser keeps a chart of his best January, February, and so on, and uses it as a composite yearly goal.

In pitching the customer, Singer Business Machines' Philip Rosell has come up with such a winning technique for selling electronic point-of-sale systems to retailers that Singer even asked him to write it up in PERT chart fashion. Salesman Rosell's opening strategy is a letter to the prospect's top operating officer, requesting a meeting. Rosell starts at the top because of the big investment involved in buying his equipment. "We seldom get turned down," Rosell says of his request for that first big meeting. Then Rosell teams up with a local salesman and system engineer, and the three go in together and discuss what the system can do for the prospect. "We don't try to sell him any hardware," Rosell says. "That's what he has a purchasing agent for."

THE LESSONS TAUGHT BY FAILURE

If the first meeting is encouraging, Rosell follows it up with store surveys and endless conferences and demonstrations for the store's credit, merchandising, data processing, and financial executives. "We infiltrate the whole company," says Rosell. "In every case where we've made a major sale, the company has felt we were part of its team."

Rosell recalls only two occasions when he did not follow his usual selling approach. This was at the insistence of the customer, who wanted a consultant to act as go-between. Both times the sale was lost.

What happens when you do blow the big sale? H. Glen Haney, a marketing director for the Univac Div. of Sperry Rand Corp., makes it a point to go back and find out why. "We lost a $4.5 million sale to a large state agency about a year ago," Haney says. "In a four-hour debriefing with the agency head, the state budget bureau people, and all other principals that were involved in the purchase, we found out that the loss of the sale really had nothing to do with the quality of our marketing effort. We lost because we had not clearly enough defined the conversion effort that the customer faced. Though our cost-performance was better than the competition, the agency decided to stay with its current vendor for that reason." Yet the lost sale was not a total loss. "As a result of that session," says Haney, "we have developed a series of conversion tools for our salesmen, aimed at solving that problem."

Owens-Corning Fiberglas Corp. took the same approach when a big customer, a thermoplastic compounder in Detroit, considered switching to an Owens-Corning competitor, which had cut its prices 1½¢ per lb. The competitor had a plant near the compounder, and the compounder decided to pick up its materials there, saving on freight. "It was a legitimate saving," says James MacLean, national sales manager for Owens-Corning's Textile & Industrial Group. "So we put our heads together." The local salesman, along with the group's marketing and packaging experts, finally developed a special package for shipping the material that the compounder could then use to ship his finished product. Savings: 2¢ per lb. for the customer and one industrial account for Owens-Corning.

Sam Jackson, an assistant sales manager

for U.S. Steel Corp. in Philadelphia, calls it the difference between moving a product for its own sake and fitting the same product to a customer's system. One of Jackson's customers was bemoaning a 10% hike in the cost of castings. "I suggested that the part could be converted from a casting to welded steel," says Jackson, "and got together with our metallurgical and research people to test the conversion." The customer finally accepted it, saving the 10% boost in cost that he would have paid had he continued to cast the part.

"What makes Jackson stand out is that he knows the different types of metals, the industry that he is selling to, and how to cut costs," says Irwin Rashkover, director of procurement for Gindy Mfg. Corp., a Budd Co. subsidiary. "Jackson knows how to help us save money by working out different tolerances for the steel we buy— for instance, by going to the high side of sheet tolerances. The supersalesman knows this. The ordinary steel salesman doesn't."

DON'T TAKE "NO" FOR AN ANSWER

Robert Hawkins, who sells radio communications systems for Motorola, Inc., has the simplest—and oldest—selling technique of all: He refuses to take "no" for an answer. When Hawkins was pitching the field service organization of a national equipment supply house, he insisted that Motorola's one-way paging system could improve service and cut manpower needs. When a purchasing agent shrugged him off, Hawkins went above him to a vice president and received grudging permission for a one-year study of the company's service coverage and performance in 20 cities. Yet when he completed the study, which showed the need for a paging system, Hawkins still did not receive an order. So he offered to follow that up with an intensive three-month test of the paging system in a single city.

"For the entire three months," says Hawkins, "a day never went by when I didn't spend some time with the prospect." Hawkins even helped the dispatcher to design more efficient routes, while soothing the ruffled nerves of its servicemen. "They were afraid of the dispatcher becoming a Big Brother and controlling their every move," he says. Finally convinced, the company has decided to go nationwide with the paging system.

Sometimes, such indecision can go too far. That is when Olivetti's James Schlinkert calls a halt. "To close a tough sale," he says, "you must establish yourself— not the buyer—as the authoritative person." Schlinkert describes just such a sale that he ran up against a few months ago. A small corporation of five people had a definite need for an accounting system. "We had them all at our office one evening and presented our solution to their problem," says Schlinkert. "They were a hard-nosed lot that had evaluated every other accounting system available. After a couple of hours of haggling over a $15,000 sale, I finally shut off the machine, put the key in my pocket, and virtually threatened to throw them out of my office. Immediately, they became very docile and signed a contract. I shocked my salesman when I did that. But I had to take a calculated risk. The need and solution had been established."

TRAINING TODAY'S SALESMAN

Developing such instincts takes years. Some salesmen never develop them, and that puts a heavier burden than ever on today's sales recruiting and training. "In years past," says Transamerica's Herb Eagle, "you figured you could take a new salesman and help him develop the qualities that he needed. With today's higher costs and greater complexity of selling, you have to look for those qualities first off. And if they aren't there, you don't hire."

Five or ten years ago, for instance, most large technical or engineering companies automatically recruited from engineering schools. Now, many of these same companies are seeking salesmen with a broader outlook and thus are looking for liberal arts, marketing, and other non-engineering backgrounds. "We have even successfully used English, history, and physical education majors," marvels Baxter T. Fullerton, sales vice president of Warner & Swasey Co.'s Cleveland Turning Machine Div. The trick, of course, is to gain a universal man with broad interests, yet avoid what one Houston educator calls "the round man who is so round that he just rolls and develops no depth or substance."

Other companies are looking less for college graduates and more for seasoned professionals. "We used to steer clear of the retreads," says Peter Warshaw, a division national products manager for Powers Regulator Co. "Today when there's a vacancy, we don't contact colleges at all. We contact employment agencies, professional societies, and use referrals within the industry. We just can't afford to take the guy, make the major investment in him for two or three years, and then have him sell the training that we gave him to someone else." The new man, Warshaw stresses, must also be productive immediately. "The sales quotas are now so large and selling costs so high that we can't afford to have the backup man or bat boy anymore."

At the same time, sales training has broadened out. A growing number of companies offer continuing instruction for all their salesmen—and for good reason. Armour-Dial, Inc., a consumer goods division of Greyhound Corp., ran a study on salesmen who had attended a recent session at its Aurora (Ill.) sales training center. The result: a boost of 12% in the number of calls per day, 25% in new-product retail placements, 100% in case sales, 62% in displays sold, and 250% in sales to direct-buying or chain accounts.

The big changes coming in sales recruiting and training—and in the salesman's whole approach to his markets—promise to usher in a broad new relationship between him and his company. Robert W. DeMott, Jr., vice president and general manager of Rex Chainbelt's Industrial Sales Div., notes that about 10 years ago, industry's overall marketing effort seemed to eclipse selling in importance. "Now, and more so in the future," he claims, "the trend will be to place selling on a par with marketing."

Wharton's Goodman goes one step further, claiming that the supersalesman of the future will even be ahead of company management when it comes to understanding his markets. "This is going to sound heretical," he admist, "but I see emerging a situation in which the salesman's function within a company is recognized as most important, with management performing a largely supportive role."

While he might get an argument on that, no one can dispute his larger point: the supersalesman is here to stay.

35

The Computer, Personal Selling, and Sales Management

James M. Comer

The computer revolution has come to the salesman and the sales manager.

Several years ago an article entitled "The Salesman Isn't Dead, He's Different" was published.[1] It is now the sales manager's turn—he is not expendable, but he must become more sophisticated. He must learn to participate not only in the development, but also in the application, of new technology. The aggressive, knowledgeable sales manager must prepare *now* for what he soon will be required to do. One important aspect of that preparation must be a thorough knowledge of, and familiarity with, computer technology and the integration of the computer into his regular activities.

The purpose of this article is to review published reports of the integration of the computer into sales management planning, organizing, and control activities. This is

[1]Carl Reiser, "The Salesman Isn't Dead, He's Different," *Fortune* (November 1962).

done: (1) to demonstrate the logical, but not necessarily inevitable, progression of a firm from simple computer-based data collection and manipulation into model building; and (2) to point out when and under what circumstances a particular system is useful to a sales manager. This latter objective is especially important since complex computer-based systems are frequently touted as the "answer" to the sales manager's problems. Often these computer-based systems are not necessary and a less complex system will suffice, or a simple system must be instituted and operated successfully *before* a more complex system can be installed.

To facilitate the review, a categorization method is suggested that divides the literature on computer applications in sales management into two general areas: (1) sales reporting and analysis systems, and (2) planning-oriented systems.

Reprinted with permission from *Journal of Marketing*, published by the American Marketing Association, 39 (July 1975), pp. 27–33.

SALES REPORTING AND
ANALYSIS SYSTEMS

Firms have had sales reporting and analysis systems for decades. Reporting has been as informal as casual verbal exchanges or as stringent as daily written reports. Sales managers, in most cases, conducted analysis by reading call reports and comparing them with actual sales. They were then expected to draw vital conclusions about such things as salesmen abilities and performance and customer response to programs. They were also required to make rational decisions about sales territory design, sales force size, and so on. Given these kinds of responsibilities and the expansion of sales forces over wider geographic areas, it is not surprising that published accounts in the 1960s about the innovative introduction of the computer into sales management were glowing.[2]

The enthusiasm of the 1960s waxed over the computer's ability to digest, consolidate, and reorganize data into meaningful reports. The first applications were on the analysis of sales by product, by account, and by salesman or territory.[3] They were designed to facilitate sales management *ex post facto* product, market, and territory analysis. With this capacity, the mechanical aspects of sales analysis were performed routinely for sales management.

However, routinized computer sales analysis proved inadequate in many cases. This led to the development of the next stage—a system that would produce data not only on account sales but also on salesmen call allocations. The immediate objective of such a system was to relieve sales

managers of their data-matching responsibility and give them more time for certain planning activities. Such a system was SOAR (Store Objectives and Accomplishments Report).

SOAR was a computer-based salesman reporting and analysis system developed at Pillsbury Company. It covered over 500 salesmen selling some 100 types, sizes, and flavors of products in 25 regions and five zones to over 40,000 retail stores plus direct accounts.[4] The impetus for the development of SOAR arose out of such problems as salesman control and the determination of which retail stores should be called upon, and how frequently, by the sales force. In system operation, the computer prints from a master customer list a SOAR form for each account. The form contains such information as region, store name and address, dollar volume, advertising group, and the like. Each salesman receives a batch of these preprinted forms which corresponds to the accounts in his territory, with one form printed for each call the salesman is to make during a given retail selling period. The salesman then sets both dollar and quantity sales objectives, preferably by store, for the subsequent two- or three-month selling period. When the salesman makes his store call, he reports day and time in hours and minutes, presentations scanned, and the results compared with the salesman's projections. The system periodically condenses these results and sends them out to the individual salesman and his immediate supervisor.

At Pillsbury, SOAR was replaced in late 1974 by REACH (Retail Achievement Report).[5] Among other things, REACH puts more emphasis on other salesman activities (such as setting up displays) and on quarterly, rather than monthly, volume goals.

---

[2]William T. Cullen, "Sales Reporting Systems," and John Lincoln, "Using the Computer for More Effective Sales Force Management," in "Marketing Harnesses the Computer," *American Management Association Bulletin*, No. 92 (1966), pp. 14–18 and 19–25. See also, Phyllis Daignault, "Marketing Management and the Computer," *Sales Management* (August 20, 1965), pp. 49–60.

[3]Cullen, *ibid.*, p. 17.

[4]Lloyd M. DeBoer and William H. Ward, "Integration of the Computer Into Salesman Reporting," *Journal of Marketing*, 35 (January 1971), pp. 41–47.

[5]From a conversation with Mr. William H. Ward at Pillsbury Company, Minneapolis, January 1975.

An interesting aspect of these modifications is that the sales department did the redesign work. Here is a case where the user, once a system had proved its worth, took over the system, adapted it, and made it his own.

SOAR, REACH, and similar systems are not the ultimate in system development. Weiss has described a direct salesman-computer communication link-up in which salesmen carry a small mobile device that instantaneously records and transmits information to a central electronic facility.[6] The picture that Weiss paints is yet to be completed, and there are many technological and human problems to be solved before it is. In the interim, sales management must clearly define its needs and role in the development of firm-wide information systems. Dodge has made a start in this direction with his enumeration of three general rules for sales management to observe in developing information systems:

1. The marketing information system should be fitted to the existing organizational structure of sales management. . . .

2. The marketing information system should reflect the operational philosophy established for field sales. Accountability at a given organization level specifies the data parameters of output.

3. The marketing information system should be thoroughly understood and accepted by all personnel in sales.[7]

Several additional lessons have been learned in this area. For example, whenever an information system of any kind is designed and installed it must be recognized that the salesman's primary responsibility is to sell, not to collect data. Furthermore, any sales system must be useful and relevant to the people most concerned, the salesman and the sales manager. Without their support and participation, the system will be useless.

Management Use of Computerized Sales Reporting and Analysis Systems

It is likely that most firms have some type of computerized sales analysis system. The question of whether the more advanced, SOAR-type system should be adopted depends on the firm's resources and the conditions it faces in its market. This step should be taken if: (1) the firm has the technical and monetary resources to do so, (2) the market is complex and geographically extensive, (3) major decisions on sales force allocation and size are made frequently, (4) the redistribution system is complex, (5) the sales force is large and organizationally "distant" from management, (6) the product line is broad, and (7) the probability is high that some of these conditions will exist in the next five years. Two characteristics of these conditions are important: (a) they are independent of the nature of a firm's business, and (b) it is not necessary that all conditions exist in order for a firm to install such a system.

A computer-based system, if correctly designed, serves several purposes. First, it relieves both sales managers and the sales force of many of the onerous, repetitive reporting and summarization responsibilities. Second, it permits a fuller application of management by exception, since highly specific limits on sales performance can be established and monitored. Last, the routinization of control functions permits sales management and salespeople to allocate more time to planning and sales effort.

PLANNING-ORIENTED SYSTEMS

Some of the first analytical attempts at solving such sales management problems as call allocation relied on operations research

---

[6]E. P. Weiss, "The Salesman Gets Hooked Into Information Systems," *Advertising Age* (June 14, 1965), pp. 84–87.

[7]H. R. Dodge, *Field Sales Management* (Dallas: Business Publications, 1973), p. 28.

(OR) techniques.[8] These early attempts were static, limited in scope, and designed solely to solve the specific problem at hand.[9] It was soon apparent that, in the dynamic environment of sales management, OR solutions might be outmoded as soon as they were discovered. The development of flexible planning systems that had the capacity to incorporate market dynamism was a solution to the static limitations inherent in OR-type approaches. However, useful planning systems are not instantaneously developed and made operational. A variety of preceding systems, perhaps analogous to SOAR, make them feasible. For example, a fully developed salesman reporting–management analysis system functions as: a data source for the construction and operation of diverse aspects of the planning system, a monitoring or control device to insure salesmen observation of planning dictums, and a measurement of the validity and reliability of the underlying planning models.

To organize discussion of the various computer applications in this area, a two-way categorization has been devised: data base systems and model base systems. These two systems represent a progression in sophistication rather than a distinction; thus, this categorization is more an organizational device than an attempt to identify unique entities.

Data Base Systems

These systems rely on an aggregated or disaggregated data base for making certain sales management decisions. Normally, these data bases are but an aspect of the firm's computerized marketing information system. Sales management usually must devise its own data extraction and manipulation routines to solve its peculiar problems.[10]

In constructing a data base, the firm will use many sources both inside and outside the firm. The internal sources normally provide microdata such as customer billing records, salesmen call activities, consumer attitudes, and the like, as well as information on potential customers and competitive activities. Outside sources, for the most part, provide macrodata on industry performance and broad-based changes in the economy, and disaggregated microdata. The composition and construction of these data are beyond the scope of this article. What is of concern is how sales management uses a data base system. Several examples demonstrate this use:

☐ Prospect Identification. One firm identifies prospects for its salesmen by collating facts about sales territories from existing data, SIC information, and various product characteristics. These various data sets are combined into a matrix so that top prospects in a territory can be identified.[11]

☐ Customer Profiles. A firm profiles each customer in its data bank. This profile includes customer features and reasons for using a competitive product. It is the feeling in this company that not only is the salesman better prepared for his calls with this kind of information, but sales forecasting and product design problems are also more easily solved when customer needs are more clearly defined.[12]

☐ An NICB report detailed a number of specific sales management applications of

[8]Arthur A. Brown, Frank T. Hulswit, and John D. Kettelle, "A Study of Sales Operations," *Operations Research*, 4 (June 1956), pp. 296–308; and Clark Ward, Donald F. Clark, and Russell Ackoff, "Allocation of Sales Effort in the Lamp Division of the General Electric Company," *Operations Research*, 4 (December 1956), pp. 629–47.

[9]For a discussion of operations research and personal selling, see David Montgomery and Frederick E. Webster, Jr., "Applications of Operations Research to Personal Selling Strategy," *Journal of Marketing*, 32 (January 1968), pp. 50–57.

[10]Two examples of methodologies that rely heavily on large data bases are: Walter J. Semlow, "How Many Salesmen Do You Need," *Harvard Business Review*, 27 (May–June 1959), pp. 126–32; and Walter J. Talley, Jr., "How to Design Sales Territories," *Journal of Marketing*, 25 (January 1961), pp. 7–12.

[11]For these examples and others, the reader is referred to Thayer C. Taylor, ed., "The Computer in Marketing—Part II: Sales Force Management," *Sales Management* (March 15, 1969), pp. 71–78.

[12]*Ibid.*

a computerized data base. Some examples are: J. T. Ryerson and Son, Inc., redesigned its sales territory structure based upon marginal profit figures; Girdwood Publishing Company reorganized its sales force in both the line and staff functions; and Diamond Crystal Salt Corporation has a wide spectrum of applications, ranging from developing salesmen call policy through analyzing individual account profitability.[13]

The foregoing are some of the applications of computer technology. These applications do not relieve either sales management or field sales personnel of many decision making responsibilities; rather, they organize data in such a way as to facilitate decision making. On the other hand, a model base system does, in a sense, substitute computerized "decisions" for personal ones.

Model Base Systems

These systems have at their heart a model or series of models for data manipulation and output generation. Often these models are designed to solve one specific class of problems or assist in making a particular type of recurring decision. Whatever the situation may be, it is the independent verified model, which manipulates data and prescribes courses of action, that distinguishes this type of system.

Work done in this area can be divided into three groups: (1) call allocation determination, (2) sales territory design, and (3) salesmen routing.

Call Allocation. Lodish, in a pioneering study, developed CALLPLAN: "an interactive computer system designed to aid salesmen or sales management in allocating sales call time."[14] The salesman or sales manager provides information for a terri-

tory on: the number of clients, prospects, and geographical subdivisions in the territory; the call length in hours; the sales response period; the effort period in months; and, for each effort period, the total number of half hours available for selling plus travel time, and the maximum number of calls to make on any account. Additional data on historical call patterns per client are used, as well as estimates of client sales response if alternative call allocations are made. Output from CALLPLAN is a series of optimal call allocations to clients and prospects by geographic area, and a comparison of estimated sales from the optimal policy with those of the present policy. Lodish reported fourteen preliminary applications of CALLPLAN. In 1974, Lodish cited additional applications of his model as part of a larger procedure for allocating sales force effort.[15]

Armstrong has also developed an interactive system (SCHEDULE) for determining optimal call policy. Like Lodish's CALLPLAN, it has the individual salesman or sales manager provide certain values. These values are transformed via a mathematical programming model into a suggested call allocation policy by account along with expected return for the call allocation. Armstrong cited one application of SCHEDULE with a small sales force. He did not present any statistical evidence that SCHEDULE had improved the sales force call policy, but he did interview the salesmen after they used SCHEDULE. They "agreed that SCHEDULE-prepared call allocation plans . . . were significantly better than the plans they were currently using."[16]

The present author has developed and tested a system entitled ALLOCATE, which

[13]National Industrial Conference Board, "Allocating Field Sales Resources," *Experience in Marketing Management*, 23 (1970), pp. 20–34.

[14]Leonard M. Lodish, "CALLPLAN: An Interactive Salesman's Call Planning System," *Management Science*, 18 (December 1971), p. 25.

[15]Leonard M. Lodish, "A 'Vaguely Right' Approach to Sales Force Allocations," *Harvard Business Review*, 52 (January–February 1974), pp. 119–24.

[16]Gary M. Armstrong, "SCHEDULE: An Interactive Computer Program for Determination of the Optimal Allocation of Personal Selling Effort," working paper (University of Illinois at Chicago Circle, 1973).

assigns effort to subsets of customers and prospects based on their progress toward the saturation state of their response curve.[17] It is a batch-processed system designed to be used by upper-level sales management either as an input device for sales management decisions, such as sales-territory-size, or as a vehicle for determining the effect of alternative call allocation strategies on territorial revenue over multiple time periods. The author tested ALLOCATE on the sales territories of a consumer products firm that was selling through a combination of wholesalers and direct retail accounts. In the test, ALLOCATE not only successfully replicated salesman behavior in selected sales territories, but also demonstrated its capacity to generate the effect of alternative call allocation strategies on revenue over time in those territories.

Sales Territory Design. Xerox Corporation developed a salesman allocation model employing a market grid approach.[18] A grid of intersecting horizontal and vertical lines is laid over a sales area, thus generating a set of cells which contain customers. Each cell must contain data on the expected number of customers, the expected revenue from each customer, and the expected number of calls per day per salesman. The model then allocates calls sequentially to the customer with the highest revenue per call value until all accounts in a cell are called on and all potential realized. Additional cells are combined until the salesman's maximum time limit is reached. This set of cells then constitutes the salesman's territory.

Hess and Samuels have developed a sales-districting model, GEOLINE, which they derived from research and application of a successful computer technique for legislative districting.[19] The model assumes an established territorial set and constructs a predetermined number of compact sales territories using an integer formulation of a linear transportation program. The solution is not optimal, because the objective of GEOLINE is to design sales territories such that the sales activity measure among the territories is approximately equal. The sales activity measure may be territory potential, salesman workload, or some other relevant criterion. However, GEOLINE output is a set of sales territories realigned quickly, efficiently, and more accurately than by noncomputer methods. Hess and Samuels cited successful field applications by CIBA Pharmaceutical Company and the IBM World Trade Corporation. Since 1970, the system has also been put into operation in a number of pharmaceutical and oil companies.

One output of Lodish's CALLPLAN program was an estimate of the marginal profit of an additional hour of allocated salesman effort in a territory. Lodish has used CALLPLAN and its output as a basis for the development of a sales districting model.[20] It is a mathematical programming model that is heuristically solved so that the marginal profit figures for each salesman are approximately equal. Output defines: (1) which salesmen are to be assigned to which area, (2) the number of trips to be made by the salesman to each area, and (3) the amount of time to be spent in each area. Lodish notes that five companies realigned territories using his procedure, and they felt the computer procedure made a positive contribution to the improved results.

Salesmen Routing. Truck routing and salesmen routing are part of the operations research touring problem. Several attempts

[17]James M. Comer, "ALLOCATE: A Computer Model for Sales Territory Planning," *Decision Sciences,* 3 (July 1974), pp. 323–39.

[18]Peter J. Gray, "Computers and Models in the Marketing Decision Process," in *Computer Innovations in Marketing,* Evelyn Konrad, ed. (New York: American Management Association, 1970), pp. 158–67.

[19]Sidney W. Hess and Stuart A. Samuels, "Experiences with a Sales Districting Model: Criteria and Implementation," *Management Science,* 18 (December 1971), pp. 41–54.

[20]Leonard M. Lodish, "Sales Territory Alignment to Maximize Profit," *Journal of Marketing Research,* 12 (February 1975), pp. 30–36.

have been made to develop computerized routing models for salesmen and sales management.

Lazer, et al., developed a simple computerized model, using Bayesian decision methodology, in which a "routing ratio" is constructed for each account on the basis of the expected values of sales from the account divided by the total time (travel, waiting, and sales) required for that account.[21] The model selects the route that maximizes the total expected value of a "trip" covering all selected accounts, subject to a time constraint. They tested their model by routing the salesmen for a wholesale liquor distributor. In the example provided, a salesman's route was improved from his selected route of $1.98 expected value per minute of selling time to an "optimum" value of $2.03.

A more complete routing system, TOURPLAN, has been developed by Cloonan.[22] TOURPLAN is a heuristic programming approach to the salesman tour problem. The TOURPLAN model employs two heuristics to arrive at an initial solution for the accounts under consideration.[23] An optimal solution is then determined using a combinatorial search routine. The system was first tested in two environments: first, in artificial territories with known and unknown optimal routings; and second, in real territories where salesman solutions were known but optimums were not. In the artificial territories, the system achieved efficiencies (ratio to optimum) of 99% to 100%. In real territories, a 90%+ efficiency rate was obtained where the corresponding field salesmen were operating at about 85% efficiency.

Shanker, et al., have developed a computer-based procedure to solve simultaneously the sales territory design problem and the salesman call frequency problem.[24] It combines and extends the Hess and Lodish methodologies in several aspects. Input consists primarily of management estimates of various problem dimensions combined with an integer-programming—set-partitioning algorithm. It is an optimizing program whose solution specifies which customers should be called on by which salesman and prescribes the call frequency. A hypothetical situation was used to illustrate the effectiveness of the procedure.

Two other computer-based systems have been developed that may be adaptable for use by sales management. DETAILER, developed by Montgomery, et al., was designed to allocate salesman time to product promotions on a sales call.[25] However, Montgomery describes DETAILER as being used by a product manager and not sales management. Winer's system is presented as a procedure for developing optimal compensation plans.[26] However, it was designed to determine the best salary career path for salesmen, not to optimize sales or profit generated for the firm.

Planning Systems and Sales Management

The traditions of the sales fraternity maintain that the personal selling function is

[21] William Lazer, Richard T. Hise, and Jay A. Smith, "Computer Routing: Putting Salesmen in Their Place," *Sales Management* (March 15, 1970), pp. 29–35. See also, James H. Donnelly and John M. Ivancevich, *Analysis for Marketing Decisions* (Homewood, Ill.: Richard D. Irwin, 1970), pp. 252–62.

[22] James B. Cloonan, "TOURPLAN: A Sales Call Routing and Scheduling Program," working paper 9-73 (DePaul University, Chicago, 1973).

[23] The first heuristic is developed in James B. Cloonan, "A Heuristic Approach to Some Sales Territory Problems," in *Proceedings of the Fourth International Conference on Operations Research*, D. B. Hertz and J. Malese, eds. (New York: John Wiley & Sons, 1966), pp. 284–92.

[24] Roy J. Shanker, Ronald E. Turner, and Andres A. Zoltners, "Sales Territory Design: An Integrated Approach," *Management Science*, [22 (November 1975), pp. 309–20].

[25] David B. Montgomery, Alvin J. Silk, and Carlos E. Zaragoza, "Multiple-Product Sales Force Allocation Model," *Management Science*, 21 (December 1974), pp. 3–24.

[26] Leon Winer and Leon Schiffman, "Developing Optimum Sales Compensation Plans with the Aid of a Simulation Model," in *1974 Combined Proceedings*, Ronald Curhan, ed. (Chicago: American Marketing Association, 1975), pp. 509–14.

strictly a person-to-person relationship and that rigorous analysis should be suspect as unrealistic and academic. Although this view is far from accurate, it is a barrier to those far-sighted corporate and sales managers who have, or intend to develop, a computer-based planning system for their firms. The fears and prejudices of more traditional sales managers and salesmen must be assuaged, because an intricate system forcibly superimposed on a complex sales force can lead to permanent damage. The problem for the manager is to get the support and cooperation of the sales force and sales managers for system development.

Several suggestions are made:

1. It is a tenet of human relations theory that involving people in the formulation/design of a project tends to invoke commitment. So, in the system design stage, solicit salesmen/sales manager participation wherever possible.

2. The development and installation of any new system, especially one such as this, is bound to cause anxiety about job loss or fears of inadequacy in dealing with the "monster." Although there is no perfect solution, familiarity can help reduce fears and anxieties. Therefore, introduce the system slowly and carefully, and hold frequent training sessions to educate your personnel in system use.

3. In tests, Lodish and Armstrong had salesmen use the systems on their own territories. Both reported salesmen conclusions that the program allocated calls better than they could. The implication is that the salesmen developed favorable attitudes toward the system because they could, on their own initiative, construct better call routines. The message to management is clear: to maintain salesman morale when you are instituting changes using a system, whenever possible have the the salesman see for himself the beneficial effects for his territory.

Planning Systems and Control

Once a firm has computerized planning systems in operation, two questions arise: "How do we know that the planned change is operating effectively?" and "How do we know when to rerun the model(s)?" Both questions reflect the necessary development

of control routines to complement the planning models. The first question may be answered in two parts. First, hard criteria for performance evaluation should be established before the change is made. Examples of criteria are average sales or cost per call and aggregate territory sales or cost. Second, after the planned changes are implemented, these changes must be monitored to ensure performance. The second question may be answered either by establishing a policy of rerunning the models at regular intervals or, in the mode of management by exception, rerunning only when behavior or events exceed certain predetermined tolerances. If management finds it is faced with consistent violations of standards, model validity may be questionable or the sales force may be playing the model instead of doing its job.

IMPLEMENTING SYSTEMS

A large-scale operating system takes years to develop. Therefore, if management wishes to have a useful system available in the future, it must start *now* to develop one. Three stages in the process can be identified: appraisal, design, and implementation.

Appraisal

Most firms who use personal selling have some type of reporting and analysis system. As there is a great diversity among firms, so too is there a broad range of complexity in system design. Each firm must weigh the pros and cons and decide which course of action it should select. Some factors to consider are: (1) the present state of sophistication of the firm's planning system, (2) current and projected product and market complexity, (3) the firm's technical and monetary resources, and (4) current and predicted competitor activities. If the firm decides to extend its present system, a gradual, carefully prepared implementation program is strongly recommended.

Design

A useful first step in system design is to identify the existing needs of your sales personnel. This can be accomplished through consultation with knowledgeable sales managers and salesmen. Succeeding steps should include an in-depth examination of the models discussed in this article to see if one or more of them is relevant, and the development of estimates of the costs and benefits of designing an original program peculiarly suited to the present and future needs of the firm.

Before full-scale implementation can occur, designed systems must be field-tested for validity and reliability. In fact, part of system design should include the establishment of routine control procedures for insuring the maintenance of validity.

Implementation

In implementing a new system, the firm should proceed carefully in step-wise fashion, adding capability only after such factors as data bases are established and users are trained. Gradual implementation may be technical in nature, progressing from the less complex to the more sophisticated; or it may progress on a geographic basis, from territory to district, region, and ultimately to the national level. Obviously, a schedule that combines geographic and technical implementation is also possible. System implementation should include procedures for involving sales managers and salesmen in the process. Formal feedback systems on problems with system operation perform two necessary functions. First, the firm can check users to be certain they are utilizing the system efficiently. Often opportunities for new applications are identified here. Second, users may not feel as threatened by the system and, in fact, may make valuable contributions if they have a question and suggestion pipeline to designers and corporate management.

CONCLUSIONS

This article reviewed published accounts of the integration of the computer into reporting, analysis, and decision making in personal selling and sales management. It was shown that, contrary to tradition, the computer has applications in this area of marketing, but so far only a few problems have been attacked beyond the routine computer-based sales reporting and analysis systems. For a firm to take that additional step requires patient development geared to the capabilities and requirements of the user. Only when the user, be it sales representative or sales manager, accepts the system as relevant to his needs and integrates it into his routine can it be truly labeled a success.

VI Controlling the Marketing Effort

Marketing strategy sets a direction for marketing programs. This part examines the implementation and controlling of these programs.

After reading this part, you should have a better understanding of:

1. Alternative ways of organizing marketing personnel.
2. The relationship between marketing and production managers.
3. The value of profitability analysis in measuring marketing performance.

36

The Changing Role of the Product Manager in Consumer Goods Companies

Victor P. Buell

A recent study examines the current status of the product manager's role and the changes it has undergone.

What the proper role of the product or brand manager should be remains a troublesome question for the managements of consumer goods companies. It is particularly a problem for packaged goods producers, who are the most frequent users of this organizational device.

The role of the product manager has undergone several changes since the product management system was first introduced. That these changes have not produced entirely satisfactory results is evident in the continuing public debate on this topic. Titles of selected articles and papers illustrate the situation:

☐ The Product Manager System Is In Trouble[1]
☐ Has the Product Manager Failed? Or the Folly of Imitation[2]

☐ Product Management—Vision Unfulfilled[3]
☐ Brand Manager vs. Creative Man: The Clash of Two Cultures[4]
☐ Brand Manager vs. Advertising Director— Must One of Them Go?[5]
☐ Product Managers and Advertising—A Study of Conflict, Inexperience and Opportunity[6]

The purpose of this article is to review the changes that have occurred in the product management form of organization since its introduction, to explore the reasons behind the continuing controversy, and to examine current changes in management

[1]Stephens W. Dietz, *Advertising Age* (June 2, 1969), pp. 43-44.

[2]*Sales Management* (January 1, 1967), pp. 27-29.

[3]David J. Luck and Theodore Nowak, *Harvard Business Review*, 43 (May–June 1965), p. 143.

[4]Ralph Leezenbaum, *Marketing Communications* (April 1970), pp. 40-43.

[5]*Advertising Age* (January 27, 1969), p. 53.

[6]James F. Pomeroy, paper presented to the Association of National Advertisers Workshop on Development and Approval of Creative Advertising, New York, April 2, 1969.

Reprinted with permission from *Journal of Marketing*, published by the American Marketing Association, 39 (July 1975), pp. 3–11.

thinking and their implications for the future. To this end, the author uses material from his recent study of several leading consumer goods manufacturers and major advertising agencies.

THE STUDY:
BACKGROUND AND APPROACH

Much of the controversy has centered on the degree of control the product manager exercises over advertising. Under a grant from the Association of National Advertisers (ANA), the author studied the advertising decision making process in companies with major advertising expenditures.[7] Although its overall purpose was broader, the study provided the opportunity to explore management attitudes toward product management and to gather information on the restructuring this system currently is undergoing.

In-depth interviews were held during the summer and fall of 1972 with 63 executives in 20 leading companies which represented ten consumer industry classifications plus one miscellaneous category. Extensive interviews were also held with 23 executives in ten major advertising agencies.

Sixteen of the companies produced packaged goods primarily and four produced consumer durables primarily. Product management was the predominant form of marketing organization in fifteen of the companies; a functional form predominated in five. Some of the companies used one organizational form in some divisions and the other form in other divisions.

Survey Sample

The combined domestic sales of the 20 companies surveyed exceeded $60 billion, and their combined advertising expenditures were over $1.5 billion. Seventeen were among the 50 largest advertisers and 10

[7]Victor P. Buell, *Changing Practices in Advertising Decision-Making and Control* (New York: Association of National Advertisers, 1973).

ranked among the top 20. The primary industry classifications of the consumer packaged goods companies included food; drugs and cosmetics; soaps, cleansers, and allied products; soft drinks; tobacco; paper; liquor; and one miscellaneous category. The consumer durable goods companies fell under the industry classifications of electric appliances, automobiles, and building products.

Participant companies were selected with the assistance of the Management Policy Committee of the Association of National Advertisers. Selection criteria included: (1) company commitment to a large advertising budget, (2) recognized leadership position in the company's industry, (3) management willingness to participate, and (4) multiple industry representation. Preference was given to companies that had extensive experience with product managers. Advertising agencies were selected from among leading agencies that served one or more of the 20 manufacturing companies. To encourage participation and frank discussion, participants were assured that neither companies nor individuals would be identified in the report.

Thirty-one corporate executives were interviewed, including chairmen, presidents, executive and group vice presidents, and staff vice presidents. Positions occupied by the 32 divisional executives interviewed included presidents, marketing vice presidents, directors of marketing or advertising, directors of brand management, and group product managers.

The 10 advertising agencies in the study were among the nation's 20 largest and had combined U.S. billings in excess of $2 billion. Agency executives interviewed included chairmen, presidents, executive and senior vice presidents, and vice presidents.

Data Collection Method

All interviews were conducted by the author. Interviews were open-ended and ranged in length from one to three hours. Policies, procedures, and files were made freely available. Interviews with agency executives provided cross-checks on information developed with their clients.

The purpose of the study was to gain understanding of the reasons behind advertising and marketing management practices rather than duplicate the quantitative data developed by the more commonly used mail questionnaire. Because of the qualitative nature of the study, findings are reported primarily as the author's interpretations of prevailing management practices, attitudes, and intentions rather than in the form of statistical summaries. The findings have been reported to the participating executives and have been discussed in depth with several of them.

While the study provides the principal data source for this article, conclusions are based also on interviews with executives during other research projects by the author, reviews of product management literature, and recent reports of mail surveys.

Because of the selective sample, the findings are not representative of all companies. The findings are important in that they represent managerial viewpoints in consumer goods companies with leadership positions, most of whom employ large numbers of product managers.

HISTORICAL DEVELOPMENTS

The product management system, although introduced nearly 50 years ago, did not come into general use until the 1950s. The Association of National Advertisers, in a recent study among its members, found that the following percentages of participating companies used product managers: packaged goods—85% (93% of those with annual advertising expenditures exceeding $10 million); other consumer goods—34%; industrial goods—55%.[8]

[8]*Current Advertising Practices: Opinions as to Future Trends* (New York: Association of National Advertisers, 1974).

Product management is a response to the organizational problem of providing sufficient management attention to individual products and brands when there are too many for any one executive to coordinate effectively all of the aspects of the marketing mix. Companies, or divisions of companies, with a limited line of products normally follow a functional plan of organization wherein departments such as sales, advertising and sales promotion, marketing research, product planning, and customer service report to a common marketing executive. When shifting from this purely functional organization, product managers are added to assist the chief marketing executive by assuming the planning and coordination for individual products or product lines.

Although the product manager has made possible greater management concentration by product, the position also has created new problems. Responsibility often has been assigned to the product manager for achievement of goals such as sales volume, share of market, and even profit in some cases; yet the product manager has no line authority over the functional departments that execute his plans.

Shift of Advertising Responsibility to the Product Manager

A key change in the original concept was made when companies shifted the management of advertising from the advertising manager to the product manager. In leading packaged goods companies that currently use product managers, one rarely finds an advertising department on the organization chart. If one is there, it is usually at the group or corporate level, where it provides services common to several divisions, such as media planning and coordinating media purchases.

The reasons for phasing out the separate advertising function were: (a) to reduce costs, which rose as the advertising department expanded to manage the advertising for increasing numbers of products and

EXHIBIT 1
Functional marketing organization

brands; and (b) to give the product manager more control over execution of a major marketing function. Such a move was possible because the advertising agency was available to develop and place advertising.

Exhibits 1 and 2 provide examples of typical functional and product management organizations. While details may vary from company to company, these charts reflect the main differences that exist between the two organizational forms in the companies studied by the author.

EXHIBIT 2
Product management organization

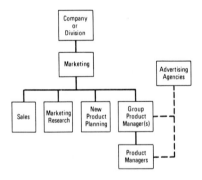

Companies Assume the Planning Function

Concurrent with the growth of the product management function, companies began to assume the marketing planning and service functions—with the exception of

creative and media—that had been performed for them by their advertising agencies.

As marketing grew in sophistication during the 1950s, much of the know-how was centered in the agencies. Gradually, however, companies expanded their own supporting service functions and the responsibility for initiating marketing plans became a key function of the product manager. This change has been made with little criticism. Agencies have accepted the idea that marketing planning should originate within the company, and they are aware of the growing effectiveness of the product manager as a planner.

Increases in Intervening Management Levels

As companies grow, the product manager becomes further removed from the real decision making levels of management. When products were fewer in number product managers reported directly to higher-level executives, who had the authority to make broad decisions and implement programs. As product lines proliferated, and the numbers of product managers grew correspondingly, intervening levels of supervision became necessary. In large companies today, product managers may be anywhere from two to four levels below the executive who has the real decision making authority and the clout to see that plans are carried out.

Due to rapid growth, companies also have shifted to filling product manager positions with younger, less experienced people. This relative inexperience, plus separation from the key decision maker, has increased management concern over the degree of authority that should be delegated to the product manager. These concerns are particularly strong with respect to advertising because of the magnitude of advertising costs and the importance of advertising to product success.

Continued Use of Functional Organization

The ANA study of its members found that 34% of the participating larger consumer durable goods companies used product managers, as compared with 85% of the packaged goods companies. Why do some companies stay with the functional form?

Pearson and Wilson believe there may be good reasons why a company should prefer the functional organization.[9] In fact, they think some companies have made a mistake in switching to product management before it was really necessary. They maintain that companies with a line of similar products, with one dominant product line, or with several large product lines (sufficient to support divisionalization) might be better off avoiding product management. It was not long after Pearson left McKinsey & Co. to become president of PepsiCo that the Pepsi-Cola division did away with product managers.[10] This division sells a related line of soft drinks with one dominant product—Pepsi-Cola.

Three of the consumer durable goods companies interviewed by the author had functional marketing setups. The major appliance group of an electrical company and the major division of an automotive manufacturer each had relatively few products although they accounted for large dollar sales. Both companies preferred to use advertising to build the overall brand name in addition to promoting individual products; they felt they could achieve better control through the functional advertising manager. The third company, a manufacturer of building products, organized its product divisions by markets and channels. Historically, the corporate advertising department has supervised the development of advertising and sales promotion for the various market sales managers, who appear to prefer this arrangement.

While there are good reasons why many companies do not use product management, there appears to be no significant defection by current users, as was implied in the article that featured the PepsiCo story.[11] Of the 211 companies surveyed by the ANA, 5% had adopted product management during the preceding three years, as compared with 1% who had abandoned it.[12] Clewett and Stasch, in a survey of 160 product managers and other marketing executives, found less than 1% who felt that product management was likely to be discontinued in their divisions.[13] In the author's study, none of the fifteen companies that used product management planned to change.

No doubt some companies will shift from product management from time to time for sound organizational reasons or out of sheer frustration. But there is no evidence of a trend in this direction. If a trend exists it would appear to be in the direction of continued adoption of product management.

CURRENT MANAGEMENT ATTITUDES

Executives interviewed by the author were concerned about the product management system but were committed to making it work better. Their attitudes appeared to be changing with respect to the question of the product manager's responsibility and authority and his role in advertising. They also expressed concern over the scarcity of advertising specialists within their companies.

[9]Andrall E. Pearson and Thomas W. Wilson, Jr., *Making Your Marketing Organization Work* (New York: Association of National Advertisers, 1967).

[10]"The Brand Manager: No Longer King," *Business Week* (June 9, 1973), pp. 58–66.

[11]*Ibid.*

[12]Same reference as footnote 8.

[13]Richard M. Clewett and Stanley F. Stasch, "Product Managers in Consumer Packaged Goods Companies," working paper (Northwestern University Graduate School of Management, March 1974).

Disaffection with the "Little President" Concept

Almost all of the executives interviewed recognized that the earlier concept of the product manager as a "little president" or "little general manager," with profit responsibility, was unrealistic. As the manager of a paper products company said:

We've gotten away from the concept of the guy who runs his own little company. We want our product managers to be profit conscious, but what we're really talking about is sales volume.

Remnants of the concept persist, however, as illustrated by excerpts from two recruiting brochures. The brochure of a household products company states:

The Product Manager has responsibility for his brand. He is not only responsible for its management, he is accountable for its overall performance. . . . The Product Manager is not just a marketing manager, but in many respects a general manager of a good size business.

When this statement was pointed out to an executive of this company the author was told that it no longer represents management opinion; that, in fact, the company's product managers have no decision making authority.

The brochure of a food company, after explaining the product manager's role in developing objectives and strategies, says: "The Product Manager is responsible for the execution and performance of the brands entrusted to him."

In describing the position, the marketing director of another food company probably came closest to prevailing management attitudes when he avoided mentioning responsibility for execution or performance:

Our product manager's job is planning—objectives and strategy—monitoring progress, coordinating budget development and control, and working with other departments—Home Economics and Manufacturing, for example—on product cost and quality.

Clarifying the Advertising Role

Packaged goods executives pretty much agree that the typical product manager has insufficient training, experience, or skill to be entrusted with important creative decisions. They tend to share the view of the agency vice president who told the author: "Advertising is too important a decision to be left in the hands of a product manager. His role should be planning and coordination—not advertising approval."

Agency critics complain that because of his inexperience the product manager is too cautious and too meticulous in judging creative work; he delays the development process and causes dilution of creative copy by requiring repeated rework; and, to compensate for his insecurity, he relies too heavily on copy testing, which normally produces inconclusive data. Company executives agree. All want the product manager involved in advertising decision making, but they are developing procedures that get agency recommendations up the line to the final decision maker as quickly as possible. Agencies, it should be noted, are reassigning responsibility for client contact to higher management levels to correspond with the client management levels making advertising decisions.

Current top management attitudes are reflected in the following comments. The president of a personal products company said:

I want the best people in a profit center working on, and approving, marketing decisions. We try to set the atmosphere and tone so that our brand manager feels important, yet knows that advertising is too important to be decided at the bottom level.

The executive vice president of a drug products company explained his company's position this way:

We give much authority to the product manager other than the copy side—sales promotion, for example. But we let him know he is not to be the final authority on advertising. We say the person who knows the most about advertising should make the ultimate decision.

EXHIBIT 3

Where advertising companies say creative decisions are made

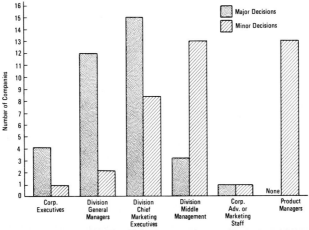

NOTE: The figures represented by the bars total more than the number of companies because decisions may be made jointly by two or more executives, decisions may be made by one executive in the absence of another, or the decision level may vary by degree of importance within the Major or Minor categories.

SOURCE: Adapted from Victor P. Buell, *Changing Practices in Advertising Decision-Making and Control* (New York: Association of National Advertisers, 1973), p. 49.

Companies, however, do make a distinction between *major* and *minor* advertising decisions. Exhibit 3 indicates the differences in executive levels that deal with decisions of varying importance. Major decisions may include almost anything to do with an important product or, for less important products, they may involve only significant matters, such as a change in strategy. The author's research showed that advertising decisions considered to be major were made most frequently at the division manager or division marketing manager levels, with some going to the corporate level. None of the companies believed *major* creative-type advertising decisions were made by the product manager. Decisions considered minor, on the other hand, most frequently were made at the product manager and division middle management (group product manager) levels. Understanding this distinction may help to clarify the sometimes confusing results of those mail surveys that indicate that the product

manager makes advertising decisions: he does make some decisions, but usually not the major ones.

Considering the past sharp criticisms by agency executives it is worth noting that these complaints have been directed primarily at the product manager's role in the advertising approval process. In contrast, they agree with his role as the authoritative source of information and as marketing planner. An agency vice president who works with both functional and product management organizations volunteered this comment:

I would rather work with a product manager than with an advertising manager. The product manager has all the information, although he may be unaware of the broader strategies. But in the vertical organization, each person has only a part of the information we require.

Need for the Advertising Specialist

After several years of operating without advertising departments, many company executives now wonder whether they have any real advertising expertise left in-house. The normal promotion route provides added experience in judging advertising, and one learns from his mistakes and successes. But experience does not necessarily develop the kind of expertise in judging creative work that comes from long and intensive involvement in the development of advertising by talented people. Some marketing executives seem to have better creative judgment than others, but promotion up the line from product manager does not automatically guarantee success in this area.

To replace the skills that were lost with the demise of the advertising department, three companies have created a new position, staff advertising director, to provide creative counsel to product managers and others concerned with advertising decisions. Whereas the former advertising manager made the advertising decision, the new advertising director provides counsel to those charged with the decision making responsibility.

Where this position has been introduced, it has usually been placed within the division marketing management organization. Executives report that product and other managers exhibit reluctance to avail themselves of staff counsel when it is located in corporate headquarters.

How Much Authority?

The persistent, unresolved question puzzling management is how much and what kind of authority the product manager needs. Luck, in discussing the many functional areas with which the product manager must interact, states: "Product managers are seriously hampered by ambiguity of authority in the execution of their plans and decisions. . . ."[14]

A common management attitude was expressed by the group vice president of a liquor company, who said: "The brand manager's authority is the authority of his influence and knowledge." While true as far as it goes, this conclusion seems oversimplified. Several studies bear on the issue.

Lucas, in a mail survey of 60 product managers, found that four in five believed their degree of control over the decision areas of advertising, marketing research, and market testing was "adequate for their assigned responsibilities."[15] Smaller proportions reported that they had adequate control over the personal selling, production, and distribution functions, and in the areas of legal affairs, advertising expenditures, and pricing. That these product managers did not consider their responsibilities insignificant is evident in the fact that two-thirds felt that they had major, or even 100%, responsibility for product profit.

The mail survey of 160 executives, primarily product managers and group product managers, conducted by Clewett and Stasch found product managers to be "less than major participants" in the decision areas of advertising, product, packaging, pricing, and personal selling.[16] They were reported to be "major participants" in marketing research and promotion. When tasks, as opposed to decision making, were considered, this study reported that product managers had a "major role" in planning, budgeting, scheduling, communicating plans and maintaining enthusiasm for them, monitoring progress, revising plans, and reporting performance. The two studies appear to disagree only in the area of advertising decision authority.

Gemmill and Wileman report that in the absence of direct authority, product managers influence action by using re-

[14]David J. Luck, "Interfaces of a Product Manager," *Journal of Marketing*, 33 (October 1969), pp. 32–36.

[15]Darrell B. Lucas, "Point of View: Product Managers in Advertising," *Journal of Advertising Research*, 12 (June 1972), pp. 41–44.

[16]Clewett and Stasch, *op. cit.*

ward power, coercive power, expert power, and referent (i.e., personal relationships) power.[17] They found that product managers who primarily employed expert/referent power were the most effective.

Dietz has identified at least two types of product managers: the *brand coordinator*, who has no entrepreneurial responsibility; and the *brand champion*, who has responsibility for making entrepreneurial recommendations.[18] Common to both types, he says, are the responsibilities for planning, securing approval of plans, coordinating the execution of plans by functional departments, and evaluating the results of the actions taken. Dietz suggests that the brand coordinator needs little authority to fulfill his responsibility but that the more aggressive brand champion reaches out for authority in frustration over the slowness with which higher levels of management arrive at decisions.

As mentioned earlier, the author's findings indicate that the product manager's authority varies with the relative importance of the decision and that his influence varies with his experience and competence. As a division president in a food products company said:

The product manager system works well for us, but we don't have a set way of working with every product manager. Some are more experienced and some are more aggressive than others.

Consensus appears to exist with respect to the product manager's responsibility for planning, coordinating, and evaluating. Differences continue with respect to the questions of authority over execution and the authority to make decisions. The present answer for the last two would seem to be "it all depends."

[17]Gary R. Gemmill and David L. Wileman, "The Product Manager as an Influence Agent," *Journal of Marketing*, 36 (January 1972), pp. 26–30.

[18]Stephens Dietz, "Get More Out of Your Brand Management," *Harvard Business Review*, 51 (July-August 1973), p. 127.

As a result of these changing management attitudes, all companies interviewed indicated that they had made, or were making, changes in their product manager setups with respect to functions, authority, management decision making levels, staffing, or length of time in the job. Eight indicated that they were acting in all of these areas.

Management accepts the system but believes it needs improvement. The president of a food company expressed the viewpoint of many when he commented: "There is nothing fundamentally wrong with the product manager system, but I don't think we operate it as well as we should."

Emphasizing Position Strengths— Deemphasizing Weaknesses

In redefining the job, management is emphasizing the functions that product managers can perform well and deemphasizing those aspects of the position with inherent weaknesses. Emphasis is being placed on the role of the product manager as the gatherer and synthesizer of all information about the product and its markets, as the developer of plans, as the communicator of approved plans, and as the monitor of performance. Management expects the product manager to have a deep personal commitment to the success of his product, while they recognize that he alone cannot be held responsible for achievement of sales and profits. Ultimate responsibility, they believe, must rest with the executive in a position to control all marketing activities.

The role of the product manager as decision maker is being deemphasized. The current trend is for decision making authority to be given in accordance with the importance of the decision area and to vary with the experience and competence of the individual product manager. The product manager will remain involved with the decision making process, but he will be encouraged to bring key decisions to his manager's attention. As one marketing director said, "The brand manager's job is to get good decisions made irrespective of who makes them."

Controlling Resource Allocation at Higher Levels

Management not only wants decisions made where the most competence exists, but it also recognizes the need to control resource allocations among products. The president of a liquor company put it this way: "Our brand managers make many decisions but they don't make the key ones. Someone at a higher level must look at the broad allocation of expenditures."

Obviously, the product manager is not in a position to see the overall picture. The more effective an individual product manager is, the better job he may do in obtaining a disproportionate share of functional resources. It is higher management's job to see that money and other resources are allocated on the basis of profit potential.

The idea that decision making should be moved up the line rather than down the line does not sit well with long-term advocates of decentralized management. However, most executives interviewed seemed to have come to terms with this issue. They recognized that on matters that have a major impact on profit, decisions should be made where all the necessary information is available and where competence exists to make the best judgment. This means that different decisions will be made at different levels, but it does not preclude participation by the product manager, who should have the most information about his product and market. Exceptions to this philosophy were found at the corporate level in three companies. Checks at the division levels in these companies indicate, however, that major advertising decisions were, in fact, being made at the marketing vice president or division president levels.

Staffing with Marketing Experience

During the 1960s and early 1970s, a number of companies sought out the recent MBA graduate to fill the assistant product manager position. The graduate schools provided a selective recruiting source of people with broad management training. Though not unhappy with the quality of these recruits, managements have found that their limited training in marketing (particularly in advertising) and the usual absence of marketing experience are drawbacks for product management. They complain, also, that higher competitive compensation levels for the MBA tend to upset established wage patterns.

With the exception of two major packaged goods producers, the companies interviewed had reduced their reliance on the graduate business school as a primary recruiting source for product management. Five had eliminated this source entirely. They were recruiting instead from advertising agencies and other companies and were making internal transfers from sales, marketing research, and the like, in order to obtain people with marketing experience. Some of these people may already have their MBA degree, which is considered a plus, but the emphasis is being placed on marketing experience.

Slowing Job Turnover

Simultaneously, eight of the companies were upgrading the position and attempting to hold incumbents in the job for longer periods. This has not been easy, since the job attracts high-potential, well-motivated individuals who consider product management a stepping stone to higher management. To attract and hold good people, companies in the past have advanced them from assistant to associate to product manager to group product manager fairly rapidly. Switching to different product groups often occurred along the way.

This "churning" is felt to be undesirable. Incumbents do not stay with a product long enough to develop the desired product and market expertise. Furthermore, short-term assignments do not encourage the long-range planning that can enhance market position. Through different hiring practices and by providing incentives to remain with a product longer, the eight companies hope to increase product manager effectiveness. Other managements that would like to increase longevity in the job explain that they have been unable to do so because of rapid company growth.

FUTURE IMPLICATIONS

In summary, over the years the product manager system has undergone a number of changes and it is still in the process of change. Because the position corresponds to none of the classic line, staff, or functional positions it has never fit neatly into traditional organizational structure. Yet for companies with many products it affords a better means of product-by-product management concentration than does functional organization. For this reason—and despite its acknowledged problems—most companies that are using the product management system plan to stay with it.

It is too early to tell whether the current trend to emphasize planning and coordina-tion, and deemphasize decision making, will resolve the major problems. The same can be said for attempts to improve staffing and to lengthen incumbent tenure.

In some ways the product manager system appears to be in tune with current organizational behavior theory, with its emphasis on group cooperation and participative decision making and its deemphasis of hierarchical authority patterns. The author found, for example, that those organizations with the longest product management experience appeared to be most happy with it, apparently because people throughout these organizations better understand the system. People seem to recognize the reasons for cooperating with the product manager in the absence of any formal authority on his part. The corporate advertising vice president of one long-time user of product management emphasized this point:

What makes our system tick is not organization or who makes the decision, but something more intangible—our people are trained in the company system and everyone knows how it works.

No doubt we have not heard the last of the product manager problem nor the last of change. Until a better idea comes along, however, we are likely to see continued use of the system and continued efforts to improve it. Product management has been, and will continue to be, an intriguing subject for organizational theorists and practicing managers alike.

37 Can Marketing and Manufacturing Coexist?

Benson P. Shapiro

The challenge is: to increase cooperation and decrease conflict between these adversary functions.

Marketing personnel in companies that manufacture industrial goods often complain about the activities and attitudes of their manufacturing counterparts with laments such as: "Why can't they become market-oriented or customer-oriented?" "Why are they so provincial?" The manufacturing people, on the other hand, lament like this: "The marketing people have no understanding of costs, profits, plants, or operations. They are just a bunch of dumb peddlers."

While some consumer goods companies, particularly those in fashion industries with broad product lines (e.g., apparel, furniture), experience antagonism between these two key functions, the need for cooperation is much greater in the typical industrial goods company.

In this article I will begin by detailing the areas of necessary cooperation but potential conflict. Then, I will consider the causes of conflict. Next, I will suggest ways of managing the conflict by increasing cooperation and minimizing antagonism between the marketing and manufacturing functions. Finally, I will recommend an approach for strengthening the two functions.

THE PROBLEM AREAS

The accompanying exhibit lists eight general areas in which there is a strong likelihood of conflict in managing the marketing/manufacturing interface in an industrial company. Let us start by taking a closer look at each of these problem areas.

1. Capacity planning and long-range sales forecasts

Beyond the day-to-day issue of what product do we make tomorrow or next week, one of the strategic areas of cooperation is capacity planning and long-range sales forecasting. It often takes a long time for a

Marketing/manufacturing areas of necessary cooperation but potential conflict

PROBLEM AREA	TYPICAL MARKETING COMMENT	TYPICAL MANUFACTURING COMMENT
1 Capacity planning and long-range sales forecasting.	"Why don't we have enough capacity?"	"Why didn't we have accurate sales forecasts?"
2 Production scheduling and short-range sales forecasting.	"We need faster response. Our lead times are ridiculous."	"We need realistic customer commitments and sales forecasts that don't change like wind direction."
3 Delivery and physical distribution.	"Why don't we ever have the right merchandise in inventory?"	"We can't keep everything in inventory."
4 Quality assurance.	"Why can't we have reasonable quality at reasonable cost?"	"Why must we always offer options that are too hard to manufacture and that offer little customer utility?"
5 Breadth of product line.	"Our customers demand variety."	"The product line is too broad—all we get are short, uneconomical runs."
6 Cost control.	"Our costs are so high that we are not competitive in the marketplace."	"We can't provide fast delivery, broad variety, rapid response to change, and high quality at low cost."
7 New product introduction.	"New products are our life blood."	"Unnecessary design changes are prohibitively expensive."
8 Adjunct services such as spare parts inventory support, installation, and repair.	"Field service costs are too high."	"Products are being used in ways for which they weren't designed."

company to change its manufacturing capacity. If such a change requires a new or enlarged building, design and construction can take several years. The addition of new equipment can take up to two years in most industries. Even the hiring and training of additional employees to staff existing physical capacity can take as long as from one year in fairly typical industries to several years in fields requiring great skill and experience such as tool and die making or advanced welding.

The problem is further exacerbated by the business cycle. Usually, most companies want to build plants, buy equipment, and hire employees at the very time when the construction industry is busiest, the equipment backlogs longest, and the labor market tightest. In addition, excess capacity is expensive. Mortgage payments, rent, taxes, depreciation, unemployment benefits, wasted training, and so on eat into profits when sales are lowest.

Thus the solution is clear: have exactly the right capacity at the right time.

But that requires precise long-term sales forecasting. And, because sales forecasting is not a science, the marketing and sales executives who forecast sales can't be expected to be right every time. In many companies, the problem is much more complex than just a gross sales forecast. In these situations, either capacity is a function of product mix, or different manufacturing processes require different facilities or labor input. Here the sales forecast must not only be precise in total, but each part must also be precise.

Capacity planning is an area in which both marketing and manufacturing are seldom perfect. The sales forecasts are often wrong partly because of the inexactness of the forecasting act itself and partly because the salespeople who are closest to the customer often react emotionally to market prospects. When business is down, the salespeople perceive it as even worse than it is; when business is good, they become ebullient.

In self-defense, manufacturing people often second-guess the marketers and operate from revised forecasts. Since the manufacturing people are insulated from the marketplace, their forecasts are often no better, and are sometimes even worse.

If capacity is too low, marketers are upset because they are losing sales. If capacity is too high relative to sales, they are upset because costs are too high.

2. Production scheduling and short-range sales forecasting

This problem area is a short-term mirror image of the longer-term situation. It is more operational and thus less likely to involve top level line executives, but the conflict between the production scheduler and the sales manager can be intense, especially due to the fact that specific customer relationships and orders are involved.

In addition, the people active in this fray usually have less perspective on the company as well as less experience and judgment. They are therefore likely to be insular in their viewpoints. Also, as in the longer term, perfection is unlikely to be achieved. The forecasts aren't perfect, and the schedules are not totally flexible. In addition, the scheduler must be responsive to needs beyond those of the sales manager and his or her customers. The scheduler often is attempting to maximize total output, minimize cost, and maintain labor stability so that he is almost forced to schedule at the convenience of the plant manager as well as of the marketers.

3. Delivery and physical distribution

This area is like the previous two in that it involves sales forecasts going from marketing to manufacturing and manufacturing's response through the management of a capability. In this instance, the response is determined by inventory availability instead of manufacturing capacity.

The nature of the company's industrial business largely determines the importance of this problem area and the degree of conflict related to it. If the company manufactures a broad line of proprietary items (as opposed to custom designed and built items) and if customers require rapid response, the inventory/distribution system is of major concern. Companies that provide replacement parts for capital equipment, for example, usually find delivery and inventory control crucial because their customers' operations are dependent on their ability to ship orders quickly.

In many companies physical distribution has been a traditional area of conflict involving frequent organizational shuffling. Usually the sequence works something like this: marketing runs physical distribution and inventory control and, while customer service is good, inventories are too high. Yet manufacturing does not gain the benefits it thinks it needs from using the inventory to smooth production and lengthen runs because marketing is always demanding small batches on short notice to keep inventories balanced.

In response to this problem, management shifts the physical distribution function from marketing to manufacturing. The result is better inventory management and coordination with production scheduling, but poorer customer service. Then, after months of organizational backbiting and bickering, management settles on a third option. It creates a separate physical distribution function. Finally, this arrangement satisfies neither marketing nor manufacturing and lasts only until the pressure gets too high, and the organization is reshuffled again.

4. Quality assurance

Because production and inspection operations are seldom perfect, products have quality problems that are obvious to customers and sources of aggravation and embarrassment to salespeople. The typical marketing expectation is that if the plant were run correctly, problems would be nonexistent or at least minimal. Sometimes that is true—quality problems are caused by poor manufacturing management.

On the other hand, quality levels are closely related to other marketing interests that involve manufacturing complexity, variety, cost, and field service. Marketers often perceive customers as desiring "advanced" features and options. These complicate the manufacturing task and increase the probability of quality and field service problems. In addition, the broader the product line, the more opportunity there is for the manufacturing operation to fail in some way because of employee unfamiliarity or system error.

Finally, because meticulous manufacturing and quality assurance are expensive, in some situations it is cheaper to fix a few problems in the field than to raise manufacturing and inspection standards throughout the production process.

5. Breadth of product line

Folklore has it that the marketers want a broad product line while manufacturers respond with the classic line attributed to Henry Ford: "You can have any color you want as long as it's black." The source of the conflict is understandable when one compares the cost (to the company) of a product line broader than optimum (from the total company's viewpoint) to one narrower than optimum.

The product line that is too narrow results in lost sales through (a) loss of competitive position as a "full line" supplier or in particular product areas and market segments, (b) loss of distributor and sales force support, and (c) loss of economies of scale.

The line that is too broad results in (a) added inventory cost of raw material on hand, work in process, and finished goods, (b) increased cost of manufacturing changeover due to loss of capacity setup changes, scrap generation, and stress and strain on equipment and employees, (c) added order processing and transportation costs, and (d) possible sales force, distributor, and customer confusion and displeasure.

Most of the costs of the narrow product line and all of the *measurable* (as distinct from actual) costs are in the marketing area. For the broader than optimum line the situation is reversed—all of the measurable costs and almost all of the actual costs are in the manufacturing area. There is therefore a natural, rational basis for conflict.

6. Cost control

Most marketers view cost as a prime determinant of price as well as, of course, of profits. Marketers tend to attribute costs that are too high to inept manufacturing management. Manufacturing personnel tend to relate high costs to "unreasonable" marketing demands such as rapid delivery, high quality, a broad line, and facile introduction of new products. Because it is inherently difficult to precisely assess either the costs or the benefits of such demands and to know what is "just enough" quality and so forth, there is often little factual data to support or refute such biases.

7. New product introduction

Although they are a prime competitive weapon in the marketplace, new products can greatly upset the manufacturing operation. They require new processes, employee training, new equipment, and trial-and-error operation until they are integrated into existing operations.

Furthermore, what is only a minor modification to a marketer may be a major operating change to a manufacturing person. Ideally, innovative new products should offer great customer benefit and little upset in the plant. All too often, the manufacturing personnel perceive little customer benefit and great upset in the plant.

8. Adjunct services

Finally, there is a range of services, which often include installation and field service or repair, that concern both marketing and manufacturing. As in the preceding areas, interests and perceptions differ, and conflict is frequent. Factory people, for example, tend to view installation as the final manufacturing operation while marketers view it as a customer service function.

THE BASIC CAUSES

The explainable reasons for conflict in the problem areas just discussed fall into two categories. One consists of basic causes found in almost every industrial goods producer. The other is complicating factors that exacerbate the basic causes in certain situations. Here, I will confine my discussion to a review of the basic causes. Then, in the following section, I will examine the complicating factors.

Evaluation and Reward. One prime reason for the marketing/manufacturing conflict is that the two functions are evaluated on the basis of different criteria and receive rewards for different activities. On the one hand, the marketing people are judged on the basis of profitable growth of the company in terms of sales, market share, and new markets entered. Unfortunately, the marketers are sometimes more sales-oriented than profit-oriented. On the other hand, the manufacturing people are often evaluated on running a smooth operation at minimum cost. Similarly unfortunately, they are sometimes more cost-oriented than profit-oriented.

This system of evaluation and reward means that the marketers are encouraged to generate change, which is one hallmark of the competitive marketplace. To be rewarded, they must generate new products, enter new markets, and develop new programs. But the manufacturing people are clearly rewarded for accepting change only when it significantly lowers their costs.

Because the marketers and manufacturers both want to be evaluated positively and rewarded well, each function responds as the system asks it to in order to protect its self-interest.

The nature of the costs involving the problem areas magnifies the differences in the evaluation and reward system. The prior discussion about breadth of product line is a good example. Because the costs of a broader line are primarily in the manufacturing area, the manufacturing manager emphasizes the advantages of a narrower line. The reverse is true for the marketer. Thus the situation literally forces each manager into an adversary position. Each creates pressure for the policy that minimizes his costs, maximizes his benefits, and leads to a positive evaluation and an appropriate reward.

Inherent Complexity. Many of the problem areas help to engender conflict by the very nature of their inherent complexity. Because they involve at least two different functions, they usually need data from two different sources. Furthermore, the data are typically a mixture of "soft" (i.e., qualitative) marketing data and "hard" (i.e., quantified) manufacturing data. With regard to capacity expansion, it is fairly easy to determine the costs of facilities and equipment but hard to forecast sales and capacity utilization.

The problem areas are also complex because of the amount of the organization they involve. In many ways, the sales and the manufacturing operations represent the real horsepower of a company. They are the line functions that support the planning, financial, control, and administrative staffs. Thus any issue at this interface involves the core of the company.

Moreover, there is inherent complexity both conceptually and operationally at the analysis, policy formulation, and implementation levels. The data are in both sides of the house. The people responsible for formulating and implementing the policies are in both places. And the effects are felt in both.

Orientation and Experience. Another basic cause of conflict relates to the exposure, both current and past, of the managers involved. By and large, the industrial marketer is most likely to have come up through the sales route. He began as a salesperson who "lived and died" by his customers, and his work experience has always emphasized the customer. As a sales manager and even as a marketing manager, he deals with customer problems. The problems may be broader and the accounts larger, but his orientation remains the same—the customer.

The top marketing people usually have offices near the more operationally oriented salespeople, work with them on an intimate basis, and even visit field sales locations

and customers. Their early biases are thus magnified by the people and situations they deal with on a day-to-day basis.

Their counterparts in manufacturing often began as foremen and worked up through the production operation. They are aware of factory problems. They understand them, and they are exposed to them every day. Even the top manufacturing executives interact with their close (organizationally and geographically) associates whose prime concern is the plant. They visit manufacturing operations much more frequently than they do customers.

Each marketing and each manufacturing manager is more aware of his own organizational situation and problems. Each is more at ease with his own function. Each is also more in tune with his own subordinates. He hires and trains them. He shares their experiences and viewpoints. He understands their orientations and attitudes. How could they be anything but right?

Cultural Differences. In most situations, the top level marketing and manufacturing managers literally live differently. As an example, consider two executives at an actual but disguised company that I will call here the Stopem Startem Controller Company (SSC). This company is a medium-sized midwestern producer of electronic flow controllers for liquids and gases sold to original equipment manufacturers, engineering contractors, and end-users in process industries such as chemicals, paper, and petroleum refining.

Sam Sell, who is vice president of sales and marketing, received a bachelor's degree in chemical engineering from Drexel Institute in Philadelphia. He began his career as a salesman and worked for several other companies before joining SSC. Bob Build, vice president of manufacturing, received a bachelor's degree in mechanical engineering from Purdue University and a master's in industrial engineering from Illinois Institute of Technology. He began as a foreman with SSC and worked his way up through line and staff production positions.

These two executives differ literally in the way they live as well as in the way in which they manage. Sam Sell has much greater ego drive and empathy (the typical salesperson's personality structure) than Bob Build. Sell drives an Oldsmobile 98 and enjoys golf, tennis, and poker. Build drives a Porsche, which he maintains himself, and his hobbies are his car, gardening, and woodworking. He is a meticulous craftsman. In short, they fulfill their different marketing and manufacturing stereotypes. But they are real people. And they are the rule rather than the exception.

In fact, despite the belief among some academics I have talked with that the differences just cited are too strongly drawn, there are data to support them. Paul R. Lawrence and Jay W. Lorsch, for example, have found significant differences in the task and social concerns of sales and production managers.[1]

It is not unlikely that Sam Sell's and Bob Build's cultural differences alone would make it hard for them to work together intimately. When this subtle but equally important source of conflict is added to the other previously described basic causes, it is easy to understand why the marketing and manufacturing people don't always see eye-to-eye.

COMPLICATING FACTORS

The situation can be even more complex because there are some additional factors that have an impact on most companies as well as a more limited set of factors that affect some companies. Let us first consider the more limited factors. In some industrial companies, the marketing and manufacturing people must also interface

with either the R&D function or the engineering function, or both. The two-party situation thus becomes a three- or four-party situation.

This interface is especially difficult in the new product area where R&D and engineering are key functions. In many companies that manufacture electrical or mechancial components and/or equipment (e.g., machine tools, drives, hydraulics), the engineering manager plays a role that coordinates manufacturing and marketing and in some cases even subordinates these functions. At times, the nature of the business and its strategy dictate that ascendency. At other times, the engineering manager by virtue of his technical knowledge and/or political strength is the only person who can manage the marketing/manufacturing interface.

Other functions enter the picture to add complexity to certain decision areas. The finance people, for example, are almost always intimately involved with capacity planning decisions. Control personnel are usually active in cost control and often in inventory control/physical distribution decisions.

Companies with large and diverse product lines have a particularly difficult job in managing the marketing/manufacturing interface. Rapidly growing companies also encounter special difficulties because the pressures for performance are greater, the resources more strained, and the organizational mechanisms often less developed. Thus, although the need for cooperation is greater, the capabilities to cooperate are sometimes more limited.

These situations affect only some companies. Almost all manufacturers, however, feel the effects of environmental changes. The economy has been more erratic than in the recent past. Since the sales cycles of most industrial goods companies are closely related to the general business cycle, they are greatly affected. Sales forecasting is more difficult, product planning is harder, and mistakes are more costly. Mistakes also

[1]Paul R. Lawrence and Jay W. Lorsch, "Differentiation and Integration in Complex Organizations," *Administrative Quarterly* (June 1967), p. 1.

contribute to long-term counterproductive antagonisms.

Technology is changing more rapidly. Products more quickly become obsolete, and then processes need to be replaced. This environmental change puts tremendous burdens on both marketers and manufacturers.

Closely related to technological change is the proliferation of automated operations, which are often much harder to change than more labor-intensive operations. Mistakes are more expensive, and response to marketing needs slower. However, even newer technologies utilizing minicomputers may allow more flexible response. But until these are developed, automation apparently makes the marketing/manufacturing interface less fluid and thus more exasperating.

Capital constraints and the high cost of capital make major manufacturing changes expensive and redeployment of plant facilities difficult. Mistakes are visible, and poor response and poor coordination can't be easily covered over by committing more dollars.

Finally, the sheer increase in the size of companies makes the marketing/manufacturing interface more difficult to manage. More people are involved. For example, if it is a multidivision corporation, both the marketing and the manufacturing managers must coordinate not only with one another, but also with divisional functional managers, the division general manager, and their corporate counterparts.

The situation is, however, not all bleak.

MANAGING THE CONFLICT

Like market competition, conflict can ensure effectiveness and efficiency. Top management's task is to maintain a constructive amount of tension by making sure that both marketing and manufacturing understand the need for a balanced situation but still strongly represent their own interests.

Explicit Policies

Top management can balance the interface with more than the traditional techniques of mediation and arbitration, which are useful and necessary. A good beginning is the development and promulgation of clear, straightforward corporate policies. For example, marketing and manufacturing are much less likely to argue about product line breadth if, as a conscious policy, the company decides to be a full-line producer, to emphasize only high-volume items, or to concentrate on some other category of products. Such policies provide a set of rules within which the marketing and manufacturing people can operate, and they encompass most, if not all, of the problem areas delineated earlier.

Illustrative Examples. Let me demonstrate the importance of explicit corporate policies covering the marketing/manufacturing interface by offering two examples.

In one situation, a manufacturer sold replacement parts for heavy construction equipment to distributors and large end-users. To the marketing people, the essence of their strategy was rapid response to orders and on-time delivery because lack of a part could keep an expensive piece of equipment out of operation. To the manufacturing people, the basis of their approach was effective asset management, which meant low inventories and high capacity utilization.

However, manufacturing's low inventories made it impossible for the company to provide rapid response to orders. High capacity utilization implied undercapacity when the highly cyclical construction industry was busiest.

Vocal dissatisfaction from key distributors and large end-users finally reached top management. After several meetings involving both marketing and manufacturing people a task force was formed to study the issue. The task force approach had two happy results. First, the people involved developed personal cross-functional relationships. Second, explicit corporate guidelines accepted by top management included the measurement of manufacturing people on service levels stressing percentage of orders shipped complete and percentage shipped on time.

In short, the guidelines clarified the trade-off between service level on the one hand and inventory size and capacity utilization on the other. The conflict problem was not "solved," but the tension was brought under control.

In the other situation, a manufacturer of office furniture was subject to frequent hassles concerning length of product line. Because no explicit goal had been established, the manufacturing vice president constantly fought to reduce the line and his marketing counterpart fought to expand it. They found it impossible to jointly analyze the financial impact of changes in product line length, and each became more strongly committed to his own belief.

The sales manager, who reported to the marketing vice president, provided ample evidence of "lost sales" because the line lacked additional "popular" styles. Similarly, the plant manager supported the manufacturing vice president with reams of data on the "cost" of the "overly long" product line. No light but much heat was generated by quarterly "planning" meetings.

Subsequently, in desperation, a team of outside experts was handed the problem. The team clarified costs, studied the market, and—as in the previous example—made explicit the trade-off between a broader product line more attuned to customer needs and a smaller product line more responsive to manufacturing constraints. In this particular example, the management decision to contract the product line in particular areas was incorporated into a revised strategic plan. Nobody was totally pleased with the solution but both functional sides viewed the result as a "sensible compromise."

Over time, the management guidelines have been adjusted to changes in customer needs, competitive activities, manufacturing capabilities, and technology. In fact, product line length is now a major parameter of the corporate business plan.

Each function should also be responsible for developing policies that relate to the total corporate strategy and to the needs of its sister function. Thus, if the manufacturing schedule and corporate policies are oriented toward large orders, the sales force can have policies limiting small orders. Or, on the other hand, if delivery is a key part of corporate and marketing policy, the manufacturing operation can emphasize high finished and semifinished inventory. Although it is poor policy to have the marketing function stressing delivery while manufacturing stresses low finished goods inventory, it is not unusual to find such situations.

Modified Measurements

To bolster common policies, the evaluation and reward system can be modified to stress interfunctional cooperation. Marketing managers might, for example, be judged on those variables viewed as important to the manufacturing operation. Good sales forecasting might be rewarded instead of going over the sales quota. If the sales people are judged on their ability to beat the quota, they will keep it low rather than realistic.

Manufacturing people might be judged on a combination of inventory size, delivery response time, and the ability to meet delivery commitment dates rather than just on asset management. Cost goals should be spelled out not only in terms of lower costs but also in terms of improved performance in quality, implementation of new product introduction, and so forth.

A common evaluation and reward system can be effective only if there are policies on which the criteria can be based and data that enable measurement against a plan. Many companies don't, for example, have planned or actual breadth of line data. All that is known is that marketing thinks the line is too narrow and manufacturing is just as sure that it is too broad.

The gathering and analysis of data concerning interfunctional problems are useful for more than measuring performance against a plan. Data are necessary to relieve some of the inherent complexity of the interfunctional situations. As an example, if a company were concerned with field service, it would have to have good data on service costs, frequency of failure, impact on the customer and/or prospects, and even the cost of tighter quality control.

It is important for the data to include quantified plans and budgets, as well as actual performance. The best way to evaluate sales forecasting is to record the forecast and compare it with actual sales. The same is true of the other problem areas.

The data to be gathered will vary with the type of industry and the situation but should in general focus as closely as possible on the basic desired parameters. As well as cost performance, these data will often emphasize customer needs such as inventory support, rapid repair service, and the like.

In fact, it is quite realistic to survey customers concerning their perceptions and to use these as a basis for analysis, planning, and evaluation. For example, while it is important to measure the cost of a service operation, average frequency of repair, and maximum time from request to repair, it is also useful to ask customers to rate the service quality, helpfulness of repair people, and so on.

People Concerns

Several people-oriented approaches can be taken, the simplest of which is to encourage informal interfunctional contact. The best sales meetings, for example, include manufacturing managers and representatives from other functional areas. This enables the manufacturers to meet informally with the marketers in both work and recreational settings. Experiences and concerns can be shared. Perhaps even more important, personal relationships can be developed. These generate mutual respect and understanding, which are particularly useful when difficult interfunctional problems are confronted.

Another people-oriented approach involves mixed career paths. If more managers cross over functional lines during their development, they will better understand the activities, concerns, and values of their sister functions. It will also lead to better balanced top managers. Most companies shy away from this approach because they fear the upset or cost. Concerns include, "I don't want a foreman-type to ruin a good customer" or "That sales-type will be eaten alive by the union."

While such concerns are valid, the problems are clearly not insurmountable— especially if the program is begun fairly early in career development and fairly low in the organization where risks are minimal. This career path approach requires a strong management commitment but the benefits can be high because it provides a solution to the orientation, experience, and cultural differences discussed earlier.

A major side benefit is the development of broad-experienced general managers. A surprisingly large proportion of outstanding division general managers has risen this way. In the past such a path often came about haphazardly. In the future, it should be part of a combined executive development program and method of coping with interfunctional conflict.

Still another people-oriented approach is less drastic than mixed career paths and perhaps less effective. Many opportunities present themselves for interfunctional task forces and committees. If these are well-developed and involve people at lower levels in the organization, they can be effective in helping each function to learn from the other. The informal contact engendered by such a program can often be as useful as the purely task-related interaction.

Mediation and arbitration cannot be neglected as useful tools in managing the interface. They are really a part of the broader, more focused program recommended here. Top management can gain much by bringing marketing and manufacturing people together in an air of cooperation to analyze, plan, and implement approaches to problem areas. These sessions will be particularly useful if, as previously mentioned, goals are explicitly specified and credible data are available.

STRENGTHENING THE FUNCTIONS

In order to lessen the amount of marketing/manufacturing conflict, management can make each function more responsive to the other's needs. Marketers should build their programs around the operational strengths of their manufacturing unit. Thus the marketing executive must not only analyze his customers and prospects to understand their needs, but also analyze the manufacturing capability to understand its competitive strengths and constraints. Then, he must divide his market into segments and select for penetration those segments whose needs he can fill. Finally, he must develop a product policy that builds on the manufacturing unit's ability to service customers in the chosen segments.

This kind of strategy is a great deal easier to describe than to implement. Few companies have explicit policies that provide a clear definition of the products and services they will offer and the benefits they will provide to the customer. Thus a product policy might state, "We will provide large volumes of a limited line of utilitarian items at low cost to customers who are capable of buying such volumes and willing to accept little variety and infrequent design change."

It requires a great deal of top management discipline to select market segments and develop product policies. Without such an explicit strategy, the company begins to be "all things to all people" and eventually becomes "nothing to everybody." The marketing function is thus given the task of selecting customers who need the company's products.

The manufacturing function should not offer the marketers a fixed capability. Instead, the productive capacity of the company should become a well-honed marketing tool. In the past 12 years two main concepts have been developed by manufacturing scholars to help to accomplish this.

Martin K. Starr has suggested that products can be designed so that they can be made of interchangeable modules. With the appropriate production process, this modular approach enables the manufacturing function to provide substantial variety to the customer at limited cost. In such a situation, argues Starr, "Marketing management supplies the consumer with apparent variety even though the production output is based on the concepts of mass production."[2]

Careful design of the manufacturing system can do even more. Wickham Skinner has shown that improved competitiveness can result from "learning to focus each plant on a limited, concise, manageable set of products, technologies, volumes, and markets" and from "learning to structure basic manufacturing policies and supporting services so that they focus on one explicit manufacturing task instead of on many inconsistent, conflicting, implicit tasks."[3] This approach enables a company to build

[2]Martin K. Starr, "Modular Production—A New Concept," *Harvard Business Review* (November-December 1965), p. 137.

[3]Wickham Skinner, "The Focused Factory," *Harvard Business Review* (May-June 1974), p. 114.

its manufacturing capability in response to the specific needs of a clearly defined market segment. In a sales sense, customer benefits are maximized while manufacturing costs are minimized.

Recent suggestions that large factories are not necessarily efficient make the Skinner concept even more implementable.[4] One large auto parts supplier, for example, has committed itself to the construction of small (no more than 500 employees) plants designed around specific customer needs and production technologies. This focused approach is a far cry from the consolidated manufacturing operations of the past.

CONCLUDING NOTE

The following advertisement appeared in a recent issue of the *Saturday Review:*

Semantic difficulty with our Osaka, Japan branch factory has resulted in 468 Concert Grand Pianos, with tonal dynamics in reverse of normal. For particulars write Weaver Piano Company, East Grand Forks, SR Box G.P.R.[5]

While this particular ad was obviously written in jest, actual problems such as this are quite common. But they can be addressed if top management understands that:

☐ The problems of marketing and manufacturing conflict are real and important.

☐ The causes are complex but understandable.

☐ The situation can be improved through carefully developed programs to foster cooperation.

☐ The company will prosper when the marketing and manufacturing functions operate in an atmosphere of cooperation with the realization that each has its role to play and its needs to fill. Neither function can subvert the other.

[4]See Roger W. Schmenner, "Before You Build a *Big* Factory," *Harvard Business Review* (July–August 1976), p. 100.

[5]*Saturday Review* (October 30, 1976), p. 60.

38 Profitability Analysis by Market Segments

Leland L. Beik
Stephen L. Buzby

The contribution approach to cost accounting serves to relate products, channels, and/or other marketing components to the profitability of market segments. Using the profit criterion, the marketing manager can plan and control his decisions for the component being analyzed and make collateral adjustments in other elements of the marketing mix.

By tracing sales revenues to market segments and relating these revenues to marketing costs, the marketing manager can improve and control his decision making with respect to the firm's profit objective.

First expressed by Smith in 1956, the concept of market segmentation has since been elaborated in many different ways.[1] It has recently been defined by Kotler as ". . . the subdividing of a market into homogeneous subsets of customers, where any subset may conceivably be selected as a market target to be reached with a distinct marketing mix."[2] The underlying logic is based on the assumption that:

. . . the market for a product is made up of customers who differ either in their own characteristics or in the nature of their environment in such a way that some aspect of their demand for the product in question also differs. The strategy of market segmentation involves the tailoring of the firm's product and/or marketing program to these differences. By modifying either of these, the firm is attempting to increase profits by converting a market with heterogeneous demand characteristics into a set of markets that although they differ from one another, are internally more homogeneous than before.[3]

The concept of market segmentation may be used for strategic alignment of the firm's productive capacities with its existing and potential markets. By analyzing market needs and the firm's ability to serve those needs, the basic long-run policies of the firm can be developed. Through choice

[1]Wendell R. Smith, "Product Differentiation and Market Segmentation as Alternative Marketing Strategies," *Journal of Marketing*, 21 (July 1956), pp. 3–8; and James F. Engel, Henry F. Fiorillo, and Murray A. Cayley, eds., *Market Segmentation: Concepts and Applications* (New York: Holt, Rinehart and Winston, Inc., 1972).

[2]Philip Kotler, *Marketing Management*, 2nd ed. (Englewood Cliffs, N.J.: Prentice-Hall, Inc., 1972), p. 166.

[3]Ronald E. Frank, "Market Segmentation Research: Findings and Implications," in *Applications of the Sciences in Marketing Management*, Frank M. Bass, Charles W. King, and Edgar A. Pessemier, eds. (New York: John Wiley & Sons, Inc., 1968), p. 39.

Reprinted with permission from *Journal of Marketing*, published by the American Marketing Association, 37 (July 1973), pp. 48–53.

of target segments, competition may be minimized; through selective cultivation, the firm's competitive posture may be greatly improved.

For both strategic and tactical decisions, marketing managers may profit by knowing the impact of the marketing mix upon the target segments at which marketing efforts are aimed. If the programs are to be responsive to environmental change, a monitoring system is needed to locate problems and guide adjustments in marketing decisions. Tracing the profitability of segments permits improved pricing, selling, advertising, channel, and product management decisions. The success of marketing policies and programs may be appraised by a dollar and cents measure of profitability by segment.

Managerial accounting techniques have dealt with the profitability of products, territories, and some customer classes; but a literature search has revealed not one serious attempt to assess the relative profitability of market segments.[4] Although the term "segment" has a history of use in accounting, this use implies a segment of the business rather than a special partitioning of consumers or industrial users for marketing analysis. Even when classifying customers, accounting classes are formed by frequency and size of order, location, credit rating, and other factors, most of which are related to controlling internal costs or to assessing financial profit.[5]

After indicating the value for marketing decision making, this article will delineate a framework for cost accounting by market segments. An industrial product example is constructed to demonstrate the process and to spell out the features of the contribution approach to cost accounting as applied to accounting for segment profitability. Further discussion extends the concept to a consumer situation and specifies difficulties that may attend full-scale application of the technique. The expectation is that the technique will better control marketing costs and improve marketing decisions.

MARKET SEGMENTATION AND ITS UTILITY

To have value for managerial judgments, Bell notes that market segments should: (1) be readily identified and measured, (2) contain adequate potential, (3) demonstrate effective demand, (4) be economically accessible, and (5) react uniquely to marketing effort.[6] For present purposes, the key criterion for choosing the bases for segmenting a given market is the ability to trace sales and costs to the segments defined. Allocating sales and costs is the most stringent requirement and limitation of profitability accounting as used to support marketing decisions.

Among the many possible bases for market segmentation, the analysis can be accomplished using widely recognized geographic, demographic, and socioeconomic variables.[7] Many of these, such as geographic units and population or income figures, provide known universe classifications against which to compare company sales and cost performance. Other bases of segmentation such as buyer usage rate, expected benefits, or psychological or sociological characteristics of consumers typically require research to match their distribution, directly or indirectly, with company sales and costs.

Given proper segmentation, separate

[4]Closest to the present analysis and perhaps the best summary of the state of the art is Charles H. Sevin, *Marketing Productivity Analysis* (New York: McGraw-Hill Book Company, 1965).

[5]Robert B. Miner, "Distribution Costs," in *Marketing Handbook*, Albert W. Frey, ed. (New York: The Ronald Press Company, 1965); see especially pp. 23–17 and 23–32.

[6]Martin L. Bell, *Marketing: Concepts and Strategy*, 2nd ed. (Boston: Houghton Mifflin Company, 1972), p. 185.

[7]See William M. Weilbacher, "Standard Classification of Consumer Characteristics," *Journal of Marketing*, 31 (January 1967), p. 27.

products (or channels or other elements of the marketing mix) can serve as the primary basis for cost and revenue allocation. Knowledge of profit by segments then contributes directly to decisions concerning the product line and adjustment of sales, advertising, and other decision variables. The process is illustrated in the following industrial example.

A matrix system can be developed as part of marketing planning to partition segments for profitability analysis.[8] A company with lines of computers, calculators, and adding machines might first divide its market into territories as in the upper section of Exhibit 1. The cell representing adding machines in the eastern market might next be sorted by product items and customer classes. The chief product preference of each company class is noted by an important benefit segmentation within the cells of the lower section of Exhibit 1.

Since the segments react differently to product variations and other marketing activities, it is advantageous to isolate profit by product for each market segment. Using this information, the marketing manager can specifically tailor product policies to particular market segments and judge the reaction of segments to increased or decreased marketing efforts over time. Decision adjustments and control of marketing costs interact to improve product line management directly and other decisions indirectly.

In theory, segment profitability analysis is worthwhile only where decisions adjusting the marketing mix add incremental profits that exceed the costs of the extra analysis. In practice, information concerning the profitability of marketing decisions has been so sparse that the analysis is likely to be profitable where allocations to mar-

[8] See William J. E. Crissy and Robert M. Kaplan, "Matrix Models for Marketing Planning," *MSU Business Topics*, 11 (Summer 1963), p. 48. The matrix "targeting" treatment is also familiar to readers of basic marketing texts by E. J. McCarthy or G. D. Downing.

EXHIBIT 1
Matrix breakdown by products and segments

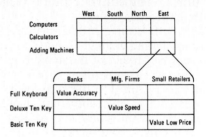

ket segments are approximate and fail to approach theoretical perfection.

MARKETING COST ANALYSIS

In its simplest form, marketing cost analysis relates the cost of marketing activities to sales revenues in order to measure profits. A profit and loss statement must be constructed for any marketing component (e.g., product, channel) being analyzed. The approach consists of dividing the firm's basic costs (e.g., salaries, rent) into their functional categories (e.g., selling, advertising). The functional category amounts are then assigned within the appropriate marketing classifications.

The actual form of the profit and loss statements will depend upon the nature of the company being analyzed, the purpose of the marketing analysis, and the records available. The form of statement will also depend upon the accounting technique used to assign costs to the marketing components under study. One might use a full-cost approach, assigning both direct and indirect costs across the marketing classifications on the best available bases. Alternatively, one might use a direct-cost approach and assign direct costs only, avoiding arbitrary assignment of fixed or overhead costs. Most marketing sources have utilized the full- and direct-cost approaches.

EXHIBIT 2

Product productivity analysis—contribution approach

	COMPANY TOTAL	FULL KEYBOARD	DELUXE TEN KEY	BASIC TEN KEY
Net sales	$10,000	$5,000	$3,000	$2,000
Variable Manufacturing Costs	5,100	2,500	1,375	1,225
Mfg. Contribution	$ 4,900	$2,500	$1,625	$ 775
Marketing Costs				
Variable:				
Sales Commissions	450	225	135	90
Variable Contribution	$ 4,450	$2,275	$1,490	$ 685
Assignable:				
Salaries—Salesmen	1,600	770	630	200
Salary—Marketing Manager	100	50	25	25
Product Advertising	1,000	670	200	130
Total	$ 2,700	$1,490	$ 855	$ 355
Product Contribution	$ 1,750	$ 785	$ 635	$ 330
Nonassignable:				
Institutional Advertising	150			
Marketing Contribution	$ 1,600			
Fixed-joint Costs				
General Administration	300			
Manufacturing	900			
Total	$ 1,200			
Net Profits	$ 400			

A third costing approach is better suited to the needs of the marketing manager and the requirements of analysis by market segments. Essentially, it is an adaptation of the contribution approach to preparing financial statements.[9] Exhibit 2 presents a simplified illustration of how the contribution approach can be adapted to break out product profitability for adding machines in the eastern market.

First, all of the variable nonmarketing costs have been assigned to products. These costs represent nonmarketing dollar expenditures which fluctuate, in total, directly in proportion to short-run changes in the sales volume of a given product. Similarly, variable marketing costs have been deducted to produce variable product contribution margins identical to those which would result from a direct costing approach.

The remaining marketing costs have been broken down into two categories—assignable and nonassignable. The assignable costs represent dollar expenditures of a fixed or discretionary nature for which reasonably valid bases exist for allocating them to specific products. For example, the assignment of salesmen's salaries in Exhibit 2 might be based on Sevin's recommendation to use "selling time devoted to each product, as shown by special sales-call reports or special studies."[10] The marketing manager's salary could be assigned on the

[9]See Charles R. Horngren, *Cost Accounting: A Managerial Emphasis*, 2nd ed. (Englewood Cliffs, N.J.: Prentice-Hall, Inc., 1967); and Ralph L. Day and Peter D. Bennett, "Should Salesmen's Compensation be Geared to Profits?" *Journal of Marketing*, 26 (October 1962), pp. 6-9.

[10]Sevin, *op. cit.*, p. 13.

basis of personal records indicating the amount of time devoted to the management of each product. Product advertising would be assigned by reference to the actual amount spent on advertising each product.

The use of the actual dollar level of sales was purposely avoided in choosing the allocation bases for the assignable costs in Exhibit 2. Horngren, among others, has stated that when dealing with fixed or discretionary costs, "The costs of efforts are independent of the results actually obtained, in the sense that the costs are programmed by management, not determined by sales."[11]

The nonassignable marketing costs represent dollar expenditures of a fixed or discretionary nature for which there are no valid bases for assignment to products. Consequently, institutional advertising has not been assigned to the products to avoid confounding the product profitability margins which would result from the arbitrary allocation of this cost. Since the primary purpose is calculating marketing-related product contribution margins, the remaining nonmarketing costs can be taken as a deduction from the total marketing contribution margin to produce a net profit figure for the firm.

Although the preceding example was purposely simplified, the framework is sufficiently flexible to handle different objectives and more complex problems. If the firm in Exhibit 2 were a single product firm, for example, the three customer classes (banks, manufacturers, and retailers) could easily be substituted for primary emphasis in place of the products. The analysis would differ only through variations in the treatment of fixed, variable, and assignable costs required by the new objective. That assignability changes with objective may be illustrated by the fact that product advertising costs can often be assigned to products but rarely to customer classes.

[11]Horngren, *op. cit.*, p. 381.

To aid in handling more complex problems, a discussion of common bases for assigning a wide range of marketing costs may be found in Sevin.[12] In some instances, the approach can be further improved by application of mathematical programming to assign costs to the marketing components.[13] Budgetary data and marketing lags could also be introduced to upgrade the analysis.[14]

COSTING BY SEGMENTS

In particular, the framework of the contribution approach may be applied to costing by segments. Exhibit 3 extends the product analysis of Exhibit 2. Recall that the segments are partitioned by territorial, customer class, and product benefit criteria although the primary customer class names are used to identify segments in the table. Instead of tracing the sales of each product to all three customer classes, one simplifying device is to identify the primary benefit sought by a customer class as segment sales and to combine sales of the given product to the other customer classes as nonsegment sales. For example, sales of the full-keyboard adding machine to banks become segment sales, while sales to large manufacturing firms or to retailers are nonsegment sales. This device is appropriate where nontarget sales are expected to be minimal; otherwise more columns can be added to the table.

Where sales revenues can be traced directly to customers, customer classes, and

[12]Sevin, *op. cit.*, Chapter 2.

[13]William J. Baumol and Charles H. Sevin, "Marketing Costs and Mathematical Programming," in *Management Information: A Quantitative Accent*, Thomas Williams and Charles Griffin, eds. (Homewood, Ill.: Richard D. Irwin, Inc., 1967), pp. 176–90.

[14]Richard A. Feder, "How to Measure Marketing Performance," in *Readings in Cost Accounting, Budgeting, and Control*, 3rd ed., W. Thomas Jr., ed. (Cincinnati, Ohio: South-Western Publishing Co., 1968), pp. 650–68.

EXHIBIT 3

Segment productivity analysis—contribution approach

	COMPANY TOTAL	FULL KEYBOARD		DELUXE TEN KEY		BASIC TEN KEY
		BANK SEG.	NONSEG.	MFG. SEG.	NONSEG.	RETAIL SEG.
Net Sales	$10,000	$3,750	$1,250	$2,550	$450	$2,000
Variable Manufacturing Costs	5,100	1,875	625	1,169	206	1,225
Mfg. Contribution	$ 4,900	$1,875	$ 625	$1,381	$244	$ 775
Marketing Costs						
Variable:						
Sales Commissions	450	169	56	115	20	90
Variable Contribution	$ 4,450	$1,706	$ 569	$1,266	$224	$ 685
Assignable:						
Salaries—Salesmen	1,600	630	140	420	210	200
Salary—Marketing Manager	100	38	12	19	6	25
Product Advertising	1,000	670	-0-	200	-0-	130
Total	$ 2,700	$1,338	$ 152	$ 639	$216	$ 355
Segment Contribution	$ 1,750	$ 368	$ 417	$ 627	$ 8	$ 330
Nonassignable:						
Institutional Advertising	150					
Marketing Contribution	$ 1,600					
Fixed-joint Costs						
General Administration	300					
Manufacturing	900					
Total	$ 1,200					
Net Profits	400					

territories and where marketing costs can be similarly traced, the analysis is straightforward. Where the less tangible benefit segmentation is used, sales analysis or marketing research must measure the degree to which benefits are related to each customer class. If sales analysis shows that banks purchase 75% of the full-keyboard sales because they value accuracy while manufacturers and retailers account for the remaining 25%, both revenues and sales commissions may be prorated accordingly. This allocation is employed in Exhibit 3.

To illustrate a few marketing implications, it might be noted that over one-half of the full-keyboard profit contribution actually comes from nonsegment sales rather than from the primary target segment. The nonsegment profitability results in part from low personal selling and absence of advertising costs. An opportunity possibly exists in further promotion, perhaps to large manufacturing firms. Had the table completed the analysis for purchases of full-keyboard machines by manufacturers and retailers, the actual segment of opportunity could be pinpointed. If institutional or other possible sales proved substantial during further classification, a new segment of opportunity might be identified.

Quite obviously, the eastern banking segment has a low profit contribution considering the level of marketing effort expended. Exhibit 3 deals with one sample area and product class, and a comparison with other area banking segments might prove enlightening. Perhaps marketing costs could be reduced in the eastern segment if sales were up to par. Or if sales were comparatively low, marketing effort (price, personal selling, advertising) could be reallocated to meet competition more effectively.

Similar analysis can be applied to the manufacturing and retailing segments of Exhibit 3, and to the territories and products not incorporated in the present illustration. The advantage over standard sales analysis is that a profit rather than a volume measure is applied and that variations in marketing costs and sales response are taken into account.

MARKETING PRODUCTIVITY: CONSUMER SEGMENTS

The previous example has been simplified so that minimum tables serve to explain the technique. Segment analysis becomes complex as more than two or three criteria are used for partitioning and as additional criteria are considered for different classes of marketing decisions. A further example adds realism and extends the concept to a consumer situation.

A company that sells snowmobiles is likely to have some special channel problems. To control channel management, meteorological data permit primary and secondary snow belts to be mapped across the U.S. and Canada. Sales analysis or research could show how to allocate purchases among consumers in major metropolitan, city, town, and rural areas. Further analysis could determine patronage among department stores, automotive dealers, farm equipment dealers, marinas, and other classes of outlets. Sales to resorts for rentals might be included as a segment or analyzed separately. Finally, the several analyses could map sales into geographical units. Segmenting by snow conditions, population density, outlets patronized, and dwelling area, and then allocating revenues and costs to the segments would

point outlet selection and channel adjustments toward the more profitable outlets in favorable population and snow-belt locations.

By collecting and analyzing warranty card information, snowmobile purchasers could be classified as to family life cycle, social status, or other variables. This data would probe the profit potential of appealing to young families, selected social classes, or possibly even to hunters, sailing enthusiasts, and other outdoor people. Dates on the warranty cards would help adjust the timing of promotions in advance of the snow season or to balance the pre-Christmas advertising in line with purchase habits of its customer segments. Having targeted promotion on the basis of past data, current warranty card information, and revenue and cost information, the profitability of each target segment could be determined.

Analyzing the profitability of advertising or price decisions involves special problems in tracing sales and costs. If segments have been defined on tangible bases, say area and dealer patronage, the difficulty might be overcome by setting up an experiment.[15] Variations of advertising messages, local media, and possible price would serve as treatments in segments matched to control other variables. Recording segment revenues and treatment costs would constitute a profit measure of selected advertising and/or price decisions. Experiments may thus be used with segment cost analysis to plan corporate marketing programs.

MANAGERIAL IMPLICATIONS

Given responsible means of partitioning market segments, major elements of the marketing mix may be segregated for analysis using the contribution approach to cost accounting. An example has been em-

[15]Sevin, *op. cit.*, Chapters 6, 7, and 8.

ployed to show how segment profitability can be measured for items in a product line thereby contributing directly to product management decisions. By analyzing the profit and loss statements for the costs of other marketing efforts, additional adjustments can be made in other decisions such as personal selling and advertising. A further example has indicated how channel and other marketing management problems can be similarly gauged by a profit measure for a consumer product and consumer segments.

Several major problems have to be met in applying costing techniques to market segments. One difficulty is choosing productive bases for segmentation, and limiting analysis to a manageable number of bases is another. Although some bases are obvious from experience, they remain product specific, and criteria for choice are not fully developed. Another major problem is obtaining data for the less tangible modes of segmentation, particularly data that permit assignment of sales revenues and costs in accord with each base used for segment definition.

Recognizing and solving problems, however, often leads to further improvements. For example, many of the behavioral applications to marketing imply use in segment analysis but are difficult to relate to other marketing variables on any basis other than judgment. As limitations of source data are overcome, profit accounting by segments may add to the marketing utility of behavioral advances.

Costing by market segments promises improvement in marketing efficiency by way of better planning of expenditures and control of costs. Upon documenting reasons for today's soaring marketing costs, Weiss comments over and over that marketing costs are resistant to sophisticated cost analysis and that marketing cost controls are inadequate in modern corporations.[16] Although not calculated to stem such pressures as inflation, cost accounting by market segments can control selling, advertising, packaging, and other marketing costs in relation to profit potentials. Perhaps even greater value stems from the potential ability to fine-tune product offerings and other marketing decisions to the requirements of well-defined consumer segments. As part of the material regularly supplied to marketing managers, market segment profitability analysis could easily become a key component of marketing information systems of the future.

[16]E. B. Weiss, "Pooled Marketing: Antidote for Soaring Marketing Costs," *Advertising Age*, 43 (November 13, 1972), pp. 63–64.

39 Improving Sales Force Productivity

William P. Hall

Increasing the productivity of salesmen is one method for boosting profits. The author discusses field cost ratios, and suggests ways to evaluate and improve sales force effectiveness.

Mention "productivity" and the typical manager thinks immediately of the manufacture of more units in less time or at less cost. Indeed, industrial engineering is a well-established profession devoted to setting work standards and constantly searching out opportunities to improve manufacturing productivity.

Less frequently does top corporate management, or marketing management, give thought to sales force productivity. Granted, most sales and marketing managers understand cost ratios and recognize the need to improve volume per salesman or territory. Yet, in attempting to achieve real breakthroughs, they typically suffer from several problems.

- ☐ Nobody is quite sure what sales cost ratios are proper for a particular business.
- ☐ Applying productivity concepts to a sales force is either unfamiliar ground, distasteful, or a "no-no" area.

- ☐ Even if the interest is there, staff support or capability is lacking.
- ☐ Solutions are applied piecemeal, or to individual territories, and are not applied as part of a total plan.

WHAT COSTS DO WE LIVE WITH?

Since most productivity improvements are geared to standards of some kind, it helps to start the exercise by giving some thought to standards. Rarely is a stopwatch applied to the activities of sales personnel. Almost never is a time study made of a salesman's day. In fact, the typical reaction of sales management may be, "Salesmen are different, so keep your stopwatch in the factory."

The closest management generally comes to worrying about a sales standard is to address the matter of cost ratios. "How do our costs compare with those of the competition? Are we above or below them?" The typical reply has been, "Well, I really don't know, but old Charlie might tell me if I spend enought time with him over a couple of martinis."

In recent years, increasingly valuable information has been developed to assist in answering the cost question. For example, the American Management Association compensation surveys provide helpful data. Surveys by The Conference Board have also advanced the cause. In recent years, *Sales Management* magazine has initiated its annual survey of selling costs. This survey provides data on levels and trends in compensation, travel, and related costs. Finally, trade associations may survey members, as often as once a year, to develop pertinent cost and other financial ratios. Many commodity line associations in wholesaling have well organized cost surveys, and such surveys have long been common in retailing.

However, in many areas of the economy, and particularly in manufacturing, good sales-cost data are either not available or are too broad in nature. That is, if available, they tend to encompass too many types of businesses and do not break down sales costs into such components as field sales force compensation, travel expenses, and supervision.

During 1974, I participated in two surveys which shed some light on how field sales costs function. Further, they provide insight into answering the perplexing question of how to know when costs are too high and, more important, what to do about it in terms of improved productivity.

Field Cost Inflation

Beginning in the early 1950s, American Supply Association (formerly Central Supply Association), which serves plumbing distributors, has been making surveys of sales compensation practices among its members. Since 1959, A. T. Kearney, Inc.,

EXHIBIT 1

Trend in salesmen's compensation cost ratios, 1959–1974

YEAR	AVERAGE SALES PER TERRITORY	AVERAGE COMPENSATION	COMPENSATION AS PERCENT OF SALES
1959	$200,000	$ 6,000	3.0%
1962	238,600	7,200	3.0
1970	322,900	11,000	3.4
1974	536,900	14,600	2.7

SOURCE: American Supply Association.

has assisted ASA in preparing and interpreting a number of these surveys. Among the findings are those shown in Exhibit 1.

Although the ratio was somewhat above 3.0 percent in 1970 and somewhat below in 1974, it is apparent that the typical ratio of sales compensation cost to sales has been very close to 3.0 percent over a long period of time. It is further apparent that, as compensation has risen with inflation, sales per territory have increased. Finally, it is clear that if sales volume lags behind salary escalation, as it did in 1970, the cost ratio increases. Or, a significant improvement in volume per territory can drive the cost ratio below the 3.0 percent average, as it did in 1974.

Looking at 1980, if the rate of inflation continues at 10 percent, then the average level of compensation will be $25,865 per salesman. The salesman, in turn, will have to generate sales per territory of $862,000, if his cost ratio is to be 3.0 percent.

In short, average volume per territory must continue to grow with inflation, and it must be carefully monitored relative to the cost ratio it produces. Further, compensation is only part of the cost of keeping a salesman on the road. Other costs include fringe benefits, travel expenses, supervision, and miscellaneous expenses, such as telephone and office expenses. Finally, the three components of the equation (volume per salesman or territory, cost of the field effort per territory, and the resulting cost ratio) can vary widely from industry to industry.

Beating the Average

A specific survey of field sales costs which I managed in 1974 provides a revealing example of how field sales costs function. Participants were manufacturers of building materials and related products. Each participant provided, among other inputs, data as to average sales volume per sales territory and field sales cost ratios (salesmen's compensation, salesmen's expense, and overhead expense). For four companies with very similar commodity lines, average sales per salesman, and average sales cost ratios were as shown in Exhibit 2. When graphed, the relationship between volume per territory and the cost ratio is rather dramatic, as shown in Exhibit 3.

Although other survey participants had results above and below the line in the graph, the conclusion is inescapable that higher volume per territory results in substantially lower field sales costs. It may be said that the results are obvious. However, I have not run into too many sales or marketing managers who have had an opportunity to view their results on such a basis. Comparative data are difficult to assemble and often show only average results (as in the ASA survey), not the dramatic differences between Company A and Company D.

Remember that these companies carry roughly similar product lines. If the difference between Company A and Company

EXHIBIT 3
Cost/volume relationship

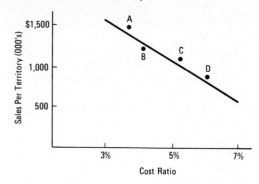

D were small, it would be easy to claim that the concept had no particular significance. However, consider the possible savings if Company D could achieve a 5.0 percent cost ratio goal (close to the average of the four companies, and yet well below the ratios of Company A and Company B).

Company D has total sales of about $57 million. One way to achieve better results would be to produce $75 million of sales with the same sales force. Since such an increase over current volume might be difficult, another possibility would be to maintain sales at the $57 million level and decrease the number of salesmen. As shown in Exhibit 4, the cost savings possibilities approach $1 million.

The point to be made is that the savings potential is very large, and it is not fictional, for competitors are already enjoy-

EXHIBIT 2
Sales per territory and sales cost ratios for four selected companies

COMPANY	SALES PER SALESMAN	FIELD COST RATIO
A	$1,500,000	3.8%
B	1,250,000	4.1
C	990,000	5.3
D	760,000	6.7

EXHIBIT 4
Savings from improved sales productivity, Company D

	AVERAGE COST RATIO	
	6.7%	5.0%
Total volume	$57,000,000	$57,000,000
Total field sales cost	3,819,000	2,850,000
Number of salesmen	75	56
Average sales per salesman	$ 760,000	$ 1,018,000
Average cost per salesman	50,920	50,920

ing such results. In fact, a 5.0 percent cost ratio is still well below the performance of Companies A and B.

Further Observations on the Cost/Volume Ratio

A number of observations should be made about the functioning of the cost/volume relationship, as illustrated in Exhibit 3.

Inflationary Impact. With inflation, the base line formed by the averages moves upward. That is, it functions as shown in Exhibit 5.

To maintain a 5.0 percent cost ratio over time and with inflation, more volume has to be sold per salesman. In other words, real improvement in the ratio will only be brought about by increasing volume per territory at a rate substantially greater than the rate of inflation.

EXHIBIT 5
Upward movement with time (inflation)

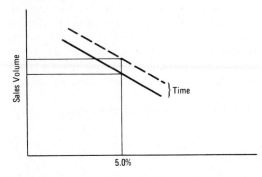

Industry Differences. From our study of five different product groups, it is clear that the general cost/volume relationship prevailed for all five. However, the fitted curve varied as shown in Exhibit 6.

Clearly, cost characteristics can differ between types of products. Hence, it is important to develop the means to compare results with industry groupings which are as similar as possible. The more disparate the

EXHIBIT 6
Difference in cost/volume relationship between industries

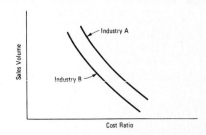

industries, the more invalid the comparison. For example, salesmen for steel mills generate very high volumes per individual, while salesmen of institutional furniture and equipment generate relatively low volumes per salesman. A comparison of these two industry groups might appear as in Exhibit 7.

Useful conclusions can be made by comparing steel companies with each other or institutional furniture companies with one another. Nothing is to be gained by comparising [sic] disparate industries, in view of the vastly different sales and product environments.

Profitability. One shortcoming of the cost/volume comparison is that it lacks any perspective on gross profit performance. It is quite valid to argue, "Sure, we have a higher field cost, but our salesmen sell a

EXHIBIT 7
Cost/volume comparison of disparate industries

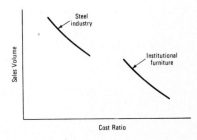

EXHIBIT 8

Comparison of sales costs to gross profit performance

	COMPANY B		COMPANY D	
	000's	MARGIN	000's	MARGIN
Sales per salesman	$1,250	100.0%	$760	100.0%
Gross profit	188	15.0	152	20.0
Field sales cost	51	4.1	51	6.7
Profit contribution	*$ 137*	*10.9%*	*$101*	*13.3%*

more profitable line than Company D." The argument is illustrated in Exhibit 8.

On the one hand, the field cost ratio for Company B is lower, but so also is the profit contribution, because of the low gross profit margin. In short, the lower field cost ratio does not result in a better profit contribution. On the other hand, the *total gross profit dollars* are higher for Company B. Unfortunately, few surveys will be able to compare both sales and gross profit results. We have been able to make some comparisons among a few wholesaler groups, but most manufacturers are reluctant to provide such data.

Accordingly, in my view, the best assumption is that, if product lines are reasonably similar, then gross profits will be sufficiently similar to allow us to return to the original premise: superior sales volume per salesman will result in a low cost ratio, and this lower ratio will favorably affect net profit.

Sales Compensation Plan. Management choice of the field sales compensation program can have an important bearing on how the cost/volume curve functions. The three forms of sales compensation are: salary (fixed), commission (variable), and salary plus incentive (fixed plus variable). To assess the impact of each type of plan on the cost curve, let us assume three salesmen on three different plans. Their results might look as shown in Exhibit 9 and Exhibit 10.

As shown, a commission plan can be considered a "variable" expense from an accounting standpoint, in that the expense dollars rise and fall directly with sales volume. However, when looked at from the standpoint of an expense ratio, it can be considered as just the opposite—the ratio remains fixed as sales rise or fall. Conversely, the fixed cost plan (salary) or fixed plus variable plan (salary plus incentive) results in significant changes in the cost ratio as sales volume rises or falls.

EXHIBIT 9

Cost impact of three compensation plans at various sales levels

	SALES VOLUME (THOUSANDS)		
TYPE OF PLAN	$250	$500	$750
Salary @ $25,000	$25,000	$25,000	$25,000
Commission @ 5% of sales	12,500	25,000	37,500
Salary @ $12,500 plus commission of 2.5%	18,750	25,000	31,250
COST RATIOS			
Salary plan	10.0%	5.0%	3.3%
Commission plan	5.0	5.0	5.0
Salary plus incentive plan	7.5	5.0	4.2

EXHIBIT 10

Sales/cost relationship based on various compensation plans

The importance of this analysis becomes clear. The sales/cost ratio relationship is influenced by the type of plan chosen. It is very difficult to drive the cost ratio down with a straight commission plan. However, the ratio is most responsive to a salary plan, and the ratio responds to a salary plus incentive plan. In view of the great popularity of salary plus incentive plans among businesses these days, it is probably fair to say that management has recognized them as an attractive trade-off. That is, they allow for the impact of ratio improvement and, at the same time, provide rewards to the sales force for good performance, albeit not as generous as with a straight commission plan.

In terms of total field expense (compensation, travel, supervision, etc.), almost all plans have both fixed and variable components. Some commission plans cover compensation only, and the company pays for travel expenses, which are fixed or semi-variable. Others are designed so that salesmen take both income and expenses from their commission check. Even in this latter case, supervision and general sales administrative costs will result in some fixed cost portion. Nonetheless, the general conclusion prevails that it becomes much more difficult to generate field sales cost ratio improvement with a commission plan. Productivity improvement under commission plans is difficult, when considered in terms of cost ratio reduction.

FIELD MANAGEMENT PROBLEMS

Before attacking the questions of why Company A produces such demonstrably better results than Company D and what management of Company D might do about it, some comments should be made about changing conditions which have resulted in the wide variations in performance between companies. Several of these problems, when faced individually or in concert, may have confounded the management of Company D.

Sales Cost Escalation. Ample discussion has already been given to the need to stay ahead of the inflation treadmill. Just to stay even with higher compensation costs and travel expenses, sales per territory must go up proportionately. When sales do not at least keep pace, trouble is abrewing.

Market Changes. Shifts in market size and characteristics call for different sales approaches. As one example, the growth of chain stores and decline of small food retailers have occasioned major shifts in sales approaches by both manufacturers and wholesalers.

Product Proliferation. As product lines have grown, the sales job has become more complex and demanding. Management is faced with the question of when to drop the generalist in favor of the specialist.

Changing Channels. The most successful channel of ten years ago may not be the best way to market today. The building material manufacturer had better have programs geared to the home improvement center chain, or he will be facing a serious loss of position.

Competitive Environment. Growth markets attract new competitors, and mature markets become fiercely price competitive. (At what level will the price of electronic calculators bottom out?)

The sales management equation is not a simple one; hence, achievement of better performance is bedeviled by numerous problems. Yet, these very complexities create an environment for markedly different results between companies in similar businesses. There is ample evidence that wide differences in performance exist.

OPPORTUNITIES FOR PROFIT IMPROVEMENT

In almost every company with conscientious sales management, some type of effort is being made to improve productivity. Each effort may have a modest effect, but, in combination, the results may be impressive. Some of the more productive approaches are worthy of comment. These can best be classified into three broad categories. Beginning with specific problems of territory management and moving towards broad sales/marketing management, these problem categories include territory management, job specialization/job simplification, and general sales management.

Territory Management

This facet of sales productivity improvement relates directly to the field sales effort in terms of what can be accomplished within each territory. It is directed towards the classical sales coverage, which is geographically oriented. Steps for improvement typically include (1) a time and duty analysis, (2) a customer/prospect audit and ABC analysis, and (3) changes in incentive compensation practices.

A time and duty analysis is essentially the function of the industrial engineer. It identifies the major functional components of the sales job (direct face-to-face selling, waiting, travel, and paperwork) and assigns time (and costs) to these elements. It is an aspect of sales management not commonly challenged and not frequently actually studied.

One analysis of sample territories for a large greetings card manufacturer revealed that a substantial portion of the time of well-paid salesmen was being spent serving distributor inventories. This time/cost analysis led to the conclusion that significant improvement in sales force productivity could be realized if the service effort were shifted to lower cost specialists.

A fundamental approach to improved geographical coverage is through application of the ABC analysis based on the customer/prospect audit. Essentially, this technique consists of an analysis of all customers and prospects in a territory, followed by a ranking in terms of their potential into A, B, and C categories. Based on several criteria, the A category could require the most concentrated sales/marketing efforts, and the C category the least. Goals are then set in terms of sales efforts (calls), with the greatest concentration on A accounts.

For example, if a salesman can make one hundred calls per month, he might allocate them as follows: category A, seventy calls per month; category B, twenty; and category C, ten. Customers ranked below C might be covered by telephone or direct mail.

A midwestern wholesaler of farm machinery has emphasized the ABC approach since the late 1960s. Salesmen covering seven territories call on farm equipment dealers. As a result of management emphasis on building volume with A and B dealers, the customer mix shifted from 1970 to 1973 as shown in Exhibit 11. It is interesting to note that the shift in emphasis resulted in the growth of average sales per territory from $368,000 in 1970 to $640,000 in 1973. The sales growth was substantially greater than the increase in field sales expense. Hence, the field cost ratio was reduced, and the savings went to net profit.

As pointed out earlier, profit pay-off from improved sales force productivity can be influenced by the type of sales compensation plan selected. Once the farm equipment wholesaler sold its sales management and sales personnel on the ABC approach, it changed sales compensation from a

EXHIBIT 11

Application of ABC analysis in seven territories, 1970–73

CUSTOMER RANKING	DEALERS		CALLS		VOLUME (THOUSANDS)	
	1970	1973	1970	1973	1970	1973
A	53	140	849	2,406	$ 609	$2,478
B	109	151	1,554	1,974	766	1,071
C	428	327	4,232	3,028	1,064	839
D	371	251	1,852	1,008	143	80
Total	*961*	*869*	*8,487*	*8,416*	*$2,582*	*$4,468*

heavy commission orientation to a salary plus incentive, with the incentive heavily weighted towards products with good profitability and of interest to A and B dealers. The plan has provided improved income to salesmen, accompanied by reduced sales cost ratios. Needless to say, tying incentives to management goals is an essential ingredient of good territory management.

Job Specialization/Job Simplification

The old adage "Don't work harder, work smarter" applies quite appropriately to a growingly complex and costly sales force. As a sales force expands, cost/effectiveness benefits based on job specialization or job simplification begin to surface. This aspect of improved productivity may combine changes in territory management with some changes in supervisory or corporate roles.

Job specialization can be directed either by product or by market. For example, AMP Incorporated may have salesmen within a territory specializing by product line. Further, they may be supported by a special task force to assist in introducing a new product or rejuvenating an old one.

Another approach is to orient salesmen by industry specialization. IBM has specialized its sales force along industry lines (banking, insurance, retailing, and wholesaling). Where market demand is shifting, the key need may be to change emphasis from one channel to another. A few years ago, Swingline shifted its sales force from heavy wholesale to retail emphasis, increased the number of calls per outlet (five to seven per day), and encouraged more effective activity per call. The shift in customer emphasis and effectiveness per call resulted in substantially higher order size and output per salesman.

Impressive improvements in productivity can be generated by changing the sales job content to allow for greater specialization by function. Such approaches typically involve shifting the expensive field sales effort away from lower value and time consuming activities towards more productive pursuits. The latter activities can be taken on by a specialist who can handle them at lower cost and often with greater skill.

One example is to cover low volume accounts by telephone or by mail. U.S. Gypsum Company has initiated such a program in one of its eastern regions. A computerized analysis of accounts identified customers with consistent purchases but low volume. These accounts were taken away from salesmen and given to a telephone sales person for regular contact. In many cases, regularity of contacts has been improved, the cost of solicitation reduced, and sales increased.

In an entirely different business, a household goods moving company developed a telephone solicitation program to generate sales appointments. When implemented by the agency sales force of over 1,000 persons, the average salesman produced 1.5 times more booked business.

Another example of productivity improvement is the provision of specialty support personnel to back up the sales effort in such areas as distributor stocking and inventory control or retail shelf service. The example has already been cited of the greetings card company which identified the opportunity to shift distributor inventory servicing from salesmen to specialists. In my experience, successful food brokers have long since learned the merits of separating the sales function from the routine tasks of retail shelf service (stock checking, stock rotation, and pricing). Large brokers typically employ a small group of sales personnel who maintain sales contacts at the buyer and store manager level. These sales persons are, in turn, supported by field personnel who perform the in-store services.

A final example of the benefits to be gained from the specialist is in terms of service or technical support personnel. For example, a regional manufacturer of prefabricated and modular housing has enjoyed significant market penetration and relatively low field sales costs because salesmen are instructed to turn all technical and service problems over to a headquarters specialist. A less effective competitor's salesmen are regularly involved in time-consuming technical and service problems.

General Sales Management

What takes place at headquarters has an important impact on sales productivity. The types of field improvement already described can best be achieved when they fit within a sound general sales management framework. Some elements include (1) a dynamic and current organization structure, (2) a good planning program, and (3) adequate analysis of territory potential and customer profitability.

A few years ago, American Seating Company made a concerted effort to improve the productivity of its sales force and reduce field costs. One major initial step in

the program was the reorganization of the field sales effort into three sales forces built along market lines—amusement, education, and transportation. Since the change, major shifts in demand have occurred in each market, and monitoring of sales productivity and costs has been greatly facilitated by the structural change.

Without adequate documentation of sales objectives, goals, and strategies at the headquarters, regional, and territory levels, it is almost impossible to mount a sustained improvement program. Invariably, the company with a well-thought-out plan has done its analytical homework. That is, it knows where it stands relative to competition and has ongoing plans to stay ahead or catch up. My own experience over the years (with companies making such diverse products as gloves, domestic water pumps, and compressor components) confirms that well-documented and implemented marketing plans produce beneficial profit results.

A final necessary ingredient at the headquarters level is adequate analysis, with two of the most important areas being territory potential analysis and customer profitability analysis. Although the customer/prospect audit of a territory is an invaluable sales tool, it often is subject to significant errors. When initiated at the territory level, the effort often identifies potential which is less than 50 percent of what is actually available. To bridge the gap between what salesmen think is present as potential and what actually exists, calls for "top down," or broad national view of potential within geographical areas (territories), wherever the exercise is practical in terms of available data. Such an analysis provides the necessary inputs for shifts in territory alignment or changes in personnel within territories. A typical type of sales performance index developed for a manufacturer of electrical parts is shown in Exhibit 12. In this instance, some thought might be given to changing personnel in Territory A. Also, although volume in Ter-

EXHIBIT 12

Sales performance index

TERRITORY	POTENTIAL	SALES AS PERCENT OF TOTAL	SALES PERFORMANCE INDEX
A	7.22%	5.77%	80
B	3.17	4.39	138
C	13.58	14.58	107
↓	↓	↓	↓
Total	*100.0 %*	*100.0 %*	*100*

ritory C is adequate relative to potential, consideration might be given to splitting the territory.

An essential requirement in guiding field efforts is customer profitability analysis. In establishing criteria to determine what should constitute an A classification for a customer, the first ingredient should be sales potential. Often, this figure can be determined quite accurately in the field, with some assistance from headquarters market research or product management personnel who are charged with potential analysis. However, the field force is totally reliant upon its accounting department to supply customer profitability data. It is clear that such analysis provides another important criterion for ranking customers on an ABC basis. A customer with an A rating in terms of sales potential, but who provides marginal profits or losses, must clearly be rerated, perhaps to the C or D categories. Here is the means to supply the missing ingredient—profitability. The final thrust then becomes one of improving sales productivity and cost ratios, but within the constraint of a profit goal.

THE SALES AUDIT

What have been described up to this point are a number of ingredients for improving sales force productivity. In almost all sales forces, some of the many ingredients are present, but if something is missing, a new program may provide improved results.

In many cases, dramatic opportunities for improvement can best be achieved by a broad overview of the field sales effort. Such an audit program can be undertaken by a specially appointed internal team, by a company's captive consulting group, by an outside consultant, or by any combination of the foregoing. In fact, the combination approach is often the most effective, and, in fact, is in keeping with modern practice in seeking productivity improvement. The audit should include the following:

☐ *Marketing Profile.* This phase involves identifying company objectives, strategies, market position, sales organization, territorial coverage, sales results, costs, and profit results. It establishes the basic framework within which improvement opportunities can be identified.

☐ *Definition of Selling Function.* This step identifies the major functional components of the field sales job in terms of current practices versus both management objectives and market requirements. The components of the job may include planning, travel, waiting, face-to-face selling, service, and paperwork.

☐ *Evaluation of Effectiveness.* Somewhat different from how a salesman is spending his time is the question of his effectiveness, again relative to company objectives, market requirements, and competitive activities.

☐ *Analysis of Territory Configuration and Coverage.* This step is concerned with the nature and rationale for the current sales territories in terms of geographical configurations, sales potentials, sales goals, and workload (time available and calls made).

☐ *Review of Information System.* It is important to determine whether information is adequate and timely to serve sales management and permit performance measurement.

☐ *Evaluation of Sales Management.* This phase calls for an evaluation of the field sales organization structure (including direct selling, supervisory, and support personnel), an appraisal of the effectiveness of personnel, and an indication as to whether the compensation plans at all levels of the sales force are supportive of management objectives and strategies.

☐ *Ranking of Improvement Opportunities.* As the result of the previous six analyses, a number of improvement opportunities are typically identified. Because, in our experience, a smorgasbord of ideas evolves, it becomes critical to rank the opportunities in terms of importance and pay-off potential. Without setting priorities, the effort can degenerate into an exercise in fighting brush fires.

☐ *Development of an Implementation Program.* The final step is to create a work plan calling for specific action within each top priority area, identifying program responsibilities, establishing time schedules, and setting up monitoring procedures.

In some cases, top management has been worried over a "high" field sales cost, only to find that costs for the particular industry are not that far out of line, and only fine tuning or modest changes are needed. In other cases, the improvement opportunities are large and very real. I am thinking of a current study where the improvement potential in terms of cost reduction is in the magnitude of $500,000.

Where significant changes are appropriate, the time span from problem identification to implementation of improvement programs can be agonizingly slow. I remember having to wait six months to revise an incentive compensation plan, while the accounting department came up with profitability data by salesman. Also, one change

which may take a year to accomplish may necessarily precede another which, in its turn, will take a year to implement.

It is my observation, as indicting as it may sound, that such audits are seldom initiated by sales management. To begin with, there is a certain untouchable mystique about marketing costs. Often, corporate or divisional managers with backgrounds in finance, production, or engineering are somewhat in awe of marketing management, and an audit is their wedge to challenge the mystique. In fairness, competent sales management will respond that the audit is not needed, because it will merely confirm superior results.

To return to the opening analysis, sales cost ratios are coming under increasing scrutiny. With inflation, sales results per salesman or per territory must be constantly improved just to maintain an even cost ratio. However, wide differences are apparent within similar industries and product groups, as to the volume that can be generated per salesman, and the results are closely correlated to cost ratios. The differences in ratio results are very large; in fact, they indicate that improvements offer substantial cost savings.

Many approaches to sales force productivity improvement are possible and have been successfully adopted by sales management. Yet, where productivity appears to be out of line, a more broad-scale attack in terms of a general audit may be appropriate. While there is some risk of only a limited pay-off, the more typical outcome is a substantial change in practices and bottom line results.

Index of Cases